Fodor's 04

ARIZONA

D1056396

Where to Stay and Eat
for All Budgets

Must-See Sights
and Local Secrets

Ratings You Can Trust

Fodor's Travel Publications   New York, Toronto, London, Sydney, Auckland
www.fodors.com

FODOR'S ARIZONA 2004

Editor: Douglas Stallings

Editorial Contributors: Matt Baatz, Satu Hummasti, David Joiner, Mara Levin, Carrie Miner, Bob and Gloria Willis

Maps: David Lindroth, *cartographer*; Bob Blake and Rebecca Baer, *map editors*

Design: Fabrizio La Rocca, *creative director*; Guido Caroti, *art director*; Melanie Marin, *senior picture editor*

Production/Manufacturing: Robert B. Shields

Cover Photo (The Mittens, Monument Valley): Rob Boudreau/Stone/Getty Images

ISBN 1-4000-1266-X

ISSN 1525-5026

SPECIAL SALES

Fodor's Travel Publications are available at special discounts for bulk purchases for sales promotions or premiums. Special editions, including personalized covers, excerpts of existing guides, and corporate imprints, can be created in large quantities for special needs. For more information, contact your local bookseller or write to Special Markets, Fodor's Travel Publications, 1745 Broadway, New York, NY 10019. Inquiries from Canada should be directed to your local Canadian bookseller or sent to Random House of Canada, Ltd., Marketing Department, 2775 Matheson Boulevard East, Mississauga, Ontario L4W 4P7. Inquiries from the United Kingdom should be sent to Fodor's Travel Publications, 20 Vauxhall Bridge Rd., London SW1V 2SA, England.

AN IMPORTANT TIP & AN INVITATION

Although all prices, opening times, and other details in this book are based on information supplied to us at press time, changes occur all the time in the travel world, and Fodor's cannot accept responsibility for facts that become outdated or for inadvertent errors or omissions. So **always confirm information when it matters,** especially if you're making a detour to visit a specific place. Your experiences—positive and negative—matter to us. If we have missed or misstated something, **please write to us.** We follow up on all suggestions. Contact the Arizona editor at editors@fodors.com or c/o Fodor's at 1745 Broadway, New York, NY 10019.

PRINTED IN THE UNITED STATES OF AMERICA

10 9 8 7 6 5 4 3 2 1

DESTINATION ARIZONA

The splendor of Arizona's natural landmarks—from the vastness of the Grand Canyon to the thousand-foot-high walls of Canyon de Chelly to the myriad shapes and spires of Monument Valley to Sedona's red rocks and the living Sonoran Desert—is reason enough to visit. But there is more to the state than beautiful vistas. Traces of a rich, layered history mark the awesome terrain and inspire artists, artisans, and the discerning shoppers who buy their work, from beautifully woven Navajo rugs to the cowboy paintings of the incomparable Lon Megargee. Arizona's cuisines are captivating, whether you enjoy spicy Sonoran Mexican or more sophisticated, contemporary Southwestern cuisine. The brilliant skies enthrall lovers of the outdoors, especially in a place where much of the state gets little rainfall to spoil outdoor endeavors. Take time to absorb the calming lessons of the heat and the majestic landscape—on the still waters of a magnificent lake at sunset or beside a fountain on an awning-shaded patio over lunch—and a bit of Arizona will stay with you forever. Have a fabulous trip!

Karen Cure, Editorial Director

CONTENTS

ABOUT THIS BOOK

There's no doubt that the best source for travel advice is a like-minded friend who's just been where you're headed. But with or without that friend, you'll have a better trip with a Fodor's guide in hand. Once you've learned to find your way around its pages, you'll be in great shape to find your way around your destination.

SELECTION

Our goal is to cover the best properties, sights, and activities in their category, as well as the most interesting communities to visit. We make a point of including local food lovers' hot spots as well as neighborhood options, and we avoid all that's touristy unless it's really worth your time. You can go on the assumption that everything you read about in this book is recommended wholeheartedly by our writers and editors. Flip to On the Road with Fodor's to learn more about who they are. It goes without saying that no property mentioned in the book has paid to be included.

RATINGS

Orange stars ★ denote sights and properties that our editors and writers consider the very best in the area covered by the entire book. These, the best of the best, are listed in the Fodor's Choice section in the front of the book. Black stars ★ highlight the sights and properties we deem Highly Recommended, the don't-miss sights within any region. Fodor's Choice and Highly Recommended options in each region are usually listed on the title page of the chapter covering that region. Use the index to find complete descriptions. In cities, sights pinpointed with numbered map bullets ❻ in the margins tend to be more important than those without bullets.

SPECIAL SPOTS

Pleasures & Pastimes focuses on types of experiences that reveal the spirit of the destination. Watch for Off the Beaten Path sights. Some are out of the way, some are quirky, and all are worth your while. If the munchies hit while you're exploring, look for Need a Break? suggestions.

TIME IT RIGHT

Wondering when to go? Check On the Calendar up front and chapters' Timing sections for weather and crowd overviews and best days and times to visit.

SEE IT ALL

Use Fodor's exclusive Great Itineraries as a model for your trip. (For a good overview of the entire destination, follow those that begin the book, or mix regional itineraries from several chapters.) In cities, Good Walks guide you to important sights in each neighborhood; ☞ indicates the starting points of walks and itineraries in the text and on the map.

BUDGET WELL

Hotel and restaurant price categories from ¢ to $$$$ are defined in the opening pages of each chapter—expect to find a balanced selection for every budget. For attractions, we always give standard adult admission fees; reductions are usually available for children, students, and senior citizens. Look in Discounts & Deals in Smart Travel Tips for information on destination-wide ticket schemes. Want to pay with plastic? AE, D, DC, MC, V following restaurant and hotel listings indicate whether American Express, Discover, Diner's Club, MasterCard, or Visa is accepted.

BASIC INFO

Smart Travel Tips lists travel essentials for the entire area covered by the book; city- and region-specific basics end each chapter. To find the best way to get around, see the transportation section; see individual modes of travel ("By Car," "By Train") for details. We assume you'll check Web sites or call for particulars.

ON THE MAPS Maps throughout the book show you what's where and help you find your way around. Black and orange numbered bullets ❻ ❻ in the text correlate to bullets on maps.

BACKGROUND In general, we give background information within the chapters in the course of explaining sights as well as in CloseUp boxes and in Understanding Arizona at the end of the book. To get in the mood, review the suggestions in Books & Movies.

FIND IT FAST Within the book, chapters are arranged in a roughly clockwise direction starting with Phoenix. Chapters are divided into small regions, within which towns are covered in logical geographical order; attractive routes and interesting places between towns are flagged as En Route. Heads at the top of each page help you find what you need within a chapter.

DON'T FORGET Restaurants are open for lunch and dinner daily unless we state otherwise; we mention dress only when there's a specific requirement and reservations only when they're essential or not accepted—it's always best to book ahead. Hotels have private baths, phone, TVs, and air-conditioning and operate on the European Plan (a.k.a. EP, meaning without meals). We always list facilities but not whether you'll be charged extra to use them, so when pricing accommodations, find out what's included.

SYMBOLS

Many Listings

★ Fodor's Choice
★ Highly recommended
⊠ Physical address
✛ Directions
⊡ Mailing address
☎ Telephone
🖷 Fax
⊕ On the Web
✑ E-mail
🖾 Admission fee
☉ Open/closed times
⚑ Start of walk/itinerary
Ⓜ Metro stations
⊟ Credit cards

Outdoors

⚲ Golf
⚠ Camping

Hotels & Restaurants

🖬 Hotel
🛏 Number of rooms
♨ Facilities
🍴 Meal plans
✕ Restaurant
✑ Reservations
🏛 Dress code
✎ Smoking
🍸 BYOB
✕🖬 Hotel with restaurant that warrants a visit

Other

☺ Family-friendly
🛈 Contact information
⇨ See also
⊠ Branch address
☞ Take note

ON THE ROAD WITH FODOR'S

A trip takes you out of yourself. Concerns of life at home completely disappear, driven away by more immediate thoughts—about, say, what marvels will beguile the next day, or where you'll have dinner. That's where Fodor's comes in. We make sure that you know all your options, so that you don't miss something that's around the next bend just because you didn't know it was there. Because the best memories of your trip might well have nothing to do with what you came to Arizona to see, we guide you to sights large and small all over the region. You might set out to see the Grand Canyon, but back at home you find yourself unable to forget the sunset from atop one of the Hopi Mesas or that great Mexican restaurant on Tucson's South 4th Avenue. With Fodor's at your side, serendipitous discoveries are never far away.

Our success in showing you every corner of the Arizona is a credit to our extraordinary writers. Although there's no substitute for travel advice from a good friend who knows your style, our contributors are the next best thing—the kind of people you would poll for travel advice if you knew them.

Flagstaff resident Matt Baatz spends most free moments mountain biking and hiking the trails near Flagstaff and Sedona. In his first year away from his native Pennsylvania, he has traversed hundreds of miles of forest, desert, and canyon, but what remains unexplored may occupy him for years to come.

Finland native Satu Hummasti came to Arizona almost seven years ago. She spent three years as an almost constant resident but now divides her time between Phoenix and New York City, where she works as a freelance writer and dancer.

David Joiner got his first taste of eastern Arizona in 1993 and has been exploring the area ever since. When not traveling around his adopted home state, he can often be found adventuring in rather obscure parts of Asia, where he helped update *Fodor's Vietnam*. He currently resides in Tucson.

Tucson updater Mara Levin divides her time among travel writing, social work, and her role as mom to two daughters. A native of California, Mara now lives in Tucson, where the grass may not be greener but the mountains, tranquility, and slower pace of desert life have their own appeal.

Carrie Miner first saw the Grand Canyon when she moved to Arizona at the age of 17. What she originally dismissed as a "big hole in the ground" soon became a challenge that she has now explored to its sublime depths. Carrie continues to seek out the past and present through the landscape and cultures of the Southwest and has written extensively about her home state in the pages of *Arizona Highways*. She has also contributed to *Fodor's Great American Vacations* and *Fodor's Travel Historic America: The Old West*.

Bob and Gloria Willis, a husband-and-wife freelance travel-writing and photography team, reside in Scottsdale. They spend time riding through, camping in, and four-wheeling through Arizona with their dog, who was adopted in one of their favorite places, Canyon de Chelly.

Time Zones

Numbers below vertical bands relate each zone
to Greenwich Mean Time (0 hrs.).
Local times frequently differ from these general indications,
as indicated by light-face numbers on map.

Arizona

WHAT'S WHERE

1 Phoenix & Central Arizona

One of America's fastest-growing metropolitan areas, Phoenix rose atop the ancient Hohokam civilization's ruins. Easterners flooded Phoenix in the 1920s in search of clean air. Rising where the Sonoran Desert butts up against the Superstition Mountains, the Phoenix metropolitan area also includes Scottsdale, Tempe, and some 20 other communities surrounded by a landscape of stunning beauty. Frank Lloyd Wright was so taken with the area when he consulted on Phoenix's Biltmore resort in 1927 that he built a sprawling winter home, Taliesin West, on 600 rugged acres outside Scottsdale. Today, visitors come to hike in the valley's superb desert parks, golf on championship courses, dine at some of the state's best restaurants, or luxuriate at pricey resorts and spas.

2 North-Central Arizona

The Sinagua built prodigiously across this area between the 8th and 15th centuries. North and south of Flagstaff, you can see their sturdy cliff dwellings at the Montezuma Castle, Walnut Canyon, and Wupatki national monuments. Today, 900 years after the last eruption of what is now Sunset Crater Volcano National Monument, the haunting bleakness of the land bespeaks the power of the Earth's inner fires, just as the blooming prickly pear cactus bespeaks the desert's power to bring forth surprising beauty. The laid-back towns of north-central Arizona are as bewitching as the landscape. Prescott's cool mountain heights and curiously New England–like architecture lure Phoenix residents fleeing southern heat. Funky Jerome, a former copper-mining boomtown now charms visitors with its bawdy history, its boutiques, and its spectacular views. Sedona's red rocks and B&Bs draw visitors looking to hike or merely to relax and enjoy the scenery. The town's "vortices" may or may not concentrate the planet's energy and create a perfect environment for the nourishment and alignment of the soul, but they certainly have their draw.

3 The Grand Canyon & Northwest Arizona

The Grand Canyon, one of nature's longest-running works in progress, both exalts and humbles the human spirit. You can view the spectacle from the South Rim, but the North Rim is the rim less traveled, and its devotees don't mind a bit. They like the elbow room and willingly travel to see views that outdazzle even the stunners farther south. As if the canyon itself weren't enough, northwestern Arizona also lures anglers with oversized trout near Lees Ferry and, in Lake Havasu City, with a bit of Britannia in the form of London Bridge—the real thing, shipped over from England in pieces to span a neck of man-made Lake Havasu. Meanwhile, Americana reigns around Kingman, a local transportation hub where you can cruise along legendary Route 66, that pre-interstate icon of American restlessness and the call of the open road. Not far from Kingman is Oatman, a ghost town with a main street straight out of a Western movie. Other destinations—Lake Mead and Hoover Dam, in Nevada—have their appeals, too.

4 The Northeast

Most residents of northeastern Arizona are Navajo and Hopi and, although computers are part of daily life now, traditions endure that predate the conquistadors. Portions of high-desert country are holy to those who live here—almost all of this land is majestic. Wind and frost have created magical effects in stone, such as the swirled rock formations (actually petrified sand dunes) in sunset-hued Antelope Canyon. In Monument Valley you'll see the starkly beautiful landscape made popular by Ansel Adams and countless Hollywood Westerns. Along with the living Navajo and Hopi communities, the White House Ruin in breathtaking Canyon de Chelly and the ruins at Betatakin and Keet Seel in Navajo National Monument are eloquent reminders of how ancient peoples wrested shelter from this fierce land. At Lake Powell, Glen Canyon Dam inverted the equation: here, humankind dominated nature, and the lake created is a spectacular meeting of earth and water.

(5) Eastern Arizona

Eastern Arizona, by turns, is verdant or stark and haunting. The White Mountains, northeast of Phoenix, contain the world's largest stand of ponderosa pines, as well as alpine meadows decked with wildflowers and some of the cleanest air you'll ever breathe. If you love the outdoor life, you may well fall in love with this place. Side by side to the northeast lie a few of the region's more interesting landmarks: Homolovi Ruins State Park is home to five ancestral Hopi pueblos. The Painted Desert assumes hues from blood red to pink, then back again, as the sun rises, climbs, and sets. And Petrified Forest National Park protects a forest of trees that stood when dinosaurs walked the earth, the pieces of petrified logs looking deceptively like driftwood cast upon an oceanless beach.

(6) Tucson

Augmented annually by legions of "snowbirds" who come for the winter, Tucson isn't that much smaller than Phoenix, yet it still retains the feel of a small Southwestern town. Claiming that Phoenix has paved over the desert in its sprawl, Tucsonans say the serenity of their mostly arid land imparts an easygoing personality to their city. A walk in verdant Sabino Canyon, a favorite of hikers that's within the city limits, does nothing to dispel that notion. Neither does a stroll among the towering cacti of Saguaro National Park. Colonial Spain and Mexico left a strong imprint on Tucson's art, architecture, cuisine, and culture. In downtown's El Presidio Historic District, traditional Mexican adobes and wide-porch Territorial homes underscore the city's Hispanic heritage. The residents of South 4th Avenue swear the best Mexican food north of the border is served here. A little farther out, city slickers enjoy daily horseback rides at some of the region's many guest ranches or luxury pampering at one of the local spas.

(7) Southern Arizona

You might be tempted to dismiss southern Arizona as a desolate, empty landscape. You'd be wrong. Mountain-and-desert scenery as splendid as any in Arizona is one reason, including the remarkable fauna and rock formations at Chiricahua National Monument. Enduring pockets of the Old West in the form of ghost towns are another. The community of Pearce died in the 1930s, when gold deposits ran dry. Douglas is also a time capsule, where local ranchers meet for drinks under the Tiffany skylights of the once-grand Gadsden Hotel. Tombstone, not in the least ghostly, hums with commerce and reenactments of gunfights, most notably the confrontation in which the Earps and Doc Holliday shot it out with the Stantons at the OK Corral. In southern Arizona, the old frontier is not the only frontier: at Kitt Peak National Observatory, astronomers gaze into the universe, joined by more than a few travelers who have made the stunning drive through the Tohono O'odham Reservation to behold the world's final frontier. And deep below the dry desert, near Benson, is Kartchner Caverns, one of the most spectacular wet cave systems in the world.

GREAT ITINERARIES

Highlights of Arizona

14 days

Ghostly Native American ruins, chamber music in Sedona, color-soaked canyons, shopping in Tucson: Arizona is full of history, culture, and good times. Start or end this survey with a few days in Phoenix.

PRESCOTT, JEROME, & SEDONA

2 days. From Phoenix, head northwest to take a look around Prescott, "Everyone's Hometown," and its old-fashioned town square, Victorian homes, and pine-covered foothills. The near–ghost town of Jerome clings to the mountainside nearby. Surrounded by windswept sandstone, Sedona is breathtaking, as well.

GRAND CANYON

2 days. The Grand Canyon is truly one of the wonders of the world. Whether you raft the Colorado, ride a mule, tackle a hike, or gaze from the terrace of a rim-side hotel, time here is always an adventure.

NAVAJO NATIONAL MONUMENT & MONUMENT VALLEY

1 day. Tram tours led by Navajo guides roll past the sandstone mesas and spires of Monument Valley, where private cars can't go. At Navajo National Monument, linger among the cliff dwellings and ponder the lives of those who came before.

CANYON DE CHELLY

2 days. Journey into magical Canyon de Chelly on foot, on horseback, or in a guided four-wheel-drive vehicle to view Native American ruins and the magnificent sandstone landscape.

THE HOPI MESAS

2 days. Rising above the desert floor, the Hopi Mesas are home to some of the oldest inhabited villages in the United States.

PAINTED DESERT & PETRIFIED FOREST

1 day. If rocks could talk, those in Petrified Forest National Park and the Painted Desert would tell how aeons of wind and rain polished the remains of a primeval swamp into gem-colored hills filled with fossils.

CORONADO TRAIL TO TUCSON

1 day. On the scenic Coronado Trail you will find treasure in abundance: aspen and fir forests, lakes stocked with trout, and wildlife.

TUCSON

2 days. While in Tucson, check out the beautiful San Xavier del Bac mission and the El Presidio Historic District surrounding the Museum of Art.

SAGUARO NATIONAL PARK

1 day. Both the east and the west sections of Saguaro National Park put you face to face with the eponymous cactus. Experience desert plants and animals at the Arizona-Sonora Desert Museum. At Old Tucson Studios, movies are still being filmed.

The Old West

12 days

Desperadoes, Indian warriors, galloping ponies, lawmen riding into the sunset: In Arizona, the Wild West is never far away. You can relive the romance at the state's historic locales, starting or ending with a stay in Tucson.

GHOST TOWNS

4 days. Guns still blaze and villains fall in Tombstone—but only during staged fights. Be sure to check out the OK Corral. Later, explore quaint Bisbee, now an artists' haven of restored Victorian homes and upscale bistros. After a morning in tumbledown Gleeson and Pearce, move on to Fort Bowie National Historic Site, where U.S. soldiers once skirmished with Cochise's Apaches. Downtown Willcox looks like the cow town it is and has two Western history museums.

SOUTH OF TUCSON

1 day. To appreciate the Spanish influence on small towns along the meandering Santa Cruz River, tour the mission at Tumacacori National Historic Park. Up the road is Tubac, site of Arizona's first European settlement and the Tubac Presidio State Historic Park and Museum.

PHOENIX

2 days. Downtown Phoenix preserves the city's first Anglo homes in Heritage Square and puts its Anglo history on display at the Phoenix Museum of History. In Scottsdale, the Buffalo Museum of America and Old Town Scottsdale preserve the Old West amid decidedly New West surroundings. And don't miss the rich Native American collection at the **Heard Museum**.

NORTH OF PHOENIX

1 day. Catch a melodrama at the opera house or hop a buckboard to tour the re-created village at the Pioneer Arizona Living History Museum. In Wickenburg, home to many fine guest ranches, you'll find a tranquil site where justice was meted out: the Jail Tree.

THE VERDE VALLEY
2 days. Gold once lured folks to Prescott, giving rise to the former red-light district known as Whiskey Row; stop at Sharlott Hall Museum for a glimpse of the town's past. Old mine tunnels honeycomb the land around Jerome, where museums memorialize the local mining bonanza.

FLAGSTAFF
1 day. The natural beauty of this area leaves no doubt as to why Anglos settled here. To see how they lived, stop in downtown's restored Historic Railroad District and at Riordan State Historic Park.

CENTRAL ARIZONA
1 day. Learn about life on an Old West military outpost at Fort Verde State Historic Park; then sample frontier fare in Tortilla Flat. Protected by two mountain ranges, once-flourishing Globe retains the charm of its mining days.

High season at the resorts of Phoenix and Tucson is winter, when cold winds are blowing in the north and the snowbirds fly south to the warmer desert. Expect the best temperatures—and the highest prices—from December through March; if you can stand the heat, the posh desert resorts drop their prices—sometimes by more than half—from June through September. The South Rim of the Grand Canyon is busy year-round, but least busy during the winter months, from January through early March; things pick up for the Christmas season and again for Spring Break.

Climate

Phoenix averages 300 sunny days and 7 inches of precipitation annually. Tucson gets all of 11 inches of rain each year, and the high mountains see about 25 inches. The Grand Canyon is usually cool on the rim and about 20°F warmer on the floor. During winter months, approximately 6–12 inches of snow falls on the North Rim; the South Rim receives half that amount. Temperatures in valley areas like Phoenix and Tucson average about 60°F to 70°F in the daytime during the winter months and between 100°F and 115°F during peak summer months. Flagstaff and Sedona stay much cooler, dropping into the 30s and 40s Fahrenheit during the winter months and leveling off at 80°F to 90°F in the summer.

Forecasts **Weather Channel Connection** ☎ 900/932-8437, 95¢ per minute from a Touch-Tone phone ⊕ www.weather.com.

PHOENIX

Jan.	65F	18C	May	93F	32C	Sept.	98F	36C
	38	3		57	14		69	20
Feb.	69F	20C	June	102F	37C	Oct.	88F	29C
	41	4		68	19		57	14
Mar.	75F	23C	July	105F	38C	Nov.	75F	23C
	45	7		78	23		45	7
Apr.	84F	28C	Aug.	102F	36C	Dec.	66F	19C
	52	11		76	24C		39	4

TUCSON

Jan.	64F	18C	May	89F	32C	Sept.	96F	36C
	37	3		57	14		68	20
Feb.	68F	20C	June	98F	37C	Oct.	84F	29C
	39	4		66	19		57	14
Mar.	73F	23C	July	101F	38C	Nov.	73F	23C
	44	7		73	23		44	7
Apr.	82F	28C	Aug.	96F	36C	Dec.	66F	19C
	51	11		71	22		39	4

FLAGSTAFF

Jan.	41F	5C	May	66F	19C	Sept.	71F	22C
	14	–10		33	1		41	5
Feb.	44F	7C	June	77F	25C	Oct.	62F	17C
	17	– 8		41	5		30	– 1
Mar.	48F	9C	July	80F	27C	Nov.	51F	11C
	23	– 5		50	10		21	– 6
Apr.	57F	14C	Aug.	78F	26C	Dec.	42F	6C
	28	– 2		48	9		15	– 9

ON THE CALENDAR

Arizona's top seasonal events are listed below, and any one of them could provide the stuff of lasting memories. Contact local tourism authorities for exact dates and further information.

ONGOING

Jan., Feb.	The Parada del Sol Rodeo and Parade, a popular state attraction on Scottsdale Road in Scottsdale, features lots of dressed-up cowboys and cowgirls, plus horses and floats.
May, June	At Flagstaff's three-week Trappings of the American West Festival, the featured attraction is cowboy art—everything from painting, sculpture, photography, and cowboy paraphernalia to cowboy poetry readings.

WINTER

Dec.	At the Arizona Temple Gardens & Visitors Center Christmas Lighting, in Mesa, more than 600,000 lights illuminate the walkways, reflection pool, trees, and plants.
Early Dec.	For the three days of Old Town Tempe Fall Festival of the Arts, the downtown area closes to traffic for art exhibits, food booths, music, and other entertainment.
Jan. 1	Tempe's nationally televised Tostitos Fiesta Bowl Footbowl Classic kicks off the year with a match between two of the top college teams in the nation.
Late Jan.	At the Phoenix Open Golf Tournament in Scottsdale, top players compete at the Tournament Players Club.
	The Quartzsite Pow Wow Gem and Mineral Show is a gigantic gem, mineral, and jewelry market, held the last Wednesday through Sunday of the month in Quartzsite, about 19 mi from the California border (take I–10 west of Phoenix, then Exit 17 or 19 in Quartzsite).
Early Feb.	The Rodeo of Rodeos, sponsored by the Phoenix Jaycees, opens with the Parada del Sol parade.
	The World Championship Hoop Dance Contest at the Heard Museum in Phoenix attracts superbly skilled native hoop dancers from across the U.S. and Canada to compete for a world champion title.
Mid-Feb.	At O'odham Tash in Casa Grande, Native American tribes from around the country, and from Canada and Mexico, host parades, native dances, a rodeo, a powwow, costume displays, and food stands.
	The huge Tucson Gem and Mineral Show, organized by the Tucson Gem and Mineral Society, attracts rock hounds—amateur and professional—from all over the world who come to buy, sell, and display their geological treasures and to attend lectures and competitive exhibits.
	History comes to life during Wickenburg Gold Rush Days, when the Old West town puts on a parade, rodeo, dances, gold-panning demonstrations, a mineral show, and other activities.

La Fiesta de los Vaqueros features the world's longest "nonmechanized" parade—horses pull floats and carry dignitaries—launching a five-day rodeo at the Tucson Rodeo Grounds. An all-women's rodeo is included in the festivities.

SPRING

Early Mar.	In Phoenix, the Heard Museum Guild Indian Fair and Market is a prestigious juried show of Native American arts and crafts. Visitors can also enjoy Native American foods, music, and dance.
Mid-Mar.	For the Lost Dutchman Gold Mine Superstition Mountain Trek in Apache Junction, the Dons of Arizona search for the legendary lost mine, pan for gold, and eat lots of barbecue to keep up their strength. There are crafts demonstrations and fireworks, too.
Mid–Late Mar.	In March, women compete in the Standard Register PING Tournament, at the Moon Valley Country Club in Phoenix.
Late Apr.	Tucson hosts the International Mariachi Conference, four days of mariachi-music workshops and performances, along with cultural and educational exhibits.
	Bisbee's La Vuelta de Bisbee is one of Arizona's largest bicycle races and attracts top racers from around the country to the hills of the historic mining town.
	Yaqui Easter is celebrated in old Pasqua Village (Tucson) with various activities taking place during the Palm Sunday and Easter weekends. Visitors are welcome to watch traditional Yaqui dances and ceremonies.
Early May	During the Route 66 Fun Run Weekend from Seligman to Topock, the longest drivable stretch of the historic road between Chicago and Los Angeles, is feted with a Show-and-Shine car rally—anyone with a vehicle can join the ride—and various activities along the route, including entertainment, barbecues, and a Miss Route 66 beauty pageant.
Late May	During the Rendezvous, the townspeople of Williams set up an interpretive village and reenact the lives of 1800s mountain traders. Events include a steak fry and a Buckskinners black powder shoot.

SUMMER

Early June	Festivities of Old West Day/Bucket of Blood Races, in Holbrook, include arts and crafts, Western dress, and Native American song and dance, in addition to the 10-km (6-mi) fun run and 20-mi bike ride from Petrified Forest National Park to Holbrook.
First Week in July	Prescott Frontier Days and Rodeo, billed as the world's oldest rodeo, finds big crowds and an equally big party on downtown Whiskey Row.
Mid-July	The Native American Arts & Crafts Festival in Pinetop-Lakeside brings storytellers, dancers, musicians, and artists together for two days in a beautiful mountain setting.

First Weekend in Aug.	Flagstaff's SummerFest is a gathering of painters, potters, musicians, and other artists from around the United States. They vie with carnival rides and food vendors for the crowd's attention.
Early Aug.	The Southwest Wings Birding Festival, held throughout Cochise County and in Bisbee, includes field trips to local canyons and forests, lectures by recognized Audubon authorities, and other avian-oriented events.
Mid-Aug.	The Payson Rodeo, known as the "World's Oldest Continuous Rodeo," draws top cowboys from around the country to compete in bull-riding and calf- and steer-roping contests.
FALL	
Sept.	Each September the Grand Canyon Chamber Music Festival is held in the Shrine of the Ages auditorium at the South Rim. Call or write for schedule information and advance tickets.
Early Sept.	The Navajo Nation Annual Tribal Fair is the world's largest Native American fair. Held in Window Rock, it includes a rodeo, traditional Navajo music and dances, food booths, and an intertribal powwow.
Late Sept.	At the Jazz on the Rocks Festival in Sedona, four or five ensembles perform in a spectacular red-rock setting.
Early Oct.	Rex Allen Days in Willcox honors the local cowboy film star and narrator for Walt Disney productions with a parade, country fair, concerts, rodeo, dances, and more.
Mid-Oct.	At Tombstone's Helldorado Days this town relives the spirited Wyatt Earp era and the shoot-out at the OK Corral.
Mid–Late Oct.	A weeklong event, London Bridge Days includes a Renaissance festival, a parade, and a variety of British-theme contests in Lake Havasu City.
Late Oct.	In late October, you can join the celebration of traditional Navajo culture at the Western Navajo Fair in Tuba City.
Early Nov.	During the Thunderbird Hot-Air-Balloon Classic, 150 or more balloons participate in Scottsdale's colorful race.
Late Nov.	At 111 mi, El Tour de Tucson is the largest perimeter bicycling event in the world, attracting international celebrity cyclists.
Last Weekend in Nov.	The waters of Lake Powell alight with the Festival of Lights Boat Parade as dozens of illuminated boats glide from Wahweap Lodge to Glen Canyon Dam and back.

PLEASURES & PASTIMES

Ballooning

Nothing is as thrilling as soaring over the desert and mountains in a hot-air balloon, and Arizona is a great location to do it. The ballooning season runs from September through May, when weather and temperatures are at their best. Several companies can take you soaring into the clouds, and there are also several competitive ballooning events during the season if being a spectator is more to your liking.

Baseball

The Arizona Diamondbacks are the big draw come April, but many fans come in March to watch professional teams warm up for the season in spring-training Cactus League games, most of them in the Phoenix area. The teams start their training camps as early as February. Free drills—held in the morning before an exhibition game—are fun to watch, and there's a good chance you might be able to chat with the players before or after these sessions. And the best part is that these games are much more affordable than they are in the major-league season. In some cases, reserved seats sell out each fall before the upcoming season, but you can almost always get general admission seats on game days.

Boating & Water Sports

You may be surprised to find so many lakes in what most consider a desert state. In fact, Arizonans own more boats per capita than residents of almost any other state. The two national recreational areas, Glen Canyon (Lake Powell), in north-central Arizona, and Lake Mead (including Lake Mohave), in the northwest, have marinas, launching ramps, and boat and ski rentals. At both lakes you can take a paddle-wheeler tour or take the wheel yourself in a fully equipped houseboat. Lake Havasu, fed by the Colorado River in the western part of the state, is another popular site for boating, waterskiing, windsurfing, and jet-skiing. London Bridge, which was moved block by block from England and reassembled here, is a surreal vision at this lakeside resort. Saguaro and Canyon lakes, just east of Scottsdale, offer good boating and waterskiing for those based in the Phoenix area looking for a convenient day trip.

Golf

Your clubs certainly won't gather dust in Arizona. Aside from attending the big-draw Phoenix Open, golfers flock to this state to tee off at the myriad top-ranked private and municipal courses. Year-round desert courses offer cheaper greens fees during the summer, while those in the northern parts usually shut down for the winter. Just about every resort has its own course or is affiliated with a private club, and the state has some of the best courses in the country.

Hiking

Throughout the state, hikers can choose from trails that wind through the desert, climb mountains, meander past supernal rock formations, delve deep into forests, or circumnavigate cities. Hiking is the best way to see Grand Canyon National Park, and a trip down to the canyon floor will reward you with a lifetime of memories. But all over the state, you'll find developed trails, in the cool mountains near Flagstaff, in the White Mountains of eastern Arizona, in Phoenix's massive park system, and in the parks and preserves of southern Arizona. Whether it's desert or mountain hiking you are looking for, you're sure to find it somewhere in the state.

Horseback Riding

Traveling by horseback through the somewhat wild West or the scenic high country is perhaps the most appropriate way to explore Arizona. Stables offer a selection of mountain or desert trail rides lasting a half day, two days, or as long as two weeks. In northern regions the season is from May through October. If riding is the focus of your Arizona holiday, you might consider staying at a dude ranch, where you can saddle up every day.

Native American Culture

Attending Native American festivals and exploring the remains of earlier settlements can be a rewarding part of a trip to Arizona. As is the case with traveling anywhere, any effort made to enhance your understanding of local culture and history will enrich all aspects of your visit. Keep in mind, too, that when you enter a reservation you are, in effect, entering another country, one governed by different laws and customs. Obey *all* posted signs (some signs on the reservations look less than official, but they mean what they say) and ask at the reservation visitor center or check with local authorities if you have any questions.

Shopping

Many tourists come to Arizona for no other reason than to purchase fine Native American jewelry and crafts. Collectibles include Navajo rugs and sand paintings, Hopi katsina dolls (intricately carved and colorful representations of Hopi spiritual beings) and pottery, Tohono O'odham (Papago) basketry, and Apache beadwork, as well as the highly prized silver and turquoise jewelry produced by several different tribes.

Skiing

Cross-country and downhill skiing are winter pastimes in Arizona, even if its mountains don't quite match the scale of the Rockies. Flagstaff Nordic Center north of Flagstaff, Mormon Lake Ski Touring Center southeast of Flagstaff, the Grand Canyon's North Rim Nordic Center, and miles of crisscrossing trails around Alpine are good places for cross-country skiing. The three peaks of Sunrise Park Resort in the White Mountains are owned and operated by the White Mountain Apache tribe and constitute the state's largest ski area. Other popular areas are Arizona Snowbowl near Flagstaff and Mt. Lemmon Ski Valley near Tucson, the continent's southernmost ski slope.

FODOR'S CHOICE

The sights, restaurants, hotels, and other travel experiences on these pages are our editors' top picks—our Fodor's Choices. They're the best of their type in the area covered by the book—not to be missed and always worth your time. In the destination chapters that follow, you will find all the details.

LODGING

$$$$	**Arizona Biltmore,** Phoenix. Phoenix's first luxury resort has maintained its high standards since 1929, with low-key elegance that makes it one of the classiest places in the Southwest.
$$$$	**The Boulders,** Carefree. The Valley's most serene and secluded luxury resort hides among hill-size granite boulders in the foothills town of Carefree.
$$$$	**White Stallion Ranch,** Tucson. Southern Arizona's best guest ranch is just a few miles from the heart of Tucson.
$$$–$$$$	**Hermosa Inn,** Paradise Valley. This small resort was once the home of cowboy artist Lon Margaree, and its understated sophistication is welcome after the other big splashy Phoenix resorts.
$$–$$$$	**Briar Patch Inn,** Sedona. It may not be in the heart of Sedona, but its lovely location in Oak Creek Canyon sets it apart.
$$$	**Arizona Inn,** Tucson. With almost all that you would want from a landmark inn—period furnishings, fireplaces, quiet and friendly service, even a midtown location—you won't be disappointed.
$$–$$$	**Red Setter Inn,** Greer. The hand-hewn log inn is the best thing going in the White Mountains of eastern Arizona.
$$	**Casa Tierra,** Tucson. In an adobe building, this fine B&B outside town is great for a desert getaway.
$–$$	**Cameron Trading Post,** Cameron. With its trading-post charm, this may well be the best base for seeing both the North and South rims of the Grand Canyon, as well as nearby Navajo-Hopi country.
$–$$	**Canyon Rose Suites,** Bisbee. Suites in this downtown B&B have full kitchens; there's even a full-service spa.
$–$$	**Grand Canyon Lodge,** North Rim. On the North Rim you can avoid the crowds as you enjoy the mighty abyss. The historic, rustic Grand Canyon Lodge has spectacular canyon views.
$–$$	**Wahweap Lodge,** Wahweap, Lake Powell. Although rooms are standard, this central source for Lake Powell recreation has cruises, river excursions, boat rentals, waterskiing, and a good restaurant—it's a nearly all-in-one resort.
$	**Clarion Hotel & Suites Santa Rita,** Tucson. The rooms are nothing fancy, but this historic hotel in downtown Tucson offers up great value as well as one of the city's best restaurants.
$	**Comfort Inn,** Scottsdale. A comfortable, clean room in a convenient, safe location costs a third less than the pricey resorts nearby.

$ **Holiday Inn Express,** Benson. The closest lodging to Kartchner Caverns is also the area's best choice and best buy.

$ **Wigwam Motel,** Holbrook. You can spend the night in this kitschy Route 66 landmark for a song. Where else can you stay in a concrete tepee?

BUDGET LODGING

¢–$ **Bright Angel Lodge,** Grand Canyon Village. Mary Jane Colter's log-and-stone lodge gives you every bit as much atmosphere as the El Tovar but for half the price.

¢–$ **School House Inn Bed & Breakfast,** Bisbee. Once a real schoolhouse, this atmospheric B&B is your best budget choice in quaint Old West town.

¢ **Reed's Lodge,** Springerville. This welcoming motel and its owner, Roxanne Knight, can make your stay in the White Mountains an exceedingly pleasant one.

RESTAURANTS

$$$$ **Marquesa,** Scottsdale. Expertly prepared Catalonian cuisine is served in this elegant Fairmont Scottsdale Princess dining room.

$$$–$$$$ **Janos,** Tucson. The innovative Southwestern cuisine of chef Janos Wilder keeps the crowds coming year-round.

$$$ **Lon's at the Hermosa,** Paradise Valley. The setting may be rustic, but the menu spans the globe with ingredients as fresh and contemporary as any in town.

$$$ **Restaurant Hapa,** Scottsdale. Thai, Chinese, and other astonishingly flavorful Asian-hybrid entrées and desserts add up to one big-time dining experience.

$$–$$$ **El Tovar Dining Room,** Tucson. A meal in this historic dining room at the canyon's edge is an elegant way to while away your evening.

$$ **Café Poca Cosa,** Tucson. Superb Moorish architecture that calls to mind the Alhambra in Granada makes this fine Spanish restaurant a sight in its own right.

$$ **Kramer's at the Manzanita,** Cornville. The sophistication of the Continental fare here is unexpected, considering the location.

BUDGET RESTAURANTS

¢–$ **Cruisers Café 66,** Williams. You might think it's still 1957 at this little diner, and it's a much cheaper and better alternative than the fast-food places at the canyon rim.

¢–$ **Mi Nidito,** Tucson. This local favorite is the best choice for Mexican on South 4th Avenue.

¢–$ **Rendezvous Diner,** Greer. Your best choice in the charming mountain town is this simply superb family restaurant.

¢–$ **Thai Spices,** Sedona. This small, unadorned restaurant is a rare, authentic find in a culinarily underwhelming town.

¢ **Carolina's,** Phoenix. As the lines at this humble spot attest, one of the culinary pleasures of coming to Phoenix is the opportunity to find delicious, authentic Sonoran Mexican cooking.

¢ **Ruiz's Mexican Food & Cantina,** Benson. A tiny, homey Mexican diner packs in the crowds all day. And it's pronounced "Reese."

ARCHAEOLOGY

Homolovi Ruins State Park, northeast of Winslow. Two of the well-preserved pueblos here have more than 1,000 rooms; the Hopi hold them sacred.

Montezuma Castle National Monument, Camp Verde. The five-story cliff dwelling is one of the best-preserved archaeological sites in North America.

Navajo National Monument, Black Mesa. Betatakin and Keet Seel, two 13th-century pueblos, are the largest ever found in Arizona and among the best preserved.

Pueblo Grande Museum and Cultural Park, Phoenix. Phoenix's only national landmark was once a Hohokam village; it's a great place for kids to learn about Native American culture.

Tusayan Ruin and Museum, Grand Canyon, South Rim. This museum on Desert View Drive is a good place to get up close and personal with some of the original canyon residents.

Wupatki National Monument, East of Flagstaff. This well-preserved Hopi tall house in the shadow of Sunset Crater has more than 100 rooms.

DRIVES

Apache Trail, southeast of Phoenix. President Theodore Roosevelt thought this route through the mountains southeast of Phoenix was the "most sublimely beautiful panorama nature ever created." He was right.

Coronado Trail, eastern Arizona, near Springerville. The steep 123-mi stretch of highway from Springerville to Clifton is dramatic as it winds from verdant meadows down into the Sonoran Desert.

Goosenecks Region, southern Utah. This twisting canyon is almost as breathtaking as the Grand Canyon, though on a smaller scale.

Oak Creek Canyon, Sedona. Another stunning canyon, this one is quiet and tree-lined on its low end near Flagstaff, towering and majestic as it looks toward Sedona.

Point Sublime, Grand Canyon, North Rim. The panorama along the dirt road leading out to the point is one of the most awesome views you'll ever witness from the comfort of your car.

Salt River Canyon, Fort Apache Indian Reservation. This scenic stretch of U.S. 60 goes through a mini–Grand Canyon of multicolored spires and buttes that you won't soon forget.

Texas Canyon, near Willcox. Is it possible to tire of canyons? Not when they are like this one—hung with massive boulders in astonishing formations apparently defying gravity.

GOLF

ASU Karsten Golf Course, Tempe. This top university course allows you to play in the footsteps of the pros for a less-than-top price.

Gold Canyon Golf Club, Gold Canyon. This resort east of Phoenix has two scenic, championship courses.

The Lodge at Ventana Canyon Golf Course, Tucson. The two courses here are scenic, challenging, and well maintained.

Randolph Park Golf Courses, Tucson. These municipal golf courses are dirt-cheap and high-quality; the North courses hosts the LPGA each year.

Sedona Golf Resort, Sedona. You might find it difficult keeping your eye on the ball at this beautiful course set against Sedona's red rocks.

Silver Creek Golf Club, Show Low. The quality and setting of this well-maintained course make it one of the state's great values.

Troon North Golf Courses, Scottsdale. Though expensive, these two courses are both tops in terms of quality, with a nod going to the Monument Course.

HISTORY

Mission San Xavier del Bac, Tucson. Built from native materials by Franciscan missionaries between 1777 and 1797, this beautiful church still serves the community.

Pipe Spring National Monument, near Fredonia. The strategically important fort in the 19th century protected one of the only reliable sources of water for miles around; the museum gives you a fascinating glimpse at how frontier life was lived.

Riordan State Historic Park, Flagstaff. A grand log-and-stone mansion designed by the same architect who built the El Tovar Hotel is furnished with original Stickley pieces.

Sharlot Hall Museum, Prescott. One of Arizona's most important history museums focuses on the town of Prescott.

Taliesin West, Scottsdale. Architect Frank Lloyd Wright's winter residence ingeniously integrates indoor and outdoor space.

NATURE

Arizona-Sonora Desert Museum, Tucson. This great zoo and botanical garden focuses on the flora and fauna of the Sonoran Desert.

Canyon de Chelly National Monument, Chinle. Thousand-foot cliffs contain ancient dwellings, including the White House, that are in profound harmony with their natural surroundings.

Chiricahua National Monument, southeast of Willcox. The pinnacles and spires in these 12,000 acres are among the most haunting and beautiful sights in the state.

Desert Botanical Garden, Phoenix. This is simply one of the greatest collections of desert flora in the Southwest.

Grand Canyon, North Rim. The only way to get to know the canyon is to hike or ride a mule down through the geological eras to the bottom of the chasm.

Kartchner Caverns State Park, Benson. One of the most spectacular wet cave systems in the entire world, the caverns were kept secret for 14 years while they were readied for visitors. But make reservations far in advance, because now the secret is out.

Monument Valley Navajo Tribal Park, Monument Valley. The cathedral-like sandstone spires will be instantly familiar if you've seen Ansel Adams's photos or John Ford's Hollywood Westerns.

Petrified Forest National Park, near Holbrook. Millions of fossilized trees, as well as animal skeletons, are spread out over what was once a forested marshland—225 million years ago, that is.

Saguaro National Park West, Tucson. You'll see the world's largest stand of saguaro cacti here, as well as fascinating petroglyphs made by the Hohokam people.

SMART TRAVEL TIPS

Finding out about your destination before you leave home means you won't squander time organizing everyday minutiae once you've arrived. You'll be more streetwise when you hit the ground as well, better prepared to explore the aspects of Arizona that drew you here in the first place. The organizations in this section can provide information to supplement this guide; contact them for up-to-the-minute details, and consult the A to Z sections that end each chapter for facts on the various topics as they relate to the Arizona's many regions. Happy landings!

AIR TRAVEL

BOOKING

When you book, **look for nonstop flights** and **remember that "direct" flights stop at least once.** Try to avoid connecting flights, which require a change of plane. Two airlines may operate a connecting flight jointly, so ask whether your airline operates every segment of the trip; you may find that the carrier you prefer flies you only part of the way. To find more booking tips and to check prices and make online flight reservations, log on to www.fodors.com.

CARRIERS

America West, the only airline calling Phoenix its hub, offers the most direct flights in and out of Phoenix, although Southwest Airlines comes in at a close second. Most of the country's other major airlines fly into Phoenix and have a few flights into Tucson as well; US Airways flies only to Phoenix.

Among the smaller airlines, Aerocalifornia flies between Tucson and Mexico only. ATA flies only to Phoenix. Frontier connects Phoenix to Denver and points beyond. Great Lakes Airlines flies to Phoenix and Page. Midwest Express connects Phoenix and Milwaukee.

Only one airline, Lufthansa, flies between continental Europe and Phoenix, and only British Airways flies direct from London to Phoenix; other airlines, however, have connecting flights to Phoenix and Tucson through their major U.S. hubs.

Within Arizona, America West Express/ Mesa Airlines flies from Phoenix to Flagstaff, Prescott, Lake Havasu, Kingman, Sierra Vista, and Yuma. Great Lakes

Aviation connects Phoenix and Page. Scenic Airlines flies from Las Vegas to the Grand Canyon.

Major Airlines Alaska Airlines ☎ 800/426-0333 ⊕ www.alaskaair.com. **America West** ☎ 800/235-9292 ⊕ www.americawest.com. **American** ☎ 800/433-7300; 0208/365-0777 in the U.K. ⊕ www.aa.com. **Continental** ☎ 800/525-0280; 0800/776-464 or 01293/776-464 in the U.K. ⊕ www.continental.com. **Delta** ☎ 800/221-1212; 0800/414-767 in the U.K. ⊕ www.delta.com. **Northwest** ☎ 800/225-2525 ⊕ www.nwa.com. **United** ☎ 800/241-6522 ⊕ www.united.com. **Southwest** ☎ 800/435-9792; 0845/844-4777 in the U.K. ⊕ www.southwest.com. **US Airways** ☎ 800/428-4322 ⊕ www.usairways.com.

Smaller Airlines Aerocalifornia ☎ 800/237-6225. **ATA** ☎ 800/225-2995 ⊕ www.ata.com. **Frontier Airlines** ☎ 800/432-1359 ⊕ www.frontierairlines.com **Great Lakes Airlines** ☎ 800/554-5111 ⊕ www.greatlakesav.com. **Midwest Express** ☎ 800/452-2022 ⊕ www.midwestexpress.com.

From Europe British Airways ☎ 0845/773-3377 reservations, 0845/779-9977 general queries, 800/247-9297 within the U.S. ⊕ www.britishairways.com. **Lufthansa** ☎ 800/645-3880, 1805/8384-2672 in Frankfurt ⊕ www.lufthansa-usa.com.

Within Arizona America West Express/Mesa ☎ 800/235-9292 ⊕ www.americawest.com. **Scenic Airlines** ☎ 800/535-4448.

CHECK-IN & BOARDING

Always **find out your carrier's check-in policy.** Plan to arrive at the airport about 2 hours before your scheduled departure time for domestic flights and 2½ to 3 hours before international flights. You may need to arrive earlier if you're flying from one of the busier airports or during peak air-traffic times. Despite its daily passenger volume, lengthy lines at the check-in counters or security checkpoints at Phoenix Sky Harbor are rarely a problem. To avoid delays at airport-security checkpoints, try not to wear any metal. Jewelry, belt and other buckles, steel-toe shoes, barrettes, and underwire bras are among the items that can set off detectors.

Assuming that not everyone with a ticket will show up, airlines routinely overbook planes. When everyone does, airlines ask for volunteers to give up their seats. In return, these volunteers usually get a several-hundred-dollar flight voucher, which can be used toward the purchase of another ticket, and are rebooked on the next flight out. If there are not enough volunteers, the airline must choose who will be denied

boarding. The first to get bumped are passengers who checked in late and those flying on discounted tickets, so **get to the gate and check in as early as possible,** especially during peak periods.

Always **bring a government-issued photo ID to the airport;** even when it's not required, a passport is best.

CUTTING COSTS

The least expensive airfares to Arizona are priced for round-trip travel and must usually be purchased in advance. Airlines generally allow you to change your return date for a fee; most low-fare tickets, however, are nonrefundable. It's smart to **call a number of airlines and check the Internet;** when you are quoted a good price, **book it on the spot**—the same fare may not be available the next day, or even the next hour. Always **check different routings** and look into using alternate airports. Also, price off-peak flights, which may be significantly less expensive than others. Travel agents, especially low-fare specialists (⇨ Discounts & Deals), are helpful.

Consolidators are another good source. They buy tickets for scheduled flights at reduced rates from the airlines, then sell them at prices that beat the best fare available directly from the airlines. Sometimes you can even get your money back if you need to return the ticket. Carefully read the fine print detailing penalties for changes and cancellations, purchase the ticket with a credit card, and **confirm your consolidator reservation with the airline.**

Consolidators AirlineConsolidator.com ☎ 888/468-5385 ⊕ www.airlineconsolidator.com; for international tickets. **Best Fares** ☎ 800/576-8255 or 800/576-1600 ⊕ www.bestfares.com; $59.90 annual membership. **Cheap Tickets** ☎ 800/377-1000 or 888/922-8849 ⊕ www.cheaptickets.com. **Expedia** ☎ 404/728-8787 or 800/397-3342 ⊕ www.expedia.com. **Hotwire** ☎ 920/330-9418 or 866/468-9473 ⊕ www.hotwire.com. **Now Voyager Travel** ✉ 45 W. 21st St., 5th fl., New York, NY 10010 ☎ 212/459-1616 🖶 212/243-2711 ⊕ www.nowvoyagertravel.com. **Onetravel.com** ⊕ www.onetravel.com. **Orbitz** ☎ 888/656-4546 ⊕ www.orbitz.com. **Priceline.com** ⊕ www.priceline.com. **Travelocity** ☎ 888/709-5983, 877/282-2925 in Canada, 0870/111-7060 in U.K. ⊕ www.travelocity.com.

ENJOYING THE FLIGHT

State your seat preference when purchasing your ticket, and then repeat it when you confirm and when you check in. For more legroom, you can request one of the few emergency-aisle seats at check-in, if you are capable of lifting at least 50 pounds—a Federal Aviation Administration requirement of passengers in these seats. Seats behind a bulkhead also offer more legroom, but they don't have underseat storage. Don't sit in the row in front of the emergency aisle or in front of a bulkhead, where seats may not recline.

Ask the airline whether a snack or meal is served on the flight. If you have dietary concerns, **request special meals when booking.** These can be vegetarian, low-cholesterol, or kosher, for example. It's a good idea to pack some healthful snacks and a small (plastic) bottle of water in your carry-on bag. On long flights, try to maintain a normal routine, to help fight jet lag. At night, **get some sleep.** By day, **eat light meals, drink water** (not alcohol), and **move around the cabin** to stretch your legs. For additional jet-lag tips consult *Fodor's FYI: Travel Fit & Healthy* (available at bookstores everywhere).

Smoking policies vary from carrier to carrier. Many airlines prohibit smoking on all of their international flights; others allow smoking only on certain routes or certain departures. Ask your carrier about its policy.

FLYING TIMES

Flying time to Phoenix or Tucson is 5½ hours from New York, 3½ hours from Chicago, 1¼ hours from Los Angeles, 11 hours from London, and 12 hours from Frankfurt.

HOW TO COMPLAIN

If your baggage goes astray or your flight goes awry, complain right away. Most carriers require that you **file a claim immediately.** The Aviation Consumer Protection Division of the Department of Transportation publishes *Fly-Rights,* which discusses airlines and consumer issues and is available on-line. You can also find articles and information on mytravelrights.com, the Web site of the nonprofit Consumer Travel Rights Center.

⚐ Airline Complaints Aviation Consumer Protection Division ⊠ U.S. Department of Transportation, C-75, Room 4107, 400 7th St. SW, Washington, DC 20590 ☎ 202/366-2220 ⊕ airconsumer.ost.dot.gov. **Federal Aviation Administration Consumer Hotline** ⊠ for inquiries: FAA, 800 Independence Ave. SW,

Washington, DC 20591 ☎ 800/322-7873 ⊕ www. faa.gov.

RECONFIRMING

Check the status of your flight before you leave for the airport. You can do this on your carrier's Web site, by linking to a flight-status checker (many Web booking services offer these), or by calling your carrier or travel agent.

AIRPORTS

Major gateways to Arizona include **Phoenix Sky Harbor International,** about 3 mi east of Phoenix city center, and **Tucson International Air Terminal,** about 8½ mi south of the central business area.

Phoenix Sky Harbor International Airport (PHX) is one of the busiest airports in the United States, but it rarely gives way to congestion or lengthy lines, and its spacious, modern terminals are easily navigable. Sky Harbor's three passenger terminals are connected by inter-terminal buses, which run regularly throughout the day. Tucson International Airport (TUS) has one terminal, and although it services far fewer passengers per day than Sky Harbor, it does offer nonstop flights to major metropolitan areas around the country.
⚐ Major Airports Phoenix Sky Harbor International ⊠ 3400 Sky Harbor Blvd., 24th and Buckeye Sts., off I-10, Exit 149 ☎ 602/273-3300 ⊕ www. phxskyharbor.com. **Tucson International Airport** ⊠ 7250 S. Tucson Blvd., at Valencia Rd. between 1-10 and I-19 ☎ 520/573-8000 ⊕ www. tucsonairport.org.

BIKE TRAVEL

⇨ *See also* the Bicycling sections under Outdoor Activities and Sports *in individual chapters.*

BIKES IN FLIGHT

Most airlines accommodate bikes as luggage, provided they are dismantled and boxed; check with individual airlines about packing requirements. Some airlines sell bike boxes, which are often free at bike shops, for about $15 (bike bags can be considerably more expensive). International travelers often can substitute a bike for a piece of checked luggage at no charge; otherwise, the cost is about $100. U.S. and Canadian airlines charge $40–$80 each way.

BUS TRAVEL

Greyhound serves many Arizona destinations from most parts of the United States but does not serve any destinations on the Navajo and Hopi reservations in northeastern Arizona.

Greyhound Lines ☎ 800/231-2222 ⊕ www.greyhound.com.

BUSINESS HOURS

MUSEUMS & SIGHTS

Most museums in Arizona's larger cities are open daily. A few are closed on Monday, and hours may vary between May and September (off-season in the major tourist centers of Phoenix and Tucson). Call ahead when planning a visit to lesser-known museums or attractions, whose hours may vary considerably. Major attractions are open daily.

SHOPS

Most retail stores are open 10 AM to 6 PM, although stores in malls tend to stay open until 9 PM. Those in the less-populated areas are likely to have shorter hours and may be closed on Sunday. Shopping centers, especially in larger cities, are also often open Sunday from noon to 5 or later.

CAMERAS & PHOTOGRAPHY

The wide-open vistas, bright sky, dramatic canyons, and desert expanses make for great pictures but call for a few extra considerations for the photographer. Even if you are keeping your equipment list minimal, consider bringing a wide-angle lens, good for capturing panoramas, and a polarizing filter, which reduces glare. When hiking, especially if your trip traverses the desert or rivers, consider bringing an older, less-valuable camera. In any case, it is a good idea to carry extra plastic bags, in case of an unexpected desert wind or rainstorm, and lens cloths, for dust. Because the light in Arizona tends to be bright, and dramatic contrasts in light and shade can over- or under-expose the entire picture, try to base the light reading on a more neutrally lit area in the picture.

The *Kodak Guide to Shooting Great Travel Pictures* (available at bookstores everywhere) is loaded with tips.

Photo Help **Kodak Information Center** ☎ 800/242-2424 ⊕ www.kodak.com.

EQUIPMENT PRECAUTIONS

Don't pack film and equipment in checked luggage, where it is much more susceptible to damage. X-ray machines used to view checked luggage are extremely powerful and therefore are likely to ruin your film. Try to **ask for hand inspection of film,** which becomes clouded after repeated exposure to airport X-ray machines, and **keep videotapes and computer disks away from metal detectors.** Always **keep film, tape, and computer disks out of the sun.** Carry an extra supply of batteries, and **be prepared to turn on your camera, camcorder, or laptop** to prove to airport security personnel that the device is real.

CAR RENTAL

Rates in Phoenix begin at $25 a day and $165 a week for an economy car with air-conditioning, an automatic transmission, and unlimited mileage. This does not include tax on car rentals, which can range anywhere from 10.10% to 18.10%, depending on pickup location. Rates in Phoenix may be higher during the winter months, which is considered the high tourist season. Check the Internet or local papers for discounts and deals, as they can significantly lower rental rates. Local rental agencies may also offer lower rates.

Major Agencies **Alamo** ☎ 800/327-9633 ⊕ www.alamo.com. **Avis** ☎ 800/331-1212, 800/879-2847 or 800/272-5871 in Canada, 0870/606-0100 in U.K., 02/9353-9000 in Australia, 09/526-2847 in New Zealand ⊕ www.avis.com. **Budget** ☎ 800/527-0700, 0870/156-5656 in the U.K. ⊕ www.budget.com. **Dollar** ☎ 800/800-4000; 0124/622-0111 in U.K., where it's affiliated with Sixt; 02/9223-1444 in Australia ⊕ www.dollar.com. **Hertz** ☎ 800/654-3131, 800/263-0600 in Canada, 0870/844-8844 in U.K., 02/9669-2444 in Australia, 09/256-8690 in New Zealand ⊕ www.hertz.com. **National Car Rental** ☎ 800/227-7368, 0870/600-6666 in U.K. ⊕ www.nationalcar.com.

CUTTING COSTS

For a good deal, **book through a travel agent who will shop around.** Also, **price local car-rental companies**—whose prices may be lower still, although their service and maintenance may not be as good as those of major rental agencies—and **research rates on the Internet.** Remember to ask about required deposits, cancellation penalties, and drop-off charges if you're planning to pick up the car in one city and leave it in another. If you're traveling during a holiday period, also make sure that a confirmed reservation guarantees you a car.

INSURANCE

When driving a rented car you are generally responsible for any damage to or loss of the vehicle. You also may be liable for any property damage or personal injury that you may cause while driving. Before you rent, see what coverage you already have under the terms of your personal auto-insurance policy and credit cards.

For about $9 to $25 a day, rental companies sell protection, known as a collision- or loss-damage waiver (CDW or LDW), that eliminates your liability for damage to the car; it's always optional and should never be automatically added to your bill. In Arizona the car-rental agency's insurance is primary; therefore, the company must pay for damage to third parties up to a preset legal limit, beyond which your own liability insurance kicks in. However, **make sure you have enough coverage to pay for the car.** If you do not have auto insurance or an umbrella policy that covers damage to third parties, purchasing liability insurance and a CDW or LDW is highly recommended.

REQUIREMENTS & RESTRICTIONS

In Arizona most agencies won't rent to you if you're under the age of 21, and several major agencies will not rent to anyone under 25.

SURCHARGES

Before you pick up a car in one city and leave it in another, **ask about drop-off charges or one-way service fees,** which can be substantial. Note, too, that some rental agencies charge extra if you return the car before the time specified in your contract. To avoid a hefty refueling fee, **fill the tank just before you turn in the car,** but be aware that gas stations near the rental outlet may overcharge. It's almost never a deal to buy the tank of gas that's in the car when you rent it; the understanding is that you'll return it empty, but some fuel usually remains. Surcharges may apply if you're under 25 or if you take the car outside the area approved by the rental agency. You'll pay extra for child seats (about $6 a day), which are compulsory

for children under five, and usually for additional drivers (about $10 per day).

CAR TRAVEL

EMERGENCY SERVICES

Dial 911 to report accidents on the road and to reach police, the Arizona Department of Public Safety (Highway Patrol), or fire department. There are no highway safety boxes or emergency phones on Arizona interstates or highways; call the highway patrol for help in any non-emergency situation.

🚗 **Arizona Department of Public Safety** ☎ 602/223–2000; 602/223–2163 Highway Patrol.

ROAD CONDITIONS

The highways in Arizona are well maintained, but there are some natural conditions you should beware of.

DESERT HEAT. Vehicles and passengers should be well equipped for searing summer heat in the low desert. If you're planning to drive through the desert, make sure you are well stocked with radiator coolant, and **carry plenty of water, a good spare tire, a jack, and emergency supplies.** If you get stranded, stay with your vehicle and wait for help to arrive.

DUST STORMS. These usually occur from May to mid-September, just before thunderstorms hit, causing extremely low visibility. Dust storms are more common on the highways and interstates that traverse the open desert (I–10 between Phoenix and Tucson, I–10 between Benson and the New Mexico state line, and I–8 between Casa Grande and Yuma). If you're on the highway, **pull as far off the road as possible, turn off your headlights to avoid being hit, and wait for the storm to subside.**

FLASH FLOODS. Warnings about flash floods should not be taken lightly. Sudden downpours send torrents of water racing into low-lying areas so dry that they are unable to absorb such a huge quantity of water quickly. The result can be powerful walls of water suddenly descending upon these low-lying areas, devastating anything in their paths. If you see rain clouds or thunderstorms in the area, stay away from dry riverbeds (also called arroyos or washes). If you find yourself in one, get out quickly. If you're with a car in a long gully, leave your car and climb out of the gully. You simply won't be able to outdrive a speeding wave. The idea is to **get to higher ground immediately when it rains.** Major highways are mostly flood-proof, but some smaller roads dip through washes; most roads that traverse through these low-lying areas will have flood warning signs, which should be seriously heeded during rainstorms. Washes filled with water should not be crossed until you can see the bottom. By all means, don't camp in these areas at any time, interesting as they may seem.

FRAGILE DESERT LIFE. The dry and easily desecrated desert floor takes centuries to overcome human damage. Consequently, it is illegal for four-wheel-drive and all-terrain vehicles and motorcycles to travel off established roadways.

🗐 Road Conditions **Arizona Department of Transportation** ☎ 511 Arizona road information from within Arizona; 888/411-7623 Arizona road information from outside the state ⊕ www.azfms.com.

RULES OF THE ROAD

During the past few years speed limits have been raised, and many stretches now permit drivers to travel at 75 mph. In the cities, freeway limits are between 55 mph and 65 mph. Seat belts are required at all times. Tickets can be given for failing to comply. Driving with a blood-alcohol level higher than 0.08 will result in arrest and seizure of your driver's license. Fines are severe.

At some point you will probably pass through one or more of the state's 23 Indian reservations. Roads and other areas within reservation boundaries are under the jurisdiction of reservation police and governed by separate rules and regulations. **Observe all signs and respect Native Americans' privacy.** Be careful not to hit any animals, which often wander onto the roads; the penalties can be very high.

Always **strap children under age 5 into approved child-safety seats.** In Arizona, children must wear seat belts regardless of where they're seated. In Arizona, you may turn right at a red light after stopping if there is no oncoming traffic. When in doubt, wait for the green.

CHILDREN IN ARIZONA

Many large resorts and dude ranches have special half-day or daylong activities for children, and many offer baby-sitting services. Children of all ages are enthralled by the Wild West flavor around Tucson and the southeastern part of the state, with Tombstone ranking as a particular favorite. If you're driving on long desert stretches, take along plenty of games and snacks.

If you are renting a car, don't forget to **arrange for a car seat** when you reserve. For general advice about traveling with children, consult *Fodor's FYI: Travel with Your Baby* (available in bookstores everywhere).

🗐 The monthly magazine *Raising Arizona Kids* focuses on Phoenix happenings but also includes a calendar of children-friendly events around the state. You can buy single copies for $3.95 each at chains like Borders, Barnes & Noble, and B. Dalton; at local bookshops; and at area retail and grocery stores in Phoenix and surrounding areas, or send $19.95 for a year's subscription. ⊠ 4545 E. Shea Blvd., Suite 168, Phoenix 85028 ☎ 602/953-5437 🖷 602/953-3305 ⊕ www.raisingarizonakids.com.

FLYING

If your children are two or older, **ask about children's airfares.** As a general rule, infants under two not occupying a seat fly at greatly reduced fares or even for free. But if you want to guarantee a seat for an infant, you have to pay full fare. Consider flying during off-peak days and times; most airlines will grant an infant a seat without a ticket if there are available seats.

Experts agree that it's a good idea to use safety seats aloft for children weighing less than 40 pounds. Airlines set their own policies: if you use a safety seat, U.S. carriers usually require that the child be ticketed, even if he or she is young enough to ride free, because the seats must be strapped into regular seats. And even if you pay the full adult fare for the seat, it may be worth it, especially on longer trips. Do **check your airline's policy about using safety seats during takeoff and landing.** Safety seats are not allowed everywhere in the plane, so get your seat assignments as early as possible.

When reserving, **request children's meals or a freestanding bassinet** (not available at all airlines) if you need them. But note that bulkhead seats, where you must sit to use the bassinet, may lack an overhead bin or storage space on the floor.

WHERE TO STAY

Most hotels in Arizona allow children under a certain age to stay in their parents' room at no extra charge, but others charge for them as extra adults; be sure to **find out the cutoff age for children's discounts.**

All **Holiday Inns** allow children under age 19 to stay free when sharing a room with an adult. The **Westin La Paloma Hotel** in Tucson has supervised activities year-round for children ages 6 months to 12 years, as well as junior tennis camps for children 5 to 14 years old in summer. The **Tanque Verde Guest Ranch,** also in Tucson, offers year-round activities for children 4 to 11, which include horseback riding, tennis, fishing, swimming, and arts and crafts. In the Phoenix area, the **Pointe Hilton Resort at Squaw Peak** runs its Southwestern-themed Coyote Camp for children ages 4 to 12 year-round. The Funicians Kids Club at the **Phoenician Resort** in Scottsdale offers activities for children 5 to 12 throughout the year; Scottsdale's **Hyatt Regency** also offers a full range of supervised daytime activities (with an emphasis on Native American crafts and stories) through its Camp Hyatt program, geared for children 3 to 12. Most of the above resorts also have baby-sitting services or can direct you to a trusted local agency.

🏠 Best Choices **Holiday Inn** ☎ 800/465-4329 ⊕ www.ichotelsgroup.com. **Hyatt Regency** ☎ 480/ 991-3388 or 800/233-1234 ⊕ www.hyatt.com. **Phoenician Resort** ☎ 800/888-8234 ⊕ www. thephoenician.com. **Pointe Hilton Resort at Squaw Peak** ☎ 602/997-2626 or 800/947-9784 ⊕ www. pointehilton.com. **Tanque Verde Ranch** ☎ 800/ 234-3833 ⊕ www.tanqueverderanch.com. **Westin La Paloma Hotel** ☎ 520/742-6000 or 800/228-3000 ⊕ www.westin.com.

SIGHTS & ATTRACTIONS

Places that are especially appealing to children are indicated by a rubber-duckie icon (🦆) in the margin.

CONSUMER PROTECTION

Whether you're shopping for gifts or purchasing travel services, **pay with a major credit card** whenever possible, so you can cancel payment or get reimbursed if there's a problem (and you can provide documentation). If you're doing business with a particular company for the first time, **contact your local Better Business Bureau and the attorney general's offices** in your state

and (for U.S. businesses) the company's home state as well. Have any complaints been filed? Finally, if you're buying a package or tour, always **consider travel insurance** that includes default coverage (⇨ Insurance).

🏠 **Council of Better Business Bureaus** ⊠ 4200 Wilson Blvd., Suite 800, Arlington, VA 22203 ☎ 703/ 276-0100 🖷 703/525-8277 ⊕ www.bbb.org.

CUSTOMS & DUTIES

IN AUSTRALIA

Australian residents who are 18 or older may bring home A$400 worth of souvenirs and gifts (including jewelry), 250 cigarettes or 250 grams of cigars or other tobacco products, and 1,125 ml of alcohol (including wine, beer, and spirits). Residents under 18 may bring back A$200 worth of goods. Members of the same family traveling together may pool their allowances. Prohibited items include meat products. Seeds, plants, and fruits need to be declared upon arrival.

🏠 **Australian Customs Service** ⊘ Regional Director, Box 8, Sydney, NSW 2001 ☎ 02/9213-2000 or 1300/363263, 02/9364-7222 or 1800/803-006 quarantine-inquiry line 🖷 02/9213-4043 ⊕ www. customs.gov.au.

IN CANADA

Canadian residents who have been out of Canada for at least seven days may bring in C$750 worth of goods duty-free. If you've been away fewer than seven days but more than 48 hours, the duty-free allowance drops to C$200. If your trip lasts 24 to 48 hours, the allowance is C$50. You may not pool allowances with family members. Goods claimed under the C$750 exemption may follow you by mail; those claimed under the lesser exemptions must accompany you. Alcohol and tobacco products may be included in the seven-day and 48-hour exemptions but not in the 24-hour exemption. If you meet the age requirements of the province or territory through which you reenter Canada, you may bring in, duty-free, 1.5 liters of wine *or* 1.14 liters (40 imperial ounces) of liquor *or* 24 12-ounce cans or bottles of beer or ale. Also, if you meet the local age requirement for tobacco products, you may bring in, duty-free, 200 cigarettes and 50 cigars. Check ahead of time with the Canada Customs and Revenue Agency or the Department of Agriculture for policies regarding meat products, seeds, plants, and fruits.

You may send an unlimited number of gifts (only one gift per recipient, however) worth up to C$60 each duty-free to Canada. Label the package UNSOLICITED GIFT—VALUE UNDER $60. Alcohol and tobacco are excluded.

Canada Customs and Revenue Agency ⊠ 2265 St. Laurent Blvd., Ottawa, Ontario KIG 4K3 ☎ 800/461-9999, 204/983-3500, 506/636-5064 ⊕ www.ccra.gc.ca.

IN NEW ZEALAND

All homeward-bound residents may bring back NZ$700 worth of souvenirs and gifts; passengers may not pool their allowances, and children can claim only the concession on goods intended for their own use. For those 17 or older, the duty-free allowance also includes 4.5 liters of wine or beer; one 1,125-ml bottle of spirits; and either 200 cigarettes, 250 grams of tobacco, 50 cigars, *or* a combination of the three up to 250 grams. Meat products, seeds, plants, and fruits must be declared upon arrival to the Agricultural Services Department.

New Zealand Customs ⊠ Head office: The Customhouse, 17–21 Whitmore St. ☐ Box 2218, Wellington ☎ 09/300–5399 or 0800/428–786 ⊕ www.customs.govt.nz.

IN THE U.K.

From countries outside the European Union, including the United States, you may bring home, duty-free, 200 cigarettes or 50 cigars; 1 liter of spirits or 2 liters of fortified or sparkling wine or liqueurs; 2 liters of still table wine; 60 ml of perfume; 250 ml of toilet water; plus £145 worth of other goods, including gifts and souvenirs. Prohibited items include meat products, seeds, plants, and fruits.

HM Customs and Excise ⊠ Portcullis House, 21 Cowbridge Rd. E, Cardiff CF11 9SS ☎ 0845/010–9000 or 0208/929–0152, 0208/929–6731 or 0208/910–3602 complaints ⊕ www.hmce.gov.uk.

IN THE U.S.

U.S. residents who have been out of the country for at least 48 hours may bring home, for personal use, $800 worth of foreign goods duty-free, as long as they haven't used the $800 allowance or any part of it in the past 30 days. This exemption may include 1 liter of alcohol (for travelers 21 and older), 200 cigarettes, and 100 non-Cuban cigars. Family members from the same household who are traveling together may pool their $800 personal exemptions. For fewer than 48 hours, the duty-free allowance drops to $200, which may include 50 cigarettes, 10 non-Cuban cigars, and 150 ml of alcohol (or 150 ml of perfume containing alcohol). The $200 allowance cannot be combined with other individuals' exemptions, and if you exceed it, the full value of all the goods will be taxed. Antiques, which the U.S. Bureau of Customs and Border Protection defines as objects more than 100 years old, enter duty-free, as do original works of art done entirely by hand, including paintings, drawings, and sculptures. This doesn't apply to folk art or handicrafts, which are in general dutiable.

You may also send packages home duty-free, with a limit of one parcel per addressee per day (except alcohol or tobacco products or perfume worth more than $5). You can mail up to $200 worth of goods for personal use; label the package PERSONAL USE and attach a list of its contents and their retail value. If the package contains your used personal belongings, mark it AMERICAN GOODS RETURNED to avoid paying duties. You may send up to $100 worth of goods as a gift; mark the package UNSOLICITED GIFT. Mailed items do not affect your duty-free allowance on your return.

To avoid paying duty on foreign-made high-ticket items you already own and will take on your trip, register them with Customs before you leave the country. Consider filing a Certificate of Registration for laptops, cameras, watches, and other digital devices identified with serial numbers or other permanent markings; you can keep the certificate for other trips. Otherwise, bring a sales receipt or insurance form to show that you owned the item before you left the United States.

U.S. Bureau of Customs and Border Protection ⊠ for inquiries and equipment registration, 1300 Pennsylvania Ave. NW, Washington, DC 20229 ⊕ www.customs.gov ☎ 877/287–8667 or 202/354–1000 ⊠ for complaints, Customer Satisfaction Unit, 1300 Pennsylvania Ave. NW, Room 5.5D, Washington, DC 20229.

DISABILITIES & ACCESSIBILITY

Local Resources **Arizona Office for Americans with Disabilities** ⊠ 100 N. 15th Ave., Suite 170, Phoenix 85007 ☎ 602/542-6276 or 800/358-3617, 602/542-6686 TTY ⊕ www.know-the-ada.com. **Sun Sound Reading Service** ☎ 602/231-0500 in Phoenix, 520/296-2400 in Tucson, 928/779-1775 in Flagstaff.

WHERE TO STAY

Despite the Americans with Disabilities Act, the definition of accessibility seems to differ from hotel to hotel. Some properties may be accessible by ADA standards for people with mobility problems but not for people with hearing or vision impairments, for example.

If you have mobility problems, ask for the lowest floor on which accessible services are offered. If you have a hearing impairment, check whether the hotel has devices to alert you visually to the ring of the telephone, a knock at the door, and a fire/emergency alarm. Some hotels provide these devices without charge. Discuss your needs with hotel personnel if this equipment isn't available, so that a staff member can personally alert you in the event of an emergency.

If you're bringing a guide dog, get authorization ahead of time and write down the name of the person with whom you spoke.

RESERVATIONS

When discussing accessibility with an operator or reservations agent, **ask hard questions.** Are there any stairs, inside *or* out? Are there grab bars next to the toilet *and* in the shower/tub? How wide is the doorway to the room? To the bathroom? For the most extensive facilities meeting the latest legal specifications, **opt for newer accommodations.** If you reserve through a toll-free number, consider also calling the hotel's local number to confirm the information from the central reservations office. Get confirmation in writing when you can.

SIGHTS & ATTRACTIONS

Many of the well-visited museums, attractions, and parks in Arizona are ADA-accessible. Grand Canyon National Park accepts the Golden Access Passport, which allows a traveler with a disability into the park free of charge; wide walkways that are wheelchair-accessible skirt several stretches of the canyon. The Petrified Forest, which stands on an open plain, can be viewed quite well from a vehicle. Kartchner Caverns offer easy access to the main areas. Larger cities in Arizona offer plenty of accessible parking.

TRANSPORTATION

Amtrak advises that you request redcap service, special seats, or wheelchair assistance when you make reservations. Also note that not all stations are equipped to provide these services. All passengers with disabilities are entitled to a 15% discount on the lowest available fare, and there are special fares for children with disabilities as well. Contact Amtrak for a free brochure that outlines services for older travelers and people with disabilities. Greyhound bus lines, which provides service to many destinations in Arizona, will assist persons with disabilities throughout their trip, with advance notice; in the case of certain disabilities, Greyhound will carry a person with disabilities and a companion for the price of a single fare. For those wishing to rent a car, Avis, Hertz, and National can provide cars with hand controls in some destinations with advance notice; call ahead to confirm that you can be accommodated at your destination.

Amtrak ⌖ National Railroad Passenger Corp., 60 Massachusetts Ave. NE, Washington, DC 20002 ☎ 800/872-7245 ⊕ www.amtrak.com. **Avis** ☎ 800/331-1212 ⊕ www.avis.com. **Greyhound** ☎ 800/229-9424, 800/752-4841 to request assistance, 800/345-3109 TTY ⊕ www.greyhound.com. **Hertz** ☎ 800/654-3131 ⊕ www.hertz.com. **National** ☎ 800/328-4567 ⊕ www.nationalcar.com.

Complaints **Aviation Consumer Protection Division** (⇨ Air Travel) for airline-related problems. **Departmental Office of Civil Rights** ⊠ for general inquiries, U.S. Department of Transportation, S-30, 400 7th St. SW, Room 10215, Washington, DC 20590 ☎ 202/366-4648 ⎙ 202/366-9371 ⊕ www.dot.gov/ost/docr/index.htm. **Disability Rights Section** ⊠ NYAV, U.S. Department of Justice, Civil Rights Division, 950 Pennsylvania Ave. NW, Washington, DC 20530 ☎ ADA information line 202/514-0301, 800/514-0301, 202/514-0383 TTY, 800/514-0383 TTY ⊕ www.ada.gov. **U.S. Department of Transportation Hotline** ☎ for disability-related air-travel problems, 800/778-4838 or 800/455-9880 TTY.

TRAVEL AGENCIES

In the United States, the Americans with Disabilities Act requires that travel firms serve the needs of all travelers. Some agencies specialize in working with people with disabilities.

Travelers with Mobility Problems Access Adventures/B. Roberts Travel ✉ 206 Chestnut Ridge Rd., Scottsville, NY 14624 ☎ 585/889-9096 ⊕ www.brobertstravel.com ✑ dltravel@prodigy. net; run by a former physical-rehabilitation counselor. **Accessible Vans of America** ✉ 9 Spielman Rd., Fairfield, NJ 07004 ☎ 877/282-8267, 888/282-8267, 973/808-9709 reservations ⌕ 973/808-9713 ⊕ www.accessiblevans.com. **CareVacations** ✉ No. 5, 5110-50 Ave., Leduc, Alberta, Canada T9E 6V4 ☎ 780/986-6404 or 877/478-7827 ⌕ 780/986-8332 ⊕ www.carevacations.com, for group tours and cruise vacations. **Flying Wheels Travel** ✉ 143 W. Bridge St. ✑ Box 382, Owatonna, MN 55060 ☎ 507/451-5005 ⌕ 507/451-1685 ⊕ www. flyingwheelstravel.com.

DISCOUNTS & DEALS

Be a smart shopper and **compare all your options** before making decisions. A plane ticket bought with a promotional coupon from travel clubs, coupon books, and direct-mail offers or purchased on the Internet may not be cheaper than the least expensive fare from a discount ticket agency. And always keep in mind that what you get is just as important as what you save.

DISCOUNT RESERVATIONS

To save money, **look into discount reservations services** with Web sites and toll-free numbers, which use their buying power to get a better price on hotels, airline tickets (⇨ Air Travel), even car rentals. When booking a room, always **call the hotel's local toll-free number** (if one is available) rather than the central reservations number—you'll often get a better price. Always ask about special packages or corporate rates.

Airline Tickets Air 4 Less ☎ 800/AIR4LESS; low-fare specialist.

Hotel Rooms Accommodations Express ☎ 800/444-7666 or 800/277-1064 ⊕ www. accommodationsexpress.com. **Hotels.com** ☎ 214/369-1246 or 800/246-8357 ⊕ www.hotels.com. **Quikbook** ☎ 800/789-9887 ⊕ www.quikbook. com. **RMC Travel** ☎ 800/245-5738 ⊕ www. rmcwebtravel.com. **Turbotrip.com** ☎ 800/473-7829 ⊕ www.turbotrip.com.

PACKAGE DEALS

Don't confuse packages and guided tours. When you buy a package, you travel on your own, just as though you had planned the trip yourself. Fly/drive packages, which combine airfare and car rental, are often a good deal. In cities, ask the local visitor's bureau about hotel packages that include tickets to major museum exhibits or other special events.

ECOTOURISM

Arizona has some of the best-preserved prehistoric sites in the world. Both federal and state laws prohibit removal or destruction of artifacts from such sites. In Arizona, it is illegal to uproot or in any way harm a saguaro, and penalties are stiff. Whatever your activity, it is a good idea to tread lightly in natural settings. Remember to extinguish campfires and return the soil to its natural condition by mixing the ashes with dirt and water and covering the site with dirt.

EATING & DRINKING

The restaurants we list are the cream of the crop in each price category. Properties indicated by an ✕▣ are lodging establishments whose restaurant warrants a special trip. Unless otherwise noted, the restaurants listed in this guide are open daily for lunch and dinner.

PRICES

CATEGORY	COST
$$$$	over $30
$$$	$20-$30
$$	$12-$20
$	$8-$12
¢	under $8

Prices are per person for a main course at dinner.

RESERVATIONS & DRESS

Reservations are always a good idea; we mention them only when they're essential or not accepted. Book as far ahead as you can, and reconfirm as soon as you arrive. (Large parties should always call ahead to check the reservations policy.) We mention dress only when men are required to wear a jacket or a jacket and tie.

SPECIALTIES

Two distinct cultures—Native American and Sonoran—have had the greatest influence on native Arizona cuisine. Chilies, beans, corn, tortillas, and squash are common ingredients for those restaurants that specialize in regional cuisine (cactus is just as tasty but less common). Mom-and-pop *taquerias* are abundant, especially in the southern part of the state.

WINE, BEER & SPIRITS

Although Arizona is not typically associated with viticulture, the region southeast of Tucson, stretching to the Mexico border, has several microclimates ideal for wine growing. The iron- and calcium-rich soil is similar to that of the Burgundy region in France and, when combined with the temperate weather and lower-key atmosphere, has enticed several independent and family-run wineries to open in the past several years. You can easily spend an afternoon touring some of the wineries in the Elgin, Sonoita, and Nogales areas, which are only minutes apart, or you can do a larger loop to include some of the wineries farther east. Most wineries are open daily and have tastings between 10 AM and 5 PM.

In Arizona, you must be 21 to buy any alcohol. Liquor stores are open daily, including Sunday, but must stop selling alcohol at 1 AM; bars also stop serving alcohol at this time. You will find beer, wine, and alcohol at most supermarkets. Possession and consumption of alcoholic beverages is illegal on Indian reservations.

Arizona Wine Growers Association Box 181, Vail 85641 www.arizonawine.org. **Callaghan Vineyards** 336 Elgin Rd., Elgin 85611 520/455-5322 www.callaghanvineyards.com. **Sonoita Vineyards** Elgin Cavelo Rd. Box 33, Elgin 85611 520/455-5893 www.sonoitavineyards.com. **The Village of Elgin Winery** 471 Elgin Rd., Elgin 85611 520/455-9309 www.elginwines.com.

E-MAIL

Checking your e-mail or surfing the Web can sometimes be done in the business centers of major hotels, which usually charge an hourly rate. Web access is also available at many fax and copy centers, many of which are open 24 hours and on weekends. In major cities look for cyber-cafés, where tabletop computers allow you to log on while sipping coffee or listening to live jazz. Whether you have e-mail at home or not, you can **arrange to have a free e-mail address** from several

services, including one available at www.yahoo.com (the site explains how to apply for an address).

GAY & LESBIAN TRAVEL

Arizona is a socially conservative state, but Phoenix has a large gay and lesbian population—one of the nation's largest—and Tucson has a visible gay scene as well. There are also quite a few gay men and lesbians in Bisbee, Sedona, and Flagstaff. Although there are no statewide gay- and lesbian-oriented organizations in Arizona, the agencies listed below can help plan gay-friendly vacations. Information on gay establishments in specific cities can be found easily on the Internet. A good place to start is www.visitgayarizona.com, the official Arizona Travel and Tourism Web site for gay and lesbian travelers. For details about the gay and lesbian scene in Bisbee, Flagstaff, Phoenix, Sedona, and Tucson, consult *Fodor's Gay Guide to the USA* (available in bookstores everywhere).

Gay- & Lesbian-Friendly Travel Agencies Different Roads Travel 8383 Wilshire Blvd., Suite 520, Beverly Hills, CA 90211 323/651-5557 or 800/429-8747 (Ext. 14 for both) 323/651-3678 lgernert@tzell.com. **Kennedy Travel** 130 W. 42nd St., Suite 401, New York, NY 10036 212/840-8659, 800/237-7433 212/730-2269 www.kennedytravel.com. **Now, Voyager** 4406 18th St., San Francisco, CA 94114 415/626-1169 or 800/255-6951 415/626-8626 www.nowvoyager.com. **Skylink Travel and Tour** 1455 N. Dutton Ave., Suite A, Santa Rosa, CA 95401 707/546-9888 or 800/225-5759 707/636-0951; serving lesbian travelers.

Local Publications *Echo* 602/266-0550 is a gay and lesbian news and entertainment magazine published biweekly that covers events throughout the state and is distributed all over Arizona. *Heat-Stroke News* 602/264-3646 is a Phoenix-based biweekly. The weekly *Observer* 520/622-7176 covers the Tucson and Phoenix area.

GUIDEBOOKS

Plan well and you won't be sorry. Guidebooks are excellent tools—and you can take them with you. You may want to check out color-photo-illustrated *Compass American Guide: Arizona,* thorough on culture and history, or *Fodor's Road Guide USA: Arizona, Colorado, New Mexico,* for comprehensive restaurant, hotel, and attractions listings for driving vacations. Both are available at on-line re-tailers and bookstores everywhere.

A useful option for touring northern Arizona is the series of Walkabout Audio Tours, which has been produced and marketed by an anthropologist and former teacher in Sedona. The driving and walking tours cover popular historic and natural areas in northern and north-central Arizona, including several tours of the Grand Canyon, the Sedona area, and other interesting places. They can be purchased directly from the company and are also sold in some bookstores and gift shops in Sedona and the region. CDs are $16, cassettes $9, or you can purchase a package of three tours at a discount.
🔲 **Walkabout Audio Tours** 🖅 Box 20436, Sedona, AZ 86341 ☎ 877/530-1030 🌐 www.walkaboutaudiotours.com

HIKING

Be sure to take the following precautions when you go for a hike of any length.

ANIMAL BITES

Wherever you're hiking, particularly between April and October, **keep a lookout for rattlesnakes.** You're likely not to have any problems if you maintain distance from snakes that you see—they can strike only half of their length, so a 6-ft clearance should allow you to stay unharmed, especially if you **don't provoke them.** If you are bitten by a rattler, don't panic. Just get to a hospital within two to three hours of the bite. Try to keep the bite below heart level, and stay calm, as increased heart rate can spread venom more quickly. Keep in mind that 30% to 40% of bites are dry bites, where the snake uses no venom (still, get thee to a hospital). **Avoid night hikes without rangers,** when snakes are on the prowl and less visible.

Scorpions and Gila monsters are really less of a concern, since they strike only when provoked. To avoid scorpion encounters, **don't put your hands where you can't see with your eyes,** such as under rocks and in holes. Likewise, if you move a rock to sit down, make sure that scorpions haven't been exposed. Campers should shake out shoes in the morning, since scorpions like warm, moist places. If you are bitten, see a ranger about symptoms that may develop. Chances are good that you won't need to go to a hospital. Children are a different

case, however: scorpion stings can be fatal for them. Always try to keep an eye on what they may be getting their hands into to avoid the scorpion's sting. Gila monsters are relatively rare and bites are even rarer, but bear in mind that the reptiles are most active between April and June, when they do most of their hunting. Should a member of your party be bitten, it is most important to release the Gila monster's jaws as soon as possible to minimize the amount of venom released. This can usually be achieved with a stick, an open flame, or immersion of the animal in water.

DEHYDRATION

This underestimated danger can be very serious, especially considering that one of the first major symptoms is the inability to swallow. It may be the easiest hazard to avoid, however; simply **drink every 10–15 minutes,** up to a gallon of water per day in summer.

HYPOTHERMIA

Temperatures in Arizona can vary widely from day to night—as much as 40°F. Be sure to **bring enough warm clothing for hiking and camping, along with wet-weather gear.** It is always a good idea to pack an extra set of clothes in a large, waterproof plastic bag (a large resealable bag will do) that would stay dry in any situation. Exposure to the degree that body temperature dips below 95°F produces the following symptoms: chills, tiredness, then uncontrollable shivering and irrational behavior, with the victim not always recognizing that he or she is cold. If someone in your party is suffering from any of this, wrap him or her in blankets and/or a warm sleeping bag immediately and try to keep him or her awake. The fastest way to raise body temperature is through skin-to-skin contact in a sleeping bag. Drinking warm liquids also helps.

POTABLE WATER

Never drink from any stream, no matter how clear it may be. Giardia organisms can turn your stomach inside out. The easiest way to purify water is to **dissolve a water purification tablet** in it. Camping-equipment stores also carry purification pumps. **Boil water for 15 minutes,** a reliable method, though time- and fuel-consuming.

SUN PROTECTION

Wear a hat and sunglasses and put on sunblock to protect against the burning Arizona sun. And **watch out for heatstroke.** Symptoms include headache, dizziness, and fatigue, which can turn into convulsions and unconsciousness and can lead to death. If someone in your party develops any of these conditions, have one person seek emergency help while others move the victim into the shade and wrap him or her in wet clothing (is a stream nearby?) to cool him or her down.

HOLIDAYS

Major national holidays are New Year's Day (Jan. 1); Martin Luther King Day (3rd Mon. in Jan.); Presidents' Day (3rd Mon. in Feb.); Memorial Day (last Mon. in May); Independence Day (July 4); Labor Day (1st Mon. in Sept.); Columbus Day (2nd Mon. in Oct.); Thanksgiving Day (4th Thurs. in Nov.); Christmas Eve and Christmas Day (Dec. 24 and 25); and New Year's Eve (Dec. 31).

INSURANCE

The most useful travel-insurance plan is a comprehensive policy that includes coverage for trip cancellation and interruption, default, trip delay, and medical expenses (with a waiver for preexisting conditions).

Without insurance you'll lose all or most of your money if you cancel your trip, regardless of the reason. Default insurance covers you if your tour operator, airline, or cruise line goes out of business. Trip-delay covers expenses that arise because of bad weather or mechanical delays. Study the fine print when comparing policies.

U.K. residents can buy a travel-insurance policy valid for most vacations taken during the year in which it's purchased (but check preexisting-condition coverage).

Always **buy travel policies directly from the insurance company**; if you buy them from a cruise line, airline, or tour operator that goes out of business you probably won't be covered for the agency or operator's default, a major risk. Before making any purchase, **review your existing health and home-owner's policies** to find what they cover away from home.

🖪 Travel Insurers In the U.S.: **Access America** ✉ 6600 W. Broad St., Richmond, VA 23230 ☎ 800/284-8300 🖷 804/673-1491 or 800/346-9265

⊕ www.accessamerica.com. **Travel Guard International** ✉ 1145 Clark St., Stevens Point, WI 54481 ☎ 715/345-0505 or 800/826-1300 🖷 800/955-8785 ⊕ www.travelguard.com.

FOR INTERNATIONAL TRAVELERS

For information on customs restrictions, *see* Customs & Duties, *above.*

CAR RENTAL

When picking up a rental car, non-U.S. residents need a reservation voucher for any prepaid reservations that were made in the traveler's home country, a passport, a driver's license, and a travel policy that covers each driver.

CAR TRAVEL

Gas prices vary widely across Arizona, but stations are plentiful, and most stay open late (24 hours along large highways and in big cities), except in rural areas, where Sunday hours are limited and where you may drive long stretches without a refueling opportunity. Highways are well paved. Interstate highways—limited-access, multi-lane highways whose numbers are prefixed by "I–"—are the fastest routes. Interstates with three-digit numbers encircle urban areas, which may have other limited-access expressways, freeways, and parkways as well. Tolls may be levied on limited-access highways. So-called U.S. highways and state highways are not necessarily limited-access but may have several lanes.

Along larger highways, roadside stops with rest rooms, fast-food restaurants, and sundries stores are well spaced. State police and tow trucks patrol major highways and lend assistance. If your car breaks down on an interstate, pull onto the shoulder and wait for help, or have your passengers wait while you walk to an emergency phone (available in most states). If you carry a cell phone, dial *55, noting your location on the small green roadside mileage markers.

Driving in the United States is on the right. Do **obey speed limits** posted along roads and highways. Watch for lower limits in small towns and on back roads. Arizona requires front-seat passengers to wear seat belts. On weekdays between 6 and 10 AM and again between 4 and 7 PM **expect heavy traffic.** To encourage carpooling, some freeways have special lanes for so-called high-occupancy vehicles (HOV)—cars carrying more than one passenger.

Bookstores, gas stations, convenience stores, and rest stops sell maps (about $3) and multiregion road atlases (about $10).

CONSULATES & EMBASSIES

Australia **Australian Consulate General & Trade Commission** ✉ 2049 Century Park E, Level 19, Los Angeles, CA 90067 ☎ 310/229-4800 🖨 310/277-2258 or 310/277-3462 ⊕ www.austemb.org/consulates/losangeles.htm.

Canada **Canadian Consulate General** ✉ 550 South Hope St., 9th floor, Los Angeles, CA 90071 ☎ 213/346-2700 🖨 213/620-8827 ⊕ www.losangeles.gc.ca.

New Zealand **New Zealand Consulate General** ✉ 12400 Wilshire Blvd., Suite 1150, Los Angeles, CA 90025 ☎ 310/207-1605 🖨 310/207-3605 ⊕ www.nzemb.org.

United Kingdom **British Consulate General** ✉ 11766 Wilshire Blvd., Suite 1200, Los Angeles, CA 90025 ☎ 310/481-0031 🖨 310/481-2960 ⊕ www.britainusa.com/la.

CURRENCY

The dollar is the basic unit of U.S. currency. It has 100 cents. Coins are the copper penny (1¢); the silvery nickel (5¢), dime (10¢), quarter (25¢), and half-dollar (50¢); and the golden $1 coin, replacing a now-rare silver dollar. Bills are denominated $1, $5, $10, $20, $50, and $100, all green and identical in size; designs vary. In addition, you may come across a $2 bill, but the chances are slim. The exchange rate at this writing was US$1.60 per British pound, 71¢ per Canadian dollar, 64¢ per Australian dollar, and 57¢ per New Zealand dollar.

ELECTRICITY

The U.S. standard is AC, 110 volts/60 cycles. Plugs have two flat pins set parallel to each other.

EMERGENCIES

For police, fire, or ambulance, **dial 911** (0 in rural areas).

INSURANCE

Britons and Australians need extra medical coverage when traveling overseas.

Insurance Information In the U.K.: **Association of British Insurers** ✉ 51 Gresham St., London EC2V 7HQ ☎ 020/7600-3333 🖨 020/7696-8999 ⊕ www.abi.org.uk. In Australia: **Insurance Council of Australia** ✉ Insurance Enquiries and Complaints, Level 3, 56 Pitt St., Sydney, NSW 2000 ☎ 1300/363683 or 02/9251-4456 🖨 02/9251-4453 ⊕ www.iecltd.com.au. In Canada: **RBC Insurance** ✉ 6880 Financial Dr., Mississauga, Ontario L5N 7Y5 ☎ 800/565-3129 🖨 905/813-4704 ⊕ www.rbcinsurance.com. In New Zealand: **Insurance Council of New Zealand** ✉ Level 7, 111-115 Customhouse Quay 🗋 Box 474, Wellington ☎ 04/472-5230 🖨 04/473-3011 ⊕ www.icnz.org.nz.

MAIL & SHIPPING

You can buy stamps and aerograms and send letters and parcels in post offices. Stamp-dispensing machines can occasionally be found in airports, bus and train stations, office buildings, drugstores, and the like. You can also deposit mail in the stout, dark blue steel bins at strategic locations everywhere as long as the parcels are affixed with proper postage and weight less than one pound. Packages weighing more than one pound must be taken to a post office or handed to a postal carrier.

For mail sent within the United States, you need a 37¢ stamp for first-class letters weighing up to 1 ounce (23¢ for each additional ounce) and 23¢ for postcards. You pay 80¢ for 1-ounce airmail letters and 70¢ for airmail postcards to most other countries; to Canada and Mexico, you need a 60¢ stamp for a 1-ounce letter and 50¢ for a postcard. An aerogram—a single sheet of lightweight blue paper that folds into its own envelope, stamped for overseas airmail—costs 70¢.

To receive mail on the road, have it sent c/o General Delivery at your destination's main post office (use the correct five-digit ZIP code). You must pick up mail in person within 30 days and show a driver's license or passport.

PASSPORTS & VISAS

When traveling internationally, **carry your passport** even if you don't need one (it's always the best form of ID) and **make two photocopies of the data page** (one for someone at home and another for you, carried separately from your passport). If you lose your passport, promptly call the nearest embassy or consulate and the local police.

Visitor visas aren't necessary for Canadian or European Union citizens, or for citizens of Australia who are staying fewer than 90 days.

Australian Citizens Passports Australia ☎ 131-232 ⊕ www.passports.gov.au. **United States Consulate General** ⊠ MLC Centre, Level 59, 19–29 Martin Pl., Sydney, NSW 2000 ☎ 02/9373-9200, 1902/941-641 fee-based visa-inquiry line ⊕ usembassy-australia.state.gov/sydney.

Canadian Citizens Passport Office ⊠ to mail in applications: 200 Promenade du Portage, Hull, Québec J8X 4B7 ☎ 819/994-3500 or 800/567-6868, 866/255-7655 TTY ⊕ www.ppt.gc.ca.

New Zealand Citizens New Zealand Passports Office ⊠ for applications and information, Level 3, Boulcott House, 47 Boulcott St., Wellington ☎ 0800/22-5050 or 04/474-8100 ⊕ www.passports.govt.nz. **Embassy of the United States** ⊠ 29 Fitzherbert Terr., Thorndon, Wellington ☎ 04/462-6000 ⊕ usembassy.org.nz. **U.S. Consulate General** ⊠ Citibank Bldg., 3rd floor, 23 Customs St. E, Auckland ☎ 09/303-2724 ⊕ usembassy.org.nz.

U.K. Citizens U.K. Passport Service ☎ 0870/521-0410 ⊕ www.passport.gov.uk. **American Consulate General** ⊠ Queen's House, 14 Queen St., Belfast, Northern Ireland BT1 6EQ ☎ 028/9032-8239 ☐ 028/9024-8482 ⊕ www.usembassy.org.uk. **American Embassy** ⊠ for visa and immigration information (enclose an SASE), Consular Information Unit, 24 Grosvenor Sq., London W1 1AE ⊠ to submit an application via mail, Visa Branch, 5 Upper Grosvenor St., London W1A 2JB ☎ 09068/200-290 recorded visa information or 09055/444-546 operator service, both with per-minute charges, 0207/499-9000 main switchboard ⊕ www.usembassy.org.uk.

TELEPHONES

All U.S. telephone numbers consist of a three-digit area code and a seven-digit local number. Within many local calling areas, you dial only the seven-digit number. Within some area codes, you must dial "1" first for calls outside the local area. To call between area-code regions, dial "1" then all 10 digits; the same goes for calls to numbers prefixed by "800," "888," "877," and "866"—all toll free. For calls to numbers preceded by "900" you must pay—usually dearly.

For international calls, dial "011" followed by the country code and the local number. For help, dial "0" and ask for an overseas operator. The country code is 61 for Australia, 64 for New Zealand, 44 for the United Kingdom. Calling Canada is the same as calling within the United States. Most local phone books list country codes and U.S. area codes. The country code for the United States is 1.

For operator assistance, dial "0." To obtain someone's phone number, call directory assistance at 555–1212 or occasionally 411 (free at public phones). To have the person you're calling foot the bill, phone collect; dial "0" instead of "1" before the 10-digit number.

At pay phones, instructions often are posted. Usually you insert coins in a slot (usually 25¢–50¢ for local calls) and wait for a steady tone before dialing. When you call long-distance, the operator tells you how much to insert; prepaid phone cards, widely available in various denominations, are easier. Call the number on the back, punch in the card's personal identification number when prompted, then dial your number.

LODGING

Arizona's hotels and motels run the gamut—from world-class resorts to budget chains and from historic inns, bed-and-breakfasts, and mountain lodges to dude ranches, campgrounds, and RV parks. **Make reservations well in advance for the high season**—winter in the desert south and summer in the high country. Tremendous bargains can be found off-season, when even the most exclusive establishments cut their rates by half.

The lodgings we list are the cream of the crop in each price category. We always list the facilities that are available, but we don't specify whether they cost extra; when pricing accommodations, always ask what's included and what costs extra. Properties are assigned price categories based on the range from their least-expensive standard double room at high season (excluding holidays) to the most expensive. Properties marked ✕☐ are lodging establishments whose restaurants warrant a special trip.

Assume that hotels operate on the **European Plan** (EP, with no meals) unless we specify that they use the **Continental Plan** (CP, with a Continental breakfast), **Breakfast Plan** (BP, with a full breakfast), **Modified American Plan** (MAP, with breakfast and dinner), or the **Full American Plan** (FAP, with all meals).

PRICES

CATEGORY	COST
$$$$	over $250
$$$	$175–$250
$$	$120–$175
$	$70–$120
¢	under $70

Prices are for two people in a double room during high season.

BED & BREAKFASTS

The Arizona Association of Bed and Breakfast Inns has member inns in most of the popular destinations in the state. The Arizona Trails Reservation Service has an extensive list of bed-and-breakfast and private home rentals throughout the state and can also help with vacation packages, tours, and golf vacations. Intimate lodgings in Arizona boast a range of styles, from Southwestern adobe haciendas in areas like Sedona and Tucson to pine cabins in the White Mountains. The Arizona Office of Tourism (⇨ Visitor Information) has a statewide list of bed-and-breakfasts.

🖪 Reservation Services **Arizona Association of Bed and Breakfast Inns** ☎ Box 22086, Flagstaff 86002 ☎ 800/284-2589 ⊕ www.arizona-bed-breakfast.com. **Arizona Trails Bed & Breakfast Reservation Service** ☎ Box 18998, Fountain Hills 85269 ☎ 480/837-4284 or 888/799-4284 ⊕ www.arizonatrails.com. **Mi Casa Su Casa** ☎ Box 950, Tempe 85280 ☎ 480/990-0682 or 800/456-0682 🖷 480/990-3390 ⊕ www.azres.com.

CAMPING

You can choose from a feast of federal, state, Native American, and private campgrounds in virtually all parts of the state. Facilities range from deluxe parks with swimming pools and recreation rooms to primitive backcountry wilderness sites. Most campgrounds provide toilets, drinking water, showers, and hook-ups. Camping is also permitted in Arizona's seven national forests, but be forewarned that they often have no facilities whatsoever; in most cases, backcountry camping permits must be reserved in advance, especially for popular backcountry trails and destinations.

Pack according to season, region, and length of trip. Basics include a sleeping bag, a tent (optional, and forbidden in some RV parks), a camp stove, cooking utensils, food and water supplies, a first-aid kit, insect repellent, sunscreen, a lantern, trash bags, a rope, and a tarp. In case you forget something, almost every camping item is available for sale or rent at one of Arizona's many sporting-goods shops.

Individual campgrounds should be contacted before travel for suggestions as to specific equipment to bring, as well as necessary reservations, advance deposits, and permits. Most state parks have a 14-day maximum-stay limit.

🖪 **Arizona State Parks Department** ✉ 1300 W. Washington St., Phoenix 85007 ☎ 602/542-4174 ⊕ www.pr.state.az.us. **Apache Sitgreaves National Forest** ✉ 309 S. Mountain Ave., Springerville 85938 ☎ 928/333-4301 ⊕ www.fs.fed.us/r3/asnf. **Bureau of Land Management** ✉ 222 N. Central Ave., Phoenix 85004 ☎ 602/417-9528 ⊕ www.az.blm.gov. **Coconino National Forest** ✉ 2323 E. Greenlaw La., Flagstaff 86004 ☎ 928/527-3600 ⊕ www.fs.fed.us/r3/coconino. **Coronado National Forest** ✉ Federal Bldg., 300 W. Congress St., Tucson 85701 ☎ 520/670-4552 ⊕ www.fs.fed.us/r3/coronado. **National Park Service** ✉ 3115 N. 3rd Ave., Suite 101, Phoenix 85013 ☎ 602/640-5250 or 202/208-6843 🖷 602/640-5265 ⊕ www.nps.gov. **Prescott National Forest** ✉ 344 S. Cortez St., Prescott 86303 ☎ 928/443-8000 ⊕ www.fs.fed.us/r3/prescott. **Tonto National Forest** ✉ 2324 E. McDowell Rd., Phoenix 85006 ☎ 602/225-5200 ⊕ www.fs.fed.us/r3/tonto. **Williams-Forest Service Visitor Center** ✉ 200 W. Railroad Ave., Williams 86046 ☎ 928/635-4061.

DUDE RANCHES

Down-home Western lifestyle, cooking, and activities are the focus of guest ranches, situated primarily in Tucson and southern Arizona and Wickenburg northwest of Phoenix. Some are resortlike properties where guests are pampered, whereas smaller, family-run ranches expect *everyone* to join in the chores. Horseback riding and other outdoor recreational activities are emphasized. Most dude ranches are closed in summer. The Arizona Dude Ranch Association can give you the names and addresses of its member ranches and their facilities and policies. Contact the Arizona Office of Tourism (⇨ Visitor Information) for the names and addresses of dude ranches throughout the state.

🖪 **The Arizona Dude Ranch Association** ☎ Box 603, Cortaro 85652 🖷 no phone ⊕ www.azdra.com.

HOME EXCHANGES

If you would like to exchange your home for someone else's, **join a home-exchange**

organization, which will send you its up-dated listings of available exchanges for a year and will include your own listing in at least one of them. It's up to you to make specific arrangements.

Exchange Clubs HomeLink International Box 47747, Tampa, FL 33647 813/975-9825 or 800/638-3841 813/910-8144 www.homelink.org; $110 yearly for a listing, on-line access, and catalog; $70 without catalog. **Intervac U.S.** 30 Corte San Fernando, Tiburon, CA 94920 800/756-4663 415/435-7440 www.intervacus.com; $105 yearly for a listing, on-line access, and a catalog; $50 without catalog.

HOSTELS

No matter what your age, you can **save on lodging costs by staying at hostels.** In some 4,500 locations in more than 70 countries around the world, Hostelling International (HI), the umbrella group for a number of national youth-hostel associations, offers single-sex, dorm-style beds and, at many hostels, rooms for couples and family accommodations. Membership in any HI national hostel association, open to travelers of all ages, allows you to stay in HI-affiliated hostels at member rates; one-year membership is about $28 for adults (C$35 for a two-year minimum membership in Canada, £13.50 in the U.K., A$52 in Australia, and NZ$40 in New Zealand); hostels charge about $10–$30 per night. Members have priority if the hostel is full; they're also eligible for discounts around the world, even on rail and bus travel in some countries.

Hostels in Arizona Hostelling International Phoenix 1026 N. 9th St., Phoenix, AZ 85006 602/254-9803 www.hiayh.org.
Organizations Hostelling International–USA 8401 Colesville Rd., Suite 600, Silver Spring, MD 20910 301/495-1240 301/495-6697 www.hiayh.org. **Hostelling International–Canada** 205 Catherine St., Suite 400, Ottawa, Ontario K2P 1C3 613/237-7884 or 800/663-5777 613/237-7868 www.hihostels.ca. **YHA England and Wales** Trevelyan House, Dimple Rd., Matlock, Derbyshire DE4 3YH, U.K. 0870/870-8808, 0870/770-8868, 0162/959-2700 0870/770-6127 www.yha.org.uk. **YHA Australia** 422 Kent St., Sydney, NSW 2001 02/9261-1111 02/9261-1969 www.yha.com.au. **YHA New Zealand** Level 4, Torrens House, 195 Hereford St. Box 436, Christchurch 03/379-9970 or 0800/278-299 03/365-4476 www.yha.org.nz.

MEDIA

NEWSPAPERS & MAGAZINES

Major Arizona-interest publications available statewide are *Arizona Business, Arizona Highways,* and *Sunset Magazine. Phoenix Magazine* and *Desert Living Magazine* focus on architecture, dining, style, arts, and events in the Phoenix area.
Web sites *Arizona Business* www.azbusinessmagazine.com. ***Arizona Highways*** www.arizhwys.com. ***Sunset Magazine*** www.sunset.com.

TELEVISION

In Phoenix, Channel 12 (KPNX) is the NBC affiliate and a site for local news. Channel 15 (KNXV) and Channel 5 (KPHO) are, respectively, the ABC and CBS affiliates in Phoenix; both carry local and national news. The ABC affiliate in Tucson is Channel 9 (KGUN), and the CBS affiliate is Channel 13 (KOLD). PBS is broadcast through Arizona State University in Tempe on Channel 8 (KAET), and through the University of Arizona on Channel 6 (KUAT) in Tucson. COX, which can be found on Channel 9 or 52, broadcasts Phoenix Suns games and other sports events. Other major stations in the state include Channel 6 (KMOH) in Kingman, Channel 2 (KNAZ) in Flagstaff, and Channel 4 (KVOA) in Tucson, all NBC affiliates.

MONEY MATTERS

Due to their relative sizes, Phoenix and Tucson tend to have the greatest variety of accommodations and restaurants in the state. There is no real "average" for restaurant or dining prices—rooms can run from $50 a night at a hotel near the airport to $800 a night in one of Phoenix's posh desert spa-resorts. Suffice to say that you'll be able to find a hotel or eatery to fit most any budget. Resorts in Sedona and in some of the smaller, more exclusive desert communities can be pricey due to their growing reputations as destinations in and of themselves, so be prepared to make a day trip of it if you don't want to drop several hundred dollars on a fancy B&B. The Grand Canyon area is equally pricey, but camping options and dorm-style resorts, such as the Phantom Ranch on the canyon floor ($65 a night), are more affordable accommodation options.

Prices throughout this guide are given for adults. Substantially reduced fees are almost always available for children, students, and senior citizens. For information on taxes, *see* Taxes.

ATMS

Most ATMs are on either the Cirrus (affiliated with MasterCard) or Plus system (affiliated with Visa).

⚡ **Cirrus** ☎ 800/424-7787 ⊕ www.mastercard. com. **Plus** ☎ 800/843-7587 ⊕ usa.visa.com.

CREDIT CARDS

⚡ Reporting Lost Cards **American Express** ☎ 800/441-0519. **Diners Club** ☎ 800/234-6377. **Discover** ☎ 800/347-2683. **MasterCard** ☎ 800/ 622-7747. **Visa** ☎ 800/847-2911.

NATIONAL & STATE PARKS

Look into discount passes to save money on park entrance fees. For $50, the National Parks Pass admits you (and any passengers in your private vehicle) to all national parks, monuments, and recreation areas, as well as other sites run by the National Park Service, for a year. (In parks that charge per person, the pass admits you, your spouse and children, and your parents, when you arrive together.) Camping and parking are extra. The $15 Golden Eagle Pass, a hologram you affix to your National Parks Pass, functions as an upgrade, granting entry to all sites run by the NPS, the U.S. Fish and Wildlife Service, the U.S. Forest Service, and the Bureau of Land Management. The upgrade, which expires with the parks pass, is sold by most national-park, Fish and Wildlife, and BLM fee stations. A percentage of the proceeds from pass sales funds National Parks projects.

Both the Golden Age Passport ($10), for U.S. citizens or permanent residents who are 62 and older, and the Golden Access Passport (free), for those with disabilities, entitle holders (and any passengers in their private vehicles) to lifetime free entry to all national parks, plus 50% off fees for the use of many park facilities and services. (The discount doesn't always apply to companions.) To obtain them, you must show proof of age and of U.S. citizenship or permanent residency—such as a U.S. passport, driver's license, or birth certificate—and, if requesting Golden Access, proof of disability. The Golden Age and

Golden Access passes are available only at NPS-run sites that charge an entrance fee. The National Parks Pass is also available by mail and via the Internet.

⚡ **National Park Foundation** ⊠ 11 Dupont Circle NW, 6th floor, Washington, DC 20036 ☎ 202/238-4200 ⊕ www.nationalparks.org. **National Park Service** ⊠ National Park Service/Department of Interior, 1849 C St. NW, Washington, DC 20240 ☎ 202/208-6843 ⊕ www.nps.gov. **National Parks Conservation Association** ⊠ 1300 19th St. NW, Suite 300, Washington, DC 20036 ☎ 202/223-6722 ⊕ www. npca.org.

⚡ Passes by Mail & On-Line **National Park Foundation** ⊕ www.nationalparks.org. **National Parks Pass** ⊘ Box 34108, Washington, DC 20043 ☎ 888/467-2757 ⊕ www.nationalparks.org; include a check or money order payable to the National Park Service, plus $3.95 for shipping and handling, or call for passes by phone.

⚡ State Parks **Arizona State Parks Department** ⊠ 1300 W. Washington St., Phoenix 85007 ☎ 602/542-4174 ⊕ www.pr.state.az.us.

PACKING

Wear casual clothing and resort wear in Arizona. When in more elegant restaurants in larger cities, as well as in dining rooms of some resorts, most men wear jackets and appropriate pants (few places require ties). Dressy casual wear is appropriate for women even in the nicest places—take along a silky blouse and chunky silver jewelry and you'll fit in almost anywhere.

Stay cool in cotton fabrics and light colors. T-shirts; polo shirts; sundresses; and lightweight shorts, trousers, skirts, and blouses are useful year-round in the south. **Bring sun hats, swimsuits, sandals, and sunscreen**—mandatory warm-weather items. **Bring a sweater and a warm jacket in winter,** particularly for high-country travel—anywhere around Flagstaff and north of it. And **don't forget jeans and sneakers or sturdy walking shoes**; they're important year-round.

In your carry-on luggage, **pack an extra pair of eyeglasses or contact lenses and enough of any medication** you take to last a few days longer than the entire trip. You may also ask your doctor to write a spare prescription using the drug's generic name, as brand names may vary from country to country. In luggage to be checked, **never pack prescription drugs, valuables, or undeveloped film.** And don't forget to carry with you the addresses of offices that handle refunds of lost traveler's checks. Check *Fodor's How to Pack* (available at on-line retailers and bookstores everywhere) for more tips.

To avoid customs and security delays, carry medications in their original packaging. Don't pack any sharp objects in your carry-on luggage, including knives of any size or material, scissors, and corkscrews, or anything else that might arouse suspicion.

To avoid having your checked luggage chosen for hand inspection, don't cram bags full. The U.S. Transportation Security Administration suggests packing shoes on top and placing personal items you don't want touched in clear plastic bags.

CHECKING LUGGAGE

You're allowed to carry aboard one bag and one personal article, such as a purse or a laptop computer. Make sure what you carry on fits under your seat or in the overhead bin. Get to the gate early, so you can board as soon as possible, before the overhead bins fill up.

Baggage allowances vary by carrier, destination, and ticket class. On international flights, you're usually allowed to check two bags weighing up to 70 pounds (32 kilograms) each, although a few airlines allow checked bags of up to 88 pounds (40 kilograms) in first class. Some international carriers don't allow more than 66 pounds (30 kilograms) per bag in business class and 44 pounds (20 kilograms) in economy. On domestic flights, the limit is usually 50 to 70 pounds (23 to 32 kilograms) per bag. In general, carry-on bags shouldn't exceed 40 pounds (18 kilograms). Most airlines won't accept bags that weigh more than 100 pounds (45 kilograms) on domestic or international flights. Check baggage restrictions with your carrier before you pack.

Airline liability for baggage is limited to $2,500 per person on flights within the United States. On international flights it amounts to $9.07 per pound or $20 per kilogram for checked baggage (roughly $640 per 70-pound bag) and $400 per passenger for unchecked baggage. You can buy additional coverage at check-in for about $10 per $1,000 of coverage, but it often excludes a rather extensive list of items, shown on your airline ticket.

Before departure, **itemize your bags' contents** and their worth, and label the bags with your name, address, and phone number. (If you use your home address, cover it so potential thieves can't see it readily.) Include a label inside each bag and **pack a copy of your itinerary**. At check-in, **make sure each bag is correctly tagged** with the destination airport's three-letter code. Because some checked bags will be opened for hand inspection, the U.S. Transportation Security Administration recommends that you leave luggage unlocked or use the plastic locks offered at check-in. TSA screeners place an inspection notice inside searched bags, which are resealed with a special lock.

If your bag has been searched and contents are missing or damaged, file a claim with the TSA Consumer Response Center as soon as possible. If your bags arrive damaged or fail to arrive at all, file a written report with the airline before leaving the airport.

🔁 **Complaints** U.S. Transportation Security Administration Consumer Response Center ☎ 866/289-9673 ⊕ www.tsa.gov.

SENIOR-CITIZEN TRAVEL

Almost all museums, cultural centers, movie theaters, attractions, and national and state parks offer senior-citizen discounts with proper ID. Sun City, a suburb of Phoenix, is a major senior-citizen retirement community.

To qualify for age-related discounts, **mention your senior-citizen status up front** when booking hotel reservations (not when checking out) and before you're seated in restaurants (not when paying the bill). Be sure to have identification on hand. When renting a car, ask about promotional car-rental discounts, which can be cheaper than senior-citizen rates.

🔁 **Educational Programs** Elderhostel ✉ 11 Ave. de Lafayette, Boston, MA 02111-1746 ☎ 877/426-8056, 978/323-4141 international callers, 877/426-2167 TTY 🖷 877/426-2166 ⊕ www.elderhostel.org. **Interhostel** ✉ University of New Hampshire, 6 Garrison Ave., Durham, NH 03824 ☎ 603/862-1147 or 800/733-9753 🖷 603/862-1113 ⊕ www.learn.unh.edu.

SPORTS & THE OUTDOORS

BICYCLING

The relatively flat terrain in the deserts and valleys, the mild winter weather, and spectacular vistas make for great biking in Arizona. Mountainous regions around Payson, Prescott, Sedona, and Tucson offer excellent mountain bike trails. If you plan on biking in the summer months, make sure you carry plenty of water and apply sunscreen regularly. Call the local or county Parks and Recreation Department in the area you're visiting for information on nearby bike paths. The Arizona Bicycle Club, Inc., publishes a schedule of the many bicycle races and tours that take place throughout the state.

F **The Arizona Bicycle Club, Inc.** ⌖ Box 7191, Phoenix, AZ 85011 ☎ 602/989-8740 or 602/279-6674 ⊕ www.azbikeclub.com.

FISHING

Fishing license are required in Arizona and can be obtained in advance of your trip from the Arizona Game and Fish Department. For permission to fish on the San Carlos Apache or White Mountain Apache reservation in eastern Arizona's White Mountains, contact the tribal office.

F **Arizona Game and Fish Department** ✉ 2222 W. Greenway Rd., Phoenix 85023 ☎ 602/942-3000 ⊕ www.gf.state.az.us. **San Carlos Apache Tribe** ⌖ Box 0, San Carlos 85550 ☎ 928/475-2343. **White Mountain Apache Tribe** Wildlife and Outdoor Recreation Division ⌖ Box 220, Whiteriver 85941 ☎ 928/338-4385 ⊕ www.wmat.nsn.us.

GOLF

Arizona has some of the best and most popular golf courses in the United States. For a list of Arizona's many courses, contact the Arizona Golf Association.

F **Arizona Golf Association** ✉ 7226 N. 16th St., Suite 200, Phoenix 85020 ☎ 602/944-3035, 800/458-8484 in Arizona ⊕ www.azgolf.org.

HIKING

The Grand Canyon's Backcountry Office provides hikers with trail details, weather conditions, and packing suggestions for canyon hikes. For hikers who prefer to travel with a group, the Sierra Club leads a variety of wilderness treks. Contact the local chapters in Phoenix, Tucson, Kingman, Prescott, Sedona, and Flagstaff for information on guided hikes in these areas.

F **Grand Canyon National Park Backcountry Office** ⌖ Box 129, Grand Canyon 86023 ☎ 928/638-7875 ⎙ 928/638-2125 ⊕ www.nps.gov/grca. **Sierra Club Grand Canyon Chapter** ⌖ 202 E. McDowell Rd., Suite 277, Phoenix 85004 ☎ 602/253-8633 ⊕ arizona.sierraclub.org.

RIVER RAFTING

The National Park Service maintains a list of outfitters that run white-water rafting trips on the Colorado. You can also contact the Grand Canyon River Permits Office for information on commercial and non-commercial river trips through the canyon. Mild to Wild Rafting and Wilderness Aware are outfitters based in Colorado that offer trips down the spectacular Salt River between March and May.

F **Grand Canyon National Park** Grand Canyon River Permits Office ⌖ Box 129, Grand Canyon 86023 ☎ 800/959-9164 or 928/638-7843 ⎙ 928/638-7844 ⊕ www.nps.gov/grca. **Mild to Wild Rafting** ⌖ 53 Rio Vista Cir., Durango, CO 81301 ☎ 800/567-6745 ⎙ 970/382-0545 ⊕ www.mild2wildrafting.com. **Wilderness Aware Rafting** ⌖ Box 1550WS, Buena Vista, CO 81211 ☎ 800/462-7238 ⎙ 719/395-6716 ⊕ www.inaraft.com/salt.htm.

ROCKHOUNDING

The Department of Mines and Mineral Resources is an excellent source of information about specimens that can be found in each part of the state. There is also a small mining and mineral museum on the first floor of the building.

F **Department of Mines and Mineral Resources** ✉ 1502 W. Washington St., Phoenix 85007 ☎ 602/255-3795 ⊕ www.admmr.state.az.us.

SKIING

F Cross-country Skiing Contacts **Flagstaff Nordic Center** ✉ U.S. 180, 16 mi north of Flagstaff, North Flagstaff ☎ 928/779-1951 ⊕ www.arizonasnowbowl.com. **Williams Valley Winter Sports Area** ✉ Forest Service Rd. 249, Alpine ☎ 928/339-4384.

F Downhill Skiing Contacts **Arizona Snowbowl** ✉ Snowbowl Rd., North Flagstaff ☎ 928/779-1951 ⊕ www.arizonasnowbowl.com. **Mt. Lemmon Ski Valley** ✉ Mt. Lemmon Hwy., Summerhaven ☎ 520/576-1321, 520/547-7510 winter road conditions ⊕ www.fs.fed.us/r3/coronado. **Sunrise Park Resort** ✉ AZ 273, 7 mi south of AZ 260 ⌖ Box 117, Greer 85927 ☎ 928/735-7669, 800/772-7669 hotel reservations and snow reports ⊕ www.sunriseskipark.com.

STUDENTS IN ARIZONA

IDs & Services STA Travel ✉ 10 Downing St., New York, NY 10014 ☎ 212/627-3111 or 800/777-0112, 24-hr service center 🖷 212/627-3387 ⊕ www.sta.com. **Travel Cuts** ✉ 187 College St., Toronto, Ontario M5T 1P7, Canada ☎ 416/979-2406, 800/592-2887 in the U.S., 866/246-9762 in Canada 🖷 416/979-8167 ⊕ www.travelcuts.com.

TAXES

SALES TAX

Arizona state sales tax (called a transaction privilege tax), which applies to all purchases except food in grocery stores, is 5.6%. Phoenix and Tucson levy city sales taxes of 1.8% and 2%, respectively, and Flagstaff taxes purchases at a rate of 1.51%. When added to county taxes, the total sales tax in Phoenix goes up to 8.1%; in Tucson, to 7.6%; and in Flagstaff, to 7.91%. Total sales taxes throughout the state range from 7.3% to 10.1%. Sales taxes do not apply on Indian reservations.

TIME

Arizona sets its clocks to mountain standard time—two hours earlier than Eastern standard, one hour later than Pacific standard. However, from April to October, when other states switch to daylight saving time, Arizona does *not* change its clocks; during this portion of the year, the mountain standard hour in Arizona is the same as the Pacific daylight hour in California. To complicate matters, the vast Navajo reservation in the northeastern section of the state *does* observe daylight saving time, so that from April to October it's an hour later on the reservation than it is in the rest of the state. Finally, the Hopi reservation, whose borders fall within those of the Navajo reservation, stays on the same non-Navajo, non–daylight saving clock as the remainder of the state.

TIPPING

At restaurants, a 15% tip is standard for waiters; up to 20% may be appropriate at more expensive establishments or for excellent service at any restaurant. The same goes for taxi drivers, bartenders, and hairdressers. Coat-check operators usually expect $1; bellhops and porters should get $1 per bag; hotel maids in upscale hotels should get about $2 per day of your stay. On package tours, conductors and drivers usually get $10 per day from the group as a whole; check whether this has already been figured into your cost. For local sightseeing tours, you may individually tip the driver-guide a few dollars if he or she has been helpful or informative. Ushers in theaters do not expect tips.

TOURS & PACKAGES

Because everything is prearranged on a prepackaged tour or independent vacation, you spend less time planning—and often get it all at a good price.

BOOKING WITH AN AGENT

Travel agents are excellent resources. But it's a good idea to collect brochures from several agencies, as some agents' suggestions may be influenced by relationships with tour and package firms that reward them for volume sales. If you have a special interest, **find an agent with expertise in that area**; the American Society of Travel Agents (ASTA; ⇨ Travel Agencies) has a database of specialists worldwide. You can log on to the group's Web site to find an ASTA travel agent in your neighborhood.

Make sure your travel agent knows the accommodations and other services of the place being recommended. Ask about the hotel's location, room size, beds, and whether it has a pool, room service, or programs for children, if you care about these. Has your agent been there in person or sent others whom you can contact?

Do some homework on your own, too: local tourism boards can provide information about lesser-known and small-niche operators, some of which may sell only direct.

BUYER BEWARE

Each year consumers are stranded or lose their money when tour operators—even large ones with excellent reputations—go out of business. So **check out the operator.** Ask several travel agents about its reputation, and try to **book with a company that has a consumer-protection program.** (Look for information in the company's brochure.) In the United States, members of the National Tour Association and the United States Tour Operators Association are required to set aside funds to cover payments and travel arrangements in the event that the company defaults. It's also a good idea to choose a company that participates in the American Society of Travel Agents' Tour Operator Program; ASTA will act as mediator in any disputes between you and your tour operator.

Remember that the more your package or tour includes, the better you can predict the ultimate cost of your vacation. Make sure you know exactly what is covered, and **beware of hidden costs.** Are taxes, tips, and transfers included? Entertainment and excursions? These can add up.

🔳 Tour-Operator Recommendations **American Society of Travel Agents** (⇨ Travel Agencies). **National Tour Association (NTA)** ✉ 546 E. Main St., Lexington, KY 40508 ☎ 859/226-4444 or 800/682-8886 🖷 859/226-4404 ⊕ www.ntaonline.com. **United States Tour Operators Association (USTOA)** ✉ 275 Madison Ave., Suite 2014, New York, NY 10016 ☎ 212/599-6599 🖷 212/599-6744 ⊕ www.ustoa.com.

PACKAGES

Like group tours, independent vacation packages are available from major tour operators and airlines. The companies listed below offer vacation packages in a broad price range.

🔳 Air/Hotel/Car **America West Vacations** ☏ 1920 W. University Dr., Tempe, AZ 85281 ☎ 800/356-6611 ⊕ www.americawest.com. **Delta Vacations** ☎ 800/872-7786 ⊕ www.delta.com. **United Vacations** ☎ 800/328-6877 ⊕ www.united.com. **US Airways Vacations** ☎ 800/455-0123 ⊕ www.usairways.com.

🔳 Custom Packages **Amtrak Vacations** ☎ 800/321-8684 ⊕ www.amtrak.com/savings/amtrakvacations.html.

THEME TRIPS

🔳 Archaeology **Archaeological Conservancy** ☏ 5301 Central Ave. NE, Suite 402, Albuquerque, NM 87108-1517 ☎ 505/266-1540. **Crow Canyon Archaeological Center** ☏ 23390 C.R. K, Cortez, CO 81321 ☎ 970/565-8975 or 800/422-8975 🖷 970/565-4859 ⊕ www.crowcanyon.org. **Earthwatch Institute** ✉ 3 Clock Tower Pl., Suite 100 ☏ Box 75, Maynard, MA 01754 ☎ 978/461-0081 or 800/776-0188 🖷 978/461-2332 ⊕ www.earthwatch.org. **Southwest Ed-Ventures** ☏ Four Corners School of Outdoor Education, Box 1029, Monticello, UT 84535 ☎ 435/587-2156 or 800/525-4456 🖷 435/587-2193 ⊕ www.sw-adventures.org.

🔳 Bicycling **Backroads** ☏ 801 Cedar St., Berkeley, CA 94710-1800 ☎ 510/527-1555 or 800/462-2848 🖷 510/527-1444 ⊕ www.backroads.com. **Cycle America** ☏ Box 485, Cannon Falls, MN 55009 ☎ 507/263-2665 or 800/245-3263 🖷 507/263-

0873 ⊕ www.cycleamerica.com. **Timberline Adventures** ☏ 7975 E. Harvard, Suite J, Denver, CO 80231 ☎ 303/368-4418 or 800/417-2453 🖷 303/368-1651 ⊕ www.timbertours.com.

🔳 Golf **Golfpac** ☏ Box 162366, Altamonte Springs, FL 32716-2366 ☎ 407/260-2288 or 800/327-0878 🖷 407/260-8989 ⊕ www.golfpactravel.com.

🔳 Motorcycling **Arizona Motorcycle Tours** ☏ 5253 E. Hilton Ave., Mesa, AZ 85206 ☎ 480/654-5045 or 480/250-8685 ⊕ www.azmctours.com.

🔳 Native American History **Journeys into American Indian Territory** ☏ Box 575, East Port, NY 11941 ☎ 631/878-8655 or 800/458-2632 🖷 631/878-4518 ⊕ www.indianjourneys.com.

🔳 Natural History **Smithsonian Journeys** ☏ 1100 Jefferson Dr. SW, Room 3077, Washington, DC 20560 ☎ 202/357-4700 or 877/338-8687 🖷 202/633-9250 ⊕ www.smithsonianjourneys.org. **Victor Emanuel Nature Tours** ☏ 2525 Wallingwood Dr., Suite 1003, Austin, TX 78746 ☎ 512/328-5221 or 800/328-8368 🖷 512/328-2919 ⊕ www.ventbird.com.

🔳 River Rafting For trips on the Colorado River: **Action Whitewater Adventures** ☏ Box 1634, Provo, UT 84603 ☎ 801/375-4111 or 800/453-1482 🖷 801/375-4175 ⊕ www.riverguide.com.

OARS Dories ☏ Box 216, Altavill, CA 95221 ☎ 209/736-0805 or 800/877-3679 🖷 209/736-2902 ⊕ www.grandcanyondories.com. **OARS** ☏ Box 67, Angels Camp, CA 95222 ☎ 209/736-4677 or 800/346-6277 🖷 209/736-2902 ⊕ www.oars.com. **World Wide River Expeditions** ☏ 625 Riversands Rd., Moab, UT 84532 ☎ 435/259-7515 or 800/231-2769 🖷 435/259-7512.

🔳 Self-Drive **Off the Beaten Path** ☏ 7 E. Beall St., Bozeman, MT 59715 ☎ 406/586-1311 or 800/445-2995 🖷 406/587-4147 ⊕ www.offthebeatenpath.com.

🔳 Spas **Spafinder** ✉ 91 5th Ave., 6th floor, New York, NY 10003-3039 ☎ 212/924-6800 or 800/255-7727 ⊕ www.spafinder.com represents numerous day and stay spas in Arizona.

TRAIN TRAVEL

The *Southwest Chief* operates daily between Los Angeles and Chicago, stopping in Kingman, Flagstaff, and Winslow. The *Sunset Limited* travels three times each week between Los Angeles and Orlando, with stops at Yuma, Tucson, and Benson. There is a connecting Amtrak bus (a 2½ hour trip) between Flagstaff and Phoenix. For details, contact **Amtrak** (☎ 800/872-7245 ⊕ www.amtrak.com).

TRAVEL AGENCIES

A good travel agent puts your needs first. Look for an agency that has been in business at least five years, emphasizes customer service, and has someone on staff who specializes in your destination. In addition, **make sure the agency belongs to a professional trade organization.** The American Society of Travel Agents (ASTA)—the largest and most influential in the field with more than 20,000 members in some 140 countries—maintains and enforces a strict code of ethics and will step in to help mediate any agent-client disputes involving ASTA members if necessary. ASTA (whose motto is "Without a travel agent, you're on your own") also maintains a Web site that includes a directory of agents. (If a travel agency is also acting as your tour operator, *see* Buyer Beware *in* Tours & Packages.)

🚩 Local Agent Referrals **American Society of Travel Agents (ASTA)** ✉ 1101 King St., Suite 200, Alexandria, VA 22314 ☎ 703/739-2782, 800/965-2782 24-hr hot line 🖷 703/739-3268 ⊕ www. astanet.com. **Association of British Travel Agents** ✉ 68-71 Newman St., London W1T 3AH ☎ 020/7637-2444 🖷 020/7637-0713 ⊕ www.abta.com. **Association of Canadian Travel Agents** ✉ 130 Albert St., Suite 1705, Ottawa, Ontario K1P 5G4 ☎ 613/237-3657 🖷 613/237-7052 ⊕ www.acta.ca. **Australian Federation of Travel Agencies** ✉ Level 3, 309 Pitt St., Sydney, NSW 2000 ☎ 02/9264-3299 🖷 02/9264-1085 ⊕ www.afta.com.au. **Travel Agents' Association of New Zealand** ✉ Level 5, Tourism and Travel House, 79 Boulcott St. ⍉ Box 1888, Wellington 6001 ☎ 04/499-0104 🖷 04/499-0786 ⊕ www. taanz.org.nz.

VISITOR INFORMATION

For general information and brochures contact the Arizona Office of Tourism; for specific information on the state's indigenous culture, contact the Native American attractions.

🚩 Tourist Information **Arizona Office of Tourism** ✉ 1110 W. Washington St., Suite 155, Phoenix 85007 ☎ 602/364-3700 or 866/298-3795 🖷 602/364-3702 ⊕ www.arizonaguide.com.

🚩 Native American Attractions **Hopi Tribe Office of the Chairman** ⍉ Box 123, Kykotsmovi 86039 ☎ 928/734-2441 🖷 928/734-2435 ⊕ www.hopi. nsn.us. **Navajo Nation Tourism Office** ⍉ Box 663, Window Rock 86515 ☎ 928/871-6436 or 928/871-7371 🖷 928/871-7942 ⊕ www.navajoland.com.

WEB SITES

Do check out the World Wide Web when planning your trip. You'll find everything from weather forecasts to virtual tours of famous cities. Be sure to **visit Fodors.com** (⊕ www.fodors.com), a complete travel-planning site. You can research prices and book plane tickets, hotel rooms, rental cars, vacation packages, and more. In addition, you can post your pressing questions in the Travel Talk section. Other planning tools include a currency converter and weather reports, and there are loads of links to travel resources.

For more specific information on Arizona, visit the following:

🚩 Grand Canyon **The Canyon** ⊕ www.thecanyon. com. **Grand Canyon National Park** ⊕ www.nps. gov/grca.

🚩 The Great Outdoors **Arizona State Parks Web Site** ⊕ www.pr.state.az.us. **Great Outdoor Recreation Page** ⊕ www.gorp.com. **National Park Service site** ⊕ www.nps.gov.

🚩 Newsweeklies *Phoenix New Times* ⊕ www. phoenixnewtimes.com. *Tucson Weekly* ⊕ www. tucsonweekly.com.

PHOENIX & CENTRAL ARIZONA

FODOR'S CHOICE

The Apache Trail, *a scenic drive southeast of Phoenix*

Arizona Biltmore, *a resort in Phoenix*

ASU Karsten Golf Course, *Tempe*

The Boulders, *a resort in Carefree*

Carolina's, *Phoenix*

Comfort Inn, *a budget hotel in Scottsdale*

Desert Botanical Garden, *Phoenix*

Gold Canyon Golf Club, *Gold Canyon*

Hermosa Inn, *Paradise Valley*

Lon's at the Hermosa, *a restaurant in Paradise Valley*

Marquesa, *a restaurant in Scottsdale*

Pueblo Grande Museum and Cultural Park, *Phoenix*

Restaurant Hapa, *Scottsdale*

Taliesin West, *Frank Lloyd Wright's winter home in Scottsdale*

Troon North, *a golf course in Scottsdale*

HIGHLY RECOMMENDED

SIGHTS   Arizona Science Center, *Phoenix*

Boyce Thompson Southwestern Arboretum, *Superior*

Heard Museum, *Phoenix*

Main Street Arts District, *Scottsdale*

Mystery Castle, *Phoenix*

Phoenix Museum of History, *Phoenix*

South Mountain Park, *Phoenix*

Many other great hotels and restaurants enliven this area. For other favorites, look for the black stars as you read this chapter.

Updated by
Bob and
Gloria Willis

IN CENTRAL ARIZONA, the great Sonoran Desert, considered by many to be the most beautiful desert in the world, provides an amazing diversity of natural environments in a relatively small area. Here, you will find some of the oldest human dwellings in the western hemisphere along with the homes of contemporary Native American tribes and one of America's fastest-growing major urban centers: metropolitan Phoenix, a melding of 22 communities, with a population of more than 3.2 million people.

The Valley of the Sun, a term synonymous with metro Phoenix, is named for its 325-plus days of sunshine each year. The Valley marks the northern tip of the Sonoran Desert, a prehistoric seabed that reaches from northwestern Mexico. The Valley's landscape offers more than cacti, surprising most visitors. Palo verde and mesquite trees, creosote bushes, palms, and aloe dot the land, which is accustomed to being scorched by temperatures in excess of 100°F for weeks at a time. Late summer brings precious rain when monsoon storms illuminate the sky with brilliant lightning shows and the desert exudes the sweet scent of creosote. Spring sets the Valley blooming, from giant saguaros crowned in white flowers to masses of vibrantly painted wildflowers dotting desert crevices and mountain landscapes.

As the Hohokam discovered 2,300 years ago, this miracle can be augmented by human hands. Having migrated north from northwestern Mexico, they cultivated cotton, corn, and beans in tilled, rowed, and irrigated fields for about 1,700 years, establishing more than 300 mi of canals—an engineering miracle, particularly when you consider the limited technology available. The Hohokam, whose name comes from the Piman word for "people who have gone before," constructed a great town upon whose ruins modern Phoenix is built, and then vanished. Drought, long winters, and other causes are suggested for their disappearance.

From the time the Hohokam left until the Civil War, the once fertile Salt River valley lay forgotten, used only by occasional small bands of Pima and Maricopa Indians. Then, in 1865, the U.S. Army established Fort McDowell in the mountains to the east, where the Verde River flows into the Salt River. To feed the men and the horses stationed there, a former Confederate army officer reopened the Hohokam canals in 1867. Within a year, fields bright with barley and pumpkins earned the area the name Punkinsville. By 1870, the 300 residents had decided that their new city would arise from the ancient Hohokam ruins, just as the mythical phoenix rose from its own ashes.

Phoenix would rise indeed. Within 20 years, it had become large enough—its population was about 3,000—to wrest the title of territorial capital from Prescott. By 1912, when Arizona was admitted as the 48th state, the area, irrigated by the brand-new Roosevelt Dam and Salt River Project, had a burgeoning cotton industry. Copper and cattle were mined and raised elsewhere but were banked and traded in Phoenix, and the cattle were slaughtered and packed here in the largest stockyards outside of Chicago.

Meanwhile, the climate, so long a crippling liability, became an asset. Desert air was the prescribed therapy for the respiratory ills rampant in the sooty, factory-filled East; Scottsdale began in 1901 as "30-odd tents and a half dozen adobe houses" put up by health-seekers. By 1930, travelers looking for warm winter recreation as well as rejuvenating aridity filled the elegant San Marcos Hotel and Arizona Biltmore, first of the many luxury retreats for which the area is now known worldwide.

If you have 3 days

See the **Heard Museum** ⑫ for its internationally acclaimed collection of Native American artifacts, and swing by the **Burton Barr Central Library** ⑩ on your way downtown to the **Arizona Science Center** ② and **Phoenix Museum of History** ③. On day two, rise early and begin your day at Frank Lloyd Wright's **Taliesin West** ㉝; then head south into Scottsdale for a day of gallery browsing and a walk through **Old Town Scottsdale** ㉘. On your final day visit the stunning **Desert Botanical Garden** ⑲, and take a detour on your way home across Lincoln Drive in northeast Phoenix. This scenic route provides the best views of the Valley's beauty, so be sure to head west as the sun descends and the sky absorbs dozens of colors, introducing the evening.

If you have 5 days

Follow the tour above, and on the fourth day, consider some hiking: even inexperienced hikers will enjoy the walk up to **Papago Park**'s ⑱ Hole-in-the-Rock or the 1¼-mi trip to the top of Piestewa (formerly Squaw) Peak, whereas the more experienced may choose to ascend Camelback Mountain. **South Mountain Park** ⑮ has many trails for hikers of all abilities. Spend the afternoon exploring the stark beauty of the surrounding desert on horseback, in a jeep, or by hot-air balloon. On your fifth day, drive the loop of the Apache Trail, enjoying breathtaking views of Fish Creek Canyon—or head north to take a tour of **Arcosanti** ㊴ or explore the Old West town of **Wickenburg** ㊳.

If you have 7 days

Expand your drive of the Apache Trail to include an overnight stay in 🚉 **Globe** ㊺. Along the way stop to enjoy the view of Weaver's Needle from the **Peralta Trail** ㊸, stroll through **Boyce Thompson Southwestern Arboretum** ㊹, or check out the ancient Hohokam ruins at **Casa Grande Ruins National Monument** ㊶ to the south of Phoenix.

The 1950s brought with them residential air-conditioning, an invention that made the summers bearable for the growing workforce of the burgeoning technology industry. The Valley is very much a work still in progress; for better or worse, Phoenix is changing, and so quickly that even longtime residents have a difficult time keeping up. Historians are quick to point out that never in the world's history has a metropolis grown from "nothing" to attain the status of Phoenix in such a short period of time. But at the heart of all the bustle is a way of life that keeps its own pace: Phoenix is, after all, the world's largest small town—where people dress informally and where the rugged, Old West ambience lives on despite the sprawling growth. If the heat can be overwhelming at noon on a summer day, at least it has the restorative effect of slowing things down to an enjoyable pace.

EXPLORING PHOENIX

Phoenix, which is in Maricopa County, has grown around what was once a cluster of independent towns. Gaps between communities that were simply open spaces of desert a few short years ago have begun to close in and blend the entire Valley into one large, sprawling community. If it were not for the welcome signs of various municipalities on roadways, you would be hard-pressed to tell where one community ends and another begins. Situated in a large valley surrounded by desert hills and mountains ranges, Metro Phoenix retains a strong Western heritage; however, don't expect to find older ethnic neighborhoods, as you would in Eastern and Midwestern cities—they just aren't here. First-time visitors are often surprised to discover that some of the area's finest restaurants and shops are situated in hotels and strip malls.

Commuting through the region can be complex and exasperating unless you have a car of your own. From Cave Creek, a suburb north of Phoenix, the one-way cab fare to the Bank One Ballpark (about 35 mi) can easily cost you more than the daily charge for a rental car. Public transit is here in varying degrees and is inexpensive, but services do not connect well within and between communities.

Getting Your Bearings

Phoenix is at the center of the Valley, with other communities radiating out from it. Due east of downtown Phoenix lie Scottsdale, Tempe, Mesa, and Apache Junction, and just beyond the last is the southern edge of the Superstition Mountains. To the southeast are Gilbert, Guadalupe, Ahwatukee, and Chandler. The west Valley includes Glendale, Peoria, Sun City, Avondale, Goodyear, and Litchfield Park. To the north are the towns of Cave Creek and Carefree.

It's actually pretty easy to get your bearings once you know how the Valley is laid out. Central Avenue, which runs north and south through the heart of downtown Phoenix, is the city's east-west dividing line. Everything east of Central is considered the East Valley and everything west of Central is the West Valley. One block east and parallel to Central Avenue is 1st Street. Avenues are on the west side of the Valley, and streets are on the east side. Street numbers increase as you drive farther from Central Ave. Thus, 40th Street is 40 blocks east of Central, while 63rd Avenue is 63 blocks west of Central. North-south increments are taken from Washington Street in downtown Phoenix, so 4002 North 36th Street is 40 blocks north of Washington.

Downtown Phoenix

Growth in the Valley over the past two decades has created new demands on the downtown area. More spaces for large conventions and trade shows, rapid growth brought on by new business development, creation of new apartments and lofts, and new cultural and sports facilities have helped create a more "real" downtown area. Downtown Phoenix is also known as Copper Square and is a mixture of Phoenix's past and present. Restored homes in Heritage Square, from the original town site, give you an idea of how far the city has come since its inception around the turn of the 20th century.

Numbers in the text correspond to numbers in the margin and on map What to See in Downtown Phoenix.

a good walk

Park your car in the garage on the southeast corner of 5th and Monroe streets or at any of the many nearby public parking facilities (they're listed on the free map provided by Downtown Phoenix Partnership and available in local restaurants). Begin your tour in the blocks known as the Heritage and Science Park; the area from 5th to 7th Street between Monroe and Adams contains **Heritage Square** ❶ ▶, the **Arizona Science Center** ❷, and the **Phoenix Museum of History** ❸. From the corner of 5th and Monroe streets, walk two blocks west to **St. Mary's Basilica** ❹, Phoenix's first Catholic church. Head north one block to Van Buren Street. On the northeast corner of the intersection, you'll see two glass-clad office towers with a lane of royal palms between them. Follow the palm

1

Food

Generations of Phoenix schoolchildren have learned about Arizona's four Cs: copper, cattle, cotton, and climate. Today, a good argument could be made for adding a fifth: cuisine. Phoenix and Scottsdale have earned a place in the lexicon of cooking; from sophisticated Southwestern cuisine to Asian to traditional Sonoran Mexican and New Mexican, top-notch restaurant choices abound, and, because greater Phoenix is truly international, you can also find good Italian, French, Spanish, Japanese, Vietnamese, Thai, and Chinese.

Golf

The Valley of the Sun is among the top U.S. golf destinations, thanks to warm temperatures, azure skies, the scenic desert backdrop, and more than 200 challenging courses. The burgeoning growth of the area has brought with it an explosion of golf courses, many of them world-class. However, there's an equally exciting range of moderate, affordable courses to satisfy all levels of play and most every pocketbook. November through April is peak season; in summer, golf fees are a fraction of the cost, and many resorts offer packages combining resort stays with golf. Each January, thousands of golf aficionados descend upon the Valley to attend the prestigious Phoenix Open at the Tournament Player's Club in Scottsdale.

Mountains

The Valley of the Sun is ringed by mountains, which provide outdoor enthusiasts with a wide variety of sporting venues. Some of these are inside the city limits. Piestewa (formerly Squaw) Peak, north of downtown, is popular with hikers. Camelback Mountain and the Papago Peaks are landmarks between Phoenix and Scottsdale. South of the city are the much less lofty peaks of South Mountain Park, which separates the Valley from the rest of the Sonoran Desert. East of the city, beyond Tempe and Mesa, the peaks of the Superstition Mountains—named for their eerie way of seeming just a few miles away—are the first of a range that stretches all the way into New Mexico. To the west, past Glendale and Litchfield Park, the formidable White Tank Mountains separate the Valley from the lands that slope steadily downward to the Mojave Desert of California. Finally, just an hour north of the Valley, the slopes of the Mogollon (pronounced *muh*-gee-on) Rim, all green with piñon, juniper, and Ponderosa pines, serve as a cool refuge for Valley dwellers, where I–17 leads tens of thousands on exodus every weekend from May to September.

Spas

The Valley has some of the best spas in the world, from destination spas where you can buy weeklong packages to day spas where both locals and visitors relax and retreat. The newest include Royal Palms Spa at the Royal Palms Resort, Willow Springs Spa at the Fairmont Scottsdale Princess, the Golden Door Spa at the Boulders, the Sanctuary Spa at Sanctuary, and the Mist Spa at the Radisson. The Spas at Camelback Inn and the Arizona Biltmore continue to be old-time favorites.

Greater Phoenix

trees: they lead to the **Arizona Center** ⑤. Leaving the Arizona Center, from the corner of 3rd and Van Buren streets, walk a block west to 2nd Street and then two blocks south, passing the 24-story Hyatt Regency hotel on your right, then another block and a half west on Adams Street to the **Museo Chicano** ⑥. You can walk to Heritage and Science Park from here, catch a DASH shuttle back, or continue on two more blocks west toward the striking facade of the **Orpheum Theatre** ⑦.

If you're really an indefatigable walker, continue south through the plaza on the Orpheum's east side to Washington Street; head east on Washington Street, passing Historic City Hall and the county courthouse on your right. At the intersection of Washington Street and 1st Avenue, you'll see Patriots Square Park on the southeast corner. Cross diagonally (southeast) through the park to the corner of Jefferson Street and Central Avenue. Another block east on Jefferson and then a block south on 1st Street will take you to the site of the **America West Arena** ⑧. From the arena, follow Jefferson Street east for two blocks to South 4th Avenue and Phoenix's newest sports venue, **Bank One Ballpark** ⑨. Afterward, catch the DASH shuttle back to your car.

TIMING   In moderate weather, this walk is a pleasant daylong tour; from late May to mid-October, when the temperatures are at their hottest, it's best to break it up over two days. Be sure to take advantage of the free DASH (Downtown Area Shuttle).

What to See

⑧ **America West Arena.** This 20,000-seat venue, known locally as the Purple Palace, is home to the Phoenix Suns NBA team, the Arizona Rattlers arena football team, the Phoenix Mercury WNBA team, and the Phoenix Coyotes NHL team. It's almost a mall in itself—with cafés and

shops, it's interesting to see. Tour availability is determined by the day's
schedule of events, and you must have a reservation. ⊠ *201 E. Jefferson St., at 2nd St., Downtown* ☎ *602/379–2000, 602/379–2060 tour
reservations only* ⊕ *www.americawestarena.com* ⊠ *Tours $3* ⊗ *Tours
weekdays by appointment only.*

⑤ Arizona Center. In an oasis of dramatic fountains, sunken gardens, and towering palm trees stands this two-tier, open-air structure, which is downtown's most attractive shopping venue. The center features about 50
shops and restaurants spread over two stories, open-air vendors, a large
sports bar, and a multiplex cinema. ⊠ *Van Buren St. between 3rd and
5th Sts., Downtown* ☎ *602/271–4000 or 480/949–4386* ⊕ *www.
arizonacenter.com.*

★ ✋ ② Arizona Science Center. With more than 300 hands-on exhibits, this
venue for science-related fun and exploration is an entertaining educational experience for children and grown-ups alike. You can pilot a simulated airplane flight, travel through the human body, navigate your way
through the solar system in the Dorrance Planetarium, and watch a movie
in the giant, five-story film theater. ⊠ *600 E. Washington St., Downtown* ☎ *602/716–2000* ⊕ *www.azscience.org* ⊠ *Museum $9; combi-
nation museum, theater, and planetarium $19* ⊗ *Daily 10–5.*

⑨ Bank One Ballpark. Known affectionately as BOB, the Valley's major-
league ballpark is home to the Arizona Diamondbacks. A retractable
roof, natural-grass playing surface, family picnic area, and even a swimming pool let Phoenicians enjoy a day at the ballpark while escaping
the summer heat. Tours are given Monday–Saturday. It's a good idea
to call ahead, since there are no tours on daytime game days. ⊠ *401 E.
Jefferson St., between S. 4th and S. 7th Sts., Downtown* ☎ *602/462–*

6000 ⊕ www.diamondbacks.mlb.com ☒ Tours $6 ⊙ Tours Mon.–Sat. at 10:30, noon, 1:30, and 3 (10:30 and noon only on evening game days).

▶ ❶ **Heritage Square.** In a parklike setting from 5th to 7th Street between Monroe and Adams streets, this city-owned block contains the only remaining houses from the original Phoenix town site. On the south side of the square, along Adams Street, stand several houses built between 1899 and 1901. The Teeter House contains a Victorian-style tearoom, and the Thomas House and Baird Machine Shop is now Pizzeria Bianco The one-story brick Stevens House holds the **Arizona Doll and Toy Museum** (☒ 602 E. Adams St., Downtown ☎ 602/253–9337), which is open Tuesday–Saturday 10–4, Sunday noon–4, and closed in August; admission is $2.50.

The queen of Heritage Square is the **Rosson House**, an 1895 Victorian in the Queen Anne style. Built by a physician who served a brief term as mayor, it is the sole survivor among fewer than two dozen Victorians erected in Phoenix. It was bought and restored by the city in 1974. ☒ 6th and Monroe Sts., Downtown ☎ 602/262–5029 ☒ $4 ⊙ Wed.–Sat. 10–4, Sun. noon–4.

---

need a break? The Victorian-style tearoom in the **Teeter House** (☒ 622 E. Adams St., Downtown ☎ 602/252–4682), which was built as a private home in 1899, serves authentic teatime fare; you'll also find heartier sandwiches and salads, ideal if you're looking for more than a snack.

---

❻ **Museo Chicano.** Works of artists from the United States and Mexico are showcased here. Exhibits include art in many media from different periods, showing both classic and modern culture and making this site a premier center for enjoying Latin American art. ☒ 147 E. Adams St., Downtown ☎ 602/257–5536 ☒ $2 ⊙ Tues.–Sat. 10–4.

❼ **Orpheum Theatre.** The Spanish colonial–revival architecture and exterior reliefs of this 1929 movie palace have long been admired; a 12-year, $14 million renovation project was completed in 2001. The eclectic ornamental details of the interior have been meticulously restored. Call for details on free guided tours and upcoming events. ☒ 203 W. Adams St., Downtown ☎ 602/534–5600 ⊙ Tours by appointment only.

❸ **Phoenix Museum of History.** This striking glass-and-steel museum offers exhibits on regional history from the 1860s (when Anglo settlement began) through the 1930s. Interactive exhibits are designed to help you appreciate the city's multicultural heritage as well as witness its growth. ☒ 105 N. 5th St., Downtown ☎ 602/253–2734 ☒ $5 ⊙ Mon.–Sat. 10–5, Sun. noon–5.

❹ **St. Mary's Basilica.** Founded in 1881, the oldest standing church in Phoenix adds historic flavor to the downtown. Inside the basilica (which Pope John Paul II visited in 1987) there's a magnificent stained-glass window designed in Munich. Mass is held daily, but call for visiting hours. ☒ N. 3rd and Monroe Sts., Downtown ☎ 602/252–7651 ☒ Free ⊙ Hrs vary; call for opening times.

The Cultural Center

The heart of Phoenix's downtown cultural center and renaissance is the Margaret T. Hance Park, also known as Deck Park. Built atop the I–10 tunnel under Central Avenue, it spreads more than 1 mi from 3rd Avenue on the west to 3rd Street on the east, and ¼ mi from Portland Street north to Culver Street. It is the city's second-largest downtown park (the largest is half-century-old Encanto Park, 2 mi northwest). Deck Park is a good place from which to survey revitalized downtown neighborhoods and to appreciate the expansions and renovations of nearly all the area's museums.

Numbers in the text correspond to numbers in the margin and on the Exploring Greater Phoenix map.

a good tour

Park free in the lot of the **Burton Barr Central Library** ⑩ ▶ at the corner of Central Avenue and East Willetta Street. Two blocks north on Central, across McDowell Road, is the modern, green-quartz **Phoenix Art Museum** ⑪. North of the museum, a slight detour brings a brief respite from the noise and traffic of Central Avenue as well as a glimpse of some lovely residential architecture: head one block east on Coronado Road to Alvarado Road, and then follow Alvarado north for two longish blocks (zigzagging a few feet to the east at Palm Lane) to Monte Vista Road; turn left onto Monte Vista and proceed 50 yards west to the entrance of the **Heard Museum** ⑫. From the Heard, head south on Central Avenue toward the red-granite Viad Tower, with its refreshing fountains and intriguing sculpture garden. If you want to visit **Encanto Park** ⑬, which is west of 7th Avenue, you may wish to drive, since it's west of 7th Avenue and a bit far away to go on foot, particularly when the temperatures top 90°F.

TIMING   Seeing all the neighborhood's attractions makes a comfortable daylong tour in moderate weather; in the warm months, it is too much for one day. Bus 0 runs up and down Central Avenue every 10 minutes on weekdays and every 20 minutes on Saturday.

What to See

▶ ⑩ **Burton Barr Central Library.** Architect Will Bruder's magnificent contribution to Phoenix has a copper exterior that evokes images of the mesas, buttes, and canyons of Monument Valley. Skylights, glass walls, and mirrors bathe the interior in natural light. The Crystal Canyon, a five-story glass atrium, is best appreciated on a swift ride in one of the glass elevators. On the top floor, a cable-suspended steel ceiling floats over the largest reading room in North America. Free one-hour tours are offered with advance reservations. ⊠ *1221 N. Central Ave., Downtown* ☎ *602/262–4636, 602/262–6582 tour reservations* ⊕ *www.phoenixpubliclibrary.org* ☉ *Mon.–Thurs. 9–9, Fri.–Sat. 9–6, Sun. noon–9.*

need a break?

Funky, friendly **Willow House** (⊠ 149 W. McDowell Rd., at 3rd Ave., Downtown ☎ 602/252–0272) is a place to people-watch from an armchair or sofa and to grab a sandwich, dessert, or coffee. Check out the various artworks on display, as well as the kaleidoscopic fish painted on the rest-room walls.

⑬ **Encanto Park.** Urban Encanto (Spanish for "enchanted") Park covers 222 acres and sits at the heart of one of Phoenix's oldest residential neighborhoods. There is a wide range of attractions here, including picnic areas, a lagoon where you can paddleboat and canoe, a municipal swimming pool, a nature trail, the Kiddieland/Enchanted Island amusement park, fishing in the park's lake, two public golf courses, and basketball and tennis courts. ⊠ *15th Ave. and Encanto Blvd., Encanto* ☎ *602/261–8993* ⊠ *Park free, Enchanted Island rides $1* ☉ *Park daily 6 AM–midnight; Enchanted Island Wed.–Fri. 10–4, weekends 7–4.*

⑫ **Heard Museum.** Pioneer settlers Dwight and Maie Heard built a Spanish colonial–revival building on their property to house their impressive collection of Southwestern art. Today, the staggering collection of this world-

KEY

▶ *Start of walk*

0 — 4 miles
0 — 6 km

renowned museum includes such exhibits as a Navajo hogan, an Apache wickie-up (a temporary Native American structure, similar to a lean-to, constructed from branches, twigs, and leaves, which was sometimes covered with locally obtained hides), and rooms filled with art, pottery, jewelry, katsinas, and textiles. Children enjoy the interactive art-making exhibits. Annual events include the Guild Indian Fair & Market and the World Championship Hoop Dance Contest. The museum has an incredible gift shop with authentic, high-quality goods purchased directly from native artists. There's a museum satellite branch in Scottsdale that has rotating exhibits. ✉ *2301 N. Central Ave., Downtown* ☎ *602/252–8848 or 602/252–8840* ⊕ *www.heard.org* 🖃 *$7* ⊙ *Daily 9:30–5.*

⓫ **Phoenix Art Museum.** The green-quartz exterior of this modern museum is an eye-catching piece of architecture. The museum has 17,000 works of art from all over the world but is perhaps best known for its extensive and popular Western American Collection, which includes sculptures by Frederic Remington and paintings by Georgia O'Keeffe, Thomas Moran, and Maxfield Parrish. Since the museum hosts more than 20 significant exhibitions annually, there's usually something special to see. Tours of the collection are given at 2 PM daily. ✉ *1625 N. Central Ave., Downtown* ☎ *602/257–1880* ⊕ *www.phxart.org* 🖃 *$7* ⊙ *Daily 10–6.*

off the beaten path	**BEAD MUSEUM –** In the historic district of downtown Glendale, this little museum attracts bead collectors from around the globe. You'll learn the intriguing story of international trade and intricate bead craft from 30,000 BC through today. There's a nice gift shop, and the 3,000-volume reference library can be perused by appointment. ✉ *5754 W. Glenn Dr., northwest corner of Glenn Dr. and 58th Ave., Glendale* ☎ *623/931–2737* 🖃 *$3, free Sun.* ⊕ *www.thebeadmuseum.com* ⊙ *Mon.–Wed. and Fri.–Sat. 10–5, Thurs. 10–8, Sun. 11–4.*

South Phoenix

A mostly residential area and home to much of Phoenix's substantial Hispanic population, South Phoenix—the area south of Buckeye Road—is worth a visit for two reasons: its family-style restaurants and roadside stands offer some of the best Mexican food in the city, and it's where you'll find South Mountain Park and one of the more unusual sights in the Valley—the Mystery Castle.

a good tour	From central Phoenix, take 7th Street south, past Baseline Road, to its junction with Mineral Road. Here you'll find the **Mystery Castle** ⓮ ▶, a decidedly original home turned museum. After a tour, follow Mineral Road west for about ½ mi to Central Avenue and the entrance to **South Mountain Park** ⓯. Take any of several scenic drives through this 16,500-acre city-owned wilderness. Dobbins Lookout, 1,120 ft above Phoenix, has spectacular views of the city. Maps of all scenic drives as well as of hiking, mountain biking, and horseback trails are available at the Gatehouse Entrance just inside the park boundary.
TIMING	Depending on how long you spend in the park, this tour can be accomplished in a couple of hours or can last an entire day. Leave about a half hour each way for driving, an hour to 90 minutes at the castle, and anywhere from a quick 20-minute drive to an all-day hike in South Mountain.

Sights to See

▶ ★ ⓮ **Mystery Castle.** At the foot of South Mountain lies a curious dwelling built from desert rocks by Boyce Gulley, who came to Arizona to cure his tuberculosis. Boyce's daughter Mary Lou lives here now and leads tours on request. Full of fascinating oddities, the castle has 18 rooms with 13 fireplaces, a downstairs grotto tavern, and a roll-away bed with a mining railcar as its frame. The pump organ belonged to Elsie, the Widow of Tombstone, who buried six husbands under suspicious circumstances. ⊠ *800 E. Mineral Rd., South Phoenix* ☎ *602/268–1581* ▭ *$5* ☾ *Oct.–June, Thurs.–Sun. 11–4.*

★ ☾ ⑮ **South Mountain Park.** This desert wonderland, the world's largest city park (almost 17,000 acres), offers a wilderness of mountain-desert trails for hikers, bikers, and horseback riders. The Environmental Center has a model of the park as well as displays detailing its history, from the time of the ancient Hohokam people to gold-seekers. Roads climb past buildings constructed by the Civilian Conservation Corps, winding through desert flora to the trailheads. Look for ancient petroglyphs, try to spot a desert cottontail rabbit or chuckwalla lizard, or simply stroll among the wondrous vegetation. ⊠ *10919 S. Central Ave., South Phoenix* ☎ *602/495-0222* ▭ *Free* ☾ *Daily 5:30 AM–10:30 PM. Environmental Center Mon.–Sat. 9–5, Sun. noon–5.*

need a break?
Carolina's (⊠ 1202 E. Mohave St., South Phoenix ☎ 602/252–1503) makes the best flour tortillas for 100 mi, and the burritos are the best way to try them. You can eat at this small establishment or just pick up some carry-out, which you can enjoy as a picnic under one of the ramadas in South Mountain Park.

Papago Salado

The word Papago, meaning "bean eater," was a name given by 16th-century Spanish explorers to the Hohokam, a vanished native people of the Phoenix area. Farmers of the desert, the Hohokam grew corn, beans, squash, and cotton. They lived in central Arizona from about AD 1 to 1450, at which point their civilization abandoned the Salt River (Rio Salado) valley and left behind remains of villages and a complex system of irrigation canals. The Papago Salado region is between Phoenix and Tempe and contains the Pueblo Grande ruins, the Desert Botanical Garden, the Phoenix Zoo, and Papago Park.

a good tour
From downtown Phoenix, take Washington Street east to the **Pueblo Grande Museum and Cultural Park** ⑯ ⌐, between 44th Street and the Hohokam Expressway (AZ 143). After a stop at the museum, follow Washington Street east 3½ mi to Priest Drive and turn north. Priest Drive becomes Galvin Parkway north of Van Buren Street; follow signs to entrances for the **Phoenix Zoo** ⑰ and **Papago Park** ⑱ or to the **Desert Botanical Garden** ⑲. Afterward, if you want to visit the **Hall of Flame** ⑳, drive south on Galvin Parkway to Van Buren Street; turn east and drive ⅛ mi, turning south onto Project Drive (at the buff-color stone marker that reads SALT RIVER PROJECT).

TIMING   Seeing all the sights requires the better part of a day. You may want to save the Desert Botanical Garden for the end of your tour, as it stays open 8–8 year-round and is particularly lovely when lighted by the setting sun or by moonlight.

Sights to See

☾ ⑲ **Desert Botanical Garden.** Opened in 1939 to conserve and showcase the ecology of the desert, these 150 acres contain more than 4,000 different species of cacti, succulents, trees, and flowers. A stroll along the ½-mi-long "Plants and People of the Sonoran Desert" trail is a fascinating lesson in environmental adaptations; children will enjoy playing the self-

Fodor'sChoice ★

guiding game "Desert Detective." The attractive Garden Shop is a wonderful place to purchase items associated with a green thumb. ✉ *1201 N. Galvin Pkwy. Papago Salado* ☎ *480/941–1225* ⊕ *www.dbg.org* ✉ *$7.50* ⊘ *Oct.–Apr., daily 8–8; May–Sept., daily 7 AM–8 PM.*

need a break? If you're headed to the Papago Salado region from downtown Phoenix, stop in **Kohnie's Coffee** (✉ 4225 E. Camelback Rd., Camelback Corridor ☎ 602/952–9948) for coffee, pastries, bagels, and scones. It's open at 7 AM (Sunday at 8 AM) and closed by 1 PM (noon on weekends and all day on Monday).

⑳ Hall of Flame. Retired firefighters lead tours through more than 100 restored fire engines and tell harrowing tales of the "world's most dangerous profession." Children can climb on a 1916 engine, operate alarm systems, and learn fire safety lessons from the pros. Helmets, badges, and other firefighting-related articles are on display, dating from as far back as 1725. ✉ *6101 E. Van Buren St., Papago Salado* ☎ *602/ 275–3473* ⊕ *www.hallofflame.org* ✉ *$5.50* ⊘ *Mon.–Sat. 9–5, Sun. noon–4.*

⑱ Papago Park. An amalgam of hilly desert terrain, streams, and lagoons, this park has picnic ramadas (shaded, open-air shelters), a golf course, a playground, hiking and biking trails, and even largemouth bass and trout fishing. (An urban fishing license is required for anglers age 15 and over.) The hike up to landmark **Hole-in-the-Rock** (a natural observatory used by the native Hohokam to devise a calendar system) is a much easier climb up than down. **Governor Hunt's Tomb,** the white pyramid at the top of Ramada 16, commemorates the former Arizona leader and provides a lovely view. ✉ *625 N. Galvin Pkwy., Papago Salado* ☎ *602/256–3220* ✉ *Free* ⊘ *Daily 6 AM–10 PM.*

⑰ Phoenix Zoo. Four designated trails wind through this 125-acre zoo, replicating such habitats as an African savannah and a tropical rain forest. Meerkats, warthogs, desert bighorn sheep, and the endangered Arabian oryx are among the unusual sights. The Forest of Uco is home to the endangered spectacled bear from South America. Harmony Farm on the Discovery Trail introduces youngsters to small mammals, and a stop at the big red barn provides a chance to groom a horse or milk a cow. Make sure to save time to walk through the enchanting Butterfly Pavilion. The 30-minute narrated safari train tour costs $2 and provides a good orientation to the park. In December, the popular "Zoo Lights" exhibit transforms the area into an enchanted forest of more than 225 million twinkling lights, many in the shape of the zoo's residents. ✉ *455 N. Galvin Pkwy., Papago Salado* ☎ *602/273–1341* ⊕ *www.phoenixzoo.org* ✉ *$12* ⊘ *Sept.–May, daily 9–5; June–Aug., daily 7 AM–8 PM.*

⑯ Pueblo Grande Museum and Cultural Park. Phoenix's only national landmark, this park (in the center of the city) was once the site of a 500-acre Hohokam village supporting about 1,000 people and containing homes, storage rooms, cemeteries, and ball courts. Three exhibition galleries hold displays on the Hohokam culture and archaeological methods. View the 10-minute orientation video before heading out on the ½-mi Ruin Trail past excavated mounds and ruins that give a hint of Hohokam savvy: there's a building whose corner doorway was perfectly placed to watch the summer solstice sunrise. Children will particularly like the hands-on, interactive learning center. ✉ *4619 E. Washington St., Papago Salado,* ☎ *602/495–0901* ⊕ *www.pueblogrande.com* ✉ *$2, free Sun.* ⊘ *Mon.–Sat. 9–4:45, Sun. 1–4:45.*

Tempe

In 1860, Charles Trumbell Hayden arrived on the east end of the Salt River, where he built a flour mill, warehouses, and a ferry across the river. This settlement and trade center became known as Hayden's Ferry. Other settlers soon arrived, including an English lord who felt—upon approaching the town from Phoenix and seeing the buttes, river, and fields of green mesquite—that the name should be changed to Tempe after the Vale of Tempe in Greece.

Today Tempe is home of Arizona State University's main campus and a thriving student population. A 20-minute drive from Phoenix, the tree- and brick-lined Mill Avenue (on which a flour mill at the site of Hayden's original still stands) is the main drag, rife with student-oriented hangouts, bookstores, boutiques, eateries, and a repertory movie house.

Tempe's banks on the Rio Salado are the future site of a commercial and entertainment district. Its first phase, Tempe Town Lake—a 2-mi-long waterway created by inflatable dams in a flood control channel—is open for boating. The lake is lined with biking and jogging paths, part of the project's design to encourage active recreation and promote development along the river.

a good walk Street parking is hard to find, but you can park in the public garage at Hayden Square, just north of 5th Street and west of Mill Avenue. Be sure to have your ticket stamped by local merchants to avoid paying parking fees. After parking, take a stroll a few minutes north to the shore of **Tempe Town Lake** ㉑ ⌐, where the new Tempe Arts Center, scheduled to open in 2006, is being built and where you can rent a boat, or you may wish to save the lake for a cool-down break later in the day. Then walk south again, toward **La Casa Vieja** ㉒, on the southwest corner of Mill Avenue and 1st Street; cross 1st Street; and enjoy your stroll through the Tempe Arts Center sculpture garden en route to the small center itself. Behind the main building, walk north to the old Mill Avenue bridge, where you can check out the Arts Center's rooftop artwork. Turn around and head to the main part of town. Walk south on Mill Avenue, passing the old Hayden flour mill—which is no longer operating—as well as "A" Mountain (so named by ASU students). Continue south along shop-lined Mill Avenue until you reach 5th Street; walk a block east on toward the inverted pyramid of **Tempe City Hall** ㉓. Follow the pathway west through the grounds of City Hall and Plazita de Descanso, back to Mill Avenue. Head two blocks south on Mill to University Drive and proceed to Gammage Parkway, where you'll find the Grady Gammage Auditorium and ASU art museums and galleries on the southwest corner of the **Arizona State University** ㉔ campus. You can walk back up Mill Avenue, catch the free FLASH shuttle northward (it stops on the north corner of Gammage Parkway and Mill Avenue), or wind your way northward through the university campus up toward ASU Sun Devil Stadium.

TIMING If you're planning to shop as well as tour the campus and museums, allow four or five hours for exploring. Stop by the Town Lake for a break during the day so that you can take a boat ride or simply soak up some sunshine.

Sights to See

㉔ **Arizona State University.** What began as the Tempe Normal School for Teachers—in 1886, a four-room redbrick building and 20-acre cow pasture—is now the 750-acre campus of ASU, the largest university in the Southwest. The **ASU Visitor Information Center** (✉ 826 E. Apache Blvd., at Rural Rd. ☎ 480/965–0100) has maps of a self-guided walking tour (it's a long walk from Mill Avenue, so you might opt for the short version suggested here). You'll wind past public art and innovative architecture—including a music building that bears a strong resemblance to a wedding cake (designed by Taliesin students to echo Frank Lloyd Wright's Gammage Auditorium) and a law library shaped like an open book—and end up at the 74,000-seat ASU Sun Devil Stadium, home to the school's Sun Devils and home field for the NFL's Arizona Cardinals. Admission to all ASU museums is free.

Heralded for its superior acoustics, the circular **Grady Gammage Auditorium** (✉ Mill Ave. at Apache Blvd. ☎ 480/965–4050) was the last public structure completed by architect Frank Lloyd Wright, who detached the rear wall from grand tier and balcony sections in an effort to surround every patron with sound. The stage can accommodate a full symphony orchestra, and there's a 2,909-pipe organ. Artwork is exhibited in the lobby and in two on-site galleries. Free half-hour tours are offered weekdays between 1 and 3:30 during the school year.

While touring the west end of campus, stop into the **Arizona State University Art Museum,** which is in the gray-purple stucco Nelson Fine Arts Center, just north of the Gammage Auditorium. The center's museum houses some fine examples of 19th- and 20th-century painting and sculpture by masters such as Winslow Homer, Edward Hopper, Georgia O'Keeffe, and Rockwell Kent; it has an extensive collection for a relatively small museum. You'll also find works by faculty and student artists and an interesting gift shop. ✉ *Mill Ave. and 10th St.* ☎ *480/ 965–2787* ⊕ *asuartmuseum.asu.edu* ✆ *Free* ☉ *Tues. 10–9, Wed.–Sat. 10–5, Sun. 1–5.*

A short walk east of the Nelson Fine Arts Center, just north of the Hayden Library, ASU's experimental gallery and collection of crockery and ceramics are in the **Matthews Center.** ✉ *Mill Ave. and 10th St.* ☎ *480/ 965–2875* ✆ *Free* ☉ *Sept.–May, Tues.–Sat. 10–5.*

In Matthews Hall, the **Northlight Gallery** (✉ Matthews Hall, Mill Ave. and 10th St. ☎ 480/965–6517 ☉ Mon.–Thurs. 10:30–4:30) exhibits works by both renowned and emerging photographers. There is no admission charge.

The **Edna Vihel Center for the Arts** (✉ 3340 S. Rural Rd., ☎ 480/350–5287) is a short drive from downtown Tempe and a major arts venue, offering rotating exhibits of paintings and photography, as well as book signings, readings, and charity events. There's also a small theater for play and dance productions.

㉒ **La Casa Vieja.** In 1871, when Tempe was still known as Hayden's Ferry, this adobe hacienda was built as the home of Charles Hayden and was the town's first building. Now a restaurant called **Monte's La Casa Vieja,** the lobby and dining rooms display historical photographs and are a good choice for lunch or a steak dinner while visiting Tempe. ✉ *3 W. 1st St.* ☎ *480/967–7594* ☉ *Sun.–Thurs. 11–11, Fri.–Sat. 11 AM–midnight.*

㉓ **Tempe City Hall.** Local architects Rolf Osland and Michael Goodwin constructed this inverted pyramid not just to win design awards (which they have) but also to shield city workers from the desert sun. The pyramid is constructed mainly of bronzed glass and stainless steel; the point disappears in a sunken courtyard lushly landscaped with jacaranda, ivy, and flowers, out of which the pyramid widens to the sky: stand underneath and gaze up for a weird fish-eye perspective. ✉ *31 E. 5th St., 1 block east of Mill Ave.* ☎ *480/967–2001* ✆ *Free.*

▶ **㉑** **Tempe Town Lake.** The Town Lake is the newest addition to the growth of Tempe and attracts college students and Valley residents of all ages. Call Rio Lago Cruises to rent your own boat or choose the Saturday sunset boat ride, which includes food, drinks, and music. Rio Lago's offices are located north of 3rd Street between Mill and Ash. ✉ *990 W. Rio Salado Pkwy., between Mill and Rural north of Arizona State University* ☎ *480/517–4050 Rio Lago Cruises* 🖾 *35-min Cruises $6, Sunset Cruises (Sat. only) $15* ☉ *Cruises Sun.–Thurs. 10–6, Fri.–Sat. 10–8.*

need a break? The outdoor patio of the **Coffee Plantation** (✉ 680 S. Mill Ave. ☎ 480/829–7878), a popular café near the ASU campus, is a lively scene—students cramming, local residents chatting over a cup of joe, and poets and musicians presenting their latest works.

Scottsdale

Historic sites, nationally known art galleries, and souvenir shops fill downtown Scottsdale; a quick walking tour can easily turn into an all-day excursion if you browse. Historic Old Town Scottsdale has the look of the Old West, and 5th Avenue is known for shopping and Native American jewelry and crafts stores. Cross onto Main Street and enter a world frequented by the international art set (Scottsdale has the third-largest artist community in the United States). Discover more galleries and interior-design shops along Marshall Way.

Numbers in the text correspond to numbers in the margin and on the What to See in Central and Downtown Scottsdale and What to See in Greater Phoenix maps.

a good tour

Park in the free public lot on the corner of 2nd Street and Wells Fargo Avenue, east of Scottsdale Road.

Start your walk by exiting the parking structure from its northeast corner, where a short brick-paved sidewalk leads northward to the plaza of Scottsdale Mall. The **Scottsdale Center for the Arts** ㉕ ▶ is right there. Be sure to check out the **Scottsdale Museum of Contemporary Art** ㉖, right next door to the main center building. Stroll counterclockwise around the mall's lovely grounds, passing Scottsdale's library and municipal buildings and ending up on the plaza's west side by **Scottsdale Historical Museum** ㉗. Continue west to the intersection of Brown Avenue and Main Street to reach the heart of **Old Town Scottsdale** ㉘, occupying four square blocks from Brown Avenue to Scottsdale Road, between Indian School Road and 2nd Street. From Main Street in Old Town, cross Scottsdale Road to the central drag of the **Main Street Arts District** ㉙. Turn north onto Goldwater Boulevard and gallery-stroll for another two blocks. At Indian School Road, head one block east to the **Marshall Way Arts District** ㉚. Continue two blocks north on Marshall Way to the fountain of prancing horses that marks **5th Avenue** ㉛. A couple of blocks north is the **Scottsdale Convention and Visitors Bureau** ㉜, on Scottsdale Road. If you return to 5th Avenue, you can catch the trolley back to Scottsdale Mall here, on the south side of the intersection of 5th Avenue and Stetson Drive, or walk the five blocks south on Scottsdale Road and one block east on Main Street.

Not far from downtown Scottsdale are two other worthy attractions worth a drive: **Taliesin West** ㉝ was Frank Lloyd Wright's winter home. In the El Pedregal Marketplace, at the Boulders Resort in Carefree, is the **Heard Museum North** ㉞. While in North Scottsdale, you might also wish to see the fascinating metal and ceramic wind chimes at Cosanti Originals studio, made by disciples of Paolo Soleri, the father of the futuristic planned community Arcosanti (⇨ *see* Shopping).

TIMING   You could easily spend a full day in downtown Scottsdale, as there's a lot to take in between the countless galleries and shops. Most galleries on Main Street and Marshall Way are open Thursday evenings until 9. Although your tour of the downtown area can easily be completed on foot, a trolley runs through the area and out to several resorts: Ollie the Trolley charges $5 for an all-day pass, although service within downtown Scottsdale is free (☎ 480/970–8130 information). If you have a limited amount of time, spend a half-day in downtown Scottsdale and the rest of the day at Taliesin West, or spend a morning at Taliesin West and then drive to El Pedregal for an afternoon of shopping and art viewing at the Heard Museum North.

What to See

㉛ 5th Avenue. For more than 40 years, this shopping stretch has been the location of boutiques and specialty shops. Whether you seek handmade Native American arts and crafts, casual clothing, or cacti, you'll find it here—plus colorful storefronts, friendly merchants, even an old "cigar-store" Indian. ⊠ *5th Ave. between Civic Center Rd. and Stetson Dr., Downtown.*

㉞ Heard Museum North. A small satellite of the big Heard in downtown Phoenix has one gallery with its own small, permanent collection of Native American art; it also hosts two rotating exhibits during the year, which may be made up of items from the parent Heard's permanent collection or exhibits on loan from other museums. The gift shop is well stocked with expensive, high-quality items. ⊠ *Boulders Shopping Mall,*

34505 N. Scottsdale Rd., at Carefree Hwy., North Scottsdale Scottsdale
☎ *480/488–9817* ⊕ *www.heard.org* ✆ *$3* ☉ *Mon.–Sat. 10–5:30, Sun.*
noon–5:30.

need a break? **Bakery Cafe at El Pedregal Marketplace** (⊠ 34505 N. Scottsdale Rd., at Carefree Hwy. ☎ 480/488–4100) is an ideal place to stop for a bite to eat and a cool drink. Sit outdoors in the beautiful garden setting of this Moroccan-inspired mall nestled at the base of 250-ft tall boulders.

★ ㉙ **Main Street Arts District.** Gallery after gallery displays artwork of myriad styles—contemporary, western realism, Native American, and traditional. Several antiques shops are also here; specialties include porcelains and china, jewelry, and Oriental rugs. ⊠ *Bounded by Main St. and 1st Ave., Scottsdale Rd. and 69th St., Downtown.*

㉚ **Marshall Way Arts District.** Galleries that exhibit predominantly contemporary art line the blocks of Marshall Way north of Indian School Road. Upscale gift and jewelry stores can be found here, too. Farther north on Marshall Way across 3rd Avenue, the street is filled with more art galleries and creative stores with a southwestern flair. ⊠ *Marshall Way, from Indian School Rd. to 5th Ave., Downtown.*

㉘ **Old Town Scottsdale.** Billed as "the West's Most Western Town," this area of Scottsdale has rustic storefronts and wooden sidewalks; it's touristy, but it's the closest you'll come to experiencing life here as it was 80 years ago. High-quality jewelry, pots, and Mexican imports are sold alongside the expected kitschy souvenirs. ⊠ *Main St. from Scottsdale Rd. to Brown Ave., Downtown.*

▶ ㉕ **Scottsdale Center for the Arts.** Galleries within this cultural and entertainment complex rotate exhibits frequently, but they typically emphasize contemporary art and artists. The airy and bright **Museum Store** (☎ 480/874–4464) has a great collection of unusual jewelry, as well as stationery, posters, and art books. ⊠ *7380 E. 2nd St., Downtown* ☎ *480/994–2787* ⊕ *www.scottsdalearts.org* ✆ *Free* ☉ *Mon.–Wed. and Fri.–Sat. 10–5, Thurs. 10–8, Sun. noon–5; also during performance intermissions.*

㉜ **Scottsdale Convention and Visitors Bureau.** Pop inside to pick up some local maps, guidebooks, and brochures. Ask the helpful staff for a walking-tour map of Old Town Scottsdale's historic sites. ⊠ *4343 Scottsdale Rd., at Drinkwater Blvd., Suite 170, Downtown* ☎ *480/421–1004 or 800/ 782–1117* ⊕ *www.scottsdalecvb.com* ✆ *Free* ☉ *Weekdays 8:30–6, Sat. 10–4.*

㉗ **Scottsdale Historical Museum.** Scottsdale's first schoolhouse, this redbrick building houses a version of the 1910 schoolroom, as well as photographs, original furniture from the city's founding fathers, and displays of other treasures from Scottsdale's early days. ⊠ *7333 Scottsdale Mall, Downtown* ☎ *602/945–4499* ✆ *Free* ☉ *Sept.–June, Wed.–Sat. 10–5, Sun. noon–5.*

㉖ **Scottsdale Museum of Contemporary Art.** This museum, next to the Scottsdale Center for the Arts, is housed in the spectacular Gerard L. Cafesjian Pavilion. When you step through the immense glass entryway designed by New York artist James Fraser Carpenter and stroll through the spaces within the five galleries, you'll realize it's not just the spacious outdoor sculpture garden that makes this a "museum without walls." New installations are planned every few months, with an emphasis on contemporary art, architecture, and design. Free, docent-led tours are conduct on Thursdays at 1:30. ⊠ *7380 E. 2nd St., Downtown* ☎ *480/ 994–2787* ⊕ *www.scottsdalearts.org* ☜ *$7, free Thurs.* ☉ *Tues.–Wed. and Fri.–Sat. 10–5, Thurs. 10–8, Sun. noon–5.*

need a break? Walk into the **Sugar Bowl Ice Cream Parlor** (⊠ 4005 N. Scottsdale Rd. ☎ 480/946–0051), and you'll swear you've been transported back in time to a 1950s malt shop. Doing business in the same building since 1958, the Sugar Bowl serves great burgers and lots of yummy ice cream confections. Valley resident Bil Keane, creator of the comic strip "Family Circus," has often used this spot as inspiration for his cartoons, many of which are on display here.

㉝ **Taliesin West.** Ten years after visiting Arizona in 1927 to consult on de-
Fodor'sChoice signs for the Biltmore hotel, architect Frank Lloyd Wright chose 600
★ acres of rugged Sonoran Desert at the foothills of the McDowell Mountains as the site for his permanent winter residence. Today the site is a National Historic Landmark and still an active community of students and architects. Wright and apprentices constructed a desert camp here, using organic architecture to integrate the buildings with their natural surroundings. In addition to the living quarters, drafting studio, and small apartments of the Apprentice Court, Taliesin West also has two theaters, a music pavilion, and the Sun Trap—sleeping spaces surrounding an open patio and fireplace. Two guided tours cover different parts of the interior, and a guided desert walk winds through the petroglyphs and landscape from which Wright drew his vision. Five guided tours are offered, ranging from a one-hour "panorama" tour to a three-hour behind-the-scenes tour, with other tours offered seasonally. Times vary, so call ahead; all visitors must be accompanied by a guide. ⊠ *12621 Frank Lloyd Wright Blvd., North Scottsdale* ☎ *480/860–8810 or 480/860–2700* ⊕ *www.franklloydwright.org* ☜ *$12.50–$45* ☉ *Sept.–June, daily 8:30–5:30; July–Aug., Thurs.–Mon. 8:30–5:30.*

WHERE TO EAT

Phoenix and its environs draw millions of visitors every year: tourists, conventioneers, and winter snowbirds who roost for months at a time. The population boom has been matched by an astonishing restaurant renaissance. Inventive local chefs have put Southwestern cuisine on the world culinary map. Travelers with sophisticated tastes will be thrilled with Phoenix's restaurants, some ranked among the country's best.

Restaurants are remarkably casual. Except for a handful of high-end spots, slacks and sports shirt are dressy enough for men; pants or a simple skirt are appropriate for women. Phoenix is a sprawling metropolis without much demarcation as to where one town stops and another starts; there are few suburban "downtown" areas. Therefore, first-time visitors to the Valley from the East and Midwest are often surprised to discover that many of the finest Valley restaurants are located in either hotels or strip malls.

Remember that restaurants change hours, locations, chefs, prices, and menus frequently, so it's best to call ahead to confirm. Show up without a reservation during tourist season, and you may find the drive-through window the only place in town without a two-hour wait. All listed restaurants are open for lunch and dinner unless otherwise specified.

Prices

	WHAT IT COSTS			
$$$$	**$$$**	**$$**	**$**	**¢**
AT DINNER	over $30	$20–$30	$12–$20	$8–$12	under $8

Prices are per person for a main course. The final tab will include sales tax of 8.1% in Phoenix, 7.7% in Scottsdale.

Downtown Phoenix

American

$$–$$$$ ✕ **Durant's Fine Foods.** Durant's has endured since 1950 in the same location, with the same menu, and even many of the original waitstaff, making it one of Phoenix's legendary eating establishments. Steaks, chops, and fresh seafood, including Florida stone crab, dominate here; when the restaurant once tried to update its menu, regulars protested so furiously, the idea was shelved. The bar is an entertaining place to partake in a lively conversation, toss down a half-dozen or so succulent oysters on the half shell, and sip a martini. This was the first Valley restaurant to ban cell phones in its dining room. Bravo! ✉ *2611 N. Central Ave., Downtown* ☏ *602/264–5967* ▤ *AE, D, DC, MC, V.*

$–$$ ✕ **Coronado Café.** You might miss this hidden treasure if it weren't for the lines of customers waiting outside at lunchtime. This charming 1950s residence in the heart of Phoenix has merely 30 seats and immediate parking for three vehicles, but you'll be happy you stopped by for such homemade favorites as chicken-corn chowder or a chicken Caesar sandwich that you need to eat with a fork. The entrées change daily, but on a hot summer day, be sure to order the homemade iced tea (it's BYOB if you desire something with a little more kick). ✉ *2201 N. 7th St., Downtown* ☏ *602/258–5149* ⚝ *Reservations not accepted* ▤ *MC, V* ◔ *Closed Sun.–Mon. No dinner Sat.*

¢–$ ✕ **Mrs. White's Golden Rule Café.** This downtown lunch spot is open only until 5 PM, but it's the best place in town for true Southern cooking. Every entrée—from fried chicken to pork chops—comes with corn bread, and the peach cobbler is legendary. You'll also find catfish, black-eyed peas, and collard greens. ✉ *808 E. Jefferson St., Downtown* ☏ *602/262–9256* ⚝ *Reservations not accepted* ▤ *No credit cards* ◔ *Closed weekends. No dinner.*

Chinese

¢–$$ ✕ **Gourmet House of Hong Kong.** This popular Chinese restaurant draws customers who are interested in such genuine Chinatown specialties as *chow fun* (thick rice noodles). Try the assorted-meat version, topped with chicken, shrimp, pork, and squid. Lobster with black bean sauce may be the world's messiest platter, but it's also one of the tastiest. Along with an extensive seafood list, such adventurous delights as five-flavor frogs' legs, duck feet with greens, and beef tripe casserole are offered. ✉ *1438 E. McDowell Rd., Downtown* ☏ *602/253–4859* ▤ *AE, D, DC, MC, V.*

Pizza

★ $ ✕ **Pizzeria Bianco.** In this small pizzeria in Heritage Square, Brooklyn native Chris Bianco makes pizza with a passion. He uses a wood-fired brick oven imported from Italy and makes his own mozzarella cheese. Other toppings include homemade fennel sausage, wood-roasted cremini mushrooms, and the freshest herbs and spices. The wine bar next door is a good place to wait for your table, as the restaurant doesn't take reservations. ✉ *623 E. Adams St., Downtown* ☏ *602/258–8300* ⚝ *Reservations not accepted* ▤ *MC, V* ◔ *Closed Mon. No lunch weekends.*

Where to Eat in Phoenix

Central Phoenix

Central Phoenix is bounded by Camelback Road on the north, Paradise Valley on the east, I–17 on the west, and Buckeye Road (excluding Papago Salado) on the south.

Chinese

¢–$$ ✕ **China Chile.** You might drive past this place hundreds of times and never be tempted to stop, but beyond the bright pink facade and windowless storefront, you'll find a busy restaurant filled with very happy diners for lunch and dinner. Start with the plump, boiled wontons in a spicy Szechuan peanut sauce. The chicken in a phoenix nest is a crisp potato nest filled with succulent chicken, crunchy vegetables, and bean sauce garnished with quail eggs. Vegetable offerings, including the crispy Szechuan-style string beans in garlic sauce and spicy eggplant braised in chili paste, are a meal unto themselves. ✉ *3501 N. Central Ave., Central Phoenix* ☎ *602/266–4463* ▭ *AE, DC, MC, V* ☉ *Closed Sun. No lunch Sat.*

Italian

$$–$$$ ✕ **Avanti.** Owners Angelo Livi and Benito Mellino have been welcoming guests to this classic Italian restaurant since 1974. For starters, try one of the house specialties, light and divine potato gnocchi paired with spinach ravioli. The veal dishes, such as saltimbocca or osso buco, are particularly memorable. Other entrées on the extensive menu include cioppino, paella, and a daily homemade pasta special. The dining room, piano bar, and dance area were remodeled in 2002 and impart a fresh, romantic atmosphere to this venerable favorite. ✉ *2728 E. Thomas Rd., Central Phoenix* ☎ *602/956–0900* ▭ *AE, D, DC, MC, V* ☉ *No lunch weekends.*

$$–$$$ ✕ **Nonni's Kitchen.** "Nonni" is what owner-chef Chrysa Kaufman called her grandmother, who no doubt would approve of the well-prepared food served here. Cozily decorated with old family photos and warm woods, this friendly, neighborhood restaurant makes you feel comfortable immediately Mesquite-grilled flatbread brushed with herb-infused olive oil is the perfect accompaniment to the outstanding vegetable antipasto—an airy potato frittata surrounded by baby beets, marinated beans, mushrooms, and other organic veggies grown locally at Victory Farms. Delicious main courses include Nonni's Sunday chicken, braised in white wine with herbs, onions, and mushrooms. Don't miss the honey-dipped doughnuts for dessert. ✉ *4410 N. 40th St., Central Phoenix* ☎ *602/977–1800* ▭ *AE, D, DC, MC, V* ☉ *Closed Sun. No lunch.*

★ $$ ✕ **La Fontanella.** Quality and value add up to a winning combination at this outstanding neighborhood restaurant. The interior is reminiscent of an Italian villa, with antiques, crisp table linens, fresh flowers, and windows dressed in lace curtains. Chef-owner Isabelle Bertuccio turns out magnificent food, often using recipes from her Tuscan and Sicilian relatives. The escargot appetizer and herb-crusted rack of lamb entrée top the list. Homemade pasta is served with Sicilian semolina bread and homemade sausages or meatballs. For dessert, Isabelle's husband, Berto, creates sumptuous gelato, which he supplies to restaurants and resorts Valley-wide. ✉ *4231 E. Indian School Rd., Central Phoenix* ☎ *602/ 955–1213* ▭ *AE, D, DC, MC, V* ☉ *No lunch weekends.*

Mexican

¢–$ ✕ **Oaxaca.** Mama's recipes for fresh tortillas, *calavasitas* (squash with melted cheese), and excellent green-corn tamales have been drawing locals to this friendly establishment since 1976. The decor is dated and the restaurant is not in the best neighborhood (just a few blocks from

ON THE MENU

ALTHOUGH YOU'LL FIND the largest concentration of good Mexican restaurants in Tucson, Phoenix has its fair share as well. Some menus are in Spanish only, so it's helpful to know the key words. The predominant cuisine is Sonoran.

Aguas frescas: A fresh-fruit drink, sort of a smoothie
Albondigas: Meatball soup
Almendrado: An almond dessert, often the colors of the Mexican flag
Atole: A sweet drink made with corn masa, milk, and crushed fruit
Birria: Traditionally stewed goat, but often made with beef
Caldo de queso: Cheese-and-potato soup
Carne asada: Grilled marinated beef
Carne seca: Sun-dried, marinated beef
Carnitas: Stewed pork
Cazuela: Machaca soup
Chorizo: Spicy pork or pork-and-beef sausage

Enchiladas: Soft corn tortillas filled with meat or cheese, covered with sauce
Flautas: Rolled, deep-fried tacos
Horchata: Rice-milk and cinnamon drink
Machaca: Dried beef cooked with tomatoes, onions, chilies, and often egg
Mariscos: shellfish
Menudo: Hominy-and-tripe stew
Mole: A sauce made from chiles, spices, crushed seeds, and flavored with chocolate
Posole: Hominy-and-pork stew
Sopa Azteca: Soup, made with chicken, avocados, and tortillas in broth
Tacos: Tortillas, briefly heated, filled and wrapped into thin cylinders
Tamales: Pockets of corn dough, with savory fillings, which are wrapped in corn husks and steamed.
Tortas: Sandwich on a white bun
Tostadas: Lightly friend, open tortillas topped with meat, lettuce, etc.
Tripitas de leche: Tripe (the stomach) of a cow

---

the state capitol), but the food is authentic and freshly prepared in the restaurant's kitchen every day. Oaxaca attracts a crowd of local politicians and men in blue. Guitarists entertain on weekends. ⊠ *1516 W. Van Buren St., Central Phoenix* ☎ *602/258–0804* ☐ *AE, D, MC, V.*

Spanish

$$–$$$ ✕ **Altos.** Sophisticated locals come here to bask in the scents of Iberia—garlic, sherry, olive oil, and saffron. *Calamari de Pedro* (tender squid dipped in a saffron batter and sizzled in olive oil) is a good appetizer for sharing. Main dishes include the *filete pelon,* a buttery filet mignon topped with Spanish cabrales blue cheese. *Lomo en adobo*—pork loin smothered in a chili, sesame seed, sugar, and peanut sauce—is reminiscent of mole dishes. The sugar-glazed chocolate espresso crème brûlée is deservedly popular. ⊠ *5029 N. 44th St., Central Phoenix* ☎ *602/808–0890* ☐ *AE, D, DC, MC, V* ☉ *No lunch weekends.*

Phoenix: Camelback Corridor

The Camelback Corridor, a veritable restaurant row, runs west to east from Phoenix to Scottsdale—the cities are divided by 64th Street.

Contemporary

$$–$$$$ ✕ **Eddie Matney's.** A Phoenix star, chef Eddie Matney delights diners with what he calls "new American" cuisine, which he defines as traditional foods prepared in unexpected ways. You can order such creative and beautifully presented comfort foods as bacon- and basil-seasoned meat loaf with country mashed potatoes and wild mushroom gravy, or a macaroni casserole baked with goat cheese and topped with Dungeness crab. Desserts like the peanut butter, chocolate, and banana Boston cream pie

are indulgent masterpieces. ✉ *2398 E. Camelback Rd., Camelback Corridor* ☎ *602/957–3214* ▤ *AE, D, DC, MC, V* ⊘ *Closed Sun. No lunch weekends.*

$$–$$$ ✕ **Tarbell's.** It's evident that cutting-edge cuisine is the star at this sophisticated, sleek neighborhood bistro. Hardwood floors, copper accents, and a curving cherry-wood and maple bar create an attractive, cosmopolitan look. The foccacia with red onion, Romano cheese, and roasted thyme is excellent. Grilled salmon served on a crispy potato cake and drizzled with molasses-lime glaze is a long-standing classic. Imaginative designer pizzas are cooked in a wood-burning oven, and desserts are wonderful here. Your sweet tooth won't be disappointed if you opt for Tarbell's warm, rich, chocolate cake topped with pistachio ice cream. ✉ *3213 E. Camelback Rd., Camelback Corridor* ☎ *602/955–8100* ⌲ *Reservations essential* ▤ *AE, D, DC, MC, V* ⊘ *No lunch.*

$$–$$$ ✕ **Tomaso's.** In a town where restaurants come and go overnight, Tomaso's has been a favorite since 1977, and for good reason. Chef Tomaso Maggiore learned to cook as a child at the family's restaurant in Palermo, Sicily, and honed his skills at the Culinary Institute of Rome. The result is authentic, classic Italian cuisine that is consistently well prepared and delicious. The house specialty, *cuscinetto di vitella* (veal stuffed with prosciutto and mascarpone cheese) is outstanding. Other notables include *crostacei fradiavolo* (mounds of shellfish heaped over linguini), as well as risotto, osso buco, and cannelloni. ✉ *3225 E. Camelback Rd., Camelback Corridor* ☎ *602/956–0836* ▤ *AE, D, DC, MC, V* ⊘ *No lunch weekends.*

French

$$–$$$ ✕ **Bistro 24.** Smart and stylish, with impeccable service, Bistro 24 greets diners with its parquet floor, colorful murals, elegant bar, and outdoor patio. Stop here for a break from shopping and enjoy the largest Cobb salad in town and a cup of French-press coffee. For dinner, try a classic French favorite such as steak au poivre with frites, cassoulet, bouillabaisse, or simply a well-prepared grilled salmon or crispy-skin whitefish. The bistro's Sunday brunch is a local favorite. ✉ *Ritz-Carlton Hotel, 2401 E. Camelback Rd., Camelback Corridor* ☎ *602/952–2424* ▤ *AE, D, DC, MC, V.*

$$–$$$ ✕ **Christopher's Fermier Brasserie & Paola's Wine Bar.** Chef Christopher Gross and wine director Paola Gross have made this spot one of the most welcoming in town by serving simple, delicious fare using the freshest ingredients and produce from local farmers. Foods are prepared in the brasserie tradition, and the salad with goat cheese, leek tart, lobster bisque, steak au poivre, and bouillabaisse are all comfort foods of the highest order. The wine bar offers more than 100 vintages by the glass and stocks an excellent selection of cigars. ✉ *Biltmore Fashion Park, 2584 E. Camelback Rd., Camelback Corridor* ☎ *602/522–2344* ▤ *AE, D, DC, MC, V.*

Greek

$$–$$$ ✕ **Greekfest.** This informal but elegant restaurant is lovingly appointed with thick, arched, whitewashed walls; tasteful bric-a-brac; hardwood floors; and attractive table settings. The food pleases as well. Among the appetizers, look for *taramasalata* (mullet roe blended with lemon and olive oil) and *saganaki* (cheese flamed with brandy and extinguished with a squirt of lemon). Entrées, such as *exohiko* (succulent chunks of lamb with cheese and roasted vegetables baked in phyllo dough) or salmon *chios* (salmon fillet baked with feta cheese, kalamata olives, and pine nuts), are equally hard-hitting. For dessert, the *galaktoboureko* (warm custard pie baked in phyllo) is a triumph of Western civilization. ✉ *1940 E. Camelback Rd., Camelback Corridor* ☎ *602/265–2990* ▤ *AE, D, DC, MC, V* ⊘ *No lunch Sun.*

Italian

$$–$$$ ✕ **Acqua E Sale.** This popular and tastefully decorated restaurant serves consistently good Italian food. In particular, the veal dishes—like scallopini with white truffle and porcini mushroom sauce—are wonderful. Ravioli stuffed with sweet butternut squash and Chilean sea bass are popular choices. Appetizers include dishes that have come to be favorites of Americans: fried calamari, duck prosciutto, and buffalo milk mozzarella and tomato salad. ⊠ *4225 E. Camelback Rd., Camelback Corridor* ☎ *602/952–1522* ▭ *AE, MC, V* ☉ *Closed Sun. No lunch.*

☾ $–$$ ✕**Tucchetti.** Straw-clad Chianti bottles, red-checkered tablecloths, strings of colorful lights, and a festive, informal (and often loud) atmosphere make dining here fun. The fare is hearty, home-style cooking and includes such Italian staples as chicken Vesuvio, veal piccata, and several mix-and-match pastas and sauces. Thin-crust pizzas are a menu highlight, and the signature dish, a baked cube of spaghetti, is presented with dramatic fanfare by the upbeat staff. There's an endless salad bar featuring antipasti, homemade minestrone soup, and bread. On Monday, the kids' menu is free for those under 13, when they are accompanied by an adult. ⊠ *2135 E. Camelback Rd., Camelback Corridor* ☎ *602/ 957–0222* ▭ *AE, D, MC, V.*

Mediterranean

★ $$$–$$$$ ✕ **T. Cook's.** One of the finest restaurants in the Valley, T. Cook's oozes ambience and romance. Floor-to-ceiling windows with dramatic views of Camelback Mountain and exquisite 1930s-style decor add up to a perfect setting for a special evening. The artistic, Mediterranean-style menu features rotisserie specialties prepared in the restaurant's lodge-style fireplace. Such delectables as lobster bisque with farm-raised Arizona shrimp, osso buco, and spit-roasted chicken with baby corn are offered. Desserts and pastries, prepared by famed pastry chef Pierino Jermonti, are nothing less than spectacular works of art. ⊠ *Royal Palms Resort & Spa, 5200 E. Camelback Rd., Camelback Corridor* ☎ *602/808–0766* ⌣ *Reservations essential* ▭ *AE, D, DC, MC, V.*

Southwestern

$$$ ✕**Vincent Guerithault on Camelback.** Chef Guerithault is best known for creating French food with a Southwestern touch. You can make a meal of his famous appetizers, duck confit tamales and salmon quesadillas. His signature crème brûlée arrives in three thin pastry cups filled with vanilla, coffee, and coconut custard. On Saturday from 9 AM to 1 PM, you'll find exotic fruits, vegetables, and cheeses at the Touch of Provence market held in the restaurant parking lot. ⊠ *3930 E. Camelback Rd., Camelback Corridor* ☎ *602/224–0225* ⌣ *Reservations essential* ▭ *AE, D, DC, MC, V* ☉ *No lunch weekends.*

Steak

$$$$ ✕ **Harris' Restaurant.** This upscale steak house serves only prime beef aged on the premises for 21 days. The elegant supper-club interior evokes the San Francisco original. Start with Harris's famous martini, and then move on to the extensive wine list. All the steak cuts are marvelous, but the fresh fish is exquisite, too. Servers are gracious and attentive. ⊠ *3101 E. Camelback Rd., Camelback Corridor* ☎ *602/502–8888* ⌣ *Reservations essential* ▭ *AE, D, DC, MC, V* ☉ *Closed Sun. No lunch Sat.*

North-Central Phoenix

North-central Phoenix is the area north of Camelback Road between I–17 and Paradise Valley.

Contemporary

$$$–$$$$ ✕ **Convivo.** This is the closest you'll get to a Manhattan dining experience in the desert: a dozen tables, a tiny kitchen, and a rotating new American menu featuring fresh seasonal produce. You'll find American standards combined with unexpected flavors such as the coconut-crusted ahi tuna topped with fried calamari and drizzled with plum-marigold-mint vinaigrette. The "Convivo collection" appetizer plate elevates vegetables to an art form and includes an ever-changing assortment of hummus, cheeses, and salads. Save room for exciting desserts like the fudgy ancho-chili brownie. The wine list is thoughtful and not overpriced. ✉ 7000 N. 16th St., North-Central Phoenix ☎ 602/997–7676 ☐ AE, D, DC, MC, V ✪ Closed Sun.–Mon. No lunch.

French

★ $$$–$$$$ ✕ **Coup Des Tartes.** This old house has lent its setting to a casual, yet attractive, country French restaurant with seating scattered among three small rooms. This is a casual BYOB place, and there's an $8 corkage fee; however, all's forgiven when you taste the delicate cuisine prepared in the restaurant's tiny kitchen. Chef-owner Natascha Ovando, who is a graduate of the French Culinary Institute in New York, changes the menu weekly, sometimes even daily. Offerings may include such dishes as baked Brie, fennel-tinged sea bass, or lemon-herb chicken on a bed of spinach basil risotto. Ovando's signature dessert, a banana brûlée tart, is absolutely delectable. ✉ 4626 N. 16th St., North-Central Phoenix ☎ 602/212–1082 ⌕ Reservations essential ☐ AE, D, DC, MC, V ✪ Closed Sun.–Mon. No lunch.

Indian

$–$$ ✕ **Taste of India.** This perennial favorite in the Valley specializes in northern Indian cuisine. Breads here—*bhatura, naan, paratha*—are superb. Just about every spice in the rack is used for the lamb and chicken dishes and vegetarians will enjoy wonderful meatless specialties. Be prepared to guzzle extra water if your server says an item is spicy. ✉ 1609 E. Bell Rd., North-Central Phoenix ☎ 602/788–3190 ☐ AE, D, MC, V.

Italian

$$–$$$ ✕ **Christo's Ristorante.** Cozy and unassuming in a Phoenix strip mall, Christo's keeps its tables filled with loyal customers for both lunch and dinner. Attentive servers ensure that your water glass never empties and that bread doesn't have enough time to cool. Folks rave about the roasted rack of lamb, the veal, and the tortellini alla papalina. All main courses come with delicious soup and salad. ✉ 6327 N. 7th St., North-Central Phoenix ☎ 602/264–1784 ☐ AE, D, DC, MC, V ✪ Closed Sun.

¢–$ ✕ **Mediterranean House.** Filled with locals at lunch and dinner, this homey neighborhood restaurant is nothing fancy. The cuisine is a bit ill-defined and seems to cover an area between Greece and the Middle East, but the Korean owners still manage to dish out tasty and well-prepared Mediterranean food. The thick, spicy lentil soup is very pleasing, and the Egyptian chicken—a huge plate of sliced chicken breast, battered and fried, is absolutely delicious. Vegetarians appreciate the combination plate piled with baba ghanouj, hummus, and falafel balls served with warm pita bread and a zesty yogurt sauce. ✉ 1588 E. Bethany Home Rd. North-Central Phoenix ☎ 602/248–8460 ☐ AE, MC, V ✪ Closed Sun. No lunch Sat.

Papago Salado

Papago Salado is the area southeast of central Phoenix near Tempe.

Barbecue

¢ ✕ **Honey Bear's BBQ.** Honey Bear's motto—"You don't need no teeth to eat our meat"—may fall short on grammar, but this place isn't packed with folks looking to improve their language skills. This is Tennessee-style barbecue, which means smoky baby back ribs basted in thick, zippy, slightly sweet sauce with a wonderful orange tang. The sausage-enhanced "cowbro" beans and scallion-studded potato salad are great sides. If a slab of ribs still leaves you hungry, finish up with the homemade sweet potato pie. ⊠ *5012 E. Van Buren St., Phoenix Papago Salado* ☎ *602/273–9148* ♿ *Reservations not accepted* ▱ *AE, D, MC, V.*

South Phoenix

South Phoenix is the area south of Buckeye Road, between 27th Avenue on the west and Tempe on the east.

Japanese

$–$$$ ✕ **Shinbay.** This small, serene spot is the perfect place to have a relaxing sushi meal, complete with flights of premium sake. The raw fish is the freshest in town, and the cooked dishes are also lovely. Three-course dinner specials change nightly. At lunch, the bento box is a good value. ⊠ *15410 S. Mountain Pkwy., South Phoenix* ☎ *602/704–1422* ▱ *AE, MC, V* ☽ *Closed Sun. No lunch Mon.*

Mexican

★ ¢–$$ ✕ **Los Dos Molinos.** In a hacienda that belonged to Tom Mix, this entertaining restaurant focuses on New Mexican–style Mexican food. And that means *hot*. Hatch, New Mexico, chilies form the backbone of the dishes here, and the green-chili enchilada and beef taco are potentially lethal. The red salsa and the stacked enchiladas with an egg on top are so good you'll beg for more. There's also a funky courtyard where you can sip margaritas while waiting for a table. This is a must-do dining experience if you want some authentic New Mexican–style food, but come prepared to swig lots of water. ⊠ *8646 S. Central Ave., South Phoenix* ☎ *602/243–9113* ♿ *Reservations not accepted* ▱ *AE, D, MC, V* ☽ *Closed Sun.–Mon.*

¢ ✕ **Carolina's.** This small, nondescript restaurant in south Phoenix makes the most delicious, thin-as-air, flour tortillas imaginable. In-the-know locals and downtown working folks have been lining up at Carolina's for years to partake of its homey and downright cheap Mexican food. Food is served on paper plates. The menu offers the standard tacos, tamales, burritos, flautas, and enchiladas, but everything here is truly delicious. You can also purchase homemade chorizo and tamales by the dozen. Or, for a couple of dollars, you can buy a package of warm tortillas to take home, but chances are they'll be gone long before you arrive. ⊠ *1202 E. Mohave St., South Phoenix* ☎ *602/252–1503* ▱ *AE, MC, V.*

Fodor'sChoice
★

Paradise Valley

Paradise Valley is a town that has been absorbed into the greater Phoenix area; it's bordered by McDonald Drive to the south, Scottsdale Road to the east, Shea Boulevard to the north, and the Phoenix Mountain Preserve to the west.

Contemporary

$$$ ✕ **elements.** Perched on the side of Camelback Mountain at the Sanctuary Resort, this spot is popular with the cocktail crowd for breath-

taking desert sunsets and city-light views. There's a cordial community table where you can sit and order such appetizers as duck spring rolls, chilled tiger shrimp with Asian slaw, and fried calamari with miso-scallion vinaigrette. Among the best main courses are rack of lamb and penne with wild mushrooms. ⊠ *Sanctuary on Camelback Mountain, 5700 E. McDonald Dr., Paradise Valley* ☎ *480/948–2100* ⊟ *AE, D, DC, MC, V.*

$$$ ✕ **Lon's at the Hermosa.** The romantic setting—in a historic adobe ha-
FodorsChoice   cienda hand-built by cowboy artist Lon Megargee—has sweeping vis-
★   tas of Camelback Mountain and a lovely patio, perfect for an after-dinner drink under the stars. The dining room is decorated with Megargee's art and other interesting cowboy memorabilia. The menu includes such appetizers as rock shrimp with roasted-corn sauce and juniper-smoked wild Chinook salmon. Main courses include the wood-grilled filet mignon over Gorgonzola-mashed potatoes, which melts in your mouth, and more exotic dishes like pecan-grilled antelope. Fresh vegetables and herbs are pulled from the property's own garden. Sunday brunch is popular with Phoenicians. ⊠ *Hermosa Inn, 5532 N. Palo Cristi Dr., Paradise Valley* ☎ *602/955–7878* ⊟ *AE, D, DC, MC, V* ⊗ *No lunch weekends.*

Scottsdale

Fast-growing Scottsdale can be broken down into roughly three neighborhoods. Downtown encompasses the small area bordered by Highland Avenue to the north, 56th Street to the west, Thomas Road to the south, and Scottsdale Road to the east; North Scottsdale includes everything north of Shea Boulevard; and Central Scottsdale is everything between Downtown and North Scottsdale. The Camelback Corridor, a veritable restaurant row, runs west–east from Phoenix to Scottsdale, with 64th Street the border between the two.

American

$$$$ ✕ **Golden Swan.** Often considered one the top five restaurants in the Southwest, this desert oasis is a great place for a special dinner or a leisurely Sunday champagne brunch. Sit outside under umbrellas or in a covered pavilion that juts into a koi-filled lagoon ringed by palms and hibiscus. The brunch concept is unusual: everything except dessert is laid out buffet-style in the kitchen under the watchful eyes of toque-clad chefs. ⊠ *Hyatt Regency at Gainey Ranch, 7500 E. Doubletree Ranch Rd., North Scottsdale* ☎ *480/991–3388* ⌂ *Reservations essential* ⊟ *AE, D, DC, MC,* ⊕ *www.scottsdale.hyatt.com.*

★ **$$$–$$$$** ✕ **The Grill at the TPC.** This is one clubhouse grill where everything is way over par, making it one of the better restaurants in Scottsdale. If you're hunting for a "melt-in-your-mouth steak," this might well be the place. There are prime steaks, both dry-aged and wet-aged beef, and the seafood, flown in fresh daily, is second to none. For proof, try the phenomenal sesame-crusted ahi tuna. ⊠ *Fairmont Scottsdale Princess Resort, 7575 E. Princess Dr., North Scottsdale* ☎ *480/585–4848* ⌂ *Reservations essential* ⊟ *AE, D, DC, MC, V.*

American/Casual

$–$$$ ✕ **Bandera.** If you're looking for a quick, tasty dinner before a night out on the town, try this casual, high-volume spot. The weekly menu includes wonderfully moist and meaty rotisserie chicken; you'll see the birds spinning in the big window before you even walk through the door. If you're not a poultry fan, salads, fresh fish, prime rib, and meat loaf usually make it onto the menu. The mashed potatoes are divine—you'll think Mom is in the kitchen peeling spuds. If you get here at prime eating hours, especially on weekends, be prepared to wait for a table. ⊠ *3821 N. Scotts-dale Rd., Central Scottsdale* ☎ *480/994–3524* ⌣ *Reservations not accepted* ⊟ *AE, MC, V* ⊙ *No lunch.*

¢–$$ ✗ **Busters.** A local favorite, situated in the Mercado del Lago Plaza, is a casual, comfortable spot for good burgers, fresh oysters, build-your-own lavosh (Armenian pizza), wood-grilled steaks, and an impressive selection of imported beers. Choose patio seating overlooking Lake Margherite, where you can enjoy the setting sun splash color over the McDowell Mountains. ⊠ *8320 N. Hayden Rd., North Scottsdale* ☎ *480/951–5850* ⊟ *AE, D, DC, MC, V.*

¢–$ ✗ **AZ 88.** This sleek, glassed-in restaurant is a great spot for people-watching. The kitchen puts out great food at rock-bottom prices. Try the wonderful shrimp ceviche, a huge Cobb salad, inventive sandwiches (Elsa's chicken, a grilled breast with pecans, peppers, and honey mustard, is a favorite), and sumptuous burgers (served with homemade waffle fries and chunks of fruit). Drinkers will find the martinis huge and exquisite. The music is usually a bit too loud inside for casual conversation, so if the weather is good, ask to dine on the beautifully appointed patio overlooking Scottsdale Mall. ⊠ *7353 E. Scottsdale Mall, North Scottsdale* ☎ *480/994–5576* ⊟ *AE, D, DC, MC, V* ⊙ *No lunch weekends.*

¢–$ ✗ **Kashman's Place.** To get a good feel for one North Scottsdale neighborhood, stop at Kashman's Place for breakfast or lunch. Brooklyn transplants Nancy and Steve Kashman serve sumptuous omelets with sides like crisp home fries, creatively blended salads, and piled-high sandwiches to a large following of locals. Their popularity is well earned, since everything here is deliciously fresh and portions are generous. The New York bagels are done the authentic way—boiled and baked on premises using filtered water they've duplicated from NYC water samples. The outside patio is dog friendly, so feel free to bring your favorite pooch. Expect lines on weekends. It's open from 6 AM to 3:30 PM daily. ⊠ *23425 N. Scottsdale Rd., at Pinnacle Peak Rd., North Scottsdale* ☎ *480/585–6221* ⊟ *AE, D, DC, MC, V* ⊙ *No dinner.*

☺ ¢–$ ✗ **Original Pancake House.** As the name suggests, this is a great spot for old-time breakfasts. Omelets are oven-baked, and everything is made by hand. Crepes, waffles, and egg dishes are good, but the flapjacks inspire worship from local admirers, who wait patiently for a table on weekends. The signature apple pancake is made from homemade batter poured over sautéed apples then baked to crispy perfection and glazed with cinnamon sugar. Other varieties, such as the Dutch Baby, an oven-baked confection served with whipped butter and powdered sugar, are also worth the wait. ⊠ *6840 E. Camelback Rd., Camelback Corridor* ☎ *480/946–4902* ⌣ *Reservations not accepted* ⊟ *No credit cards.*

Chinese

☺ ¢–$ ✗ **Flat Wok.** You can be as decadent or calorie-conscious as you want at this all-you-can-eat Mongolian grill. Once you choose your own meat, seafood, vegetables, rice noodles, and sauces, the chef will wok what you build. A salad bar and pasta buffet round out the experience. ⊠ *6501 E. Greenway Pkwy., North Scottsdale* ☎ *480/948–5544* ⊟ *AE, D, DC, MC, V.*

Contemporary

$$$–$$$$ ✗ **Acacia.** This restaurant—in the foothills of Pinnacle Peak—is in far north Scottsdale, but it's still worth the drive. The menu includes some exotic offerings like spiced venison chops with potato hash, but most folks come for the steaks (try the 18-ounce bone-in rib eye), fresh fish (including an outstanding pan-seared Chilean sea bass), and side dishes, such as the crispy steak-cut fries and the rich, creamed spinach. But also consider the cold seafood platter, with an array of prawns, oysters,

Alaskan king crab, and fresh steamed lobster accompanied by a trio of dipping sauces. ⊠ *Four Seasons Scottsdale at Troon North, 10600 E. Crescent Moon Dr., North Scottsdale* ☎ 480/515–5700 ⌕ *Reservations essential* ▤ *AE, D, MC, V* ☉ *No lunch.*

$$$–$$$$ ✕ **Rancho Pinot Grill.** The attention to quality paid by the husband-and-wife proprietors here—he manages, she cooks—has made this one of the town's top dining spots. The inventive menu changes daily, depending on what's fresh. If you're lucky, you might come on a day when the kitchen has made *posole,* a mouthwatering broth with hominy, salt pork, and cabbage. Entrées might include quail with soba noodles, rosemary-infused chicken with Italian sausage, and grilled sea bass atop basmati rice. ⊠ *6208 N. Scottsdale Rd., Central Scottsdale* ☎ 480/367–8030 ⌕ *Reservations essential* ▤ *AE, D, MC, V* ☉ *Closed Sun.–Mon. and mid-Aug.–mid-Sept. No lunch.*

$$–$$$$ ✕ **Cowboy Ciao.** Looking for a culinary kick? This kitchen weds Southwestern fare and Italian flair, and it's no shotgun wedding, either. Main dishes, such as the Chianti-marinated filet mignon, fennel-seasoned meat loaf, and wild mushrooms in an ancho chili cream sauce heaped over polenta, are creative without going off the deep end. The chocolate lottery—complete with an actual lottery ticket—is a dessert hoot. You can also order one of several affordable flights of wine, which will give you a different glass with each course. ⊠ *7133 E. Stetson Dr., Central Scottsdale* ☎ 480/946–3111 ▤ *AE, D, DC, MC, V* ☉ *No lunch Sun.–Mon.*

$$–$$$$ ✕ **Michael's at the Citadel.** One of this town's best-looking places has a two-story sandstone waterfall, warm fireplaces, and lush desert landscaping. The contemporary American fare is simply elegant. Entrées are the real stars here: roast salmon mignon on vegetable ribbons; grilled lamb with a goat-cheese potato tart; Niçoise-style roasted Chilean sea bass. Sunday brunch showcases offerings like rolled Swedish pancakes with cinnamon apples and mascarpone. If you're celebrating a special occasion, Michael's is the spot. ⊠ *8700 E. Pinnacle Peak Rd., North Scottsdale* ☎ 480/515–2575 ▤ *AE, DC, MC, V* ☉ *No lunch weekends.*

$$–$$$$ ✕ **Roaring Fork.** Elk-antler chandeliers, earth-tone fabrics and leathers, barbed-wire accessories. and a buffalo skull above the bar add up to a comfortable, rustic ambience in this restaurant named after a Colorado river. Chef Robert McGrath calls his creations "American Western" cuisine, which includes such interesting dishes as mustard-crusted trout, a pork porterhouse steak, and fun side dishes like smoked-tomato grits and green-chili macaroni. For dessert, "Lucky 7" is a chocolate tart filled with chocolate silk and smothered in (you guessed it) chocolate ice cream and milk chocolate sauce. The reasonably priced saloon menu is served in the bar from 7 to 10 PM. ⊠ *Finova Building, 4800 N. Scottsdale Rd., Central Scottsdale* ☎ 480/947–0795 ▤ *AE, D, DC, MC, V* ☉ *No lunch.*

$$–$$$ ✕ **Razz's Restaurant and Bar.** There's no telling what part of the globe chef-proprietor Erasmo "Razz" Kamnitzer will use for culinary inspiration. However, you can count on his creations to give dormant taste buds a wake-up call: black bean paella is a twist on a Spanish theme; South American bouillabaisse is a fragrant fish stew, stocked with veggies; and *bah mie goreng* teams noodles with fish, meat, and vegetables, perked up with dried cranberries and almonds. Count on it—Razz'll dazzle. ⊠ *10321 N. Scottsdale Rd., North Scottsdale* ☎ 480/905–1308 ▤ *AE, D, DC, MC, V* ☉ *Closed Sun.–Mon. No lunch.*

$$ ✕ **L'Ecole.** You'll have no regrets putting yourself in the talented hands of the student chefs at the Valley's premier cooking academy. You'll get a complete dinner for as little as $25 and lunch for around $13, a real bargain. The three-course prix-fixe dinner menu selections change fre-

quently, as the restaurant is taken over by a different class each week. You can expect inventive appetizers like ginger-soy marinated gravlax, entrées such as fillet Rossini (with foie gras, truffles, and a demi-glace sauce), and such desserts as crème brûlée. Because the students also pull server duty, you can count on being pampered, too. ⊠ *Scottsdale Culinary Institute, 8100 E. Camelback Rd., Central Scottsdale* ☎ *480/990–7639* ⌕ *Reservations essential* ▭ *D, MC, V* ✆ *Closed weekends.*

$ ✕ **L'Academie Café.** It hard to find a better bargain in Scottsdale than the newest student-run restaurant of the Scottsdale Culinary Institute. The bistro-style café's à la carte menu focuses on the cuisine of the Mediterranean, particularly the Italian and French rivieras. The student chefs in pursuit of their degrees in culinary arts create selections of fresh fish and veal, panini, salads, and desserts. Although menus rotate regularly, diners clamor to try such offerings as Italian sausage, Portobello, and mozzarella pizza; seafood lasagna filled with plump pieces of fresh fish, shrimp, and clams; and decadent desserts like a chocolate flourless torte with raspberry coulis. ⊠ *Scottsdale Culinary Institute, 4301 N. Scottsdale Rd., Central Scottsdale* ☎ *480/941–0229* ▭ *D, MC, V* ✆ *Closed weekends.*

French

★ $$$$ ✕ **Mary Elaine's.** Formal and elegant, this is the Valley's finest high-end dining experience. Mary Elaine's austere ambience is a perfect backdrop for dramatic city-light views of Scottsdale from every table. The French-inspired menu offers an à la carte menu as well as two distinctive tasting menus each evening. Offerings may include fricassee of lobster, foie gras drizzled with maple syrup and 100-year-old balsamic vinegar, and a pan-roasted wild turbot with black truffle–lobster sauce. Desserts like the warm chocolate soufflé tart are breathtaking. An extensive wine cellar, impeccable service, and a pleasant jazz vocalist make this an exceptional dining experience. ⊠ *The Phoenician, 6000 E. Camelback Rd., Camelback Corridor* ☎ *480/941–8200* ⌕ *Reservations essential* ⌂ *Jacket required* ▭ *AE, D, DC, MC, V* ✆ *Closed Sun. No lunch.*

Italian

$$$$ ✕ **Leccabaffi Ristorante.** Leccabaffi (which means "lick your mustache") is on many lists of Valley favorites, and you will be licking your chops the minute you walk through the door. The temptation begins just inside the entrance, where an antipasto table is heaped with grilled and roasted vegetables. But the stars here are the lusty, northern Italian meat, fish, and poultry dishes. Fresh fish is flown in daily, and the *vitello alla Valdostana* (a bone-in veal chop with a pocket of Fontina cheese) is a triumph. For dessert, the *formaggio di pecora e mielesoft* (sheep cheese and honey) is a delicious choice. ⊠ *9719 N. Hayden Rd., North Scottsdale* ☎ *480/609–0429* ▭ *AE, D, MC, V* ✆ *Closed Mon. No lunch.*

★ $$–$$$ ✕ **Maria's When in Naples.** In a town teeming with Italian restaurants, this is a standout. The antipasto spread laid out just inside the entrance tastes as good as it looks. Maria, herself, makes all of the homemade pasta. Check out the *salsiccia Pugliese* (fettuccine topped with homemade sausage, leeks, porcini mushrooms, and white wine sauce) or the *orecchiette Barese* (ear-shape pasta tossed with cauliflower, pancetta, sun-dried tomatoes, olive oil, and cheese). ⊠ *7000 E. Shea Blvd., North Scottsdale* ☎ *480/991–6887* ▭ *AE, D, DC, MC, V* ✆ *No lunch weekends.*

Japanese

$–$$$ ✕ **Sushi on Shea.** You may be in the middle of the desert, but the sushi here will make you think you're at the ocean's edge. Yellowtail, toro, shrimp, scallops, freshwater eel, and even monkfish liver pâté are among the long list of delights. *Nabemono* (hot pot or meals-in-a-bowl) are prepared at your table. The best dish? Maybe it's the *una-ju* (broiled freshwater eel with a sublime smoky scent), served over sweet rice. The fact that some people believe eel is an aphrodisiac only adds to its charm. ⊠ *7000 E. Shea Blvd., North Scottsdale* ☎ *480/483–7799* ▤ *AE, D, DC, MC, V* ☉ *No lunch.*

Latin

$$–$$$ ✕**Havana Patio Cafe.** Tapas are marvelous here, particularly the shrimp pancakes, potato croquettes, and Cuban tamales. There's an intoxicating choice of entrées including paella heaped with a whole Maine lobster. And there's even something for vegetarians: *cho cho*, a fresh chayote squash stuffed with loads of veggies and topped with a Jamaican curry sauce. ⊠ *6245 E. Bell Rd., North Scottsdale* ☎ *480/991–1496* ▤ *AE, D, DC, MC, V.*

Mexican

★ $$$ ✕**La Hacienda.** Situated in a turn-of-the-20th-century ranch house setting, La Hacienda is widely considered to be among the finest Mexican restaurants in North America. To ensure authentic cuisine, chef Reed Groban took tasting tours through Mexican villages and towns. You'll find no burritos or tacos here, just magnificent appetizers like the ancho chili stuffed with dried fruit, nuts, and chicken, or such incredible entrées as *camarones salteados* (braised, sautéed shrimp) with a poblano rice casserole and tamarind sauce, or *cochinillo asado*, La Hacienda's signature dish—spit-roasted suckling pig marinated in tamarind and bitter orange, wheeled up to the table and carved to order. ⊠ *Fairmont Scottsdale Princess Resort, 7575 E. Princess Dr., North Scottsdale* ☎ *480/585–4848* ▤ *AE, D, DC, MC, V* ☉ *Closed Wed. No lunch.*

¢–$$ ✕**Carlsbad Tavern.** This casual and busy New Mexico–style eatery serves up big portions of such tasty dishes as a half-pound burger grilled over pecan wood, green-chili mashed potatoes, chipotle barbecue baby-back ribs, and a spicy chorizo meat loaf on focaccia with brown gravy. They'll custom-mix your margarita with fresh lime and lemon juice and blend it with your choice of some 35 tequilas. There's a late-night menu for the after 10 PM crowd. ⊠ *3313 N. Hayden Rd., Central Scottsdale* ☎ *480/ 970–8164* ▤ *AE, D, MC, V.*

Pan-Asian

$$$ ✕**Restaurant Hapa.** Hapa, meaning "half" in Hawaiian, is a salute to the
FodorśChoice Asian-American ancestry of chef-owner James McDevitt. The Pan-Asian
★ contemporary fare served here has received national recognition and with good reason. McDevitt is masterful at fusing exotic flavors and textures and wrapping them into such offerings as skillet-roasted mussels in a Thai-style coconut broth scented with lemongrass, mint, basil, and ginger, or into the superb house specialty—beef tenderloin brushed with hot mustard and caramelized sugar. If you'd like to sample more than just one entrée, the three-course chef's tasting menu paired with flights of wine is highly recommended. ⊠ *6204 N. Scottsdale Rd., Central Scottsdale* ☎ *480/998–8220* ▤ *AE, MC, V* ☉ *Closed Sun. No lunch.*

Seafood

$$–$$$$ ✕**Salt Cellar.** It's rare to find a restaurant in a cellar, especially in the desert. This unusual place, near the Salt River, was originally an ASU hamburger joint—purposely built underground with concrete walls and floors. Today, it has been transformed with crisp linen tablecloths and nautical decor. The kitchen dishes out straightforward, fresh seafood. For starters try Chesapeake Bay crab cakes, oysters Rockefeller, or turtle soup. Then move on to well-prepared entrées such as Idaho trout, Yakimono Hawaiian ahi, or charcoal-broiled king salmon. If you're really

hungry, splurge and order a gigantic 5-pound live Maine lobster. ✉ *550 N. Hayden Rd., South Scottsdale* ☎ *480/947–1963* 🖃 *AE, D, DC, MC, V* 🕒 *Closed Mon. No Lunch.*

Southwestern

$$–$$$ ✕ **Old Town Tortilla Factory.** Aside from the tasty Sonoran cuisine and the best homemade tortillas in Scottsdale, the draw here is the ambience. The restaurant is in the heart of Old Town Scottsdale, constructed from a historic adobe home. Hundred-year-old pecan trees shade the large flagstone patio, which is a popular spot for alfresco dining or for sipping a margarita made with one of the premium tequilas. Signature dishes include ancho raspberry–encrusted pork chops and Shawnee sea bass—pan-seared and served with a rock shrimp and cheese quesadilla, topped with shoestring sweet potatoes. Save room for dessert: the banana crisp wrapped in a sweet tortilla with blackberry compote is out of this world. ✉ *6910 E. Main St., Downtown Scottsdale* ☎ *480/945–4567* 🖃 *AE, D, DC, MC, V* 🕒 *No lunch.*

Spanish

$$$$
Fodor'sChoice
★
✕ **Marquesa.** Upon entering this gem of a restaurant, you'll know you're in for an amazing experience. The Spanish-colonial setting has polished marble, antiques, and floor-to-ceiling oil paintings. Diners here partake of Catalonian cuisine seasoned with herbs and flavors indigenous to the region. Appetizers are extraordinary, including *anec d' Napoléon,* phyllo dough pouches stuffed with duck, foie gras, and mushrooms. Main courses include expertly prepared seafood, meats, and poultry; however, the real triumph is the paella, bursting with lobster, chicken, mussels, shrimp, escargots, pork, and mussels. Marquesa also serves a wonderful market-style Sunday brunch that can be enjoyed alfresco on the garden patio. ✉ *Fairmont Scottsdale Princess Resort, 7575 E. Princess Dr., North Scottsdale* ☎ *480/585–4848* 🗠 *Reservations essential* 🖃 *AE, D, DC, MC, V* 🕒 *No lunch.*

Steak

$$$ ✕ **Don & Charlie's.** A favorite with major-leaguers in town for spring training, this venerable chophouse specializes in prime-grade steak and baseball memorabilia—the walls are covered with pictures, autographs, and uniforms. The New York sirloin, prime rib, and double-thick lamb chops are a hit; sides include au gratin potatoes and creamed spinach. Serious carnivores will not strike out here. ✉ *7501 E. Camelback Rd., Camelback Corridor* ☎ *480/990–0900* 🖃 *AE, D, DC, MC, V* 🕒 *No lunch.*

$$–$$$$ ✕ **Morton's of Chicago.** The Windy City chain is famous for exceptional service, immense steaks, and entertaining tableside presentations, but most of all for consistency. The monstrous 24-ounce porterhouse or 14-ounce double-cut fillet can satisfy the hungriest cowpoke. If you've been hankerin' for a great aged prime steak, you won't go wrong here. The seafood is excellent, too, but plays second fiddle to the beef. ✉ *15233 N. Kierland Blvd., North Scottsdale* ☎ *480/951–4440* 🗠 *Reservations essential* 🖃 *AE, DC, MC, V* 🕒 *No lunch.*

Thai

$–$$ ✕ **Malee's on Main.** This fashionable, casual eatery in the heart of Scottsdale's Main Street Arts District serves sophisticated, Thai-inspired fare. The recommended *ahoi phannee* is a medley of seafood in a bamboo-leaf bowl moistened with red curry sauce, coconut, lime leaf, and Thai basil. The Thai barbecued chicken, grilled to a sizzle and coated with rum, is a house favorite. Everything is made to order here, so you specify the spiciness—from mild to flaming. But even the "mild" dishes have a bite. ✉ *7131 E. Main St., Downtown* ☎ *480/947–6042* 🖃 *AE, DC, MC, V* 🕒 *No lunch Sun.*

East Valley: Tempe, Mesa, Chandler

The East Valley includes those communities—all separate municipalities—south and east of Phoenix and Scottsdale.

American

$$-$$$ ✕ **Gordon Biersch.** This branch of the San Francisco chain serves up mugs of sophisticated house brews along with relatively sophisticated food. Big picture windows and balcony seating allow great views of Tempe from the second-story dining room, and the food is just as visually pleasing. Smoked salmon hand-rolls, a skillet of roasted mussels, and beer-batter onion rings are good munchies, and finishing an order of garlic fries requires the help of several friends. The cioppino, oyster pan roast, New York steak, and peppered ahi tuna are winning entrées. And drink up: the brewmaster follows the *Reinheitsgebot,* 500-year-old German purity guidelines for beer making. ⊠ *420 S. Mill Ave., Tempe* ☎ *480/736–0033* 🖃 *AE, D, DC, MC, V.*

$-$$$ ✕ **Landmark.** In a 1908 building that was originally a Mormon church, this family-run restaurant serves the kind of all-American home cooking that Norman Rockwell would've loved. In fact, the dining room decorated with lace curtains, chandeliers, and white linens looks like it could be a backdrop for one of his paintings. The food is straightforward, comfy home cooking—roast turkey, chicken potpie, fried chicken, and baked fish. However, the real draw is the salad *room,* probably the largest salad bar you'll ever see, featuring nearly 100 items that include soups, breads, salad fixings, and hot dishes. Don't forget to save room for apple pie with a slice of cheddar on top. ⊠ *809 W. Main St., Mesa* ☎ *480/962–4652* 🖃 *AE, D, MC, V* ☺ *No lunch Sun.*

Chinese

$-$$ ✕ **C-Fu Gourmet.** This is serious Chinese food, the kind you'd expect to find on Mott Street in New York City's Chinatown or Grant Avenue in San Francisco. C-Fu's specialty is fish, and you can see several species in big holding tanks. If you've ever wondered why shrimp is a delicacy, it will be clear once you bite into these crustaceans. After they're fished out of the tank, they're steamed and bathed in a potent garlic sauce. Clams in black bean sauce and tilapia in a ginger-scallion sauce also hit all the right buttons. There's a daily dim sum brunch, too. ⊠ *2051 W. Warner Rd., Chandler* ☎ *480/899–3888* 🖃 *AE, D, DC, MC, V.*

Contemporary

$$-$$$ ✕ **House of Tricks.** There's nothing up the sleeves of Robert and Robin Trick, who work magic on their eclectic menu emphasizing the freshest available seafood. A towering, old elm tree is the focal point of the outdoor bar and patio at this intimate restaurant converted from a 1920s home. The appetizer list is known for its offbeat creations, such as cheese and avocado blintzes and stuffed grape leaves in chipotle plum sauce. Main dishes are just as clever. The roasted eggplant–and–goat cheese lasagna and grilled rack of pork with jalapeño-orange marmalade, scallops, saffron, and Pernod get high marks. ⊠ *114 E. 7th St., Tempe* ☎ *480/968–1114* 🖃 *AE, D, DC, MC, V* ☺ *Closed Sun.*

French

★ **$$-$$$** ✕ **Citrus Cafe.** Elegant yet casual, this small restaurant does everything right to create an inviting atmosphere, from the romantic candlelit dining room to a daily menu featuring what's freshest from the market (it's written out on a board). For starters, try the baked Brie with almonds and apples or the superb leek and potato soup. The main dishes are pure French comfort food: veal kidneys, sweetbreads, leg of lamb, roast pork, and occasionally even rabbit. ⊠ *2330 N. Alma School Rd., Chandler* ☎ *480/899–0502* ▤ *AE, D, DC, MC, V* ☉ *Closed Mon. No lunch.*

Japanese

$–$$ ✕**Yamakasa.** One of the Valley's top Japanese restaurants and its next-door neighbor, C-Fu Gourmet, order their ocean fare in tandem, so you can be sure the high-quality sushi here is fresh. The skilled sushi masters display particular artistry in the hand-rolls. The *nabemono* (literally, "hot pot") dishes are also worth investigating. Another specialty is *shabu-shabu*, thin-sliced beef that you swish in a boiling, sake-seasoned broth. ("Shabu-shabu" is the hissing sound the meat makes when it hits the liquid.) ⊠ *2051 W. Warner Rd., Chandler* ☎ *480/899–8868* ▤ *AE, D, DC, MC, V* ☉ *Closed Mon. No lunch Sun.*

Mexican

★ ¢–$$ ✕**Los Sombreros Mexican Cantina.** An unlikely location in the middle of a strip mall does not prepare you for the delicious, freshly prepared food inside. Jeffrey Smedstad and his wife, Azucena, create dishes not found in the typical Mexican restaurant. Start with the grilled vegetable gorditas perched on a bed of shredded lettuce and paired with roasted tomato–chipotle salsa, or *nopales queso fundido* (tender cactus in a mix of Monterey Jack cheese, onions, and tomatoes). Fish is especially good, such as the pan-roasted salmon atop a decorative corn husk with delicious, zesty vegetables. Ice creams are house-made, and the flan is the best you'll find this side of Mexico City. ⊠ *1849 N. Scottsdale Rd. Tempe* ☎ *480/994–1799* ▤ *AE, D, DC, MC, V* ☉ *Closed Mon. No lunch.*

↻ ¢–$ ✕**Rosa's Mexican Grill.** This festive, family-friendly restaurant summons up images of a Baja beach taqueria. The tacos are Rosa's true glory: beef, pork, and chicken are marinated in fruit juices and herbs for 12 hours, slowly oven-baked for another 10, then shredded and charbroiled. The fish taco, pepped up with cabbage, radishes, and lime, is also in a class by itself. Spoon on one of Rosa's five fresh homemade salsas. But beware the fiery habanero version—it can strip the enamel right off your teeth. ⊠ *328 E. University Dr., Mesa* ☎ *480/964–5451* ▤ *No credit cards* ☉ *Closed Sun.–Mon.*

Middle Eastern

¢–$ ✕**Tasty Kabob.** The Persian food here is heavily seasoned, but never spicy hot. Perfumed basmati rice is often teamed with several grilled kabobs—skewers of ground beef, lamb, chicken, or beef tenderloin. The stews, called *khoresht* and *polo*, give you a taste of authentic Persian fare. If *baghali polo*—dill-infused rice tossed with lima beans and lamb shank—is on the menu, don't hesitate to order it. ⊠ *1250 E. Apache Blvd., Tempe* ☎ *480/966–0260* ▤ *AE, D, MC, V* ☉ *Closed Mon.*

West Valley: West Phoenix, Glendale, Litchfield Park

The West Valley includes the parts of West Phoenix that are west of I–17 and north of Buckeye Road plus the separate municipalities of Glendale and Litchfield Park.

Chinese

★ $$ ✕**Silver Dragon.** This is one of the best Chinese restaurants in town—as long as you order properly. Insist on sitting in the big room to the left as you walk in the door, and ask for the Chinese menu (it has brief English descriptions). Your boldness will be rewarded with some of the best Hong Kong–style Chinese fare between the two coasts. Crispy Hong Kong–Style Chicken is a plump whole bird steamed, flash-fried, and cut into bite-size pieces. Hot-pot dishes, noodles, fish, and vegetarian dishes—the Buddhist-Style Rolls are outstanding and make it hard to eat Chinese food anyplace else in the Valley. ✉ *8946 N. 19th Ave., West Phoenix* ☎ *602/674–0151* ☰ *AE, MC, V* ☉ *No lunch Sat.*

German

$–$$ ✕ **Haus Murphy's.** On weekends, kick back with the old-country accordionist, knock back some old-country brews, and devour the hearty dishes in this charming storefront restaurant situated in a 1985 building in the heart of downtown Glendale. Schnitzel is a specialty, especially the spicy paprika version, teamed with crispy chunks of fried potatoes and green beans. Sauerbraten, paired with tart red cabbage and two huge potato dumplings, is not for the faint of appetite. Wash everything down with a variety of German beers, including a couple on tap, and save room for the sweet, homemade desserts—apple strudel and hazelnut torte. ✉ *5819 W. Glendale Ave., Glendale* ☎ *623/939–2480* ☰ *AE, D, MC, V.*

Mexican

¢–$ ✕ **Lily's Cafe.** Friendly mom-and-pop proprietors, a jukebox with south-of-the-border hits, and low-priced, fresh Mexican fare have kept patrons coming here for almost 50 years. Beef is the featured ingredient. The chimichanga is world-class, stuffed with tender beef and covered with cheese, guacamole, and sour cream. Fragrant tamales, spunky red chili beef, and chiles rellenos right out of the fryer also shine. ✉ *6706 N. 58th Dr., Glendale* ☎ *623/937–7757* ⌔ *Reservations not accepted* ☰ *No credit cards* ☉ *Closed Mon.–Tues. and Aug.*

¢–$ ✕ **Pepe's Taco Villa.** The neighborhood's not fancy, and neither is this restaurant. But in a town filled with gringo-ized, south-of-the-border fare, this is the real deal. Tacos *rancheros*—spicy, shredded pork pungently lathered with adobo paste—are a dream. So are the green corn tamales, *machacado* (air-dried beef), and chiles rellenos. But don't leave here without trying the sensational mole, a rich, exotic sauce fashioned from chilies and chocolate. ✉ *2108 W. Camelback Rd., West Phoenix, Phoenix* ☎ *602/242–0379* ☰ *No credit cards* ☉ *Closed Tues.*

Southwestern

$$–$$$$ ✕ **Arizona Kitchen.** With the help of a historian of Native American foods, the chef here has put together a bold Southwestern menu. Appetizers such as blue corn *piki* rolls, stuffed with capon and goat cheese, and the wild boar Anasazi bean chili give you an indication of what's to come. Entrées include grilled sirloin of buffalo and venison medallions in a blackberry-zinfandel cocoa sauce. For dessert, try the chili-spiked ice cream in the striking turquoise "bowl" of hardened sugar. It's worth the 20-minute drive from downtown Phoenix. ✉ *Wigwam Resort, 300 E. Indian School Rd., Litchfield Park* ☎ *623/935–3811* ☰ *AE, D, DC, MC, V* ☉ *Closed Sun.–Mon. and July–Aug. No lunch.*

Vietnamese

$–$$ ✕ **Pho Bang.** What makes this little hole-in-the-wall restaurant so appealing—aside from price—is the simplicity and freshness of the food: rice, noodles, vegetables, beef, seafood, pork, and chicken. If you order the house specialty, *tom va bo nuong vi* (#35 on the menu), the server returns with three plates: one with transparently thin slices of marinated beef and raw shrimp; one with piles of mint, lettuce, cilantro, pickled leeks, cucumber, and carrot; and one with rice paper. You fire up the portable grill and cook the beef and shrimp. When they're done, combine with the veggies, fold into rice paper, and start dunking. ✉ *1702 W. Camelback Rd., West Phoenix* ☎ *602/433–9440* ⌔ *Reservations not accepted* ☰ *MC, V.*

WHERE TO STAY

Historic resorts, including the Arizona Biltmore, Camelback Inn, and Royal Palms—all in Phoenix—are still among the Valley's most popular getaways. Most others are in the neighboring, tourist-friendly city of Scottsdale, a destination in its own right. A few are scattered 20 to 30 mi to the north in the quickly expanding communities of Carefree and Cave Creek. Guest-ranch territory is 60 mi northwest, in the town of Wickenburg.

Most downtown Phoenix properties are business and family hotels, closer to the heart of the city—and to the average vacationer's budget. Many properties cater to corporate travelers during the week but lower their rates on weekends to entice leisure travelers. Ask about weekend specials when making reservations.

Many people flee snow and ice to bask in the Valley of the Sun. As a result, winter is the high season, peaking in January through March. Summer season—mid-May through the end of September—is giveaway time, when a night at one of the fanciest resorts often goes for a quarter of the winter price.

With more than 55,000 hotel rooms in the metro area, you have a wide range of lodging choices, including everything from world-class resorts to chain motels to guest ranches and extended-stay hotels.

WHAT IT COSTS				
$$$$	**$$$**	**$$**	**$**	**¢**
FOR 2 PEOPLE over $250	$175–$250	$120–$175	$70–$120	under $70

Prices are for two people in a standard double room in high season.

Phoenix: Camelback Corridor

$$$$ **Arizona Biltmore.** Designed by Frank Lloyd Wright's colleague Albert
Fodor\'sChoice Chase McArthur, the Biltmore has been Phoenix's premier resort since
★ it opened in 1929. The hotel sits on 39 acres of impeccably manicured grounds, and the dramatic lobby, which fills with piano music each evening, has dramatic, stained-glass skylights. Spacious guest rooms (the smallest is 400 square ft) are tastefully appointed with Southwestern-print fabrics and Mission-style furniture; each has a sitting area and desk, while bathrooms have marble sinks. Accommodating, guest-focused staff are unobtrusive. A special dinner or Sunday brunch at Wright's will surround you with old-time Arizona ambience. ⊠ *24th St. and Missouri Ave., Camelback Corridor, 85016* ☎ *602/955–6600 or 800/950–0086* ☄ *602/381–7600* ⊕ *www.arizonabiltmore.com* ☞ *720 rooms, 50 villas* ♨ *4 restaurants, minibars, cable TV, golf privileges, miniature golf, putting green, 7 tennis courts, 8 pools, health club, hair salon, 3 outdoor hot tubs, spa, bicycles, badminton, croquet, horseshoes, lobby lounge, children's programs (ages 6–12), laundry service, concierge, business services, car rental, free parking* ☰ *AE, D, DC, MC, V.*

★ **$$$$** **Ritz-Carlton.** The sand-colored neo-Federal facade facing Biltmore Fashion Park hides a graceful, beautifully appointed luxury hotel well known for impeccable service. Exuding old-world charm, large public rooms are decorated with 18th- and 19th-century European paintings and a handsome china collection. Guest rooms are bright and airy and have stocked refrigerators, feather and foam pillows, and marble baths. There's twice-daily maid service as well. Both mountain and city vistas can be best appreciated from the rooftop terrace, where the heated pool

Where to Stay in Phoenix

is found. The Town and Country Club is open to guests in the evenings. ⊠ *2401 E. Camelback Rd., Camelback Corridor, Phoenix 85016* ☎ *602/468–0700 or 800/241–3333* 🖷 *602/468–0793* ⊕ *www.ritzcarlton. com* 🖘 *281 rooms, 14 suites* ↻ *Restaurant, room service, in-room safes, refrigerators, cable TV, pool, gym, 2 saunas, bicycles, 3 bars, shop, laundry service, concierge floor, Internet, business services, meeting rooms, parking (fee)* ⊟ *AE, D, DC, MC, V.*

★ **$$$$** ⊡ **Royal Palms Resort & Spa.** Once the home of Cunard Steamship executive Delos T. Cooke, this Mediterranean-style resort has beautifully maintained courtyards with antique fountains, a stately row of the namesake palms at its entrance, and individually designed, stylish rooms. The deluxe casitas are each done in a different style—trompe l'oeil, romantic retreat, Spanish colonial—by members of the American Society of Interior Designers. The restaurant, T. Cook's, is renowned in the Valley, and the Alzadora Spa, which opened in late 2002, is spectacular. ⊠ *5200 E. Camelback Rd., Camelback Corridor, 85018* ☎ *602/840–3610 or 800/ 672–6011* 🖷 *602/840–6927* ⊕ *www.royalpalmshotel.com* 🖘 *116 rooms and casitas, 4 suites* ↻ *Restaurant, room service, in-room safes, refrigerators, cable TV, golf privileges, tennis court, pool, gym, spa, bicycles, croquet, hiking, bar, laundry service, business services, meeting rooms, parking (fee), no-smoking rooms* ⊟ *AE, D, DC, MC, V.*

$$$ ⊡ **Phoenix Inn Suites Phoenix.** A block off a popular stretch of Camelback Road, this three-story hotel, part of an Arizona chain, is a remarkable bargain, considering it has amenities not generally seen in properties of the same price category—including leather love seats, microwaves, refrigerators, and coffeemakers in each room. Several rooms have corner jetted tubs. Continental breakfast is served each morning from 6 to 10 in a pleasant breakfast room. Local calls are free. ⊠ *2310 E. Highland Ave., Camelback Corridor, 85016* ☎ *602/956–5221 or 800/956–5221* 🖷 *602/468–7220* ⊕ *www.phoenixinn.com* 🖘 *120 suites* ↻ *Some in-room hot tubs, microwaves, refrigerators, pool, gym, hair salon, hot tub, shop, laundry facilities* ⊟ *AE, D, DC, MC, V* ⊚I *CP.*

$–$$$ ⊡ **Homewood Suites Phoenix-Biltmore.** This all-suites chain is a major value, especially considering its location in the heart of the upscale Biltmore District. Suites, which have a spacious living and working area with a sleeper-sofa and one or two separate bedrooms, were given a face-lift in 2003; each has a full kitchen. A breakfast buffet is served each morning, and from Monday to Thursday evening there's a "manager's reception," a mini-feast featuring anything from a taco bar to baked potatoes with all the trimmings. Add to the list free passes to a nearby fitness club and transportation within a 5-mi radius of the hotel. ⊠ *2001 E. Highland Ave., Camelback Corridor, 85016* ☎ *602/508–0937* 🖷 *602/ 508–0854* ⊕ *www.homewood-suites.com* 🖘 *124 rooms* ↻ *In-room data ports, kitchens, cable TV with movies, laundry facilities, laundry service, pool, gym, no-smoking rooms* ⊟ *AE, D, DC, MC, V* ⊚I *BP.*

$$ ⊡ **Courtyard Phoenix Camelback.** Public areas in this four-story hotel are mostly glass and tile, filled with plenty of greenery. The comfortable rooms are equipped with desks and data ports, complimentary coffee as well as irons and ironing boards. King suites have microwaves and refrigerators. A lap pool and Jacuzzi await in the landscaped courtyard. You won't go hungry staying here—there's a small café on premises that serves breakfast, lunch, and dinner or, if you prefer, there are more than 50 restaurants within a 1½-mi radius. ⊠ *2101 E. Camelback Rd., Camelback Corridor, 85016* ☎ *602/955–5200 or 800/321–2211* 🖷 *602/955– 1101* ⊕ *www.marriott.com* 🖘 *155 rooms, 12 suites* ↻ *In-room data ports, some microwaves, some refrigerators, cable TV with movies, pool, gym, hot tub, restaurant, bar, laundry facilities, laundry service, meeting rooms, free parking* ⊟ *AE, D, DC, MC, V.*

Paradise Valley

★ **$$$$**   ⚏ **Marriott's Camelback Inn.** This historic resort is a swank oasis of comfort and relaxation in the gorgeous valley between Camelback and Mummy mountains. Built on 125 acres in the mid-1930s, the latilla beam–kiva log buildings ooze Southwestern charm; the grounds are adorned with stunning cacti and desert flowers. Rooms are notably spacious, and seven suites even have private swimming pools. A gallery exhibits Barry Goldwater's photographs, which display a real talent with a camera. Visit the acclaimed spa, where you can indulge in a massage or in something more exotic such as a para-joba body wrap or an adobe mud purification treatment. ⊠ *5402 E. Lincoln Dr., Paradise Valley 85253* ☎ *480/948–1700 or 800/242–2635* ⊞ *480/951–8469* ⊕ *www. camelbackinn.com* ⇋ *453 rooms, 27 suites* ♨ *5 restaurants, coffee shop, in-room fax, some kitchenettes, 2 18-hole golf courses, 6 tennis courts, 3 pools, spa, hiking, lounge, shops, children's programs (ages 5–12), Internet, business services, meeting rooms, free parking* ⊟ *AE, D, DC, MC, V.*

★ **$$$$**   ⚏ **Sanctuary on Camelback Mountain.** This luxurious boutique hotel is the only resort perched on the north slope of Camelback Mountain. Secluded casitas are painted in desert hues and furnished in contemporary style; beds are covered with luxury linens and custom duvets. Bathrooms are travertine marble with elegant sinks, custom cabinetry, and roomy tubs. An infinity-edged pool, tennis courts, Zen meditation garden, and Asian-inspired Sanctuary Spa make this property a welcoming oasis on the desert. The hotel's restaurant, elements, is deservedly popular and an enchanting spot for dinner or a cocktail at sunset. ⊠ *5700 E. McDonald Dr., Paradise Valley 85253* ☎ *480/948–2100 or 800/245–2051* ⊞ *480/607–3386* ⊕ *www.sanctuaryoncamelback.com* ⇋ *98 casitas* ♨ *Restaurant, room service, in-room data ports, some kitchenettes, minibars, cable TV, 6 tennis courts, 3 pools, gym, massage, spa, bar, shop, business services, meeting rooms, free parking* ⊟ *AE, D, DC, MC, V.*

$$$–$$$$
FodorsChoice
★   ⚏ **Hermosa Inn.** The ranch-style lodge at the heart of this small resort was the home and studio of cowboy artist Lon Megargee in the 1930s; today the adobe structure houses Lon's at the Hermosa, justly popular for its new American cuisine. The inn, on 6 acres of lushly landscaped desert, is a hidden jewel of hospitality and low-key luxury. Villas as big as private homes and individually decorated casitas hold an enviable collection of art. A blessedly peaceful alternative to some of the larger resorts, the Hermosa offers serenity, attention to detail, and alluring accommodations. ⊠ *5532 N. Palo Cristi Rd., Paradise Valley 85253* ☎ *602/955–8614 or 800/241–1210* ⊞ *602/955–8299* ⊕ *www. hermosainn.com* ⇋ *4 villas, 3 haciendas, 22 casitas, 17 ranchos* ♨ *Restaurant, in-room data ports, some kitchenettes, minibars, cable TV, 3 tennis courts, pool, 2 hot tubs, massage, bar, free parking* ⊟ *AE, D, DC, MC, V* ⍝ *BP.*

Downtown

$$$$ ⚏ **Wyndham Phoenix.** When Wyndam took over this hotel in 2003, the chain immediately invested $6 million into renovations. It sits in the center of bustling Copper Square within 1 mi of performing arts venues, major-league sports arenas, museums, and more than 135 restaurants. Rooms are attractively furnished and feature new mattresses and bedding, high-speed Internet access, large desks, ergonomic desk chairs, and premium bath amenities. Although this hotel is geared primarily toward the needs of the business traveler, children under the age of 18 stay free with parents, a real bonus to families willing to stay in the downtown area. ⊠ *50*

E. Adams St., Downtown, 85004 ☎ *602/333–0000* ⊕ *www.wyndham. com* ➥ *445 room, 87 suites* ⚬ *Restaurant, room service, in-room data ports, some refrigerators, cable TV with movies, pool, gym, hair salon, sauna, bar, comedy club, shop, laundry service, Internet, business services, airport shuttle, car rental, parking (fee)* ⊟ *AE, D, DC, MC, V.*

$$–$$$$ ▧ **Hyatt Regency Phoenix.** A quintessential Hyatt, this convention-oriented hotel has a seven-story atrium with huge sculptures, colorful tapestries, potted plants, and comfortable seating areas. Rooms are spacious, and there's a revolving restaurant with panoramic views of the Phoenix area. The hotel efficiently handles the arrival and departure of hundreds of business travelers each day. Note: the atrium roof blocks east views on floors 8 through 10. ✉ *122 N. 2nd St., Downtown, 85004* ☎ *602/252–1234* 🖷 *602/254–9472* ⊕ *www.hyatt.com* ➥ *667 rooms, 45 suites* ⚬ *4 restaurants, in-room data ports, cable TV with movies, pool, wading pool, gym, outdoor hot tub, 2 bars, concierge, business services, meeting rooms, car rental, parking (fee)* ⊟ *AE, D, DC, MC, V.*

$$ ▧ **Hotel San Carlos.** Built in 1928 in an Italian Renaissance design, this is the only historic hotel still operating in downtown Phoenix. The seven-story San Carlos is a step back in time: big-band music, wall tapestries, Austrian crystal chandeliers, shiny copper elevators, and an accommodating staff transport you to a more genteel era. Among other distinctions, the San Carlos was the Southwest's first air-conditioned hotel, and suites bear the names of such movie-star guests as Marilyn Monroe and Spencer Tracy. The rooms are snug by modern standards but have attractive period furnishings, coffeemakers and complimentary movies. ✉ *202 N. Central Ave., Downtown, 85004* ☎ *602/253–4121 or 800/ 678–8946* 🖷 *602/253–6668* ⊕ *www.hotelsancarlos.com* ➥ *133 rooms* ⚬ *In-room data ports, cable TV with movies, pool, meeting rooms, dry cleaning, laundry service, parking (fee)* ⊟ *AE, D, DC, MC, V.*

Central Phoenix

$$$–$$$$ ▧ **Hilton Suites.** This practical and popular hotel with an 11-story atrium is a model of excellent design within tight limits. It sits off Central Avenue, 2 mi north of downtown amid the Central Corridor cluster of office towers. The marble-floor, pillared lobby opens into an atrium containing palm trees, natural boulder fountains, glass elevators, and a lantern-lighted café. Each room has an exercise bike and VCR and a large walk-through bathroom between the living room and bedroom. ✉ *10 E. Thomas Rd., Central Phoenix, 85012* ☎ *602/222–1111* 🖷 *602/ 265–4841* ⊕ *www.hilton.com* ➥ *226 suites* ⚬ *Restaurant, room service, in-room data ports, kitchenettes, cable TV with movies and video games, in-room VCRs, indoor pool, exercise equipment, gym, hot tub, sauna, bar, shop, laundry facilities, laundry service, concierge, business services, free parking, some pets allowed* ⊟ *AE, D, DC, MC, V.*

$$–$$$ ▧ **Embassy Suites Phoenix Airport West.** Just minutes from downtown, this four-story all-suites hotel has lush palms and olive trees surrounding bubbling fountains and a sunken pool in its enclosed atrium. Complimentary breakfast (cooked to order) and an evening social hour are offered in the spacious atrium lounge. Suites have hair dryers, irons and ironing boards, and kitchenettes. ✉ *2333 E. Thomas Rd., Central Phoenix, 85016* ☎ *602/957–1910* 🖷 *602/955–2861* ⊕ *www.embassy- suites.com* ➥ *183 suites* ⚬ *Restaurant, kitchenettes, pool, gym, hot tub, lounge, laundry service, airport shuttle, free parking* ⊟ *AE, D, DC, MC, V* ⏉❶ *BP.*

$ ▧ **Sunshine Hotel & Suites.** With a 1½-acre Getaway Lagoon ringed by exotic palms and bamboo, this is central Phoenix's best bargain oasis.

Rooms and public areas are simply furnished, whereas the VIP floor offers cabana suites and a private rooftop pool with views of downtown's ever-changing skyline. Be prepared for occasional lapses in service, however, but at these prices, you are getting your money's worth. ✉ *3600 N. 2nd Ave., Central Phoenix, 85013* ☎ *602/248–0222* 🖷 *602/265–6331* ⊕ *www.getawayresort.com* ⏎ *257 rooms, 23 suites* ♨ *Restaurant, cable TV with movies and video games, putting green, 4 pools, gym, hot tub, basketball, shuffleboard, volleyball, bar, video game room, playground, laundry facilities, laundry service, business services, free parking* ☐ *AE, D, DC, MC, V.*

North-Central Phoenix

☾ **$$$–$$$$** 🖼 **Pointe Hilton at Squaw Peak.** The real highlight of the Squaw Peak, the more family-oriented of the two Pointe Hiltons in Phoenix, is a 9-acre recreation area known as the Hole-in-the-Wall River Ranch, with swimming pools fed by man-made waterfalls, a 130-ft water slide, and a 1,000-ft "river" that winds past a miniature golf course, tennis courts, outdoor decks, and artificial buttes with stunning mountain vistas. Accommodations in the pink stucco buildings vary in size from standard two-room suites to a grand three-bedroom house; all have two or more TVs, wet bars, and balconies. ✉ *7677 N. 16th St., North-Central Phoenix, 85020* ☎ *602/997–2626 or 800/876–4683* 🖷 *602/997–2391* ⊕ *www.pointehilton.com* ⏎ *431 suites, 130 casitas, 1 house* ♨ *3 restaurants, some kitchens, minibars, golf privileges, miniature golf, 3 tennis courts, 7 pools, gym, spa, mountain bikes, hiking, Ping-Pong, 2 lounges, shops, children's programs (ages 6–12), meeting rooms, parking (fee)* ☐ *AE, D, DC, MC, V.*

North-East Phoenix

☾ **$$$$** 🖼 **JW Marriott Desert Ridge Resort & Spa.** The Valley's newest resort, which opened in late 2002, and the largest resort in Arizona is in the burgeoning northeastern corridor. The immense entryway has floor-to-ceiling windows that allow the sandstone lobby, the Sonoran Desert, and the resort's amazing water features to meld together, creating a feast for the eyes. Rooms are fresh with bright decor and balconies or patios. The 4 acres of water fun include the "lazy river," where you can flop on an inner tube and float the day away. There are two outstanding golf courses. Roy Yamaguchi's newest Phoenix restaurant is just one of nine restaurants on property that offer distinctive dining. ✉ *5350 E. Marriott Dr., 85054* ☎ *480/293–5000, 888/236–2427 for reservations only* 🖷 *480/905–0032* ⊕ *www.marriott.com* ⏎ *950 rooms, 85 suites* ♨ *9 restaurants, coffee shop, room service, in-room data ports, minibars, some refrigerators, in-room safes, 2 18-hole golf courses, 8 tennis courts, 5 pools, spa, 2 lounges, shops, hair salon, children's programs (ages 5–12), baby-sitting, Internet, business services, meeting rooms, free parking, no-smoking rooms* ☐ *AE, D, DC, MC, V.*

South Phoenix

☾ **$$$–$$$$** 🖼 **Pointe South Mountain Resort.** This all-suites resort next to South Mountain Park was spiffed up in 2003, adding a redesigned golf course and the largest water park in Arizona. At the Oasis, you can tube down a river, splash in the wave pool, or zoom down the nation's tallest water slide. When you've had your fill of the wet and wild, there's a four-story sports center, golf, tennis, horseback riding, and mountain biking. Each suite has two TVs, a living room (with sofa bed), and a separate bedroom. For an extra $15 a night per suite, you can have up to four kids in the room. ⊠ *7777 S. Pointe Pkwy., South Phoenix, 85044* ☎ *602/438–9000 or 877/800–4888* 🖷 *602/431–6535* ⊕ *www.pointesouthmtn.com* ⇔ *640 suites* ⚷ *6 restaurants, room service, data ports, minibars, 18-hole golf course, 10 tennis courts, pro shop, 6 pools, health club, hair salon, sauna, mountain bikes, hiking, horseback riding, racquetball, volleyball, laundry facilities, meeting rooms, free parking* ⊟ *AE, D, DC, MC, V.*

West Valley

$$$$ ▦ **Wigwam Resort.** Built in 1918 as a retreat for executives of the Goodyear Company, the Wigwam has the pleasing feel of an upscale lodge. Casita-style rooms, situated along paths overflowing with cacti, palms, and huge bougainvillea, are decorated in a tasteful Southwestern style: distressed-wood furniture, iron lamps, pastel walls, and brightly patterned spreads. Local art adorns the walls, and all rooms have patios. It's easy to see how this isolated world of graciousness inspires a fierce loyalty in its guests, some of whom have been returning for more than 50 years. ⊠ *300 Wigwam Blvd., Litchfield Park 85340* ☎ *623/935–3811 or 800/327–0396* 🖷 *623/935–3737* ⊕ *www.wigwamresort.com* ⇔ *261 rooms, 70 suites* ⚷ *3 restaurants, 3 18-hole golf courses, 9 tennis courts, pro shop, 2 pools, gym, hair salon, 2 hot tubs, basketball, croquet, Ping-Pong, shuffleboard, volleyball, 3 bars, children's programs (ages 6–12), business services, meeting rooms, free parking* ⊟ *AE, D, DC, MC, V.*

Near Sky Harbor Airport

$$$ ▦ **Doubletree Phoenix Gateway Center Suites.** In the Gateway Center, just 1½ mi north of the airport, this honeycomb of six-story towers is the best of a dozen choices for anyone who just wants to get off the plane and into a comfortable, centrally located hotel. Two-room suites have wet bars with microwave ovens and refrigerators. Vacationers, beware: bedroom furnishings definitely cater to the corporate crowd who are traveling light—two-drawer credenzas serve as bureaus, and dinky wardrobes function as closets. ⊠ *320 N. 44th St., Airport, 85008* ☎ *602/225–0500* 🖷 *602/225–0957* ⊕ *www.doubletree.com* ⇔ *242 suites* ⚷ *Restaurant, room service, in-room data ports, microwaves, refrigerators, cable TV with movies, pool, gym, sauna, bar, laundry facilities, laundry service, Internet, meeting rooms, free parking* ⊟ *AE, D, DC, MC, V.*

$–$$ ▦ **Hampton Inn Airport.** More affordable than many of the other airport options, this accommodating, four-story hotel is 9 mi from downtown. Rooms are moderate in size and appointed with handsome armoires and bright-colored prints for drapes and bedspreads. Free Continental breakfast is available in the lobby, where a good-size TV is tuned to the local wake-up news show. Take advantage of the hotel airport shuttle, running from 5 AM to midnight. ⊠ *4234 S. 48th St., Airport, 85040* ☎ *602/438–8688 or 800/426–7866* 🖷 *602/431–8339* ⊕ *www.hamptoninn.com* ⇔ *130 rooms, 4 suites* ⚷ *Restaurant, refrigerators, in-room VCRs, pool, gym, hot tub, bar, laundry facilities, laundry service, meeting rooms, airport shuttle, free parking* ⊟ *AE, D, DC, MC, V* ⑩ *CP.*

Tempe

$$$ ▦ **Tempe Mission Palms Hotel.** Between the Arizona State University campus and Old Town Tempe, this three-story courtyard hotel is handy to the East Valley. The tone is set by a handsome, casual lobby—Matisse-inspired upholstery on overstuffed chairs—and an energetic young staff.

It's a particularly convenient place to stay if you're attending ASU sports and pro-football Cardinals events (the stadium is virtually next door). Rooms are bright, simple Southwestern in style, and comfortable. The hotel's Harry's Bar becomes a lively sports lounge at game time. ✉ *60 E. 5th St., Tempe 85281* ☎ *480/894–1400 or 800/547–8705* 🖷 *480/ 968–7677* ⊕ *www.missionpalms.com* ➾ *303 rooms* ⚅ *Restaurant, room service, 3 tennis courts, pool, gym, sauna, bar, business services, meeting rooms, airport shuttle, free parking; no smoking* ▤ *AE, D, DC, MC, V.*

$$–$$$ ▣ **Twin Palms Hotel.** Across the street from ASU's Gammage Auditorium and minutes from Old Town Tempe shopping, dining, and entertainment venues, this seven-story high-rise has a domed-window facade. Faux finishes creatively mask dated, textured walls in the rooms, and corner basins strike strategic blows to cramped bathrooms. Hotel guests receive free admission to facilities at the nearby ASU Recreation Complex, with three Olympic-size pools, badminton and squash courts, and aerobics classes. ✉ *225 E. Apache Blvd., Tempe 85281* ☎ *480/967–9431 or 800/367–0835* 🖷 *480/303–6602* ⊕ *www.twinpalmshotel.com* ➾ *140 rooms, 1 suite* ⚅ *Restaurant, room service, in-room data ports, cable TV with movies, pool, bar, laundry facilities, laundry service, concierge floor, 24-hr airport shuttle, free parking, no-smoking rooms* ▤ *AE, D, DC, MC, V.*

$$–$$$ ▣ **Wyndham Buttes Resort.** Two miles east of Sky Harbor airport, nestled in desert buttes at I–10 and AZ 60, this hotel joins dramatic architecture (the lobby's back wall is the volcanic rock itself) and classic Southwest design (pine and saguaro-rib furniture, works by major regional artists) with stunning Valley views. "Radial" rooms are largest, with the widest views; inside rooms face the huge free-form pools, with waterfall, hot tubs, and poolside cantina. The elegant Top of the Rock restaurant is a definite plus. ✉ *2000 Westcourt Way, Tempe 85282* ☎ *602/ 225–9000 or 800/843–1986* 🖷 *602/438–8622* ⊕ *www.wyndham.com* ➾ *353 rooms* ⚅ *2 restaurants, in-room data ports, minibars, cable TV with movies, 4 tennis courts, 2 pools, gym, 4 hot tubs, massage, sauna, bicycles, hiking, 3 bars, shop, laundry service, concierge floor, business services, meeting rooms, free parking, no-smoking rooms* ▤ *AE, D, DC, MC, V.*

Scottsdale

★ ☾ $$$$ ▣ **Fairmont Scottsdale Princess.** Home of the TPC Stadium golf course, this resort covers 450 breathtakingly landscaped acres of desert. Rooms are Southwestern in style, with walk-around tile showers and immense closets. Kids will love the fishing pond and water slides. Willow Stream Spa has a dramatic rooftop pool and is being hailed as one of the top spots in the country. Service is what you'd expect at a resort of this caliber, both excellent and unobtrusive. The restaurants are notable as well. To fully appreciate the resort's luxurious amenities and ambience, take a free-guided tour. ✉ *7575 E. Princess Dr., North Scottsdale, 85255* ☎ *480/585–4848 or 800/344–4758* 🖷 *480/585–0091* ⊕ *www.fairmont. com* ➾ *650 rooms, 21 suites, 125 casitas, 75 villas* ⚅ *5 restaurants, 3 bars, some in-room data ports, in-room safe, minibars, cable TV with movies and video games, 2 18-hole golf courses, 7 tennis courts, racquetball, squash, pro shop, 4 gift shops, 4 pools, 2 water slides, health club, spa, children's programs (ages 6–12), business services, free parking* ▤ *AE, D, DC, MC, V.*

$$$$ ▣ **Four Seasons Scottsdale at Troon North.** This is a logical choice for serious golfers, as it's adjacent to two Troon North premier courses, where guests receive preferential tee times and free shuttle service. However, you don't have to be a golfer to luxuriate in the world-class amenities and service offered at this resort tucked in the shadows of Pinnacle Peak. Large, casita-style rooms are sumptuously furnished and have separate sitting and sleeping areas as well as garden showers, fireplaces, and balconies or patios. Suites come with telescopes and star charts, and techno-savvy guests enjoy the in-room WebTV. A smart destination on Sunday morning is Acacia, the hotel's main restaurant, for one of the best brunches in town. ⊠ *10600 E. Crescent Moon Dr., North Scottsdale, 85255* ☎ *480/515–5700 or 888/207–9696* 🖶 *480/515–5599* ⊕ *www.fourseasons.com* 🔊 *210 rooms, 22 suites* ⊘ *3 restaurants, in-room data ports, in-room safes, minibars, cable TV, golf privileges, 4 tennis courts, 2 pools, gym, hair salon, sauna, spa, steam room, bicycles, hiking, 2 lounges, shops, children's programs (ages 5–12), laundry service, business services, meeting rooms, parking (fee), no-smoking rooms* 🖃 *AE, D, DC, MC, V.*

🖐 **$$$$** 🏨 **Hyatt Regency Scottsdale at Gainey Ranch.** When you stay here, it's easy to imagine that you're relaxing at an oceanside resort instead of the desert. Shaded by towering palms, with manicured gardens and walking paths, you'll find water everywhere—a large pool area has waterfalls, a lagoon, and even a sandy beach, and if you want, you can take a ride in a *sandolo* (small gondola). The dramatic, two-story lobby, filled with stunning Native American art, opens to outdoor conversation areas where cozy fires burn in huge stone fireplaces on cool desert nights. Large rooms with all the amenities have balconies or patios. Three golf courses will suit any duffer's fancy. ⊠ *7500 E. Doubletree Ranch Rd., North Scottsdale, 85258* ☎ *480/991–3388 or 800/233–1234* 🖶 *480/483–5550* ⊕ *www.hyatt.com* 🔊 *493 rooms, 7 casitas* ⊘ *4 restaurants, bars, in-room data ports, cable TV with movies, 3 18-hole golf courses, 8 tennis courts, 10 pools, health club, hair salon, sauna, spa, bicycles, croquet, bar, children's programs (ages 6–12), concierge floor, business services, free parking* 🖃 *AE, D, DC, MC, V.*

★ **$$$$** 🏨 **The Phoenician.** Where luxurious, expensive resorts are the rule, the Phoenician still stands apart, primarily in the realm of service. The gilded, marbled lobby with towering fountains is the perfect backdrop for the $8 million collection of authentic Dutch masters. Rooms have private patios and are large and tastefully decorated with rattan furniture and oversize marble bathrooms. The secluded tennis garden, 27 holes of premier golf, the Center for Well Being Spa with its inspiring meditation atrium and pool lined with mother of pearl tiles—everything here is world-class. And Mary Elaine's is one of the finest (and most expensive) restaurants in the state. ⊠ *6000 E. Camelback Rd., Camelback Corridor, 85251* ☎ *480/941–8200 or 800/888–8234* ⊕ *www. thephoenician.com* 🔊 *581 rooms, 73 suites* ⊘ *4 restaurants, room service, in-room data ports, in-room safes, minibars, 18-hole golf course, 9-hole golf course, 12 tennis courts, pro shop, 9 pools, health club, hair salon, sauna, steam room, archery, badminton, basketball, billiards, croquet, Ping-Pong, volleyball, children's programs (ages 5–12), business services, meeting rooms, parking (fee)* 🖃 *AE, D, DC, MC, V.*

$$$–$$$$ 🏨 **Radisson Resort and Spa.** One of the biggest and most affordable tennis resorts in Scottsdale, this hotel is the perfect match for active types who desire the facilities of a low-key, but upscale, hotel along with excellent tennis facilities. The Mist Spa makes it an even more attractive destination. The large, airy lobby has massive fountains. Spacious rooms, which are bright and airy, have patios or balconies as well as sitting areas; oversize beds, minibars, and high-speed Internet access are all pluses. And you will enjoy convenient room service and a complimentary newspaper delivered to your door. The "Fun Factory" is a recommendable children's program. ⊠ *7171 N. Scottsdale Rd., Central Scottsdale,*

85253 ☎ 480/991–3800 or 800/333–3333 ⊟ 602/948–1381 ⊕ *www. radisson.com* ⇆ *318 rooms, 34 suites* ⚴ *Restaurant, patisserie, in-room data ports, cable TV with movies, golf privileges, 21 tennis courts, 3 pools, health club, hair salon, sauna, spa, steam room, volleyball, 2 bars, shop, children's programs (ages 3–11), Internet, parking (fee)* ⊟ *AE, D, DC, MC, V.*

$$–$$$$ 🏨 **JAMES Hotel Scottsdale.** Situated on Scottsdale's Civic Center Mall, the JAMES (formerly the Old Town Hotel & Conference Center) is the first of a new brand of stylish urban resorts. All rooms have pillow-top mattresses and expensive linens for comfort, as well as the latest high-tech toys, including wireless Internet access and 42-inch plasma TVs with DVD players; there's even curbside check-in. The hotel's northern Italian restaurant, Fiamma, which provides 24-hour room service, is overseen by celebrity chef Michael White. The convenient location is a short stroll from the arts district, museums, Fashion Square, swanky Fifth Avenue boutiques, nightclubs, and restaurants. ⊠ *7353 E. Indian School Rd., Downtown, 85251* ☎ *480/994–9203* ⊕ *www.jameshotels.com* ⇆ *206 rooms, 17 suites* ⚴ *Restaurant, room service, minibars, cable TV, in-room VCR, 2 pools, gym, outdoor hot tub, spa, laundry service, shop, bar, dance club, business services, convention center, Internet, free parking, some pets allowed, no-smoking rooms* ⊟ *AE, D, DC, MC, V.*

☾ $$–$$$ 🏨 **Hotel Waterfront Ivy.** Centrally located near downtown shopping and attractions, the Ivy is a boutique extended-stay hotel geared to business travelers that also serves families well with its reasonably priced suites and extensive recreational facilities. Studios have mini-fridges and microwaves; one- and two-bedroom suites have full kitchens with dishwashers and unexpected amenities like coffee grinders and fresh coffee beans. There's a free social hour each evening, full breakfast buffet each morning, fresh-baked cookies at night, and free shuttle service from 8 AM to 8 PM to within 5 mi of the hotel. Kids will enjoy the out-of-doors play area and in-room TV video games. ⊠ *7445 E. Chaparral Rd., Central Scottsdale, 85250* ☎ *480/994–5282 or 877/284–3489* ⊟ *480/994–5625* ⊕ *www.hotelwaterfrontivy.com* ⇆ *25 studios, 80 suites* ⚴ *In-room data ports, some kitchens, some microwaves, some refrigerators, in-room safes, cable TV with movies and video games, 2 tennis courts, 5 pools, gym, hot tub, bicycles, laundry facilities, playground, meeting rooms* ⊟ *AE, D, DC, MC, V* ⦿ *BP.*

$ 🏨 **Comfort Inn.** This may be one of the nicest Comfort Inns you ever laid

★ your eyes on, and it's in a quiet, upscale North Scottsdale neighborhood along the Scottsdale Road corridor. The two-story glass entryway is as welcoming as the enthusiastic staff inside. Rooms are utilitarian but clean and have irons and ironing boards, refrigerators, and free HBO. There are several trendy restaurants and lots of shopping opportunities within easy walking distance. It's a comfortable, affordable, and family-friendly alternative in a town filled with expensive resorts. ⊠ *7350 E. Gold Dust Rd., at Scottsdale Rd., North Scottsdale, 85258* ☎ *480/596–6559; 888/ 296–9776 reservations only* ⊟ *480/596–0554* ⊕ *www.comfortinn.com* ⇆ *123 rooms, 3 suites* ⚴ *In-room data ports, refrigerators, cable TV with movies, pool, gym, hot tub, business services, Internet, free parking* ⊟ *AE, D, DC, MC, V* ⦿ *CP.*

$ 🏨 **Ramada Limited Scottsdale.** There are two attractive things about this exterior-corridor, three-story motel, formerly an EconoLodge: the location, which is within walking distance of Scottsdale's Old Town and the boutique/gallery enclave, and the price, which is hard to beat in the heart of Scottsdale. Renovated in 2003, the simple but clean rooms have standard but serviceable furnishings, so don't come expecting luxury; what you will find is a friendly welcome and a chance to leave the car behind for an hour or two, which is rare in this city. ⊠ *6935 E. 5th Ave., Downtown, 85251* ☎ *480/994–9461 or 800/528–7396* 🖷 *480/947–1695* ⊕ *www.ramada.com* ⤶ *92 rooms* ⚮ *Some microwaves, refrigerators, cable TV, pool, gym, hot tub, laundry facilities, free parking, no-smoking rooms* ▤ *AE, D, DC, MC, V* ⏐◯⏐ *CP.*

¢–$ 🖾 **Motel 6 Scottsdale.** The best bargain in Scottsdale lodging is easy to miss, but it's worth hunting for, because it's close to the specialty shops of 5th Avenue and Scottsdale's Civic Plaza Mall. Rooms are small and spare with few amenities, but the price is remarkable for the area. Anyway, how many Motel 6 properties have a pool surrounded by palms and rooms with a view of Camelback Mountain? ⊠ *6848 E. Camelback Rd., Downtown, 85251* ☎ *480/946–2280 or 800/466–8356* 🖷 *480/949–7583* ⊕ *www.motel6.com* ⤶ *122 rooms* ⚮ *In-room data ports, cable TV, pool, hot tub, free parking, some pets allowed, no-smoking rooms* ▤ *AE, D, DC, MC, V.*

Carefree

$$$$ 🖾 **The Boulders.** One of the country's top resorts hides within hill-sized, 12-million-year-old granite boulders and the lush Sonoran Desert in the town of Carefree, just north of Scottsdale. Casitas snuggled into the rocks have exposed log-beam ceilings and curved, pueblo-style half-walls and shelves. Each has a patio with a view, a wood-burning fireplace, and a spacious bathroom with deep soaking tub. El Pedregal Market Place, an upscale mall, adjoins the resort. Golfers come from far and wide to play on the two premier courses. The Golden Door spa, which opened in 2002, is one of the best in the state. ⊠ *34631 N. Tom Darlington Dr., 85377* ☎ *480/488–9009 or 800/553–1717* 🖷 *480/488–4118* ⊕ *www.wyndham.com* ⤶ *160 casitas, 46 patio homes* ⚮ *5 restaurants, room service, in-room data ports, in-room safes, some kitchens, minibars, cable TV, 2 18-hole golf courses, 6 tennis courts, 2 pools, gym, hair salon, spa, hiking, horseback riding, concierge, Internet, business services, meeting rooms, car rental, free parking* ▤ *AE, D, DC, MC, V.*

FodorsChoice ★

NIGHTLIFE & THE ARTS

The Arts

For weekly listings of theater, arts, and music events, check out "The Rep Entertainment Guide" in Thursday's *Arizona Republic*; pick up a free issue of the independent weekly *New Times* from street-corner boxes; or check out *Where Phoenix/Scottsdale Magazine,* available free in most hotels. A good on-line source of information on events in the Valley is **Digital City** (⊕ www.digitalcity.com). The on-line arm of the *Arizona Republic* (⊕ www.azcentral.com) has extensive nightlife and arts listings.

TICKETS **Arizona State University Public Events Box Office** (☎ 480/965–6447, ⊕ www.herbergercollege.asu.edu) sells tickets for events performed at ASU through the Herberger College of Fine Arts. **Tickets.com** (⊕ www.tickets.com) sells tickets for ASU Public Events at Gammage Theatre, Kerr Theatre, and the ASU Sundome. **Ticketmaster** (☎ 480/784–4444, ⊕ www.ticketmaster.com) sells tickets for nearly every event in the Valley and has outlets at all Robinsons-May department stores, Fry's, Wherehouse, and Tower Records stores.

Major Performance Venues

Major performance venues in the Valley are proliferating. Arizona State University's music and performing arts departments offer top-notch programs including dance, opera, music, and drama during the school year. Performances are either free or very reasonably priced. The Orpheum Theatre, Herberger TheatER, and Symphony Hall are home to the Arizona Opera, Phoenix Symphony, and Ballet Arizona while the new Dodge Theatre flexes between an intimate Broadway stage set-up to a concert hall seating 5,000.

PHOENIX The **Celebrity Theatre** (⊠ 440 N. 32nd St., Central Phoenix ☎ 602/267–4882 ⊕ www.celebritytheatre.com) is a 2,600-seat theater-in-the-round hosting concerts and other live performances. **Cricket Pavilion** (⊠ 2121 N. 83rd Ave. West Valley ☎ 602/254–7599 ⊕ www.cricket-pavilion.com) books shows like *Prairie Home Companion* and *Wheel of Fortune* as well as live concerts. The **Dodge Theatre** (⊠ 400 W. Washington St., Downtown ☎ 602/379–2800 ⊕ www.dodgetheatre. com) is Phoenix's new high-tech, state-of-the-art entertainment venue designed for concerts, Broadway plays, and boxing.The permanent home of the Arizona Theatre Company, Actors Theatre of Phoenix, is **Herberger Theater Center** (⊠ 222 E. Monroe St., Downtown ☎ 602/534–5600 ⊕ www.herbergertheater.org), which also hosts performances of visiting dance troupes and orchestras. The **Orpheum Theatre** (⊠ 203 W. Adams St., Downtown ☎ 602/252–8497) showcases various performing arts, the Arizona Ballet, children's theater, and film festivals. Facing the Herberger Theater, **Symphony Hall** (⊠ 225 E. Adams St., Downtown ☎ 602/534–5600) is the home of the Phoenix Symphony and Arizona Opera as well as a venue for pop concerts by top-name performers.

SCOTTSDALE **Kerr Cultural Center** (⊠ 6110 N. Scottsdale Rd., Central Scottsdale ☎ 480/965–5377) showcases smaller theater and dance performances. **Scottsdale Center for the Arts** (⊠ 7380 E. 2nd St., Downtown ☎ 480/994–2787 ⊕ www.scottsdalearts.org) hosts cultural events on the Scottsdale Mall as well as year-round performances in two intimate theater settings.

ARIZONA STATE **Gammage Auditorium** (⊠ Arizona State University, Mill Ave. at Apache
UNIVERSITY Blvd., Tempe ☎ 480/965–3434 ⊕ www.asugammage.com), which was designed by Frank Lloyd Wright, is where you can see most Broadway shows that reach the area. The box office is open weekdays 10–6. **Herberger College of Fine Arts at Arizona State University** (⊠ Arizona State University, Mill Ave. at Apache Blvd., Tempe ☎ 480/965–8863 ⊕ www.herbergercollege.asu.edu) includes Katzin Concert Hall and the Evelyn Smith Music Theatre and Organ Hall, which houses an 1,800-pipe Fritts Organ. Numerous performances are offered during the school year, from September through April, and many are free. Box office hours are Tuesday–Friday 10:30–6 and Saturday noon–4. The **Sundome Center** (⊠ 19403 R. H. Johnson Blvd., Sun City West ☎ 623/975–1900) sits in the far West Valley but manages to attract national tours of comedians and musicians. The box office hours are weekdays 9–3.

Classical Music

Arizona Opera (⊠ 4600 N. 12th St., Downtown, Phoenix ☎ 602/266–7464 ⊕ www.azopera.com), one of the nation's most respected regional companies, stages an opera season, primarily classical, in both Tucson and Phoenix. The Phoenix season runs from October to March at Symphony Hall. The box office is open weekdays 10–3:30.

Phoenix Symphony Orchestra (Box Office ⊠ Arizona Center, 455 N. 3rd St., Suite 390, Downtown, Phoenix ☎ 602/495–1999 ⊕ www. phoenixsymphony.org), the resident company at Symphony Hall, has reached the top rank of American regional symphonies. Its season, which runs September through May, includes orchestral works from classical and contemporary literature, a chamber series, composer festivals, and outdoor pops concerts. Tickets may be purchased at the Symphony Box Office without a service charge. The box office is open weekdays 9–4.

Dance

Ballet Arizona (✉ 3645 E. Indian School Rd., Central Phoenix, Phoenix ☎ 602/381–1096 ⊕ www.balletaz.org), the state's professional ballet company, presents a full season of classical and contemporary works (including pieces commissioned for the company) in Tucson and Phoenix, where it performs at Symphony Hall and the Orpheum Theater. The ballet's season runs from October through May. The ballet box office is open weekdays 9–4:30.

Film

Valley Art Theatre (✉ 509 S. Mill Ave., Tempe ☎ 480/829–6668) shows major foreign releases and domestic art films if you're looking for something besides the latest blockbuster.

Theater

Actors Theatre of Phoenix (✆ Box 1924, Phoenix 85001 ☎ 602/253–6701 ⊕ www.atphx.org) is the resident theater troupe at the Herberger Theater Center. The theater presents a full season of drama, comedy, and musical productions; it runs from September through May.

Arizona Theatre Company (✆ 808 N. 1st St. ☎ 602/252–8497 ⊕ www.aztheatreco.org) is the only resident company in the country with a two-city (Tucson and Phoenix) operation. Productions, held from September through June, range from classic dramas to musicals and new works by emerging playwrights.

Black Theater Troupe (✉ 333 E. Portland St., Downtown, Phoenix ☎ 602/258–8128) performs at its own house, the Helen K. Mason Center, a half-block from the city's Performing Arts Building on Deck Park. It presents original and contemporary dramas and musical revues, as well as adventurous adaptations, between September and May.

Childsplay (✆ Box 517, Tempe 85280 ☎ 480/350–8101 ⊕ community.tempe.gov/childsplay) is the state's nationally acclaimed theater company for young audiences and families, which runs during the school year. Rotating through many a venue—Herberger Theater Center, Scottsdale Center for the Arts, and Tempe Performing Arts Center—these players deliver colorful, high-energy performances.

Great Arizona Puppet Theatre (✉ 302 W. Latham St., Downtown, Phoenix ☎ 602/262–2050 ⊕ www.azpuppets.org), which performs in a historic building featuring lots of theater and exhibit space, mounts a year-long cycle of inventive puppet productions that change frequently; it also offers puppetry classes.

DINNER THEATER **Broadway Palm Dinner Theatre** (✉ 5247 E. Brown Rd., Mesa ☎ 480/325–6700 or 888/504–7256 ⊕ www.broadwaypalmwest.com) offers a buffet dinner followed by a live, full-length Broadway-style musical in its 500-seat theater.

Farrelli's Cinema Supper Club (✉ 14202 N. Scottsdale Rd., North Scottsdale ☎ 480/905–7200 ⊕ www.farrellis.com) offers dinner, a movie, and art deco ambience. Watch new releases on a big screen while dining on contemporary American cuisine.

WILD WEST SHOWS At **Rawhide Western Town & Steakhouse** (✉ 23023 N. Scottsdale Rd., North Scottsdale, Scottsdale ☎ 480/502–1880 ⊕ www.rawhide.com), the false fronts on the dusty Main Street contain a train depot, saloons, gift shops, and craftspeople. Reenacted Old West shoot-outs and cheesy souvenirs make this a venue for down-home, but tacky, fun. City slickers can take a ride on a stagecoach or gentle burro, and children enjoy the Petting Ranch's barnyard animals. Hayrides travel a short distance into the desert for nightly Sundown Cookouts under the stars.

✺ **Rockin' R Ranch** (✉ 6136 E. Baseline Rd., Mesa ☎ 480/832–1539 ⊕ www.rockinr.net) includes a petting zoo, a reenactment of a wild shoot-out, and—the main attraction—a nightly cookout with a Western stage show. Pan for gold or take a wagon ride until the "vittles" are served, followed by music and entertainment. Similar to its competitor, Rawhide, Rockin' R is a better deal because of its all-inclusive pricing.

Nightlife

From brewpubs, sports bars, and coffeehouses to dance clubs, mega-concerts, and country venues, the Valley of the Sun offers nightlife of all types. Nightclubs, comedy clubs, and upscale lounges abound in downtown Phoenix; along Camelback Road in north-central Phoenix; and in Scottsdale and Tempe, as well as other suburbs.

Among music and dancing styles, country-and-western has the longest tradition here. Jazz venues, rock clubs, and hotel lounges are also numerous and varied. Phoenix is getting hipper and more cosmopolitan as it gets older: cigar lovers and martini sippers will find plenty of places to indulge their tastes. There are also more than 30 gay and lesbian bars, centered primarily on 7th Avenue, 7th Street, and the stretch of Camelback Road between the two.

You can find listings and reviews in the *New Times* free weekly newspaper, distributed Wednesday, and "The Rep Entertainment Guide" of the *Arizona Republic*. *PHX Downtown*, a free monthly available in downtown establishments, has an extensive calendar for the neighborhood's events from art exhibits and poetry readings to professional sporting events. The local gay scene is covered in *Echo Magazine*, which you can pick up all over town.

Bars & Lounges

America's Original Sports Bar (✉ Arizona Center, 455 N. 3rd St., Downtown, Phoenix ☎ 602/252–2112) offers more than 40,000 square ft of boisterous fun, with more than 60 TVs (seven giant screens among them).

Buddah Bar (✉ 7419 E. Indian Plaza, Central Scottsdale Scottsdale ☎ 480/970–1945) is a sophisticated hangout with a large center bar, a tasting-dipping menu, and a DJ-controlled dance wing.

The **Famous Door** (✉ 7419 E. Indian Plaza, Central Scottsdale, Scottsdale ☎ 480/970–1945) specializes in martinis and cigars. Relax to the sounds of local jazz artists on weekends.

Fox Sports Grill (✉ 16203 N. Scottsdale Rd., North Scottsdale, Scottsdale ☎ 480/368–0369) is a sports bar where you can watch live Fox Sports broadcasts while you're drinking and dining. It's the first of its kind.

Jilly's American Grill (✉ 7301 E. Butherus, North Scottsdale, Scottsdale ☎ 480/368–8663) is the new "in" place to watch sports on 45 monitors or at a private TV booth. The weeknight TV clientele turns into a nightclub scene on weekends with music and dancing for a thirty- to fortysomething crowd.

Majerle's Sports Grill (✉ 24 N. 2nd St., Downtown, Phoenix ☎ 602/253–9004), operated by former Suns basketball player Dan Majerle, is within striking distance of the major sports facilities and offers a comprehensive menu as well as a bar for pre- and post-game celebrations.

Seamus McCaffrey's Irish Pub (✉ 18 W. Monroe St., Downtown Phoenix ☎ 602/253–6081) is a fun and friendly place to enjoy a joke, a song, or one of the dozen European brews on draft. A small kitchen turns out traditional Irish fare.

Top of the Rock Bar (✉ 2000 W. Westcourt Way, Tempe ☎ 602/431–2370), the lounge in Top of the Rock restaurant at the Buttes, attracts an older, professional crowd to drink in cocktails and spectacular views.

Casinos

Casino Arizona at Indian Bend (✉ 9700 E. Indian Bend Rd., North Scottsdale, Scottsdale ☎ 480/850–8642) has 200 slot machines and musical entertainment nightly.

Casino Arizona at Salt River (✉ Loop 101 and McKellips Rd., South Scottsdale, Scottsdale ☎ 480/850–7777, 480/850–7790 for free transportation) is the largest casino in the area, with five restaurants, four lounges, a sports bar, a 250-seat theater featuring live performances, a 50-table card room, a keno parlor, and a bingo hall. The off-track betting room features wide-screen TVs.

Fort McDowell Casino (✉ AZ 87 at Fort McDowell Rd., Fountain Hills ☎ 602/843–3678 or 800/843–3678) is popular with the Scottsdale resort crowd. In addition to the cards, slot machines, and keno games, off-track greyhound wagering takes place in a classy mahogany room with 18 giant video screens. Take advantage of the casino's free Valley-wide shuttle.

Gila River Casino (✉ AZ 87 at Fort McDowell Rd., Fountain Hills ☎ 602/843–3678 or 800/843–3678) is popular with the Scottsdale resort crowd. In addition to the cards, slot machines, and keno games, off-track greyhound wagering takes place in a classy mahogany room with 18 giant video screens. Take advantage of the casino's free Valley-wide shuttle.

Coffeehouses

Willow House (✉ 149 W. McDowell Rd., Downtown Phoenix ☎ 602/252–0272) is a self-described artists' cove that draws artsy bohemian types—a uniquely fun and funky spot in a city not overflowing with great coffeehouses. Thursday-night poetry readings are a big draw. The espresso flows until midnight on weeknights, 1 AM on weekends.

Comedy

The **Comedy Spot at Farrelli's** (✉ 14202 Scottsdale Rd. North Scottsdale, Scottsdale ☎ 480/905–7200) offers stand-up and improv on Friday and Saturday nights at Scottsdale's only comedy venue. There is a $10 cover with a $10 food and drink minimum.

The **Improv** (✉ 930 E. University Dr., Tempe ☎ 480/921–9877), part of a national chain, showcases better-known headliners from Thursday to Sunday; shows cost between $10 and $20.

The **Jester'Z Live Improv Comedy Show** (✉ 7117 E. McDowell Rd., Central Scottsdale, Scottsdale ☎ 480/423–0120) has clean, family-friendly comedy shows, performed by Jester'Z Improvisational Troupe on Thursday and Friday nights. There is a cover charge of $5 to $10.

Rascal's (✉ 100 N. 1st St., Wyndham Hotel, Downtown Phoenix, Phoenix ☎ 602/254–0999) is part of a national chain that features headlining comics. Cover is $9–$20 Thursday–Saturday and $7 on Sunday for open-mike night.

Country & Western

Buffalo Chip Saloon (✉ 6811 E. Cave Creek Rd., Cave Creek ☎ 480/488–9118) gives you a chance to see real cowboys and cowgirls doing the two-step at this fun Western bar with live music and great bratwurst.

★ **Greasewood Flats** (✉ 27500 N. Alma School Pkwy., North Scottsdale, Scottsdale ☎ 480/585–7277) is one of the best places in the Valley to have a unique Western experience under the stars. The place isn't fancy;

in fact, it's downright ramshackle, but the burgers are delicious and the crowds friendly. There's a dance floor with live music from Thursday through Sunday. In winter, wear jeans and a jacket here, since everything is outside; to keep warm, folks congregate around fires burning in halved 42-gallon oil drums.

Handlebar-J (⊠ 7116 E. Becker La., Central Scottsdale, Scottsdale ☎ 480/948–0110) has a lively, 10-gallon-hat–wearing crowd.

Harold's Cave Creek Corral (⊠6895 E. Cave Creek Rd., Cave Creek ☎480/488–1906) is just across the dirt parking lot from the Buffalo Chip Saloon. Harold's has two full bars, a restaurant, a huge dance floor with live bands on weekends, a game room, and 15 TVs.

Mr. Lucky's (⊠ 3660 N.W. Grand Ave., West Phoenix, Phoenix ☎ 602/246–0686) is the granddaddy of Phoenix Western clubs, where you can dance the two-step all night (or learn how, if you haven't before).

Red River Music Hall (⊠ 730 N. Mill Ave., Tempe ☎ 480/829–6779) is a theater venue that hosts all kinds of performances, including a jazz series, country music concerts, and special Christmas shows.

Dance Clubs

Axis and Radius (⊠ 7340 E. Indian Plaza Rd., Central Scottsdale, Scottsdale ☎ 480/970–1112) is the dressed-to-kill locale where you can party and hobnob with celebrities. Michael Jordan, George Clooney, and Cher are just some of the beautiful people who've rocked at these side-by-side clubs connected by a glass catwalk. The laser light show is astounding.

Bash on Ash (⊠ 230 W. 5th St., Tempe ☎ 480/966–8200) is where a college crowd dances to alternative and indie rock.

Cajun House (⊠ 7117 E. 3rd Ave., Downtown, Scottsdale ☎ 480/945–5150), currently one of the hottest spots in the Valley, is a Louisiana-themed venue decorated as a two-story block of Bourbon Street. Join locals who sip Hurricanes while listening to touring acts that play rock, jazz, and Cajun music. On weekends there's a line.

Sanctuary (⊠ 7340 E. Shoeman La., North Scottsdale, Scottsdale ☎ 480/970–5000) is an ultra-swanky dance club where lasers flash to the DJ's tunes and the bartender lights your martini with a blow torch. There's a cigar bar, too.

Gay & Lesbian Bars

Ain't Nobody's Business (⊠ 3031 E. Indian School Rd., Central Phoenix, Phoenix ☎602/224–9977) is the most popular lesbian bar in town; you'll also find a few gay men at this male-friendly establishment, well known as one of the most fun in town.

Amsterdam (⊠ 718 N. Central Ave., Downtown, Phoenix ☎ 602/258–6122) attracts a young crowd that wants to see and be seen; it's where Phoenix's beautiful (gay) people hang out.

B. S. West (⊠ 7125 E. 5th Ave., Downtown, Scottsdale ☎ 480/945–9028) draws a stylish, well-heeled crowd to this location tucked in a shopping center on Scottsdale's main shopping drag.

Charlie's (⊠ 727 W. Camelback Rd., West Phoenix, Phoenix ☎ 602/265–0224), a longtime favorite of local gay men, has a country-western look (cowboy hats are the accessory of choice) and friendly staff.

Jazz

A League of Our Own (⊠ 40 E. Camelback Rd., Camelback Corridor, Phoenix ☎ 602/265–2354), a large club filled with oversized booths and vintage furniture, has cool jazz and blues Tuesday–Saturday 4 PM–1 AM.

J. Chew & Co. (⊠ 7320 Scottsdale Mall, Downtown Scottsdale, Scottsdale ☎ 480/946–2733) is a popular spot for listening to live jazz and sipping a drink. Patio seating centers on a cozy wood-burning fireplace.

Leland's House of Fine Food & New Orleans Jazz (✉ 37433 Cave Creek Rd., Cave Creek ☎ 480/488–4094) features New Orleans and Chicago-style jazz Thursday–Saturday. The Sunday jazz brunch is deservedly popular.

★ **Remington's Lounge** (✉ Scottsdale Plaza Resort, 7200 N. Scottsdale Rd., North Scottsdale, Scottsdale ☎480/948–5000) has a popular piano player, Danny Long, who delivers jazz standards as well as ballads to a very appreciative following from Tuesday to Saturday night. This is one of the most popular piano bars in the East Valley.

Microbreweries

Bandersnatch Brew Pub (✉ 125 E. 5th St., Tempe ☎ 480/966–4438) is a popular pre- and post-game hangout for Arizona State University Sun Devils' fans. It brews several *cervezas* daily.

Crazy Ed's Satisfied Frog (✉ 6245 E. Cave Creek Rd., Cave Creek ☎ 480/488–3317) is a fun spot to grab a sandwich and a bottle of locally brewed chili-pepper beer.

Rock Bottom Brewery (✉ 8668 E. Shea Blvd., North Scottsdale, Scottsdale ☎ 480/998–7777) has casual dining and beer brewed on the premises.

The **Unlikely Cowboy** (✉ 20751 N. Pima Rd., North Scottsdale, Scottsdale) serves award-winning, brewed-on-the-premises, German-style beers as well as good food in an upscale atmosphere.

Rock & Blues

The **Blue Note** (✉ 8040 E. McDowell Rd., Central Scottsdale, Scottsdale ☎ 480/945–9573) is a blues club with live shows every night.

Char's Has the Blues (✉ 4631 N. 7th Ave., Central Phoenix, Phoenix ☎ 602/230–0205) is the Valley's top blues club, with nightly bands.

Long Wong's on Mill (✉ 701 S. Mill Ave., Tempe ☎ 480/966–3147) may not be the most elegant joint you'll ever see, but huge crowds of students and other grungy types pack the crowded, graffiti-covered room to catch the sounds of local musicians playing raw rock and roll.

Mason Jar (✉2303 E. Indian School Rd., Central Phoenix, Phoenix ☎602/956–6271) has nightly shows, mostly hard rock.

Rhythm Room (✉ 1019 E. Indian School Rd., Central Phoenix, Phoenix ☎ 602/265–4842) hosts local and touring blues artists. On Saturday night, there's barbecue in the parking lot.

Sugar Daddy's Blues (✉ 3102 N. Scottsdale Rd., North Scottsdale, Scottsdale ☎ 480/970–6556) serves up rhythm, blues, and food nightly until 1 AM.

SPORTS & THE OUTDOORS

Central Arizona has ample opportunity for outdoor recreation, but the area's dry desert heat imposes particular restraints—even in winter, hikers and cyclists should wear lightweight opaque clothing, a hat or visor, and high-UV-rated sunglasses and should carry a quart of water for each hour of activity. The intensity of the sun makes strong sunscreen (SPF 15 or higher) a must, and don't forget to apply it to your hands and feet. From May 1 to October 1, you shouldn't jog or hike from one hour after sunrise until a half hour before sunset. During those times, the air is so hot and dry that your body will lose moisture at a dangerous, potentially lethal rate. Don't head out to desert areas at night to jog or hike in summer; that's when rattlesnakes and scorpions are on the prowl. Tickets for most sporting events can be purchased from **Ticketmaster** (☎ 480/784–4444 ⊕ www.ticketmaster.com), which sells tickets either on the phone, on its Web site, or at its venues Valley-wide.

Auto Racing

Phoenix International Raceway (✉ 11901 W. Baseline Rd., Avondale ☎ 602/252–2227 ⊕ www.phoenixintlraceway.com), the Valley's NASCAR track south of Litchfield Park, hosts the Skoal Bandit Copper World Classic, Phoenix 200 Indy Car race, and Phoenix 500 NASCAR race.

Baseball

Take one step outside during March and you'll realize why many of the major-league baseball teams choose Phoenix for spring training. It can't get much better. The 12 teams of the Cactus League start playing in late February and reside in the Valley through March. Games start at the end of February. Additionally, the Arizona Diamondbacks major-league team is based in Phoenix and holds spring training games at Tucson's Electric Park. The **Cactus League** has an information Web site (⊕ www. cactus-league.com). You can information on teams on the Web site of **Major League Baseball** (⊕ www.mlb.com), where you can also buy tickets to games.

LOCAL TEAMS The **Arizona Diamondbacks** (✉ Bank One Ballpark, 401 E. Jefferson St., between S. 4th and S. 7th Sts., Downtown, Phoenix ☎ 602/462–6000 team offices, 602/514–8400 Bank One Ballpark Ticket Office ⊕ www. azdiamondbacks.com), the 2001 World Series Champions, play at the 48,500-seat Bank One Ballpark, which has a retractable roof, a natural-grass playing surface, and a slew of restaurants, luxury boxes, and party suites. Their Cactus League spring training takes place in Tucson's Electric Park.

SPRING **Anaheim Angels** (✉ Tempe Diablo Stadium, Tempe ☎ 602/784–4444
TRAINING TEAMS ⊕ www.angelsbaseball.com).
Chicago Cubs (✉ HoHoKam Park, Mesa ☎ 480/503–5555 ⊕ www.cubs. com).
Kansas City Royals (✉ Surprise Stadium, 15754 N. Bullard Ave., West Valley, Surprise ☎ 623/594–5600 ⊕ www.kansascityroyals.com).
Milwaukee Brewers (✉ Maryvale Baseball Park, West Phoenix, Phoenix ☎ 602/895–1200 ⊕ www.milwaukeebrewers.com).
Oakland A's (✉ Phoenix Municipal Stadium, Downtown, Phoenix ☎ 602/392–0217 ⊕ www.oaklandathletics.com).
San Diego Padres (✉ Peoria Sports Complex, Peoria ☎ 800/409–1511 ⊕ www.padres.com).
San Francisco Giants (✉ Scottsdale Stadium, Downtown Scottsdale, Scottsdale ☎ 480/990–7972 ⊕ www.sfgiants.com).
Seattle Mariners (✉ Peoria Sports Complex, Peoria ☎ 800/409–1511 ⊕ www.mariners.com).
Texas Rangers (✉ Surprise Stadium, 15754 N. Bullard Ave., West Valley, Surprise ☎ 623/594–5600 ⊕ www.texasrangers.com).

Basketball

Phoenix Mercury (✉ America West Arena, 201 E. Jefferson St., at 2nd St., Downtown, Phoenix ☎ 602/379–7867 team offices, 602/379–2000 America West Arena Ticket Office ⊕ www.wnba.com/mercury) are active during the summer Women's NBA (WNBA) season. The Mercury draw among the top crowds in the league.
Phoenix Suns (✉ America West Arena, 201 E. Jefferson St., at 2nd St., Downtown, Phoenix ☎ 602/379–7867 team offices, 602/379–2000 America West Arena Ticket Office ⊕ www.suns.com) often fill all 19,000 spectator seats in the America West Arena on game nights, and they remain the Valley's marquee pro team.

CloseUp

BASEBALL'S THREE SEASONS

F YOU'RE A DYED-IN-THE-WOOL *baseball fan, there's no better place for you to visit than the Valley of the Sun. Baseball has become nearly a year-round activity in the Phoenix area, beginning with Spring Training in late February and continuing through the Arizona Fall League championships in mid-November.*

Professional baseball sunk its roots in the warm Sonoran Desert more than a half-century ago, in 1947, when Bill Veeck brought his Cleveland Indians to Arizona (Tucson) and Horace Stoneham brought the New York Giants to Phoenix for spring training. Before 1947, only a few exhibition games had been played in Arizona. Most spring training games took place in the Florida Grapefruit League, as they had since 1914. Some teams trained in California in the 1930s, and a few teams played in such places as San Antonio, Savannah, Puerto Rico, and even Havana, Cuba. But Veeck's move was the catalyst. In 1951, baseball fans in Arizona watched Joe DiMaggio and rookie Mickey Mantle train and play at the Phoenix Municipal Stadium, when the New York Yankees came over from Florida for a year, brought by owner—and Phoenix resident—Del Webb.

Spring

In 2003, the Texas Rangers and the Kansas City Royals both began holding Spring Training at the West Valley's newest baseball complex in Surprise. This new state-of-the-art facility seats more than 10,000 fans, and the field is actually below street level. The batting cages are located on the main concourse, allowing fans to watch their favorite stars while bellying up to the concession stands.

Today, the Cactus League consists of 12 major league teams (nine in The Valley and three in Tucson). Ticket prices are reasonable, around $7–$8 for bleacher seats to $15 for reserved seats. Many of the stadiums have lawn-seating areas in the outfield, where you can spread a blanket and bring a picnic. Cactus League stadiums are more intimate than big-league parks, and often players come right up to the stands to say hello to fans

and to sign autographs. Special events such as fireworks nights, bat and T-shirt giveaway nights, and visits from sports mascots add to the festive feeling during spring training. A Cactus League game allows a family to enjoy nine innings of baseball, a hotdog, and some peanuts without absorbing the national debt.

Tickets for some teams go on sale as early as December. Brochures listing game schedules and ticket information are available by calling the Arizona teams' venues or checking the Cactus League's Web site. You'll find complete Cactus League spring training schedules, news, features, and even stadium maps.

Summer

During the regular major league season, Bank One Ballpark (BOB), in the heart of Phoenix's Copper Square, is a lively spot to watch the hometown Arizona Diamondbacks play (the team does spring training in Tucson). The stadium is a technological wonder, and in addition to the excitement on the natural-grass diamond, there's a constant barrage of lights and sights and sounds, not to mention more concession stands than you can imagine. If the weather's a little too warm outside, they simply close the roof, turn on the gigantic air-conditioners, and keep you as cool as a cucumber while you enjoy the game. You can tour the stadium, except on afternoon-game days and holidays.

Fall

At the conclusion of the regular season, the Arizona Fall League runs until the week before Thanksgiving. Each major league team sends six of their most talented young prospects to compete with other young promising players—180 players in all. There are six teams in the league, broken down into two divisions. In the past few years, many of today's superstars played in the Fall League. It's a great way to see future Hall of Famer's in their early years. Tickets for Fall League games are $5 for adults, $4 for kids and seniors, or you can get season tickets.

Bob and Gloria Willis

Bicycling

The desert climate can be tough on cyclists. Be sure to have a helmet and a mirror when riding in the streets: there are few adequate bike lanes in the Valley.

Scottsdale's Indian Bend Wash (along Hayden Road, from Shea Boulevard south to Indian School Road) has paths suitable for bikes winding among its golf courses and ponds. **Pinnacle Peak,** about 25 mi northeast of downtown Phoenix, is a popular place to take bikes for the ride north to Carefree and Cave Creek, or east and south over the mountain pass and down to the Verde River, toward Fountain Hills. Mountain bikers will want to check out the **Trail 100,** which runs throughout the Phoenix Mountain preserve (enter at Dreamy Draw park, just east of the intersection of Northern Avenue and 16th Street). **Cave Creek** and **Carefree,** in the foothills about 30 mi northeast of Phoenix, offer pleasant riding with plenty of places to stop to catch your breath. **South Mountain Park** is the prime site for mountain bikers, with its 40-plus mi of trails—some of them with challenging ascents and all of them quiet and scenic. **Phoenix Parks and Recreation** (☎ 602/262–6861 ⊕ www.ci.phoenix.az.us/parks) has detailed maps of Valley bike paths.

ABC/Desert Biking Adventures (☎ 602/320–4602 or 888/249–2453 ⊕ www.desertbikingadventures.com) provides transportation from Scottsdale hotels and offers two-, three-, and four-hour mountain-biking excursions through the McDowell Mountains and the Sonoran Desert.

Wheels N' Gear (✉ 7607 E. McDowell Rd., Central Scottsdale, Scottsdale ☎ 480/945–2881) rents bikes by the day or the week.

Four-Wheeling

Taking a jeep or a wide-track Humvee through the backcountry has become a popular way to experience the desert terrain's saguaro-covered mountains and curious rock formations.

Arizona Desert Mountain Jeep Tours (✉ 6303 E. Cochise, Scottsdale ☎ 480/860–1777 ⊕ www.azdesertmountain.com) ventures down to the Verde River on its own trail and offers wilderness cookouts.

Arrowhead Desert Jeep Tours (✉ 841 E. Paradise La., Phoenix ☎ 602/942–3361 or 800/514–9063 ⊕ www.azdeserttours.com), run by a self-described "hard-core prospector who fell in love with tourism," offers adventures that include gold-panning on a private claim, cookouts, cattle drives, river crossings, and Native American dance demonstrations.

Desert Dog Hummer Adventures (✆ Box 17647, Fountain Hills 85268 ☎ 480/837–3966) offers half- and full-day Hummer tours to the Four Peaks Wilderness Area in Tonto National Forest as well as Sonoran Desert adventures.

Desert Storm Hummer Tours (✉ 15525 N. 83rd Way, No. 8, Scottsdale 85260 ☎ 480/922–0020 ⊕ www.dshummer.com) conducts four-hour nature tours for $90 per person, climbing 4,000 ft up the rugged trails of Tonto National Forest via Hummer.

Wild West Jeep Tours (✉ 7127 E. Becker La., Scottsdale ☎ 480/922–0144 ⊕ www.wildwestjeeptours.com) has special permits that allow it to conduct four-wheeler excursions in the Tonto National Forest and to visit thousand-year-old Indian ruins listed on the National Register of Historic Places.

Football

The **Arizona Cardinals** (✉ Sun Devil Stadium, Stadium Dr., Tempe ☎ 602/379–0102 ⊕ www.azcardinals.com), the area's professional football team, play at ASU's outdoor Sun Devil Stadium in Tempe.

Golf

Arizona has more golf courses per capita than any other state west of the Mississippi River, making it one of the most popular golf destinations in the United States. It's also one of Arizona's major industries, as greens fees can run from $35 at a public course to more than $500 at some of Arizona's premier golfing spots. New courses seem to pop up monthly: there are more than 200 in the Valley (some lighted at night), and the PGA's Southwest section has its headquarters here. Call well ahead for tee times during the cooler months. During the summer, it's not uncommon to schedule a round before dawn. For a copy of the *Arizona Golf Guide,* contact the **Arizona Golf Association** (⌖ 7226 N. 16th St., Phoenix 85020 ☎ 602/944–3035 or 800/458–8484 ⊕ www.azgolf.org).

Arizona Biltmore Country Club (⊠ Arizona Biltmore Resort & Spa, 24th St. and Missouri Ave., Camelback Corridor, Phoenix ☎ 602/955–9655 ⊕ www.arizonabiltmore.com), the granddaddy of Valley golf courses, has two 18-hole PGA championship courses, lessons, and clinics.

FodorsChoice ★ **ASU Karsten Golf Course** (⊠ 1125 E. Rio Salado Pkwy., Tempe ☎ 480/921–8070) is the Arizona State University golf course where NCAA champions train.

The **Boulders Resort Golf Club** (⊠ The Boulders, 34831 N. Tom Darlington Dr., Carefree ☎ 480/488–9028 ⊕ www.wyndham.com) has two 18-hole, par-72 courses.

Encanto Park (⊠ 2775 N. 15th Ave., West Phoenix, Phoenix ☎ 602/253–3963) has an attractive, affordable public course with a 9- and 18-hole course.

FodorsChoice ★ **Gold Canyon Golf Club** (⊠ 6100 S. King's Ranch Rd., Gold Canyon ☎ 480/982–9449), near Apache Junction in the East Valley, offers fantastic views of the Superstition Mountains and challenging golf. Don't miss this one.

★ **Grayhawk Country Club** (⊠ 8620 E. Thompson Peak Pkwy., North Scottsdale, Scottsdale ☎ 480/502–1800) is always in excellent condition and has beautiful mountain views and lots of challenge.

Hillcrest Golf Club (⊠ 20002 Star Ridge Dr., Sun City West ☎ 623/584–1500) is the best course in the Sun Cities development, with 179 acres of well-designed turf.

Lookout Mountain Golf Club (⊠ Pointe Hilton at Tapatio Cliffs, 1111 N. 7th St., North-Central Phoenix, Phoenix ☎ 602/866–6356 ⊕ www.pointehilton.com) has one 18-hole, par-72 course.

Marriott's Camelback Golf Club (⊠ Marriott's Camelback Inn, 7847 N. Mockingbird La., Paradise Valley ☎ 480/596–7050 ⊕ www.camelbackinn.com) has two 18-hole courses.

Ocotillo Golf Resort (⊠ 3751 S. Clubhouse Dr., Chandler ☎ 480/917–6660 ⊕ www.ocotillogolf.com) is designed around 95 acres of man-made lakes; there's water in play on nearly all 27 holes.

Papago Golf Course (⊠ 5595 E. Moreland St., North-Central Phoenix, Phoenix ☎ 602/275–8428) is a low-priced, scenic public course and Phoenix's best municipal course.

★ The **Phoenician Golf Club** (⊠ The Phoenician, 6000 E. Camelback Rd., Camelback Corridor, Scottsdale ☎ 480/423–2449 ⊕ www.thephoenician.com) has a 27-hole course that plays up against the mountains.

Raven Golf Club at South Mountain (⊠ 3636 E. Baseline Rd., South Phoenix, Phoenix ☎ 602/243–3636) has thousands of drought-resistant Aleppo pines and Lombardy poplars, making it a cool, shady haven for summertime golfers.

Sun Ridge Canyon (⊠ 13100 N. Sun Ridge Dr., Fountain Hills ☎ 480/837–5100), east of Scottsdale, is a great course for both the low handicapper and those who score above 100. The incredible mountain views are almost distracting.

★ **Tournament Players Club of Scottsdale** (⊠ Fairmont Scottsdale Princess Resort, 17020 N. Hayden Rd., North Scottsdale, Scottsdale ☎ 480/585–3600 ⊕ www.fairmont.com), a 36-hole course by Tom Weiskopf and Jay Morrish, is the site of the PGA Phoenix Open each January.

Fodor'sChoice ★ **Troon North** (⊠ 10320 E. Dynamite Blvd., North Scottsdale, Scottsdale ☎ 480/585–5300) is a challenge for the length alone (7,008 yds). The million-dollar views add to the experience at this perfectly maintained course.

Wigwam Golf and Country Club (⊠ Wigwam Resort, 300 Wigwam Blvd. Litchfield Park ☎ 623/935–3811 ⊕ www.wigwamresort.com) is the home of the famous Gold Course, as well as two other 18-hole courses.

Health Clubs

Valley of the Sun YMCA (⊕ www.valleyymca.org ⊠ Chandler/Gilbert ⊠ 1655 W. Frye Rd., Chandler ☎ 480/899–9622 ⊠ Downtown ⊠ 350 N. 1st. Ave., Phoenix ☎ 602/257–5138 ⊠ Glendale/Peoria ⊠ 14711 N. 59th Ave., Glendale ☎ 602/588–9622 ⊠ Mesa ⊠ 207 N. Mesa Dr., Mesa ☎ 480/969–8166 ⊠ Scottsdale/Paradise Valley ⊠ 6869 E. Shea Blvd., Scottsdale ☎ 480/951–9622 ⊠ Tempe ⊠ 7070 S. Rural Rd., Tempe ☎ 480/730–0240) offers full facilities—including weight rooms, aerobics classes, pool, and racquetball privileges—to nonmembers at several Valley locations.

Hiking

One of the best ways to see the beauty of the Valley is from above. Fortunately, the flat Valley is circled by mountains that are inviting to hikers of all calibers. No matter the season, be sure to bring sunscreen, plenty of water, and a camera to capture a dazzling sunset. The city's **Phoenix Mountain Preserve System** (⊡ Phoenix Mountain Preservation Council, Box 26121, Phoenix 85068 ☎ 602/262–6861 ⊕ www.phoenixmountains. org) administers the mountainous regions that surround the city and has its own park rangers who can help plan your hikes. It also publishes a book, *Day Hikes and Trail Rides in and around Phoenix.*

Camelback Mountain and Echo Canyon Recreation Area (⊠ Tatum Blvd. and McDonald Dr., Paradise Valley ☎ 602/256–3220 Phoenix Parks & Recreation Dept.) offers intermediate to difficult hikes up the Valley's most outstanding landmark. This is a must-see for out-of-towners.

The **Papago Peaks** (⊠ Van Buren St. and Galvin Pkwy., Central Scottsdale, Scottsdale ☎ 602/256–3220 Phoenix Parks & Recreation Dept., Eastern and Central District) were sacred sites for the Tohono O'odham and probably the Hohokam before them. The soft-sandstone peaks contain accessible caves, some petroglyphs, and splendid views of much of the Valley. This is a good spot for family hikes.

Piestewa Peak Summit Trail (⊠ 2701 E. Piestewa Peak Dr., Paradise Valley ☎ 602/262–7901 North Mountain Preserves Ranger Station), just north of Lincoln Drive, ascends the landmark mountain at a steep 19% grade, but children can handle the 1¼-mi hike if adults take it slowly— allow about 1½ hours for each direction.

★ **South Mountain Park** (⊠ 10919 S. Central Ave., South Phoenix, Phoenix ☎ 602/261–8457) is the jewel of the city's Mountain Park Preserves. Its mountains and arroyos contain more than 40 mi of marked and maintained trails—all open to hikers, horseback riders, and mountain bikers. It also has three auto-accessible lookout points, with 65-mi sight lines. Rangers can help you plan hikes to view some of the 200 petroglyph sites.

Hockey

The **Phoenix Coyotes** (✉ America West Arena, 201 E. Jefferson St., at 2nd St., Downtown, Phoenix ☎ 602/379–7825 team offices, 602/379–2000 American West Arena Ticket Office ⊕ www.phoenixcoyotes.com) are the NHL team in Phoenix. In 2000, hockey great Wayne Gretzky became managing partner of the Coyotes.

Horseback Riding

More than two dozen stables and equestrian tour outfitters in the Valley attest to the saddle's enduring importance in Arizona—even in this auto-dominated metropolis. Stables offer rides for an hour, a whole day, and even some overnight adventures.

All Western Stables (✉ 10220 S. Central Ave., South Phoenix, Phoenix ☎ 602/276–5862), one of several stables at the entrance to South Mountain Park, offers rentals, guided rides, hayrides, and cookouts.
Cowboy College (✉ 30208 N. 152nd St., Scottsdale ☎ 480/471–3151 or 888/330–8070 ⊕ www.cowboycollege.com) has wranglers who will teach you everything you need to know about ridin', ropin', and ranchin'.
MacDonald's Ranch (✉ 26540 N. Scottsdale Rd., North Scottsdale, Scottsdale ☎ 480/585–0239 ⊕ www.macdonaldsranch.com) offers one- and two-hour trail rides and guided breakfast, lunch, and dinner rides through desert foothills above Scottsdale.
Spur Cross Stable (✉ 44029 Spur Cross Rd., Cave Creek ☎ 480/488–9117 or 800/758–9530 ⊕ www.horsebackarizona.com) has well-cared-for horses that will take you on one- to seven-hour rides to the high Sonoran Desert of the Spur Cross Preserve and the Tonto National Forest. Longer rides include visits to petroglyphs sites and a saddlebag lunch.

Hot-Air Ballooning

A sunrise or sunset hot-air-balloon ascent is a remarkable desert sightseeing experience. The average fee—there are more than three dozen Valley companies to choose from—is $135 per person, and hotel pickup is usually included. Since flight paths and landing sites vary with wind speeds and directions, a roving land crew follows each balloon in flight. Time in the air is generally between 1 and 1½ hours, but allow 3 hours for the total excursion. Be prepared for changing temperatures as the sun rises or sets, but it's not actually any colder up in the balloon.

Adventures Out West (☎ 602/996–6100 or 800/755–0935 ⊕ www. adventuresoutwest.com) will send you home with a free video of your flight taped from the balloon.
Hot Air Expeditions (☎ 480/502–6999 or 800/831–7610 ⊕ www. hotairexpeditions.com) offers the best ballooning in Phoenix. Flights are long, the staff is charming, and the gourmet snacks are out of this world.
Unicorn Balloon Company (☎ 480/991–3666 or 800/468–2478 ⊕ www. unicornballoon.com), operating since 1978, is run by the state's ballooning examiner for the FAA. Headquartered at Scottsdale Airport, it offers free pickup at many area hotels.

Sailplaning

Arizona Soaring Inc. (✉ Maricopa ☎ 480/821–2903 or 800/861–2318 ⊕ www.azsoaring.com), at the Estrella Sailport in Maricopa, 35 mi south of Phoenix, off I–10, gives sailplane rides in a basic trainer or high-performance plane. The adventuresome can opt for a wild 15-minute acrobatic flight.
Turf Soaring School (✉ 8700 W. Carefree Hwy., Peoria ☎ 602/439–3621 ⊕ www.turfsoaring.com) is open daily for glider rides and also offers group rates.

Tennis

Kiwanis Park Recreation Center (✉ 6111 S. All America Way, Tempe ☎ 480/350–5201 Ext. 5) has 15 lighted premier-surface courts (all for same-day or one-day-advance reserve). Before 5 PM, courts rent for $4.50; after 5 PM, the rate is $6, and $2 drop-in programs are offered for single players weekdays, 10:30–noon.

Mountain View Tennis Center (✉ 1104 E. Grovers Ave., Phoenix ☎ 602/ 534–2500), just north of Bell Road, has 20 lighted courts, a pro shop, and lessons.

Phoenix Tennis Center (✉6330 N. 21st Ave., West Phoenix, Phoenix ☎602/ 249–3712), a city facility with 22 lighted hard courts, charges $11 per hour per court for doubles.

Village Camelback Racquet & Health Club (✉ 4444 E. Camelback Rd., Camelback Corridor, Phoenix ☎ 602/840–6412 ⊕ www.dmbclubs. com) is a private tennis facility, health club, and spa featuring lighted courts, ball-machine clinics, and lessons. Out-of-towners can enjoy club amenities for $17 a day.

Tubing

The Valley may not be known for its wealth of water, but locals manage to make the most of whatever they can. A popular summer stop is the northeast side of the Salt River, where sun worshipers can rent an inner tube and float down the river for an afternoon. Several Valley outfitters rent tubes. **Salt River Recreation** (✉Usery Pass and Power Rds., Mesa ☎480/ 984–3305 ⊕www.saltrivertubing.com), conveniently located and offering shuttle-bus service to and from your starting point, rents tubes for $9 for the day; tubing season runs from May to September.

SHOPPING

Since its number of resorts began multiplying in the 1930s and 1940s, Phoenix has acquired a healthy share of high-style clothiers and leisure-wear boutiques. But long before that, Western clothes dominated fashion here—jeans and boots, cotton shirts and dresses, 10-gallon hats and bola ties (the state's official neckwear). In many places around town, they still do.

On the scene as well, of course, were the arts of the Southwest's true natives—Navajo weavers, sand painters, and silversmiths; Hopi weavers and katsina-doll carvers; Pima and Tohono O'odham (Papago) basket makers and potters; and many more. Inspired by the region's rich cultural traditions, contemporary artists have flourished here, making Phoenix—and in particular Scottsdale, a city with more art galleries than gas stations—one of the Southwest's largest art centers (alongside Santa Fe, New Mexico).

Today's shoppers will find the best of the old and the new—all presented with Southwestern style. Cowboy collectibles, handwoven rugs, traditional Mexican folk art, contemporary turquoise jewelry . . . you'll find them all in the Valley of the Sun. One-of-a-kind shops, upscale stores, and outlet malls offer shoppers everything from cutting-edge, contemporary fashion to more relaxed, down-home styles.

Most of the Valley's power shopping is concentrated in central Phoenix, downtown Scottsdale, and the Kierland area in North Scottsdale. But auctions and antiques shops cluster in odd places—and as treasure hunters know, you've always got to keep your eyes open.

Antiques & Collectibles

The central Phoenix corridor, between 7th Street and 7th Avenue, is where you will find many antiques stores. Most shops sit north of Thomas and south of Camelback. Prices, though reasonable, are firm at most shops. A surprise to many visitors is the old-town district of suburban Glendale, with more than 80 antiques and collectible shops nestled around Historic Old Towne and Catlin Court, which are listed on the National Register of Historic Places.

Antique Centre (⊠ 2012 N. Scottsdale Rd., Central Scottsdale, Scottsdale ☎ 480/675–9500) has a hodgepodge of collectibles and trinkets. **Antique Trove** (⊠ 2020 N. Scottsdale Rd., Central Scottsdale, Scottsdale ☎ 480/947–6074), next door to Antique Centre, has similar "you never know what you might find" merchandise. **Central Antiques** (⊠ Uptown Plaza, Central Ave. and Camelback Rd., Camelback Corridor, Phoenix ☎ 602/241–1174) is one of the best places in the Valley to find fine china and silver and high-end antiques. **Glendale Old Towne & Catlin Court** (⊠ 59th and Glendale Aves., Glendale) is a quaint antiques district with more than 80 shops and restaurants in colorful, century-old bungalows. Stop in at antiques-filled Aunt Pittypat's Kitchen for breakfast or lunch or have a cup of tea at the Spicery, which is in an 1895 Victorian home.

Arts & Crafts

The best option, if you're interested in touring Scottsdale's galleries, is the **Art Walk** (⊠ Main St., Downtown, Scottsdale ☎ 480/990–3939), held from 7 to 9 PM each Thursday year-round (except Thanksgiving). Main Street and Marshall Way, the two major gallery strips, take on a party atmosphere during the evening hours when tourists and locals are browsing.

Art One (⊠ 4120 N. Marshall Way, Central Scottsdale, Scottsdale ☎ 480/946–5076) carries works by local art students; much of what is found here is quite interesting. **Cosanti Originals** (⊠ 6433 Doubletree Ranch Rd., North Scottsdale, Scottsdale ☎ 480/948–6145) is the studio where architect Paolo Soleri's famous bronze and ceramic wind chimes are made and sold. You can watch the craftspeople at work, then pick out your own—prices are surprisingly reasonable. The **Heard Museum Shop** (⊠ 22 E. Monte Vista Rd., Downtown, Phoenix ☎ 602/252–8344) is hands-down the best place in town for Southwestern Native American and other crafts, both traditional and modern. Prices tend to be high, but quality is assured, with many one-of-a-kind items among the collection of rugs, katsina dolls, pottery, and other crafts; there's also a wide selection of lower-priced gifts. **Suzanne Brown Galleries** (⊠ 7156 Main St., Downtown, Scottsdale ☎ 480/945–8475) has a fabulous collection of innovative glasswork, painting, and other fine arts. **Trailside Gallery** (⊠ 7330 Scottsdale Mall Downtown, Scottsdale ☎ 480/945–7751) has been showcasing works by members of the Cowboy Artists of America for more than 40 years and specializes in traditional American paintings and sculptures. **Xanadu Gallery** (⊠ Shops at Gainey Village, 8977 N. Scottsdale Rd., North Scottsdale, Scottsdale ☎ 480/368–9929) specializes in paintings and sculptures of desert scenes, children, and flower gardens by internationally renowned artists.

Books

Barnes and Noble (⊠ Metrocenter, I–17 and Peoria Ave., West Phoenix, Phoenix ☎ 602/678–0088 ⊠ 4847 E. Ray Rd., South Phoenix, Phoenix

☎ 480/940–7136 ✉ 10500 N. 90th St., North Scottsdale, Scottsdale ☎ 480/391–0048) has the most stores in Arizona of any chain.

Bookstar (✉ 2073 E. Camelback Rd., Camelback Corridor, Phoenix ☎ 602/957–2001 ✉ 12863 N. Tatum Blvd., North-Central Phoenix, Phoenix ☎ 602/953–8066) is a good place to find deep discounts on popular books.

B. Dalton (✉ Metro Center, I–17 and Peoria Ave., West Phoenix, Phoenix ☎ 602/997–5847 ✉ Paradise Valley Mall, Cactus Rd. and Tatum Blvd., Paradise Valley ☎ 602/996–7430) has two stores in the Valley.

Borders Books and Music (✉ 2402 E. Camelback Rd., Camelback Corridor, Phoenix ☎ 602/957–6660 ✉ 4555 E. Cactus Rd., North-Central Phoenix, Phoenix ☎ 602/953–9699) is a popular chain with a good music selection.

Brentano's Bookstore (✉ Scottsdale Fashion Square South, 7014-590 E. Camelback Rd., Camelback Corridor, Scottsdale ☎ 480/423–8717) is a small bookstore with a nice assortment of stationery and cards.

Changing Hands Bookstore (✉ 6428 S. McClintock Dr., Tempe ☎ 480/730–0205) has three stories of new and used books and an inviting atmosphere that will tempt you to linger.

Gifts Anonymous (✉ 4524 N. 7th St., Central Phoenix, Phoenix ☎ 602/277–5256) carries books and small gifts exclusively for those in 12-step programs.

The **Poisoned Pen** (✉ 4014 N. Goldwater Blvd., Central Scottsdale, Scottsdale ☎ 480/947–2974) specializes in mysteries.

Those Were the Days (✉ 516 S. Mill Ave., Tempe ☎ 480/967–4729) sells used and rare books.

Waldenbooks (✉ Metrocenter, I–17 and Peoria Ave., West Phoenix, Phoenix ☎ 602/997–8861 ✉ Paradise Valley Mall, Cactus Rd. and Tatum Blvd., Paradise Valley ☎ 602/953–2407 ✉ 302 E. Bell Rd., North-Central Phoenix, Phoenix ☎ 602/863–2424) is a large, primarily mall-based chain scattered throughout the Valley.

Markets

Two of metropolitan Phoenix's best markets can be found in the tiny town of Guadalupe, which is tucked between I–10, Baseline Road, and Warner Road, almost entirely surrounded by Tempe. Take I–10 south to Baseline Road, go east ½ mi, and turn south on Avenida del Yaqui to find open-air vegetable stalls, roadside fruit stands, and tidy houses covered in flowering vines.

Guadalupe Farmer's Market (✉ 9210 S. Ave. del Yaqui, Guadalupe ☎ 480/730–1945) has all the fresh ingredients you'd find in a rural Mexican market—tomatillos, varieties of chili peppers (fresh and dried), fresh-ground *masa* (cornmeal) for tortillas, spices like cumin and cilantro, and on and on.

Mercado Mexico (✉ 8212 S. Ave. del Yaqui, Guadalupe ☎ 480/831–5925) carries ceramic, paper, tin, and lacquerware, all at unbeatable prices.

Patriot's Square Marketplace (✉ Patriot's Square Park, Washington St. and Central Ave., Downtown, Phoenix ☎ 623/848–1234) sells arts and crafts, locally grown produce, baked goods, and homemade jams and salsas, livening up downtown every Wednesday 10–2, from October through April.

Scottsdale Downtown Farmer's Market (✉ 6th Ave. between Scottsdale Rd. and Stetson Dr., Downtown Scottsdale, Scottsdale). Listen to music as you shop for fresh produce, flowers and a host of specialty items every Saturday morning from 9 to 1.

Shopping Centers

Arizona Mills (✉ 5000 Arizona Mills Circle, I–10 and Superstition Fwy., Tempe ☎ 480/491–9700), the leader in the local discount-shopping competition, is a mammoth center featuring almost 200 outlet stores, a food court, cinemas, and a faux rain forest.

Biltmore Fashion Park (✉ 24th St. and Camelback Rd., Camelback Corridor, Phoenix ☎ 602/955–8400) has posh shops in a parklike setting. Macy's and Saks Fifth Avenue are the anchors for more than 60 internationally famous stores and boutiques and 12 renowned restaurants. The **Borgata** (✉ 6166 N. Scottsdale Rd., Central Scottsdale, Scottsdale ☎ 480/998–1822), a re-creation of the Italian village of San Gimignano, is a lovely outdoor setting in which to shop for upscale merchandise or to merely sit at one of the outdoor cafés and enjoy the ambience.

Cofco Chinese Cultural Center (✉ 2425 E. Camelback Rd., Central Phoenix, Phoenix ☎ 602/955–7229) is adorned by beautiful replicas of pagodas, statutes, and traditional Chinese gardens. It's the place to find Asian restaurants, gift shops, and the 99 *Market,* an Asian grocery store. Make sure to take a stroll through the market's fish department—you'll forget you're on the desert.

ⓒ **Desert Ridge Marketplace** (✉ Tatum Blvd. and Loop 101, North Phoenix, Phoenix ☎ 480/513–7586), an out-of-doors megamall, has more than 1 million square ft of shops, restaurants, and entertainment venues, but it's also an important destination for family fun. The District is the mall's focal point for entertainment and includes an 18-theater cineplex, bowling alley, rock-climbing wall, and Jillian's, a multivenue entertainment center with a virtual-reality game room and dance club.

El Pedregal Festival Marketplace (✉ Scottsdale Rd. and Carefree Hwy., North Scottsdale, Scottsdale ☎ 480/488–1072) is an attractive two-tiered shopping plaza at the foot of a 250-ft boulder formation. In the spring and summer there are open-air Thursday-night concerts in the courtyard amphitheater. In addition to its posh boutiques, El Pedregal contains the Heard Museum North, a satellite of the downtown Heard with its own gift shop.

Kierland Commons (✉ Greenway Pkwy. at Scottsdale Rd., North Scottsdale, Scottsdale ☎ 480/348–1577) is one of the city's newest shopping areas. Designed as an "urban village," it has a range of upscale specialty retailers and restaurants in an out-of-doors pedestrian-mall setting.

★ **Scottsdale Fashion Square** (✉ Scottsdale and Camelback Rds., Central Scottsdale, Scottsdale ☎ 480/941–2140), with a retractable roof, is undoubtedly the Southwest's finest destination for upscale shopping. Nordstrom, Dillard's, Neiman Marcus, Macy's, Robinsons-May, and many specialty shops unique to Arizona are here as well as a huge food court, fine restaurants, and a luxury cineplex.

SIDE TRIPS NEAR PHOENIX

All the following sights are within a 1½-hour drive of Phoenix. To the north, Arcosanti and Wickenburg make satisfying half-day or day trips from Phoenix. Stop along the way to visit the petroglyphs of Deer Valley Rock Art Center and the reenactments of Arizona territorial life at the Pioneer Arizona Living History Museum. You also might consider Arcosanti and Wickenburg as stopovers on the way to or from Flagstaff, Prescott, or Sedona.

South of Phoenix, an hour's drive takes you back to prehistoric times and the site of Arizona's first known civilization, as well as one of its major pioneer Western towns. Florence, one of central Arizona's first

Side Trips Near Phoenix

ALT 89
17
260
Mingus Mountain
89
ALT 89
69
Dewey
Humboldt
169
Mayer
Verde Valley
Strawberry
260
Prescott National Forest
69
39 Arcosanti
Cordes Junction
Payson
260
Crown King
Bumblebee
Sunset Point Rest Area
Tonto National Forest
Horse Thief Basin
Hassayampa River
Black Canyon City
Verde River
188
38 Wickenburg
Sunflower
Lake Pleasant
New River
Pioneer Arizona Living History Museum
Carefree
Four Peaks
74
37 Carefree Rd.
Pinnacle Peak
87
Theodore Roosevelt Lake Reservoir & Dam **47**
93
60
Adobe Mountain
17
Paradise Valley
Tonto National Monument **46** ◆ Upper Ruins
36 Deer Valley Rock Art Center
Sun City
Piestewa Peak
Camelback Mountain
Salt R.
88
48 Tortilla Flat
Glendale
Phoenix
Scottsdale
Mesa
88
◆ Fish Creek Canyon
Apache Junction
Globe **45**
Guadalupe
SOUTH MTN. PARK
Tempe
60
Superstiton Mountains
42
60 89
Peralta Trail **43**
Gila River
Chandler
Florence Junction
44
10
89
Boyce Thompson Southwestern Arboretum
Montezuma Peak
GILA RIVER INDIAN RESERVATION
Casa Grande Ruins National Monument
60
238
387 **87** **41**
287 **40**
Florence
8
87
89
PAPAGO INDIAN RESERVATION
10

| 0 | 20 miles |
| 0 | 30 km |

TO TUCSON ↓

cities, is rich in examples of territorial architecture. The Casa Grande Ruins National Monument captures vivid reminders of the Hohokam, who began farming this area more than 1,500 years ago.

Deer Valley Rock Art Center

36 *15 mi north of downtown Phoenix on I–17. Exit at W. Deer Valley Rd. and drive 2 mi west.*

On the lower slopes of the Hedgepeth Hills, Deer Valley Rock Art Center has the largest concentration of ancient petroglyphs in the metropolitan Phoenix area. Some 1,500 of the cryptic symbols are found here, left behind by various Native American cultures that have lived in the Valley (or passed through) during the past thousand years. After watching one of the videos about the petroglyphs, pick up a pair of binoculars for $1 and an informative trail map and set out on the ¼-mi path. Telescopic tubes point to some of the most well-formed petroglyphs, but you'll soon be picking them out everywhere: mysterious, enduring, and beautiful, they range from human and animal forms to more abstract figures. Even the cars whizzing by in the distance can't spoil this trip through ancient art and culture. ⊠ *3711 W. Deer Valley Rd., North Phoenix, Phoenix* ☎ *623/582–8007* ⊕ *www.asu.edu* ⊠ *$6* ⊙ *Tues.–Sat. 9–5, Sun. noon–5.*

Pioneer Arizona Living History Museum

37 *25 mi north of downtown Phoenix on I–17 (Exit 225 [Pioneer Rd.]), just north of the Carefree Highway (AZ 74).*

The Pioneer Arizona Living History Museum contains 28 original and reconstructed buildings from throughout territorial Arizona. Costumed guides filter through the bank, schoolhouse, and print shop, as well as the Pioneer Opera House, where classic melodramas are performed daily. This museum is popular with the grade-school field-trip set, and it's your lucky day if you can tag along for their tour of the site—particularly when John the Blacksmith forges, smelts, and answers sixth-graders' questions that adults are too know-it-all to ask. For an extra $5 per adult, tour the grounds via a reproduction Conestoga wagon. ⊠ *3901 W. Pioneer Rd., North Phoenix, Phoenix* ☎ *623/465–1052* ⊕ *www.pioneer-arizona.com* ⊠ *$5.75* ⊙ *Wed.–Sun. 9–5.*

Wickenburg

38 *70 mi from Phoenix. Follow I–17 north for about 25 mins to the Carefree Hwy. (AZ 74) junction. About 30 mi west on AZ 74, take U.S. 89/ 93 north and go another 10 mi to Wickenburg.*

This town, land of guest ranches and tall tales, is named for Henry Wickenburg, whose nearby Vulture Mine was the richest gold strike in the Arizona Territory. By the late 1800s, the banks of the Hassayampa River hosted a booming mining town with a seemingly endless supply of gold, copper, and silver. Resident miners developed a reputation for waxing overenthusiastic about the area's potential wealth, helping to coin the term "Hassayamper" for tellers-of-tales throughout the Old West. Legend has it that a drink from the Hassayampa River will cause one to fib forevermore—a tough claim to test, since for most of the river's 100-mi course it flows underground. Nowadays, Wickenburg's Old West atmosphere attracts visitors with its sleepy downtown and Western museum. There is a group of good antiques shops, most of which are found on Tegner and Frontier streets. Maps for self-guided walking tours of the town's historic buildings are available at the **Wickenburg Chamber of Commerce** (⊠ 216 N. Frontier St. ☎ 928/684–5479 ⊕ www. wickenburgchamber.com), in the city's old Santa Fe Depot.

The **Desert Caballeros Western Museum** (⊠ 21 N. Frontier St. ☎ 928/684–7075 or 928/684–2272) is a worthwhile stop, especially if you are interested in the lore of the American West; children enjoy re-creations of a turn-of-the-20th-century general store and local street scene. On the northeast corner of Wickenburg Way and Tegner Street, check out the **Jail Tree**, to which prisoners were chained, the desert heat sometimes finishing them off before their sentences were served.

The self-guided trails of **Hassayampa River Preserve** wind through lush cottonwood-willow forests, mesquite trees, and around a 4-acre, spring-fed pond and marsh habitat. You'll spot wildlife aplenty, but it's rare birds that abound here, including waterfowl, herons, and Arizona's rarest raptors. ⊠ *3 mi southeast of Wickenburg on U.S. 60* ☎ *928/684–2772* ☞ *$5* ⊘ *Mid-Sept.–mid-May, Wed.–Sun. 8–5; mid-May–mid-Sept., Fri.–Sun. 8–5.*

The **Vulture Mine** (⊠ Vulture Mine Rd., Vulture Mine ☎ 520/859–2743) was once the largest producing gold mine in Arizona, though its vein has long since run out. A small town originally grew up around the mine, but the only thing left today are a few storage buildings and a home where caretakers live. The self-guided tour through this "ghost town" wanders past mining memorabilia (still in place on the grounds); old buildings including bunkhouses, the jail, and a blacksmith shop; the mine shaft itself; and the infamous hanging tree where some of the town's more notorious residents were hanged. The raw ore was crushed in the Hassayampa River about 10 mi away, and the town of Wickenburg sprung up there to provide services to miners working at the Vulture operation. Head west from Wickenburg on U.S. 60 for about 6 mi; then turn left onto Vulture Mine Road and travel 12 mi to the mine at the end of the pavement.

Where to Stay & Eat

For approximate costs, *see* the dining and lodging price charts at the beginning of this chapter.

¢–$$ ✕ **Anita's Cocina.** Reliable Tex-Mex fare is featured here. Fresh, steaming tamales are especially tasty, for either lunch or dinner. Try a fruit burrito for dessert. ⊠ *57 N. Valentine St.* ☎ *928/684–5777* ☐ *MC, V.*

$$$$ ▦ **Kay El Bar Ranch.** Tucked into a hollow by the Hassayampa River, this is what guest ranches used to be—personable, low-key, and remote, and John and Nancy Loftis accept only 24 guests at a time. Some of the biggest mesquite trees in Arizona shade the lodge, a family cottage with private patio (built in 1914), two separate casitas, and charming adobe cookhouse, where family-style meals are served. Each compact room in the lodge—designed for sleeping rather than hanging out—has a small, modern bathroom. In the evening everyone gathers in the living room for cocktails and homemade hors d'oeuvres by the stone fireplace. ⊠ *37500 S. Rincon Rd.* ✆ *Box 2480, 85358* ☎ *928/684–7593* ⊕ *www. kayelbar.com* ⇥ *8 rooms, 1 house, 2 casitas* ♨ *Dining room, golf privileges, pool, hot tub, horseback riding, Ping-Pong, volleyball, library; no room phones, no room TVs* ☐ *MC, V* ⊘ *Closed May–mid-Oct.* ⎟◯⎟ *FAP.*

$$$$ ▦ **Rancho de los Caballeros.** This 20,000-acre property combines the guest-ranch experience with first-class amenities. Meals are served in the lodge's bright, festive dining room, and everyone is asked to dress for each night's sit-down dinner—jackets or Western vests for men. Rooms

are spacious, done in low-key Southwestern style. Some contain two queen-size beds and can be creatively configured—through a system of adjoining doors—to annex separate living rooms or sleeping quarters for children. The Los Caballeros Golf Club course is considered one of the country's top resort courses. ⊠ *1551 S. Vulture Mine Rd., 85390* ☎ *928/684–5484* 🖷 *928/684–2267* ⊕ *www.guestranches.com/caballeros* ➷ *79 rooms* ♨ *Dining room, driving range, 18-hole golf course, 4 tennis courts, pool, massage, bicycles, horseback riding, lounge, children's programs (ages 5–12)* 🖃 *No credit cards* ⊘ *Closed mid-May–Oct.*

Nightlife

The **Rancher Bar** (⊠ 910 W. Wickenburg Way ☎ 928/684–5957) is a modern-day saloon where real live wranglers and cowboys meet up to shoot some pool after a hard day's work. A live country-music combo plays weekend nights, when the two-stepping locals really file in.

Arcosanti

39 *65 mi north of Phoenix on I–17, near the exit for Cordes Junction (AZ 69).*

Two miles down a partly paved road northeast from the gas stations and cafés, the evolving complex and community of Arcosanti was masterminded by Italian architect Paolo Soleri to be a self-sustaining habitat in which architecture and ecology function in symbiosis. Arcosanti is a bit tired-looking these days and hasn't quite achieved Soleri's original vision. However, it's still worth a stop to take a tour, have a bite at the café, and purchase one of the hand-cast bronze wind-bells made at the site. The town is off I–17 at Cordes Junction, near the town of Mayer. ☎ *928/632–7135* ⊕ *www.arcosanti.org* 🖃 *Tour $8* ⊘ *Daily 9–5; tours hourly 10–4.*

> en route
>
> If you're continuing from Arcosanti to Prescott, consider stopping in at **Young's Farm** (⊠ AZ 69 at AZ 169, Dewey ☎ 928/632–7272). Family run since 1947, Young's sells fresh turkeys for the holidays, has hayrides and a pumpkin festival in October, a petting zoo, and a restaurant serving hearty lunches and dinners. The store has become a beloved purveyor of fresh vegetables, potpies and pumpkins, sweet corn and cider, honey and fresh bread.

Florence

40 *Take U.S. 60 east (Superstition Freeway) to Florence Junction (U.S. 60 and AZ 79) and head south 16 mi on AZ 79 to Florence.*

This Old West town southeast of Phoenix is distinguished by an American Victorian courthouse and more than 150 other sites listed on the National Register of Historic Places. You may recognize Florence as the location where *Murphy's Romance* was filmed. The **Pinal County Visitor's Center** (⊠ 330 W. Butte St. ☎ 520/868–4331 ⊕ www.co.pinal.az. us/visitorcenter) answers questions and provides brochures September–May, weekdays 8–3, and June–August, weekdays 9–2.

The **Pinal County Historical Society** (⊠ 715 S. Main St. ☎ 928/868–4382), a free museum open Tuesday–Saturday 11–4 and Sunday noon–4, displays furnishings from 1900s houses and Native American crafts and tools. Open Thursday–Monday 8–5, **McFarland State Historic Park** (⊠ Main and Ruggles Sts. ☎ 928/868–5216 ⊕ www.florenceaz.org/ mcfarlandstatepark) houses memorabilia of former governor and U.S. senator Ernest W. McFarland in the circa-1878 Pinal County Courthouse.

Where to Eat

For approximate costs, *see* the dining and lodging price charts at the beginning of this chapter.

¢–$$ ✕ **Old Pueblo Restaurant.** Of the down-home Mexican and American fare served in this simple restaurant, the steak fajita burros, chimichangas, and *carne asada* (grilled beefsteak) are favorites. ⊠ *505 S. Main St.* ☎ *520/ 868–4784* ⊟ *AE, D, DC, MC, V* ☉ *Closed Sat.*

Casa Grande Ruins National Monument

🏚 *9 mi west of Florence on AZ 287 or, from I–10, 16 mi east on AZ 387 and AZ 87. Note: follow the signs to the ruins, not to the town of Casa Grande. When leaving the ruins, take AZ 87 north 35 mi back to U.S. 60.*

The ruins of Casa Grande were unknown to European explorers until Father Kino, a Jesuit missionary, first recorded their existence in 1694. The ruins were named a national monument in 1918. Allow an hour to explore the site, longer if park rangers are giving a talk or leading a tour.

Start at the visitor center, where a small museum displays artifacts and information on the Hohokam, who lived here and farmed irrigated fields of corn, beans, squash, cotton, tobacco, and other crops until they vanished mysteriously in about AD 1450. Begin your self-guided tour with an inspection of the 35-ft-tall (that's four stories, folks) Casa Grande (Big House), the tallest Hohokam building known, built in the early 14th century. It sits underneath a modern roof erected on posts to protect it from sun and wind, but the grandeur of the centuries shines through. Neighboring structures are much smaller, and only a bit of the 7-ft wall around the compound is still in evidence. The original purpose of Casa Grande still eludes archaeologists; some think it was an ancient astronomical observatory or a center of government, religion, trade, or education. On your way out, cross the parking lot by the covered picnic grounds and climb the platform for a view of a ball court and two platform mounds, said to date from the 1100s. Although only a few prehistoric sites can be viewed, more than 60 are included in the monument area. ⊠ *AZ 87, Coolidge* ☎ *520/723–3172* ⊕ *www.nps.gov/cagr* ⊠ *$3* ☉ *Daily 8–5.*

THE APACHE TRAIL

Fodor'sChoice Making a large loop east of Phoenix, this 150-mi drive was called by Pres-
★ ident Theodore Roosevelt "the most awe-inspiring and most sublimely beautiful panorama nature ever created." A stretch of winding highway, the AZ 88 portion of the Apache Trail follows closely the route forged through wilderness in 1906 to move construction supplies to build Roosevelt Dam, which lies at the northernmost part of the loop. Take a day to drive the trail, drink in the marvelous vistas, and stop to explore along the way.

From the town of Apache Junction, you can choose to drive the trail in either direction; there are advantages to both. If you begin the loop going clockwise—heading eastward on AZ 88—your drive may be more relaxing; you'll be on the farthest side of this narrow dirt road some refer to as the "white-knuckle route," with its switchbacks and drop-offs straight down into spectacular Fish Creek Canyon. But if you follow the route counterclockwise—continuing on U.S. 60 past the town of Apache Junction—you'll be able to appreciate each attraction better.

The tour below follows the route counterclockwise. Although the drive itself can be completed in one day, it's advisable to consider spending a night in Globe and continuing the loop back to Phoenix the following day.

Superstition Mountains

㊷ *From Phoenix, take I–10 and then U.S. 60 (the Superstition Freeway) east through the suburbs of Tempe, Mesa, and Apache Junction.*

As the Phoenix metro area gives way to cactus- and creosote-dotted desert, the massive escarpment of the Superstition Mountains heaves into view and slides by to the north. The Superstitions are supposedly where the legendary Lost Dutchman Mine is, the location—not to mention the existence—of which has been hotly debated since pioneer days. The best place to learn the history of the area and about the "Dutchman" Jacob Waltz and the Lost Dutchman Mine is at **Goldfield Ghost Town and Superstition Mountain Museum** (✉ 4650 N. Mammoth Mine Rd., 4 mi northeast of Apache Junction on AZ 88, Goldfield ☎ 480/983–0333 ⊕ www.goldfieldghosttown.com). The ghost town's shops are open daily 10–5, the saloon daily 10–8, the museum daily 10–5. The ghost town's shops are free; admission to the museum is $2.

Peralta Trail

㊸ *About 11½ mi southeast of Apache Junction, off U.S. 60, take the Peralta Trail Rd. (just past King's Ranch Rd.), an 8-mi, rough gravel road that leads to the start of the Peralta Trail.*

The 4-mi round-trip Peralta Trail winds 1,400 ft up a small valley for a spectacular view of **Weaver's Needle,** a monolithic rock formation that is one of Arizona's more famous sights. Allow a few hours for this rugged and challenging hike, bring plenty of water and a snack or lunch, and don't hike it in the middle of the day in summer.

Boyce Thompson Southwestern Arboretum

★ **㊹** *12 mi east of Florence Junction (U.S. 60 and AZ 79).*

At the foot of Picketpost Mountain, the Boyce Thompson Southwestern Arboretum is one of the treasures of the Sonoran Desert. From the visitor center, well-marked, self-guided trails traverse 35 acres, winding through all of the desert's varied habitats—from gravelly open desert to lush creekside glades. Native flora coexists alongside exotic specimens such as Canary Islands date palms and Australian eucalyptus. The Smith Interpretive Center, a National Historic Site, has two greenhouses and displays on geology, plant propagation, and native basketry. Benches with built-in misting machines are a relief on hot days, and natural exhibits illustrate such subjects as herbs used in traditional Sonoran healing. Bring a picnic lunch and enjoy the arboretum's lovely picnic grounds. ✉ 37615 U.S. 60, *Superior* ☎ 520/689–2811 ⊕ www.ag.arizona.edu/bta ▢ $5 ☉ Daily 8–5.

en route A few miles farther past the arboretum, **Superior** is the first of several modest mining towns and the launching point for a dramatic winding ascent through the Mescals to a 4,195-ft pass that affords panoramic views of this copper-rich range and its huge, dormant, open-pit mines. Collectors will want to watch for antiques shops through these hills, but be forewarned that quality varies considerably. A gradual descent will take you into **Miami** and **Claypool,** once-thriving boomtowns that have carried on quietly since major-corporation mining ground to a halt in the 1970s. Working-class buildings are dwarfed by the mountainous piles of copper tailings to the north. At a stoplight in Claypool, AZ 88 splits off northward to the Apache Trail, but continue on U.S. 60 another 3 mi to make the stop in the city of Globe.

Globe

45 *U.S. 60, 51 mi east of Apache Junction, 25 mi east of Superior, and 3 mi east of Claypool's AZ 88 turnoff.*

On the southern reaches of Tonto National Forest, Globe is the most cosmopolitan of the area's mining towns. Initially, it was gold and silver that brought miners here—the city allegedly got its name from a large, circular boulder of silver, with lines like continents, found by prospectors—although the region is now renowned as one of North America's richest copper deposits. If you're driving the Apache Trail loop, be sure to stop in Globe to fill up the tank, as it is the last chance to gas up until looping all the way back to U.S. 60 at Apache Junction. But Globe is worth more than a quick pit stop; its charm is its lack of prestige—and, in some cases, modernity. At the **Globe Chamber of Commerce** (✉ 1¼ mi north of downtown on U.S. 60 ☎ 928/425–4495 or 800/804–5623 🌐 www.globemiamichamber.com), open weekdays 9–5, you can pick up brochures detailing the self-guided Historic Downtown Walking Tour.

A good place to begin a visit to Globe is the **Gila County Historical Museum** (✉ 1330 N. Broad St. ☎ 928/425–7385) to see the collection of memorabilia from the area's mining days. The museum, which is free, is open weekdays 9–5. The restored late-19th-century Gila County Courthouse houses the **Cobre Valley Center for the Arts** (✉ 101 N. Broad St. ☎ 928/425–0884), showcasing works by local artists. Also visit the ladies and their looms in the basement Weaver's Studio, open Thursday–Saturday 10–3.

For a step 800 years back in time, tour the 2 acres of excavated Salado Indian ruins on the southeastern side of town at the **Besh-Ba-Gowah Archaeological Park.** After a trip through the small museum and a video introduction, enter the area full of remnants of more than 200 rooms occupied here by the Salado during the 13th and 14th centuries. You'll also see public areas such as the central plaza (also the principal burial ground; archaeologists have uncovered more than 150 burials), roasting pits, and open patios. Besh-Ba-Gowah is a name given by the Apaches, who, arriving in the 17th century, found the pueblo abandoned and moved in. Loosely translated, the name means "metal camp," as remains left on the site point to it as part of an extensive commerce and trading network. ✉ *150 N. Pine St.* ☎ *928/425–0320* 🌐 *www.jqjacobs. net/southwest/besh_ba_gowah.html* 🎟 *$3* 🕐 *Daily 9–5.*

Where to Stay & Eat

For approximate costs, *see* the dining and lodging price charts at the beginning of this chapter.

¢–$ ✕ **Chalo's.** This casual roadside spot offers top-notch Mexican food. Try an order of the savory stuffed sopaipillas, which are filled with pork and beef, beans, and red or green chilies. ✉ *902 E. Ash St.* ☎ *928/425–0515* 🖃 *MC, V.*

¢–$ 🛏 **Noftsger Hill Inn.** Built in 1907, this bed-and-breakfast was originally the North Globe Schoolhouse; now classrooms serve as guest rooms with private baths, filled with mining-era antiques and affording fantastic views of the Pinal Mountains and historic Old Dominion Mine. Innkeepers Rosalie and Dom Ayala promise you'll enjoy walking off "miner-size" breakfasts with a hike through the scenic Copper Hills behind the old school. ✉ *425 North St., 85501* ☎ *928/425–2260 or 877/780–2479* 🌐 *www.noftsgerhillinn.com* 🛏 *6 rooms* ⚪ *No smoking* 🖃 *MC, V* 🍴 *BP.*

¢ ⊡ **El Rey Motel.** Hosts Rebecca and Ricardo Bernal lovingly operate this quintessential roadside motel, where wagon wheels and potted plants dot the grounds. This vintage motor court offers small, immaculate rooms; covered parking spaces; and a shared central picnic and barbecue area. ⊠ *1201 E. Ash St., 85501* ☎ *928/425–4427* 🖷 *928/402–9147* ⤴ *23 rooms* ⊟ *AE, D, MC, V.*

Nightlife

Run by the San Carlos Apache tribe, **Apache Gold** (⊠ U.S. 70, 5 mi east of Globe ☎ 928/425–7800 or 800/272–2433) has more than 500 slots, keno, and video and live poker. Call about the free shuttle from most of Globe's hotels and motels.

Shopping

Broad Street, Globe's main drag, is lined with a number of antiques and gift shops.On Ash, between Hill and South East streets, **Copper City Rock Shop** (⊠ 566 Ash St. ☎ 928/425–7885) specializes in mineral products, many from Arizona. **Past Times** (⊠ 1068 Adonis Ave. ☎ 928/473–3791) carries antiques. **Simply Sarah** (⊠ 294 N. Broad St. ☎ 928/425–2248), with its ornately carved stone arch, has upscale ladies' clothing in predominantly natural fibers and high-quality accessories. **True Blue Jewelry** (⊠ 200 N. Willow St. Globe ☎ 928/425–8361) carries high-quality jewelry made with turquoise supplied by Globe's Sleeping Beauty Mine. Ask to watch the five-minute video about turquoise mining and preparing it for use. Try **Turquoise Ladies** (⊠ 996 N. Broad St. ☎ 928/425–6288) for owner June Stratton's collection of uniquely Globe souvenirs and stories.

| en route | At the stoplight 3 mi south of Globe on U.S. 60, AZ 88 splits off to the northwest. About 25 mi later on AZ 88, heading toward the Tonto National Monument, you'll see towering quartzite cliffs about 2 mi in the distance—look up and to the left for glimpses of the 40-room **Upper Ruins**, 14th-century condos left behind by the Salado people. They can't be seen from within the national monument, so make sure you've got binoculars. |

Tonto National Monument

🐾 *30 mi northwest of U.S. 60 on AZ 88.*

This well-preserved complex of 13th-century Salado cliff dwellings is worth a stop. The self-guided walking tour of the Lower Cliff Dwellings is interesting, but if you have time, take a ranger-led tour of the 40-room Upper Cliff Dwellings, offered on selected mornings from November to April. Tour reservations are required and should be made as far as a month in advance. To reach Tonto National Monument, go northwest on AZ 88, 30 mi beyond the intersection of U.S. 60 and AZ 88. ⊠ *AZ 88, Roosevelt* ✪ *HC 02, Box 4602, 85545* ☎ *928/467–2241* ⊕ *www.nps.gov/ tont* ☒ *$3* ☺ *Daily 8–5; Nov.–Apr., tours Thurs. and weekends at 9:30 AM; May–Oct., tours Tues., Thurs., and weekends at 9:30 AM.*

Theodore Roosevelt Lake Reservoir & Dam

🐾 *5 mi northwest of Tonto National Monument on AZ 88.*

Flanked by the desolate Mazatzal and Sierra Anchas mountain ranges, this aquatic recreational area is a favorite with bass anglers, water-skiers, and boaters. Not only is this the largest masonry dam on the planet, but the massive bridge is the longest two-lane, single-span, steel-arch bridge in the nation.

> **en route**   Past the reservoir, AZ 88 turns west and becomes a meandering dirt road, eventually winding its way back to Apache Junction via the magnificent, bronze-hued volcanic cliff walls of **Fish Creek Canyon**, with views of the sparkling lakes, towering saguaros, and, in the springtime, vast fields of wildflowers.

Tortilla Flat

48 *AZ 88, 38 mi southwest of Roosevelt Dam; 18 mi northeast of Apache Junction.*

Close to the end of the Apache Trail, this old-time restaurant and country store are what is left of an authentic stagecoach stop. This is a fun place to stop for a well-earned rest and refreshment—miner- and cowboy-style grub, of course—before heading back the last 18 mi to civilization. Enjoy a hearty bowl of killer chili and some prickly-pear-cactus ice cream while sitting at the counter on a saddle barstool.

PHOENIX & CENTRAL ARIZONA A TO Z

To research prices, get advice from other travelers, and book travel arrangements, visit ⊕ www.fodors.com.

AIR TRAVEL

Phoenix Sky Harbor International Airport is served by most major airlines, including Aeromexico, Air Canada, Alaska Air, Aloha Airlines, America West Airlines, American Airlines, ATA, Arizona Express, British Airways, Continental, Delta, Frontier, Great Lakes, Hawaiian Airlines, Lufthansa, Midwest Express, Northwest, Southwest, Sun Country, United, and US Airways. It's a major hub for both America West and Southwest.

AIRPORTS & TRANSFERS

Most air travelers visiting Arizona fly into Phoenix Sky Harbor International Airport. Just 3 mi east of downtown Phoenix, it is surrounded by freeways linking it to almost every part of the metro area.

🖪 **Sky Harbor International Airport** ☎ 602/273-8863 ⊕ www.phxskyharbor.com.

AIRPORT TRANSFERS   It's easy to get from Sky Harbor to downtown Phoenix (3 mi west) and Tempe (3 mi east). The airport is also only about 30 minutes by freeway from Glendale (to the west) and Mesa (to the east). Scottsdale (to the northeast) runs north and south for 33 mi and can be reached by AZ 101; depending on your destination, expect the trip to take anywhere from 25 minutes to downtown Scottsdale to an hour to North Scottsdale.

Valley Metro buses will get you directly from Terminal 2, 3, or 4 to the bus terminal downtown (at 1st and Washington streets) or to Tempe (Mill and University avenues). With free transfers, the bus can take you from the airport to most other Valley cities (Glendale, Sun City, Scottsdale, etc.), but the trip is likely to be slow unless you take an express line.

The Red Line runs westbound to Phoenix every half hour from about 6 AM until after 9 PM weekdays. Saturday, take Bus 13 and transfer at Central Avenue to Bus 0 north. The Red Line runs eastbound to Tempe every half hour from 3:30 AM to 7; in another 25 minutes, it goes to downtown Mesa (Center and Main streets).

A few limousine firms cruise Sky Harbor, and many more provide airport pickups by reservation. Scottsdale Limousine requires reservations but offers a toll-free number; rates start at $65 (plus tip).

The blue vans of SuperShuttle cruise Sky Harbor, each taking up to seven passengers to their individual destinations, with no luggage fee or airport surcharge. Wheelchair vans are also available. Drivers accept credit cards and expect tips. Fares are $6 to downtown Phoenix, around $16 to most places in Scottsdale, and $18 to $35 to places in far north Scottsdale or Carefree.

Only a few taxi firms are licensed to pick up at Sky Harbor's commercial terminals. All cabs add a $1 surcharge for airport pickups, do not charge for luggage, and are available 24 hours a day. A trip to downtown Phoenix can range from $8 to $12. The fare to downtown Scottsdale averages about $18. If you're heading to the East Valley, expect to shell out more than $20. Checker/Yellow Cab and Courier Cab are the Valley's main taxi services and charge about $3 for the first mile and $1.50 per mile thereafter (not including tips).

🚖 **Checker/Yellow Cab** ☎ 602/252-5252. **Courier Cab** ☎ 602/232-2222. **Scottsdale Limousine** ☎ 480/946-8446 or 800/747-8234. **SuperShuttle** ☎ 602/244-9000 or 800/258-3826 ⊕ www.supershuttle.com. **Valley Metro buses** ☎ 602/253-5000.

BUS TRAVEL TO & FROM PHOENIX
Greyhound Lines has statewide and national routes from its main terminal near Sky Harbor airport.

🚌 **Greyhound Lines** ✉ 2115 E. Buckeye Rd., Phoenix ☎ 602/389-4200 ⊕ www.greyhound.com.

BUS TRAVEL WITHIN PHOENIX
Valley Metro routes service most of the Valley suburbs, but these routes are not really suitable for vacationers and offer limited service evenings and weekends. Fares are $1.25 for regular service, $1.75 for express, with free transfers. The city of Phoenix also runs a free Downtown Area Shuttle (DASH), with purple minibuses circling the area between the Arizona Center and the state capitol at 15-minute intervals from 6:30 AM to 11 PM weekdays and from 11 AM to 11 PM weekends; this system also serves major thoroughfares in several suburbs—Glendale, Scottsdale, Tempe, Mesa, and Chandler. The city of Tempe operates the Free Local Area Shuttle (FLASH), which serves the downtown Tempe and Arizona State University area from 7 AM until 8 PM.

🚌 **Valley Metro** ☎ 602/253-500 ⊕ www.valleymetro.org.

BUSINESS HOURS
BANKS Generally, banks are open Monday–Thursday 9–4, Friday 9–6. Selected banks have Saturday-morning hours, and a few large grocery stores have bank windows that stay open until 9 PM.

POST OFFICES Post offices are open weekdays 9–5; some open Saturday morning.

SHOPS Most enclosed shopping malls are open weekdays 10–9, Saturday 10–6, and Sunday noon–5; some of the major centers are open later on weekends. Many grocery stores are open 7 AM–9 PM, but several major chain stores throughout the Valley are open 24 hours.

CAR RENTALS
To get around Phoenix, *you will need to rent a car* if you arrive by air. Only the major downtown areas (Phoenix, Scottsdale, Tempe) are pedestrian-friendly. There is no mass transit beyond a commuter bus system. At the airport most rental companies offer shuttle services to their lots. Don't expect to nab a car without a reservation, however, especially in the high season, from January to April. Most companies keep nearly all of their stock on the roads.

🚗 **Alamo** ☎ 602/244-0897. **Avis** ☎ 602/273-3222. **Budget** ☎ 602/267-1717. **Dollar** ☎ 602/224-2349. **Enterprise** ☎ 602/225-0588. **Hertz** ☎ 602/267-8822. **National** ☎ 602/275-4771. **Thrifty** ☎ 602/244-0311.

CAR TRAVEL

If you're coming to Phoenix from the west, you'll probably come in on I–10. The trip from the Los Angeles basin, via Palm Springs, takes six to seven hours, depending on where you start. From San Diego, I–8 slices across the low desert to Yuma and on toward the Valley on what the Spanish called El Camino del Diablo (the Devil's Highway); at Gila Bend, take AZ 85 up to I–10. The trip takes a total of six to seven hours. From the east, I–10 takes you from El Paso, across southern New Mexico, and through Chiricahua Apache country into Tucson, then north to Phoenix (a total of about 9–11 hours).

From the northwest, I–40 crosses over from California and runs along old Route 66 to Flagstaff. East of Kingman, however, U.S. 93 branches off diagonally to the southeast, becoming U.S. 60 at Wickenburg and continuing into Phoenix.

The northeastern route, I–40 from Albuquerque, crosses Hopi and Navajo historic lands to Flagstaff, where I–17 takes you south to Phoenix—an eight-hour journey. For a scenic shortcut, take AZ 377 south at Holbrook to Heber and the pines of the Mogollon Rim; then take AZ 260 down the 2,000-ft drop to Payson and AZ 87 through the forests of saguaro cactus into Phoenix.

Around downtown Phoenix, AZ 202 (Papago Freeway), AZ 143 (Hohokam Freeway), and I–10 (Maricopa Freeway) make an elongated east–west loop, encompassing the state capitol area to the west and Tempe to the east. At midloop, AZ 51 (Piestewa Peak Parkway) runs north into Paradise Valley. From AZ 202 east, the AZ 101 runs north to Scottsdale and makes a loop west to Sun City. And from the loop's east end, I–10 runs south to Tucson, 100 mi away (although it's still referred to as I–10 east, as it is eventually headed that way); U.S. 60 (Superstition Freeway) branches east to Tempe and Mesa.

Roads in Phoenix and its suburbs are laid out on a single, 800-square-mi grid. Even the freeways run predominantly north–south and east–west. (Grand Avenue, running about 20 mi from northwest downtown to Sun City, is the *only* diagonal.)

Central Avenue is the main north–south grid axis: all roads parallel to and west of Central are numbered *avenues*; all roads parallel to and east of Central are numbered *streets*. The numbering begins at Central and increases in each direction.

GASOLINE Gasoline prices stay fairly comparable to the national average. Expect summer prices to rise as the fuel is oxygenated to fight pollution.

ROAD In the Valley of the Sun, rain and fog are rare, and snow gets major head-
CONDITIONS lines. Most metro-area streets are well marked and well lighted, and the freeway system links Valley areas.

RULES OF THE Camera devices are mounted on several streetlights to catch speeders
ROAD and red-light runners, and their locations are constantly changing. You may think you've gotten away with a few miles over the limit and return home only to find a ticket waiting for you. To avoid tickets, drive within the speed limit.

Many accidents in the Valley are created as a result of confusion in the left-turn lanes. Each individual jurisdiction varies. In some jurisdictions, the left-turn arrow precedes the green light and in other jurisdictions it follows the green light. As well, the yellow lights tend to be shorter than most drivers are accustomed to. Therefore, be prepared for sudden stops and watch intersections for yellow-light runners. Weekdays 6 AM–9 AM and 4 PM–6 PM, the center or left-turn lanes on the major surface arteries of 7th Street and 7th Avenue become one-way traffic-flow lanes between McDowell Road and Dunlap Avenue. These specially marked lanes are dedicated mornings to north–south traffic (into downtown) and afternoons to south–north traffic (out of downtown).

Arizona requires seat belts on front-seat passengers and children 16 and under.

EMERGENCIES

🔳 Emergencies **Ambulance, Fire, and Police Emergencies** ☎ 911.

🔳 Hospitals **Maricopa County Medical Center** ⊠ 2601 E. Roosevelt St., Central Phoenix, Phoenix ☎ 602/344-5011. **Scottsdale Memorial Hospital** ⊠ 7400 E. Osborn Rd., Central Scottsdale, Scottsdale ☎ 480/481-4000 or 480/860-3000.

🔳 Pharmacies **Osco Drug** ⊠ 3320 N. 7th Ave., Central Phoenix, Phoenix ☎ 602/266-5501 ⊠ 35th and Glendale Aves., West Phoenix, Phoenix ☎ 602/841-7861 ⊠ Scottsdale and Shea Rds., North Scottsdale, Scottsdale ☎ 480/998-3500 ⊠ 1836 W. Baseline Rd., Mesa ☎ 480/831-0212. **Walgreens** ⊠ 4114 N. 24th St., Central Phoenix, Phoenix ☎ 602/381-0275 ⊠ 3605 E. Thomas Rd., Central Phoenix, Phoenix ☎ 602/267-0648 ⊠ 1120 S. 16th St., South Phoenix, Phoenix ☎ 602/252-8758 ⊠ 4006 E. Bell Rd., North-Central Phoenix, Phoenix ☎ 602/971-1096 ⊠ 8449 E. MacDonald Dr., Paradise Valley ☎ 480/483-0628 ⊠ 3420 N. Scottsdale Rd., Central Scottsdale, Scottsdale ☎ 480/941-0525.

SIGHTSEEING TOURS

Reservations for tours are a must all year, with seats often filling up quickly in the busy season, October through April. All tours provide pickup services at area resorts, but some offer lower prices if you drive to the tour's point of origin.

ORIENTATION TOURS
Gray Line Tours gives seasonal, three-hour narrated tours including downtown Phoenix, the Arizona Biltmore hotel, Camelback Mountain, mansions in Paradise Valley, Arizona State University, Papago Park, and Scottsdale's Old Town; the price is about $30.

Open Road Tours offers excursions to Sedona and the Grand Canyon, Phoenix city tours, and Native American–culture trips to the Salt River Pima–Maricopa Indian Reservation.

For $38, Vaughan's Southwest Custom Tours gives a 4½-hour city tour for 11 or fewer passengers in custom vans, stopping at the Pueblo Grande Museum, the Arizona Biltmore, and the state capitol. Vaughan's will also take you east of Phoenix on the Apache Trail. The tour is offered on Tuesday, Friday, and Saturday; the cost is $69.

🔳 **Gray Line Tours** ✉ Box 21126, Phoenix 85036 ☎ 602/495-9100 or 800/732-0327 ⊕ www.graylinearizona.com. **Open Road Tours** ⊠ 522 E. Dunlap Ave., No. 2, Phoenix 85020 ☎ 602/997-6474 or 800/766-7117 ⊕ www.openroadtours.com. **Vaughan's Southwest Custom Tours** ✉ Box 31250, Phoenix 85046 ☎ 602/971-1381 or 800/513-1381 ⊕ www.southwesttours.com.

SPECIAL-INTEREST TOURS
Cimarron Adventures and River Co. arranges half-day float trips down the Salt and Verde rivers. Trips cost about $35 per person.

🔳 **Cimarron Adventures and River Co.** ⊠ 7901 E. Pierce St., Scottsdale ☎ 480/994-1199 ⊕ www.thetent.com/arcadia/az/azcr_cimarron.htm.

TAXIS

Taxi fares are unregulated in Phoenix, except at the airport. The 800-square-mi metro area is so large that one-way fares in excess of $50 are not uncommon; you might want to ask what the damages will be before you get in, since it will often be cheaper to rent a car, even if you are renting for only a day. Except within a compact area, such as central Phoenix, travel by taxi is not recommended.

TRAIN TRAVEL

Amtrak provides train service in Arizona with bus transfers to Phoenix. Eastbound train passengers will stop in Flagstaff, where Amtrak buses depart daily for Phoenix each morning. Westbound train travelers will likely make the transfer in Tucson, where Amtrak-run buses have limited service to Phoenix on Sunday, Tuesday, and Thursday nights. What used to be Phoenix's downtown train terminal is now the Amtrak Thruway Bus Stop.

Amtrak ⊠ 4th Ave. and Harrison St. ☎ 602/253-0121 ⊕ www.amtrak.com.

VISITOR INFORMATION

The Arizona Office of Tourism is open weekdays 8–5. The Native American Tourism Center aids in arranging tourist visits to reservation lands; it can't afford to send information packets, but you can call or stop in weekdays 8–5. You can find more information at the Greater Phoenix Convention and Visitors Bureau and at the Phoenix Chamber of Commerce. The Scottsdale Convention and Visitors Bureau is open weekdays 8:30–6:30, Saturday 10–5, and Sunday 11–5.

Before You Leave **Arizona Office of Tourism** ⌂ 1110 W. Washington, Suite 155, Phoenix 85007 ☎ 602/364-3730 or 888/520-3444 ⊕ www.arizonaguide.com. **Native American Tourism Center** ☎ 480/945-0771 🖶 480/945-0264.

In Phoenix & Central Arizona **Greater Phoenix Convention and Visitors Bureau** ⊠ Arizona Center, 2nd and Adams Sts., Downtown, Phoenix ☎ 602/254-6500 ⊕ www.phoenixcvb.com. **Scottsdale Convention and Visitors Bureau** ⊠ 4343 N. Scottsdale Rd., at Drinkwater Blvd., Downtown, Scottsdale ☎ 480/421-1004 or 800/782-1117 ⊕ www.scottsdalecvb.com.

NORTH-CENTRAL ARIZONA

2

FODOR'S CHOICE

Briar Patch Inn, *Sedona*

Kramer's at the Manzanita Restaurant & Lounge, *a restaurant in Cornville*

Montezuma Castle National Monument, *Camp Verde*

Oak Creek Canyon, *a scenic drive beginning in Sedona*

Riordan State Historic Park, *Flagstaff*

Sedona Golf Resort, *a top course in Sedona*

Sharlot Hall Museum, *Prescott*

Thai Spices, *a budget restaurant in Sedona*

Wupatki National Monument, *in the San Francisco Volcanic Field*

HIGHLY RECOMMENDED

RESTAURANTS
Cottage Place, *Flagstaff*

Dahl & DiLuca, *Sedona*

Heartline Café, *Sedona*

L'Auberge, *Sedona*

Pietro's, *Sedona*

HOTELS
Alma de Sedona, *Sedona*

The Canyon Wren, *Sedona*

Enchantment Resort, *Sedona*

Graham Inn and Adobe Village, *Sedona*

Hassayampa Inn, *Prescott*

Inn at 410, *Flagstaff*

L'Auberge de Sedona, *Sedona*

Little America of Flagstaff, *Flagstaff*

Surgeon's House, *Jerome*

Many great sights also enliven this area. For our favorites, look for the black stars as you read this chapter.

Updated by
Matt Baatz

RICH IN NATURAL attractions, north-central Arizona is also rich in artifacts from its earliest inhabitants: several national and state parks—among them Walnut Canyon, Wupatki, Montezuma Castle, and Tuzigoot national monuments—hold well-preserved evidence of the architectural accomplishments of Native American Sinagua and other ancestral Puebloans who made their homes in the Verde Valley and the region near the San Francisco Peaks. Flagstaff, the largest city in north-central Arizona and gateway to fathomless pine forests, is a convenient jumping-off point for tours.

Those interested in exploring the West's wild and woolly days will enjoy a visit to the preserved fort at Camp Verde, which gives an excellent feel for frontier life, and the funky former mining town of Jerome. The many Victorian houses in temperate Prescott attest to the attempt to bring "civilization" to Arizona's territorial capital.

The Verde Valley towns of Cornville, Clarkdale, and Cottonwood are as sleepy as their names suggest. Sedona couldn't provide a greater contrast, with its sophisticated restaurants, upscale shops and accommodations, and New Age entrepreneurs. Drive just a few miles, though, and you're among soaring red rocks. AZ 89A, which heads north out of Sedona through wooded Oak Creek Canyon en route to Flagstaff, is one of the most scenic drives in the state.

Exploring North-Central Arizona

The landscape of north-central Arizona is a series of vast plateaus punctuated by steep ridges and canyons. To the north of Flagstaff, a string of tall volcanic mountains, the San Francisco Peaks, rises above 12,000 ft, tapering to 9,000-ft Mt. Elden and a scattering of diminutive cinder cones. To the south, a seemingly endless stand of ponderosa pines covers this part of the Colorado Plateau before the terrain plunges dramatically into Oak Creek Canyon. The canyon then opens up to reveal red buttes and mesas in the high-desert areas surrounding Sedona. The desert gradually descends to the Verde Valley, crossing the Verde River before reaching the 7,000-ft Black Range, over which lies the Prescott Valley. When touring, avoid the interstates as much as possible; the back ways are sometimes the most direct and usually provide the best vantage points from which you can view the stunning contrasts of the landscape. It's wise, especially if you are an outdoors enthusiast, to start in the relatively lowland areas of Prescott and the Verde Valley, climbing gradually into Sedona and Flagstaff. It can take several days to grow accustomed to high elevation here. If you can, plan to be in Sedona mid-week, when the perennial weekend crowds aren't around to crowd the streets.

About the Restaurants

Sedona and Flagstaff have the largest number of good, multiethnic restaurants in the region, but even little Cottonwood has become more food conscious in the last couple of years. Prescott and Jerome have their share of good cafés, but beyond the main streets of these four towns, restaurants tend toward standard American and Mexican road food, some of which is homey and delicious.

About the Hotels

Flagstaff has many comfortable motels (most of the familiar U.S. chains are represented) and pleasant bed-and-breakfasts, but no real luxury. There's a nearly continuous string of motels lining Route 66 once you're within the city limits, and if you aren't too particular about accommodations and rumbling trains, you can usually book a room on the fly even during the busy summer season. Otherwise, it's good to make reservations, if only a day or two ahead of your arrival. You'll find stunning settings and outstanding amenities in Sedona but few bargains. Book rooms in Sedona well ahead of time in the busy spring and fall seasons; you might find some relative bargains in winter and summer, when tourism in the area isn't quite as brisk. Sedona has spring-like temperatures even in January, when it's sure to be snowing in Flagstaff, but summer temperatures well above 100°F are common. Many of Prescott's hotels have fabled pasts. Little Jerome has one historic hotel, along with a few reliable B&Bs, but it's smart to call ahead if you think you might want to spend the night here.

WHAT IT COSTS					
	$$$$	$$$	$$	$	¢
RESTAURANTS	over $30	$20–$30	$12–$20	$8–$12	under $8
HOTELS	over $250	$175–$250	$120–$175	$70–$120	under $70

Restaurant prices are per person for a main course at dinner. Hotel prices are for two people in a standard double room in high season, excluding taxes and service charges.

Timing

Autumn, when the wet season ends, the stifling desert temperatures moderate, and the mountain aspens reach their full golden splendor, is a great time to visit. Hotel rooms in Prescott and Flagstaff are less expensive in winter, but mountain temperatures often dip below zero, and snowstorms often occur weekly, especially near Flagstaff. Prescott and Flagstaff hold most of their festivals and cultural events in summer. Sedona's biggest event, the Jazz on the Rocks Festival, takes place in September.

Exploring North-Central Arizona

The Verde Valley, in the southern part of the area covered in this chapter, is undervisited, but nearby Prescott, which has always been a Phoenician beat-the-heat getaway, is becoming popular among out-of-towners. It's hard to believe that Sedona, which is adding movie screens, chic restaurants, and B&Bs at an alarming rate, was fairly sedate in the late 1980s. Flagstaff has long been the population hub for north-central Arizona.

Numbers in the text correspond to numbers in the margin and on the North-Central Arizona, Prescott, Sedona and Flagstaff maps.

THE VERDE VALLEY, JEROME, PRESCOTT & SEDONA

About 90 mi north of Phoenix, as you round a curve approaching Exit 285 of I–17, the valley of the Verde River suddenly unfolds in a panorama of grayish-white cliffs, tinted red in the distance and dotted with desert scrub, cottonwood, and pine. For hundreds of years many Native American communities, especially those of the southern Sinagua people, lined the Verde River. Rumors of great mineral deposits brought Europeans to the Verde Valley as early as 1583, when Hopi Indians guided Antonio de Espejo here, but it wasn't until the second half of the 19th century that this wealth was commercially exploited. The discovery of silver and gold in the Black Hills, which border the valley on the southwest, gave rise to such boomtowns as Jerome—and to military installations such as Fort Verde, set up to protect the white settlers and wealth seekers from the Native American tribes they displaced. Mineral wealth was also the impetus behind the establishment of Prescott, across the

A short stay can give you a little taste of this rich part of the state, but at least five days are necessary for the full flavor. Linger longer if you want to savor the region's history and landscape or enjoy some outdoor activities. The following itineraries assume you'll start out in Phoenix, as most folks do, and head north.

2

If you have 3 days

Spend the first two nights in ▦ **Sedona** ⑬ ⮕ – ⑮. Take a jeep tour or a hike in **Red Rock State Park** ⑫, and then explore the town's shops and sights. On the next day, visit the ghost town of **Jerome** ⑥. On your third day, drive through scenic **Oak Creek Canyon** ⑰ to ▦ **Flagstaff** ⑱ – ㉗, where you can visit the **Riordan State Historic Park** ㉑ or the **Museum of Northern Arizona** ㉔ in the afternoon and the **Lowell Observatory** ⑳ at night.

If you have 5 days

Expand your time in ▦ **Sedona** ⑬ ⮕ – ⑮ by exploring Oak Creek Canyon and Red Rock State Park on the first day and shopping or exploring the town on the second. Enjoy a good part of the third day in **Jerome** ⑥; then continue on to ▦ **Prescott** ⑦ – ⑪, where you can spend the night in one of the many Victorian-era lodgings. Next day, poke around the town's antiques shops and **Sharlot Hall Museum,** and in the late afternoon drive up to ▦ **Flagstaff** ⑱ – ㉗. Then make excursions to the adjacent **Sunset Crater** ㉙ and **Wupatki** ㉛ national monuments, where Native American artifacts may be explored in an inactive volcanic field.

If you have 7 days

Take your time driving up from Phoenix to Sedona, spending the morning of the first day at **Fort Verde State Historic Park** ① ⮕ and **Montezuma Castle National Monument** ②. In the afternoon, ride the **Verde Canyon Railroad** and spend the night in ▦ **Jerome** ⑥. Continue on to ▦ **Prescott** ⑦ – ⑪ for a day or two before heading over to ▦ **Flagstaff** ⑱ – ㉗, where you can ski in the winter or view the entire San Francisco Peaks region from the Agassiz ski lift in summer. If you conclude your trip in ▦ **Sedona** ⑬ – ⑮, you'll have made a very satisfying circle of the area.

Mingus Mountains from Verde Valley, as a territorial capital by President Lincoln and other Unionists who wanted to keep the riches out of Confederate hands.

Camp Verde

94 mi north of Phoenix on I–17.

⮕ ❶ The military post for which **Fort Verde State Historic Park** is named was built between 1871 and 1873 as the third of three fortifications in this part of the Arizona Territory. To protect the Verde Valley's farmers and miners from Tonto Apache and Yavapai raids, the fort's administrators oversaw the movement of nearly 1,500 Native Americans to the San Carlos and Fort Apache reservations. A museum details the history of the area's military installations, and three furnished officers' quarters show the day-to-day living conditions of the top brass. Signs from any of I–17's three Camp Verde exits will direct you to the 10-acre park. ⊠ *125 Hollomon St.* ☎ *928/567–3275* ⊕ *www.pr.state.az.us* ⊡ *$3* ☉ *Daily 8–5.*

② The five-story 20-room cliff dwelling at **Montezuma Castle National Mon-**

FodorsChoice **ument** was named by explorers who believed it had been erected by the
★ Aztecs. Southern Sinagua Native Americans actually built the structure,
one of the best-preserved prehistoric ruins in North America—and one
of the most accessible. An easy paved trail (⅓ mi round-trip) leads to
the dwelling and to adjacent Castle A, a badly deteriorated six-story living space with about 45 rooms. No one is permitted to enter the ruins,
but the viewing area is very close by. From Camp Verde, take Main Street
to Montezuma Castle Road.

Somewhat less accessible than Montezuma's Castle—but equally striking—
is the **Montezuma Well** (☎ 928/567–4521) unit of the national monument.
Although there are some Sinagua and Hohokam ruins here, the limestone
sinkhole with a limpid blue-green pool lying in the middle of the desert is
the park's main attraction. This cavity—55 ft deep and 365 ft across—is
all that's left of an ancient subterranean cavern; the water remains at a constant 76°F year-round. It's a short hike up here, but the peace, quiet, and
the views of the Verde Valley reward the effort. To reach Montezuma Well
from Montezuma Castle, return to I–17 and go north to Exit 293; you'll
see the signs for the well, which is 4 mi east of the freeway. The drive includes a short section of dirt road. ✉ *Montezuma Castle Rd., 7 mi northeast of Camp Verde* ☎ *928/567–3322 Montezuma Castle, 928/567–3322
Ext. 15 bookstore* ⊕ *www.nps.gov/moca* ✉ *$3 per person* �)= *Labor
Day–Memorial Day, daily 8–5; Memorial Day–Labor Day, daily 8–7.*

Sports & the Outdoors
The **Verde Ranger District** office of the **Prescott National Forest** (✉ 300
E. AZ 260, Camp Verde ☎ 928/567–4121 ⊕ www.fs.fed.us/r3/prescott)
is a good resource for places to hike—as well as to fish and boat—along
the Verde River.

Dead Horse Ranch State Park

③ *20 mi northwest of Montezuma Castle National Monument; 1 mi north
of Cottonwood, off Main St.*

In the late 1940s, when Calvin "Cap" Ireys asked his family to help him
choose among the ranches he was thinking about buying in the Verde
Valley, his son immediately picked "the one with the dead horse on it."
Ireys sold the land to the state in 1973 at one-third of its value, with
the stipulation that the park into which it was to be converted retain
the ranch's colorful name.

The 423-acre spread, which combines high-desert and wetlands habitats, is a pleasant place to wile away the day. You can fish in the Verde
River or the well-stocked Park Lagoon, or hike on some 6 mi of trails
that begin in a shaded picnic area and wind along the banks of the river;
adjoining forest service pathways are available for those who enjoy longer
treks. Birders can check off more than 100 species from the Arizona
Audubon Society lists provided by the rangers. Many people are especially eager to see the bald eagles that perch along the Verde River in
winter and the common black hawks—a misnomer for these threatened
avians—that nest here in summer. ✉ *675 Dead Horse Ranch Rd., Cottonwood* ☎ *928/634–5283* ⊕ *www.pr.state.az.us* ✉ *Day use $5 per
car; camping without electricity $12, with electricity $19* ☉ *Daily 8–5.*

Where to Eat
For approximate costs, *see* the dining price chart at the beginning of this
chapter.

2

Camping

The Prescott and Coconino national forests cover a large part of north-central Arizona. Campgrounds close to Sedona often fill up in summer, especially those along Oak Creek in Oak Creek Canyon; if you want to camp near the red rocks, two good places to try are Manzanita and Banjo Bill. In Coconino National Forest near Flagstaff, the campgrounds near Mormon Lake and Lake Mary—including Pinegrove, Lakeview, Forked Pine, Double Springs, and Dairy Springs—are popular to the point of overcrowding in summer. Sites near Prescott and Jerome in the Prescott National Forest are generally less visited; Potato Patch and Granite Basin are both scenic, and sleeping out on top of Mingus Mountain is unforgettable.

Hiking

You can hike through thickly wooded areas in the Verde Valley and the Prescott National Forest in the state's highest alpine region (and even ascend a volcano), and among the rock formations around Sedona. National Forest Service offices in Camp Verde, Prescott, Sedona, and Flagstaff direct trekkers to the best trails.

Native American Culture

The achievements of the Sinagua people, who lived in north-central Arizona from the 8th through the 15th centuries, reached their height in the 12th and 13th centuries, when various related groups occupied most of the San Francisco Volcanic Field and a large portion of the upper and middle Verde Valley. The Sinagua sites around modern-day Camp Verde, Clarkdale, and Flagstaff provide a window onto this remarkable culture. Some of the best examples of surviving Sinagua architecture can be found at Wupatki National Monument, northeast of Flagstaff.

$$ ✕ **Kramer's at the Manzanita Restaurant & Lounge.** You wouldn't expect

Fodor'sChoice to find sophisticated cooking in Cornville, 6 mi east of Cottonwood,

★ but here a European-born chef (who came to the Verde Valley via Los Angeles) prepares Continental fare, using organic produce and locally raised meat whenever possible. Roast duckling à l'orange and rack of lamb are beautifully presented; try the mushroom soup if it's available. The hours here are not as cosmopolitan as the food: dinner ends at 8. ✉ *11425 E. Cornville Rd., Cornville* ☎ *928/634–8851* ▤ *MC, V* ☾ *Closed Mon.–Tues.*

¢–$$ ✕ **Page Springs Restaurant.** Come to these two rustic, wood-paneled rooms in Cornville, on the loop to the town of Page Springs, off AZ 89A for down-home Western chow: great chili, burgers, and steaks. You'll get an Oak Creek view for a lot less than you'd pay closer to Sedona. ✉ *1975 N. Page Springs Rd., Cornville* ☎ *928/634–9954* ▤ *No credit cards.*

¢ ✕ **Gabriela's Mexican Food.** You'll find traditional Mexican food served in this tiny eatery off the main Camp Verde drag. Try the *carne asada* (marinated, grilled beef) tacos and the chicken burros (what burritos are often called in this part of Arizona). ✉ *522 W. Finnie Flats Rd., Camp Verde* ☎ *928/567–4484* ▤ *No credit cards* ☾ *Closed Sun.*

Tuzigoot National Monument

4 *3 mi north of Cottonwood.*

Not as well preserved as Montezuma Castle but more impressive in scope, Tuzigoot is another complex of ruins of the Sinagua people, who lived on this land overlooking the Verde Valley from about AD 1000 to 1400. Items used for food preparation, as well as jewelry, weapons, and farming tools excavated from the site, are displayed in the visitor center. Within the ruins, you can step into a reconstructed room. ⊠ *Broadway Rd., between Cottonwood's Old Town and Clarkdale, Clarkdale* ☎ *928/634-5564* ⊕ *www.nps.gov/tuzi* ⊠ *$3* ⊙ *Labor Day–Memorial Day, daily 8–5; Memorial Day–Labor Day, daily 8–7.*

Clarkdale

5 *19 mi northwest of Camp Verde, via AZ 260 and AZ 89A; 23 mi southwest of Sedona on AZ 89A; 2 mi southwest of Tuzigoot National Monument.*

There's little to see in Clarkdale, but the town once provided the smelter for copper mines in nearby Jerome. Its current incarnation is said to have arisen from a colony of prostitutes and hard-core gamblers who were tossed out of a rowdy mining camp in one of its periodic purges of "sinners."

★ ⊙ Train buffs come to catch the 22-mi **Verde Canyon Railroad** (⊠ Arizona Central Railroad, 300 N. Broadway, Clarkdale ☎ 800/320–0718 ⊕ www.verdecanyonrr.com), whose knowledgeable announcers regale riders with the area's colorful history and point out natural attractions along the way—in winter, you're likely to see bald eagles. This trip, which takes about four hours, is especially popular in fall-foliage season and in the spring, when the desert wildflowers bloom; make reservations well in advance. Round-trip rides cost $39.95. For $59.95 you can ride the living room–like and much more comfortable first-class cars, where hot hors d'oeuvres, coffee, and a cocktail are included in the price.

Jerome

★ **6** *3½ mi southwest of Clarkdale, 20 mi northwest of Camp Verde, 33 mi northeast of Prescott, 25 mi southwest of Sedona on AZ 89A.*

Jerome was once known as the Billion Dollar Copper Camp, but after the last mines closed in 1953, the booming population of 15,000 dwindled to 50 determined souls, earning Jerome the "ghost town" designation it still holds, although its population has risen back to almost 500. It's hard to imagine that this town, which doesn't have a single convenience store, once was the location of Arizona's largest JCPenney department store and one of the state's first Safeway supermarkets. Jerome saw its first revival during the mid-1960s, when hippies arrived and turned it into an art colony of sorts, and it's now becoming a tourist attraction. In addition to its shops and historic sites, Jerome is worth visiting for its scenery: it's built into the side of Cleopatra Hill, and from here you can see Sedona's red rocks, Flagstaff's San Francisco Peaks, and even eastern Arizona's Mogollon Rim country.

Jerome is about a mile above sea level, but structures within town sit at elevations that vary by as much as 1,500 ft, depending on whether they're on Cleopatra Hill or at its foot. Blasting at the United Verde (later Phelps Dodge) mine regularly shook buildings off their foundations— the town's jail slid across a road and down a hillside, where it sits today. That's not all that was unsteady about Jerome. In 1903 a reporter from a New York newspaper called Jerome "the wickedest town in America" due to its abundance of drinking and gambling establishments; town records from 1880 list 24 saloons. Whether by divine retribution or drunken accidents, the town burned down several times. The mine's financial backers were a bit more respectable: Eugene Jerome, for whom the town was named, was first cousin to Jenny Jerome, Winston Churchill's mother.

Jerome has around 50 retail establishments (that's more than one for every 10 residents). You can get a map of the town's shops and its attractions at the visitor-information trailer on AZ 89A. Except for the state-run historic park, attractions and businesses don't always stay open as long as their stated hours when things are slow.

Of the three mining museums in town, the most inclusive is part of **Jerome State Historic Park.** Just outside town, signs on AZ 89A will direct you to the turnoff for the park, reached by a short, precipitous road. The museum occupies the 1917 mansion of Jerome's mining king, Dr. James "Rawhide Jimmy" Douglas Jr., who purchased Little Daisy Mine in 1912. You can see some of the tools and heavy equipment used to grind ore, but accounts of the town's wilder elements—such as the House of Joy brothel—are not so prominently displayed. ⊠ *State Park Rd.* ☎ *928/ 634–5381* ⊕ *www.pr.state.az.us* 🖻 *$4* ⊘ *Daily 8–5.*

The **Mine Museum** in downtown Jerome is staffed by the Jerome Historical Society. The museum's collection of mining stock certificates alone is worth the (small) price of admission—the amount of money that changed hands in this town 100 years ago boggles the mind. ⊠ *200 Main St.* ☎ *928/634–5477* 🖻 *$2* ⊘ *Daily 9–4:30.*

Where to Stay & Eat

For approximate costs, *see* the dining and lodging price charts at the beginning of this chapter.

$–$$ ✕ **Haunted Hamburger/Jerome Palace.** After the climb up the stairs from Main Street to this former boardinghouse, you'll be ready for the hearty burgers, chili, cheese steaks, and ribs that dominate the menu. Lighter fare, including such meatless selections as the guacamole quesadilla, is also available. An outdoor deck that overlooks Verde Valley helps to overcome the often indifferent service. ⊠ *410 Clark St.* ☎ *928/634– 0554* ▤ *MC, V.*

¢ ✕ **English Kitchen.** One of the oldest restaurants in the country, this space has housed some kind of restaurant since 1899, when Chinese immigrant Charley Hong arrived in Jerome and set up shop. Nearly 100 years later, in 1986, Tim and Jayne Toth bought the restaurant, and they serve salads, burgers, and sandwiches at lunch, as well as the best breakfast in town, to residents who might prefer to keep this place a secret. ⊠ *416 Main St.* ☎ *928/634–2132* ▤ *MC, V* ⊘ *Closed Mon. No dinner.*

¢ ✕ **Flatiron Cafe.** Ask where to have lunch or a late-afternoon snack, and nearly every Main Street shop owner will direct you to a tiny eatery at the fork in the road. The menu includes healthful sandwiches, such as black-bean hummus with feta cheese, and many coffee drinks. Breakfast is also served here. ⊠ *416 Main St.* ☎ *928/634–2733* ▤ *No credit cards* ⊘ *Closed Wed.–Thurs. No dinner.*

¢ ✕ **Red Rooster Café.** The old Safeway is now a café with tin ceilings and country accents, yet the delicious meat-loaf sandwich is nontraditional, served on whole wheat bread with Dijon mustard *sans* mashed potatoes. A compact but eclectic lunch menu includes green-chili quiche and a turkey wrap topped with bacon, avocado, and chipotle mayonnaise. On the weekends, live music rounds out the homey atmosphere. ⊠ *363 Main St.* ☎ *928/634–7087* ▤ *MC, V* ⊘ *Closed Tues. No dinner.*

$–$$ ⊡ **Ghost City Inn.** The outdoor verandah at this 1898 B&B affords sweeping views of the Verde Valley and Sedona. Most rooms are decorated in Victorian style, but one has contemporary Western touches and another has a rustic appeal. Afternoon tea with cookies is an unexpected luxury for this formerly rough-and-ready town. ⊠ *541 N. Main St., 86331* ☎▦ *928/634–4678* ⊕ *www.ghostcityinn.com* ↩ *6 rooms, 2 with bath* ▤ *AE, D, MC, V* ⧖*◯l BP.*

$–$$ ⊡ **Jerome Grand Hotel.** This full-service hotel is housed in a former hospital built by the United Verde Mine Company in 1927. It's on Cleopatra Hill, so many rooms have splendid views, and all rooms have TVs with VCRs. ⊠ *200 Hill St., 86331* ☎ *928/634–8200 or 888/817–6788* ▦ *928/639–0299* ⊕ *www.jeromegrandhotel.net* ↩ *22 rooms, 1 suite* ⧗ *Restaurant, in-room VCRs, lounge* ▤ *AE, D, MC, V.*

★ $–$$ ⊡ **Surgeon's House.** Abundant plants, knickknacks, bright colors, and plenty of sunlight make this Mediterranean-style home, which once belonged to Jerome's sawbones, a most welcoming place to stay. The friendly ministrations of innkeeper Andrea Prince enhance the experience. Her multicourse breakfasts might include potato–sour cream soup, overstuffed burritos, or a marinated fruit compote. There are two suites and two rooms, including a former chauffeur's quarters, which has a skylight and private patio. All have private bathrooms. You'll enjoy knockout vistas from almost everywhere in the house. A plus: pets are welcome. ⊠ *101 Hill St., 86331* ☎ *928/639–1452 or 800/639–1452* ⊕ *www.surgeonshouse.com* ↩ *2 rooms, 2 suites* ⧗ *Some kitchenettes, some pets allowed (fee)* ▤ *MC, V* ◯l *BP.*

Nightlife

Paul & Jerry's Saloon (⊠ Main St. ☎ 928/634–2603) attracts a rowdy crowd to its two pool tables and old wooden bar. On weekends there's live music and a lively scene at the **Spirit Room** (⊠ Main St. and AZ 89A ☎ 928/634–8809); the mural over the bar harks back to the days when it was a dining spot for the prostitutes of the red-light district.

Shopping

Jerome has its share of art galleries (some perched precariously on Cleopatra Hill), along with boutiques, but they're funkier than those in Sedona. Main Street and Hull Avenue, just around the bend from Main, are Jerome's two main shopping streets. Your eyes may begin to glaze over after browsing through one boutique after another, most offering tasteful Southwestern paraphernalia.

Aurum (⊠ 369 Main St. ☎ 928/634–3330) focuses on contemporary art jewelry in silver and gold; about 30 artists are represented. **Designs on You** (⊠ 233 Main St. ☎ 928/634–7879) carries attractively styled women's clothing. **Jerome Artists Cooperative Gallery** (⊠ 502 Main St. ☎ 928/639–4276) specializes in jewelry, sculpture, painting, and pottery by local artists. The **Jewel** (⊠ 420 Hull Ave. ☎ 928/639–0259) specializes in Australian opals. **Nellie Bly** (⊠ 136 Main St. ☎ 928/634–0255) stocks perfume bottles and outstanding kaleidoscopes. Among the work of 300 artists at the **Raku Gallery** (⊠ 250 Hull Ave. ☎ 928/634–2876) you'll find wrought-iron furniture, free-blown glass, and fountains. **Sky Fire** (⊠ 140 Main St. ☎ 928/634–8081), the most sophisticated shop in Jerome, has two floors of items to adorn your person and your house, from Southwestern-pattern dishes to handcrafted Mission-style hutches.

<table>
<tr><td>

en route

</td><td>

The drive down a mountainous section of AZ 89A from Jerome to Prescott is gorgeous (if somewhat harrowing in bad weather), filled with twists and turns through **Prescott National Forest.** If you're coming from Phoenix, the route that crosses the Mogollon Rim, overlooking the Verde Valley, is scenic but less precipitous.

</td></tr>
</table>

Sports & the Outdoors

CAMPING For information about camping near Jerome at Mingus Mountain, Playground, or Potato Patch—all open May–October—contact the Prescott National Forest's **Verde Ranger District** (✉ 300 E. AZ 260, Camp Verde ☎ 928/567–4121 ⊕ www.fs.fed.us/r3/prescott).

Prescott

33 mi southwest of Jerome on AZ 89A to AZ 89, 100 mi northwest of Phoenix via I–17 to AZ 69.

In a forested bowl 5,300 ft above sea level, Prescott is a prime summer refuge for Phoenix-area dwellers. It was proclaimed the first capital of the Arizona Territory in 1864 and settled by Yankees to ensure that gold-rich northern Arizona would remain a Union resource. (Tucson and southern Arizona were strongly pro-Confederacy.) It is believed that ancestors of the Yavapai, whose reservation is today on the outskirts of town, were the area's original inhabitants, but early territorial settlers thought that ruins in the area were of Aztec origin. You can see the results of this notion—inspired by *The History and Conquest of Mexico,* a popular book by historian William Hickling Prescott, for whom the town was named—in such street names as Montezuma, Cortez, and Alarcon.

Despite a devastating downtown fire in 1900, Prescott remains the Southwest's richest store of late-19th-century New England–style architecture (some have called it the "West's most Eastern town"). With two institutions of higher education, Yavapai College and Prescott College, Prescott could be called a college town, but it doesn't really feel like one, perhaps because so many retirees also reside here, drawn by the temperate climate and low cost of living.

The city's main drag is Gurley Street, named after John Addison Gurley, who was slated to be the first governor but died days before he was to move to the Arizona Territory. Those interested in architecture should be sure to get a map of the town's Victorian neighborhoods. Most are within walking distance of the chamber office. Many Queen Annes have been beautifully restored, and a number of them are now B&Bs. Antiques and collectibles shops line both sides of Cortez Street to the north of the courthouse.

❼ **Courthouse Plaza** is the heart of Prescott. Here the 1916 Yavapai County Courthouse stands, guarded by an equestrian bronze of turn-of-the-20th-century journalist and lawmaker Bucky O'Neill, who died while charging San Juan Hill in Cuba with Teddy Roosevelt during the Spanish-American War. At the south end of the plaza, across from the courthouse's main entrance, the Chamber of Commerce is a good place to get your bearings. ✉ *Bounded by Gurley and Goodwin Sts. to the north and south and by Cortez and Montezuma Sts. to the west and east, Downtown.*

❽ **Whiskey Row** got its name because it once held 20 saloons and houses of pleasure. Social activity is more subdued these days, and the historic bars provide an escape from the street's many boutiques. ✉ *Montezuma St. along west side of Courthouse Plaza, Downtown.*

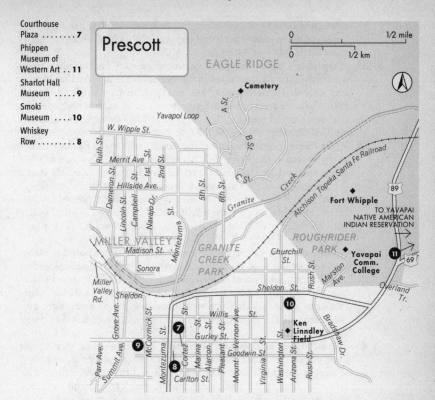

⑨ The remarkable **Sharlot Hall Museum** documents local history. Along with the original ponderosa-pine log cabin, which housed the territorial governor, and the museum, named for historian and poet Sharlot Hall, the parklike setting contains three fully restored period homes and a transportation museum. Territorial times are the focus, but natural history and artifacts of the area's prehistoric peoples are also on display. ⊠ *415 W. Gurley St., 2 blocks west of Courthouse Plaza, Downtown* ☎ *928/445–3122* ⊕ *www.sharlot.org* ⊠ *$5 donation requested per family* ☉ *Apr.–Oct., Mon.–Sat. 10–5, Sun. 1–5; Nov.–Mar., Mon.–Sat. 10–4, Sun. 1–5.*

Fodor'sChoice
★

⑩ The 1935 stone-and-log **Smoki Museum** is almost as interesting as the Native American artifacts inside. Priceless baskets and katsinas, as well as pottery, rugs, and beadwork, make up this fine collection, which represents Native American culture from the pre-Columbian period to the present. ⊠ *147 N. Arizona St., Downtown* ☎ *928/445–1230* ⊕ *www.smokimuseum.org* ⊠ *$4* ☉ *Mid Apr.–Oct., Mon.–Sat. 10–4, Sun. 1–4; Nov.–mid Apr., Fri.–Sat. and Mon. 10–4, Sun. 1–4.*

⑪ Included in the permanent collection of the respected **Phippen Museum of Western Art,** about 5 mi north of downtown, is work by many prominent artists of the West, along with the paintings and bronze sculptures of George Phippen. ⊠ *4701 AZ 89 N, Hwy. 89* ☎ *928/778–1385* ⊕ *www.phippenartmuseum.org* ⊠ *$3* ☉ *Mon.–Sat. 10–4, Sun. 1–4.*

Where to Stay & Eat

For approximate costs, *see* the dining and lodging price charts at the beginning of this chapter.

$$–$$$ ✕ **Murphy's.** Mesquite-grilled meats and beer brewed exclusively for the restaurant are the specialties here. The baby-back ribs, fresh steamed clams, and fresh fried catfish are your best bets. The bar has a good selection of microbrewed beers and imports. ⊠ *201 N. Cortez St., Downtown* ☎ *928/445–4044* ⊟ *AE, D, MC, V.*

$–$$$ ✕ **Agostino's Italian Cucina.** A quaint restaurant on Prescott's main square, Agostino's specializes in the standard fare of the Italian-American kitchen. Chicken parmigiana, spaghetti with meatballs, and calamari marinara are all solid choices. Pasta can be overcooked, so order it al dente if you prefer it that way. ⊠ *107 S. Cortez St., Downtown* ☎ *928/778–6818* ⊟ *AE, D, MC, V.*

$$ ✕ **The Palace.** Legend has it that the patrons who saved the Palace's ornately carved 1880s Brunswick bar from a Whiskey Row fire in 1900 continued drinking at it while the rest of the row burned across the street. Whatever the case, the bar remains the centerpiece of the beautifully restored turn-of-the-20th-century structure, with a high, pressed-tin ceiling. Steaks and chops are the stars here, but the grilled fish and hearty corn chowder are fine, too. ⊠ *120 S. Montezuma St., Downtown* ☎ *928/541–1996* ⊟ *AE, MC, V.*

$–$$ ✕ **Genovese.** Low-priced, classic southern Italian fare makes this restaurant near Courthouse Plaza a local favorite. Try the cannelloni stuffed with shrimp, crab, ricotta cheese, and spinach. The cheese-and-sauce-laden lasagna will satisfy the largest appetite. Toppings on the crispy thin-crust pizza include Gorgonzola, artichokes, and ham along with the standards. ⊠ *217 W. Gurley St., Downtown* ☎ *928/541–9089* ⊟ *AE, MC, V.*

$–$$ ✕ **Prescott Brewing Company.** Good beer, good food, good service, and good prices—for a casual meal, it's hard to beat this cheerful, multilevel restaurant. In addition to the chili, fish-and-chips, and British-style bangers (sausage) and mash, you'll also find vegetarian enchiladas made with tofu and a pasta salad with sun-dried tomatoes, avocado, broccoli, and two types of cheese. Fresh-baked beer bread comes with many of the entrées. ⊠ *130 W. Gurley St., Downtown* ☎ *928/771–2795* ⊟ *AE, D, DC, MC, V.*

$–$$ ✕ **Zuma's Woodfire Café.** One of the more sophisticated restaurants in town, Zuma's offers pizzas made in a wood-burning oven, with such toppings as goat cheese, grilled onions, and fresh basil. The large menu also includes salads, pastas, and grilled meats and fish. The current chef moved here from the Hassayampa Inn, Zuma's biggest competition. ⊠ *124 N. Montezuma St., Downtown* ☎ *928/541–1400* ⊟ *AE, D, MC, V.*

¢–$ ✕ **El Charro Restaurant.** This is where you'll find the best Mexican food in town, mostly heavy Sonoran food, and most of it homemade. The restaurant has been open since 1959, and the enchiladas, fajitas, and basic soft tacos are perennial customer favorites. The salsa has been tamed over the years, but ask for hot sauce and your wish will be granted. ⊠ *120 N. Montezuma St., Downtown* ☎ *928/445–7130* ⊟ *AE, MC, V.*

¢ ✕ **Kendall's Famous Burgers and Ice Cream.** A great diner in the middle of downtown, Kendall's serves hamburgers cooked to order with your choice of 14 condiments. Be sure to try the homemade french fries. ⊠ *113 S. Cortez St., Downtown* ☎ *928/778–3658* ⊟ *No credit cards.*

¢ ✕ **Plaza Café.** A bustling lunch place, the Plaza, as the locals call it, serves some of the healthiest meals in town. Light pasta dishes, homemade soups, veggie burgers, and rice bowls are just a few of the selections on the lengthy menu. Service is homey and brisk. ⊠ *106 W. Gurley St., Downtown* ☎ *928/445–3234* ⊟ *AE, MC, V.*

★ $$–$$$ ⌂ **Hassayampa Inn.** Built in 1927 for early automobile travelers, the Hassayampa Inn oozes character (be sure to look up at the hand-painted ceiling in the lobby), and some rooms still have the original furnishings. A complimentary cocktail at the lounge and free breakfast at the restaurant gild the lily of reasonable rates. The Peacock Room, the hotel's pretty—if overly formal—dining room, has tapestried booths, dim lighting, and better than average Continental food. ✉ *122 E. Gurley St., Downtown, 86301* ☎ *928/778–9434 or 800/322–1927* 🖷 *928/445–8590* ⊕ *www.hassayampainn.com* 📤 *58 rooms, 10 suites* ⚄ *Restaurant, cable TV, bar* ▭ *AE, D, DC, MC, V* ⦿ *BP.*

$$–$$$ ▣ **Prescott Resort Conference Center and Casino.** On a hill on the outskirts of town, this upscale property has views of the mountain ranges surrounding Prescott or the Valley. Many guests hardly notice, so riveted are they by the poker machines and slots in Arizona's only hotel casino. There are plenty of recreational facilities to occupy those able to resist the one-armed bandits. ✉ *1500 AZ 69, Hwy. 69, 86301* ☎ *928/776–1666 or 800/967–4637* 🖷 *928/776–8544* ⊕ *www.prescottresort.com* 📤 *161 rooms* ⚄ *Restaurant, coffee shop, refrigerators, cable TV, 4 tennis courts, pool, gym, hot tub, sauna, racquetball, piano bar, casino* ▭ *AE, D, DC, MC, V.*

$–$$ ▣ **Marks House Victorian Bed and Breakfast.** Victoria still reigns at this B&B, once owned by the mayor of territorial Prescott. It now belongs to Beth Maitland, a star of the daytime soap *The Young and the Restless*, and is ably managed by her parents. Rooms are impeccably furnished with period antiques: the suite in the circular turret, overlooking Thumb Butte, is particularly impressive. Breakfast is served in the formal dining room. ✉ *203 E. Union St., Downtown, 86303* ☎ *928/778–4632 or 800/370–6275* 📤 *2 rooms, 2 suites* ⚄ *Dining room* ▭ *D, MC, V* ⦿ *BP.*

$ ▣ **Hotel Vendome.** This World War I–era hostelry has seen miners, health seekers, and such celebrities as cowboy star Tom Mix walk through its doors. Old-fashioned touches, including the original claw-foot tubs, remain. Like many other historic hotels, the Vendome has its obligatory resident ghost (her room costs slightly more). Only a block from Courthouse Plaza, this is a good choice for those who want to combine sightseeing, modern comforts, and good value. ✉ *230 Cortez St., Downtown, 86303* ☎ *928/776–0900 or 888/468–3583* 🖷 *928/771–0395* ⊕ *www.vendomehotel.com* 📤 *16 rooms, 4 suites* ⚄ *Cable TV, fans, bar* ▭ *AE, D, DC, MC, V* ⦿ *CP.*

¢–$ ▣ **Hotel St. Michael.** Don't expect serenity on the busiest corner of Courthouse Plaza, but for low rates and historic charm it's hard to beat this hotel. In operation since 1900, the inn has rooms with 1920s wallpaper and furnishings; some face the plaza and others look out on Thumb Butte. The first-floor Café St. Michael serves great coffee and croissants. ✉ *205 W. Gurley St., Downtown, 86303* ☎ *928/776–1999 or 800/678–3757* 🖷 *928/776–7318* 📤 *71 rooms* ⚄ *Coffee shop, cable TV, shop* ▭ *AE, D, MC, V.*

Nightlife & the Arts

Prescott's popular **Bluegrass Festival on the Square** takes place in June. The town, which had its first organized cowboy competition in 1888, lays claim to having the world's oldest rodeo: the annual **Frontier Days** roundup, held on the Fourth of July weekend at the Yavapai County Fairgrounds. In August, the **Cowboy Poets Gathering** brings together campfire bards from around the country. The major event in December is the **Christmas Parade and Courthouse Lighting.**

Montezuma Street's Whiskey Row, just off the central Courthouse Plaza, is nowhere near as wild as it was in its historic heyday, but most bars have live music—and a lively collegiate crowd—on the weekends. The **Cadillac Bar and Grill** (✉ 216 W. Gurley St., Downtown ☎ 928/777–0018) offers live blues, jazz, rock, and pop Friday and Saturday at 9 PM. It also has "Fat Tuesday" happy-hour entertainment from 5 PM. For

RODEO LESSON

RODEOS WERE ORIGINALLY developed by cowboys to show off the skills they learned on the job herding cattle during the heydey of the big cattle drives of the late 19th century. Rodeo developed as a sport when cowboys gathered at the end of cattle-driving trails and vied for the unofficial titles of best bucking-horse rider, roper, and so on. As their day jobs were curtailed in scope by the railroads and by fencing, the contests became regular, formal contests.

The five standard events in contemporary rodeo are calf roping, bull riding, steer wrestling, saddle bronc-riding, and bareback bronc-riding. ("Bronc" is short for bronco, an unbroken range horse with a tendency to buck, or throw, a rider.) Two other events are recognized in championship competitions: single-steer roping and team roping. The barrel race,

a saddle horse race around a series of barrels, is a popular contest for women.

Participants pay entry fees, and the prize money won is their only compensation. More than half of all rodeos are independent of state and county fairs, livestock shows, or other attractions, and many are held in arenas devoted to the purpose. The equipment, however, is simple and may be improvised.

In 1929 the Rodeo Association of America was formed to regulate the sport. The contestants themselves took a hand in 1936 after a strike in Boston Garden and organized the Cowboy Turtles Association—"turtles" because they had been slow to act. This group was renamed the Rodeo Cowboys Association (RCA) in 1945 and the Professional Rodeo Cowboys Association (PRCA) in 1975. Its rules became accepted by most rodeos.

a more refined atmosphere, head over to the art nouveau piano bar at the **Hassayampa Inn** (⊠ 122 E. Gurley St., Downtown ☎ 928/778–9434); there's always someone tickling the ivories on the weekend. The bar at **Lyzzard's Lounge** (⊠ 120 N. Cortez St., Downtown ☎ 928/778–2244) was shipped from overseas via the Colorado River.

The **Prescott Fine Arts Association** (⊠208 N. Marina St., Downtown ☎928/445–3286) sponsors musicals and dramas, a series of plays for children, and a concert series. The association's gallery also presents rotating exhibits by local, regional, and national artists. The **Prescott Jazz Society** (⊠ 129½ N. Cortez St., Downtown ☎ 928/445–0000) has an intimate storefront lounge. The **Yavapai Symphony Association** (⊠ 107 N. Cortez St., Suite 105B, Downtown ☎ 928/776–4255) hosts performances by the Phoenix and Flagstaff symphonies; call ahead for schedules and venues.

Sports & the Outdoors

HIKING & CAMPING More than a million acres of national forest land surround Prescott. Thumb Butte is a popular hiking spot, but there are lots of other trekking and overnighting options. Contact the **Bradshaw Ranger District** (⊠ 2230 E. AZ 69, Hwy. 69 ☎ 928/445–7253 ⊕ www.fs.fed.us/r3/prescott) for information about hiking trails and campgrounds in the Prescott National Forest south of town down to Horse Thief Basin. Campgrounds near Prescott are generally not crowded.

HORSEBACK RIDING **Granite Mountain Stables** (⊠ 2400 W. Shane Dr., 7 mi northeast of Prescott, Hwy. 89 ☎ 928/771–9551) has daily guided rides as well as group specials, such as hay-wagon outings.

Shopping

Shops selling antiques and collectibles line Cortez Street, just north of Courthouse Plaza. You'll find fun stuff—especially Western kitsch—and some good buys on valuable pieces. Many of the stores gather together groups of retailers. Courthouse Plaza, especially along Montezuma Street, is lined with specialty and gift shops. Many match those in Sedona for quality and price. Be sure to check out **Arts Prescott** (⊠ 134 S. Montezuma St., Downtown ☏ 928/776–7717), a cooperative gallery of talented local craftspeople and artists. **Bashford Courts** (⊠ 130 Gurley St., Downtown ☏ 928/445–9798) has three floors of artsy stores. At 14,000 square ft, the **Merchandise Mart Antique Mall** (⊠ 205 N. Cortez St., Downtown ☏ 928/776–1728) is the largest of the town's collections of collectors. To get your fill of Old West kitsch, stop at **Prescott Museum & Trading Company** (⊠ 142 S. Montezuma St., Downtown ☏ 928/776–8498), which also displays a large variety of vintage boots, saddles, and taxidermy. **Sun West Gallery** (⊠ 152 S. Montezuma St., Downtown ☏ 928/778–1204) has artwork, furnishings, and Zapotec rugs.

Sedona

▶ *119 mi north of Phoenix, I–17 to AZ 179 to AZ 89A; 60 mi northeast of Prescott, AZ 89 to AZ 89A; 27 mi south of Flagstaff on AZ 89A.*

It's easy to see what draws so many people to Sedona. Red-rock buttes—Cathedral Rock, Bear Mountain, Courthouse Rock, and Bell Rock, among others—reach up into an almost always clear blue sky, both colors intensified by dark-green pine forests. The rugged landscape, at the north rim of the Verde Valley, once attracted surrealist Max Ernst, writer Zane Grey, and many filmmakers (more than 80 Westerns were shot in the area in the 1940s and '50s alone).

These days, Sedona lures enterprising restaurateurs and gallery owners from the East and West coasts. New Age followers, who believe that the area contains some of the Earth's more important vortices (energy centers), also come in great numbers in the belief that the area's "vibe" confers a sense of balance and well-being and enhances creativity. Several entrepreneurs have set up crystal shops and New Age bookshops that cater to the curious and true devotees.

Although the Sedona area has been inhabited by Native Americans for centuries, the town itself is relatively new—it wasn't even incorporated until 1988—so there are few historic sights. The town's main activity is shopping, mostly for Southwestern-style paintings, clothing, rugs, jewelry, and Native American artifacts. During warmer months visit air-conditioned shops at midday and do hiking and jeep tours in the early morning or late afternoon, when the light is softer and the heat less oppressive.

Expansion since the early 1980s has been rapid, and lack of planning has taken its toll in unattractive developments and increased traffic, especially on weekends and during busy summer months, when Phoenix residents flee north to cooler elevations. Still, the future looks promising. The town has been chosen to take part in the federally sponsored Main Street program, which means, among other things, that a number of Red Rock Territorial–style buildings in the Uptown section will be preserved and that a separate parking district will be built. A proposed bridge over Oak Creek should help alleviate some of the traffic, but it will also impinge on the natural glory of Red Rock Crossing, one of the town's most-photographed vistas.

Canyons, creeks, Indian ruins, and the red rocks are readily accessible on foot; the area is thrilling and easy to hike. Another option is to take one of the ubiquitous jeep tours.

Those with their own wheels might want to take the drive out to **Boynton Canyon,** sacred to the Yavapai Apache, who believe it was their ancient birthplace. It's where you'll find the Enchantment Resort, where all are welcome to hike the canyon and stop in for lunch or a late-afternoon drink. Weather permitting, the rather bumpy **Schnebly Hill Scenic Drive** is another inspiring option too rocky for anything but all-terrain vehicles. The vistas of Sedona from **Airport Mesa** at sunset can't be beat. The **Upper Red Rock Loop** will likely consume a roll or two of film. Many of the most picturesque spots in Sedona are considered energy centers; vortex maps of the area are available at most of Sedona's New Age stores.

You needn't be religious to be inspired by the setting and the architecture of the **Chapel of the Holy Cross.** Built in 1956 by Marguerite Brunwige Staude, a disciple of Frank Lloyd Wright, this modern landmark, with a huge cross on the facade, rises between two red-rock peaks. Vistas of the town and the surrounding area are spectacular. There are no regular services, but anyone is welcome for quiet meditation. A small gift shop sells religious artifacts and books. A trail east of the chapel leads you—after a 20-minute walk over occasional loose-rock surfaces—to a seat surrounded by voluptuous red-limestone walls, worlds away from the bustle and commerce around the chapel. ✉ *Chapel Rd., off AZ 179, Central* ☎ *928/282–4069* ✆ *Free* ☉ *Daily 9–5.*

Whether you want to swim, hike, picnic, or enjoy beautiful scenery framed through a car window, head north through the wooded **Oak Creek Canyon.** It's the most scenic route to Flagstaff and the Grand Canyon and worth a drive-through even if you're not heading north. Although the forest is primarily evergreen, the fall foliage is glorious. The road winds through a steep-walled canyon, and you'll crane your neck for views of the dramatic rock formations above. Oak Creek, which runs along the bottom, is lined with tent campgrounds, fishing camps, cabins, motels, and restaurants. ⊠ *AZ 89A, beginning 1 mi north of Sedona, Oakcreek Canyon.*

🖐 ⑮ Anglers young and old will enjoy the sure catch at the **Rainbow Trout Farm.** For $1 you'll get a cane pole with a hook and bait. There's no charge if your catch is under 8 inches; above that it's $2.85 to $5.85, depending on the length. The real bargain is that the staff will clean and pack your fish for 50¢ each. ⊠ *3500 N. AZ 89A, 3 mi north of Sedona, Oakcreek Canyon* ☎ *928/282–3379* ⊠ *$1* ☉ *Daily 9–5.*

🖐 ⑰ **Slide Rock State Park,** 7 mi north of Sedona, is a good place for a picnic. On a hot day, you can plunge down a natural rock slide into a swimming hole (bring an extra pair of jeans to wear on the slide). The only downside to this trip is the traffic, particularly on summer weekends; you might have to wait to get in. ⊠ *6871 N. AZ 89A, Oakcreek Canyon* ☎ *928/282–3034* ⊕ *www.pr.state.az.us* ⊠ *$8 per vehicle for up to 4 persons* ☉ *Labor Day–Memorial Day, daily 8–5; Memorial Day–Labor, daily Day 8–7.*

⑬ The **Cathedral Rock Trail** is a vigorous but nontechnical 1½-mi scramble up the slick rock, to a nearly 360-degree view of red-rock country. Follow the cairns, the rock piles marking the trail, faithfully, and look for the footholds in the rock. Carry plenty of water. Though short, the trail offers little shade and the pitch is steep. You can see the Verde Valley and Mingus Mountain in the distance. Look for the barely discernible "J" etched on the hillside marking the ghost town of Jerome 30 mi distant. The trail begins about ½ mi down Back O' Beyond Road off of AZ 179, 3 mi south of Sedona.

⑫ Two miles west of Sedona via AZ 89A is the turnoff for the 286-acre **Red Rock State Park,** a less-crowded alternative to the popular Slide Rock State Park, though without the possibility for swimming. The 5 mi of interconnected park trails are well marked and provide beautiful vistas. There are daily ranger-guided nature walks, bird-watching excursions on Wednesday and Saturday, and a guided hike to Eagle's Nest scenic overlook—the highest point in the park—every Saturday. Call ahead for times, which change with the season. ⊠ *4050 Red Rock Loop Rd., West* ☎ *928/282–6907* ⊕ *www.pr.state.az.us* ⊠ *$6 per car* ☉ *Daily 8–5.*

Where to Stay & Eat

Some Sedona restaurants close in January and February, so call before you go; make reservations in high season (April to October). Sedona is roughly divided into three neighborhoods: Uptown, which is a walkable shopping district; West Sedona, which is a 4-mi-long commercial strip; and Central Sedona, which encompasses everything south of the "Y" where AZ 179 and AZ 89A intersect. For approximate costs, *see* the dining and lodging price charts at the beginning of this chapter.

★ **$$$–$$$$** ✕ **L'Auberge.** The most formal dining room in Sedona promises a quiet, civilized evening of indulgence. Chef Mark May's specialties include inventive twists on traditional French cuisine, such as chilled mango soup with champagne and mint, foie gras with prosciutto, striped bass with haricot verts, and rack of lamb with goat cheese gnocchi and artichokes. Save room for the chocolate soufflé at all costs. The restaurant has one of the best (and priciest) wine lists in Arizona. Don't miss the lavish Sunday brunch. ⊠ *L'Auberge de Sedona, 241 AZ 89A, Uptown* ☎ *928/282–4200* ⊟ *AE, D, DC, MC, V.*

$$$–$$$$ ✕ **Shugrue's Hillside.** Almost everything is good here, which has made this one of the most popular restaurants in Sedona, but the salads and

VORTEX TOUR

WHAT IS A VORTEX? *The word "vortex" comes from the Latin* vertere, *which means "to turn or whirl." In Sedona, a vortex is a funnel created by the motion of spiraling energy. Sedona has long been believed to be a center for spiritual power because of the vortices of subtle energy in the area. This energy isn't described as electricity or magnetism, though it is said to leave a slight residual magnetism in the places where it is strongest.*

New Agers believe there are four major vortices in Sedona: Airport, Red Rock Crossing/Cathedral Rock, Boynton Canyon, and Bell Rock. Each manifests a different kind of energy, and this energy interacts with the individual in its presence. People come from all over the world to experience these various energy forms, hoping for guidance in spiritual matters, health, and relationships.

Juniper trees, which are all over the Sedona area, are said to respond to vortex energy in such a way that reveals where this energy is strongest. The stronger the energy, the more axial twist the junipers bear in their branches.

Airport Vortex is said to strengthen one's "masculine" side, aiding in self-confidence and focus. Red Rock Crossing/Cathedral Rock Vortex nurtures one's "feminine" aspects, such as patience and kindness. You'll be directed to Boynton Canyon Vortex if you're seeking balance between the masculine and feminine. And finally, Bell Rock Vortex, the most powerful of all, strengthens all three aspects: masculine, feminine, and balance.

These energy centers are easily accessed, and vortex maps are available at crystal shops all over Sedona.

meats are particularly good. The Caesar salad is refreshingly traditional, the inventive ginger-walnut chicken salad large enough to share. First-class rack of lamb and filet mignon are prepared and presented simply. There's a small, thoughtful, and well-priced wine list as well. Don't be confused: Shugrue's Hillside is not owned by the same folks who own Shugrue's West, a less appealing restaurant. ⊠ *671 AZ 179, Central* ☎ *928/282–5300* ⊟ *AE, DC, MC, V.*

$$–$$$$ ✕ **Cowboy Club.** One of Sedona's newest upscale restaurants, this space is divided into two rooms, the casual Cowboy Club and the more formal Silver Saddle Room. High-quality cuts of beef are the specialty, but the fried chicken served with cumin mashed potatoes is good, too. The wine list, however, is surprisingly meager. ⊠ *241 AZ 89A, Uptown* ☎ *928/282–4200* ⊟ *AE, D, DC, MC, V.*

$$–$$$$ ✕ **Sasaki.** Somewhat off the tourist path, this understated restaurant serves a limited selection of impeccably fresh sushi and sashimi. There's a full Japanese menu, too. Pork *katsu* (lightly battered and fried cutlets of pork) and *ten-zura* (cold buckwheat noodles with tempura) are good cooked options. The service couldn't be friendlier. ⊠ *65 Bell Rock Rd., Village of Oak Creek* ☎ *928/284–1757* ⊟ *AE, MC, V.*

$$–$$$$ ✕ **Takashi.** Those seeking some serenity and a respite from heavy meals will enjoy this Japanese restaurant, which provides aesthetic pleasure in everything from tea (with little bits of floating popcorn and brown rice) to dessert (sweet ginger or red-bean ice cream). Salads include a spicy sushi tuna with Japanese mayonnaise on a bed of cabbage and fresh vegetables. Combination dinners such as sashimi with tempura or teriyaki let you sample a little bit of everything. ⊠ *465 Jordan Rd., Uptown* ☎ *928/282–2334* ⊟ *AE, DC, MC, V* ⊘ *Closed Mon. No lunch Sun.*

$$$ ✕ **René at Tlaquepaque.** Ease into the plush banquettes of this pretty, lace-curtained restaurant for classic Continental dishes. Recommended starters include a delicate French onion soup and the salade Walter—baby spinach leaves and sautéed mushrooms in a hazelnut vinaigrette. Rack of lamb is the house specialty, and the true Dover sole is a real find, far from the white cliffs. Service is formal, as befits the room and menu, but casual attire is acceptable. Crêpes suzette for two, prepared tableside, is an impressive dessert. There's a well-selected wine list, too. ⊠ *Tlaquepaque Arts & Crafts Village, Unit B–117, AZ 179, Central* ☎ *928/282–9225* ⊟ *AE, MC, V.*

★ **$$–$$$** ✕ **Heartline Café.** Fresh flowers and innovative, modern Southwestern cuisine are this attractive café's hallmarks. The oak-grilled salmon marinated in tequila and lime and the chicken breast with prickly-pear sauce are two options. Appealing vegetarian plates are also on the menu. On nice days grab a seat on the rosebush-lined terrace. Desserts include a phenomenal crème brûlée, as well as homemade truffles at the chef's whim. ⊠ *1610 W. AZ 89A, West* ☎ *928/282–0785* ⊟ *AE, D, MC, V* ⊘ *No lunch Tues.–Thurs. and Sun.*

★ **$$–$$$** ✕ **Pietro's.** Good northern Italian cuisine plus a friendly and attentive staff have made this lively and casual dining spot one of Sedona's most popular. Don't miss anything made with buffalo mozzarella from Naples, which the owner secures from a distributor in Phoenix. Homemade soups are always fabulous, and owner Jon Leon is almost always on hand to help you decide on your *secondi piatti* if you can't make up your mind. ⊠ *2445 W. AZ 89A, West* ☎ *928/282–2525* ⊟ *AE, D, DC, MC, V* ⊘ *No lunch.*

★ **$–$$$** ✕ **Dahl & DiLuca.** A husband-and-wife team—Andrea DiLuca and Lisa Dahl—has created one of the most popular Italian restaurants in town with this colorful, eclectic space. Andrea runs the kitchen, and Lisa meets and greets diners as they enter. Lisa also slips into the kitchen every day to make delicious homemade soups like white bean with ham and hearty minestrone. ⊠ *2321 W. AZ 89A, West* ☎ *928/282–5219* ⊟ *AE, D, MC, V* ⊘ *No lunch.*

$–$$$ ✕ **Robert's.** A long-standing favorite on the banks of Oak Creek gained notoriety when Regis Philbin breezed through town and fell in love with the restaurant's peach cobbler. It's quite good, as are the grilled salmon, baby-back ribs, and prime rib. Nightly specials, such as fresh mako shark, are always intriguing. ⊠ *251 AZ 179, Central* ☎ *928/282–3671* ⊟ *AE, MC, V.*

¢–$ ✕ **Mesquite Tree Barbecue.** Although it offers limited indoor seating, this Uptown hideaway behind a long row of tourist shops is worth a visit. Follow your nose to the mesquite-burning grill, where you can watch beef, chicken, and pork cook slowly and fall off the bone. The sauce has a slight kick, and the homemade french fries are fabulous. ⊠ *250 Jordan Rd., No. 9, Uptown* ☎ *928/282–6533* ⊟ *MC, V.*

¢ ✕ **Sedona Coffee Roasters.** Not only does this café serve the best coffee in town by a mile, but the lunch sandwiches are perfect fare before or after a red-rock hike. Daily specials might include a healthful chicken salad with sprouts, as well as the more decadent jumbo beef Polish hot dog. You can also choose your own sandwich fixings from a list of fresh ingredients. More than 20 house-roasted coffees are sold by the pound. ⊠ *2155 W. AZ 89A, West* ☎ *928/282–0282* ⊟ *No credit cards.*

¢–$ ✕ **Thai Spices.** This small, unadorned restaurant has a loyal following of vegetarians and health-food enthusiasts, though not everything is meatless. If you call a day ahead, chef Pearl will create a special macrobiotic platter. The curries, especially red curry with tempeh, are delicious and can be prepared at the spice level of your choice. There's plenty here for carnivores, too: traditional pad thai with chicken is satisfyingly homey, and the spicy beef salad will make your hair stand on end. ⊠ *2986 W. AZ 89A, West* ☎ *928/282–0599* ⊟ *MC, V.*

FodorśChoice
★

★ $$$–$$$$ 🏨 **Enchantment Resort.** This world-class resort's Southwest-style rooms and suites are tucked into pueblo-style buildings in serene Boynton Canyon. Accommodations come in a wide variety of configurations, some with kitchens, separate living and dining areas, and multiple bedrooms, which can be joined to create large, elaborate suites. All have beehive gas fireplaces and superb views. Fresh-squeezed orange juice and a newspaper greet you each morning. The Yavapai Room serves excellent Southwestern cuisine. The resort's full-service spa, Mii Amo, offers cutting-edge treatments like hot stone massage and myo-facial release. ✉ *525 Boynton Canyon Rd., West, 86336* 📞 *928/282–2900 or 800/826–4180* 📠 *928/282–9249* 🌐 *www.enchantmentresort.com* 🛏 *107 rooms, 115 suites ♿ 2 restaurants, in-room safes, some kitchens, some kitchenettes, putting green, 12 tennis courts, pro shop, 4 pools, health club, spa, mountain bikes, boccie, croquet, hiking, Ping-Pong, bar, children's programs (ages 4–12)* 🖃 *AE, D, MC, V.*

★ $$$–$$$$ 🏨 **L'Auberge de Sedona.** This hillside resort consists of a central lodge building; a motel-style structure called the Orchards, reached by means of an incline railway; and—the major attraction—cabins in the woods along Oak Creek. Rooms in the Orchards are less expensive—and more standard-motel issue—while rooms in the lodge are decorated in lush Provençal style. The large cabins along the creek have wood-burning fireplaces. Phoenix couples flock to these country-French hideaways and dine in the hotel's French restaurant, one of the most romantic eateries in Arizona. ✉ *L'Auberge La., Uptown* 🏤 *Box B, 86336* 📞 *928/282–1661 or 800/272–6777* 📠 *928/282–2885* 🌐 *www.lauberge.com* 🛏 *69 rooms, 32 cottages ♿ 2 restaurants, minibars, refrigerators, cable TV, pool, hot tub* 🖃 *AE, D, DC, MC, V.*

★ $$–$$$$ 🏨 **Alma de Sedona.** One of Sedona's most enchanting B&Bs, this family operation, run by Lynn McCarroll, has large rooms with spectacular views and ultracomfortable beds. Decor is understated, elegant, and inviting. All rooms have private entrances and patios, and you'll find bath salts and candles in the bathrooms. When Lynn and her husband, Ron, were planning the inn, they told their architect that their top priorities were views and privacy; they've achieved both unequivocally. ✉ *50 Hozoni Dr., West, 86336* 📞 *928/282–2737 or 800/923–2282* 📠 *928/203–4141* 🌐 *www.almadesedona.com* 🛏 *12 rooms ♿ Some in-room hot tubs, cable TV, pool, meeting room; no smoking* 🖃 *AE, MC, V* 🍴 *BP.*

$$–$$$$ 🏨 **Briar Patch Inn.** In a verdant canyon with a rushing creek, this B&B
Fodor's Choice has rooms in wooden cabins (in Native American and Mexican styles),
★ some with decks overlooking Oak Creek. On summer mornings you can sit outside and enjoy home-baked breads and fresh egg dishes while listening to live classical music. New Age and crafts workshops are sometimes held on the premises. Winter is equally beautiful; request a cabin with a fireplace and wake to see icicles hanging from the trees. If you're lucky, the resident shih tzu, Brittany, will greet you. ✉ *3190 N. AZ 89A, Oakcreek Canyon, 86336* 📞 *928/282–2342* 📠 *928/282–2399* 🌐 *www.briarpatchinn.com* 🛏 *13 two-person cabins, 4 four-person cabins ♿ Fans, some kitchenettes, massage, fishing, library, meeting room* 🖃 *MC, V* 🍴 *BP.*

★ $$–$$$$ 🏨 **Graham Inn and Adobe Village.** Some of the attractive rooms at this inn south of Sedona have Jacuzzi tubs and balconies that look out onto the red rocks. Four large, individually decorated casitas, all with gas fireplaces that open into both the sitting area and the bathroom and two-person Jacuzzi tubs—are on a lot next door. What makes this place special, though, is the impeccable yet casual service. Innkeeper Elaine is the best in the business, and the French chef makes breakfasts worth the price of admission. The owners are committed to always having at least one room under $200. ✉ *150 Canyon Circle Dr., Village of Oak Creek, 86351*

☎ 928/284–1425 or 800/228–1425 🖷 928/284–0767 ⊕ *www.sedonasfinest.com* ➷ *4 rooms, 2 suites, 4 casitas △ Some in-room hot tubs, some kitchenettes, some refrigerators, in-room VCRs, cable TV, pool, hot tub, mountain bikes, library, Internet* ⊟ *D, MC, V* ⱺ *BP.*

$$–$$$$ 🏠 **Junipine Creekside Retreat.** These one- and two-bedroom cabins—here called creek houses—nestled in a juniper and pine forest (hence the name) are spacious and airy, with vaulted ceilings and fireplaces. They are an excellent value for groups of four or more, and some of the cabins comfortably sleep six. But Junipine's most enchanting feature is the sound of Oak Creek roaring below, lulling you to sleep by the fire. ✉ *8351 N. AZ 89A, Oakcreek Canyon, 86336* ☎ *928/282–3375* 🖷 *928/282–7402* ⊕ *www.junipine.com* ➷ *50 suites △ Restaurant, kitchens, outdoor hot tub* ⊟ *AE, D, MC, V.*

$$$ 🏠 **Garland's Oak Creek Lodge.** In the heart of Oak Creek Canyon, this 1930s lodge and its 16 comfortably furnished cabins—some with fireplaces and pullout beds—are owned by Gary and Mary Garland. This mile-high, 17-acre spread has its own apple orchard, and accommodations look out over the rugged cliffs of the canyon or the creek. Excellent daily breakfast and dinner are included in the room price, along with afternoon tea. It's often booked solid a year in advance, but it's worth a call to check for vacancies. ✉ *AZ 89A, Oakcreek Canyon, 8 mi north of Uptown* ⎙ *Box 152, 86339* ☎ *928/282–3343* ⊕ *www.garlandslodge.com* ➷ *16 cabins △ Restaurant, tennis court, fishing, croquet, volleyball; no room phones, no room TVs* ⊟ *MC, V* ⊘ *Closed late Nov.–Mar.* ⱺ *MAP.*

$$–$$$ 🏠 **Apple Orchard Inn.** Within walking distance of Uptown, nestled among pine and juniper trees, Apple Orchard Inn is an affordable choice. Each room has a different theme, and the inn can provide you with a personal guide to the area. The massage room is an especially nice feature. ✉ *656 Jordan Rd., Uptown, 86336* ☎ *928/282–5328 or 800/663–6968* 🖷 *928/204–0044* ⊕ *www.appleorchardbb.com* ➷ *7 rooms △ Pool* ⊟ *AE, MC, V* ⱺ *BP.*

$$–$$$ 🏠 **Boots & Saddles.** John and Linda Steele are generous hosts at this quiet inn tucked behind the main street in West Sedona. The rooms are decorated in an upscale Western motif, complete with genuine cowboy artifacts, and the Gentleman Cowboy room has unparalleled red-rock views and a telescope for stargazing. Linda serves hearty, innovative breakfasts each morning, and John knows every hiking trail in the area like the back of his hand. ✉ *2900 Hopi Dr., West, 86336* ☎ *928/282–1944 or 800/201–1944* ⊕ *www.oldwestbb.com* ➷ *4 rooms △ Refrigerators, in-room VCRs, hot tub* ⊟ *AE, D, MC, V* ⱺ *BP.*

$$–$$$ 🏠 **Lodge at Sedona.** Rooms in this rambling wood-and-stone house run in a Mission-style motif; some have fireplaces, redwood decks, or hot tubs. For solitude, walk the seven-path classic labyrinth (made of local rock) and through the gardens outside. A chef prepares a five-course breakfast each morning, which you can linger over either inside or on the outdoor terrace with a view of the red rocks in the distance. ✉ *125 Kallof Pl., West, 86336* ☎ *928/204–1942 or 800/619–4467* 🖷 *928/204–2128* ⊕ *www.lodgeatsedona.com* ➷ *6 rooms, 8 suites △ Dining room, some in-room hot tubs, some in-room VCRs, pool, gym, massage, library, meeting room, concierge; no room phones, no TV in some rooms, no smoking* ⊟ *D, MC, V* ⱺ *BP.*

★ $$ 🏠 **The Canyon Wren.** The best value in the Oak Creek Canyon area, this small B&B has free-standing cabins with views of the canyon walls. Milena and Mike (she's Slovenian, he's Floridian) are consummate hosts, regarding guests' privacy first and foremost. It's likely that their two lovable dogs, Nasa and Stubby, will greet you on arrival. Cabins have private decks and fireplaces. Breakfast is a selection of delicious baked goods from Milena's kitchen. ⊠ *6425 N. AZ 89A, Oakcreek Canyon, 86336* ☎ *928/282–6900 or 800/437–9736* 🖷 *928/282–6978* ⊕ *www. canyonwrencabins.com* ↪ *4 cabins* ⚲ *In-room hot tubs, kitchens; no room phones, no room TVs* ▤ *AE, D, MC, V* ⊠⊙⊠ *CP.*

$–$$ 🏨 **Sky Ranch Lodge.** There may be no better vantage point in town from which to view Sedona's red-rock canyons than the private patios and balconies at Sky Ranch Lodge, near the top of Airport Mesa. Some rooms have stone fireplaces and some have kitchenettes; a few are a bit worn, but all are very clean. Paths on the grounds wind around fountains and, in summer, through colorful flower gardens. This is an excellent value, primarily because of the views. ⊠ *Airport Rd., West, 86339* ☎ *928/ 282–6400* 🖷 *928/282–7682* ⊕ *www.skyranchlodge.com* ↪ *92 rooms, 2 cottages* ⚲ *Some kitchenettes, some refrigerators, cable TV, pool, hot tub, no-smoking rooms* ▤ *AE, MC, V.*

$ 🏨 **Desert Quail Inn.** Close to a lion's share of the trailheads, but out of the main flow of tourist traffic, the motel is a good base for outdoor adventures. The front desk is well stocked with maps and advice. The rooms are spacious and bright, and a few are done up in a Western motif. ⊠ *6626 AZ 179, Village of Oak Creek, 86351* ☎ *800/385–0927 or 928/ 284–1433* 🖷 *928/284–0487* ⊕ *www.desertquailinn.com* ↪ *41 rooms* ⚲ *Some in-room hot tubs, some microwaves, refrigerators, cable TV, pool, laundry facilities* ▤ *AE, D, DC, MC, V.*

¢–$ 🏨 **Sedona Motel.** A typical motel in most other aspects, the structure is built on a terrace removed from the highway, affording it the very same expansive, red-rock views as the much more expensive resorts. Almost at the exact center of the "Y," it is within easy reach of most of Sedona's attractions. The rooms, which have coffeemakers, are new-looking and well kept. ⊠ *218 AZ 179, Central, 86336* ☎ *928/282–7187* ↪ *16 rooms* ⚲ *Microwaves, refrigerators, cable TV* ▤ *D, MC, V.*

Nightlife & the Arts

Nightlife in Sedona tends to be fairly sedate. On high-season weekends, there's usually live music at the Enchantment Resort. Shugrue's Hillside presents local musicians regularly as well. Offerings vary from jazz to rock and pop; in all cases, call ahead. **Casa Rincon** (⊠ 2620 W. AZ 89A, West ☎ 928/282–4849) hosts an otherworldly dance party along with local bands and open-mike nights. The closest you'll come to a rollicking cowboy bar in Sedona is **Rainbow's End** (⊠ 3235 W. AZ 89A, West ☎ 928/282–1593), a steak house with a large dance floor and country-and-western bands on weekends.

Find out about cultural events in Sedona at the **Book Loft** (⊠ 175 AZ 179, just south of the "Y," Central ☎ 928/282–5173), which often hosts poetry readings, theatrical readings, book signings, and lectures. The Sedona **Jazz on the Rocks Festival** (☎ 928/282–1985 ⊕ www.sedonajazz. com), held every September, always attracts a sellout crowd that fills the town to capacity. The **Sedona Arts Center** (⊠ N. AZ 89A and Art Barn Rd., Uptown ☎ 928/282–3809) sponsors events ranging from classical concerts to plays; there's an innovative and growing film festival every March. The **Sedona Heritage Day Festival** (☎ 928/282–7038), a family-oriented event in early October, includes pioneer storytellers, square-dance exhibitions, music, and a barbecue.

Sports & the Outdoors

GOLF The **Oak Creek Country Club** (⊠ 690 Bell Rock Blvd., Village of Oak Creek
Fodor'sChoice ☎ 928/284–1660) is a good semiprivate course. The 18-hole **Sedona Golf**
★ **Resort** (⊠ 7260 AZ 179, Village of Oak Creek ☎ 928/284–9355) was designed by Gary Panks to take advantage of the many changes in elevation and scenery. The 10th hole, said to be the most-photographed

hole in all of Arizona, takes in a sweeping view of the Sedona Valley's red rocks.

HIKING & CAMPING For free detailed maps, hiking advice, and information on campgrounds, contact the rangers of the **Coconino National Forest** (⊠ Sedona Ranger District, 250 Brewer Rd., West, 86339 ☎ 928/282–4119 ⊕ www.fs.fed. us/r3/coconino), which is open weekdays 8–4:30. Ask here or at your hotel for directions to trailheads for Doe's Mountain (an easy ascent, with many switchbacks), Loy Canyon, Devil's Kitchen, and Long Canyon. Among the forest service paths you can hike in the Oak Creek Canyon is the popular West Fork Trail. A walk through the woods and a dip in the stream make a great summer combination. You'll find the trailhead about 3 mi north of Slide Rock State Park.

HORSEBACK RIDING Among the equine tour options at **Trail Horse Adventures** (⊠ 5 J La., Lower Red Rock Loop Rd., West ☎ 928/282–7252) are a midday picnic and an Oak Creek swim and a full-moon ride with a campfire cookout.

Shopping

SHOPPING AREAS & MALLS Most stores in what is known as the **Uptown** area, north of the "Y," running along AZ 89A to the east of its intersection with AZ 179, cater to the tour-bus trade. There are several exceptions, though. The largest concentration of stores and galleries is in **Central** Sedona, along AZ 179, south of the "Y." **West** Sedona, the more residential area that stretches west of the "Y" along AZ 89A, doesn't have such concentrated areas of shops as Uptown and Central.

It's worth a trip over to **Artisans Galleria** (⊠ 1420 W. AZ 89A, West ☎ 928/ 284–0077), which showcases the output of more than 100 artists and craftspeople. A minute or two south of the Hozho Center on AZ 179 is the **Hillside Courtyard & Marketplace** (⊠ 671 AZ 179, Central ☎ 928/ 282–4500). The **Hozho Center** (⊠ 431 AZ 179, Central ☎ 928/204–2257) is a small, upscale complex in a beige Santa Fe–style building. Inveterate bargain hunters will want to head south on AZ 179, 2 mi past Chapel of the Holy Cross, to the village of Oak Creek. At the **Oak Creek Factory Outlets** (⊠ 6601 S. AZ 179, Village of Oak Creek ☎ 928/284–2150) are such stores as Corning/Revere, Mikasa, Anne Klein, Bass, Jones New York, and Van Heusen. **Tlaquepaque Arts & Crafts Village** (⊠ AZ 179, just south of the "Y," Central ☎ 928/282–4838) gathers together more than 100 artisans, many of them painters and sculptors. The complex of red-tile-roof buildings arranged around a series of courtyards shares its name and architectural style with a crafts village just outside Guadalajara. It's a lovely place to browse, but prices tend to be high; locals joke that it's pronounced "to-lock-your-pocket."

STORES & GALLERIES **Clay Pigeon** (⊠ Hillside Courtyard & Marketplace, 671 AZ 179, Central ☎ 928/282–2845) carries boldly designed dishes and sculptures with a Western accent. A good bet for Southwestern art is **El Prado Gallery by the Creek** (⊠ Tlaquepaque, AZ 179, No. 101, Bldg. E, Central ☎ 928/282–7390). **Esteban's** (⊠ Tlaquepaque, AZ 179, No. 103, Bldg. B, Central ☎ 928/282–4686) focuses on ceramics and Native American crafts. **Garland's Navajo Rugs** (⊠ 411 AZ 179, Central ☎ 928/282–4070) has a dazzling collection of new and antique carpets, as well as Native American katsina dolls, pottery, and baskets. **Isadora** (⊠ Tlaquepaque, AZ 179, No. 120, Bldg. A, Central ☎ 928/282–6232) has beautiful handwoven jackets and shawls. **James Ratliff Gallery** (⊠ 431 AZ 179, Central ☎ 928/282–1404) has fun and functional pieces by not-yet-established artists. **Kuivato** (⊠ Tlaquepaque, AZ 179, No. 122, Bldg. B, Central ☎ 928/282–1212) carries gorgeous glassware. **Lanning Gallery** (⊠ Hozho Center, 431 AZ 179, Central ☎ 928/282–6865) sells attractive Southwestern art and jewelry. **Looking West** (✉ 242 N. AZ 89A, Uptown ☎ 928/282–4877) sells the spiffiest cowgirl-style getups in town. **Robert Shields Design** (✉ Sacajawea Plaza, 301 N. AZ 89A, Uptown ☎ 928/204–9253) carries colorful clay snakes and unusual silver jewelry. (If you still remember them, it's the same Shields who used to perform with Yarnell.) **Sedona Pottery** (✉ 411 AZ 179, Central ☎ 928/282–1192) sells unusual pieces, including flower-arranging bowls, egg separators, and life-size ceramic statues by shop owner Mary Margaret Sather.

FLAGSTAFF

146 mi northwest of Phoenix, 27 mi north of Sedona via Oak Creek Canyon.

Few travelers slow down long enough to explore Flagstaff, a town of 54,000, known locally as "Flag." Most stop only to spend the night at one of the town's many motels before making the last leg of the trip to the Grand Canyon, 80 mi north. But the city, set against a lovely backdrop of pine forests and the snowcapped San Francisco Peaks, retains a frontier flavor downtown. Flag makes a good base for day trips to Native American ruins and the Navajo and Hopi reservations, as well as to the Petrified Forest National Park and the Painted Desert.

Flagstaff has more fast-food outlets than most cities, no doubt because of the incredible demand for them: two major interstate highways crisscross the town; thousands of tourists drive through; thousands of students attending Northern Arizona University reside here; and many Native Americans come in from nearby reservations. During the summer, Phoenix residents head here, seeking relief from the desert heat. At any time of the year, temperatures in Flagstaff are about 20°F cooler than in Phoenix.

Phoenicians also come to Flagstaff in winter to ski at the small Arizona Snowbowl, about 15 mi northeast of town among the San Francisco Peaks. Accommodation rates are low at this time of year, making winter visits an excellent option for downhill and cross-country enthusiasts. Flagstaff has many accommodations (although no major hotels or resorts), but you should make reservations, especially during the summer.

Exploring Flagstaff

a good
tour

Start your exploration of Flagstaff in the **Historic Downtown District** 🔞 ▶, the heart of which is the restored Santa Fe Depot on Route 66, still a functioning train station and also a visitor center. Drive east (right) from here to reach the raucous **Museum Club** 🔟 and then head west to reach the **Lowell Observatory** 🔟. To the southwest, Route 66 branches off into Milton Road, which will take you to a turnoff for **Riordan State Historic Park** ㉑ and, a little farther to the south, one for the **Northern Arizona University Observatory** ㉒. Drive back across Route 66 and then north on Humphreys Street, a major downtown thoroughfare; about a mile after it becomes Fort Valley Road, you'll reach Fort Valley Park, where you will find the **Pioneer Museum** ㉓. Continue north for just a few minutes on Fort Valley Road to reach the **Museum of Northern Arizona** ㉔. On the opposite side of Fort Valley Road, a few hundred yards farther down, is the turnoff for Schultz Pass Road, which leads to a number of the trailheads for the **Mt. Elden Trail System** ㉕. Five miles farther along the same road is the turnoff for **Arizona Snowbowl** ㉖. Drive another 6 mi north on Fort Valley Road, keeping a close eye out for FR 245, the easily missed turnoff leading to the **Lava River Cave** ㉗.

TIMING You can see almost all of Flagstaff's attractions in a single day if you can visit the Lowell Observatory or the Northern Arizona University Observatory in the evening—which is also when the Museum Club is best experienced. Consult the schedule of tour times if you want to visit the Riordan State Historic Park. Plan on devoting at least an hour to the excellent Museum of Northern Arizona. The Historic Railroad District is a good place to have lunch. If you're a skier, you might be spending a good part of a winter's day at Arizona Snowbowl; in summer, allot a couple of hours to the sky ride and scenic trails at the top. You'll want to take your time enjoying the trails on Mt. Elden, and you should remember to pace yourself in the higher elevations; allow a full day if you decide to hike these trails. The Lava River Cave is an easy—if dark— hike that can be comfortably completed in an hour.

Sights to See

26 The **Arizona Snowbowl,** one of Flagstaff's most popular winter attractions, also lures patrons in the summer, when the Agassiz ski lift, which climbs to a height of 11,500 ft in 25 minutes, doubles as a sky ride through the Coconino National Forest. From this vantage point, you can see up to 70 mi; views may even include the North Rim of the Grand Canyon. There's a lodge nearby with a restaurant and bar. To reach the ski area, take U.S. 180 north from Flagstaff; it's 7 mi from the Snowbowl exit to the skyride entrance. ⊠ *Snowbowl Rd., North Flagstaff* ☎ *928/ 779–1951* ⊕ *www.arizonasnowbowl.com* ☎ *Skyride $9* ☉ *Skyride mid-June–early Sept., daily 10–4; early Sept.–mid-Oct., Fri.–Sun. (weather permitting) 10–4.*

▶ 18 Flagstaff's **Historic Downtown District** includes a section of historic Route 66. Some excellent examples of late Victorian, Tudor Revival, and early art deco architecture in this district give a feel for life in Flagstaff during the town's heyday as a logging and railroad center. A walking-tour map of the area is available at the visitor center in the Tudor Revival–style **Santa Fe Depot** (⊠ 1 E. Rte. 66, Downtown), an excellent place to begin sightseeing.

Highlights include the 1927 **Hotel Monte Vista** (⊠ 100 N. San Francisco St., Downtown), built after a community drive raised $200,000 in 60 days. The 1888 **Babbitt Brothers Building** (⊠ 12 E. Aspen Ave., Downtown) was constructed as a building-supply store and then turned into a department store by David Babbitt, the mastermind of the Babbitt empire. One of Flagstaff's wealthiest founding families, the Babbitts include former Arizona governor and Secretary of the Interior Bruce Babbitt, who was the most recent member of the family to wield power and influence. Most of the area's first businesses were saloons catering to railroad construction workers, which was the case with the 1888 **Vail Building** (⊠ 1 N. San Francisco St., Downtown), a brick art deco–influenced structure covered with stucco in 1939. It now houses the Sweet Life ice cream parlor.

The town's most interesting shops are concentrated downtown, and there are a couple of brewpubs and some spots where you can grab a quick bite. Students, skiers, new and aging hippies, and just about everyone else who likes good coffee jam into **Macy's** (⊠ 14 S. Beaver St., Downtown ☎ 928/774–2243) for the best cup in town. The **Black Bean** (⊠ 12 E. Rte. 66, Downtown ☎ 928/779–9905) is the place for do-it-yourself burritos, as healthful or as guacamole-smothered as you like.

27 Subterranean lava flow formed the mile-long **Lava River Cave** (⊠ FR 171B) roughly 700,000 years ago. Once you descend into its boulder-strewn maw, the cave is spacious, shaped like a railroad tunnel with 40-ft ceil-

ings. But claustrophobes take heed: about halfway through the cave tapers to a 4-ft-high squeeze that can be a bit unnerving. Pack an extra flashlight and warm clothing. A yearlong 40°F chill pervades the cave. To reach the turnoff for the cave, go approximately 14 mi north of Flagstaff on U.S. 180, and then turn west onto FR 245. Turn left at the intersection of FR 171 and look for the sign to the cave. Although the cave is on National Forest Service property, the only thing here are an interpretive sign, so it's definitely something you tackle at your own risk.

Boston businessman, author, and scientist Percival Lowell founded the **Lowell Observatory** in 1894 and studied the planet Mars from here. His predictions of the existence of a ninth planet led to the discovery of Pluto at Lowell in 1930 by Clyde Tombaugh. V. M. Slipher's observations here between 1912 and 1920 led to the theory of the expanding universe. The 6,500-square-ft Steele Visitor Center hosts exhibits and lectures and has a gift shop; a "Tools of the Astronomer" display explains what professional stargazers do. Several interactive exhibits—among them the Pluto Walk, a scaled-down version of the solar system—will interest children. On some evenings the public is invited to peer through the 24-inch Clark telescope or through a more up-to-date 16-inch reflecting telescope. Four viewings a week are offered from June through August; call ahead for a schedule. The observatory dome is open and unheated, so dress for the outdoors. To reach the observatory, which is less than 2 mi from downtown, drive west on Route 66, which resumes its former name, Santa Fe Avenue, before it merges into Mars Hill Road. ⊠ *1400 W. Mars Hill Rd., West Flagstaff* ☎ *928/774–2096* ⊕ *www.lowell.edu* ⊠ *$3* ⊙ *Visitor center and night viewing hrs change seasonally; call ahead.*

㉕ Most trails in the 35-mi-long **Mt. Elden Trail System** lead to prodigious views from the dormant volcanic field, across the vast ponderosa pine forest, all the way to Sedona. The most challenging trail in the Mt. Elden system, which happens to be the route with the most rewarding views, is along the steep switchbacks of the **Elden Lookout Trail** (⊠ off U.S. 89, 3 mi east of downtown Flagstaff). If you traverse the full 3 mi to the top, keep your focus on the landscape rather than the tangle of antennae and satellite dishes that greet you at the top. The 4-mi-long **Sunset Trail** (⊠ off U.S. 180, 3 mi north of downtown Flagstaff, then 6 mi east on FR 420 [Schultz Pass Rd.]) proceeds with a gradual pitch through the pine forest, finally emerging onto a narrow ridge nicknamed the Catwalk. By all means take pictures of the stunning valley views, but make sure your feet are well placed. This trail is closed in winter.

⑲ For real Route 66 color, don't miss the **Museum Club**, a local institution fondly known as the Zoo because the building housed an extensive taxidermy collection in the 1930s. Luckily, most of the stuffed animals—including such bizarre specimens as a one-eyed sheep—are gone, but some owls still perch above the dance floor of what is now a popular country-and-western club. Even if you don't like crowds or country music, it's worth coming to see this gigantic log cabin constructed around five trees; the entryway consists of a huge wishbone-shaped pine. ⊠ *3404 E. Rte. 66, Downtown* ☎ *928/526–9434* ⊕ *www.museumclub.com* ⊠ *Free* ⊙ *Sun.–Thurs. noon–1 AM, Fri.–Sat. noon–3 AM.*

★ ㉔ Visiting the **Museum of Northern Arizona** is worthwhile, if only to see the striking native-stone building in a cool, tree-shaded site. But the institution, founded in 1928, is also respected worldwide for its research and its collections centering on the natural and cultural history of the Colorado Plateau; only 1% of its vast holdings on the archaeology, ethnology, geology, biology, and fine arts of the region is on display at any given time. Among the permanent exhibitions are an extensive collection of Navajo rugs and an authentic Hopi kiva (men's ceremonial chamber).

A gallery devoted to area geology is usually a hit with children: it includes a life-size model dilophosaurus, a carnivorous dinosaur that once roamed northern Arizona. Outdoors, a life-zone exhibit shows the changing vegetation from the bottom of the Grand Canyon to the highest peak in Flagstaff. A nature trail, open only in summer, heads down across a small stream into a canyon and up into an aspen grove. In summer the museum hosts exhibits and the works of Native American artists, whose wares are also sold in the museum gift shop. The museum's education department sponsors excellent tours of the area and as far away as New Mexico and Utah. ⊠ *3101 N. Fort Valley Rd., University* ☎ *928/774–5213* ⊕ *www.musnaz.org* ⊠ *$5* ⊙ *Daily 9–5.*

22 The **Northern Arizona University Observatory**, with its 24-inch telescope, was built in 1952 by Dr. Arthur Adel, a scientist at Lowell Observatory until he joined the college faculty as a professor of mathematics. His work on infrared astronomy pioneered research into molecules that absorb light passing through the earth's atmosphere. Today's studies of Earth's shrinking ozone layer rely on some of Dr. Adel's early work. Visitors to the observatory—which houses one of the largest telescopes that the public is allowed to move and manipulate—are usually hosted by friendly students and faculty members of the university's Department of Physics and Astronomy. ⊠ *Bldg. 47, Northern Arizona Campus Observatory, Dept. of Physics and Astronomy, S. San Francisco St., just north of Walkup Skydome, University* ☎ *928/523–8121 weekdays, 928/523–7170 Fri. night* 🖃 *Free* ☉ *Viewings Fri. 7:30–10 PM, weather permitting.*

Operated by the Arizona Historical Society in a volcanic-rock building constructed in 1908—Coconino County's first hospital for the poor—

23 the **Pioneer Museum** includes among its displays one of the depressingly small nurses' rooms, an old iron lung, and a reconstructed doctor's office. But most of the exhibits touch on more cheerful aspects of Flagstaff history—for example, road signs and children's toys. The museum holds a folk-crafts festival on the 4th of July, complete with blacksmiths, weavers, spinners, quilters, and candle makers at work. Their crafts, and those of other local artisans, are sold in the museum's gift shop, a tiny space filled with teddy bears, dolls, hand-dipped candles, and the like. The museum is part of the Fort Valley Park complex, in a wooded residential section at the northwest end of town. ⊠ *2340 N. Fort Valley Rd., North Flagstaff* ☎ *928/774–6272* 🖃 *$1 suggested donation per individual, $3 per family* ☉ *Mon.–Sat. 9–5.*

21 Near Northern Arizona University, **Riordan State Historic Park** is a must-

Fodor'sChoice see artifact of Flagstaff's logging heyday. Its centerpiece is a mansion
★ built in 1904 for Michael and Timothy Riordan, lumber-baron brothers who married two sisters. The 13,300-square-ft, 40-room log-and-stone structure—designed by Charles Whittlesley, who was also responsible for the El Tovar Hotel at the Grand Canyon—contains furniture by Gustav Stickley, father of the American Arts and Crafts design movement. Fascinating details abound: one room holds "Paul Bunyan's shoes," a 2-ft-long pair of boots made by Timothy in his workshop. Everything on display is original to the house, half of which was occupied by members of the family until 1986. The mansion may be explored on a guided tour only. ⊠ *1300 Riordan Ranch St., University* ☎ *928/779–4395* ⊕ *www.pr.state.az.us* 🖃 *$6* ☉ *May–Oct., daily 8:30–5, with tours on the hr 9–4; Nov.–Apr., daily 10:30–5, with tours on the hr 11–4.*

Where to Stay & Eat

By city ordinance, all restaurants in Flagstaff forbid smoking. For approximate costs, *see* the dining and lodging price charts at the beginning of this chapter.

$$–$$$ ✕ **Black Bart's Steakhouse Saloon & Old West Theater.** The Wild West atmosphere at this rollicking, brightly lit barn of a restaurant is a rather cornball creation. However, the barbecued chicken is tender and flavorful, and the biscuits stick to your ribs. Just don't expect to see any vegetables on your plate unless they're deep-fried. Northern Arizona University music students entertain while they wait on tables, so don't be surprised if your server suddenly jumps onstage to belt out a couple of show tunes. ⊠ *2760 E. Butler Ave., Downtown* ☎ *928/779–3142* 🍴 *Reservations not accepted* 🖃 *AE, MC, V* ☉ *No lunch.*

★ **$$–$$$** ✕ **Cottage Place.** An unexpectedly elegant spot in a town known for heavy food and drive-through service, this cozy restaurant in a 50-year-old cottage has intimate dining rooms and an extensive wine list. The menu strays only slightly from Continental to include some classic American dishes, such as charbroiled lamb chops. Try the artichoke chicken breast or chateaubriand for two carved tableside. Dinner includes soup and salad, but save room for Chocolate Decadence and other desserts. ⊠ *126 W. Cottage Ave., Downtown* ☎ *928/774–8431* ▭ *AE, MC, V* ☉ *Closed Mon. No lunch.*

$$–$$$ ✕ **Sakura Restaurant.** The excellent fish at this Japanese restaurant in the Radisson is flown in every other day from the West Coast, but if sushi doesn't entice you, dine at a large grill table where you'll probably enjoy watching the well-seasoned, large portions of steak or seafood with vegetables being flipped in front of you. ⊠ *Radisson Woodlands Plaza Hotel, 1175 Rte. 66, East Flagstaff* ☎ *928/773–9118* ▭ *AE, D, DC, MC, V* ☉ *No lunch Sun.*

$$ ✕ **Pasto.** This downtown Italian restaurant—two intimate dining rooms in adjacent historic buildings—is popular with a young crowd for good food at reasonable prices. Such southern Italian standards as lasagna and spaghetti with meatballs appear on the menu along with more innovative fare, such as artichoke orzo and salmon Caesar salad. A courtyard in the back, tucked away among higher buildings, has a romantic urban feel. ⊠ *19 E. Aspen St., Downtown* ☎ *928/779–1937* ▭ *MC, V* ☉ *No lunch Sept.–May.*

$–$$ ✕ **Buster's Restaurant.** At lunchtime, families and students from nearby Northern Arizona University settle into the comfortable booths and enjoy fresh seafood, homemade soups, salads, giant burgers, and mesquite-grilled steaks. Try the *lahvosh* appetizer—a giant cracker heaped with toppings ranging from smoked salmon to mushrooms—or the Caesar salad with grilled Cajun chicken. At night, single professionals and skiers crowd the bar and work through its impressive beer selection. ⊠ *1800 S. Milton Rd., Downtown* ☎ *928/774–5155* ▭ *AE, D, DC, MC, V.*

$ ✕ **Beaver Street Brewery.** Popular among the wood-fired pizzas here is the Enchanted Forest, with Brie, artichoke pesto, Portobello mushrooms, roasted red peppers, and spinach. Whichever pie you order, expect serious amounts of garlic. Sandwiches, such as the Southwestern chicken with three types of cheese, come with a hefty portion of tasty fries. You won't regret ordering one of the down-home desserts, such as the super-gooey chocolate bread pudding. Among the excellent microbrews usually on tap, the raspberry ale is a local favorite. An outdoor beer garden opens up in summer. ⊠ *11 S. Beaver St., Downtown* ☎ *928/779–0079* ▭ *AE, D, DC, MC, V.*

¢–$ ✕ **Café Espress.** The menu is largely vegetarian at this natural-foods restaurant. Stir-fried vegetables, pasta dishes, Mediterranean salads, tempeh burgers, pita pizzas, fish or chicken specials, and wonderful baked goods made on the premises all come at prices that will make you feel good, too. This is an artsy and hip place (the work of local artists hangs on the walls) but friendly, and it's open for breakfast every day at 7. ⊠ *16 N. San Francisco St., Downtown* ☎ *928/774–0541* ▭ *MC, V.*

¢–$ ✕ **Salsa Brava.** This cheerful Mexican restaurant, with light-wood booths and colorful designs, eschews heavy Sonoran-style fare in favor of the grilled dishes found in Guadalajara. The fish tacos are particularly good, and this place has the only salsa bar in town. On weekends, come for a huevos rancheros breakfast. ⊠ *1800 S. Milton Rd., Downtown* ☎ *928/774–1083* ▭ *AE, MC, V.*

¢–$ ✕ **Tea and Sympathy.** This is Flagstaff's most civilized spot, where you can sink down into an overstuffed chair and enjoy an assortment of tea services—a breakfast tea with granola and fruit, or a "Sand and Sea" tea, with smoked salmon pâté, fruit, and dessert. There's almost any variety of tea you can imagine; if you like what you've tried, you can buy it loose. It's open until 6 every day. ⊠ *409 N. Humphreys St., Downtown* ☎ *928/779–2171* ▭ *AE, D, MC, V* ⊙ *No dinner.*

¢ ✕ **La Bellavia.** At this favorite bohemian breakfast nook, the trout and eggs platter is the standard—two eggs served with Idaho trout flavored with a hint of lemon, and rounded off by a buttermilk pancake gilded to perfection. Other savory options include Swedish oat pancakes, seven-grain French toast, and nine varieties of eggs Benedict. A palette of creative sandwiches and familiar salads makes this a worthwhile lunch stop as well. The café doubles as a gallery for local artists whose artwork hangs on the walls beneath an azure-painted ceiling scattered with, perhaps, the few clouds you'll see that day. ⊠ *18 S. Beaver St., Downtown* ☎ *928/774–8301* ▭ *No credit cards* ⊙ *No dinner.*

¢ ✕ **Bun Huggers.** The best burger in town is flipped over a mesquite-fired grill. Also try the tasty, if decadent, deep-fried zucchini served with shredded cheddar cheese and ranch dressing. There is a small salad bar here, but it seems like an afterthought, existing only to heal guilty consciences. ⊠ *901 S. Milton Rd., Downtown* ☎ *928/779–3743* ▭ *AE, D, MC, V.*

★ $$–$$$ ▥ **Inn at 410.** An inviting alternative to the chain motels in Flagstaff, this B&B has a quiet but convenient downtown location. All the accommodations in the beautifully restored 1907 residence are suites with private baths. Some have private entrances and fireplaces; all have coffeemakers. Monet's Garden is a lovely Jacuzzi suite with fireplace. The breakfasts are delicious and healthful; in the afternoon fresh-baked cookies are served. The innkeepers, Sally and Howard Krueger, offer concierge service akin to that of a small boutique hotel. ⊠ *410 N. Leroux St., Downtown, 86001* ☎ *928/774–0088 or 800/774–2008* 🖷 *928/774–6354* ⊕ *www.inn410.com* ↩ *9 suites* ⌂ *Some in-room hot tubs, refrigerators; no kids in some rooms, no smoking* ▭ *MC, V* ¶⊙¶ *BP.*

$$ ▥ **Jeanette's.** If you prefer the clean lines of 1920s design to Victorian froufrou, consider staying at this stylish B&B. Rooms in this residence on the city's east side are all beautifully appointed with art deco pieces; one room has a private porch, another a fireplace. Details such as handmade soap and fine china at breakfast enhance the time-travel experience, as does owner Jeanette's devotion to antique clothing, which she often dons. ⊠ *3380 E. Lockett Rd., East Flagstaff, 86004* ☎ *928/527–1912 or 800/752–1912* ⊕ *www.jeanettesbb.com* ↩ *4 rooms* ⌂ *No smoking* ▭ *D, MC, V* ¶⊙¶ *BP.*

$–$$ ▥ **Birch Tree Inn.** This historic home in a tree-filled neighborhood near downtown is nicely appointed with antiques. The place feels relaxed, in part because the hosts (two friendly couples who trade off inn-keeping stints) enjoy chatting with their guests. The billiard table adjoining the living room gets people talking to each other, too. You'll start your day well fueled for sightseeing: the morning meal might consist of a cheese, sausage, and potato casserole accompanied by fresh fruit and banana bread made on the premises. ⊠ *824 W. Birch Ave., Downtown, 86001* ☎ *928/774–1042 or 800/645–5805* ⊕ *www.birchtreeinn.com* ↩ *5 rooms, 3 with bath* ⌂ *Outdoor hot tub* ▭ *AE, MC, V* ¶⊙¶ *BP.*

★ $–$$ ▥ **Little America of Flagstaff.** The biggest hotel in town is a deservedly popular place. It's far from the roar of the trains, the grounds are surrounded by evergreen forests, and it's one of the few places in Flagstaff with room service. Plush rooms have brass chandeliers, comfortable sitting areas with French provincial–style furniture, phones in bathrooms, and large stereo TVs. Other pluses are courtesy van service to the airport and the Amtrak station and a gift shop with great Southwestern stuff. ⊠ *2515 E. Butler Ave., Downtown, 86004* ☎ *928/779–2741 or 800/352–4386* 🖷 *928/779–7983* ⊕ *www.flagstaff.littleamerica.com*

🛏 *248 rooms ᕦ Restaurant, coffee shop, room service, kitchenettes, refrigerators, pool, gym, hair salon, hiking, bar, playground, laundry facilities, airport shuttle ⊟ AE, D, DC, MC, V.*

$–$$ 🏨 **Sled Dog Inn.** This inn is on just 4 acres, but its grounds seem vastly larger, since the land borders the immense Coconino National Forest. A big draw here is, as the name implies, the owners' Siberian huskies, which are lovingly cared for. Sometimes during the winter you can even accompany the owners on a dog-sled run, but they no longer offer regular rides to guests. Rooms are contemporary rustic. ⊠ *10155 Mountainaire Rd., South Flagstaff, 86001* ☎ *928/525–6212 or 800/754–0064* ⊕ *www.sleddoginn.com* 🛏 *8 rooms, 2 suites ᕦ Hot tub, sauna, some pets allowed; no kids under 6, smoking ⊟ AE, MC, V* ❍| *CP.*

¢–$$ 🏨 **Hotel Monte Vista.** Over the years many Hollywood stars, including Bob Hope and Spencer Tracy, have stayed at this historic downtown hotel built in 1926; some of the guest rooms bear their names. The restored Southwestern-deco lobby, with its shoe-shine stand and curved archways, is appealing, and rates are low, but rooms and hallways are somewhat dark. Bunk beds in hostel-style dorm rooms are available for less than $15 per person. ⊠ *100 N. San Francisco St., Downtown, 86001* ☎ *928/779–6971 or 800/545–3068* 🖷 *928/779–2904* ⊕ *www.hotelmontevista. com* 🛏 *48 rooms ᕦ Restaurant, room service, cable TV, 2 bars, laundry service ⊟ AE, D, DC, MC, V.*

¢ 🏨 **Hotel Weatherford.** With a columned veranda that wraps around the block, this hotel, built in 1897, makes a dramatic presence at the hub of town. Imbued with a creaky charm, the rooms are spartan and a bit worn around the edges but comfortable nonetheless. You'll forgo TV and a telephone for a taste of the Old West. The Exchange Pub downstairs has a bustling nightlife scene. ⊠ *23 N. Leroux St., Downtown, 86001* ☎ *928/779–1919* 🖷 *928/773–8951* ⊕ *www.weatherfordhotel. com* 🛏 *8 rooms, 5 with bath ᕦ Restaurant, 2 bars; no a/c, no room phones, no room TVs ⊟ AE, D, DC, MC, V.*

Nightlife & the Arts

Flagstaff's large college contingent has plenty of places to gather after dark, most of them in the historic downtown district and most of them charging little or no cover. It's easy to walk from one rowdy spot to the next. For current information on what's going on in town, pick up the free *Flagstaff Live.* There's also no shortage of cultural entertainment in Flagstaff, not to mention summer festivals.

The **Alley** (⊠ 22 E. Rte. 66, Downtown ☎ 928/774–7929) books live music, from alternative to world-beat. The ground floor of the **Hotel &Weatherford** (⊠23 N. Leroux St., Downtown ☎928/779–1919) is where you'll find both Charly's, which has late-night jazz and blues bands, and the Exchange Pub, which tends to attract folksy ensembles. Dark, smoky, and decked with a neon sign, **Joe's Place** (⊠ 200 E. Rte. 66, Downtown ☎ 928/774–6281) is a Route 66 classic and a favorite place for locals to shoot pool. The **Mogollon Brewing Company** (⊠15 N. Agassiz St., Downtown ☎ 928/773–8950) rolls out live music and hardy stout. The **Monte Vista Lounge** (⊠ 100 N. San Francisco St., Downtown ☎ 928/774–2403) packs them in with nightly live blues, jazz, classic rock, punk, and an open mike on Wednesday.

Northern Arizona University's **College of Creative and Performing Arts** (⊠Ardrey Auditorium, Knoles and Riordan Rds., University ☎928/523–5661) is a top-quality performance venue. The **Flagstaff Symphony Orchestra** (☎ 928/774–5107) offers year-round musical events. **Theatrikos Theater Company** (⊠ 11 W. Cherry Ave., Downtown ☎ 928/774–1662) is a highly regarded troupe, featuring an eclectic lineup of plays.

A Celebration of Native American Art (✉ 3101 N. Fort Valley Rd., University ☎ 928/774–5211), featuring exhibits of work by Zuni, Hopi, and Navajo artists, is held at the Museum of Northern Arizona from late May through September. During the month of August, the **Flagstaff Festival of the Arts** (☎ 928/774–7750 or 800/266–7740) fills the air with the sounds of classical music and pops performances, many by world-renowned artists. **Flagstaff SummerFest** (✉ Fort Tuthill Coconino County Park, S. AZ 89A, South Flagstaff ☎ 928/774–5130), held the first weekend in August, includes an arts-and-crafts fair. Flagstaff's observatories help make September's **Festival of Science** (☎ 800/842–7293) a stellar attraction.

Sports & the Outdoors

BIKING With more than 30 mi of challenging trails a short ride from town, one of Flagstaff's best-kept secrets is inevitably leaking out. The mountain biking on Mt. Elden is on par with that of more celebrated trails in Colorado and Utah. A good place to start is the **Lower Oldham Trail,** which originates on the north end of Buffalo Park; there's a large meadow with picnic areas and an exercise path. The terrain is rolling and technical in spots but easy enough to test your tolerance of the elevation.

The **Sunset Trail,** near the summit of Mt. Elden, affords amazing views off the ridge rendered barren by a 1977 fire. Check your bearings before proceeding. The trail narrows into the aptly nicknamed Catwalk, with precipitous drops a few feet on either side. Vertigo, either from the 9,000-ft elevation or the sheer exposure, is not an option. You need to be an at least moderately experienced mountain biker to attempt this trail.

The very popular **Schultz Creek Trail** is very fun and suitable for strong beginners, though seasoned experts will be thrilled as well. Most opt to start at the top and swoop down the smooth, twisting path through groves of wildflowers and stands of ponderosa pines and aspens.

You can rent mountain bikes at **Absolute Bikes** (✉ 18 N. San Francisco St., Downtown ☎ 928/779–5969). From mid-June through mid-October, the **Flagstaff Nordic Center** (✉ U.S. 180, 16 mi north of Flagstaff, North Flagstaff ☎ 928/779–1951), which is operated by the Arizona Snowbowl, opens its cross-country trails to mountain bikers, gratis if you bring your own wheels; rentals are also available. **Mountain Sports** (✉ 1800 S. Milton Rd., University ☎ 928/779–5156 or 800/286–5156) offers competitive rates for bike rentals. A map of the **Urban Trails System** (✉ 1 E. Rte. 66, Downtown ☎ 928/774–9541 or 800/842–7293), available at the Flagstaff Visitor Center, details biking options in the area.

CAMPING Contact the **Coconino National Forest** (✉ Peaks Ranger Station, 5075 N. U.S. 89, North Flagstaff ☎ 928/526–0866 ⊕ www.fs.fed.us/r3/coconino) for information on campgrounds in the area.

HIKING & ROCK You can explore Arizona's alpine tundra in the San Francisco Peaks, where
CLIMBING more than 80 species of plants grow on the upper elevations. The habitat is fragile, so hikers are asked to stay on established trails (and there are lots of them). The altitude here will make even the hardiest hikers breathe a little harder, so individuals with cardiac or respiratory problems should be cautious about overexertion. The **Humphreys Peak Trail** is 9-mi round-trip, with a vertical climb of 3,843 ft to the summit of Arizona's highest mountain (12,643 ft). Those who don't want a long hike can do just the first mile of the 5-mi-long **Kachina Trail;** completely flat, this route is surrounded by huge stands of aspen and offers fantastic vistas. It's particularly worthwhile in fall, when changing leaves paint the landscape shades of yellow, russet, and amber. You'll find the

Humphreys Peak and Kachina trailheads at the Arizona Snowbowl. Others, such as the short but rewarding **Fatmans Loop** on Mt. Elden, can be accessed in town.

The rangers of the **Coconino National Forest** (✉ 2323 Greenlaw La., North Flagstaff ☎ 928/527–3600 ✉ Peaks Ranger Station, 5075 N. U.S. 89, North Flagstaff ☎ 928/527–3630 ⊕ www.fs.fed.us/r3/coconino) maintain many of the region's trails and can provide you with details on hiking in the area; the forest's main office is open weekdays 7:30–4:30, and the ranger station has excellent hiking and recreation guides. **Flagstaff Mountain Guides** (☎ 928/635–0145) organizes peak rock-climbing trips around town or as far away as Sedona. If you'd prefer to hone your skills first, **Vertical Relief Rock Gym** (✉ 205 S. San Francisco St., Downtown ☎ 928/556–9909) provides the tallest indoor climbing walls in the Southwest.

HORSEBACK RIDING The wranglers at **Hitchin' Post Stables** (✉ 4848 Lake Mary Rd., South Flagstaff ☎ 928/774–1719) lead rides into Walnut Canyon and operate horseback or horse-drawn wagon rides with sunset barbecues. In winter, they'll take you through Coconino National Forest on a sleigh—bells and all.

SKIING & SNOWBOARDING The ski season usually starts in mid-December and ends in mid-April. The **Arizona Snowbowl** (✉ Snowbowl Rd., North Flagstaff ☎ 928/779–1951, 928/779–4577 snow report ⊕ www.arizonasnowbowl.com), 7 mi north of Flagstaff off U.S. 180, has 30 downhill runs (37% beginner, 42% intermediate, and 21% advanced), four chairlifts, and a vertical drop of 2,300 ft. Those who have skied Colorado's Rockies might find Snowbowl disappointing—there are a couple of good bump runs, but it's better for beginners or those with moderate skill. Still, it's a fun place to spend the day. Snowboarders share trails with downhill skiers. The Hart Prairie Lodge has an equipment-rental shop and a SKIwee center for ages 4 to 8. All-day adult lift tickets are $35. Half-day discounts are available, and group-lesson packages (including two hours of instruction, an all-day lift ticket, and equipment rental) are a good buy at $47. A children's program (which includes lunch, progress card, and full supervision 9–3:30) runs $50. Many Flagstaff motels offer ski packages, including transportation to Snowbowl. The **Flagstaff Nordic Center** (✉ U.S. 180, 16 mi north of Flagstaff, North Flagstaff ☎ 928/779–1951, 928/779–4577 snow report ⊕ www.arizonasnowbowl.com), owned and operated by Arizona Snowbowl, is 9 mi north of Snowbowl Road. There are 25 mi of well-groomed cross-country trails here. Instruction packages and rental combinations are available.

Shopping

Flagstaff's prime shopping area is downtown. Even if you're not looking for anything in particular, it's fun to stroll along San Francisco Street and Route 66. The **Flagstaff Mall** (✉ 4650 N. U.S. 89, East Flagstaff ☎ 928/526–4827) is just east of town off I–40 at Exit 201. This mall has the greatest number of department and specialty stores in the area, including Dillard's, Sears Roebuck, and JCPenney. There's also a food court and a two-screen cinema.

For fine arts and crafts—everything from ceramics and stained glass to weaving and painting—visit the **Artists Gallery** (✉ 17 N. San Francisco St., Downtown ☎ 928/773–0958), a local artists' cooperative. You can pick up sporting goods at **Babbitt's Backcountry Outfitters** (✉ 12 E. Aspen Ave., Downtown ☎ 928/774–4775). The **Black Hound Gallerie** (✉ 120 N. Leroux St., Downtown ☎ 928/774–2323) specializes in posters, prints, and funky kitsch of all kinds. **Candles by Night** (✉ 113 W. Phoenix

Ave., Downtown ☎ 928/774–1461) displays whimsical handcrafted candles. The 20-odd vendors at **Carriage House Antique and Gift Mall** (✉ 413 N. San Francisco St., Downtown ☎ 928/774–1337) sell vintage clothing and jewelry, furniture, fine china, and other collectibles. The **Museum of Northern Arizona Gift Shop** (✉ 3101 N. Fort Valley Rd., University ☎ 928/774–5213) carries high-quality jewelry and crafts. **Winter Sun Trading Company** (✉ 107 N. San Francisco St., Downtown ☎ 928/774–2884) sells medicinal herbs, jewelry, and crafts. **Zani** (✉ 111-C S. San Francisco St., Downtown ☎ 928/774–9409) stocks hip home furnishings and greeting cards in addition to futons.

SIDE TRIPS NEAR FLAGSTAFF

Travelers who head straight through town, bound for the Grand Canyon, often neglect the area north and east of Flagstaff. But a detour has its rewards. If you don't have enough time to do everything, take a quick drive to Walnut Canyon—only about 15 minutes out of town.

East of Flagstaff

★ ㉘ **Walnut Canyon National Monument** consists of a group of cliff dwellings constructed by the Sinagua people, who lived and farmed in and around the canyon starting around AD 700. The more than 300 dwellings here were built between 1080 and 1250 and abandoned, like those at so many other settlements in Arizona and New Mexico, around 1300. The Sinagua traded far and wide with other Native Americans, including people at Wupatki. Even macaw feathers, which would have come from tribes in what is now Mexico, have been excavated in the canyon. The area wasn't explored by Europeans until 1883, when early Flagstaff settlers shamelessly looted the site for pots and "treasure." Woodrow Wilson declared the site a national monument in 1915, which began a 30-year process of stabilizing the ruins.

Walnut Canyon is fascinating, in part because of the opportunity to enter the dwellings and feel ancient life at close range. Some of the Sinagua homes are in near-perfect condition, in spite of all the looting, because of the dry, hot climate and the protection of overhanging cliffs. You can reach them by descending 185 ft on the 1-mi stepped **Island Trail,** which starts at the visitor center. As you follow the trail, look across the canyon for other dwellings not accessible on the path.

Island Trail takes about an hour to complete at a normal pace. Those with health concerns should opt for the easier ½-mi **Rim Trail,** which has overlooks from which dwellings, as well as an excavated, reconstructed pit house, can be viewed. Attractive picnic areas dot the grounds and line the roads leading to the park. Guides conduct tours on Wednesday, Saturday, and Sunday from late May through early September. You are permitted to enter about two dozen ruins. ✉ *Walnut Canyon Rd., Winona, 3 mi south of I–40, Exit 204* ☎ *928/526–3367* ⊕ *www.nps. gov/waca* ✍ *$3* ⊙ *Sept.–May, daily 9–5; June–Aug., daily 9–6.*

🖑 ㉙ **Meteor Crater,** a natural phenomenon, set in a privately owned park 43 mi east of Flagstaff, is impressive if for no other reason than its sheer size. A hole in the ground 600 ft deep, nearly 1 mi across, and more than 3 mi in circumference, Meteor Crater is large enough to accommodate the Washington Monument or 20 football fields. It was created when a meteorite came hurtling through space at a speed of 43,000 mph and crashed here 49,000 years ago. The area looks so much like the surface of the moon that NASA made it one of the official training sites for the Project Apollo astronauts. You can't descend into the crater because of the efforts of its owners to maintain its condition—scientists consider this to be the best-preserved crater on Earth—but guided rim tours, given every hour on the hour from 9 to 3, give you some useful background information. There's a small snack bar, and rock hounds will enjoy the Rock Shop's raw specimens from the area and jewelry made from native stones. Take I–40 east of Flagstaff to Exit 233, then 6 mi south on Meteor Crater Road. ☒ *Meteor Crater Rd., 43 mi east of Flagstaff* ☎ *928/289–2362* ⊕ *www.meteorcrater.com* ☎ *$8* ⊙ *Mid-May–mid-Sept., daily 6–6; mid-Sept.–mid-May, daily 8–5.*

San Francisco Volcanic Field

The San Francisco Volcanic Field north of Flagstaff encompasses 2,000 square mi of fascinating geological phenomena—ancient volcanoes, cinder cones, and valleys carved by water and ice, and the San Francisco Peaks themselves, some of which soar to almost 13,000 ft—as well as some of the most extensive Native American ruins in the Southwest: don't miss Sunset Crater and Wupatki. These national monuments can be explored in relative solitude during much of the year. The area is short on services, so fill up on gas and consider taking along a picnic. A good source for hiking and camping information in the San Francisco Volcanic Field area are the rangers of **Coconino National Forest** (☒Peaks Ranger Station, 5075 N. U.S. 89, North Flagstaff ☎ 928/526–0866 ⊕ www. fs.fed.us/r3/coconino). If you camp, do not pitch your tent in a low-lying area, where dangerous flash floods can literally wipe you out.

★ ③⓪ **Sunset Crater Volcano National Monument** lies 14 mi northeast of Flagstaff off U.S. 89. Sunset Crater, a cinder cone that rises 1,000 ft, was an active volcano 900 years ago. The final eruption contained iron and sulfur, which gives the rim of the crater its glow and thus its name. You can walk around the base, but you can't descend into the huge, fragile cone. If you take the **Lava Flow Trail,** a half-hour, mile-long, self-guided walk, you'll have a good view of the evidence of the volcano's fiery power: lava formations and holes in the rock where volcanic gases vented to the surface. Three smaller cones to the southeast were formed at the same time and along the same fissure.

If you're interested in hiking a volcano, head to **Lenox Crater,** about 1 mi east of the visitor center, and climb the 280 ft to the top of the cinder cone. Wear closed, sturdy shoes; the cinder is soft and crumbly. From **O'Leary Peak,** 5 mi from the visitor center on Forest Route 545A, great views can be had of the San Francisco Peaks, the Painted Desert, and beyond. The road is unpaved and rutted, however, so it's advisable to take only high-clearance vehicles, especially in winter. In addition, there's a gate, about halfway along the route, that is usually closed. This will mean a steep 2½-mi hike to the top on foot. To get to the area from Flagstaff, take Santa Fe Avenue east to U.S. 89, and head north for 12 mi; turn right onto the road marked Sunset Crater and go another 2 mi to the visitor center. ☒ *Sunset Crater–Wupatki Loop Rd., 14 mi northeast of Flagstaff* ☎ *928/556–7042* ⊕ *www.nps.gov/sucr* ☎ *$3, including Wupatki National Monument and Doney Mountain* ⊙ *Daily 8–5; hrs may be extended in summer.*

③① Families from the Sinagua and other ancestral Puebloans are believed to have lived together in harmony on the site that is now **Wupatki National Monument,** farming and trading with one another and with those who passed through their "city." The eruption of Sunset Crater may have caused migration to this area—and may have disrupted the settlement more than once around AD 1064. Although there is evidence of earlier habitation, most of the settlers moved here around 1100 and left the

FodorsChoice
★

pueblo by about 1250. The 2,700 identified sites contain archaeological evidence of Native American settlement.

The site for which the national monument was named, the Wupatki (meaning "tall house" in Hopi), was originally three stories high, built above an unexplored system of underground fissures. The structure had almost 100 rooms and an open ball court—evidence in itself of Southwestern trade with Mesoamerican tribes for whom ball games were a central ritual. Next to the ball court is a blowhole, a geologic phenomenon in which air is forced upward by underground pressure; scientists speculate that early inhabitants may have attached some spiritual significance to the region's many blowholes.

Other ruins to visit are Wukoki, Lomaki, and the Citadel, a pueblo on a knoll above a limestone sink. Although the largest remnants of Native American settlements at Wupatki National Monument are open to the public, other sites are off-limits to casual visitors. Rules regarding entering closed sites are strictly enforced. If you are interested in an in-depth tour, consider taking a ranger-led overnight hike to the **Crack-in-Rock Ruin.** The 14-mi (round-trip) trek covers areas marked by ancient petroglyphs and dotted with well-preserved ruins. The trips are conducted in April and October; call by February or August if you'd like to take part in the lottery for one of the 100 available places on these $25 hikes. Between the Wupatki and Citadel ruins, the **Doney Mountain** affords 360-degree views of the Painted Desert and the San Francisco Volcanic Field. It's a perfect spot for a sunset picnic. In summer, rangers give lectures. ⊠ *Sunset Crater–Wupatki Loop Rd., 19 mi north of Sunset Crater visitor center* ☎ *928/556-7040* ⊕ *www.nps.gov/wupa* ✉ *$3, including Wupatki National Monument and Doney Mountain* ☉ *Daily 8–5; hrs may be extended in summer.*

NORTH-CENTRAL ARIZONA A TO Z

To research prices, get advice from other travelers, and book travel arrangements, visit www.fodors.com.

AIR TRAVEL

America West flies frequently from Phoenix into Prescott Municipal Airport and to Flagstaff Pulliam Airport. Sedona Airport is a base for several air tours and has no regularly scheduled flights.

🛂 **America West** ☎ 800/235-9292 ⊕ www.americawest.com.

AIRPORTS

Prescott Municipal Airport is 8 mi north of town on U.S. 89. Flagstaff Pulliam Airport is 3 mi south of town off I–17 at Exit 337. Sedona Airport is in West Sedona.

🛂 **Flagstaff Pulliam Airport** ☎ 928/556-1234. **Prescott Municipal Airport** ☎ 928/445-7860. **Sedona Airport** ☎ 928/282-1046.

FLAGSTAFF
AIRPORT
TRANSFERS
A taxi ride from the airport to the downtown area should cost about $9–$11. Cabs are not regulated; some, but not all, have meters. It's wise to agree on a rate with a driver before you leave for your destination.
🛂 **A Friendly Cab** ☎ 928/774-4444. **Sun Taxi** ☎ 928/774-7400.

BUS TRAVEL

Greyhound Lines has daily connections from throughout the West to Flagstaff but none to Sedona. Buses also run between Prescott and Phoenix Sky Harbor International Airport.

The Sedona/Phoenix Shuttle Service makes six trips daily between those cities; the fare is $40 one-way, $65 round-trip. You can also get on or off at Camp Verde or Cottonwood. The bus leaves from three terminals of Sky Harbor International Airport in Phoenix. Reservations are required.

🚌 **Greyhound Lines** ✉ 399 S. Malpais La., Flagstaff ☎ 928/774-4573 or 800/231-2222 ✉ 820 E. Sheldon Ave., Prescott ☎ 928/445-5470 ⊕ www.greyhound.com **Sedona/Phoenix Shuttle Service** ☎ 928/282-2066, 800/448-7988 in Arizona ⊕ www.sedona-phoenix-shuttle.com.

CAR RENTALS

It makes sense to rent a car in this region. You'll find major rental agencies in Flagstaff, Prescott, and Sedona. If you want to explore the red rocks of Sedona, you can even rent a four-wheel drive.

🚗 Flagstaff **Avis** ✉ Flagstaff Pulliam Airport, Flagstaff ☎ 928/774-8421. **Budget** ✉ Flagstaff Pulliam Airport, Flagstaff ☎ 928/779-0306. **Enterprise** ✉ 800 W. Rte. 66, Flagstaff ☎ 928/774-9407. **Hertz** ✉ Flagstaff Pulliam Airport, Flagstaff ☎ 928/774-4452. **National** ✉ Holiday Inn, 2320 E. Lucky La., Flagstaff ☎ 928/779-1975. **Sears** ✉ 100 N. Humphreys St., Flagstaff ☎ 928/774-1879 or 800/527-0770.

🚗 Prescott **Budget** ✉ 1031 Commerce Dr. ☎ 928/778-3806. **Enterprise** ✉ 202 S. Montezuma St. ☎ 928/778-6506. **Hertz** ✉ Prescott Municipal Airport ☎ 928/776-1399.

🚗 Sedona **Budget** ✉ Sedona Airport, Sedona ☎ 928/282-4602. **Canyon Jeep Rentals** ✉ Oak Creek Terrace Resort, 4548 AZ 89A, Sedona ☎ 928/282-6061 or 800/224-2229. **Sedona Jeep Rentals** ✉ Sedona Airport, Sedona ☎ 928/282-2227 or 800/879-5337.

CAR TRAVEL

Flagstaff lies at the intersection of I–40 (east–west) and I–17 (running south from Flagstaff), 134 mi north of Phoenix via I–17. The most direct route to Prescott from Phoenix is to take I–17 north for 60 mi to Cordes Junction and then drive northwest on AZ 69 for 36 mi into town. I–17, a four-lane divided highway, has several steep inclines and descents (you'll see a number of runaway-truck ramps). However, it's generally an easy and scenic thoroughfare. If you want to take the more leisurely route through Verde Valley to Prescott, continue north on I–17 another 25 mi past Cordes Junction until you see the turnoff for AZ 260, which will take you to Cottonwood in 12 mi. Here you can pick up AZ 89A, which leads southwest to Prescott (41 mi) or northeast to Sedona (19 mi).

Sedona stretches along AZ 89A (also called Highway 89A), its main thoroughfare, which runs roughly east–west through town. AZ 89A is bisected by AZ 179. The more commercial section of AZ 89A east of AZ 179 is known as Uptown; locals tend to frequent the shops on the other side, called West Sedona. To the south of AZ 89A, AZ 179 is lined with upscale retailers for a couple of miles. To reach Sedona more directly from Phoenix, take I–17 north for 113 mi until you come to AZ 179; it's another 15 mi on that road into town. The trip should take about 2½ hours. The 27-mi drive from Sedona to Flagstaff on AZ 89A, which winds its way through Oak Creek Canyon, is breathtaking.

EMERGENCIES

🚑 Ambulance & Fire **Ambulance and Fire Emergencies** ☎ 911.

🏥 Hospital in Flagstaff **Flagstaff Medical Center** ✉ 1200 N. Beaver St., Flagstaff ☎ 928/779-3366.

🏥 Hospital in Prescott **Yavapai Regional Medical Center** ✉ 1003 Willow Creek Rd., Prescott ☎ 928/445-2700.

🏥 Hospital in Sedona **The Sedona Medical Center** ✉ 3700 W. AZ 89A, Sedona ☎ 928/204-4900.

💊 Pharmacies in Flagstaff **Flagstaff Medical Center Pharmacy** ✉ 1200 N. Beaver St., Flagstaff ☎ 928/779-3366. **Fry's Food and Drug** ✉ 201 N. Switzer Canyon Dr., at Rte. 66, Flagstaff ☎ 928/774-3389. **Walgreens** ✉ 1500 E. Cedar Ave., Flagstaff ☎ 928/773-1011.

📱 Pharmacy in Prescott **Goodwin Street Pharmacy** ✉ 406 W. Goodwin St., Prescott ☎ 928/776-9939.

📱 Pharmacies in Sedona **Rite Aid** ✉ 2350 W. AZ 89A, Sedona ☎ 928/282-9734. **Walgreens** ✉ 1995 W. AZ 89A, Sedona ☎ 928/282-2528.

📱 Police **Police Emergencies** ☎ 911.

SIGHTSEEING TOURS

IN FLAGSTAFF   The Ventures program, run by the education department of the Museum of Northern Arizona, offers tours of the area led by local scientists, artists, and historians. Trips might include rafting excursions down the San Juan River, treks into the Grand Canyon or Colorado Plateau backcountry, or bus tours into the Navajo reservation to visit with Native American artists. Prices start at about $400 and go up to $1,200, with most tours in the $500–$600 range.

📱 **Museum of Northern Arizona** ☎ 928/774-5213 ⊕ www.musnaz.org.

IN PRESCOTT   On Monday and Friday at 10 AM from late May through early September, volunteer guides offer free orientation tours of Prescott that leave from the Chamber of Commerce. The rest of the year, tours can be booked directly with Melissa Roughner, who'll be wearing period clothing from Arizona's territorial days when she guides you around town.

📱 **Melissa Roughner** ☎ 928/445-4567. **Prescott Chamber of Commerce** ✉ 117 W. Goodwin St., 86303 ☎ 928/445-2000 or 800/266-7534 ⊕ www.prescott.org.

IN SEDONA   Sedona Trolley offers two types of daily orientation tours, both departing from the main bus stop in Uptown and lasting less than an hour. One goes along AZ 179 to the Chapel of the Holy Cross, with stops at Tlaquepaque and some galleries; the other passes through West Sedona to Boynton Canyon (Enchantment Resort). Rates are $7 for one or $11 for both.

Several jeep-tour operators headquartered along Sedona's main Uptown drag conduct various excursions, some focusing on geology, some on astronomy, some on vortices, some on all three. You can even find a combination jeep tour and horseback ride. The ubiquitous Pink Jeep Tours are a popular choice. Sedona Adventures offers both full- and half-day options. Sedona Red Rock Jeep Tours is also a reliable operator. Prices start at about $22 per person for one hour and go up to $65 per person for four hours. Although all the excursions are safe, many are not for those who dislike heights or bumps.

Prices for hot-air-balloon tours generally start at $135 per person for a one- to two-hour tour. The only two companies with permits to fly over Sedona are Northern Light Balloon Expeditions, open since 1974 and the longest operating in northern Arizona, and Red Rock Balloon Adventures.

Sedona Art Tours guides visitors through the town's art galleries. Sedona Photo Tours will take you to all the prime spots and help you take your best (photographic) shot. Rates are $35 per person for a basic two-hour tour.

📱 **Northern Light Balloon Expeditions** ☎ 928/282-2274 or 800/230-6222 ⊕ www.sedona.net/fun/balloon. **Pink Jeep Tours** ✉ 204 N. AZ 89A, Sedona ☎ 928/282-5000 or 800/873-3662 ⊕ www.pinkjeep.com. **Red Rock Balloon Adventures** ☎ 928/284-0040 or 800/258-3754 ⊕ www.redrockballoons.com. **Sedona Adventures** ✉ 276 N. AZ 89A, Suite A, Sedona ☎ 928/282-3500 or 800/888-9494 ⊕ www.sedonaadventures.com. **Sedona Art Tours** ☎ 928/282-0788. **Sedona Photo Tours** ✉ 252 N. AZ 89A, Sedona ☎ 928/282-4320 or 800/973-3662. **Sedona Red Rock Jeep Tours** ✉ 270 N. AZ 89A, Sedona ☎ 928/282-6826 or 800/848-7728 ⊕ www.redrockjeep.com. **Sedona Trolley** ☎ 928/282-6826 or 928/282-5400 ⊕ www.sedonatrolley.com.

TAXIS

In Sedona, try Bob's Sedona Taxi. A–1 Quick Cab & Tours in Flagstaff provides local and long-distance service.

🚖 **A-1 Quick Cab & Tours** ☎ 928/214-8294. **Bob's Sedona Taxi** ☎ 928/282-1234.

TRAIN TRAVEL

Amtrak comes into the downtown Flagstaff station twice daily. There is no rail service into Prescott or Sedona.

🚉 **Amtrak** ✉ 1 E. Rte. 66 ☎ 928/774-8679.

VISITOR INFORMATION

🏛 **Camp Verde Chamber of Commerce** ✉ 435 S. Main St., 86322 ☎ 928/567-9294 ⊕ www.insightable.com/cvcc. **Clarkdale Chamber of Commerce** ⬩ Box 161, 86324 ☎ 928/634-3382 ⊕ www.clarkdalechamber.com. **Cottonwood/Verde Valley Chamber of Commerce** ✉ 1010 S. Main St., Cottonwood 86326 ☎ 928/634-7593 ⊕ chamber. verdevalley.com. **Flagstaff Visitors Center** ✉ 1 E. Rte. 66, 86001 ☎ 928/774-9541 or 800/842-7293. **Jerome Chamber of Commerce** ⬩ Box K, 86331 ☎ 928/634-2900. **Prescott Chamber of Commerce** ✉ 117 W. Goodwin St., 86303 ☎ 928/445-2000 or 800/266-7534 ⊕ www.prescott.org. **Sedona–Oak Creek Canyon Chamber of Commerce** ✉ 331 Forest Rd., at N. AZ 89A, Sedona 86339 ☎ 928/282-7722 or 800/288-7336 ⊕ www. sedona.net/chamber.html.

THE GRAND CANYON & NORTHWEST ARIZONA

3

FODOR'S CHOICE

Bright Angel Lodge, *the best budget choice in Grand Canyon Village*

Cameron Trading Post, *Cameron*

Cruisers Café 66, *a budget restaurant in Williams*

El Tovar Dining Room, *Grand Canyon Village*

Grand Canyon Lodge, *North Rim*

North Rim, Grand Canyon National Park, *the best place to view the canyon*

Pipe Spring National Monument, *Fredonia*

Point Sublime, *a scenic drive at the Grand Canyon, North Rim*

Tusayan Ruin and Museum, *South Rim*

HIGHLY RECOMMENDED

SIGHTS Bright Angel Point, *South Rim*

Bright Angel Trailhead, *South Rim*

Canyon View Information Plaza, *South Rim*

Cape Royal, *North Rim*

El Tovar Hotel, *Grand Canyon Village*

Hermits Rest, *South Rim*

Hoover Dam, *Boulder City*

Lees Ferry

Lookout Studio, *South Rim*

Powell Memorial, *South Rim*

Vermilion Cliffs, *near Lees Ferry*

Many other great hotels and restaurants enliven this area. For other favorites, look for the black stars as you read this chapter.

Updated by
Carrie Miner

THE GRAND CANYON is far more than an experience. It's an emotion. Ask anyone who's visited, hiked, worked, or lived hereabouts. Many think it deserves a greater superlative than just "Grand." The locals are about the most appreciative and vocal canyon enthusiasts. Each can refer you to dozens of favorite sites, trails, and scenic overlooks. Their lists may occasionally overlap, but rarely are they identical.

Although it's easy to list the statistics of the canyon—both geological and historical—that all becomes immaterial as you lose your breath when standing at the edge for the first sunrise or the thousandth sunset. As you gaze out from the rim, you're viewing 2 billion years of geologic history, exposed for all to see in the canyon's rock walls. There is more Paleozoic and Pre-Cambrian earth history on view here than anywhere else on the planet. As the river has carved its course through the canyon's walls, it has exposed fossil records that date from the very earliest living organisms.

Far below the rim, the Colorado River continues its timeless carving process. Prior to the completion of the Glen Canyon Dam in the 1960s, it's been estimated that an average of 400,000 tons of silt was carried away every day. That equates to 80,000 5-ton dump-truck loads—one per second, nonstop. During the last million years—give or take a few—some experts believe the Colorado may have actually flowed north instead of south.

If you were to travel from one end of the Grand Canyon to the other, you would journey just under 280 mi from Lees Ferry near the junction of the Paria and Colorado rivers in northern Arizona to the western border shared by Arizona and Nevada. At its deepest point, the canyon is nearly 6,000 ft. From the North Rim to the South Rim, the distance across varies from 18 mi to less than half a mile. However, to travel between rims by car requires a journey of 200 mi. Hiking steep and arduous trails from rim to rim is a strenuous trek of at least 21 mi. The earliest trails into the canyon were animal trails that were used and modified by the native people and later upgraded by miners. A rim-to-rim hike for the very fit is well worth the effort, though. You'll travel through four of the seven life zones—that is, regions sharing the same climate and plant and animal life—found in North America. To otherwise witness this, you'd need to travel south to north from the Mexican desert to the Canadian woods.

There is ample evidence of early habitation from ruins that are between 8,000 and 10,000 years old in some of the highest, most inaccessible areas of the canyon. The earliest inhabitants from Asia traveled over an ancient land bridge across the Bering Strait some 11,000 years ago. These Paleo-Indians were nomadic peoples known as Elephant Hunters, whose existence depended upon hunting large prehistoric elephants, mastodons, and mammoths. Then, about 1,500 years ago, the Puebloan people more popularly known as the Anasazi (a name that means both "ancient ones" and "enemy ancestors") arrived on the scene. More than 2,000 of their sites have been found, including Tusayan Pueblo, some 3 mi west of Desert View in the South Rim. The last of the Native Americans to occupy the region were the Navajo, who came into the area some 600 years ago. Their heritage can be traced back to the Athabascans of Canada.

The first Europeans to view the canyon were Spanish Conquistadors, who were more interested in finding the fabled Cíbola, the Seven Cities of Gold. Don Garcia Lopez de Cardenas's band spent four days vainly searching for a path to the bottom of the canyon. They were not able to reach the Colorado River to obtain the water they so desperately needed and left uninspired and disappointed.

The first recorded Americans to visit the region were an army survey party seeking an alternate southern supply route to Utah. They, too, left in despair and recorded that the canyon was of dubious value. Then, in 1869, John Wesley Powell undertook a famous voyage down the Colorado that created the first everlasting interest in the Grand Canyon. In 1908 the area was declared a national monument, and in 1919 Congress passed legislation making it a national park.

Today, less than a century later, millions of people each year stand in awe at the canyon and leave with a sense of fulfillment and realization that they have witnessed nature at her finest. "Leave it as it is," President Teddy Roosevelt proclaimed. "You can not improve on it. Keep it for your children, your children's children, and for all who come after you as the one great sight which every American should see."

Exploring the Grand Canyon

Although the average length of stay for the South Rim is about a half-day, you'll need to spend several days here if you want to get the real "feel" of this very special place. A word of caution is in order though— *plan ahead*. Each year, fewer than 30,000 folks can be accommodated on rafting trips, and the famous mule rides into the canyon require at least a six-month advance reservation. The same is often true of lodging facilities, especially at the South Rim. Although there are cancellations, don't count on it.

Because the North Rim is less crowded than its southern counterpart, a trip here allows you to explore the Grand Canyon in a more pleasant and leisurely way. The terrain at North Rim and the surrounding Kaibab Plateau create an outdoor playground for all ages. Although there are lodgings available, your best bet is to pack your camping gear and hiking boots and take several days to explore the lush Kaibab Forest and the highest, most dramatic rim views.

If you wish to explore the rest of northwestern Arizona, give yourself another day or two at the least. Kingman and Lake Havasu are a bit farther off the beaten path. Lake Mead, however, is on the way to Las Vegas from the Grand Canyon, so it's possible to make a quick stop at Hoover Dam or in Boulder City if you are driving back to Las Vegas to catch your flight home.

About the Restaurants

Throughout the Grand Canyon region, most visitors seek out restaurants that offer fast food, standard American fare, and Native American specialties at reasonable prices, all of which exist in great abundance. One exception to this rule is El Tovar, the oldest existing hotel in the canyon and a pleasant surprise for anyone expecting traditional National Park Service dining. Though dress is casual, you might want to don your best jeans for a meal in its dining room.

About the Hotels

As you might expect, the large number of visitors touring Grand Canyon National Park makes room reservations a must, especially during the busy summer season when rooms on both rims book up fast. You might find a last-minute cancellation, but you shouldn't count on it. If you can't find accommodations on the South Rim or in Tusayan (the development of hotels and restaurants 7 mi south of Grand Canyon Village), you can find lodging 60 mi south in Williams or 80 mi southeast in Flagstaff. While lodging in Tusayan and at the South Rim will keep you close to the action, the frenetic activity and crowded facilities are off-putting to

3

If you have 2 or 3 days

Begin your adventure in 🏠 **Williams** ㉓ ▶, west of Flagstaff on I–40, which runs roughly parallel to the old Route 66. It's fun to stay overnight in this lively western town with some good shopping and dining. Next morning, board the Grand Canyon Railway, which will carry you to the South Rim of the canyon. You'll want several hours to explore the South Rim area and Canyon Village. Taxis and shuttle buses can transport you into Tusayan to view the Grand Canyon IMAX film. There's authentic Native American entertainment each weeknight at the Grand Hotel In Tusayan. You can spend the night here or in one of the lodges in 🏠 **Grand Canyon Village.** The next morning, take a tour of the **Village Rim** ⑩– ⑱; then take the afternoon train back to Williams. If you decide to spend the evening in Tusayan, you'll have time the next morning for a hike or an exciting airplane or helicopter tour.

If you are more adventurous and a hardy hiker, you might consider going to 🏠 **Havasu Canyon.** Hike 8 mi down into the canyon to the small village of Supai and the Havasupai Lodge. It's a healthy drive to the trailhead, and you'll need a Havasupai tribal permit to hike here; however, it's an unforgettable hike. Reservations are required for staying at the lodge and are highly recommended for the backpacker's campground. You'll need plenty of time and water for your rigorous climb back to the rim. You might even consider returning to the top by mule.

If you have 4 or 5 days

To capture the full "canyon" experience, absorb it from above and from within. This trip will require reservations many months in advance. After spending your first night in one of the lodges at 🏠 **Grand Canyon Village,** ▶ take the mule-pack journey from the **Trailhead** ⑭, which stops on an especially scenic plateau and includes a trailside lunch. Arrive at 🏠 **Phantom Ranch** for dinner and a welcome night's rest. Next morning, return by mule to the South Rim. Another day or two at the canyon's rim, staying in 🏠 **Tusayan** or at the 🏠 **Cameron Trading Post** ㉕, will round out your experience.

If you have 7 to 10 days

If you've set aside a week or more, you can create a lifetime of memories by hiking, flightseeing, and mule-touring into the canyon and white-water rafting along the Colorado River. As time permits, try to schedule a trip to the North Rim for an entirely different view and "feel" of the canyon, or go northwest and visit **Lake Mead** ㊵ and view **Hoover Dam** ㊴.

some people. If you don't mind the hour-long jaunt to and from Williams, the cozy mountain town can give you a respite from the multitudes at the South Rim and also a break on prices for food and lodging. Even though the North Rim is dramatically less crowded than the South Rim, the number of rooms is severely limited. With short notice, the best time to find a room on the South Rim is during the winter months (the North Rim is closed from mid-October through mid-May). The snow only increases the canyon's sublime beauty, which makes up for the chance of encountering icy roads and chilly winds.

WHAT IT COSTS				
$$$$	**$$$**	**$$**	**$**	**¢**
RESTAURANTS over $30	$20–$30	$12–$20	$8–$12	under $8
HOTELS over $250	$175–$250	$120–$175	$70–$120	under $70

Restaurant prices are per person for a main course at dinner. Hotel prices are for two people in a standard double room in high season, excluding taxes and service charges.

Timing

There's not a bad time to visit the canyon, though summer and spring-break season are the busiest times. Each season brings new delights. Spring heralds colorful blankets of wildflowers. In summer, afternoon thunderstorms paint the canyon walls, darkening the colorful strata. Autumn color on the canyon oaks and snow-capped stone create images of change and peace in the fall and winter months. March is the month with the best chance for snow at the South Rim. Since the North Rim gets considerable snowfall, the highways and facilities are closed from mid-October until mid-May. The South Rim, open year-round, is an exposed high-desert region, where the weather changes on a whim. Thanksgiving, Christmas, and New Year's can also get quite busy; this also marks the time of year when you will most likely find a room on short notice.

The Grand Canyon covers 1,900 square mi on the Colorado Plateau; elevations range from 1,200 to 9,100 ft, which means that climatic conditions in the region vary immensely. Rainfall, for example, reaches more than 25 inches annually at the North Rim, while the South Rim collects but 16 inches in a typical year. The North Rim accumulates considerably more snow—about 130 inches per year—compared to less than half of that at the South Rim. Temperatures vary widely, too. In summer, the canyon floor may easily reach 115°F, at the South Rim temperatures rarely exceed 90°F, and it's seldom more than 80°F at the North Rim.

Numbers in the text correspond to numbers in the margin and on the Grand Canyon South Rim, Grand Canyon North Rim, and Northwest Arizona, & Lake Mead Maps.

Exploring the Grand Canyon & Northwest Arizona

The Grand Canyon encompasses 277 mi of the Colorado River, cutting 1 mi deep along Arizona's northwestern corner. Popular attractions on the heavily visited South Rim include Grand Canyon Village, Village Rim, Desert View Drive, and Hermit Road. Westward from Page you'll find the 14,000-square-mi Arizona Strip, an isolated region separated from the rest of the state by the immense gorge. From Fredonia, at Arizona's northern border, you're less than 35 mi to Zion National Park, yet you'd have to drive nearly 350 mi across three states to get from Fredonia to the county seat in Kingman. Because this region is so isolated, it is less visited than the easily accessible South Rim. Havasu Canyon, near the center of the park on the southern side, offers another respite from the crowds. Finally, at the western end of the Grand Canyon, the Colorado pauses at Hoover Dam and Lake Mead, the largest man-made body of water in the United States, which is known for its plentiful recreation areas.

THE SOUTH RIM & ENVIRONS

Traveling the final 7 mi across the Coconino Plateau past the village of Tusayan, you won't be aware of the canyon until you are nearly on top

3

Hiking

Hikers can choose from a plethora of canyon trails including everything from an easy rim hike to a strenuous trek into the depths of this massive gorge. Even though an immense network of trails winds through the Grand Canyon, the popular corridor trails are recommended for the first overnight trip in the canyon for hikers new to the region. Although permits are not required for day hikes, you must have a backcountry permit for longer trips. Some of the more popular paths and trails are listed in this chapter, and more detailed information and maps can be obtained from the Backcountry Information Center.

Mountain Biking

Bikers wanting to see the South Rim of the Grand Canyon on two wheels might be disappointed by the experience due to the narrow shoulders on park roads and the heavy traffic. Bicycles are prohibited on park trails with the exception of the Greenway System, which is currently under development on the South Rim, so the opportunities for off-road biking are also limited here. However, mountain bikers heading to the North Rim will enjoy testing the many dirt access roads, including the 17-mi trek to Point Sublime. It's a rarity to spot other people any time of the year on these primitive roads. Rangers say the best bet for mountain bikers is the Rainbow Rim Trail, which goes along the North Rim of the canyon; the 18-mi, one-way trail begins at Parissawampitts and then travels past four other fantastic viewpoints—Fence, Locust, North Timp, and Timp—winding through a ponderosa pine forest and up and down through side canyons, aspen groves, and pristine meadows.

Rafting

Those who have taken a white-water raft trip down the Colorado River often list it as one of their most memorable lifetime experiences. Trips begin at Lees Ferry, a few miles below the Glen Canyon Dam near Page. There are tranquil half- and full-day float trips from the Glen Canyon Dam to Lees Ferry as well as raft trips that run from three days to three weeks. Many of these voyages end at Phantom Ranch at the bottom of the Grand Canyon at river mile 87. You'll encounter some good white water along the way, including Lava Falls, which is considered by many to be the wildest navigable rapids on the continent.

of it. However, once you arrive, you'll understand why the National Park Service is working to improve shuttle service and parking conditions. But don't be too discouraged by the unsettled parking conditions; there are shuttles to most of the scenic overlooks, the visitor center, to Tusayan, and most of the points of interest within the park. You may not be able to park within a block or two of your destination if you visit during peak periods, but didn't you come here for some exercise, too?

A fee of $20 per vehicle (regardless of the number of passengers) is collected at the East Entrance near Cameron and also at the South Entrance near Tusayan; pedestrians and cyclists pay $10 per person. In all cases, this fee is for one week's access. The entrance gates are open 24 hours but are generally staffed from about 7 AM to 7 PM. If you arrive when there's no one at the gate, you may enter legally without paying. A word

BEATING THE CROWDS AT THE CANYON

T'S HARD TO COMMUNE with nature when you've spent time searching for a parking place, dodging video cams, and stepping away from strollers. However, this scenario is only likely to occur during the very peak months of mid-May through mid-October. In peak season, avoid the noon inbound rush at the South Rim by getting an early start. For the most part, challenges will be finding lodging within the park and reserving a saddle for the mule trek down the canyon trails. Make your reservations well in advance, especially in the summer. If you want to escape the crowds that gather at the South Rim in summer, here are a few alternative suggestions.

Take another route

You might simply choose to take another route to the South Rim, avoiding the traditional highways AZ 64 and U.S. 180 from Flagstaff. U.S. 89 north from Flagstaff takes you past the Sunset Crater and Wupatki national monuments. When you reach the Cameron Trading Post at U.S. 64, take a break (you can even stay here). This is a good place to shop, as there's a large selection of Native American artifacts, souvenirs and the usual postcards, dream-catchers, recordings, and T-shirts. There's also high-quality Navajo rugs, jewelry, and other authentic handicrafts. You can sample Navajo tacos before heading out. U.S. 64 to the west takes you directly into the park at the East Entrance, and en route you're be treated to some eye-popping scenery along the Little Colorado River Gorge. It's 25 mi from the Grand Canyon East Entrance to the visitor center at Canyon View Information Plaza.

Bypass the South Rim altogether

When you reach Cameron, continue north on U.S. 89 and left onto U.S. 89A at Bitter Springs. En route you'll pass the area known as Vermilion Cliffs. At Jacob Lake, take AZ 67 directly to the Grand Canyon North Rim. As the crow flies, its 10 mi across the canyon; however, by car, it's an additional 210 mi—but well worth the effort. The road to the North Rim closes in mid-October because of heavy snow, but in summer months and early fall, it's a wonderful alternative to beat the crowds at the South Rim. Those who make the North Rim trip will insist it offers the most beautiful scenic views and the best hiking.

Take the Grand Canyon Railway

Many visitors decide to add another ingredient to their Grand Canyon visit by taking the historic Grand Canyon Railway from the western town of Williams. The train departs from the depot every morning at 9:30 sharp (except Christmas Eve and Christmas Day) and makes the 65-mi journey in 2¼ hours. There's entertainment aboard and other unexpected adventures en route. You can do the round-trip in a single day; however, you may choose to stay overnight at the South Rim and return to Williams the following afternoon.

---

to the wise—there are no refunds for bad weather, something to keep in mind if you are traveling during the unpredictable winter months.

Tusayan

81 mi northwest of Flagstaff on U.S. 180.

The village of Tusayan, the gateway to the South Entrance of the national park, is 7 mi from Grand Canyon Village on the South Rim. Here you'll find basic amenities, including restaurants and motels, an IMAX theater, several stores, and an airport that serves as a starting point for airplane and helicopter tours of the canyon.

At the **Grand Canyon IMAX Theater** you can watch river runners battle rapids, experience the Grand Canyon from the air, and discover the canyon's natural history in a 34-minute film, *Grand Canyon—The Hid-*

den Secrets, on an 82-ft-wide screen that stands six stories high. At the theater, you'll also find an **Arizona Tourist Information Center,** where you can schedule and purchase air tours and daily Colorado River trips. ⊠ *AZ 64/U.S. 180* ☎ *928/638–2203 or 928/638–2468* ⊕ *www. grandcanyonimaxtheater.com* ☞ *$10* ⊙ *Mar.–Oct., daily 8:30–8:30; Nov.–Feb., daily 10:30–6:30; shows every hr on the ½ hr.*

Where to Stay & Eat

For approximate costs, *see* the dining and lodging price chart at the beginning of this chapter.

$$–$$$ ✕ **The Coronado Room.** When pizza and burgers just won't do, the restaurant at the Best Western Grand Canyon Squire Inn is the best upscale choice in Tusayan. The menu is primarily Continental with some Southwestern touches, and you'll find everything from escargots to elk steak. But only dinner is served, from 5 to 10 PM daily. Even though the Coronado Room takes pride in its fine-dining atmosphere, dress is casual and comfortable, as is most everything about the Grand Canyon. Reservations are usually a good idea, particularly in the busy season. ⊠ *AZ 64/ U.S. 180* ☎ *928/638–2681* ⊟ *AE, D, DC, MC, V* ⊙ *No lunch.*

$$–$$$ ▣ **Holiday Inn Express Hotel and Suites.** The main building of this hotel at the south end of Tusayan contains most of the rooms, which are modern but plain. You'll get a better deal at the Arizona Rooms, an adjacent all-suites annex, which has Western-theme suites with separate sitting rooms, coffeemakers, and VCRs—amenities you won't find next door. ⊠ *AZ 64/U.S. 180* ⌂ *Box 3251, Grand Canyon 86023* ☎ *928/ 638–3000 or 888/538–5353* 🖷 *928/638–2747* ⊕ *www.hiexpress.com* ⇥ *163 rooms, 30 suites* ⌂ *Some microwaves, some refrigerators, cable TV, some in-room VCRs, pool* ⊟ *AE, MC, V.*

★ $–$$$ ▣ **Best Western Grand Canyon Squire Inn.** About 2 mi south of the park's South Entrance, this motel lacks the historic charm of the older lodges at the canyon rim, but it has more amenities, including a small cowboy museum in the lobby, a bowling alley, and an upscale gift shop. The rooms are spacious and furnished in Southwestern style. Those in the rear have a view of the woods. The Coronado Dining Room has an adventurous menu and good service. ⊠ *AZ 64/U.S. 180* ⌂ *Box 130, Grand Canyon 86023* ☎ *928/638–2681 or 800/622–6966* 🖷 *928/638–2782* ⊕ *www. bestwestern.com* ⇥ *250 rooms, 4 suites* ⌂ *Restaurant, coffee shop, 2 tennis courts, pool, gym, hair salon, sauna, billiards, bowling, bar, laundry facilities, concierge, meeting rooms, travel services* ⊟ *AE, D, DC, MC, V.*

★ $–$$ ▣ **The Grand Hotel.** At the south end of Tusayan, this popular hotel has bright, clean rooms decorated in Southwestern colors. The warm lobby area has a stone and timber design and cozy seating areas. The restaurant offers good steaks, Mexican fare, and barbecue. At the bar, you can sit on a saddle that was once used for the canyon mule trips. Don't miss the well-stocked, reasonably priced gift shop. ⊠ *AZ 64/U.S. 180* ⌂ *Box 3319, Grand Canyon 86023* ☎ *928/638–3333* 🖷 *928/638–3131* ⊕ *www.gcanyon.com* ⇥ *120 rooms* ⌂ *Restaurant, pool, gym, hot tub, bar, meeting rooms, no-smoking rooms* ⊟ *AE, DC, MC, V.*

$–$$ ▣ **Quality Inn & Suites Grand Canyon.** The airy atrium here, which has a hot tub and lounge, distinguishes this chain motel. You can access first-floor rooms from the atrium or from the parking lot. All the rooms, in soothing shades of light blue, peach, or tan, have coffeemakers and two sinks. A buffet breakfast at the restaurant will fortify you for a day at the canyon. ⊠ *AZ 64/U.S. 180* ⌂ *Box 520, Grand Canyon 86023* ☎ *928/638–2673 or 800/221–2222* 🖷 *928/638–9537* ⊕ *www. hotelchoice.com* ⇥ *176 rooms, 56 suites* ⌂ *Restaurant, some minibars, pool, lounge* ⊟ *AE, D, DC, MC, V.*

¢–$$ ▦ **Rodeway Inn Red Feather Lodge.** Some of the rooms here are worn around the edges, but this motel is still a good value, largely because of the pool, whirlpool, and game room for children. A restaurant serves standard American food. ⊠ *AZ 64/U.S. 180* ⌾ *Box 1460, Grand Canyon 86023* ☎ *928/638–2414 or 800/538–2345* 🖷 *928/638–9216* ⊕ *www.redfeatherlodge.com* ↩ *230 rooms* ♿ *Restaurant, cable TV with movies and video games, pool, hot tub, video game room* ▭ *AE, DC, MC, V.*

¢ ⛺ **Grand Canyon Camper Village.** More a city than a village, this popular RV park and campground has 200 utility hook-ups and 50 tent sites. Hook-ups for two people run $22 for electric, $24 for water and electric, and $26 for full. There is an additional fee of $2 for each additional person over the age of 12. Tent sites are $18. Reservations are a good idea during the busy spring and summer seasons. ♿ *Flush toilets, full hook-ups, dump station, showers, picnic tables, general store, playground* ↩ *200 full hook-ups, 50 tent sites* ⊠ *Off AZ 64/U.S. 180, Grand Canyon* ⌾ *Box 490, 86023* ☎ *928/638–2887* ⊠ *$18–$26* ☼ *Open Mar.–Nov.*

¢ ⛺ **Ten X Campground.** Two miles south of Tusayan, this campground offers 70 sites with water and pit toilets but no electrical hook-ups or showers. Unlike in campgrounds in the Grand Canyon National Park itself, campfires are allowed. Learn about the surrounding ponderosa pine forest on a self-guided nature trail or check out one of the evening, ranger-led weekend programs. No reservations are accepted, except for groups of six or more. ♿ *Pit toilets, drinking water, fire pits, grills, picnic tables* ↩ *70 tent sites* ⊠ *Kaibab National Forest, 9 mi south of Grand Canyon National Park east of AZ 64/U.S. 180* ⌾ *Tusayan Ranger District, Box 3088, Grand Canyon 86023* ☎ *928/638–2443* ⊕ *www. fs.fed.us/r3/kai* ⊠ *$10* ♿ *Reservations not accepted* ☼ *Open May–Oct.*

Sports & the Outdoors

HORSEBACK RIDING   You can rent gentle horses at the **Apache Stables** (⊠ U.S. 180 ☎ 928/ 638–2891 ⊕ www.apachestables.com), at the former Moqui Lodge, which is now closed, for $30.50 an hour or $55.50 for a two-hour guided tour of the Kaibab National Forest. A four-hour Desert View ride along the South Rim goes for $95.50; a campfire trail ride is $40.50; and the campfire wagon ride is $12.50. The stables open in March, and rides are offered, weather permitting, through the end of November.

Grand Canyon Village

⚑   Most of the services at the South Rim are concentrated in Grand Canyon Village, where you'll find accommodations and dining as well as many attractions. Grand Canyon Village and the Village Rim can be explored on foot via a paved footpath that runs along the rim, about 1 mi round-trip. You can leave your car at the El Tovar parking lot, but more often than not, this lot is full, so try parking along the railroad tracks below the historic hotel.

⓯   **Bright Angel Lodge** was built in 1935 from Oregon pine logs and native stone; rustic cabins are set off from the main building. The rocks used to make the "geologic" fireplace are arranged in the order in which they are layered in the Grand Canyon, and the history room displays memorabilia from the South Rim's early years. The lodge's soda fountain has the distinction of selling the most Breyer's ice cream in the United States.

★ ⓮   **Bright Angel Trailhead** is the starting point for one of America's most famous hiking trails. It began as a path used by bighorn sheep, later used by the Havasupai, and was improved and widened in the late 1800s for

Grand Canyon South Rim

GRAND CANYON NATIONAL PARK

4 miles
6 km

KEY

▲ Start of itinerary

Venus Temple

Cape Royal

Vishnu Temple

Rama Shrine

Krishna Shrine

Shiva Temple

Solomon Temple

Wotans Throne

Colorado River

INNER GORGE

Deva Temple

Zoroaster Temple

Brahma Temple

Buddha Temple

North Kaibab Trail

Bright Angel Creek

Phantom Ranch

Cheops Pyramid

Newton Butte

Yaki Point ③

South Kaibab Trail

Tonto Trail

Bright Angel Trail

Indian Gardens

Grand Canyon Village ①②⑩⑱

See Inset

DESERT VIEW DRIVE

PARK BOUNDARY

Grandview Point ④

Moran Point ⑤

⑥

Lipan Point ⑦

Navajo Point ⑧

⑨ Desert View and the Watchtower

Tusayan Ruin and Museum

64 East Entrance

TO CAMERON

64

South Entrance

Tusayan

64

180

Grand Canyon Airport

⑳⓸ Williams

Osiris Temple

Tower of Ra

Granite Rapids

Boucher Rapids

Hermit Rapids

Colorado River

Hopi Point ⑲

⑳ Mohave Point

Abyss ㉑

Pima Point ㉒

Hermits Rest ㉓
(closed to private vehicles in summer)

Hermit Rd.

GRAND CANYON VILLAGE

Mather Point ①

Canyon View Information Plaza ②

Village Loop Drive

Park Headquarters

Hopi House ⑩

Lookout Studio ⑫

El Tovar Hotel ⑪

Kalb Studio

⑬

Bright Angel Lodge ⑮

Backcountry Information Center

Bright Angel Trail

180

Maswik Lodge

Bright Angel Trailhead ⑭

Powell Memorial ⑱

Maricopa Point ⑰

Trailview Overlook ⑯

1200 yards

1200 meters

prospectors. It's now a well-maintained path for foot and mule traffic. Before you start your trek to the bottom, keep in mind that the trail descends 5,510 ft to the Colorado River. Be certain to have an adequate supply of water, food, and sunscreen before you begin. Rangers discourage hikers from attempting to make it to Phantom Ranch on the river and back up to the South Rim as a day hike. Permits are required for overnight hikes. Directly south of Trailhead are rails once used by the Santa Fe trains and the barn that houses the famous mules.

★ ❷ The National Park Service's **Canyon View Information Plaza,** near Mather Point, cannot be reached by private vehicle. It's just a short walk from Mather Point, or you can take one of the free shuttle buses from anywhere in the village area. Here, park rangers can answer questions and assist in planning your excursions. This orientation center has the usual— rest rooms, bookstore, and a schedule for ranger-led hikes and lectures. ⊠ *East side of Grand Canyon Village, about 2 mi east of El Tovar Hotel* ☏ *928/638–7888* ✉ *Free after $20 per vehicle park admission* ☉ *Late May–early Sept., daily 8–6; early Sept.–late May, daily 8–5.*

★ ⓫ **El Tovar Hotel** has been the man-made focal point of a visit to the South Rim since it opened in 1905, when it was recognized as the most elegant hotel west of the Mississippi. Built of Oregon pine logs at a cost of $250,000, it was designed as a cross between a Swiss chalet and a Norwegian villa. Originally, the hotel had a coal-fired generator for electricity, a greenhouse to supply fresh vegetables, a henhouse for eggs, and its own diary herd for milk. When the weather gets chilly, you'll be glad to sit for a spell in front of the rustic lobby's stone fireplace for some good people-watching.

⓾ **Hopi House,** a multi-story structure of rock and mortar, was modeled after buildings found in the Hopi village of Oraibi, Arizona, the oldest continuously inhabited community in the United States. An attempt by the Fred Harvey Company to encourage Southwest Native American crafts at the turn of the 20th century, Hopi House was one of the first gift shops to open in the Grand Canyon, where it catered to the desires of early westbound rail passengers.

⓭ **Kolb Studio,** built in 1904, was the Grand Canyon's original photo studio. The Kolb brothers, Ellsworth and Emery, bought a photo studio in Flagstaff and moved the equipment to the canyon. Since there was no water available at the rim, the brothers would photograph those taking the mule trip into the canyon. Then they would travel 4½ mi to the Indian Garden (visible from the studio window), where they set up a lab with the available water to process the film and prints, returning to the rim in time to sell the finished images to the mule riders. Emery operated the studio until his death in 1976 at age 95. The gallery displays photography, paintings, and crafts exhibits year-round. There's also a bookstore.

★ ⓬ Built in 1914 to compete with the Kolbs' photographic studio, **Lookout Studio** was designed by architect Mary Jane Colter to blend into the surrounding landscape. A paved trail at the rim leads here from El Tovar Hotel. The upstairs loft provides an excellent overlook into the gorge below and a good photo spot.

❶ **Mather Point,** about 4 mi north of the South Entrance, gives you the first glimpse of the canyon from one of the most impressive and accessible vista points on the rim—you can see nearly one quarter of the Grand Canyon. This overlook, named for the National Park Service's first director, Stephen Mather, yields extraordinary views of the Inner Gorge and the numerous buttes that rise out of the eroded chasm: Wotan's

Throne, Brahma Temple, Zoroaster Temple, and many others. This overlook can be very busy—to the point of overcrowding—during peak periods. The Grand Canyon Lodge, on the North Rim, is almost directly north from Mather Point and only 10 mi away—yet you have to drive nearly 210 mi to get from one spot to the other.

Where to Stay & Eat

If you want to get your first choice (especially the Lodge or El Tovar), it's a very good idea to make reservations as far in advance as possible, but there is often some option available even nearing the last minute. For approximate costs, *see* the dining and lodging price charts at the beginning of this chapter.

$$-$$$ ✕ **El Tovar Dining Room.** Modeled after a European hunting lodge, this FodorsChoice rustic 19th-century dining room built of hand-hewn logs and beamed ★ ceiling is worth a visit in itself. The cuisine is modern Southwestern, and it's open for breakfast, lunch, and dinner. El Tovar dishes up some fantastic food, which includes such dishes as hickory-smoked rainbow trout served with a wild rice salad and topped with an apple pine nut salsa and a New York strip steak framed with buttermilk-battered onion rings and pepper jack au gratin potatoes. ⊠ *El Tovar Hotel, West Rim Dr., Grand Canyon Village* 🕾 *928/638–2631* ⚮ *Reservations essential* 🖃 *AE, D, DC, MC, V.*

$$-$$$ ✕ **Arizona Room.** This casual Southwestern-style steak house serves chicken, steak, and seafood on a first-come, first-served basis. The food is standard fare and includes such steak-house favorites as prime rib, New York strip steak, and baby back ribs. The quality is no more than what you might expect at a mid-range steak house, though the prices reflect the restaurant's choice location. Nevertheless, the canyon views from the dining room are the best of any restaurant at the South Rim, which makes the experience worthwhile. The restaurant opens for dinner at 4:30; come early if you want to avoid the crowds. ⊠ *Lodge, West Rim Dr., Grand Canyon Village* 🕾 *928/638–2631* ⚮ *Reservations not accepted* 🖃 *AE, D, DC, MC, V* ☉ *Closed Jan.–mid-Feb.*

¢ ✕ **Yvapai Lodge Cafeteria.** Locals and park employees favor the homestyle food at Yavapai Lodge in Grand Canyon Village, which offers dining on a budget. Fast-food favorites here include the pastries, burgers, and pizza. Open for breakfast, lunch, and dinner, the cafeteria also serves up other basics including pasta, chicken potpie, fried catfish, and fried chicken. ⊠ *Grand Canyon Village* 🕾 *928/638–2631* ⚮ *Reservations not accepted* 🖃 *AE, D, DC, MC, V.*

$$-$$$$ 🏨 **El Tovar Hotel.** A registered National Historic Landmark, El Tovar was built in 1905 of Oregon pine logs and native stone. The hotel's proximity to all of the canyon's facilities, its European hunting-lodge atmosphere, and its renowned dining room make it the best place to stay on the South Rim. It's usually booked well in advance (up to nine months ahead), though it's easier to get a room here during winter months. Only three suites have canyon views—the Fred Harvey, Mary Jane Colter, and El Tovar suites—and these are usually booked two years in advance, but you can enjoy the view anytime from the cocktail-lounge back porch. ⊠ *West Rim Dr., Grand Canyon Village* 🕾 *Box 699, Grand Canyon 86023* 🕾 *303/297–2757 reservations only; 928/638–2631 direct to hotel (no reservations)* 🖷 *303/297–3175 reservations only; 928/638–2855 direct to hotel (no reservations)* ⊕ *www.grandcanyonlodges.com* ⇆ *70 rooms, 8 suites* ⚭ *Restaurant, room service, some in-room hot tubs, some refrigerators, bar; no room phones, no room TVs, no smoking* 🖃 *AE, D, DC, MC, V.*

$-$$ 🏨 **Kachina Lodge.** This contemporary motel-style lodge is next to the El Tovar Hotel in Grand Canyon Village. Half of the rooms have a partial canyon view ($10 extra). The rooms with two queen beds are your best bet for families and for people with physical disabilities. Check in at El Tovar to the east. Kids under 16 are free. ⊠ *West Rim Dr., Grand Canyon Village* ☎ *Box 699, Grand Canyon 86023* ☏ *303/297–2757 reservations only; 928/638–2631 direct to hotel (no reservations)* 🖷 *303/297–3175 reservations only* ⊕ *www.grandcanyonlodges.com* ⇥ *50 rooms* ♿ *No-smoking rooms; no a/c, no room phones, no room TVs* ▭ *AE, D, DC, MC, V.*

$–$$ ▦ **Thunderbird Lodge.** This motel-style lodge is next to Bright Angel Lodge in Grand Canyon Village. For $10 more, you can get a room with a partial view of the canyon. All rooms have two queen beds. Check in at Lodge, the next hotel to the west. Kids under 16 stay free. ⊠ *West Rim Dr., Grand Canyon Village* ☎ *Box 699, Grand Canyon 86023* ☏ *303/297–2757 reservations only, 928/638–2631 direct to hotel (no reservations)* 🖷 *303/297–3175 reservations only* ⊕ *www.grandcanyonlodges. com* ⇥ *55 rooms* ♿ *No-smoking rooms; no a/c, no room phones, no room TVs* ▭ *AE, D, DC, MC, V.*

¢–$ ▦ **Bright Angel Lodge.** Famed architect Mary Jane Colter designed this
1935 log-and-stone structure, which sits within a few yards of the canyon rim and blends superbly with the natural environment. It offers as much atmosphere as El Tovar for about half the price. Accommodations are in motel-style rooms or cabins. Most rooms in the main lodge share baths; cabins, some with fireplaces and/or canyon views (No. 6158 has both), are scattered among the pines. Expect historic charm and bargain prices but not luxury. The restaurant serves family-style meals all day; the Arizona Room serves dinner only. ⊠ *West Rim Dr., Grand Canyon Village* ☎ *Box 699, Grand Canyon 86023* ☏ *303/297–2757 reservations only, 928/638–2631 direct to hotel (no reservations)* 🖷 *303/297–3175 reservations only; 928/638–2876 direct to hotel (no reservations)* ⊕ *www.grandcanyonlodges.com* ⇥ *30 rooms, 6 with shared bath; 42 cabins* ♿ *Restaurant, coffee shop, bar; no a/c, no room phones, no TV in some rooms* ▭ *AE, D, DC, MC, V.*

¢–$ ▦ **Maswik Lodge.** At the southwest end of Grand Canyon Village, the lodge, named for a Hopi Kachina who is said to guard the canyon, is ¼ mi from the rim. Accommodations, nestled in the ponderosa pine forest, range from rustic cabins to more modern rooms. The rustic log cabins are the cheapest option but are available only in summer. Make sure to bring layered clothing if you stay here, because the rustic log cabins have neither heat nor a/c; regular rooms have heat but no a/c. Maswik cafeteria offers typical national park fare; there's a lounge here, too, where you can shoot pool, throw darts, or watch the big-screen TV. Kids under 16 stay free. ⊠ *Grand Canyon Village* ☎ *Box 699, Grand Canyon 86023* ☏ *303/297–2757 reservations only, 928/638–2631 direct to hotel (no reservations)* 🖷 *303/297–3175 reservations only* ⊕ *www.grandcanyonlodges.com* ⇥ *250 rooms, 28 cabins* ♿ *Cafeteria, lounge, shop, no-smoking rooms; no a/c, no room phones, no room TVs* ▭ *AE, D, DC, MC, V.*

$ ▦ **Yavapai Lodge.** The largest motel-style lodge in the park is tucked in a piñon and juniper pygmy forest at the eastern end of Grand Canyon Village, near the RV park. The basic rooms are conveniently near the park's general store, the visitor center (½ mi), and the rim (¼ mi). The cafeteria, open for breakfast, lunch, and dinner, serves standard park service food. ⊠ *Grand Canyon Village* ☎ *Box 699, Grand Canyon 86023* ☏ *303/297–2757 reservations only, 928/638–2631 direct to hotel (no reservations)* 🖷 *303/297–3175 reservations only* ⊕ *www. grandcanyonlodges.com* ⇥ *358 rooms* ♿ *Cafeteria, shop, no-smoking rooms; no a/c, no room phones, no room TVs* ▭ *AE, D, DC, MC, V* ☉ *Closed Jan.–Feb.*

¢–$ ▥ **Phantom Ranch.** Phantom Ranch, in a grove of cottonwood trees on the canyon floor, is accessible only to hikers, mule trekkers, or rafters. The wood-and-stone buildings were originally a hunting camp built in 1922. For hikers, there are 40 dormitory beds and 14 beds in cabins, all with shared baths. Seven additional cabins are reserved for mule riders, who buy their trips as a package. The restaurant at Phantom Ranch, probably the most remote eating establishment in the United States, serves family-style meals, with breakfast, dinner, and box lunches available. Food and lodging reservations should be made 9 to 11 months ahead. ⊠ *On canyon floor at intersection of the and Kaibab trails* ☎ *303/297–2757 reservations only (no direct phone)* 🖷 *303/297–3175 reservations only* ⊕ *www.grandcanyonlodges.com* ⇨ *4 dormitories and 2 cabins for hikers, 7 cabins with outside showers for mule riders* ⚿ *Dining room; no a/c, no phones, no TVs* 🖃 *AE, D, DC, MC, V.*

¢ ⛺ **Campground.** This free campground is near Phantom Ranch on the South and North Kaibab trails, at the bottom of the canyon. There are toilet facilities and running water but no showers. A backcountry permit, which serves as your reservation, is required to stay here. ⚿ *Flush toilets, drinking water, picnic tables* ⇨ *32 tent sites* ⊠ *Intersection of South and North Kaibab trails, Grand Canyon* ✆ *Backcountry Office, Box 129, Grand Canyon 86023* ☎ *928/638–7875* 🖃 *Free* ⚒ *Reservations essential* ⊙ *Open year-round.*

¢ ⛺ **Indian Garden.** About halfway down the canyon is this free campground, located en route to Phantom Ranch on the Trail. Running water and toilet facilities are available, but there are no showers. A backcountry permit, which serves as a reservation, is required. ⚿ *Pit toilets, drinking water, picnic tables* ⇨ *15 tent sites* ⊠ *Trail, Grand Canyon* ✆ *Backcountry Office, Box 129, Grand Canyon 86023* ☎ *928/638–7875* 🖃 *Free* ⚒ *Reservations essential* ⊙ *Open year-round.*

¢ ⛺ **Mather Campground.** Mather is a National Park Service campground with both RV and tent sites but no hook-ups; it has flush toilets, water, showers, and a coin laundry. No reservations are accepted from December to March, but during the rest of the year they are a good idea, especially during the busy spring and summer seasons. ⚿ *Flush toilets, grills, picnic tables* ⇨ *97 RV sites, 190 tent sites* ⊠ *Off Village Loop Dr., Grand Canyon Village* ✆ *National Park Reservation Service, Box 1600, Cumberland, MD 21501* ☎ *800/365–2267* ⊕ *reservations.nps.gov/index.cfm* 🖃 *$15* ⊙ *Open year-round.*

¢ ⛺ **Trailer Village.** This campground in Grand Canyon Village has RV sites with full hook-ups and bathroom facilities, though they are ½ mi from the campground. The fee is good for two people; there is an extra fee of $2 for each additional person over the age of 16. No reservations are accepted from December to March, but they are a good idea the rest of the year, especially during the busy spring and summer seasons. ⚿ *Flush toilets, full hook-ups, drinking water, laundry facilities, showers* ⇨ *78 RV sites* ⊠ *Off Village Loop Dr., Grand Canyon Village* ☎ *303/297–2757 reservations only, 928/638–2631 direct to village (no reservations)* 🖷 *303/297–3175 reservations only* ⊕ *www.xanterra.com* 🖃 *$25* ⊙ *Open year-round.*

Nightlife & the Arts

If you are looking for exciting nightlife of any variety, you're in the wrong place. Nightlife in these parts consists of watching a full moon above the soaring buttes of the Grand Canyon, crawling into your bedroll beside some lonely canyon trail, or attending a free evening program on area lore. The following Grand Canyon properties have cocktail lounges: **El Tovar Hotel** (upstairs piano bar), **Lodge** (occasional live entertainment), ★ **Maswik Lodge** (sports bar). The **Grand Canyon Chamber Music Festival**

(☎ 928/638–9215 or 800/997–8285) is held each September at the Shrine of Ages amphitheater and features nearly a dozen concerts. In the early 1980s, music aficionados Robert Bonfiglio and Clare Hoffman hiked through the Grand Canyon and decided the stunning spectacle should be accompanied by the strains of a symphony. One of the park rangers agreed, and the wandering musicians performed an impromptu concert. Encouraged by the experience, Bonfiglio and Hoffman started up the Grand Canyon Music Festival in 1984. Concerts are held Friday and Saturday evenings and several other nights during the course of the three-week event.

Sports & the Outdoors

HIKING It's important to remember that there are large elevation changes and, in summer, extreme temperature ranges in the Grand Canyon. **Carry plenty of water** and energy foods. Each year there are scores of unnecessary rescues simply because hikers underestimate the enormous size of the canyon, hike beyond their ability, or do not take with them sufficient quantities of food and water. Overnight hikes into the canyon require a backcountry permit (*see* Hiking Permits *in* the A to Z section at the end of this chapter).

If you've been driving too long and want some exercise along with great views of the canyon, it's an easy mile-long hike from the **Information Plaza to El Tovar Hotel**. There's a quiet wooded area for about ½ mi, and then the path runs along the rim for another ¾ mi.

The well-maintained **Bright Angel Trail** is one of the most popular and scenic hiking paths from the South Rim to the bottom of the canyon (9 mi). Rest houses are equipped with water at the 1½- and 3-mi points from May through September and at Indian Gardens year-round. Water is also available at Campground, 9¼ mi below the trailhead. Plateau Point, about 1½ mi below Indian Garden, is as far as you should attempt to go on a day hike. Trail is the easiest of all the footpaths into the canyon, but because the climb out from the bottom is an ascent of 5,510 ft, the trip should be attempted only by those in good physical condition and should be avoided in midsummer due to extreme heat. The top of the trail, a tight set of switchbacks called Jacob's Ladder, can be icy in winter. Note that you will be sharing the trail with mule trains, which have the right-of-way and sometimes leave unpleasant surprises in your path.

MULE TOURS Mule trips, which are run by **Xanterra Parks & Resorts** (☎ 303/297–2757 🖷 303/297–3175 ⊕ www.grandcanyonlodges.com), go down the precipitous trails to the Inner Gorge of the Grand Canyon and are nearly as well known as the canyon itself. But it's hard to get reservations unless you make them months in advance, especially in summer; write to the Reservations Department. These trips have been conducted since the early 1900s, and no one has ever been killed by a mule falling off a cliff. Nevertheless, the treks are not for the faint of heart or people in questionable health. Riders must be at least 4 ft 7 inches tall, weigh less than 200 pounds, and understand English. Pregnant women are not allowed to ride, and children under 15 must be accompanied by an adult. The all-day ride to Plateau Point costs $129.12 (lunch included). An overnight with a stay at Phantom Ranch at the bottom of the canyon is $350.39 ($623.30 for two) for one night, $493.76 ($832.55 for two) for two nights; meals are included in these prices.

SKIING Although you can't schuss down into the Grand Canyon, you can cross-country ski in the woods near the rim when there's enough snow. At the South Rim, **Delaware North General Store** (✉ Grand Canyon Village

☎ 928/638–2234 or 928/638–2262) rents equipment and can guide you to the best trails.

Shopping

Nearly every lodging facility and retail store at the South Rim stocks Native American arts and crafts and Grand Canyon books and souvenirs. **El Tovar Hotel Gift Shop** (✉ West Rim Dr., Grand Canyon Village ☎ 928/638–2631) carries Native American jewelry, rather expensive casual wear, and souvenir gifts. **Hopi House** (✉ West Rim Dr., east of El Tovar Hotel, Grand Canyon Village ☎ 928/638–2631) has the widest selection of Native American handicrafts in the vicinity. **Verkamp's** (✉ West Rim Dr., across from El Tovar Hotel, Grand Canyon Village ☎ 928/638–2242) is the best place on the South Rim to buy inexpensive souvenirs of your Grand Canyon adventure.

Desert View Drive

The breathtaking Desert View Drive proceeds east for about 25 mi along the South Rim from Grand Canyon Village to Desert View. Before beginning the drive, consider stopping to see the exhibits and attend the free lectures offered by park naturalists at Yavapai Observation Station. There are four marked picnic areas along the route and rest rooms at Tusayan Museum and Desert View. This is the road you come into the park on if you enter at the East Entrance.

A fee of $20 per vehicle (regardless of the number of passengers) is collected at the East Entrance near Cameron and also at the South Entrance near Tusayan. This fee is for one week's access. The entrance gates are open 24 hours but are generally staffed from about 7 AM to 7 PM. If you arrive when there's no one at the gate, you may enter legally without paying.

⑨ Desert View and the Watchtower make for a climactic final stop if you are driving Desert View Drive from Grand Canyon Village. They are also a dramatic beginning if you enter the park through the East Entrance. From the top of the 70-ft stone-and-mortar Watchtower even the muted hues of the distant Painted Desert to the east and the 3,000-ft-high Vermilion Cliffs rising from a high plateau near the Utah border are visible. In the chasm below, angling to the north toward Marble Canyon, you can see an imposing stretch of the Colorado River. The Watchtower houses a glass-enclosed observatory with powerful telescopes. Desert View originally served as a trading post; now the building is a small museum and information center. ✉ Desert View Dr., Grand Canyon ☎ 928/638–2736, 928/638–2360 trading post ⌨ Watchtower 25¢ ☉ Daily 8–7 or 8–8 in summer, daily 9–5 in winter.

④ About 7 mi east of Yaki Point, **Grandview Point** (✉ Desert View Dr., Grand Canyon), at an altitude of 7,496 ft, has large stands of ponderosa pine, piñon pine, oak, and juniper. The view from here is one of the finest in the canyon. To the northeast is a group of dominant buttes, including Krishna Shrine, Vishnu Temple, Rama Shrine, and Shiva Temple. A short stretch of the Colorado River is also visible. Directly below the point and accessible by the rugged Grandview Trail is Horseshoe Mesa, where you can see ruins of the Last Chance Copper Mine. Grandview Point was also the site of the Grandview Hotel, constructed in the late 1890s but closed in 1908; logs salvaged from the hotel were used for the Kiva Room of the Desert View and the Watchtower.

⑦ Lipan Point (✉ Desert View Dr., Grand Canyon), a mile northeast of Tusayan Ruin, is the canyon's widest point. From here you can get an astonishing visual profile of the gorge's geologic history, with a view of every eroded layer of the canyon. You can also see Unkar Delta, where a wide creek joins the Colorado to form powerful rapids and a broad beach. Ancestral Puebloan farmers worked the Unkar Delta for hundreds of years, growing corn, beans, squash, and melons.

⑤ Moran Point (⊠ Desert View Dr., Grand Canyon), about 5 mi east of Grandview Point, was named for American landscape artist Thomas Moran, who painted Grand Canyon scenes from many points on the rim but was especially fond of the play of light and shadows from this location. He first visited the canyon with John Wesley Powell in 1873, and his vivid canvases helped persuade Congress to create a national park at the Grand Canyon. "Thomas Moran's name, more than any other, with the possible exception of Major Powell's, is to be associated with the Grand Canyon," wrote the noted canyon photographer Ellsworth Kolb. It's fitting that Moran Point is a favorite spot for photographers and painters.

⑧ Just over 1 mi east of Lipan Point lies 7,461-ft-high **Navajo Point** (⊠ Desert View Dr., Grand Canyon), the probable site of the first Spanish descent into the canyon, in 1540. Just west of Navajo Point—the highest natural elevation on the South Rim, at 7,498 ft—is the head of the unmaintained Tanner Trail, a rugged route once favored by prospectors, rustlers (it's also called Horsethief Trail), and bootleggers.

⑥ Tusayan Ruin and Museum. Three miles east of Moran Point on the south

Fodor's Choice
★

side of the highway is this archaeological site, which contains evidence of early habitation in the Grand Canyon, and the accompanying museum, which provides plenty of information about ancestral Pueblo people who once lived here. *Tusayan* comes from a Hopi phrase meaning "country of isolated buttes," which certainly describes the scenery. The partially intact rock dwellings here were occupied for roughly 20 years around AD 1200 by 30 or so Native American hunters, farmers, and gatherers. They eventually moved on like so many others, perhaps pressured by drought and depletion of natural resources. The museum displays artifacts, models of the dwellings, and exhibits on modern tribes of the region. Free 30-minute guided tours—as many as five during the summer, fewer in winter—are given daily. ⊠ *Desert View Dr., 3 mi east of Moran Point, Grand Canyon* ☎ *928/638–2305* ⊠ *Free* ☺ *Daily 9–5.*

③ At **Yaki Point** (⊠ Desert View Dr., Grand Canyon), east of Grand Canyon Village on AZ 64, you can get an exceptional view of Wotan's Throne, a majestic flat-top butte named by François Matthes, a U.S. Geological Survey scientist who developed the first topographical map of the Grand Canyon. Due north is Buddha Temple, capped by limestone. Newton Butte, with its flat top of red sandstone, lies to the east. At Yaki Point the popular South Kaibab Trail starts the descent to the Inner Gorge, crosses the Colorado over a steel suspension bridge, and wends its way to rustic Phantom Ranch, the only lodging facility at the bottom of the Grand Canyon. If you plan to go more than a mile, carry water with you. If you encounter a mule train, the animals have the right-of-way. Move to the inside of the trail and wait as they pass. Yaki Point is accessible only by the park shuttle bus most of the year. Sometimes, during winter months when visitation is low, the road is open to private vehicles.

Where to Stay

¢ ⛺ **Desert View Campground.** Fifty RV (without hook-ups) and tent sites, flush toilets, and water are available on a first-come, first-served basis. ⛺ *Flush toilets, drinking water, grills, picnic tables* ⮫ *50 campsites*

WHAT'S FREE AT THE CANYON

WHILE YOU'RE HERE, *make sure you take advantage of the many freebies offered at Grand Canyon National Park. The most useful of these services is the system of free shuttle buses at the South Rim that will ease the road-weary with three routes winding through the park—Hermits Rest Route, Village Route, and Kaibab Trail Route. Of the bus routes, the Hermits Rest Route runs only from March through November; the other two run year-round, and the Kaibab Trail Route provides the only access to Yaki Point. Hikers coming or going from the Kaibab Trailhead can catch the Hikers Express, which departs three times each morning from the Bright Angel Lodge, makes a quick stop at the Backcountry Office, and then heads out to the South Kaibab Trailhead.*

Ranger-led programs are always free and are offered year-round, though more

programs are scheduled during the busy spring and summer seasons. These might include such activities as stargazing and topics as geology and the cultural history of prehistoric peoples. Some programs are held during the day and others in the evening. Some of the more in-depth programs include a fossil walk and a condor talk. Also make sure to check with the visitor center for seasonal programs including wildflower walks and fire ecology.

Kids ages 4 to 14 can get involved as well with the park's Junior Ranger program, with activities including a ranger-led rim hike and hands-on experiments detailing how the Grand Canyon was formed.

However, rangers will tell you that the best free activity in the canyon is watching the magnificent splashes of color on the canyon walls during sunrise and sunset.

✉ *Desert View Dr., 23 mi east of Grand Canyon Village off AZ 64* ⌂ *Box 129, Grand Canyon 86023* ☎ *928/638–7875* 🖃 *$10* ⚓ *Reservations not accepted* ☾ *Mid-May–mid-Oct.*

Sports & the Outdoors

HIKING   The **South Kaibab Trail,** starting near Yaki Point on Desert View Drive near Grand Canyon Village, connects at the bottom of the canyon (after the Kaibab Bridge across the Colorado River) with the **North Kaibab Trail.** Plan on two to three days if you want to hike the gorge from rim to rim (it's easier to descend from the North Rim, as it is more than 1,000 ft higher than the South Rim). The South Kaibab Trail is steep, descending 4,800 ft in just 7 mi, with no water or campgrounds and very little shade. There are portable toilets at Cedar Ridge 1½ mi from the trailhead. Toilets and an emergency phone are also located at the Tipoff, 4½ mi down the trail (3 mi past Cedar Ridge). The trail corkscrews down through some spectacular geology, closely following the 300-million-year-old Supai and Redwall formations. Look for (but don't remove) fossils in the limestone when you take your frequent water breaks. If you're going back up to the South Rim, ascend **Trail.** Accommodations along the way include the backcountry campgrounds at Indian Garden and Phantom Ranch (reservations are required far in advance for the latter). Overnight hikes into the canyon require a backcountry permit (*see* Hiking Permits *in* the A to Z section at the end of this chapter).

Shopping

Desert View Trading Post (✉ Desert View Dr., near the Watchtower at Desert View, Grand Canyon ☎ 928/638–2360) sells a mix of traditional Southwestern souvenirs and authentic Native American arts and crafts.

Hermit Road

The Santa Fe Company built Hermit Road, formerly known as West Rim Drive, in 1912 as a scenic tour route. There are 10 scenic overlooks along this 8-mi stretch, each worth a visit. Hermit Road is filled with hairpin turns; be certain to adhere to posted speed limits. Hermit Road is usually closed to auto traffic from March through November because of congestion; during this period, a free shuttle bus will carry you to all the overlooks.

㉑ The **Abyss** (✉ Hermit Rd., Grand Canyon), at an elevation of 6,720 ft, is one of the most awesome stops on Hermit Road, revealing a sheer drop of 3,000 ft to the Tonto Platform. From the Abyss you'll also see several isolated sandstone columns, the largest of which is called the Monument.

★ ㉓ **Hermits Rest** (✉ Hermit Rd., Grand Canyon), the westernmost viewpoint, and the Hermit Trail that descends from it were named for the "hermit" Louis Boucher, a 19th-century French-Canadian prospector who had a number of mining claims and a roughly built home down in the canyon. Canyon views from here include Hermit Rapids and the towering cliffs of the Supai and Redwall formations. The stone building at Hermits Rest sells curios and refreshments and—more important—has the only rest rooms on Hermit Road.

⑲ From **Hopi Point** (✉ Hermit Rd., Grand Canyon), at an elevation of 7,071 ft, you can see a large section of the Colorado River; although it appears as a thin line, the river is nearly 350 ft wide below this overlook. Across the canyon to the north is Shiva Temple, which remained an isolated section of the Kaibab Plateau until 1937. In that year, Harold Anthony of the American Museum of Natural History led an expedition to the rock formation in the belief that it supported life that had been cut off from the rest of the canyon. Imagine the expedition members' surprise when they found an empty Kodak film box on top of the temple. Directly below Hopi Point lies Dana Butte, named for a prominent 19th-century geologist. In 1919 an entrepreneur proposed connecting Hopi Point, Dana Butte, and the Tower of Set across the river with an aerial tramway, a technically feasible plan that, fortunately, has not been realized.

⑰ Less than a mile north of Trailview Overlook, **Maricopa Point** (✉ Hermit Rd., Grand Canyon) merits a stop for its arresting scenery and a view of the Colorado River below. On your left as you face the canyon are the Orphan Mine and (below) a mine shaft and cable lines leading up to the rim. The Orphan Mine was operated briefly as a copper mine around the beginning of the 20th century. In the 1950s, it was reopened as a uranium mine and closed again in the late '60s. It was one of the few profitable mines in the region.

⑳ Four-fifths of a mile to the west of Hopi Point, **Mohave Point** (✉ Hermit Rd., Grand Canyon) also has striking views of the Colorado River and of 5,401-ft Cheops Pyramid, the grayish rock formation behind Dana Butte. Granite and Salt Creek rapids can also be seen from this spot.

㉒ **Pima Point** (✉ Hermit Rd., Grand Canyon) provides a bird's-eye view of the Tonto Platform and the Tonto Trail, which wends its way through the canyon for more than 70 mi. Also to the west, two dark cone-shaped mountains—Mt. Trumbull and Mt. Logan—are visible on clear days. They rise in stark contrast to the surrounding flat-top mesas and buttes. From here you can see the scars from Hermit Camp, which can be seen up close if you hike the Hermit Trail.

★ ⑱ About ½ mi beyond Maricopa Point, the large granite **Powell Memorial** (⊠ Hermit Rd., Grand Canyon) stands as a tribute to the first man to ride the wild rapids of the Colorado River through the canyon in 1869. John Wesley Powell measured, charted, and named many of the canyons and creeks along the river. It was here that the dedication ceremony for Grand Canyon National Park took place on April 3, 1920.

⑯ **Trailview Overlook** (⊠ Hermit Rd., Grand Canyon) provides a dramatic view of the and Plateau Point trails as they zigzag down the canyon. Across the canyon, in the deep gorge to the north, flows Creek, one of the permanent tributary streams of the Colorado River in the region. Toward the south is an unobstructed view of the distant San Francisco Peaks, Arizona's highest mountains (the tallest is 12,633 ft), as well as of Bill Williams Mountain (on the horizon) and Red Butte (about 15 mi south of the canyon rim).

Sports & the Outdoors

HIKING The steep, 9-mi **Hermit Trail** beginning just west of Hermits Rest (8 mi west of Grand Canyon Village) is recommended for experienced long-distance hikers only. For much of the year, no water is available along the way; ask a park ranger about the availability of water at Santa Maria Springs and Hermit Creek before you set out. But all water from these sources should be treated before drinking. The route leads down to the Colorado River and has inspiring views of Hermit Gorge and the Redwall and Supai formations. Six miles from the trailhead you'll come across the scattered ruins of Hermit Camp, which the Santa Fe Railroad ran as a tourist camp from 1911 until 1930. Hiking here requires a backcountry permit (*see* Hiking Permits *in* the A to Z section at the end of this chapter).

Williams

▶ ㉔ *55 mi south of Grand Canyon Village, 30 mi west of Flagstaff on I–40 and AZ 64. Use I–40 Exit 161, 163, or 165.*

At the turn of the 20th century, Williams was a rough-and-tumble town replete with saloons and bordellos. Today, it reflects a much milder side of the Wild West, with 2,900 residents and some 1,400 motel rooms. Wander along main street named, like the town, after mountain man Bill Williams, and you'll enjoy memories from the past of America's favorite road, Route 66. There are some interesting antiques shops, cozy eateries, and the ever-present souvenir and T-shirt stores.

The town sits at 6,700 ft in the world's largest stand of ponderosa pines. Often considered just a jumping-off point for the Grand Canyon (it's only an hour away from the South Rim by car and a little more than two hours by train), Williams is temperate in summer, offers skiing in the winter, and is within minutes of seven mountain lakes.

☾ Children enjoy the **Grand Canyon Deer Farm**, a petting zoo with pygmy goats, llamas, and deer, including fawns born every June and July. ⊠ *6752 E. Deer Farm Rd., 8 mi east of Williams off I–40, Exit 171* ☎ *928/635–4073* ⊕ *www.deerfarm.com* ☏ *$5.95* ☾ *Mar.–May and Sept.–Oct., daily 9–6; June–Aug., daily 8–7; Nov.–Feb., daily 10–5 (weather permitting).*

In 1989 service on the **Grand Canyon Railway** was reinaugurated along a route first established in 1901. The 65-mi trek from Williams Depot to the South Rim (2¼ hours each way) takes the vintage train through prairie, ranch, and national park land to the log-cabin train station in Grand Canyon Village. The ride includes refreshments, commentary, and corny but fun onboard entertainment by Wild West characters. Passengers ride in restored 1923 cars and enjoy complimentary soft drinks in Coach Class. Club Class, with its fully stocked mahogany bar and complimentary morning pastries and coffee, costs an additional $20. A First-Class ($55 upgrade), Deluxe Observation Class, or Luxury Parlor Car ($75–$85 upgrade) ticket gets you Continental breakfast and complimentary afternoon champagne and snacks. Both Coach and Club Classes provide the basics, with padded benches to sit on and ceiling fans to keep you cool; the other three classes provide much more comfortable seating and air-conditioning.

Even if you don't take the train, it's worth visiting the **Williams Depot,** where the trains depart. It was built in 1908 to replace the terminal where the Williams Visitor Center now resides. Attractions here include a passenger car and the locomotive of a turn-of-the-20th-century steam train, a gift shop where you can find bizarre souvenirs such as a tie that plays "I've Been Working on the Railroad," and Max and Thelma's, a full-service restaurant. A small **Railroad Museum** is next to the depot in the original dining room of the former Harvey House hotel. The museum holds an interesting collection of old railroad and Harvey-girl photographs and is a good place to learn about the history of the Grand Canyon Railway, which once carried American presidents, Franklin D. Roosevelt among them, on their whistle-stop campaigns through the West. ⊠ *Williams Depot, N. Grand Canyon Blvd. at Fray Marcos Blvd.* ☎ *800/843–8724 railway reservations and information* ⊕ *www.thetrain. com* ▣ *$54.95–$139.95 round-trip, not including 8.8% tax and $10 national park entrance fee* ⊗ *Departs daily from Williams at 10 AM, from the South Rim at 3:30 PM.*

The **Williams Visitor Center,** also housing the Chamber of Commerce and Forest Service office, is the former passenger-train depot, which was built in 1901. Its brick walls still show graffiti scrawled by early railroad workers and hobos. ⊠ *200 W. Railroad Ave., at Grand Canyon Blvd.* ☎ *928/635–1418 or 800/863–0546* ⊕ *www.williamschamber.com* ⊗ *Daily 8–5.*

Where to Stay & Eat

For approximate costs, *see* the dining and lodging price charts at the beginning of this chapter.

★ **$–$$** ✕**Pancho McGillicuddy's.** Originally the Cabinet Saloon, this restaurant is on the National Register of Historic Places. Gone are the spittoons and pipes—the smoke-free dining area now has a Mexican decor, which sets the scene for such specialties as "armadillo eggs," the local name for deep-fried jalapeños stuffed with cheese. ⊠ *141 Railroad Ave.* ☎ *928/635–4150* ▤ *MC, V.*

$–$$ ✕**Rod's Steak House.** You can't miss this steak house with the plastic Angus cow out front. Obviously the emphasis here is on meat—sizzling mesquite-broiled steaks, prime rib, and the like. You may wish to try the local favorite—Rod's special charred steak, a hefty sirloin dipped in sugar and grilled over mesquite. ⊠ *301 E. Rte. 66* ☎ *928/635–2671* ▤ *MC, V.*

¢–$ ✕**Cruisers Café 66.** Talk about nostalgia. This fun place reminds you Fodor'sChoice of your favorite 1950s high school hangout—with cocktail service. It's ★ right out of Route 66, with good burgers, steaks, ribs, pizzas, salads, and, of course, malts. ⊠ *233 W. Rte. 66* ☎ *928/635–2445* ▤ *AE, DC, MC, V.*

¢–$ ✕**Pine Country Restaurant.** This cozy and spotless restaurant, a popular local spot, is across from the Grand Canyon Railway Depot. Owner Dee Seehorn serves up homemade pies and ample, hearty meals. The crafts that make up most of the decor are all for sale and are created by local artists. Open daily at 5:30 AM, the restaurant serves breakfast, lunch, and dinner. The best thing about this homey diner is that, for an extra 15% charge, it will deliver to any hotel in town. ⊠ *107 N. Grand Canyon Blvd.* ☎ *928/635–9718* ⊟ *D, MC, V.*

¢ ✕**Grand Canyon Coffee Café.** You'll find good espresso drinks here, along with wonderful sandwiches on homemade focaccia. This is the home of the mountain man sandwich (piled-high roast beef with cheddar cheese and onions on Italian bread). Try an egg-cream soda with Ghirardelli chocolate if you're feeling nostalgic. Harley-Davidson artifacts fill the space, and some of them are for sale. ⊠ *125 W. Rte. 66* ☎ *928/635–1255* ⊟ *AE, MC, V* ☽ *No dinner Jan.–Feb.*

★ **$$–$$$** 🏠**Sheridan House Inn.** This B&B provides a more civilized alternative to crowded Grand Canyon National Park or Tusayan lodgings. The inn, nestled among pine trees just a few blocks from Route 66, has large, quiet rooms decorated with taste. Outside there are decks looking out to the tall ponderosa pines and a flagstone patio with a hot tub. Hearty breakfasts (such as eggs Benedict or buttermilk pancakes) will ready you for the hour-long drive to the canyon. Steve and Evelyn Gardner are gracious hosts, who happily help guests plan their itineraries. Steve, a former restaurant chef, prepares a casual buffet dinner every evening for an additional cost. ⊠ *460 E. Sheridan Ave., 86046* ☎ *928/635–9441 or 888/635–9345* ⊕ *www.thegrandcanyon.com/sheridan* ⇌ *6 rooms, 2 suites* ♨ *Dining room, gym, hot tub* ⊟ *AE, MC, V* ⦿ *BP.*

★ **$$** 🏠**Fray Marcos Hotel.** This hotel was designed to resemble the train depot's original Fray Marcos lodge. Neoclassical Greek columns flank the grand entrance leading into a lobby with maplewood balustrades, an enormous flagstone fireplace, and oil paintings of the Grand Canyon by local artist Kenneth McKenna. Original bronzes by Frederic Remington, from the private collection of hotel owners Max and Thelma Biegert, also adorn the lobby. The Southwestern-style accommodations are well appointed and have large bathrooms. Adjacent to the lobby is Spenser's, a pub with an ornate 19th-century hand-carved bar. ⊠ *235 N. Grand Canyon Blvd., 86046* ☎ *928/635–4010 or 800/843–8724* ⊕ *www.thetrain.com* ⇌ *196 rooms* ♨ *Cable TV, indoor pool, gym, hot tub, bar, no-smoking rooms* ⊟ *AE, D, MC, V.*

$–$$ 🏠**Mountainside Inn Gateway to the Grand Canyon.** At the east entrance to town, this motel has comfortable rooms, a good American restaurant called Miss Kitty's Steakhouse, and country-and-western bands in summer. ⊠ *642 E. Rte. 66, 86046* ☎ *928/635–4431 or 800/462–9381* 🖶*928/635–2292* ⇌*95 rooms, 1 suite* ♨ *Restaurant, pool, hot tub* ⊟*AE, D, DC, MC, V.*

$–$$ 🏠**Quality Inn Mountain Ranch & Resort.** Seven miles east of town, off Exit 171, the warm lights and friendly staff of this motel beckon. Rooms are basic and predictable; however, included with the room rate is a full breakfast in the coffee shop, which has views of the San Francisco Peaks. In season, evening hay rides—complete with singing cowboys, staged gunfights, and a cookout—are offered. The motel gives a 10% discount to senior citizens. ⊠ *6701 E. Mountain Ranch Rd., 86046* ☎ *928/635–2693 or 800/228–5151* 🖶 *928/635–4188* ⇌ *73 rooms* ♨ *Restaurant, coffee shop, 2 tennis courts, pool, hot tub, horseback riding, bar, no-smoking rooms* ⊟ *AE, D, DC, MC, V* ☽ *Closed Nov.–Feb.* ⦿ *BP.*

$ 🏠**Red Garter.** A restored bordello dating from 1897 now houses a small B&B with an old-fashioned feel. Ask for the Best Gal's room, with its own sitting room overlooking the train tracks. Despite the inn's location, all four rooms (two are interior, with skylights but no windows) are very quiet, as the only train traffic is the Grand Canyon Railway, with one daily arrival and departure. Even if you don't stay here, the fresh goodies at the on-site bakery are worth a stop. ⊠ *137 W. Railroad Ave., 86046* ☎ *928/635–1484 or 800/328–1484* ⊕ *www.redgarter. com* ⊃ *4 rooms* ⊟ *AE, D, MC, V* ⦿ *CP* ⊘ *Closed Dec.–mid-Feb.*

¢ ▦ **Red Lake Arizona Campground and Hostel.** On AZ 64, 10 mi north of Williams, this campground has 14 tent campsites ($10) and 14 RV sites with full hook-ups ($14). There's a convenience store, gift shop, gasoline, and propane. In addition, the apartment-style on-premise hostel can accommodate 32 people. Dorm beds are $11 and private rooms are $33. ⊠ *AZ 64, 10 mi north of Williams, 86046* ☎ *928/635–4753, 800/ 581–4753 reservations* ⊃ *32 beds in 8 dorm-style rooms with shared bath* ⊟ *D, MC, V.*

Sports & the Outdoors

CAMPING Both developed and undeveloped campsites can be reserved in the **Kaibab National Forest** (☎ *928/635–4061* ⊕ *www.fs.fed.us/r3/ka*), which surrounds the Williams area and goes up to the Grand Canyon itself.

SKIING The **Williams Ski Area** (⊠ *Off I–40* ✉ *Box 953, 86046,* ☎ *928/635– 9330* ⊕ *www.williamsskiarea.com*) is usually open from mid-December through much of March; from Williams, take South 4th Street for 2 mi, and then turn right at the sign and go another 1½ mi. There are four groomed runs (including one for beginners) and other downhill trails as well as areas suitable for cross-country enthusiasts.

Havasu Canyon

141 mi from Williams (to head of the Hualapai Trail), west on I–40 (to Seligman) and AZ 66, north on Indian Hwy. 18. Note: Last gas is at the junction of AZ 66 and Indian Hwy. 18.

Havasu Canyon, south of the middle part of the national park and away from the crowds, is uncommonly beautiful and undoubtedly the most scenic stretch of Route 66. It is the home of about 500 Havasupai, a tribe that has lived in this isolated area for centuries. Their name means "people of the blue water," and you'll know why when you see the canyon's waterfalls, as high as 200 ft, cascading over red cliffs into travertine pools surrounded by thick foliage and sheltering trees. Eight-mile-long Hualapai Trail twists into the canyon along the edges of sheer rock walls. Be sure to call ahead if you plan to hike the trail; you can ride a horse down for $120 round-trip, or $70 one way. You'll need to spend the night if you're hiking or riding. All visitors are charged a $20 fee to enter the Havasupai tribal lands. You are expected to respect the land and its people. If you are in a hurry, you can take a helicopter ride into the canyon with **Air West Helicopters** (☎ *623/516–2790*). Flights leave from Hualapai Hilltop and cost $85 per person each way. From March 15 through October 15, flights are between 10 AM and 1 PM on Thursday, Friday, Sunday, and Monday; from October 16 through March 14, the flights are from Friday to Sunday only. ⊠ *Havasupai Tourist Enterprise, Supai 86435* ☎ *928/448–2141 general information, 928/448– 2111 lodging reservations* ✉ *$20.*

Where to Stay & Eat

For approximate costs, *see* the dining and lodging prices chart at the beginning of this chapter.

¢–$ ✕▦ **Havasupai Lodge.** These are fairly spartan accommodations, but you won't notice it too much when you see all of the natural beauty surrounding you. The lodge and restaurant are at the bottom of Havasu Canyon and are operated by the Havasupai tribe. The restaurant serves three meals a day, mostly sandwiches and fast-food-type fare, and a daily special; dinner main-course prices are about $8–$10. ⊠ *Supai 86435*

toiletry bag you left at day spa: $72
coral necklace you lost at the Grand Canyon: $40
climbing shoes you forgot in Tucson: $89

replacing your card anywhere:
priceless

For everything from card replacement to cash advances
to locating the nearest ATM, call 1-800-MasterCard.

there are some things money can't buy.
for everything else there's MasterCard.®

Find America *with a Compass*

Written by local authors and illustrated throughout
with spectacular color images, Compass American
Guides reveal the character and culture of more than
40 of America's most fascinating destinations. Perfect
for residents who want to explore their own backyards
and for visitors who want an insider's perspective
on the history, heritage, and all there is to see and do.

Fodor's COMPASS AMERICAN GUIDES

At bookstores everywhere.

☎ 928/448–2111 ↻ *24 rooms* ⅃ *Restaurant; no room phones, no room TVs* ▭ *MC, V.*

CAMPING For information about camping in Havasu Canyon, call the **Havasupai Tourist Enterprise** (☎ 928/448–2141) You can stay in the primitive campgrounds for $10 per person per night, which is in addition to your $20 entry fee.

Cameron Trading Post

㉕ *53 mi north of Flagstaff on U.S. 89, 57 mi east of Grand Canyon Village on AZ 64.*

Most of the jewelry, rugs, baskets, and pottery sold at the historic **Cameron Trading Post** (✉ U.S. 89 ☎ 928/679–2231 or 800/338–7385) is made by Navajo and Hopi artisans, but some is created by New Mexico's Zuni and Pueblo Indians. Come armed with knowledge of Native American artisanship if you're looking at high-ticket items, some of which are sold at a separate gallery. Also at the post are a restaurant, cafeteria, grocery store, butcher shop, and post office. An outlet of the **Navajo Arts and Crafts Enterprises** (✉ AZ 64/U.S. 89 ☎ 928/679–2244) stocks authentic Navajo products.

Where to Stay & Eat

For approximate costs, *see* the dining and lodging price charts at the beginning of this chapter.

$–$$ ✕▤ **Cameron Trading Post.** Fifty-four miles north of Flagstaff, this his-
Fodor'sChoice toric trading post dates back to 1916. Southwestern-style rooms have
★   carved-oak furniture, tile baths, and balconies overlooking the Colorado River. Native-stone landscaping—including fossilized dinosaur tracks—and a small, well-kept garden with lilacs, roses, and crab-apple trees are pleasant. Make your reservations far in advance for high season. The dining room (¢–$) serves a delicious homemade green chili and fry bread that is worth the stop alone. ✉ *U.S. 89* ⌂ *Box 339, Cameron 86020* ☎ *928/679–2231 or 800/338–7385 Ext. 414* 🖨 *928/679–2350* ⊕ *www.camerontradingpost.com* ↻ *62 rooms, 4 suites* ⅃ *Restaurant, cafeteria, grocery* ▭ *AE, DC, MC, V.*

$ △ **Cameron RV Park.** This park, open year-round, is adjacent to the Cameron Trading Post. There are 60 spaces with hook-ups for $15 a day. There are no public rest rooms or showers, however. ⅃ *Full hookups, dump station, drinking water, restaurant, general store* ↻ *60 RV sites* ✉ *U.S. 89* ⌂ *Box 339, Cameron 86020* ☎ *928/679–2231 or 800/338–7385* 🖨 *928/679–2350* ⊕ *www.camerontradingpost.com* 🖃 *$15* ⌖ *No reservations accepted* ☉ *Open year-round.*

en route The route north from Cameron Trading Post on U.S. 89 offers a stunning view of the **Painted Desert** to the right. The desert, which covers thousands of square miles and stretches to the south and east, is a vision of subtle, almost harsh beauty, with windswept plains and mesas, isolated buttes, and barren valleys in pastel patterns. The sparse vegetation is mostly desert scrub, which provides sustenance for only the hardiest wildlife. Most of the undulating hills belong to the 200-million-year-old Chinle formation, the depository of countless fossil records.

About 30 mi north of Cameron Trading Post, the Painted Desert country gives way to sandstone cliffs that run for miles off to the right. Brilliantly hued and ranging in color from light pink to deep orange, the **Echo Cliffs** rise to more than 1,000 ft in many places.

They are essentially devoid of vegetation, but in a few places high up, thick patches of tall cottonwood and poplar trees, nurtured by springs and water seepage from the rock escarpment, manage to thrive.

At Bitter Springs, 60 mi north of Cameron, U.S. 89A branches off from U.S. 89, running north and providing views of **Marble Canyon**, the geographical beginning of the Grand Canyon. Like the Grand Canyon, Marble Canyon was formed by the Colorado River. Traversing a gorge nearly 500 ft deep is **Navajo Bridge**, a narrow steel span built in 1929 and listed on the National Register of Historic Places. Formerly used for car traffic, it now functions only as a pedestrian overpass. The visitor center is informational and handy.

THE NORTH RIM & ENVIRONS

The North Rim, within the 14,000-square-mi Arizona Strip, draws only about 10% of the Grand Canyon's visitors but is, many believe, even more gorgeous than the South Rim. There's plenty to see on the long drive to the North Rim, which is about 210 mi whether you start out from the South Rim of the Grand Canyon or from Flagstaff. Heavy snows block highway access and close facilities anytime after October 15 until mid- to late May.

Lees Ferry Area

76 mi north of Cameron Trading Post, U.S. 89 to U.S. 89A.

★ ❷ A turnoff at Marble Canyon Lodge, about 1 mi past Navajo Bridge in the small town of Marble Canyon, leads to historic **Lees Ferry**, 3 mi away. On a sharp bend in the Colorado River where Echo Cliffs and Vermilion Cliffs intersect, Lees Ferry is considered "mile zero" of the river—the point from which all distances on the rivers system in the Grand Canyon are measured. This spot, one of the last areas in the mainland United States to be completely charted, was first visited by non–Native Americans in 1776, when Spanish priests Fray Francisco Atanasio Domínguez and Fray Silvestre Velez de Escalante tried, but failed, to cross the Colorado. Explorer John Wesley Powell also visited in 1870 on an expedition with Mormon leaders. After the ferry was established, it became part of the Honeymoon Trail, a gateway to Utah for young couples who wanted their civil marriages in Arizona sanctified at the Latter-Day Saints temple in St. George. It also became a crossing and a supply point for miners and other pioneers who shaped the American West.

Lees Ferry retains a number of vestiges of the mining era, but it's now primarily known as the spot where most of the Grand Canyon river rafts put into the water. In addition, huge trout lurk in the river near here, so there are several places to pick up angling gear and/or a guide.

★ ❷ West from the town of Marble Canyon, rising to the right of the highway, are the sheer, spectacular **Vermilion Cliffs**, in many places more than 3,000 ft high. Keep a sharp eye out for condors; these giant endangered birds were reintroduced into the area in the winter of 1996–97. Reports suggest that the birds, once in captivity, are surviving well in the wilderness.

Where to Stay & Eat

For approximate costs, *see* the dining and lodging price charts at the beginning of this chapter.

Grand Canyon North Rim

UTAH

Lake Powell

TO
FREDONIA,
COLORADO CITY

Glen Canyon Dam

Lees
Ferry (26)

Page

98

Marble Canyon

Navajo
Bridge

34 **Toroweap Overlook**

35 **Pipe Spring National Monument**

Vermilion
Cliffs (27)

ARIZONA

House Rock
Valley

ALT
89

STRIP

ALT
89

28 **Jacob Lake**

San Bartolome
Historic Site

Colorado River

ALT
89

Bitter
Springs

KAIBAB

89

NATIONAL

ECHO CLIFFS

FOREST

Cedar
Ridge

67

The Gap

PAINTED DESERT

31 **Point Imperial**

Point Sublime 33

Grand Canyon Lodge 29

Marble Canyon

30 **Bright Angel Point**

GRAND CANYON NATIONAL PARK

32 **Cape Royal**

Colorado River

Desert
View

Grand Canyon
Village

Little Colorado River

89

Tusayan

64

KAIBAB NATIONAL FOREST

25 **Cameron Trading Post**

64

180

Valle

0   10 miles

0   15 km

24 **Williams**

★ ¢–$$$ ✕⚏ **Marble Canyon Lodge.** This Arizona Strip lodge opened in 1929 on the same day the Navajo Bridge was dedicated. Three types of accommodations are available: rooms in the original building; standard motel rooms in the newer building; and two-bedroom apartments. You can sit on the porch swing of the native-rock lodge and look out on Vermilion Cliffs and the desert or play the 1920s piano. Zane Grey and Gary Cooper are among the well-known past guests. The restaurant ($–$$) serves steaks, seafood, pasta, and sandwiches. ⊠ *¼ mi west of Navajo Bridge on U.S. 89A* ⚏ *Box 6001, Marble Canyon 86036* ☎ *928/355-2225 or 800/726-1789* ⚏ *928/355-2227* ⚏ *52 units* ⚬ *Restaurant, laundry facilities, airstrip* ⊟ *AE, D, MC, V.*

¢ ✕⚏ **Lees Ferry Lodge.** Geared toward the Lees Ferry trout-fishing trade, this lodge will outfit you, guide you, and freeze your catch. At the end of the day you can sit out on one of the garden patios of this rustic 1929 building, constructed of native stone and rough-hewn beams. Rooms are charming, if a bit quirky in their plumbing. The hotel's Vermilion Cliffs Bar and Grill ($–$$) is a popular gathering spot for river raft guides, and it serves good American fare—especially the steaks and seafood—in an authentic western setting. ⊠ *4 mi west of Navajo Bridge on U.S. 89A* ⚏ *HC 67, Box 1, Marble Canyon 86036* ☎ *928/355-2231 or 800/451-2231* ⊕ *www.leesferrylodge.com* ⚏ *9 rooms, 1 5-person trailer* ⚬ *Restaurant* ⊟ *MC, V.*

¢–$ ⚏ **Cliff Dwellers Lodge.** Built in 1949, this dining and lodging complex sits at the foot of Vermilion Cliffs. Rooms in the modern motel building are attractive and clean. ⊠ *U.S. 89A, 9 mi west of Navajo Bridge* ⚏ *HC 67, Box 30, Marble Canyon 86036* ☎ *928/355-2228 or 800/433-2543* ⚏ *928/355-2229* ⚏ *22 rooms* ⚬ *Restaurant, grocery, bar* ⊟ *D, MC, V.*

Sports & the Outdoors

FISHING The Colorado River in the Lees Ferry area is known for good-size German brown and rainbow trout. Marble Canyon Lodge sells Arizona fishing licenses. **Lees Ferry Anglers** (⊠ Milepost 547, N. U.S. 89A, Marble Canyon ☎ 928/355-2261, 800/962-9755 outside Arizona ⊕ www.leesferry.com) operates guided fishing trips, starting from $280 per day; it practices year-round catch and release.

en route As you continue the journey to the North Rim, the immense blue-green bulk of the Kaibab Plateau stretches out before you. About 18 mi past Navajo Bridge, a sign directs you to the **San Bartolome Historic Site**, an overlook with plaques that tell the story of the Domínguez-Escalante expedition of 1776. At **House Rock Valley**, a large road sign announces the House Rock Buffalo Ranch, operated by the Arizona Game and Fish Department. A 23-mi dirt road leads to the home of one of the largest herds of American bison in the Southwest. You may drive out to the ranch, but be aware that you may not see any buffalo—the expanse of their range is so great that they frequently cannot be spotted from a car.

As it nears its junction with AZ 67, U.S. 89A starts climbing to the top of the **Kaibab Plateau**, heavily forested, filled with animals and birds, and more than 9,000 ft at its highest point. The rapid change from barren desert to lush forest is dramatic.

Jacob Lake

㉘ *25 mi west of town of Marble Canyon on U.S. 89A, at AZ 67.*

Jacob Lake junction is a good base camp for exploring the beautiful Kaibab Plateau. Sometimes referred to as an "island in the sky," it is home to a wide-ranging collection of wildlife, including the unique Kaibab squirrel. The U.S. Forest Service's **Kaibab Plateau Visitor's Center** (✉ U.S. 89A/AZ 67 ☎ 928/643–7298) is open May–mid-October and offers several interpretive displays, books, and educational gifts. Gas and groceries are also available in the area.

Where to Stay & Eat

For approximate costs, *see* the dining and lodging price charts at the beginning of this chapter.

¢–$ ✕🏨 **Jacob Lake Inn.** Basic cabins and standard motel rooms—without telephones or televisions—are available at this modest 5-acre complex in Kaibab National Forest. All rooms overlook the highways. The bustling lodge center, a popular stop for those heading to the North Rim, has a grocery store, a coffee shop, a restaurant (¢–$), and a large gift shop. Even if you don't play to stay here, make sure to stop for one of their famous malts or milk shakes. ✉ *AZ 67/U.S. 89A, 86022* ☎ *928/643–7232* ⊕ *www.jacoblake.com* ⤶ *14 rooms, 22 cabins* ⬧ *Restaurant, café, grocery; no room phones, no room TVs* ▤ *AE, D, DC, MC, V.*

¢ ⛺ **Demotte Campground.** This U.S. Forest Service campground, 29 mi south of Jacob Lake, is open from late May or early June through October. It has 23 single-unit (RV or tent) sites but no hook-ups, for $12 per day. There are interpretive campfire programs in summer. No reservations are accepted. ⬧ *Flush toilets, fire pits, grills, picnic tables* ⤶ *23 campsites* ✉ *Off AZ 67* ⬧ *North Kaibab Ranger District, Box 248, Fredonia 86022* ☎ *928/643–7395* ⬧ *$12* ⬧ *Reservations not accepted* ☉ *Open June–Oct.*

¢ ⛺ **Jacob Lake Campground.** Fifty-three family and group RV and tent sites (no hook-ups) are available for $12 per vehicle per day at this U.S. Forest Service campground. On summer evenings, rangers present interpretive programs. No reservations are accepted (except for groups of 10 or more). It's open year-round, but there are no facilities or running water in winter; fees are charged only from mid-April through October. ⬧ *Flush toilets, grills, picnic tables* ⤶ *53 campsites* ✉ *U.S. 89A/AZ 67* ⬧ *North Kaibab Ranger District, Box 248, Fredonia 86022* ☎ *928/643–7395* ⬧ *$12* ⬧ *Reservations not accepted* ☉ *Open year-round.*

¢ ⛺ **Kaibab Camper Village.** This campground has 50 tent sites ($12 for two people) and 80 RV and trailer sites ($22 for a pull-through with full hook-up, $12 without hook-up). Fire pits and more than 70 picnic tables are spread out in this wooded spot, which is near a gas station, store, and restaurant. Reservations are accepted and recommended, particularly during the height of the busy summer season. ⬧ *Portable toilets, full hook-ups, showers, drinking water, picnic tables, fire pits* ⤶ *80 hook-up sites, 50 tent sites* ✉ *AZ 67, ¼ mi south of U.S. 89A* ⬧ *Box 3331, Flagstaff 86003* ☎ *928/643–7804 in season, 928/526–0924, 800/525–0924 outside Arizona in winter* 🖷 *928/527–9398* ⊕ *www.canyoneers.com* ⬧ *$12–$22* ☉ *Open mid-May–mid-Oct.*

en route AZ 67 runs south from U.S. 89A to the North Rim; the route passes through one of the thickest stands of ponderosa pine in the United States. You'll frequently see mule deer and Kaibab squirrels, which live only on this plateau. You can recognize the squirrels by their all-white tails and the long tufts of white hair on their ears. The mule deer are recognizable by their large antlers. Keep an eye out for mountain lions, elk, and black bear . . . they're here, but seeing them is rare. You're more likely to see wild turkeys.

The North Rim

44 mi south of Jacob Lake on AZ 67.

A fee of $20 per vehicle (regardless of the number of passengers) is collected as you enter the North Entrance. Those on foot, bicycle, or motorcycle pay $10 per person. In all cases, this fee is for one week's access. The entrance gates are open 24 hours but are generally staffed from about 7 AM to 7 PM. If you arrive when there's no one at the gate, you may enter legally without paying. Arizona 67 from Jacob Lake is often closed due to snowfall from mid-May to mid-October, and during these times all facilities at the North Rim are closed. The park, however, is open for day use.

㉙ The historic **Grand Canyon Lodge** (✉ AZ 67, Grand Canyon) is literally at the end of the road. Built in 1928 by the Union Pacific Railroad, the massive stone structure is listed on the National Register of Historic Places. Its huge sunroom has hardwood floors, high-beam ceilings, and a marvelous view of the canyon through plate-glass windows. Don't forget to pay your respects to Brighty, the faithful burro of children's-book fame, honored by a bronze sculpture near the lounge's west entrance. On warm days visitors sit in the sun and drink in the surrounding beauty at an equally spacious outdoor viewing deck, where National Park Service employees deliver free lectures on geology and history. Lunch, dinner, or a snack in the lodge's rock-and-log dining room is an integral part of the North Rim experience; the food is good and reasonably priced. If you don't want a full meal, just buy a soda at Pizza Place or a drink at the saloon and sit out on the west veranda to watch the sun set over the canyon.

The **Transept Trail** (✉ AZ 67, Grand Canyon) begins near the corner of the Grand Canyon Lodge's east patio. This 3-mi (round-trip) trail stays near the rim for part of the distance before it plunges into the forest, ending at the North Rim Campground and General Store, 1½ mi from the lodge.

★ ㉚ The trail to **Bright Angel Point** (✉ North Rim Dr., Grand Canyon), one of the most awe-inspiring overlooks on either rim, starts on the grounds of the Grand Canyon Lodge and runs along the crest of a point of rocks that juts into the canyon for several hundred yards. The walk is only 1 mi round-trip, but it's an exciting trek accented by sheer drops just a few feet away on each side of the trail. In a few spots where the route is extremely narrow, metal railings ensure visitors' safety. The temptation to clamber out to precarious perches to have your picture taken could get you killed. Every year several people die from falls at the Grand Canyon.

Eleven miles northeast of Grand Canyon Lodge is one of the North Rim's **㉛** most popular lookouts, **Point Imperial** (✉ AZ 67, Grand Canyon), the highest vista point (elevation 8,803 ft) at either rim, offering magnificent views of both the canyon and the distant country: the Vermilion Cliffs to the north, the 10,000-ft Navajo Mountain to the northeast in Utah, the Painted Desert to the east, and the Little Colorado River canyon to the southeast.

★ ㉜ **Cape Royal** (✉ AZ 67, Grand Canyon) is about 23 mi southeast of Grand Canyon Lodge. A short walk on a paved road from the parking lot leads to this southernmost viewpoint on the North Rim. In addition to a large slice of the Grand Canyon, Angels Window, a giant, erosion-formed hole, can be seen through the projecting ridge of Cape Royal. At Angels Window Overlook, ⅓ mi north of here, Cliff Springs Trail starts its 1-mi route (round-trip) through a forested ravine. The trail, narrow and precarious in spots, passes ancient dwellings, winds beneath a limestone overhang, and terminates at Cliff Springs, where the forest opens on another impressive view of the canyon walls.

33 Talk about solitude. There's plenty of it at **Point Sublime** (⊠ North Rim Dr., Grand Canyon), where you can camp within a few feet of the canyon's edge. Sunrises and sunsets are spectacular and worth a roll or two of film every day. The winding road, through gorgeous high country, to Point Sublime is only 17 mi, but it will take you at least an hour, more if you want to absorb the scenery en route. The road is intended only for vehicles with high road clearance (pickups and four-wheel-drive vehicles). It is also necessary to be properly equipped for wilderness road travel. Check with a park ranger or at the information desk at Grand Canyon Lodge before taking this journey. You may camp here only with a permit from the Backcountry Office at the park ranger station.

FodorsChoice
★

Where to Stay & Eat

For approximate costs, *see* the dining and lodging price charts at the beginning of this chapter.

$ ×⊞ **Grand Canyon Lodge.** This historic property, constructed mainly in the 1920s and '30s, is the premier lodging facility in the North Rim area. The main building has limestone walls and timbered ceilings. Lodging options include small, rustic cabins; larger cabins (some with a canyon view and some with two bedrooms); and newer, traditional motel rooms. You might find marinated pork kebabs or linguine with cilantro on the dining room's dinner menu ($$). Dining room reservations are essential and should be made as far in advance as possible. ⊠ *AZ 67, Grand Canyon National Park, North Rim 86052* ☎ *303/297–2757 reservations only, 928/638–2611 direct to hotel (no reservations)* 🖷 *303/297–3175 reservations only* ⊕ *www.grandcanyonnorthrim.com* 🛏 *44 rooms, 157 cabins* 🍴 *Cafeteria, dining room, bar* ▭ *AE, D, MC, V.*

FodorsChoice
★

$–$$ ⊞ **Kaibab Lodge.** In the woods 5 mi north of the North Rim entrance, this 1920s property contains rustic cabins with simple furnishings. The lodge has a cozy fireplace that's often enjoyed by lodge guests in the early evening, as the chill can be felt shortly after the sun sets—even in summer. This is a popular base for cross-country skiers in winter. ⊠ *AZ 67, Grand Canyon* 🖃 *HC 64, Box 30, Fredonia 86022* ☎ *928/638–2389* 🛏 *24 cabins* 🍴 *Restaurant* ▭ *D, MC, V* 🕐 *Closed mid-Oct.–mid-May.*

$ ⚠ **North Rim Campground.** The only designated campground at the North Rim of Grand Canyon National Park, 3 mi north of the rim, has 83 RV and tent sites (no hook-ups) for $15 per day. On-site are laundry facilities, rest rooms, showers, picnic sites, and a small grocery store. 🍴 *Flush toilets, dump station, drinking water, laundry facilities, showers, fire grates, picnic tables, general store* 🛏 *83 campsites* ⊠ *AZ 67, Grand Canyon* 🖃 *National Park Reservation Service, Box 1600, Cumberland, MD 21501* ☎ *800/365–2267* ⊕ *reservations.nps.gov/index.cfm* 🖷 *$15* 🍴 *Reservations essential* 🕐 *Open mid-May–mid-Oct.*

Sports & the Outdoors

MULE RIDES **Canyon Trail Rides** (☎ 435/679–8665 ⊕ www.canyonrides.com) conducts ☁ short mule rides suitable for children on the easier trails along the North Rim. A one-hour ride, available to those six and older, runs about $20. Half-day trips on the rim or into the canyon (minimum age 8) cost $45; full-day trips (minimum age 12), which include lunch and water, go for $95. These excursions are very popular, so try to make reservations in advance. Rides are available daily from May 15 to October 15.

Elsewhere in the Arizona Strip

The Arizona Strip—the part of the state directly north of Grand Canyon National Park—is sometimes called the American Tibet because of its isolation; it has only two small towns, Fredonia and Colorado City. The combined population of these two towns is less than 7,000, and fewer than 700 permanent residents—including 150 members of the Kaibab-Paiute tribe—live in the rest of the strip. Services in this part of the state are extremely limited; top off your tank when you find a gas station, and keep an ample supply of drinking water in your car. Once you get away from the paved highways in this region, roadways tend to be rough and may be impassable when wet.

③⑤ **Pipe Spring National Monument.** Ninety miles from the North Rim and

Fodor'sChoice 14 mi from Fredonia, the spring here is one of the few reliable sources

★ of water in the Arizona Strip. The park contains a restored rock fort and ranch, with exhibits of Southwestern frontier life. In summer there are living-history demonstrations that focus on such things as ranching operations or weaving. The fort was intended to fend off Native American attacks (which never came because a peace treaty was signed before the fort was finished). It ended up functioning mainly as headquarters for a dairy operation and in 1871 became the first telegraph station in the Arizona Territory. About ½ mi north of the monument is a campground and picnic area. While you're here check out the expanded museum and visitor center, which is now operated jointly by the National Park Service and the Kaibab-Paiute tribe. ✉ *401 N. Pipe Spring Rd.* ✎ *HC 65, Box 5, Fredonia 86022* ☏ *928/643–7105* ⊕ *www.nps.gov/ pisp* 🎟 *$4* ⊙ *Historic structures daily 8:30–4:30, visitor center and museum daily 8–5.*

Six miles back toward Fredonia from Pipe Spring on AZ 389, a dirt road leads 50 mi south through starkly beautiful, uninhabited country to

③④ **Toroweap Overlook,** a lonely and awesome viewpoint over one of the narrowest stretches of the canyon (less than 1 mi across). The overlook also contains the deepest sheer cliff (more than 3,000 ft straight down). From this vantage point, you can see upstream to sedimentary ledges, cliffs, and talus slopes. Looking downstream, you can see miles of the lava flow that forms steep deltas, some of which look like black waterfalls frozen on the cliff. Be sure you have plenty of gas, drinking water, good tires, and a reliable car; a high-clearance vehicle (one that sits high up off the ground, like a pickup truck) is best for this trip. Don't try to go in wet weather, when the dirt road is likely to be washed out. There's a ranger station near the rim as well as a primitive campground. If you plan to return the same day, you should make motel reservations in advance at an Arizona Strip motel.

NORTHWEST ARIZONA

If the Grand Canyon is the most dramatic natural attraction in northwest Arizona, it's by no means all there is to see. Towns such as Kingman hark back to the glory days of the old Route 66, and the ghost towns of Chloride and Oatman bear testament to the mining madness that once reigned in the region. Water-sports fans, or those who just want to laze on a houseboat, will enjoy Lake Havasu, where you'll find the misplaced English icon London Bridge.

Kingman

36 *112 mi west of Williams via I–40 or Rte. 66.*

The highway past Kingman may seem desolate at first, but the mountains that surround the area offer lots of outdoor activities, including those along the Kingman and Colorado rivers. Water sports play a big part in the area's recreation simply because about 1,000 mi of freshwater shoreline lies within the county along the Colorado River and around Lakes Havasu, Mohave, and Mead. Fish and boating are very popular activities here. With a little exploring, you'll also find some scattered "ghost" towns in the area, including Chloride.

Western character actor Andy Devine was from Kingman; it's obvious the moment you drive into town, as the fact is mentioned everywhere. The longest remaining stretch of Route 66 runs through Kingman. It's worth a short visit to take a walking tour past many of the historic buildings.

The **Kingman Area Chamber of Commerce** (⊠ 333 W. Andy Devine Ave. ☎ 928/753–6106 ⊕ www.kingmanchamber.org) carries T-shirts, postcards, and the usual brochures to acquaint you with local attractions. The **Bonelli House** (⊠ 430 E. Spring St. ☎ 928/753–1413), an excellent example of the Anglo-Territorial architecture popular in the early 1900s, is one of 62 buildings in the business district listed on the National Register of Historic Places. The **Mohave County Museum of History and Arts** (⊠ 400 W. Beale St. ☎ 928/753–3195 ⊕ www.ctaz.com/~mocohist/museum/index.htm) includes an Andy Devine Room with memorabilia from Devine's Hollywood years and, incongruously, a portrait collection of every president and first lady. There's also an exhibit of carved Kingman turquoise and a diorama depicting the expedition of Lt. Edward Beale, who led his ill-fated camel-cavalry unit to the area in search of a wagon road along the 35th parallel. Follow the White Cliffs Trail from downtown, and you'll see the deep ruts cut into the desert floor by the wagons that eventually came to Kingman after Beale's time.

A 15-mi drive from town up Hualapai Mountain Road will take you to **Hualapai Mountain Park** (☎ 928/757–3859 or 877/757–0915 for cabin reservations ⊕ www.hualapaimountainpark.com), where more than 2,300 wooded acres at elevations ranging from 4,984 to 8,417 ft hold 10 mi of hiking trails as well as picnic areas, rustic cabins, and RV and tenting areas.

off the beaten path

CHLORIDE – If you take U.S. 93 north from Kingman, in about 12 mi you'll come to a marked turnoff for the ghost town of Chloride, which takes its name from a type of silver ore mined in the area. Chloride is Arizona's oldest silver-mining camp. During its heyday, from 1900 to 1920, there were some 75 mines operating in the area: silver, gold, lead, zinc, molybdenum, and even turquoise were mined here. Today, you'll find about 500 folks living in Chloride; there are three cafés, two saloons, a grocery store, a B&B, and two RV parks. Some of the residents are artists and craftspeople who have small studios and shops in the historic buildings. Sights include the old jail, Chloride Baptist Church, Silverbelle Playhouse, and the Jim Fritz Museum. As you leave town, stop and take a photo of the large murals painted on the rocks by western artist Roy Purcell.

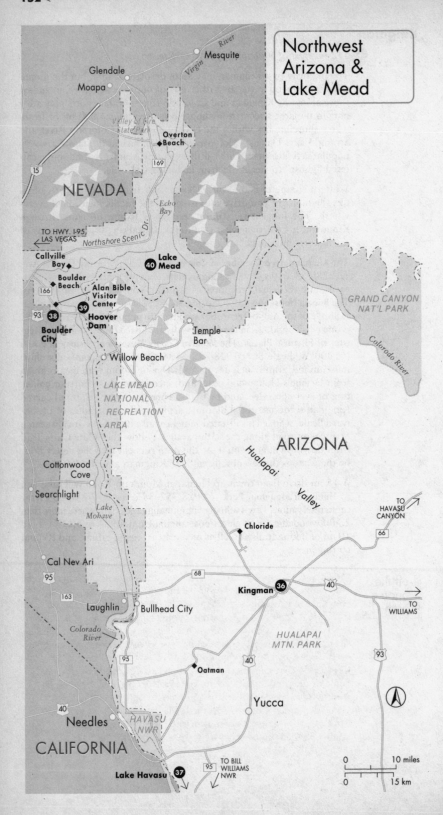

Northwest Arizona & Lake Mead

Virgin River

Mesquite

Glendale

Moapa

Valley of Fire State Park

Overton Beach

NEVADA

169

Echo Bay

TO HWY. I-95, LAS VEGAS

Northshore Scenic Dr.

Callville Bay

40 Lake Mead

Boulder Beach

166

Alan Bible Visitor Center

93 **38** **39**

Hoover Dam

Boulder City

Temple Bar

Willow Beach

GRAND CANYON NAT'L PARK

Colorado River

LAKE MEAD NATIONAL RECREATION AREA

ARIZONA

93

Hualapai

Cottonwood Cove

Valley

Searchlight

Lake Mohave

Chloride

TO HAVASU CANYON

66

Cal Nev Ari

95

163

68

Kingman **36**

40

TO WILLIAMS

Laughlin

Bullhead City

HUALAPAI MTN. PARK

Colorado River

95

93

40

Oatman

40

Yucca

Needles

HAVASU NWR

CALIFORNIA

95

TO BILL WILLIAMS NWR

Lake Havasu **37**

0   10 miles

0   15 km

Where to Stay & Eat

Kingman has several decent places to eat and about three dozen motels, most of them along Andy Devine Avenue. Most of the major chains are represented, including Days Inn, Motel 6, and Super 8. For approximate costs, *see* the dining and lodging price charts at the beginning of this chapter.

$–$$ ✕ **Hubb's Bistro.** In the Brunswick Hotel, this bustling eatery caters to most tastes and does a wonderful job with everything from burgers to seafood, including some traditional French dishes. The owner is from France and very proud of his café. ⊠ *315 E. Andy Devine Ave.* ☎ *928/718–1800* ⊟ *AE, D, MC, V* ☉ *Closed Sun.*

¢–$ 🏨 **Brunswick Hotel.** The hotel opened its doors in 1909 and was the first three-story building in town. Rooms have antique furnishings. You'll enjoy the early-1900s ambience coupled with courtesy and today's amenities. ⊠ *315 E. Andy Devine Ave., 86401* ☎ *928/718–1800* ⊕ *www.hotel-brunswick.com* ⤳ *18 rooms, 9 with shared bath; 6 suites* ♨ *Restaurant, massage, bar, no-smoking rooms; no TV in some rooms* ⊟ *AE, D, MC, V* ⬝❷❶ *CP.*

¢ 🏨 **Quality Inn.** This chain motel has comfortable rooms and a small gift display with an impressive collection of Route 66 whiskey jiggers. There's complimentary Continental breakfast, too. ⊠ *1400 E. Andy Devine Ave., 86401* ☎ *928/753–4747 or 800/228–5151* ⊕ *www.hotelchoice.com* ⤳ *98 rooms* ⊟ *AE, D, DC, MC, V* ⬝❷❶ *CP.*

en·route A worthwhile stop on your way from Kingman to Lake Havasu, the ghost town of **Oatman** is reached via old Route 66 (now AZ 68). It's a straight shot across the Mojave Desert valley for a while, but then the road narrows and winds precipitously for about 15 mi through the Black Mountains. (This road is public, but beyond a narrow shoulder, the land is privately owned and heavily patrolled, thanks to still-active gold mines throughout these low but rugged hills.) Oatman's main street is right out of the Old West; scenes from a number of films, including *How the West Was Won*, were shot here. It still has a remote, old-time feel: many of the natives carry side arms, and they're not acting. You can wander into one of the three saloons or visit the **Oatman Hotel**, where Clark Gable and Carole Lombard honeymooned in 1939 after they were secretly married in Kingman; the burros that often come in from nearby hills and meander down the street, however, are the town's real draw. A couple of stores sell hay to folks who want to feed these "wild" beasts, which at last count numbered about a dozen and which leave plenty of evidence of their visits in the form of "road apples"—so watch your step. For information about the town and its attractions, contact the **Oatman Chamber of Commerce** (☎ 928/768–6222 ⊕ www.route66azlastingimpressions.com).

Lake Havasu

➌➐ *60 mi southwest of Kingman.*

Remember the old nursery rhyme "London Bridge Is Falling Down"? Well, it was. After about 150 years of constant use, the 294-ft-long landmark was sinking into the Thames. When Lake Havasu City founder heard about this predicament, he set about actually to buy the bridge and have it disassembled, shipped 10,000 mi to western Arizona, and rebuilt, stone by stone. The bridge was reconstructed on mounds of sand and took three years to complete. When it was finished, a mile-long channel was dredged under the bridge and water was diverted from Lake Havasu through the Bridgewater Channel.

Today, the entire city is centered on this unusual attraction. If there's an Arizona Riviera, this is it. No doubt, Lake Havasu City attracts the water lovers. With its more than 45 mi of lake shoreline, you can imagine how popular water sports are here. You can rent everything from water skis to Jet Skis, small fishing boats to large houseboats.

Below the lake, the Colorado River marks the western boundary of Arizona—more than 300 mi long—all the way to the Mexican border. There are no fewer than 13 RV parks and campgrounds, about 125 boat-in campsites, and hundreds of hotel and motel rooms for additional creature comforts. The area gets less than 4 inches of rain annually, which means it's almost always sunny. Spring, winter, and fall are the best times to visit. In summer, temperatures often exceed 100°F. There are golf and tennis facilities, as well as fishing guides who'll help you find, and catch, the big ones.

If you're interested in exploring nearby old mines, a wildlife sanctuary and the desert in general, join up with a four-wheel driving tour created by **Outback Adventures** (☎ 928/680–6151 ⊕ www.outbackadventures. com).

If you have an interest in wildlife-watching—especially bird-watching—you can visit the **Havasu National Wildlife Refuge** (✉ off I–40, south of Needles ☎ 760/326–3853 ⊕ southwest.fws.gov), between Needles and Lake Havasu City, a 44,371-acre refuge for wintering Canada geese and other waterfowl. Follow the signs on I–40, south of Needles near the California border. **Bill Williams River National Wildlife Refuge** (✉ AZ 95, 23 mi south of Lake Havasu City ☎ 928/667–4144 ⊕ southwest.fws. gov), south of Lake Havasu City, is a 6,000-acre preserve where you'll be able to walk through the largest surviving cottonwood-willow woodland in the region. To reach the refuge, travel south on AZ 95; the entrance is between mileposts 160 and 161.

Where to Stay & Eat

Many tourists make this stop a day trip on their way to Laughlin or Las Vegas, but there are plenty of accommodations if you'd like to stay more than a night. Of the chain hotels in town, the Best Western and the Holiday Inn are your best bets. For approximate costs, *see* the dining and lodging price charts at the beginning of this chapter.

$$–$$$ ✕ **Shugrue's.** If you've dined at the Sedona restaurant, you know what to expect here. Shugrue's features hand-cut steaks, very fresh seafood, salads, and other well-prepared American fare. The baked desserts are worth saving room for. Most tables offer good bridge views. ✉ *1425 McCulloch Blvd.* ☎ *928/453–1400* ⊟ *AE, MC, V.*

$–$$$ ✕ **London Arms Pub and Restaurant.** Remodeled in 2002 to present dinner theater on the weekends, this traditional-looking pub offers more than the traditional fish-and-chips. Along with the standard salads and burgers, you can also order Cornish game hen, lobster ravioli, and prime rib. If you opt for an evening in the Theatre Banquet Room, you'll be served a four-course feast for $19.95, prior to the performances held at 5:30 and 7 on Friday and Saturday and on noon Sunday. The cost of the show is additional and varies. ✉ *422 English Village* ☎ *928/855–8782* ⊟ *AE, D, MC, V.*

$–$$ ✕ **Juicy's River Café.** This is a favorite hangout for the local folks who know good food when they taste it. The Sunday breakfast is especially popular. It's a small and cozy place (14 tables inside, 4 more outside) with a varied menu that includes such standbys as corned beef and cabbage, smoked prime rib, meat loaf, pot roast and vegetables, and homemade soups and desserts. ✉ *25 N. Acoma Blvd.* ☎ *928/855–8429* ▭ *AE, D, MC, V.*

¢ ✕ **Chico's Tacos.** This is a decent Mexican fast-food choice. The salsa bar offers several fresh salsas of various degrees of spiciness. ✉ *1641 McCulloch Blvd.* ☎ *928/680–7010* ▭ *D, MC, V.*

$–$$ ▦ **London Bridge Resort.** If you want to be close to the bridge, this interesting hotel is a dependable choice. The decor is a strange mix of Tudor and Southwestern; other than that, studios are standard motel rooms with kitchenettes. One-bedroom condos have separate living and dining areas as well as full kitchens; two-bedroom condos have balconies. There's a serviceable restaurant. ✉ *1477 Queen's Bay, 86403* ☎ *928/855–0888 or 800/624–7939* ☐ *928/855–9209* ⊕ *www.londonbridgeresort.com* ⇗ *4 studios, 72 1-bedroom condos, 46 2-bedroom condos* ♨ *Restaurant, some kitchenettes, some kitchens, cable TV, golf privileges, 3 pools, beach* ▭ *AE, D, MC, V.*

$ ▦ **Havasu Springs Resort.** Four hotels at this lakeside resort accommodate a wide variety of needs. In addition to the standard hotel rooms, the resort also offers suites and apartments. For the adventurous willing to plunk down a chunk of change for the three-night minimum (ranging from $1,035 to $1,650 depending on the size), houseboats provide a very popular Lake Havasu vacation option. These portable lodgings are good choices for large groups, as they sleep up to 12 people. ✉ *2581 AZ 95, Parker 85344* ☎ *928/667–3361* ☐ *928/667–1098* ⊕ *www.havasusprings.com* ⇗ *38 rooms, 4 suites, 3 apartments* ♨ *Restaurant, lounge, beach* ▭ *AE, D, MC, V.*

¢–$ ▦ **Island Inn.** Fido is welcome here, if he's small, that is. And together, you can walk to London Bridge and London Bridge Beach. There are 117 rooms, a pool, hot tub, and meeting rooms. Rooms are large and basic. ✉ *1300 W. McCulloch Blvd., 86403* ☎ *928/680–0606 or 800/243–9955* ☐ *928/680–4218* ⇗ *117 rooms* ♨ *Pool, hot tub, meeting rooms, some pets allowed (fee)* ▭ *AE, D, MC, V.*

off the beaten path

'AHAKHAV TRIBAL PRESERVE – The 2,500-acre preserve is on the Colorado Indian Tribes Reservation and is a top spot in the area for bird-watching and hiking. From AZ 95 in Parker, which is at the southern end of Lake Havasu, head west on Mohave Road for about 2 mi. When you reach the PARKER INDIAN RODEO ASSOCIATION sign, continue ½ mi farther and turn left at the TRIBAL PRESERVE sign at Rodeo Drive. There are several campgrounds, parks, and recreation areas along the Colorado River. Rent a canoe ($10 an hour or $25 a day) and bird-watch along the shoreline of the backwater area branching off the Colorado River. Some 350 species of migratory and native birds live around the region or visit on their annual migrations. The 3-mi hiking trail offers exercise stations along the way, and a trail extension will lead you to the tribal historical museum and gift shop. ✉ *25401 Rodeo Dr., Parker* ☎ *928/669–2664* ☐ *928/669–8024* ⊕ *www.ahakhav.com.*

SOUTHEAST NEVADA

There's quite a change between the natural beauty of the Grand Canyon area and the man-made spectacles of eastern Nevada. However, the mammoth Hoover Dam and huge Lake Mead are definitely worth including on your itinerary.

Boulder City, Nevada

㊳ *76 mi northwest of Kingman via U.S. 93.*

Like so many other small Western towns, Boulder City was created for the needs of a nearby construction or mining project, in this case the construction of nearby Hoover Dam, whose builders needed to house thousands of workers and to deter them from spending their hard-earned dollars on wine, women, and Las Vegas. After the project was completed, these towns were usually left to wither and die or make it on their own, and Boulder City was no exception. Developed in the 1930s, the town once housed 5,000 construction personnel; after the dam was finished, the town lost half of its population. Slowly it began a come-back and now enjoys a pleasant standard of living; it is still home to some of the dam builders, known locally as the "31ers." The town is 5 mi from Lake Mead and 8 mi from Hoover Dam. If you're looking for glitz and glamour, you're in the wrong place, and you're better off making the 21-mi trek into Las Vegas. Indeed, Boulder City is the only community in Nevada where gambling is illegal. However, it is worth a brief stopover for those who wish to spend an enjoyable couple of hours strolling the main streets downtown and popping into Native American and Mexican gift shops, antiques and jewelry stores, and galleries.

Don't miss the historic **Boulder Dam Hotel** (✉ 1305 Arizona St. ☎ 702/293–3510), built in 1932, which houses a bookstore, art gallery, and restaurant. The **Boulder City/Hoover Dam Museum** (☎ 702/294–1988), which preserves and displays artifacts relating to the workers and construction of Boulder City and Hoover Dam, is in the Boulder Dam Hotel. The **Boulder City Chamber of Commerce** (☎ 702/293–2034 ⊕ www.bouldercitychamber.com) is a good place to gather information on the history of Hoover Dam and other historic sights around town.

Hoover Dam

★ **㊴** *67 mi northwest of Kingman via U.S. 93.*

The power of humanity to hold sway over the natural world—for good or ill, depending on your viewpoint—is powerfully evident in the Hoover Dam. Simply put, it's incredible. Completed in 1935, the dam is 727 ft high (the equivalent of a 70-story building) and 660 ft thick at the base (more than the length of two football fields). Its construction required 4.4 million cubic yards of concrete, enough to build a two-lane highway from San Francisco to New York.

Equally amazing are the relatively minuscule construction costs. Congress authorized just $175 million to build the dam in 1928 to control floods and generate electricity.

Originally referred to as Boulder Dam, the structure was officially named Hoover Dam in recognition of President Herbert Hoover's role in the project. More than 700,000 people a year (34 million since the tours began in 1937) take tours of the dam. The Discovery Tour is a self-paced, self-guiding tour, but staff guides provide information and answer questions at various locations. Talks, by the guides, are presented every 15 minutes from 9 AM until 4:30 PM. You are allowed to take elevators down into the dam to visit the power-plant generators, and you will find historical exhibits on the construction of Hoover Dam and displays on the region's natural history on the Plaza level of the visitor center. A visitor center on the Nevada side contains a theater with three revolving sections, an exhibition gallery, an observation tower, and a five-story parking garage. Due to heightened security requirements,

RVs and trailers are now subject to inspection. ✉ *U.S. 93, east of Boulder City* ☎ *702/293–8321 or 702/294–3523* ⊕ *www.hooverdam.usbr. gov* ⊠ *$10* ☉ *Tours daily 9–4:30.*

Lake Mead

40 *67 mi northwest of Kingman on U.S. 93.*

It makes sense that a dam as monstrous as the Hoover creates an ocean of water behind it. Lake Mead is the largest man-made reservoir in the country, covering 229 square mi. **Lakeshore Scenic Drive** (NV 166) meanders along the beautiful shore of Lake Mead. An hour's drive will take you along the north side of the lake, where you'll find several recreation areas and marinas. If you are coming from Arizona and want to swim in Lake Mead, **Boulder Beach,** on the Nevada side of the lake, is the closest swimming beach to Arizona and only a mile or so from the dam visitor center. **Echo Bay,** roughly 40 mi northeast of Boulder Beach, is the best place to swim in the lake because it has better sand and fewer rocks—and visitors—than the other beaches. All over the lake, anglers fish for largemouth bass, catfish, trout, and black crappie, but striped bass are the feistiest and most prevalent. Houseboating is a favorite pastime; you can rent houseboats, along with speedboats, ski boats, and Jet Skis at the various marinas. Divers have a fantastic choice of underwater sights to explore, including the entire town of St. Thomas, a farming community that was inundated by the lake in the 1930s. Other activities abound, such as waterskiing, sailboarding, and snorkeling.

You can get information on the lake's history, ecology, and recreational activities, as well as driving maps and accommodations information, at the **Alan Bible Visitors Center** (✉ U.S. 93 and NV 166, Boulder City ☎ 702/293–8990), the National Park Service's visitor center for the Lake Mead area. It's just northeast of the town proper and is open daily 8:30–4:30.

Where to Stay

For approximate costs, *see* the lodging price chart at the beginning of this chapter.

$$$$ ⊞ **Seven Crown Resorts.** This is a good resource for houseboat rentals, an increasingly popular vacation option, especially for large groups. The boats come equipped with full kitchens and air-conditioning, and they can sleep up to 14 people. The beauty of renting a houseboat is that you can cruise down the lake and park where you please for as long as you like. The minimum rental is for three days, two nights; you get the best rates on a one-week rental. ✉ *Box 16247, Irvine, CA 92623* ☎ *800/752–9669* ⊕ *www.sevencrown.com* ⚹ *Kitchens; no TV* ⊟ *D, MC, V.*

¢–$ ⊞ **Temple Bar Resort.** This upgraded motel right on the Arizona shore of the lake is a good choice if you want a quiet room; the hotel's remote location ensures peace. The restaurant, which serves typical American fare, has outdoor seating overlooking the water. ✉ *Temple Bar, AZ 86643* ☎ *928/767–3211 or 800/752–9669* ⊷ *18 rooms, 4 cabins* ⚹ *Restaurant* ⊟ *D, MC, V.*

¢ ⊞ **Hacienda Resort.** Even though there is no gambling allowed within the city limits of Boulder City, this large, Vegas-style casino sits outside the city limits and is your best option for gambling in the immediate area. Close to Lake Mead and Hoover Dam, this resort has seven restaurants, live entertainment, and more than 800 slot machines. ✉ *U.S. 93, Boulder City, NV 89005* ☎ *702/293–5000* ⊷ *375 rooms* ⚹ *7 restaurants, casino* ⊟ *D, MC, V.*

¢ ⚠ **Temple Bar Campground.** Space is available on a first-come, first-served basis at this 153-site campground on the Arizona shore of the lake, but there are usually plenty of unoccupied sites on all but the busiest holiday weekends. All sites have a picnic table and fire ring. The nightly fee is $10. ⚆ *Flush toilets, dump station, running water (non-potable), fire grates, picnic tables* ⤴ *153 sites* ⊠ *Temple Bar, AZ 86643* ☎ *928/767–3401 or 800/752–9669* ☉ *Open year-round.*

Sports & the Outdoors

BOATING Rental options include houseboats, patio boats, fishing boats, and ski boats—pick up a list of marinas at the Alan Bible Visitors Center. Powerboats as well as houseboats are available at **Callville Bay Resort and Marina** (⊠ Callville Bay ☎ 702/565–8958 or 800/255–5561). **Echo Bay Resort** (⊠ Echo Bay ☎ 702/394–4000 or 800/752–9669) is a popular choice for Lake Mead houseboat rentals; the company also rents ski boats, fishing boats, and other personal watercraft. You'll find boat rentals, a beach, camping facilities, a gift shop, and a restaurant at **Lake Mead Marina** (⊠ Boulder Beach, Boulder City ☎ 702/293–3484).

CRUISES **Lake Mead Cruises** (⊠ Lake Mead Marina, near Boulder Beach, Boulder City ☎ 702/293–6180 ⊕ www.lakemeadcruises.com) offers 1½-hr cruises of the Hoover Dam area on the 300-passenger *Desert Princess* every two hours from 10 AM to 4 PM daily. Also offered are breakfast buffet cruises and early dinner and dinner-dance cruises. **Gray Line Tours** (☎ 702/384–1234 or 800/634–6579 ⊕ www.pcap.com/grayline.htm) offers a 15-mi motorized raft trip on the Colorado from the base of Hoover Dam down Black Canyon to Willow Beach.

THE GRAND CANYON & NORTHWEST ARIZONA A TO Z

To research prices, get advice from other travelers, and book travel arrangements, visit ⊕ *www.fodors.com*

AIR TRAVEL

Several carriers fly to the Grand Canyon Airport from Las Vegas, including Air Vegas, Scenic Airlines, and Vision Air, which offer service from North Las Vegas Airport to the Grand Canyon.

🛪 **Air Vegas** ☎ 800/255-7474 ⊕ www.airvegas.com. **Scenic Airlines** ☎ 800/634-6801 ⊕ www.scenic.com. **Vision Air** ☎ 702/261-3850.

AIRPORTS

North Las Vegas Airport in Las Vegas is the primary air hub for flights to Grand Canyon Airport. You can also make connections into the Grand Canyon from Sky Harbor International Airport in Phoenix.

🛪 **Grand Canyon Airport** ☎ 928/638-2446. **North Las Vegas Airport** ☎ 702/261-3806. **Sky Harbor International Airport** ☎ 602/273-3300.

AIRPORT The Tusayan/Canyon Airport Shuttle operates between Grand Canyon
TRANSFERS Airport and the nearby towns of Tusayan and Grand Canyon Village; it makes hourly runs daily between 8:15 AM and 5:15 PM, with additional trips in the summer months.

Fred Harvey Transportation Company offers 24-hour taxi service at Grand Canyon Airport, Grand Canyon Village, and the nearby village of Tusayan. Taxis also make trips to other destinations in and around Grand Canyon National Park.

🛪 **Fred Harvey Transportation Company** ☎ 928/638-2822. **Tusayan/Canyon Airport Shuttle** ☎ 928/638-0821.

BIKE & MOPED TRAVEL

Bicycles are not permitted on any of the Grand Canyon's designated trails, but there are miles of scenic paved thoroughfares in the national park. The park roads have narrow shoulders and are heavily trafficked, so if you ride on them use extreme caution. There are no rentals or tours available at either North or South Rim, however.

BUS TRAVEL

There is no public bus transportation to the Grand Canyon. Greyhound Lines provides bus service to Flagstaff, Williams, and Laughlin. Schedules change frequently; call or check the Web site for information.
🚍 **Greyhound Lines** ☎ 800/231-2222 ⊕ www.greyhound.com.

PUBLIC TRANSIT WITHIN THE GRAND CANYON

Within the park, there are three shuttle routes: Hermits Rest Route operates from March through November between Grand Canyon Village and Hermits Rest. You can catch this shuttle every 15 minutes at one hour before sunrise until one hour after sunset. The Village Route operates year-round in the village area and offers shuttles from one hour before sunrise until after dark. This shuttle service is the easiest access to the Canyon View Information Center. The Kaibab Trail Route travels from Canyon View Information Center to Yaki Point, including a stop at the South Kaibab Trailhead.

From mid-May to late October, the Trans Canyon Shuttle leaves Lodge at 1:30 PM and arrives at the North Rim's Grand Canyon Lodge about 6 PM. The return trip leaves the North Rim each morning at 7 AM, arriving at the South Rim at about noon. One-way fare is $65, round-trip $110. A 50% deposit is required two weeks in advance.
🚍 **Trans Canyon Shuttle** ☎ 928/638-2820.

BUSINESS HOURS

BANKS There is a 24-hour teller machine at the Bank One South Rim office in Market Plaza near the General Store. There are also ATM machines at several hotels and stores in Tusayan. No banking facilities are located within Grand Canyon National Park at the North Rim.
🚍 **Bank One** ☎ 928/638-2437.

POST OFFICES There's a U.S. Post Office in the Market Plaza shopping center near Yavapai Lodge. It's open weekdays 9–4:30 and Saturday 11–3.

CAMPING SUPPLIES

Delaware North General Store has three locations in the South Rim area: at Grand Canyon Village, in the nearby village of Tusayan, and at Desert View near the park's east entrance. The main store, in Grand Canyon Village, is a department store that has a deli and sells a full line of camping, hiking, and backpacking supplies, in addition to groceries.

The North Rim General Store, inside the park at the North Rim Campground, carries groceries, some clothing, and travelers' supplies.
🚍**Delaware North General Store** ✉Grand Canyon Village ☎928/638-2262 ✉Tusayan ☎ 928/638-2854 ✉ Desert View ☎ 928/638-2393. **North Rim General Store** ✉ North Rim Campground, Grand Canyon North Rim ☎ 928/638-2611.

CAR TRAVEL

Most of Arizona's scenic highlights are many miles apart, and a car is essential for touring the state. However, you won't really need one if you're planning to visit only the Grand Canyon's most popular area, the South Rim. Some people choose to fly to the Grand Canyon and then hike, catch a shuttle or taxi, or sign on for bus tours or mule rides in Grand Canyon Village.

If you are driving to Arizona from the east, or coming up from the southern part of the state, the best access to the Grand Canyon is from Flagstaff. You can take U.S. 180 northwest (81 mi) to Grand Canyon Village on the South Rim. Or, for a scenic route with stopping points along the canyon rim, drive north on U.S. 89 from Flagstaff, turn left at the junction of AZ 64 (52 mi north of Flagstaff), and proceed north and west for an additional 57 mi until you reach Grand Canyon Village on the South Rim.

To visit the North Rim of the canyon, proceed north from Flagstaff on U.S. 89 to Bitter Springs. Then take U.S. 89A to the junction of AZ 67. Travel south on AZ 67 for approximately 40 mi to the North Rim, which is 210 mi from Flagstaff.

If you are crossing Arizona on I–40 from the west, your most direct route to the South Rim is on AZ 64 (U.S. 180), which runs north from Williams for 58 mi to Grand Canyon Village.

GASOLINE The only gas station inside the national park is at Desert View, and this station operates only from March 31 to September 30 dependent on snowfall. Gas is available year-round near the South Entrance at Moqui Lodge (though the lodge itself is now closed), in Tusayan, and at Cameron, to the east.

At the South Rim, in Grand Canyon Village, the Public Garage is a fully equipped AAA garage that provides auto and RV repair daily 8–noon and 1–5 as well as 24-hour emergency service. This is a garage for repairs only and does not sell gasoline.

At the North Rim, the Chevron service station, which repairs autos, is located inside the park on the access road leading to the North Rim Campground. No diesel fuel is available at the North Rim.
🛈 **Chevron** ☎ 928/638-2611. **Public Garage** ☎ 928/638-2225.

ROAD CONDITIONS When driving off major highways in low-lying areas, watch for rain clouds. Flash floods from sudden summer rains can be deadly.

The South Rim stays open to auto traffic year-round, although access to Hermits Rest is limited to shuttle buses in summer because of congestion. Roads leading to the South Rim near Grand Canyon Village and the parking areas along the rim are badly congested in summer as well. However, if you visit from October through April, you should experience only light to moderate traffic and have no problem with parking.

Reaching elevations of 8,000 ft, the more remote North Rim has no services available from late October through mid-May. AZ 67 south of Jacob Lake is closed by the first heavy snowfall in November or December and remains closed until early to mid-May.

EMERGENCIES
There are no pharmacies at the North or South Rim. Prescriptions can be delivered daily to the South Rim Clinic from Flagstaff.
🛈 Ambulance, Fire & Police **Emergency services** ☎ 911, 9–911 from in-park lodgings.
🛈 Hospitals **Grand Canyon Walk-in Clinic** ✉ Grand Canyon Village ☎ 928/638-2551. **North Rim Clinic** ✉ Grand Canyon Lodge, Cabin 1, Grand Canyon North Rim ☎ 928/638-2611 Ext. 222.

HEALTH
HIKING SAFETY TIPS The Grand Canyon is unforgiving, and it claims several lives each year. Most of those deaths are avoidable.

The trek down into the canyon appears deceptively easy; the route back up is much longer than most other mountain day hikes and is very fatiguing. Before hiking into the canyon, assess the proposed hiking conditions versus your physical condition. During summer months, temperatures inside the canyon can climb to 105°F. Carry water on hikes to the Inner Canyon—at least 1–1½ gallons per day. To avoid dehydration, drink frequently, about every 10 minutes, especially during summer months. Likewise, take food—preferably salty energy snacks such as trail mix and pretzels, along with bananas, fig bars, and other fructose-rich foods. Do not drink alcohol or caffeine, which accelerate dehydration; for the same reason, avoid processed sugar. Wear hiking boots that have been broken in and proven on previous hikes. Also wear sunscreen and a hat. Carry a first-aid kit. In case of a medical emergency, stay with the distressed person and ask the next hiker to go for help. Do not attempt to make the round-trip to the Colorado River in one day.

Be careful when you or your children are near the edge of the canyon or walking along any of the trails that descend into it. Guardrails exist only on portions of the rims. Before engaging in any strenuous exercise, be aware that the canyon rims are more than 7,000 ft in altitude. Being at this height can cause some people—even those in good shape—to become dizzy, faint, or nauseated.

HIKING PERMITS

Overnight hikes in the Grand Canyon require a permit that can be obtained by written or faxed requests to the Backcountry Information Center. Permits cost $10, plus $5 per person, per night. The free Backcountry Trip Planner should answer all of your hiking questions. Permits are limited; however, reservations can be made up to four months in advance. If you arrive at the canyon without a permit, go to the Backcountry Office at either rim—at the South Rim near Maswik Lodge, at the North Rim at the Ranger Station. Space may be available due to a last-minute cancellation—but don't count on it.

🚩 **Backcountry Office** ⌂ Box 129, Grand Canyon 86023 ☎ 928/638-7875 🖶 928/638-2125.

SIGHTSEEING TOURS

AIR TOURS Flights by plane and helicopter over the canyon are offered by a number of companies, departing for the Grand Canyon Airport at the south end of Tusayan. Prices and lengths of tours vary, but you can expect to pay about $75 per adult for short plane trips and approximately $100 for a brief helicopter tour.

🚩 **Air Grand Canyon** ⌧ Grand Canyon Airport, Tusayan ☎ 928/638-2686 ⊕ www.airgrandcanyon.com. **AirStar Helicopters/Airlines** ⌧ Grand Canyon Airport, Tusayan ☎ 928/638-2622 or 800/962-3869 ⊕ www.airstar.com. **Grand Canyon Airlines** ⌧ Grand Canyon Airport, Tusayan ☎ 928/638-2407 or 800/528-2413 ⊕ www.grandcanyonairlines.com. **Kenai Helicopters** ⌧ Grand Canyon Airport, Tusayan ☎ 928/638-2764 or 800/541-4537 ⊕ www.flykenai.com. **Papillon Helicopters** ⌧ Grand Canyon Airport, Tusayan ☎ 928/638-2419 or 800/528-2418 ⊕ www.papillon.com.

BUS TOURS The Fred Harvey Transportation Company in Grand Canyon Village operates daily motor-coach sightseeing trips along the South Rim. Prices range from $13 for shorter trips to $32 for the longer ones. Children under 16 ride free with an adult.

🚩 **Fred Harvey Transportation Company** ⌧ Grand Canyon Village ☎ 928/638-2631.

HIKING TOURS The Grand Canyon Field Institute leads a full program of educational guided hikes around the canyon from April through October. Tour topics include everything from archaeology and backcountry medicine to photography and landscape painting. For a personalized tour of the Grand

Canyon and surrounding sacred sites, contact Marvelous Marv, the Indiana Jones of Williams, whose knowledge of the area is as extensive as his repertoire of local legends.

🎦 The **Grand Canyon Field Institute** ⬜ Box 399, Grand Canyon 86023 ☎ 928/638-2485 ⊕ www.grandcanyon.org. **Marvelous Marv** ⬜ Box 544, Williams 86046 ☎ 928/635-4948.

RAFTING TOURS

Although more than 25 companies currently offer excursions, reservations for raft trips (excluding smooth-water, one-day cruises) often need to be made more than six months in advance. A complete list of concessionaires offering trips on the Colorado River is available on the Grand Canyon National Park Web site. National Park Service white-water concessionaires include Arizona River Runners, Canyoneers, Diamond River Adventures, Grand Canyon Expeditions, Outdoors Unlimited, and Tour West. For a smooth-water, one-day trip check out Wilderness River Adventures. Prices for river-raft trips vary greatly, depending on type and length. Half-day trips on smooth water run as low as $54 per person. Trips that negotiate the entire length of the canyon and take as long as 12 days can cost close to $2,000.

🎦 **Arizona River Runners** ☎ 602/867-4866 or 800/477-7238 ⊕ www.raftarizona.com. **Canyoneers, Inc.** ☎ 928/526-0924, 800/525-0924 outside Arizona ⊕ www.canyoneers. com. **Diamond River Adventures, Inc.** ☎ 928/645-8866 or 800/343-3121 ⊕ www. diamondriver.com. **Grand Canyon Expeditions** ☎ 435/644-2691 or 800/544-2691 ⊕ www.gcex.com. **Outdoors Unlimited** ☎ 928/526-2852 or 800/637-7238. **Tour West, Inc.** ☎ 801/225-0755 or 800/453-9107 ⊕ www.twriver.com. **Wilderness River Adventures** ☎ 928/645-3279 or 800/992-8022.

VISITOR INFORMATION

Every person arriving at the South or North Rim is given a detailed map of the area. Centers at both rims also publish a free newspaper, the *Guide*, which contains a detailed area map; it is available at the visitor center, entrance stations, and many of the lodging facilities and stores. The park also distributes *Accessibility Guide,* a free newsletter that details the facilities accessible to travelers with disabilities. Grand Canyon National Park is the contact for general information. Write ahead for a complimentary *Trip Planner,* updated regularly by the National Park Service.

Several Web sites are useful for trip-planning information, including the National Park Service's Web site, which has information on fees and permits. Try thecanyon.com, a commercial site where you'll find information on lodging, dining, and general park information. You can use the Xanterra Parks & Resorts Grand Canyon Web site to make reservations for park lodging, mule rides, bus tours, and some smooth-water rafting trips. The park service allows camping reservations to be made online as well, through the campground reservation vendor.

In summer, transportation-services desks are maintained at Lodge, Maswik Lodge, and Yavapai Lodge in Grand Canyon Village; in winter, the one at Yavapai is closed. The desks provide information and handle bookings, sightseeing tours, taxi and bus services, mule and horseback rides, and accommodations at Phantom Ranch (at the bottom of the Grand Canyon). The concierge at El Tovar can also arrange most tours, with the exception of mule rides and lodging at Phantom Ranch.

Grand Canyon Lodge has lodging and general information about the North Rim year-round, but you cannot make reservations for the lodge directly through the hotel. For information on local services during the season in which the North Rim is open, generally mid-May–late October, depending on the weather, you can phone the lodge directly.

The Williams and Forest Service Visitor Center, run jointly by the U.S. Forest Service and the Williams Chamber of Commerce, offers information on the Kaibab National Forest and the entire Grand Canyon region.

Some other regional resources include the Flagstaff Visitor Center, Boulder City Chamber of Commerce, Kingman Area Chamber of Commerce, Lake Havasu Tourism Bureau, Laughlin Chamber of Commerce, and Laughlin Visitors Bureau.

🗂 Grand Canyon Contacts **Grand Canyon Lodge** ☎ 928/638–2611 direct to hotel. **Grand Canyon National Park** ✍ Box 129, Grand Canyon 86023 ☎ 928/638–7888 recorded message 🖷 928/638–7797 ⊕ www.nps.gov/grca. **Grand Canyon National Park Lodges** ✍ Xanterra Parks and Resorts, 14001 E. Iliff Ave., Suite 600, Aurora, CO 80014 ☎ 303/297–2757 🖷 303/297–3175 ⊕ www.grandcanyonlodges.com. **North and South Rim Camping** ✍ National Park Reservation Service, Box 1600, Cumberland, MD 21501 ☎ 800/365–2267 ⊕ reservations.nps.gov/index.cfm. **The Canyon.com** ⊕ www.thecanyon.com. **Williams and Forest Service Visitor Center** ✉ 200 W. Railroad Ave., at Grand Canyon Blvd., Williams 86046 ☎ 928/635–4061.

🗂 Other Arizona Contacts **Boulder City Chamber of Commerce** ✉ 1305 Arizona St., Boulder City, NV 89005 ☎ 702/293–2034 ⊕ www.bouldercitychamber.com. **Kingman Area Chamber of Commerce** ✉ 120 W. Andy Devine Ave., Kingman 86402 ☎ 928/753–6106. **Lake Havasu Tourism Bureau** ✉ 314 London Bridge Rd., Lake Havasu City 86403 ☎ 928/453–3444 or 800/242–8278 ⊕ www.golakehavasu.com. **Laughlin Chamber of Commerce** ✉ 1585 Casino Dr. ✍ Box 77777, Laughlin, NV 89028 ☎ 702/298–2214 or 800/227–5245 ⊕ www.laughlinchamber.com. **Laughlin Visitors Bureau** ✉ 1555 S. Casino Dr., Laughlin, NV 89029 ☎ 702/298–3022 ⊕ www.visitlaughlin.com.

THE NORTHEAST

4

FODOR'S CHOICE
Canyon de Chelly, *Chinle*
Goosenecks Region, Utah, *a scenic drive*
Monument Valley Navajo Tribal Park, *Monument Valley*
Navajo National Monument, *Black Mesa*
Wahweap Lodge, *Wahweap*

HIGHLY RECOMMENDED
HOTELS   Goulding's Lodge, *Monument Valley*
San Juan Inn & Trading Post, *Mexican Hat, Utah*
Uncle Bill's Place, *Page*

SIGHTS   Antelope Canyon, *Page*
First Mesa, *First Mesa*
Rainbow Bridge National Monument, *Wahweap*

Updated by
Bob and
Gloria Willis

NORTHEAST ARIZONA is a vast and magnificent land of lofty buttes, towering cliffs, and turquoise skies so clear that horizons appear endless. Most of the land in the area belongs to the Navajo and Hopi peoples, who cling to ancient traditions based on spiritual values, kinship, and an affinity for nature. In many respects life on the Hopi Mesas has changed little during the last two centuries, and visiting this land can feel like traveling to a foreign country. Native American arts and crafts can be found in shops and trading posts, and in towns such as Tuba City and Window Rock it's not uncommon to hear the gliding vowels and soft consonants of the Navajo language, a tongue as different from Hopi as English is from Chinese. As you drive in the vicinity, tune your AM radio to 660 KTNN, the Voice of the Navajo Nation. You'll quickly understand why the U.S. Marine Navajo "code talkers" communicating in their native tongue were able to devise a code within their language that was never broken by the Japanese.

The Navajo Nation encompasses more than 27,000 square mi, an area that would rank it larger than 10 of the 50 states. In its approximate center sits the 4,000-square-mi Hopi Reservation, a series of adobe villages built on high mesas overlooking cultivated land. On Arizona's northern and eastern borders, where the Navajo Nation continues into Utah and New Mexico, the Navajo National Monument and Canyon de Chelly contain haunting cliff dwellings of ancient people who lived in the area 1,500 years ago. Glen Canyon Dam, which abuts the far northwestern corner of the reservation on U.S. 89, holds back more than 200 mi of emerald waters known as Lake Powell.

Most of northeast Arizona is desert country, but it is far from boring: eerie and spectacular rock formations as colorful as desert sunsets highlight immense mesas, canyons, and cliffs; towering stands of ponderosa pine cover the Chuska Mountains to the north and east of Canyon de Chelly. Navajo Mountain to the north and west in Utah soars more than 10,000 ft, and the San Francisco Peaks climb to similar heights to the south and west by Flagstaff. According to the Navajo creation myth, these are two of the four mountainous boundaries of the sacred land where the Navajo first emerged from the Earth's interior.

Exploring the Northeast

The Navajo Nation, which encircles the Hopi Reservation, occupies most of northeastern Arizona. Canyon de Chelly is in the eastern part of the reservation. The Navajo National Monument and Monument Valley are in north-central "Navajoland" (a term used by the Navajo in promotional material). In the northwestern corner of the Arizona portion of the reservation are Lake Powell and Glen Canyon Dam. Note: Northeastern Arizona is a sparsely inhabited area with few roads and services. Rarely do establishments have numbered street addresses; even the post office operates on the basis of landmarks. Don't count on using your cell phone in many portions of the region, though talks are under way with the Navajo Nation to install cell phone towers in some areas.

Numbers in the text correspond to numbers in the margin and on the Northeast Arizona map.

About the Restaurants

Few communities in northeast Arizona have public eating establishments, but restaurants can be found in several towns discussed in this chapter. Fine dining is even more scarce, but you'll find very good Native

American, Mexican, and Southwestern cuisine, as well as standard American fare. Basic Navajo and Hopi food consists mainly of fry bread, Indian-style tacos, mutton stew, and Hopi "piki"—a paper-thin blue-corn bread. In the smaller reservation communities, only fast food may be available.

About the Hotels

One of the most important things to know when traveling in northeastern Arizona is which of the scattered communities have motels. Most motels throughout the northeast are clean, comfortable, and well maintained. Bed-and-breakfasts have begun to proliferate in Page. Contact the Page/Lake Powell Chamber of Commerce or the Navajo Nation Visitors Center for a list of area B&Bs, campgrounds, RV facilities, and Native American hogan accommodations. During summer months, it is especially wise to make reservations. Unless otherwise indicated, all rooms have air-conditioning, private baths, telephones, and TVs.

WHAT IT COSTS				
	$$$$	$$$	$$	$	¢
RESTAURANTS	over $30	$20–$30	$12–$20	$8–$12	under $8
HOTELS	over $250	$175–$250	$120–$175	$70–$120	under $70

Restaurant prices are per person for a main course at dinner. Hotel prices are for two people in a standard double room in high season, excluding taxes and service charges.

Timing

Summer is a busy time in the Lake Powell area, and reservations for accommodations are essential. Travelers seeking a quieter vacation should plan to visit between early November and late March, when the crowds—and the prices—ebb. The first weekend of September after Labor Day is a good time to be at Window Rock, when the Navajo Nation Annual Tribal Fair takes place. It's the world's largest Native American fair and includes a rodeo, traditional Navajo music and dances, food booths, and an intertribal powwow. August and September bring the Hopi Harvest Festival, a celebration featuring Harvest and Butterfly social dances.

NAVAJO NATION EAST

Land has always been central to the history of the Navajo people: it's embedded in their very name. The Tewa were the first to call them *Navahu*—which means "large area of cultivated land." But according to the Navajo creation myth, they were given the name *ni'hookaa diyan diné*—"holy earth people"—by their creators. Today, among tribal members, they call themselves the Diné. The eastern portion of the Arizona Navajo Nation (in Navajo, *diné bikéyah*) is a dry but often surprisingly green land, especially in the vicinity of the aptly named Beautiful Valley, south of Canyon de Chelly along U.S. 191. A landscape of rolling hills, wide arroyos, and small canyons, the area is dotted with traditional Navajo hogans (eight-side domed houses made of mud, logs, or even contemporary building materials), sheepfolds, cattle tanks, and wood racks. The region's easternmost portion is marked by tall mountains and towering sandstone cliffs cut by primitive roads that are generally accessible only by horse or four-wheel-drive vehicles.

4

If you have 2 days

If you are just driving through the area on your way west, you might start off in ► ▦ **Window Rock ①**, from which you'll have an easy drive to some of the most interesting sights in northeastern Arizona. On your first day, visit **Canyon de Chelly ②**. On the second, set out for the **Hopi Mesas ⑤–⑦**, stopping along the way at **Hubbell Trading Post National Historic Site ③** and, perhaps, **Keams Canyon Trading Post ④** for a mid-morning snack.

If you have 5 days

If you plan to spend a bit more time exploring the region after a trip to the Grand Canyon, head north on U.S. 89 on your first day to ► ▦ **Tuba City ⑧**. Along the way, you might wish to stop by ► ▦ **Cameron Trading Post ⑨**. Explore the area, and relax for the night. On the second day, head east at Moenkopi on AZ 264 for the **Hopi Mesas ⑤–⑦**. (And fill your tank before you leave since Tuba City is the last stop for gas before the mesas.) Have lunch at the **Hopi Cultural Center,** then return to Tuba City and head northeast on U.S. 160 toward ▦ **Kayenta ⑩**, where you can spend your second night. Get up early the next day to visit the **Navajo National Monument ⑭** and hike to Beta-Takin or Keet Seel pueblo (if you have made reservations in advance). Spend your third night at the lodge at ▦ **Goulding's Trading Post ⑬** in Monument Valley. The next day, visit **Monument Valley Navajo Tribal Park ⑪**, and then take U.S. 160 north to where it connects with U.S. 191 near the town of Mexican Water. Head south for Chinle, a good base for touring ▦ **Canyon de Chelly ②**.

Window Rock

► **①** *192 mi from Flagstaff, east on I–40 and north on Indian Hwy. 12; 26 mi from Gallup, New Mexico, north on U.S. 666 and west on NM and AZ 264.*

Named for the immense arch-shaped "window" in a massive sandstone ridge above the city, Window Rock is the capital of the Navajo Nation and the center of its Tribal Government. With a population of fewer than 5,000, this community serves as the business and social center for Navajo families throughout the reservation. Window Rock is a good place to stop for food, supplies, and gas. The **Navajo Nation Council Chambers** is a handsome structure that resembles a large hogan. Visitors can observe sessions of the council, where 88 delegates representing 110 reservation chapters meet on the third Monday of January, April, July, and October. Turn east off Indian Highway 12, about ½ mi north of AZ 264, to reach the Council Chambers. **Window Rock Navajo Tribal Park,** near the Council Chambers, is a memorial park honoring Navajo veterans, including the famous World War II code talkers. ⊠ *AZ 264* ☎ *928/871–6417.*

The **Navajo Nation Museum,** on the grounds of the former Tse Bonito Park off AZ 264, is devoted to the art, culture, and history of the Navajo people and has an excellent selection of books on the Navajo Nation. The museum hosts exhibitions of native artists each season; call for a listing of shows. Housed in the same building as the Navajo Nation Museum is the **Navajo Nation Visitor Center,** a great resource for all sorts of information on reservation activities. Within walking distance of the Navajo Nation Museum, the **Navajo Arts and Crafts Enterprises** displays local artwork, including pottery, jewelry, and blankets. ⊠ *AZ 264, next to Navajo Nation Inn,* ☎ *928/871–6673 museum, 928/ 871–7371 visitor center* 🎟 *Free* ⊙ *Weekdays 1–5.*

If you're curious about wildlife in northeastern Arizona and its ties to Navajo culture and religion, stop at the **Navajo Nation Zoological and Botanical Park.** Amid the sandstone monoliths on the border of Arizona and New Mexico, this unusual zoo and garden displays indigenous birds and animals that figure in Navajo legends—golden eagles, elk, and coyotes—as well as examples of plants used by traditional people. It's the only Native American–owned-and-operated zoo in the United States. ⊠ *AZ 264, northeast of Navajo Nation Museum* ☎ *928/871–6573* 🎟 *Free* ⊙ *Daily 8–5.*

Many all-Indian rodeos are held near the center of downtown at the **Navajo Tribal Fairgrounds.** The community hosts the annual Fourth of July celebration, with a major rodeo, ceremonial dances, and a parade. The Navajo Nation Tribal Fair, much like a traditional state fair, is held in early September. It offers standard county-fair rides, midway booths, contests, shows, and an all-Indian rodeo. ⊠ *AZ 264* ☎ *928/871–6282 Navajo Nation Fair Office.*

Where to Stay

For approximate costs, *see* the lodging chart at the beginning of this chapter.

¢ 🏨 **Navajo Land Day's Inn.** This motel in St. Michaels, 4 mi west of Window Rock, offers standard rooms appointed with Southwestern-style decor. A Blimpie's sandwich shop is in the lobby, and a Denny's restaurant is also on the property. ⊠ *392 W. AZ 264, St. Michaels 86511* ☎ *928/ 871–5690 or 800/329–7466* 🖶 *928/871–5699* ⊕ *www.daysinn.com* ⇨ *65 rooms, 8 suites* ⌂ *Restaurant, pool, gym, hot tub, sauna, meeting rooms, some pets allowed* ⊟ *AE, DC, MC, V.*

¢ 🏨 **Navajo Nation Inn.** Rooms in this two-story beam-and-stucco motel are decorated with a Navajo-style palette of tan, orange, and yellow that complements the basic pine furniture. The upstairs Haskeneini Restaurant serves Navajo cuisine in addition to regular American fare (you can build your own Navajo tacos), and the gift shop sells authentic Navajo jewelry. ⊠ *48 W. AZ 264, at Indian Hwy. 12, 86515* ☎ *928/871–4108 or 800/662–6189* 🖶 *928/871–5466* ⇨ *56 rooms* ⌂ *Restaurant, meeting rooms, some pets allowed* ⊟ *AE, D, MC, V.*

Shopping

An outlet of the **Navajo Arts and Crafts Enterprises** (⊠ AZ 264 at Indian Hwy. 12, next to Navajo Nation Inn ☎ 928/871–4090) stocks authentic tribal artworks purchased from craftspeople across the reservation. You'll occasionally find local artisans at work here. Major credit cards are accepted.

Canyon de Chelly

② *25 mi west of Window Rock on AZ 264, then north on U.S. 191.*

FodorsChoice
★

The nearly 84,000-acre Canyon de Chelly (pronounced d'*shay*) is one of the most spectacular natural wonders in the Southwest. On a smaller scale, it rivals the Grand Canyon for beauty. Its main gorges—the 26-mi-long Canyon de Chelly ("canyon in the rock") and the adjoining 35-mi Canyon del Muerto ("canyon of the dead")—have sheer, heavily eroded sandstone walls that rise to 1,100 ft. Ancient pictographs and petroglyphs decorate some of the cliffs, and within the canyon complex there are

Fishing

Lake Powell, known for its bass fishing, also holds other varieties including bluegill and pike, and the Colorado River below Glen Canyon Dam is known for its large trout. Keep in mind that Lake Powell stretches into Utah; a fishing license is required for each state. The eastern region of the Navajo reservation has scattered lakes, most of them remote and small, but two of the more popular and accessible lakes are near Canyon de Chelly: Wheatfields Lake, on Indian Highway 12 about 11 mi south of the community of Tsaile, and Many Farms Lake, near the community of Many Farms, on U.S. 191. Permits are required for fishing on the reservation.

Hiking

Some of the best hikes in this region are in Canyon de Chelly, up the streambed between the soaring orange-and-white sandstone cliffs, with the remains of the ancient ancestral Puebloan communities frequently in view. Mummy Cave is especially worth a look, its three-story watchtower nearly perfectly preserved. The more weathered Antelope House and White House stand against the sweeping canyon cliffs as impressive reminders of a bygone era. Be reminded, there is but one area in Canyon de Chelly where you can hike without a Navajo guide—from the overlook at White House Ruins, down the canyon's trail and to the ruins themselves about a 2½-mi round-trip. The Navajo National Monument offers impressive hikes to two ruins: Beta-Takin, a settlement dating back to AD 1250, and Keet Seel, which dates back as far as AD 950. Both are in alcoves at the base of gigantic overhanging cliffs. Remember, you cannot hike on private property or tribal land without permission; it's important to be respectful of this law.

Hopi Ceremonies

The Hopi are well known for colorful ceremonial dances, many of which are supplications for rain, fertile crops, and harmony with nature. Most of these ceremonies take place in village plazas and kivas (underground ceremonial chambers) and last two days or longer; outsiders are sometimes permitted to watch segments of some ceremonies but are never allowed into kivas unless invited. Seasonal katsina dances performed at agricultural ceremonies may be restricted, so it's best to inquire upon arrival. Each clan has its own sacred rituals, starting times, and dates, which are determined by tribal elders. Outsiders should be respectful, dress appropriately (no baseball caps), and adhere to the proper etiquette while observing dances.

Shopping

Most visitors to the area are tempted by the beautiful pottery, turquoise and sterling-silver jewelry, handwoven baskets, Navajo wool rugs, and other examples of Native American crafts. Many trading posts also carry the work of some New Mexico tribes, including exquisite inlaid Zuni jewelry and the world-acclaimed pottery of the Pueblo people. A vast majority of the products sold on the Hopi and Navajo reservations are authentic, but the possibility of imitations does exist. Trading posts are very reliable, as are most roadside stands, which can offer some outstanding values, but be wary of solo vendors hanging around parking lots. If you're planning on shopping on the Hopi Reservation or elsewhere outside the Navajo trading posts, it's a good idea to carry cash or traveler's checks. Phone lines in the region are sometimes unreliable, which can make credit-card use impossible.

Northeast Arizona

Glen Canyon
National Recreation
Area

19 **Rainbow Bridge
National Monument**

MO

18 **Wahweap**

17 **15** **Page**

Gou
Tradin

Glen Canyon
National
Recreation
Area

16 **Antelope
Canyon**

16

NAVAJO
INDIAN
RESERVATION

14

Navajo
National
Monument

Inscription
House ◆

564

Vermilion
Cliffs

Kaibab
National
Forest

Bitter
Springs

Echo Cliffs

98

Kaibito

Colorado River

21

◆ **White Mesa
Natural Bridge**

160

The
Gap

Elephant
Feet ◆

Red
Lake

HOPI
INDIAN
RESERVATION

Grand Canyon
National Park

160

Dinosaur
Tracks ◆

8 ⚑ **Tuba City**

Moenkopi

Coal Canyon ◆

264

Hotevilla

Bacovi

PAINTED

89

Kaibab
National
Forest

180

64

**Cameron
Trading Post**

9

DESERT

Third Mesa **7**

Kykotsmo

Old Oraibi ◆
Hopi Cultural Center
Shungopavi

6

See
Me

2

Valle

Gray
Mountain

89

180

◆ **Wapatki National
Monument**

Little Colorado R.

15

Kaibab
National
Forest

180

San Francisco
Peaks

◆ **Sunset Crater
National Monument**

Leupp

99

Williams

Winona

Twin
Arrows

Two Guns

87

Flagstaff

Homolovi
State Par

Winslow

89A

Coconino
National
Forest

Sedona

17

CloseUp

RESERVATION RULES

VISITORS TO THE NAVAJO NATION and Hopi Reservation should observe several rules when visiting either reservation.

Alcohol & Drugs

The possession and consumption of alcoholic beverages or illicit drugs is illegal on both Hopi and Navajo land. You will not be able to purchase alcohol legally while you are on the reservations, and you should not bring any alcohol onto the reservations with you.

Camping

No open fires are allowed in reservation campgrounds; you must use grills or fireplaces. You may not gather firewood on the reservation—bring your own. Camping areas have quiet hours from 11 PM to 6 AM. Pets must be kept on a leash or confined. Pick up after yourself and don't litter.

Hopi Shrines

Don't touch shrines. Hopi spirituality is intertwined with daily life, and objects that seem ordinary to you might have deeper significance. If you come upon a collection of objects at or near the Hopi Mesas, respect the person who left the offerings and do not disturb them.

Permits & Permissions

No off-trail hiking or rock climbing is allowed unless you are accompanied by a local guide. A tribal permit is required for fishing in lakes or streams. Violations of fish and game laws are punishable by heavy fines, imprisonment, or both. Off-road travel is not allowed unless accompanied by a local tour guide. Respect private property by not wandering across or through residential areas.

Photography

Always ask permission before taking photographs of the locals. You may have to pay to take the picture, and even if no money is requested, consider offering a dollar or two to the person whose photograph you have taken. The Navajo are very open about photographs; the Hopi do not allow photographs at all, including videos, tape recordings, notes, and even sketches.

Religious Ceremonies

Should you see a ceremony in progress while traveling, look for posted signs indicating who is welcome. If there are no signs, check with local shops or the village community to see if the ceremony is open to the public. Unless you are specifically invited, stay out of kivas (ceremonial rooms) and stay on the periphery of dances or processions.

Respect for the Land

Do not wander across or through residential areas or disturb property. Do not disturb or remove animals, plants, rocks, petrified wood, or artifacts. They are protected by Tribal Antiquity and federal laws, which are strictly enforced.

more than 7,000 archaeological sites. Gigantic stone walls rise hundreds of feet above streams, hogans, tilled fields, peach orchards, and sheep-grazing lands.

The first inhabitants of the canyons arrived more than 2,000 years ago. In AD 750, these Basket Makers disappeared and were replaced by Pueblo tribes who constructed stone cliff dwellings. The departure of the Pueblo people around AD 1300 is widely believed to have resulted from changing climatic conditions, soil erosion, dwindling local resources, disease, and internal conflict. Present-day Hopis see these people as their ancestors who, quite simply, left to find a better place to live. Beginning around AD 780, Hopi farmers settled here, followed by the Navajo around 1300. (The Navajo migrated from far northern Canada; no one is sure when they arrived in the Southwest.) Despite evidence to the contrary, most Navajos hold that their people have always lived here and that the Diné people passed through three different worlds before emerging into the fourth, the Glittering World. Centuries-old traditions have been passed down to the Navajo families who now live, farm, and raise sheep in the area.

Both Canyon de Chelly and Canyon del Muerto have a paved rim drive with turnoffs and parking areas. Each drive takes about two hours and displays magnificent canyon views. Prehistoric ruins can be found near the base of cliffs and perched on high, sheltering ledges. The dwellings and cultivated fields of the present-day Navajo lie in the flatlands between the cliffs, and those who inhabit the canyon today farm much the way their ancestors did. Most residents leave the canyon in winter but return in early spring to farm and tend their sheep.

The **visitor center** has exhibits on the history of the cliff dwellers and provides information on scheduled hikes, tours, and other programs within the national monument.

The **South Rim Drive** (36 mi round-trip) of Canyon de Chelly starts at the visitor center and ends at **Spider Rock Overlook,** where cliffs plunge 1,000 ft to the canyon floor. Here you'll have a view of two pinnacles, Speaking Rock and Spider Rock; the latter rises about 800 ft from the canyon floor and is considered a sacred place. Other highlights on the South Rim Drive are Junction Overlook, where Canyon del Muerto joins Canyon de Chelly; White House Overlook, from which a trail leads to the **White House Ruin,** with dwelling remains of nearly 60 rooms and several kivas; and Sliding House Overlook, where you can see ruins on a narrow, sloped ledge across the canyon. The carved and sometimes narrow trail down the canyon side to White House Ruin is the only access to Canyon de Chelly without a guide. If you have a fear of heights, this may not be a hike you want to make.

The **North Rim Drive** (34 mi round-trip) of Canyon del Muerto also begins at the visitor center and continues northeast on Indian Highway 64 toward the town of Tsaile. Major stops include Antelope House Overlook, the site of a large ruin named for the animals painted on an adjacent cliff; the Mummy Cave Overlook, where two mummies were found inside a remarkably unspoiled pueblo dwelling, the monument's largest; and Massacre Cave Overlook, the last stop, which marks the spot where an estimated 115 Navajo were killed by the Spanish in 1805. (The rock walls of the cave are still pockmarked from the Spaniards' ricocheting bullets.) ⊠ *Indian Hwy. 7, 3 mi east of U.S. 191, Chinle* ☎ *928/674–5500 visitor center* ⊕ *www.nps.gov/cach* ☒ *Free* ⊙ *Daily 8–5.*

In Tsaile, Navajo medicine men worked in conjunction with architects to design the town's six-story **Diné College.** Because all important Navajo activities traditionally take place in a circle (a hogan is essentially circular), the campus was laid out in the round, with all of the buildings inside its perimeter. Diné College's **Hatathli Museum** is actually two museums in one: one concentrates on Navajo culture, and the other contains intertribal exhibits from across the United States. ⊠ *Indian Hwy. 12, south of Indian Hwy. 64, Tsaile* ☎ *928/724–3311 college, 928/724–6653 museum* ☒ *By donation* ⊙ *Museum weekdays 8:30–4.*

To the north of Tsaile are the impressive **Chuska Mountains,** covered with sprawling stands of ponderosa pine. There are no established hiking trails in the Chuska Mountains, but up-to-date hiking information and backcountry-use permits (rarely granted if a Navajo guide does not accompany the trip) can be obtained through the Navajo Nation. ⊠ *Navajo Nation Parks and Recreation Department, Bldg. 36A, E.*

AZ 264, Window Rock ☎ Box 2520, 86515 ☎ 928/871–6647 ⊕ www. navajonationparks.org.

Where to Stay & Eat

Chinle is the closest town to Canyon de Chelly. There are several comfortable and good lodgings with restaurants as well as a supermarket and a campground. (You'll probably be approached by panhandlers in the grocery store parking lot, as well as hungry, forlorn, homeless dogs.) In late August each year, Chinle is host to the Central Navajo Fair, a public celebration complete with a rodeo, carnival, and traditional dances.

For approximate costs, *see* the dining and lodging prices chart at the beginning of this chapter.

$ ✕☐ **Best Western Canyon de Chelly Inn.** This two-story motel about 3 mi from Canyon de Chelly has cheerful rooms with modern oak furnishings and Native American–print bedspreads and drapes. All rooms have coffeemakers. The on-site Junction restaurant (¢–$$) opens for breakfast at 6:30 AM; traditional Navajo, Mexican, and American fare is served until 9 PM. ⊠ *Indian Hwy. 7 ☎ Box 295, Chinle 86503 ☎ 928/674–5875 or 800/327–0354 ☎ 928/674–3715 ⊕ www.canyondechelly.com* ➯ *102 rooms ⚭ Restaurant, cable TV, pool, some pets allowed, no-smoking rooms ⊟ AE, D, DC, MC, V.*

$ ✕☐ **Holiday Inn Canyon de Chelly.** Once Garcia's Trading Post, this motel near Canyon de Chelly is less generic than you might expect: the territorial fort–style exterior gives an authentic, rustic feel to the inn. Rooms, on the other hand, are predictably pastel and contemporary. The lobby restaurant (¢–$$), low-key by most standards, is the most upscale eatery in the area, serving well-prepared specialties such as delicious mutton stew with fry bread and honey. The hotel restaurant offers a box picnic ($5.95) for its guests and has a gift shop stocked with local Native American arts and crafts. ⊠ *Indian Hwy. 7 ☎ Box 1889, Chinle 86503 ☎ 928/674–5000 ☎ 928/674–8264 ⊕ www.sixcontinentshotels. com* ➯ *108 rooms ⚭ Restaurant, pool, shop ⊟ AE, D, DC, MC, V.*

$ ✕☐ **Thunderbird Lodge.** In an ideal location within the national monument's borders, this pleasant establishment has stone-and-adobe units that match the architecture of the site's original 1896 trading post. Rooms have rough-hewn beam ceilings, rustic wooden furniture, and Navajo-style decor. The cafeteria (¢–$) is in the original trading post and serves reasonably priced soups, salads, sandwiches, and entrées, including charbroiled steaks. The lodge also offers truck tours of Canyon de Chelly and Canyon del Muerto. ⊠ *Indian Hwy. 7 ☎ Box 548, Chinle 86503 ☎ 928/674–5841 or 800/679–2473 ⊕ www.tbirdlodge. com* ➯ *74 rooms ⚭ Cafeteria, cable TV ⊟ AE, D, DC, V.*

$ ☐ **Coyote Pass Hospitality.** You're not likely to encounter a more unusual lodging than this roving, Navajo-run B&B. It's not for everyone: you sleep on bedding on the dirt floor of a hogan (the location depends on the season, but it's usually set up near Canyon de Chelly), use an outhouse, and eat a Navajo-style breakfast—blue-corn pancakes and herbal tea, for instance—prepared on a wood-burning stove. If you don't mind roughing it a bit, this is a rare opportunity to immerse yourself in beautiful surroundings and Native American culture: the clan gives presentations on Navajo life every night. *Contact Will Tsosie ☎ Box 91-B, Tsaile 86556 ☎ 928/724–3383 ⊟ No credit cards* ⑩ *BP.*

$ ☐ **Many Farms Inn.** Many Farms High School runs this facility, which is staffed by Navajo students of hotel management. It's not fancy, but rooms are pleasant and contain two single beds, which means single or double occupancy only. Bathrooms are shared, and you'll have to go to the first floor to use pay phones or watch TV. ✉ *U.S. 191 and Indian Hwy. 59* ✆ *Box 307, Many Farms 86538* ☎ *928/781–6362* 🖨 *928/ 781–6355* ☞ *30 rooms with shared bath* �б *Refrigerators; no room phones, no room TVs* ▤ *No credit cards* ⊙ *Closed weekends Aug.–May.*

¢ ⚠ **Cottonwood Campground.** This sometimes cramped and noisy campground has 52 RV sites (maximum length 35 ft; no hook-ups) and 95 tent sites that are available free, on a first-come, first-served basis. Cottonwood trees shade the sites. Although it's open year-round, there are limited facilities from November to March. �б *Flush toilets, drinking water, picnic tables, grills* ☞ *52 RV sites, 95 tent sites* ✉ *Indian Hwy. 7, near Canyon de Chelly visitor center, Chinle 86503* ☎ *928/674–5501* ⊕ *www.nps.gov/cach* ⚿ *No reservations* ⊙ *Open year-round.*

¢ ⚠ **Spider Rock Campground.** Cordial Navajo owner Howard Smith makes everyone feel comfortable at this informal campground nestled in low piñons within a few hundred yards of the canyon. There's a nice hiking trail to the canyon's edge, and Howard occasionally offers "sweat lodges." The hand-hewn hogans have interior fire pits and are ideal for winter camping. The camp is just a short drive from the famous Spider Rock site and overlook. Howard sells firewood and limited food and camping items. He can also arrange tours. �б *Pit toilets, fire pits, showers, drinking water, dump station, picnic tables* ☞ *30 camp sites, 2 hogans* ✉ *Indian Hwy. 7, 10 mi east of Canyon de Chelly Visitor Center* ✆ *Box 2509, Chinle 86503* ☎ *928/674–8261 or 877/910–2267* ⊕ *www. home.earthlink.net/~spiderrock* 🖼 *Tent sites $10, partial hook-ups (electricity) $15, hogans $25* ⊙ *Open year-round.*

Sports & the Outdoors

HIKING Only one hike within Canyon de Chelly National Monument—the **White House Ruin Trail** on the South Rim Drive—can be done without an authorized guide. The easy trail starts near White House Overlook and runs along sheer walls that drop about 550 ft. If you have concerns about height, be aware that the path gets narrow and somewhat slippery along the way. The hike is 2½ mi round-trip, and hikers should carry their own drinking water. From late May through early September, free three-hour ranger-led hikes depart from the visitor center at 9 AM. Also in summer, two four-hour hikes (about $10 per person) leave from the visitor center in the morning and afternoon. Some trails are strenuous and steep; others are easy or moderate. Regardless, those with health concerns or a fear of heights should proceed with caution. Call ahead if you are interested in a hike: they're canceled occasionally due to local customs or events.

Private, guided hikes to the interior of the canyons cost about $15 per hour with a three-hour minimum for groups of up to four people. (Don't venture into the canyon without a guide, or you'll face a stiff fine.) For overnights, you'll need a guide as well as permission to stay on private land. If you have a four-wheel-drive vehicle and want to drive yourself, guides will accompany you for a charge of about $10 an hour with a three-hour minimum for up to three vehicles. All Navajo guides are members of the **Tsegi Guide Association** (✉ Canyon de Chelly Visitor Center, Indian Hwy. 7, Chinle ☎ 928/674–5500 ⊕ www.nps.gov/cach). You can hire a guide on the spot at the visitor center, or you can call ahead and make a reservation.

HORSEBACK **Totsonii Ranch** (✉ South Rim Dr. ✆ Box 434, Chinle 86503 ☎ 928/755–
RIDING 6209), 1½ mi beyond the end of the pavement, offers four-hour round-trip horseback rides 1,000 ft down Bat Trail to Spider Rock. Contact Lee Bigwater for more information. **Twin Trail Tours** (✉ North Rim Dr., Chinle ☎ 928/674–8425), 8 mi north of the visitor center, offers rides lasting from two hours to the entire day as well as overnight camping trips. Contact the proprietor, Lorrain Izzo, for more information.

JEEP TOURS **De Chelly Tours** (☎ 928/674–3772) offers private jeep tours into Canyon de Chelly and arranges group tours and overnight camping in the canyon as well as late day and evening tours. Entertainment such as story-tellers, music, and Navajo legends can be arranged with advance reservation. Treks with **Thunderbird Lodge Canyon Tours** (✉ Thunderbird Lodge Gift Shop, Indian Hwy. 7, Chinle ☎ 928/674–5841 or 800/679–2473), in six-wheel-drive vehicles, are available from late spring to early fall. Half-day tours are $39.50 and start at 9 AM and 2 PM daily; all-day tours cost $64.50 and include lunch.

Hubbell Trading Post National Historic Site

③ *40 mi south of Canyon de Chelly, off AZ 264; 32 mi west of Window Rock.*

John Lorenzo Hubbell, a merchant and friend of the Navajo, established this trading post in 1878. Hubbell taught, translated letters, settled family quarrels, and explained government policy to the Navajo, and during an 1886 smallpox epidemic, he turned his home into a hospital and ministered to the sick and dying. Hubbell died in 1930 and is buried near the trading post.

The National Park Service Visitor Center exhibits illustrate the post's history, and you can take a self-guided tour of the grounds and visit the Hubbell Trading Post, which contains a fine display of Native American artistry. The visitor center has a fairly comprehensive bookstore specializing in Navajo history, art, and culture; often you'll find local weavers demonstrating their craft.

The **Hubbell Trading Post Store** is famous for "Ganado red" Navajo rugs, which are sold at the store here. The quality is outstanding and prices are high but fair—rugs can cost anywhere from $100 to around $30,000. Considering the time that goes into weaving each one, the prices are quite reasonable. It is hard to resist these beautiful designs and colors, and it's a pleasure just to browse around this rustic spot, where Navajo artists frequently show their work. Documents of authenticity are provided for all works. Note: When photographing weavers, ask permission first. They expect a few dollars in return. ✉ *AZ 264, Ganado, 1 mi west of town* ☎ *928/755–3475 park office, 928/755–3254 store* ⊕ *www.nps.gov/hutr or navajorugs.spma.org* ✉ *Free* ☉ *Daily 8–5.*

en route About 20 mi west of Hubbell Trading Post on AZ 264, you'll reach **Steamboat Rock,** an immense, jutting peninsula of stone that resembles an early steamboat, complete with a geologically formed waterline. At Steamboat Rock you are only 5 mi from the eastern boundary of the Hopi Reservation.

THE HOPI MESAS

The Hopi Mesas and the small villages that line their tops have a feel of unfathomable antiquity. Generations of Hopitu, "the peaceful people," much like their ancestral Puebloan ancestors, have lived in these settlements of stone-and-adobe houses, which blend in with the earth so well that they appear to be natural formations. Television aerials, satellite dishes, and automobiles notwithstanding, these Hopi villages still impart the air of another time.

While you do not need permission before entering the Hopi Reservation, you must obtain a permit to visit certain areas. Since all Hopi villages are separate and autonomous, each has the authority to establish

RESERVATION REALITIES

BOTH THE NAVAJO AND HOPI *base their culture on the land around them, but they are two distinct peoples, as different from each other as the French are from the Germans. The similarities and contrasts between them are reflected in the harsh realities of life on the reservation.*

The Navajo refer to themselves as the Diné (pronounced din-eh)—"the people"—and live on 17 million acres in Arizona, New Mexico, Utah, and Colorado. Although it is not officially part of the reservation, many Navajo consider southwestern Colorado part of their sacred land. The Hopi trace their roots back to the original settlers of the area, whom they call the Hisatsinom, or "people of long ago." But these ancestral Puebloans are also popularly known as Anasazi, a Navajo word meaning both "ancient ones" and "ancient enemies." Hopi culture is far more formal and structured than that of the Navajo, and their religion has remained much stronger and purer. But for both tribes, unemployment is very high on the reservation, and poverty is a constant presence.

Most Navajo and Hopi disapprove of the practice, but some panhandlers nevertheless cluster at shopping centers and view sites, hoping to glean a few tourist dollars. Visitors should respond to panhandlers with a polite but firm "no." The phrases "she bay-so at-den" or "dough-da" (roughly translated, "no money") generally work. If you wish to help, make a donation to one of the legitimate organizations that raise funds at reservation grocery stores.

The sight of stray dogs, both starving and dead, is another unpleasant fact of life on the reservation. Among the Navajo in particular, dogs have never been held in high esteem, and in Navajo mythology dogs represent chaos and mischief. On both reservations, federal funding for animal control has been cut, and people struggling to make ends meet have few resources to devote to animal care. Visitors are encouraged not to feed the dogs, as this just exacerbates the problem.

Hopi mythology holds that a white-skinned people will save the tribe from its difficult life. Long ago, however, in the face of brutal treatment by whites, most Hopi became convinced that their salvation would originate elsewhere. (Some Hopi now look to the Dalai Lama of Tibetan Buddhism for redemption.) Although not easy to witness, the disappointment of the Hopi and the despair of the Navajo are easy to understand after a visit to the reservation.

To learn more about the Navajo, visit ⊕ www.navajocentral.org, ⊕ www.navajoland.comor ⊕ www.navajo.org to learn more about the Hopi, visit ⊕ www.hopi.nsn.us

— Ed Tomchin

its own governing policies, which are sometimes posted at the entrance to the village. Many villages don't allow cars, and some close to the public when they are participating in religious ceremonies. Lodging is available on Second Mesa and recommended if you wish to see the Hopi Mesas at a leisurely pace.

For approximate costs, *see* the dining and lodging prices chart at the beginning of this chapter.

Keams Canyon Trading Post

❹ *48 mi west of Hubbell Trading Post on AZ 264.*

The trading post established by Thomas Keam in 1875 to do business with local tribes is now the area's main tourist attraction, offering a primitive campground, restaurant, service station, and gift shop and ersatz shopping center. An administrative center for the Bureau of Indian Affairs, Keams Canyon also has a number of government buildings. The first 3 mi of the 8-mi wooded canyon running toward the northeast can be seen by car. At **Inscription Rock,** about 2 mi down the road, frontiersman Kit Carson engraved his name in stone. There are several picnic spots in the canyon.

Where to Eat

¢ ✕ **Keams Canyon Restaurant.** This typical roadside diner with Formica tabletops offers both American and Native American dishes, including Navajo tacos made with Indian fry bread heaped with ground beef, chili, beans, lettuce, and grated cheese. Daily specials, offered at $1 to $2 off the regular price, may include anything from barbecued ribs to lamb chops to crab legs. ⊠ *Keams Canyon Shopping Center, AZ 264, Keams Canyon* ☎ 928/738–2296 ▭ *D, MC, V* ⊘ *No dinner weekends.*

Shopping

Keams Canyon Arts and Crafts and McGee's Art Gallery (⊠ AZ 264, Keams Canyon ☎ 928/738–2295), upstairs from the Keams Canyon Restaurant, sells first-rate, high-quality Hopi crafts such as handcrafted jewelry, pottery, beautiful carvings, basketry, and artwork.

First Mesa

★ ❺ *11 mi west of Keams Canyon, on AZ 264.*

On First Mesa you will initially approach Polacca; the older and more impressive villages of Hano, Sichomovi, and Walpi are at the top of the mesa. First Mesa villages are world renowned for their hand-coiled pottery. From Polacca, a paved road (off AZ 264) angles up to a parking lot near the village of Sichomovi, where there is a visitor center. You must get permission at the Ponsi Hall Visitor Center to visit Hano, Sichomovi, and Walpi, and it's recommended that you call ahead to determine that guided walking tours of the villages will be available during the time you'll be traveling through the area. If they are being offered, then permission is readily granted when you pay the tour fee.

All the older Hopi villages have structures built of rock and adobe mortar in a simple architectural style. **Hano** actually belongs to the Tewa, a New Mexico Pueblo tribe that fled from the Spanish in 1696 and secured permission from the Hopi to build a home on First Mesa. **Sichomovi** is built so close to Hano that only the residents can tell where one ends and the other begins. Constructed in the mid-1600s, this village is believed to have been built to ease overcrowding at Walpi, the highest point on the mesa. **Walpi,** built on solid rock and surrounded by steep cliffs, frequently hosts ceremonial dances and can be visited only when you are accompanied by a Hopi guide. It is the most pristine of the Hopi villages, with cliff-edge houses and vast scenic vistas. Inhabited for more than 1,000 years, Walpi's cliff-edge houses—the mesa measures only 15 ft across at its narrowest point—seem to grow out of the nearby terrain. Today, only about 10 residents occupy this settlement, which has neither electricity nor running water. Walpi's surroundings make it a less than ideal destination for acrophobes. ⊠ *Ponsi Hall Visitor Center, First Mesa* ☎ 928/737–2262 ⊠ *Guided tours $8* ⊘ *Tours Nov.–mid-Mar., daily 9:30–4:30; mid-Mar.–Oct., daily 8:30–4:30, except when ceremonies are being held.*

Second Mesa

❻ *10 mi southwest of First Mesa, on AZ 264.*

Shungopavi, the largest and oldest village on Second Mesa, which was founded by the Bear Clan, is reached by a paved road angling south off AZ 264, between the junction of AZ 87 and the Hopi Cultural Center. The village is well known for its silver overlay jewelry and coiled plaques. The famous Hopi snake dances (closed to the public) are held here in August during even-numbered years. Two smaller villages are off a paved road that runs north from AZ 264, about ⅓ mi east of the Hopi Cultural Center. **Mishongnovi,** the easternmost settlement, was built in the late 1600s. If you'd like to visit **Sipaulovi** (☎ 928/737–2570), the most recently established village, call the Sipaulovi Village Community Center for permission.

Ideally located on the Second Mesa "at the Center of the Universe" is the **Hopi Cultural Center,** where you can stop for the night, learn about the people and their reservation, and eat authentic Hopi cuisine. The museum here is dedicated to preserving the Hopi traditions and to presenting those traditions to non-Hopi visitors. A gift shop sells works by local Hopi artisans at reasonable prices, and a modest picnic area on the west side of the building is a pleasant spot for lunch with a view of the San Francisco Peaks. ✉ *AZ 264, Second Mesa* ☎ *928/734–6650* ⊕ *www.psv.com/hopi.html* ✑ *Museum $3* ⊙ *Mid-Mar.–Oct., weekdays 8–5 and weekends 9–3; Nov.–mid-Mar., weekdays 8–5.*

Where to Stay & Eat

¢ ✕⌂ **Hopi Cultural Center Restaurant and Motel.** This Hopi-run establishment is the only place to eat or sleep in the immediate area, but because of its remote location it almost always has vacant rooms. The restaurant (¢–$) serves traditional Hopi dishes, including Indian tacos, Hopi blue-corn pancakes, fry bread (delicious with honey or salsa), and *nok qui vi* (a tasty stew made with tender bits of lamb, hominy, and mild green chilies). The motel offers clean, quiet rooms at reasonable rates. ✉ *5 mi west of AZ 87 on AZ 264, Second Mesa 86403* ☎ *928/734–2401* ⊕ *www.psv.com/hopi.html* ⇋ *33 rooms* ▤ *DC, MC, V.*

Shopping

The **Hopi Arts and Crafts/Silvercrafts Cooperative Guild** (✉ AZ 264, Second Mesa ☎ 928/734–2463), west of the Hopi Cultural Center, hosts craftspeople selling their wares; you might even see silversmiths at work here. Shops at the **Hopi Cultural Center** (✉ AZ 264, Second Mesa ☎ 928/734–2401) carry the works of local artists and artisans. At **Hopi Fine Arts** (✉ AZ 264 at AZ 87, Second Mesa ☎ 928/737–2222 ⊕ www.hopifinearts.com), proprietor Alph Secakuku is a native of the Hopi Pueblo of Supawlavi on the Second Mesa and an authority on all arts and crafts of the Hopi people. He represents about 75 active artisans in this user-friendly gallery. **Tsakurshovi** (✉ AZ 264, Second Mesa ☎ 928/734–2478), 1½ mi east of the Hopi Cultural Center, is a small shop where Hopi come to buy bundles of sweet grass and sage, deer hooves with which to make rattles, and ceremonial belts adorned with seashells. The proprietor's wife, Janice Day, is a renowned Hopi basket maker. Not surprisingly, the shop has one of the largest collections of Hopi baskets in the Southwest.

Third Mesa

❼ *10 mi northwest of Second Mesa, on AZ 264.*

At the eastern base of Third Mesa is the village of **Kykotsmovi,** known for its greenery and peach orchards. Hopi, from Old Oraibi, descended from the mesa to build this village in a canyon where it's perennially spring-time. Along AZ 264 are crafts shops and art galleries, as well as occa-sional roadside vendors. Third Mesa villages are known for their agricultural accomplishments, textile weaving, wicker baskets, and plaques.

Kykotsmovi, at the base of Third Mesa, is literally translated as "ruins on the hills" for the many ruin sites on the valley floor and in the sur-rounding hills. Present-day Kykotsmovi was established by Hopi peo-ple from Oraibi who either converted to Christianity or who wished to attend school and be educated. Kykotsmovi is the seat of the Hopi Tribal Government. The Hopi Tribal Headquarters and Office of Pub-lic Relations in this village should be visited first so that you can obtain any necessary permissions and arrange walking tours.

Old Oraibi, a few miles west and on top of Third Mesa, is believed to be the oldest continuously inhabited community in the United States, dating from around AD 1150. It was also the site of a rare, bloodless conflict between two groups of the Hopi people; in 1906, a dispute, set-tled uniquely by a "push of war" (a pushing contest), sent the losers off to establish the town of Hotevilla. Oraibi is a dusty spot, and, as an act of courtesy, tourists are asked to park their cars outside and approach the village on foot.

Hotevilla and **Bacavi** are about 4 mi west of Oraibi, and their inhabi-tants are descended from the former residents of that village. The men of Hotevilla continue to plant crops and beautiful gardens along the mesa slopes. ✉ *Cultural Preservation Office, AZ 264, Kykotsmovi* ☎ *928/734–2441* ⊕ *www.hopi.nsn.us* ⊙ *Weekdays 8–5.*

> en route

Beyond Hotevilla, AZ 264 descends from Third Mesa, exits the Hopi Reservation, and crosses into Navajo territory, past **Coal Canyon**, where Native Americans have long mined coal from the dark seam just below the rim. The colorful mudstone, dark lines of coal, and bleached white rock have an eerie appearance, especially by the light of the moon. Twenty miles west of Coal Canyon, at the junction of AZ 264 and U.S. 160, is the town of Moenkopi, the last Hopi outpost. Established as a farming community, it was settled by the descendants of former Oraibi residents.

Tuba City

▶ **8** *50 mi northwest of Third Mesa on AZ 264.*

Tuba City, with about 12,000 permanent residents, is the administra-tive center for the western portion of the Navajo Nation. In addition to a motel, hostel, and a few restaurants, this small town has a hospital, a bank, a trading post, and a movie theater. In late October, Tuba City hosts the Western Navajo Fair, a celebration combining traditional Navajo song and dance with a parade, pageant, and countless arts-and-crafts exhibits. The octagonal **Tuba City Trading Post** (✉ Main St. ☎ 928/283–5441), founded in the early 1870s, sells groceries and authentic, reasonably priced Navajo rugs, pottery, baskets, and jewelry.

About 5½ mi west of Tuba City, between mileposts 316 and 317 on U.S. 160, is a small sign for the **Dinosaur Tracks.** More than 200 million years ago, dilophosaurus—a carnivorous bipedal reptile more than 10 ft tall—left tracks in soft mud that subsequently turned to sandstone. There's no charge for a look. Ask the locals about guiding you to the nearby petroglyphs and freshwater springs. Four miles west of the dinosaur tracks on U.S. 160 is the junction with U.S. 89. This is one of the most colorful regions of the **Painted Desert,** with amphitheaters of maroon, orange, and red rocks facing west; it's especially glorious at sunset.

Where to Stay & Eat

For approximate costs, *see* the dining and lodging prices chart at the beginning of this chapter.

$-$$ ✕ **Hogan Restaurant.** The main fare at this spot next to the Quality Inn Tuba City is Southwestern and Mexican, but the menu also lists basic American and Navajo dishes. The chicken enchiladas and beef tamales are as good as any you'll find south of the border. The large dining room looks like a Western coffee shop but incorporates such Native American touches as pottery chandeliers. Breakfast is served here, too. ⊠ *Main St. (AZ 264)* ☎ *928/283–5260* ▤ *AE, D, DC, MC, V.*

¢-$ ✕ **Kate's Cafe.** A favorite of locals, this all-American café serves breakfast—try the vegetarian omelet—lunch, and dinner. Choose from hearty burgers, Kate's club sandwich, grilled chicken, or salads at lunchtime; dinner selections include five daily pasta specials and a charbroiled New York strip steak. There may be a wait, but for local color and fine food at reasonable prices, this is the place. ⊠ *Main St. (AZ 264)* ☎ *928/ 283–6773* ▤ *No credit cards.*

¢-$ ✕ **Tuba City Truck Stop Cafe.** Home cooking is what you'll get at this small, conveniently located fast-service restaurant. The popular Navajo vegetarian taco, available for lunch and dinner, is a mix of beans, lettuce, sliced tomato, shredded cheese, and green chilies served open face on succulent fry bread. Meatier options include mutton stew served with fry bread and hominy. It's open at 6 AM for breakfast and closes at 10 PM every day. ⊠ *Main St. (AZ 264) at U.S. 160* ☎ *928/283–4975* ▤ *MC, V.*

¢-$ ▦ **Quality Inn Navajo Nation.** This motel has a trading post and shops for essentials, gifts, and souvenirs. The standard rooms are spacious and well maintained, fine for an overnight stop before or after a visit to the Hopi Mesas. The on-site Hogan Restaurant serves basic fare. ⊠ *Main St. at Moenave Rd.* ◌ *Box 247, 86045* ☎ *928/283–4545 or 800/644–8383* ▦ *928/283–4144* ⊕ *www.choicehotels.com* ↩ *78 rooms, 2 suites* ◌ *Restaurant, some in-room data ports, cable TV, shop, laundry facilities, some pets allowed, no-smoking rooms* ▤ *AE, D, DC, MC, V.*

¢ ▦ **Grey Hills Inn.** Hotel management students at Grey Hills High School run this unusual lodging, a former dormitory with large, clean rooms and comfortable beds. Paintings and other eclectic touches add character to the otherwise plain rooms. Bathrooms and showers are down the hall, and it's hard to find the inn's entrance in the large high school complex at night, but the rates are reasonable. A share of the inn's profits helps support the students' class. ⊠ *Grey Hills High School, U.S. 160, ½ mi north of AZ 264* ◌ *Box 160, 86045* ☎ *928/283–6271 Ext. 141, 928/283–4450 weekends and after school hrs* ↩ *32 rooms with shared bath* ▤ *MC, V.*

¢ △ **Quality Inn Tuba City Campground.** This park adjacent to the Quality Inn (check in at the front desk) has some shaded sites and is geared towards RVs. Several tent sites are situated along the perimeter of the campground. Reservations are accepted through the hotel's 800 number. ◌ *Flush toilets, showers, laundry facilities, full hook-ups, drinking water, grills, picnic tables, dump station* ↩ *25 RV sites, 6 tent sites* ⊠ *Main St. (AZ 264)* ◌ *Box 247, 86045* ☎ *928/283–4545 or 800/644–8383* ▦ *928/283–4144* ▤ *AE, D, DC, MC, V* ☉ *Open year-round.*

Shopping

The **Native American swap meet** (⊠ Main St.), behind the community center and next to the baseball field, held every Friday from 8 AM on, has great deals on jewelry, jewelry-making supplies, semiprecious stones, rugs, pottery, and other arts and crafts; there are also food concessions and booths selling herbs. The **Toh Nanees Dizi Shopping Center** (⊠ U.S. 160), ½ mi northeast of town, has a pizza parlor, supermarket, and the Silver Screen Twin Theaters.

Cameron Trading Post

❾ *25 mi southwest of Tuba City on U.S. 89*

Cameron Trading Post and Motel, established in 1916, is one of the few remaining authentic trading posts in the Southwest. A convenient stop if you're driving from the Hopi Mesas to the Grand Canyon, it has reasonably priced dining, lodging, camping, and shopping (⇨ *see* the listing in Chapter 3 for more detailed information). Fine authentic Navajo products are sold at an outlet of the **Navajo Arts and Crafts Enterprises** (⊠ U.S. 89 at AZ 64, Cameron ☎ 928/679–2244). ⊠ *U.S. 89, Cameron* ☎ *928/679–2231.*

en route | As you proceed toward Kayenta, 22 mi northeast of Tuba City on U.S. 160, you'll come to the tiny community of Red Lake. Off to the left of the highway is a geologic phenomenon known as **Elephant Feet.** These massive eroded sandstone buttes offer a great family photo opportunity, posing beneath these enormous columns. Northwest of here at the end of a graded dirt road in Navajo backcountry is **White Mesa Natural Bridge,** a massive arch of white sandstone that extends from the edge of White Mesa. The long **Black Mesa** plateau runs for about 15 mi along U.S. 160. Above the prominent escarpments of this land formation, mining operations—a major source of revenue for the Navajo Nation—delve into the more than 20 billion tons of coal deposited there.

NAVAJO NATION NORTH

The magnificent Monument Valley stretches to the northeast of Kayenta into Utah. At a base altitude of about 5,500 ft, the sprawling, arid expanse was once populated by ancestral Puebloan people (more popularly known by the Navajo word *Anasazi,* which means both "ancient ones" and "enemy ancestors") and in the last few centuries has been home to generations of Navajo farmers. The soaring red buttes, eroded mesas, deep canyons, and naturally sculpted rock formations of Monument Valley are easy to enjoy on a leisurely drive. Scenes from many movies— among them *National Lampoon's Vacation, How the West Was Won, Forrest Gump, Stagecoach, 2001: A Space Odyssey,* and *Wind Talkers*— have been filmed here. As well, Monument Valley is the world's most popular backdrop for TV and magazine advertisements. At U.S. 163 and the Monument Valley entrance you'll see a street of disheveled buildings called Vendor Village. Here you can purchase trinkets and souvenirs without paying sales tax. Bartering is perfectly acceptable and expected.

For approximate costs, *see* the dining and lodging prices chart at the beginning of this chapter.

Kayenta

❿ *80 mi northeast of Tuba City, on U.S. 160, 25 mi south of Monument Valley*

Kayenta, a small town with a few grocery stores, a handful of chain motels, and a hospital, is a good base for exploring nearby Monument Valley Navajo Tribal Park and the Navajo National Monument. The Burger King in town has an excellent Navajo Code Talker exhibit with lots of memorabilia relative to this heroic World War II marine group.

Take a self-guided walking tour through the small outdoor cultural park, the **Navajo Cultural Center of Kayenta**, and see the way of life, beliefs, and traditions that have shaped North America's largest Native American tribe. ⊠ *U.S. 160 between Hampton Inn and Burger King,* ☎ *928/697-3170* ☒ *Free* ☉ *Daily 7 AM–sunset.*

Where to Stay & Eat

¢–$ ✕ **Amigo Cafe.** The tables here are packed with locals who frequent this small, clean establishment where everything on the menu is made from scratch. The delicious fry bread is the real drawing card. If you've never had a Navajo taco or Navajo hamburger, this is a good place to be initiated. ⊠ *U.S. 163* ☎ *928/697-8448* ☐ *MC, V* ☉ *Closed Sun.*

¢–$ ✕ **Golden Sands.** The decor and the service at this local café next to the Best Western Wetherill Inn are equally unrefined, but you can fuel up on hamburgers, Navajo tacos, and other regional specialties. It's also a good place to learn about the area from residents who stop in for coffee. ⊠ *U.S. 163* ☎ *928/697-3684* ☐ *No credit cards* ☉ *Closed Mon.*

$–$$ ✕⌂ **Hampton Inn of Kayenta.** This warm and inviting lodgepole-style motel is a good spot to get a night's rest. The simple rooms and lobby are tastefully decorated with Southwest textures, and the on-site restaurant (¢–$) is staffed by Native Americans wearing traditional Navajo garb. Stick with the Native American cuisine; a good choice is the Sheepherder's Taco. There's a free Continental breakfast bar, patio with a beehive fireplace, and fantastic gift shop with a large selection of top-quality Native American art and unique gifts. ⊠ *U.S. 160* ⟟ *Box 1217, 86033* ☎ *928/697-3170* ☐ *928/697-3189* ⊕ *www.hamptoninn.com* ⇆ *73 rooms* ♨ *Restaurant, pool, shop* ☐ *AE, D, DC, MC, V* ⌁ *CP.*

$–$$ ✕⌂ **Holiday Inn Monument Valley.** This contemporary motel has everything you would expect from a Holiday Inn. The on-site Wagonwheel Restaurant ($–$$) offers both standard and Native American fare, and the gift shop offers traditional local arts and crafts. ⊠ *U.S. 160 at U.S. 163* ⟟ *Box 307, 86033* ☎ *928/697-3221 or 800/465-4329* ☐ *928/697-3349* ⊕ *www.holiday-inn.com* ⇆ *164 rooms* ♨ *Restaurant, pool, shop* ☐ *AE, D, DC, MC, V.*

$ ⌂ **Best Western Wetherill Inn.** Named for John Wetherill, an early area trader and the brother of the frontiersman who discovered prehistoric Native American ruins in Arizona, this clean two-story motel has Southwestern decor and a well-stocked gift shop. ⊠ *U.S. 163* ⟟ *Box 175, 86033* ☎ *928/697-3231 or 800/528-1234* ⊕ *www.bestwestern.com* ⇆ *54 rooms* ♨ *Pool, shop* ☐ *AE, D, DC, MC, V.*

Monument Valley Navajo Tribal Park

⑪ *24 mi northeast of Kayenta, off U.S. 163.*

Fodor's Choice
★

For generations, the Navajo have grown crops and herded sheep in Monument Valley, considered to be one of the most scenic and mesmerizing destinations in the Navajo Nation. Director John Ford made this amazing land of buttes, towering rock formations, and mesas popular by filming *Stagecoach* here in 1938. Within Monument Valley lies the 30,000-acre Monument Valley Navajo Tribal Park. A 17-mi self-guided driving tour on a dirt road (there's only one road, so you can't get lost) passes the memorable **Mittens** and **Totem Pole** formations, among others. Drive slowly, and be sure to walk (15 minutes round-trip) from North Window around the end of Cly Butte for the views. The park has a 99-site campground, which closes from early October through April. Be sure to call ahead for road conditions in winter. The Monument Valley **visitor center** holds a small crafts shop and exhibits devoted to ancient and modern Native American history. Most of the independent guided tours here use enclosed vans and charge about $20 for 2½ hours; you can generally find Navajo Native American guides in the center or through the booths in the parking lot. They will escort you to places that you are not allowed to visit on your own. Bring plenty of extra film and batteries to capture this surreal landscape that constantly changes with the rising and setting sun. ✉ *Visitor Center, off U.S. 163, 24 mi north of Kayenta, Monument Valley* 🖃 *Box 2520, Window Rock 86515* ☎ *435/ 727–3353 park visitor center, 928/871–6647 Navajo Parks & Recreation Dept.* ⊕ *www.navajonationparks.org* 🖭 *$3* ☉ *Visitor center May–Sept., daily 7–7; Oct.–Apr., daily 8–5.*

Camping

¢ ⚠ **Mitten View Campground.** This RV and tent campground is located within the Navajo Tribal Park and situated next to the park headquarters at an elevation of 5,500 ft. The sites here are crowded together, but most offer spectacular views of Monument Valley. Rest rooms and showers are open in summer only. Only group sites can be reserved. ♿ *Flush toilets, showers, drinking water, picnic tables, dump station* ⤳ *99 sites* ✉ *Monument Valley Navajo Tribal Park, near visitor center, off U.S. 163, 25 mi north of Kayenta, 86003* ☎ *435/727–3287* 🖭 *$10 summer, $5 winter, $20 group site* 🖃 *No credit cards* ☉ *Open May–Oct; some sites year-round.*

Sports & the Outdoors

HORSEBACK RIDING & TOURS **Homeland Horseback Tours** (✉ Monument Valley Tribal Park Visitor Center, off U.S. 163, 24 mi north of Kayenta ☎ 435/727–3227), at the Monument Valley visitor center, offers 1½-hour, half-day, full-day, and overnight tours into Monument Valley. Have you ever wanted to ride off into the sunset into the land of sandstone spires and sweeping red rock? Jeep tours of the valley from hour-long to overnight can be arranged through Roland Cody Dixon at **Roland's Navajoland Tours** (🖃 Box 1542, Kayenta 86033 ☎ 928/697–3524); he offers cultural tours with crafts demonstrations, camping, and photography. **Totem Pole Tours** (🖃 Box 360306, Monument Valley, UT 85436 ☎ 435/727–3313 or 800/ 345–8687 ⊕ moab-utah.com/totempole) offers jeep tours, some that include entertainment and outdoor barbecues.

off the beaten path

FOUR CORNERS MONUMENT – An inlaid concrete slab marks the only point in the United States where four states meet: Arizona, New Mexico, Colorado, and Utah. Most visitors—in summer, nearly 2,000 a day—stay only long enough to snap a photo; you'll see many a twisted tourist trying to get an arm or a leg in each state. The monument, a 75-mi drive from Kayenta, is administered by the Navajo Nation Parks & Recreation Department. ✉ *7 mi northwest of the U.S. 160 and NM 502 junction, Teec Nos Pos* 🖃 *Box 9000, Window Rock 86515* ☎ *928/871–6647 Navajo Parks & Recreation Dept.* ⊕ *www.navajonationparks.org* 🖭 *Free.*

Goosenecks Region, Utah

⑫ *33 mi north of Monument Valley Navajo Tribal Park, on UT 316.*

FodorsChoice
★

Monument Valley's scenic route, U.S. 163, continues from Arizona into Utah, where the land is crossed, east to west, by a stretch of the San Juan River known as the Goosenecks—so named for the myriad twists and curves it takes at the bottom of a wildly carved canyon. This barren, erosion-blasted gorge has a stark beauty that is nearly as awesome as that of the Grand Canyon. The scenic overlook for the Goosenecks is reached by turning west from U.S. 163 onto UT 261, 4 mi north of the small community of **Mexican Hat** (named for the sombrero-like rock formation you'll see on the hills to your right as you drive north), then proceeding on UT 261 for 1 mi to a directional sign at the road's junction with UT 316. Turn left onto UT 316 and proceed 4 mi to the vista-point parking lot.

Where to Stay & Eat

★ ¢ ✕▣ **San Juan Inn & Trading Post.** This spot is a well-known take-out point for white-water runners on the San Juan, a river that vacationing sleuths will recognize as the setting of many of Tony Hillerman's Jim Chee mystery novels. The inn's Southwestern-style, rustic rooms overlooking the river at Mexican Hat are clean and well maintained. Diners can watch the river flow by at the Old Bridge Bar & Grill ($–$$), which serves great grilled steak and juicy hamburgers. Fresh trout and inexpensive Navajo dishes add variety to the menu. ⊠ *U.S. 163* ⌖ *Box 310276, Mexican Hat, UT 84531* ☎ *435/683–2220 or 800/447–2022* 🖷 *435/683–2210* ⊅ *36 rooms* ⚘ *Restaurant* ⊟ *AE, D, DC, MC, V.*

Goulding's Trading Post

⑬ *1 mi west of Monument Valley Navajo Tribal Park, off U.S. 163 on Indian Hwy. 42.*

Established in 1924 by Harry Goulding and his wife, this historic spot was used as a headquarters by director John Ford when he filmed the Western classic *Stagecoach*. Numerous Westerns shot in the area have brought the site a measure of international fame. The Goulding Museum displays Native American artifacts and Goulding family memorabilia as well as Navajo artifacts and an excellent multimedia show about Monument Valley.

Where to Stay & Eat

★ $–$$ ✕▣ **Goulding's Lodge.** With spectacular views of Monument Valley from each room's private balcony, this motel often serves as headquarters for film crews. The lodge has handsome stucco buildings and all the rooms have balconies, coffeemakers, and hair dryers. The on-premises Stagecoach restaurant, serving American fare, is decorated with Western movie memorabilia. Goulding's also conducts custom guided tours of Monument Valley and provides Navajo guides into the backcountry. The lodge is 2 mi off U.S. 163, at the Monument Valley Tribal Park turnoff. ⊠ *Off U.S. 163, 24 mi north of Kayenta* ⌖ *Box 360001, Monument Valley, UT 84536* ☎ *435/727–3231* ⊕ *www.gouldings.com* ⊅ *62 rooms* ⚘ *Restaurant, grocery, cable TV, in-room VCRs, pool, shop, laundry facilities, travel services* ⊟ *AE, D, DC, MC, V.*

¢ ⚠**Goulding's Good Sam Campground.** This is a clean, modern campground with views of Monument Valley. Check in at Goulding's grocery store (in Goulding's Trading Post). If you camp here, you'll also get access—at no additional charge—to the 17-mi loop drive around Monument Valley. Shuttle vans provide free transportation to Gouldings' restaurant and museum. ⚘ *Flush toilets, laundry facilities, full hook-ups, showers, grills, grocery store, playground, indoor pool* ⊅ *66 RV sites, 50 tent sites* ⊠ *Off U.S. 163, 24 mi north of Kayenta* ⌖ *Box 360001, Monument Valley, UT 84536* ☎ *435/727–3231* ⊠ *$26 full hook-ups, $16 tent sites* ⊟ *AE, D, DC, MC, V* ⊙ *Open year-round; limited service Nov.–Mar. 15.*

Navajo National Monument

14 *53 mi southwest of Goulding's Trading Post. From Kayenta, take U.S.*
Fodor'sChoice *160 southwest to AZ 564, and follow signs 9 mi north to monument.*
★

At the Navajo National Monument, two unoccupied 13th-century cliff
pueblos, Keet Seel and Betatakin, stand under the overhang of orange
and ocher cliffs. The largest ancient dwellings in Arizona, these stone-
and-mortar complexes were built by ancestral Puebloans, obviously for
permanent occupancy, but abandoned after less than half a century.

The well-preserved, 135-room **Beta-Takin** (Navajo for "ledge house")
seems to hang in midair before a sheer sandstone wall. When discovered in 1907 by a passing American rancher, the apartments were full
of baskets, pottery, and preserved grains and ears of corn—as if the occupants had been chased away in the middle of a meal. For an impressive view of Betatakin, walk to the rim overlook about ½ mi from the
visitor center. Ranger-led tours (a 5-mi, four-hour, strenuous round-trip
hike including a 700-ft descent into the canyon) leave once a day from
late May to early September at 8 AM. No reservations are accepted; groups
of no more than 25 form on a first-come, first-served basis.

Keet Seel (Navajo for "broken pottery") is also in good condition in a
serene location, with 160 rooms and five kivas. Explorations of Keet
Seel, which lies at an elevation of 7,000 ft and is 8½ mi from the visitor center by foot, are restricted: only 20 people are allowed to visit per
day, and only between late May and early September, when a ranger is
present at the site. A permit—which also allows campers to stay overnight
near the ruins—is required. Those interested in horseback trips can
make arrangements at the visitor center to rent horses and guides from
a Navajo family. Trips to Keet Seel are very popular, so reservations are
taken up to two months in advance. Anyone who suffers from vertigo
might want to avoid this trip: the trail leads down a 1,100-ft near-ver-
tical rock face.

The **visitor center** houses a small museum, exhibits of prehistoric pottery, and a good crafts shop. Free campground and picnic areas are nearby,
and rangers sometimes present campfire programs in summer. No food,
gasoline, or hotel lodging is available at the monument. AZ 564 turns
north off U.S. 160 at the Black Mesa gas station and convenience store
and leads to the visitor center. ✉ *AZ 564, Black Mesa* ✆ *HC 71, Box
3, Tonalea 86044* ☎ *928/672-2700* 🖷 *928/672-2703* ⊕ *www.nps.
gov/nava* ✉ *Free* ☉ *Daily 8–5; tours late May–early Sept.*

Camping

¢ ⚠ **Navajo National Monument Campground.** Beautiful and serene with
no fee, this campground has no hook-ups, and open fires are not allowed
(you must use camp stoves). Because of its remote locale, the campground,
¼ mi west of the visitor center, usually has available sites. Winter snows
can block the road. ⚥ *Flush toilets, drinking water* ⬢ *30 sites* ✉ *AZ
564, Black Mesa* ☎ *928/672-2366* ⚑ *Reservations not accepted*
☉ *Open year-round, weather permitting.*

Sports & the Outdoors

HIKING Now that horseback tours have been suspended in the area, **hiking** is
the best way for adventurous souls to see Keet Seel at the Navajo National Monument. It's a pretty strenuous hike to the ruins, but if you're
fit and leave early enough, it's well worth it to visit some of the best-
preserved ruins in the Southwest. It's free, but the trail is open only from
late May through early September, and you need to call ahead to make
a reservation, usually at least two months in advance. ✆ *Navajo Na-*

tional Monument, HC 71, Box 3, Tonalea 86044 ☎ *928/672–2366*
✉ *Free* ☉ *Daily 8–5; tours late May–early Sept.*

GLEN CANYON DAM & LAKE POWELL

Lake Powell, 185 mi long with 2,000 mi of shoreline—longer than America's Pacific coast—is the heart of the huge 1,255,400-acre Glen Canyon National Recreation Area. Created by the barrier of Glen Canyon Dam—a 710-ft wall of concrete—Lake Powell took 17 years to fill. The second-largest man-made lake in the nation, Lake Powell extends through terrain so rugged it was the last major area of the United States to be mapped. It's ringed by red cliffs that twist off into 96 major canyons and countless inlets (most accessible only by boat) with huge, red-sandstone buttes randomly jutting from the sapphire waters. You could spend 30 years exploring the lake and still not experience everything there is to see. The Sierra Club has started a movement to drain the lake in order to restore water-filled Glen Canyon, which some believe was more spectacular than the Grand Canyon, but the lake is likely to be around for years to come, regardless of the final outcome of this plan.

South of Lake Powell the landscape gives way to **Echo Cliffs,** orange sandstone formations rising 1,000 ft and more above the highway in places. At **Bitter Springs,** the road ascends the cliffs and provides a spectacular view of the 9,000-square-mi Arizona Strip to the west and the 3,000-ft Vermilion Cliffs to the northwest.

For approximate costs, *see* the dining and lodging prices chart at the beginning of this chapter.

Page

⑮ *96 mi west of the Navajo National Monument, 136 mi north of Flagstaff on U.S. 89.*

Built in 1957 as a Glen Canyon Dam construction camp, Page is now a tourist spot and a popular base for day trips to Lake Powell; it has become a major point of entry to the Navajo Nation. The nearby Vermilion Cliffs are where the California condor, an endangered species, has been successfully reintroduced into the wild. The town's human population of 10,000 makes it the largest community in far-northern Arizona, and most of the motels, restaurants, and shopping centers are concentrated along **Lake Powell Boulevard,** the name given to U.S. 89 as it loops through the business district. Each year, more than 3 million people come to play at Lake Powell.

At the corner of North Navajo Drive and Lake Powell Boulevard is the **John Wesley Powell Memorial Museum,** whose namesake led the first known expeditions down the Green River and the rapids-choked Colorado through the Grand Canyon between 1869 and 1872. Powell mapped and kept detailed records of his trips, naming the Grand Canyon and many other geographic points of interest in northern Arizona. Artifacts from his expeditions are displayed in the museum, which has a good selection of regional books and maps. The museum also doubles as the town's visitor information center. A travel desk dispenses information and allows you to book boating tours, raft trips, scenic flights, accommodations in Page, or Antelope Canyon tours. When you sign up for tours here, concessionaires give a donation to the nonprofit museum with no extra charge to you. ✉ *6 N. Lake Powell Blvd.* ☎ *928/*

645–9496 ⊕ *www.powellmuseum.org* ⊡ *$1* ⊙ *Weekdays 8:30–5:30; Memorial Day–Labor Day also open Sat. (call for hrs).*

Where to Stay & Eat

$–$$$ ✕ **Dam Bar and Grille.** Although the interior looks more like a construction site than a restaurant, the food is good, well prepared, and imaginative for the all-purpose palate. It's general American with good steaks and a few touches that take you south of the border; you'll enjoy it. ⊠ *644 N. Navajo Dr.* ☎ *928/645–2161* ⊟ *AE, MC, V.*

$–$$ ✕ **Dos Amigos & Cantina** This small, cheerful spot with a simple but authentic Mexican look offers familiar, satisfying Mexican and American fare. It's well known around Page for its fajitas, chiles rellenos (cheese-stuffed peppers), and *arroz con pollo* (chicken and rice). ⊠ *287 N. Lake Powell Dr* ☎ *928/645–3036* ⊟ *AE, MC, V.*

$–$$ ✕ **Zapata's.** Specials include green-chili and home-style enchiladas, not to mention very good margaritas. Everything is made from "scratch" from family recipes. The basic, clean restaurant is decorated with Mexican blankets, *ristras* (strings of dried red-chili peppers), and pottery. ⊠ *614 N. Navajo Dr.* ☎ *928/645–9006* ⊟ *AE, D, MC, V.*

$–$$ ▦ **Days Inn & Suites.** One of the newer hotels in the area has views of Lake Powell, the Vermilion Cliffs, and Glen Canyon Dam. Standard rooms are spacious, and 22 suites have wet bars, microwaves, refrigerators, and data ports. All are decorated in a pleasant Southwestern motif. Continental breakfast is included in the rates. ⊠ *961 N. Hwy. 89, 86040* ☎ *928/645–2800* 🖷 *928/645–2604* ⊕ *www.daysinn.com* ⊲ *82 rooms* ♨ *Pool, some in-room data ports, some microwaves, some refrigerators, laundry facilities, shop* ⊟ *AE, D, DC, MC, V* ⦿| *CP.*

¢–$$ ▦ **Courtyard by Marriott.** An attractive motel on the grounds of Lake Powell National Golf Course, the Courtyard has comfortable rooms decorated in a Southwestern motif, health and fitness facilities, and on-premises dining in Peppers, an eatery specializing in American fare. ⊠ *600 Clubhouse Dr.* ⬠ *Box 4150, 86040* ☎ *928/645–5000* ⊕ *www.courtyard. com* ⊲ *153 rooms* ♨ *Restaurant, pool, gym, sauna, bar, shop, meeting rooms* ⊟ *AE, D, DC, MC, V.*

★ **¢–$$** ▦ **Uncle Bill's Place.** Most guests who've written in the journals here regret not being able to stay longer. Interesting books to skim, witty and well-traveled hosts, and a lovely garden complete with a grill make this the homiest motel in town. A humorous list of house rules ensures harmonious living in the one- to three-bedroom, suitelike apartments, in which guests often share a bathroom, living room, and full kitchen (you can rent a room or an entire apartment). Uncle Bill gives a good briefing on area attractions and eateries and will lend you a discount card for the supermarket. ⊠ *117 8th Ave., 86040* ☎ *928/645–1224* 🖷 *928/645–3937* ⊕ *www.canyon-country.com/unclebill* ⊲ *12 rooms in 5 apartments* ♨ *Grill, picnic area, kitchens, cable TV, library, travel services; no kids under 8, no smoking* ⊟ *AE, DC, MC, V.*

$ ▦ **Best Western Arizona Inn.** This modern, well-run motel on a high bluff at the northern end of Page has large rooms with queen-size beds and Southwestern-print bedspreads. Butterfield Steakhouse serves Southwestern and standard American fare. ⊠ *716 Rim View Dr.* ⬠ *Box 250, 86040* ☎ *928/645–2466 or 800/826–2718* ⊕ *www.bestwestern.com* ⊲ *103 rooms* ♨ *Restaurant, pool, hot tub, bar, meeting rooms* ⊟ *AE, D, DC, MC, V.*

$ ▦ **Best Western at Lake Powell.** You'll awake to dazzling views of the Vermilion Cliffs in this modern, three-story motel on a high bluff overlooking Glen Canyon Dam. The large rooms are functional, and the beds are comfortable. Continental breakfast is offered in the lobby. Deluxe rooms have microwave ovens and refrigerators. ⊠ *208 N. Lake Powell Blvd.,*

86040 ☎ 928/645–5988 or 888/794–2888 ⊕ *www.bestwestern.com/ atlakepowell* ➾ *132 rooms* ⟁ *Some microwaves, some refrigerators, pool, gym, hot tub, meeting rooms* ▤ *AE, D, DC, MC, V* ❍| *CP.*

$ ▦ **Canyon Colors B&B.** Run by New England transplants Bev and Rich Jones, this desert-country B&B offers travelers a personal touch. The Sunflower and Paisley rooms, which can accommodate up to five and four, respectively, have queen beds and futons. The cozier Canyon Room accommodates only two. All have private baths. The B&B also has an extensive video library, including many videos of Lake Powell and the Navajo Nation. Reservations, necessary in summer, can be made up to a year in advance. ⊠ *225 S. Navajo Dr.* ⟟ *Box 3657, 86040* ☎ *800/ 536–5230* 📠 *928/645–5979* ⊕ *www.canyon-country.com/colors* ➾ *3 rooms* ▤ *AE, D, MC, V* ❍| *BP.*

$ ▦ **Ramada Inn Lake Powell.** This modern hotel offers rooms with views of the Vermilion Cliffs adjacent to Page's 18-hole, par-72 golf course. All accommodations are decorated in a territorial motif but have the expected conveniences of a Ramada Inn. The on-site Family Tree Restaurant serves Navajo and American breakfast, lunch, and dinner. The inn also has a cocktail lounge and picnic area. ⊠ *287 N. Lake Powell Blvd., off U.S. 89* ⟟ *Box 1867, 86040* ☎ *928/645–8851* ⊕ *www. ramada.com* ➾ *129 rooms* ⟁ *Restaurant, pool, bar, meeting rooms* ▤ *AE, D, DC, MC, V.*

¢ ▦ **Thatcher's.** Nita Thatcher runs this inexpensive B&B. There is a common living room–lounge area to relax in. The room with a king-size bed has its own bath; the other two rooms share a bath. And Nita makes a hearty American breakfast each morning. Summer reservations should be made at least three months in advance. ⊠ *7 N. 16th Ave.* ⟟ *Box 421, 86040* ☎ *928/645–3335* ➾ *3 rooms, 2 with shared bath* ⟁ *No room TVs, no room phones* ▤ *No credit cards* ❍| *BP.*

¢ ⚠ **Page–Lake Powell Campground.** Lake Powell is a popular destination and very busy in summer months. It's wise to make reservations well ahead if you're planning to stay at this campground. You can make reservations on-line as well as by phone. ⟁ *Flush toilets, showers, laundry facilities, picnic tables, grocery store, indoor pool* ➾ *85 RV sites, 20 tent sites* ⊠ *849 S. Coppermine Rd., 86040* ☎ *928/645–3374* ⊕ *www. campground.page-lakepowell.com* ▤ *$26 full hookup, $20 partial hookup, $17 tent site.* ▤ *MC, V* ⊙ *Open year-round.*

Nightlife

The **Bowl** (⊠ 24 N. Lake Powell Blvd. ☎ 928/645–2682) is a 10-lane bowling alley with an outdoor patio, billiards, and coffee shop. **Gunsmoke Saloon & Eatery** (⊠ 644 N. Navajo Dr. ☎ 928/645–1888) is a spot where you can dance to live music, play billiards and video games, and munch on chicken wings until 1 AM. **Ken's Old West Restaurant & Lounge** (⊠ 718 Vista Ave. ☎ 928/645–5160) has country-and-western music and dancing; you can also get a pretty good steak, prime rib, seafood, or barbecued-chicken dinner. **Mesa Theater** (⊠ 42 S. Lake Powell Blvd. ☎ 928/645–9565) is Page's movie house.

Sports & the Outdoors

FLOAT TRIPS **Wilderness River Adventures** (☎ 928/645–3296 or 800/992–8022) offers waterborne tours, including a 4½-hour guided rafting excursion down a calm portion of the Colorado River on comfortable, safe J boats ($52). The scenery—multicolor sandstone cliffs adorned with Native American petroglyphs—is spectacular. The point of departure in Page is the Wilderness Outfitters Store at 50 South Lake Powell Boulevard, but transportation is furnished both to the launch site and back from Lees Ferry, where the trip ends.

GOLF **Lake Powell National Golf Course** (✉ 400 Clubhouse Dr., off U.S. 89 ☎ 928/
645–2023 ⊕ www.lakepowellgolf.com) has wide fairways, tiered greens
with some of the steepest holes in the Southwest, and a generous lack
of hazards. An 18-hole, par-72 and a 9-hole, par-36 municipal course
overlook Glen Canyon Dam and Lake Powell.

HIKING The **Horse Shoe Bend Trail** (✉ Off U.S. 89) has some steep up and down
paths and a bit of deep sand to maneuver; however, the views are well
worth the hike. The trail leads up to a bird's-eye view of Glen Canyon
and the Colorado River downstream from Glen Canyon Dam. There
are some sheer drop-offs here, so watch children. To reach the trail, drive
4 mi south of Page on U.S. 89 and turn west onto a blacktop road located ²⁄₁₀ mi south of mile marker 545. It's a ¾-mi hike from the parking area to the top of the canyon.

Shopping

There are numerous gift shops and clothing stores in the downtown area
along Lake Powell Boulevard. **Big Lake Trading Post** (✉ 1501 AZ 98 ☎ 928/
645–2404) has Native American artifacts and a hobby shop. The post
also has a gas station, convenience store, car wash, and coin laundry.
Blair's Dinnebito Trading Post (✉ 626 Navajo Dr. ☎ 928/645–3008
⊕ www.blairstradingpost.com) has been around for more than half a
century. Authentic Native American arts and crafts are only a small part
of what this store sells. Need tack equipment, rodeo ropes, rugs, sad-
dlery, pottery? It's all here and reasonably priced. Take time to wander
upstairs and visit the Elijah Blair collection and memorabilia rooms.

Antelope Canyon

★ ⓰ *4 mi east of Page on the Navajo reservation, on AZ 98.*

You've probably seen dozens of photographs of Antelope Canyon, a narrow, red-sandstone slot canyon with convoluted corkscrew formations,
dramatically illuminated by a ray of light streaming down from above.
And you're likely to see assorted shutterbugs waiting patiently for just
the right shot of these colorful, photogenic rocks, which are actually petrified sand dunes of a prehistoric ocean that once filled this portion of
North America. The best photographs are taken at high noon, when light
filters through "the slot" in the canyon surface to create a breathtaking display of form and color. Take a tripod and use a slow shutter speed.
This is one place that you'll definitely need to protect your camera
equipment against blowing dust. Access to the canyon is limited to
those on licensed tours. ✉ AZ 98, Page ☎ Box 2520, Window Rock
86515 ☎ 928/871–6647 Navajo Parks & Recreation Dept. ⊕ www.
navajonationparks.org ☎ $5 (included in tour cost).

Antelope Canyon Tours

Access to Antelope Canyon is restricted by the Navajo Tribe to licensed
tour operators. The tribe charges a $5 per-person fee—which is in-
cluded in the price of tours offered by the licensed concessionaires in
Page. The easiest way to book a tour of Antelope Canyon is in town at
the John Wesley Powell Memorial Museum Visitor's Center. You'll pay
nothing extra for the museum's service; however, if you'd like to go directly to the tour operators, you can do that, too. Most companies offer
1½-hour sightseeing tours for $27 or longer photography tours for $48.
The best time to see the canyon is between 8 AM and 2 PM.

Antelope Canyon Adventures (✉ 108 S. Lake Powell Blvd., Page ☎ 928/
645–5501 ⊕ www.jeeptour.com) offers 1½-hour sightseeing tours. **John
Wesley Powell Museum Visitor Center** (✉ 6 N. Lake Powell Blvd., Page
☎ 928/645–9496 ⊕ www.powellmuseum.org) arranges 1½-hour tours

and 5-hour photography tours. Photo tours leave from various locations in Page at 8 and 9:30 AM and return about 2 PM. The shorter sightseeing tours leave frequently between 8 AM and 4 PM. **Overland Canyon Tours** (✉ 18 N. Lake Powell Blvd., Page ☎ 928/608–4072 ⊕ www.overlandcanyon.com) is the only Native American–operated tour company in Page. Tours include a narrative explaining the canyon's history and geology. **Roger Ekis' Antelope Canyon Tours** (✉ 22 S. Lake Powell Blvd., Page ☎ 928/645–9102 ⊕ www.antelopecanyon.com) offers several tours daily from 8 AM to 3 PM for sightseers and photographers. The photo tour gives serious and amateur photographers the opportunity to wait for the "right light" to photograph the canyon and get some basic information on equipment setup. Tickets can be purchased at the John Wesley Powell Museum Visitor Center.

Glen Canyon National Recreation Area

⑰ *2 mi west of Page on U.S. 89.*

Once you leave the Page business district heading northwest, the Glen Canyon Dam and Lake Powell behind it immediately become visible. This concrete-arch dam—all 5 million cubic ft of it—was completed in September 1963, its power plant an engineering feat that rivaled Hoover Dam. The dam's crest is 1,560 ft across and rises 710 ft from bedrock and 583 ft above the waters of the Colorado River. When Lake Powell is full, it is 560 ft deep at the dam. The plant generates some 1.3 million kilowatts of electricity when each generator's 40-ton shaft is generating nearly 200,000 horsepower. Power from the dam serves a five-state grid consisting of Colorado, Arizona, Utah, California, and New Mexico and provides energy for some 1.5 million users.

With only 8 inches of annual rainfall, the Lake Powell area enjoys blue skies nearly year-round. Summer temperatures range from the 60s to the 90s (occasionally rising to 100°F). Fall and spring are usually balmy, with daytime temperatures often in the 70s and 80s, but chilly weather can set in. Nights are cool even in the summer, and in winter the risk of a cold spell increases, but all-weather houseboats and tour boats make for year-round cruising.

Boaters and campers should note that regulations require the use of portable toilets on the lake and lakeshore. Park authorities vigorously enforce this rule to prevent water pollution.

Just off the highway at the north end of the bridge is the **Carl Hayden Visitor Center,** where you can learn about the controversial creation of Glen Canyon Dam and Lake Powell and enjoy panoramic views of both. To enter the visitor center, you must go through a metal detector. Absolutely no bags are allowed inside. ✉ *U.S. 89, Page, 2 mi west of town* ☎ *928/608–6404* ⊕ *www.nps.gov/glca* ▦ *$10 per vehicle, $10 per week boating fee* ☉ *Visitor Center Memorial Day–Labor Day, daily 8–6; Labor Day–Memorial Day, daily 8–5.*

Wahweap

⑱ *5 mi north of Glen Canyon Dam on U.S. 89.*

Most waterborne recreational activity on the Arizona side of the lake is centered on this vacation village, where everything needed for a lakeside holiday is available: tour boats, fishing, boat rentals, dinner cruises, and much more. Stop at Wahweap Lodge for an excellent view of the lake area. You can take a boat tour of Lake Powell from the Wahweap Marina.

★ ⑲ The best way to appreciate the stunning scenery of Lake Powell is by boat. If you don't have access to your own, a boat tour to **Rainbow Bridge National Monument** is a great way see the enormity of the lake and its incredible, rugged beauty. This 290-ft red-sandstone arch is the world's largest natural bridge and can be reached only by boat or viewed by air. To the Navajos, this is a sacred area with deep religious and spiritual significance, so outsiders are asked not to hike underneath the arch itself.

Where to Stay & Eat

$$ ✕▢ **Wahweap Lodge.** The lodge, on a promontory above Lake Powell,
Fodor'sChoice serves as the center for recreational activities in the area. The brightly
★ colored Southwestern-style suites in the newest building are particularly attractive. The lodge's semicircular Rainbow Room restaurant ($–$$) offers an extensive Southwestern, American, and Continental menu and breakfast buffet, all with panoramic views of Lake Powell. In season, there are also decent pizzas from Itza Pizza. ✉ *100 Lake Shore Dr., Wahweap, 7 mi north of Page off of U.S. 89* ⬤ *Box 1597, Page 86040* ☎ *928/645–2433 or 800/528–6154* ⬅ *350 rooms* ⬥ *Restaurant, pizzeria, 2 pools, boating, waterskiing, fishing, bar, travel services* ⊟ *AE, D, DC, MC, V.*

¢ ⛰ **Wahweap Campground.** This campground offers nice views of the lake and is located in the Wahweap Marina complex, which is run by the National Park Service Concessionaire. There are showers and coin-laundry services nearby at the Wahweap Trailer Village. ⬥ *Flush toilets, drinking water, picnic tables* ⬅ *112 tent sites, 94 full hook-ups* ✉ *U.S. 89, Wahweap 86040, 5 mi north of Page near shore of Lake Powell* ☎ *928/645–1059* ⬜ *$15 tent site, $28 full hook-up* ⊟ *AE, D, DC, MC, V* ⊙ *Open year-round.*

¢ ⛰ **Wahweap Trailer Village.** This RV park has 120 full-service hook-ups, showers, and a coin laundry. It's open year-round, and reservations are accepted. ⬥ *Flush toilets, full hook-ups, dump station, drinking water, showers, laundry facilities, picnic tables* ⬅ *120 RV sites* ✉ *U.S. 89, Wahweap 86040, 5 mi north of Page near shore of Lake Powell* ☎ *928/645–1004 or 800/528–6154* ⬜ *$28* ⊟ *AE, D, DC, MC, V* ⊙ *Open year-round.*

Sports & the Outdoors

BOATING Lake Powell Resorts offers full marina services at Wahweap and State Line—including rental of small excursion boats, pontoon and deck boats, houseboats, water-sports toys, fishing boats, and personal watercraft.

At **Aramark's Lake Powell Resorts & Marinas** (⬤ Box 56909, Phoenix 85079 ☎ 800/528–6154 central reservations, 928/645–1004 direct to hotel ⬛ 602/331–5258 ⬥ www.visitlakepowell.com) houseboats rentals range widely in size, amenities, and price, depending upon season. One that sleeps eight (four double beds) can run about $900 for three nights. Larger, 59-ft Admiral Class luxury houseboats may cost as much as $3,200 for three nights; an 18-ft powerboat for eight passengers runs from approximately $139 to $232 per day. **State Line Marina** (✉ U.S. 89, State Line, UT ☎ 928/645–1111), 1½ mi north of Wahweap Lodge, is part of Aramark's Lake Powell Resorts and Marina concession and site of the boat rental office. It's here that you pick up rental houseboats, powerboats, kayaks, Jet Skis, and personal watercraft. There's also a public launch ramp in the event you're towing your own boat. **Wahweap Marina** (✉ 100 Lake Shore Dr., Wahweap ☎ 928/645–2433) is the largest of the four full-service Lake Powell marinas run by Lake Powell Resorts and Marinas. There are 850 slips and the most facilities, including a decent diner, public launch ramp, fishing dock, and a marina store where you can buy fishing licenses and other necessities. It's the only full-service marina on the Arizona side of the lake (the other three marinas—Hite, Bullfrog, and Halls Crossing—are in Utah).

BOAT TOURS Excursions on double-decker scenic cruisers piloted by experienced guides leave from the dock of Lake Powell's **Wahweap Lodge** (⊠ 100 Lake Shore Dr., Wahweap ☎ 928/645–2433 or 800/528–6154). The most popular tour is the half-day trip to Rainbow Bridge National Monument for $80 (lemonade, water, and coffee are included, and you can bring your own snacks or lunch). The full-day cruise visits several side canyons as well as Rainbow Bridge and costs about $109; this one includes a box lunch, lemonade, water, and coffee. A 2½-hour sunset dinner cruise costs about $63 and also departs from Wahweap Lodge: a prime-rib dinner—vegetarian lasagna dinners are available if ordered in advance—is served on the fully enclosed decks of the 95-ft *Canyon King* paddle wheeler, a reproduction of a 19th-century bay boat. The dinner cruise is a 2½-hour tour with the captain's choice of routes.

CAMPING Beautiful campsites are abundant on Lake Powell, from large beaches to secluded coves, with the most desirable areas accessible only by boat. You are allowed to camp anywhere along the shores of the lake unless it's restricted by the National Park Service; however, camping within ¼ mi of the shoreline requires a portable toilet or bathroom facilities on your boat. Campfires are allowed on the shoreline, but since there's little firewood available around the lake, you'll need to bring your own.

FISHING Fishing licenses for the Lake Powell area are available at the **Marina Store at Wahweap Marina** (⊠ 100 Lake Shore Dr., Wahweap ☎ 928/645–1136). **Stix Market** (⊠ 5 S. Lake Powell Blvd., Page ☎ 928/645–2891) can recommend local fishing guides.

HIKING Bring plenty of water and electrolyte-rich beverages such as Gatorade when hiking, and drink often. It is important to remember when hiking at Lake Powell to watch the sky for storms. It may not be raining where you are; however, flooding can occur in downstream canyons—particularly slot canyons—from a storm miles away.

Only seasoned hikers in good physical condition will want to try either of the two trails leading to **Rainbow Bridge**; both are about 26–28 mi round-trip through very challenging and rugged terrain. This site is considered sacred by the Navajo, and it's requested that visitors show respect by not walking under the bridge. Take Indian Highway 16 north toward the Utah state border. At the fork in the road, take either direction for about 5 mi and you'll come to a trailhead leading to Rainbow Bridge. Excursion boats pull in at the dock at the arch, but no supplies are sold there.

Navajo Nation Parks and Recreation Department (⊠ Bldg. 36A, E. AZ 264 ⊕ Box 2520, Window Rock 86515 ☎ 928/871–6647 ⊕ www. navajonationparks.org) provides backcountry permits (a slight fee is charged), which must be obtained in order to hike to Rainbow Bridge. Write to the office, and allow about a month to process the paperwork.

THE NORTHEAST A TO Z

To research prices, get advice from other travelers, and book travel arrangements, visit www.fodors.com.

AIR TRAVEL

No major airlines fly directly to northeastern Arizona. To get closer to this part of the state, you can fly into Sky Harbor International Airport in Phoenix and take a small plane operated by Denver-based Great Lakes Aviation to Page Municipal Airport.

Great Lakes Aviation ☎ 800/554-5111 ⊕ www.greatlakesav.com.

AIRPORTS
Page Municipal Airport ☎ 928/645-4337 ⊕ www.cityofpage.org.

BANKS
Wells Fargo has branch offices with ATMs in Window Rock, Kayenta, and Tuba City on the Navajo reservation. Near the reservation, Flagstaff, Page, Winslow, Chinle, and Holbrook have banks and ATMs.

BUS TRAVEL
Greyhound Lines has numerous Arizona destinations, but there is no service into the reservations. Once on the reservation, you will find that the Navajo Transit System has extensive, fixed routes throughout the Navajo reservation as well as charter service; write or phone for schedules. The buses are modern, in good condition, and generally on time, but they do not make frequent runs, and when they do run they can be slow. Fares range from 50¢ for local rides to a high of $13.05 (Window Rock to Tuba City). This can be an up-close-and-personal way to travel the Navajo Nation and meet the people who live here as they go about their daily business.

Navajo Transit System ⌂ Drawer 1330, Window Rock 86515 ☎ 928/729-4002 ⊕ www.navajotransitsystem.com.

CAR TRAVEL
The only practical way to tour the Navajo and Hopi nations is by car. If you are arriving from southern California or southern Arizona, Flagstaff is the best jumping-off point into northeastern Arizona. If you are traveling from Utah or Nevada, you might choose to come in from Utah on U.S. 89, starting your tour at Page. For those driving south from Colorado, logical entry points are Farmington and Shiprock, New Mexico, via U.S. 64 (what looks like a more direct route to Canyon de Chelly through Red Rock ends up crossing an unimproved road). Gallup, New Mexico, to the east, is also a convenient starting point for exploring the area.

Because a tour of Navajo-Hopi country involves driving long distances among widely scattered communities, a detailed, up-to-date road map is absolutely essential. A wrong turn could send you many miles out of your way. Gas stations carry adequate state maps, but two other maps are particularly recommended: the AAA (Automobile Association of America) guide to Navajo-Hopi country and the excellent map of the northeastern region prepared by the Navajo Nation Tourism Office.

Road service, auto repairs, and other automotive services are few and far between, so service your vehicle before venturing into the Navajo and Hopi Reservations, and carry emergency equipment and supplies. If you need assistance, ask a local for the nearest auto repair service. Diamond Towing offers a 24-hour emergency road service.

Diamond Towing ✉ Kayenta ☎ 928/697-8437.

ROAD CONDITIONS Most of the 27,000 square mi of the Navajo reservation and other areas of northeastern Arizona are off the beaten track. Many travelers in northeastern Arizona generally stay on the well-maintained paved thoroughfares, which are patrolled by police officers. If you don't have the equipment for wilderness travel—including a four-wheel-drive vehicle and provisions—and do not have backcountry experience, stay off the dirt roads unless they are signed and graded and the skies are clear. Seek weather information if you see ominous rain clouds in summer or signs of snow in winter. Never drive into dips or low-lying road areas during a heavy rainstorm; they could be flooded or could flood suddenly. If you heed these simple precautions, car travel through the region will be as safe as anywhere else. While driving around the Navajo Nation, tune in to 660 AM (KTNN) for local news and weather.

EMERGENCIES

Ambulance and Fire Kayenta Ambulance ☎ 928/697–4074. **Page Ambulance** ☎ 928/645–2461

Hospitals Monument Valley Health Center ✉ 4 Rock Door Canyon, Monument Valley, UT 84536 ☎ 801/727–3241. **Page Hospital** ✉ 501 N. Navajo Ave., Page ☎ 928/645–2424. **Sage Memorial Hospital** ✉ Ganado ☎ 928/755–3411. **U.S. Public Health Service Indian Hospital** ✉ Chinle ☎ 928/674–7001 ✉ Fort Defiance ☎ 928/729–5741 ✉ Keams Canyon ☎ 928/738–2211 ✉ Tuba City ☎ 928/283–2501.

Pharmacies Safeway Pharmacy ✉ Page Plaza, Page ☎ 928/645–5714 or 928/645–5068. **Wal-Mart Pharmacy** ✉ Gateway Plaza, Page ☎ 928/645–2917.

Police Canyon de Chelly Police ☎ 928/674–2111 or 928/674–2112. **Hopi tribal police: Hopi Mesas** ☎ 928/738–2233 or 928/738–2234. **Navajo tribal police** ✉ Chinle ☎ 928/674–2111 or 928/674–2112 ✉ Tuba City ☎ 928/283–3111 or 928/283–3112 ✉ Window Rock ☎ 928/871–6111 or 928/871–6112 ✉ Kayenta ☎ 928/697–5600 ✉ **Page Police** ☎ 928/645–2463.

MEDIA

RADIO KTNN radio (660 AM), the Voice of the Navajo Nation, serves the Hopi and Navajo reservations from studios in Window Rock. Some programming is in Navajo, but there are news and weather reports in English; its "sister" station is KWRK, at 106.1 on the FM dial. Another radio station you might tune to for news and weather is KOB (770 AM, 107.3 FM, or 97.9 FM). For the boater's emergency band, dial Channel 16 on the marine band.

SIGHTSEEING TOURS

AIR TOURS Gallup Flying Service offers photo and scenic aerial tours of Navajoland from Gallup, New Mexico. Classic Helicopters, at the Page Airport, can show you a bird's-eye view of Lake Powell and Rainbow Bridge.
Classic Helicopters ✉ Page Municipal Airport, Page ☎ 928/645–5356 ⊕ www.helicoptours.com. **Gallup Flying Service** ✉ West Hwy. 66, Gallup, NM ☎ 505/863–6606.

CANYON X TOURS On private property, the isolated slot canyon known as Canyon X slot can be toured only by Navajo guide Harley Klemm and his company, Overland Canyon Tour, which also operates popular tours to Antelope Canyon. Tours depart from Page at approximately 8 AM and return at 3 PM, by advance reservation only. The six-hour tour for serious shutterbugs ($135 per person) offers treks to three different, off-the-beaten-track canyons and is guided by a professional slot-canyon photographer. The four-hour guided hiking tour ($85 per person) is limited to groups of 16. Because the area is rugged, children are not allowed, and participants should have good physical mobility to climb crevasses and some rough terrain.
Overland Canyon Tours ✉ 18 Lake Powell Blvd., Page ☎ 928/608–4072 ⊕ www.overlandcanyon.com.

TIME

Unlike the rest of Arizona (including the Hopi Reservation), the Navajo reservation observes daylight saving time. Thus for half the year—April to October—it's an hour later on the Navajo reservation than everywhere else in the state.

TRAIN TRAVEL

No passenger trains enter the interior of the Navajo or Hopi Reservation or stop at any of the other towns along its perimeter. Amtrak serves Flagstaff.

VISITOR INFORMATION

🚩 **Glen Canyon Recreation Area** ✈ National Park Service, Box 1507, Page 86040–1507 ☎ 928/608–6200 or 928/608–6404 ⊕ www.nps.gov\glca. **Hopi Tribe Office of Public Relations** ✈ Box 123, Kykotsmovi 86039 ☎ 928/734–2441 ⊕ www.hopi.nsn.us. **Native American Tourism Center** ✉ 4130 N. Goldwater Blvd., Scottsdale 85251 ☎ 480/945–0771. **Navajo Nation Tourism Office** ✈ Box 663, Window Rock 86515 ☎ 928/871–7371 ⊕ www.navajoland.com. **Page/Lake Powell Chamber of Commerce** ✉ 644 N. Navajo Dr., at Dam Plaza, Page ✈ Box 727, 86040 ☎ 928/645–2741 ⊕ www.pagelakepowellchamber.org.

EASTERN ARIZONA

5

FODOR'S CHOICE

Coronado Trail, *a National Scenic Byway*

Homolovi Ruins State Park, *northeast of Winslow*

Petrified Forest National Park, *east of Holbrook*

Red Setter Inn, *Greer*

Reed's Lodge, *Springerville*

Rendezvous Diner, *Greer*

Salt River Canyon, *a scenic drive on the Fort Apache Indian Reservation*

Silver Creek Golf Club, *Show Low*

Wigwam Motel, *a budget choice in Holbrook*

HIGHLY RECOMMENDED

RESTAURANTS Annie's Gift Shop and Tea Room, *Lakeside*

HOTELS Hannagan Meadow Lodge, *Hannagan Meadow*

Paisley Corner Bed & Breakfast, *Springerville*

SIGHTS Greer

Hannagan Meadow

Updated by
David Joiner

IN A STATE OF DRAMATIC NATURAL WONDERS, eastern Arizona is often overlooked—truly a tragedy, as it is one of Arizona's great outdoor playgrounds. In the White Mountains, northeast of Phoenix, you can hike amid the largest stand of ponderosa pine in the world, fish for trout in babbling brooks, swim in clear reservoirs fed by unsullied mountain streams, and, at night, camp under millions of twinkling stars. The region's winter sports are just as varied: you can ski downhill or cross country, snowboard, snowshoe, and snowmobile on hundreds of miles of designated trails. And while some regions were burned in the devastating Rodeo-Chediski wildfire of 2002, visitor services were disrupted only temporarily, though the effects are still evident.

An unparalleled natural beauty, however, is what really makes the region remarkable—the White Mountains are unspoiled high country at its best. Certain areas have been designated as primitive wilderness, removed from the touch of people. In these vast tracts, the air is rent with piercing cries of hawks and eagles, and majestic herds of elk graze in verdant, wildflower-laden meadows. Past volcanic activity has left the land strewn with cinder cones, and the whole region is bounded by the Mogollon Rim (pronounced *muh*-gee-on)—a 200-mi geologic upthrust that splits the state—made famous as the "Tonto Rim" in Zane Grey's books. Much of the plant life is unique to this region; this is one of the few places in the country where such desert plants as juniper and manzanita grow intermixed with mountain pines and aspen.

The human aspects of the landscape are equally appealing. Historic Western towns are friendly outposts of down-home hospitality, and the region's many prehistoric ruins are reminders of the rich native cultures that once flourished here. Native Americans are still a vital presence in the region: nearly half of the White Mountains is Apache reservation. Visitors are welcome to explore most reservation lands. All that's required is a permit—easily obtained from tribal offices.

There's more to eastern Arizona than the White Mountains, however. To the north, along historic Route 66, you'll find the Painted Desert and Petrified Forest National Park and Homolovi Ruins State Park—extraordinary attractions in their own right. The austere mesas of the Painted Desert are world famous for their multihued sedimentary layers. Nature has also worked its wonders on the great fallen logs of the Petrified Forest National Park. In Triassic times, the park was a great, steamy swampland; some 225 million years ago, seismic activity forced the swamp's decaying plant matter (and a number of deceased dinosaurs) deep underground, where it eventually turned to stone. Fifty miles west of these unusual geologic remains, Homolovi Ruins State Park marks the site of four major ancestral Hopi pueblos, two of which contain more than 1,000 rooms. Between these artifacts of times past and the recreational bounty of the White Mountains wilderness, eastern Arizona offers a cultural and outdoor experience that defines the pleasures of Arizona.

Exploring Eastern Arizona

Eastern Arizona spans the gamut of high-desert wonders and in doing so offers the still-infrequent traveler abundant opportunities to delve into unspoiled nature and a surprising variety of outdoor recreation. In the northern part of the region is the Petrified Forest National Park, covering 93,000 acres and including a portion of the Painted Desert; a straight shot west on I–40 leads to important ancestral Hopi pueblos at Homolovi Ruins State Park. South of here, on the western edge of the region, is Salt River Canyon, known to many as the mini–Grand Canyon, where

5

Your White Mountains experience can vary greatly, depending on the season of your visit and your personal interests. The itineraries below assume that you're traveling between March and October, when both primary and secondary roads are passable. If you're visiting during the winter, you may have to rearrange your trip to accommodate seasonal road closures and chain requirements.

If you have 3 days

Your options are limited if you have only three days to explore the mountains, given the distance from Phoenix and the condition of the roads much of the year. Drive up to ▣ **Pinetop-Lakeside** ❸ ⌐, ▣**Greer** ❺, or ▣**Springerville-Eagar** ❼ and take advantage of a day or two of hiking, fishing, or biking. In winter, snow enthusiasts commonly make the pilgrimage to **Sunrise Park Resort** ❹ for just a day or two.

If your main priority is visiting the **Petrified Forest National Park** ⓫ and the **Painted Desert,** spend the first night in ▣ **Pinetop-Lakeside** ❸. On day two tour the park; spend the night in nearby ▣ Holbrook, or make the scenic 75-mi drive southeast into ▣ **Springerville-Eagar** ❼, where you'll find several lodging options. Another option is to retrace your route back on AZ 77 and head east for accommodations in ▣ **Show Low** ❷. Spend your third day driving back to Phoenix. You can return via U.S. 60 or opt for the day-long trip down the Coronado Trail, one of the state's most scenic byways.

If you have 5 days

After exploring the **Painted Desert** and **Petrified Forest National Park** ⓫ ⌐, head south to the White Mountains and spend the night in either ▣**Springerville-Eagar** ❼ or ▣ **Pinetop-Lakeside** ❸, depending on whether you take AZ 77 or U.S. 180. Indulge in a day of local sightseeing in either pair of twin towns, and then spend the following day working your way across east–west AZ 260 through the Apache Sitgreaves National Forest and parts of the White Mountain Apache Reservation, stopping for the night in tiny ▣ **Greer** ❺. On the last day, retrace your route back to Phoenix via U.S. 60 or, if departing from Springerville-Eagar, via the Coronado Trail. If you're looking for solitude and remote beauty, skip poking along AZ 260's towns and head straight from the Petrified Forest down U.S. 180 to **Hannagan Meadow** ❾, returning on the remainder of the Coronado Trail for day five.

If you have 7 or more days

Spend two nights in ▣ Holbrook, devoting a full day to visiting the **Painted Desert** and **Petrified Forest National Park** ⓫ ⌐ and the next half day to touring the **Homolovi Ruins State Park** ❿ and enjoying the drive south to ▣ **Pinetop-Lakeside** ❸ or ▣ **Springerville-Eagar** ❼. From either of these points, take advantage of the multitude of recreational opportunities that line east–west AZ 260. Return to Phoenix via the Coronado Trail, stopping for at least one night in ▣ **Alpine** ❽ or ▣ **Hannagan Meadow** ❾. If you don't want to repeat portions of the drive on AZ 260 and you enjoy scenic back roads, pick up a map of Forest Service routes from any ranger station and meander toward Hannagan Meadow and U.S. 191 on Forest Service roads that sprout south and east from AZ 373 and AZ 261.

the San Carlos and Fort Apache Reservations abut. The mountain towns of Pinetop-Lakeside, Greer, and Springerville-Eagar are all connected by AZ 260. At Springerville, you can connect to U.S. 191, also known as the Coronado Trail Scenic Byway. Towering over this southern part of the White Mountains is Mt. Baldy, an 11,590-ft extinct volcano considered sacred by the Apache. Of note—and definitely worth exploring— is the Mogollon Rim, a limestone escarpment that extends 200 mi from southwest of Flagstaff to the White Mountains in eastern Arizona. In the winter months, you'll have to stick to major thoroughfares, as many Forest Service roads are closed, and be sure to call for a road and weather report before setting off during this time.

About the Restaurants

Dining in eastern Arizona offers visitors a range of exciting opportunities. In the White Mountains, you might settle in for a relaxing evening of fine dining at a candlelit restaurant in the pines. Or, if cowboy-size steaks and Old West atmosphere are what you seek, choose a more rustic setting at one of the area's many Western-style cafés. In and around the Navajo and Hopi reservations, be sure to sample Indian tacos, an authentic treat made with scrumptious fry bread, beans, and chilies.

About the Hotels

The communities of Pinetop-Lakeside, Greer, Show Low, and Springerville-Eagar offer a variety of lodging choices, including modern resorts, rustic cabins, and small bed-and-breakfasts. Closer to the Navajo and Hopi reservations, you'll find many establishments run by Native Americans, tribal enterprises intent on offering first-class service and hospitality.

WHAT IT COSTS				
$$$$	**$$$**	**$$**	**$**	**¢**
RESTAURANTS over $30	$20–$30	$12–$20	$8–$12	under $8
HOTELS over $250	$175–$250	$120–$175	$70–$120	under $70

Restaurant prices are per person for a main course at dinner. Hotel prices are for two people in a standard double room in high season, excluding taxes and service charges.

Numbers in the text correspond to numbers in the margin and on the Eastern Arizona map.

Timing

If you're a skier, winter is definitely the time to tour the White Mountains. Those visiting in the beginning of January who want to witness some real-life mushing should check out the Alpine Annual Sled Dog Races.

During warmer months, take advantage of the wide variety of outdoor activities in the area. In mid-May, the tiny hamlet of Greer comes alive to celebrate Greer Days with a parade, crafts, dances, and a fishing derby. Crowds begin converging on the White Mountains starting in late June, when school is out and Valley of the Sun temperatures start to become uncomfortably warm.

Autumn is a splendid time for a drive down the Coronado Trail, with hairpin turns winding through the yellows and golds of aspen and oak. The Pinetop-Lakeside Fall Festival is held the last weekend of September, with a parade and an impressive assortment of crafts booths. The White Mountain Apache Tribal Fair is celebrated Labor Day weekend with a parade and professional Native American rodeo.

Hiking & Biking

Hikers and mountain bikers of all abilities enjoy the White Mountains' interconnecting loop trails, which are open to those on foot or on two nonmotorized wheels. Be sure to stop at ranger stations for maps and tips on trails and overnight hikes. When planning your hike, allow one hour for each 2 mi of trail covered, plus an additional hour for every 1,000 ft gained in altitude. Farther north, day hikes through the Painted Desert Wilderness are a great way to explore the park's backcountry. Mountain bikers will thrill over the White Mountain Trail System's 225 mi of interconnecting multi-use trails. Many bike routes follow narrow Forest Service roads, which carry heavy traffic during the logging season from April to November. Be especially cautious when biking on reservation roads, as bicyclists are generally unexpected. Always carry ample water and be aware that poison ivy grows in White Mountain wilderness areas.

Fishing

Anglers flock to the more than 65 lakes, streams, and reservoirs in the White Mountains, where they hook German browns, rainbow, and brook trout, as well as the occasional arctic grayling or native Apache trout, the official state fish, which is unique to Arizona. Early spring is prime trout-fishing season, but even in the winter, devoted anglers can be found ice-fishing on Nelson Reservoir or Hawley Lake. High-country warm-water fishing consists mostly of largemouth bass, bluegill, catfish, and walleye, hailed as the tastiest catch in the region. During winter months only artificial lures and flies are permitted. An Arizona fishing license is required at these sites; on tribal land, an additional White Mountain Apache fishing license is required.

Golf

The High Country's links draw golfers from the Valley of the Sun and Tucson. These mountain fairways, with their cool temperatures and thin, pine-scented air, angle through lush forests of aspen, blue spruce, and ponderosa pine and wind past numerous lakes, streams, and springs. Pinetop-Lakeside has three championship courses, and Alpine has the highest golf course in the Southwest, at 8,500 ft above sea level. All of these clubs have practice greens and driving ranges, and most offer golf instruction for individuals as well as small groups.

Native American Ruins

North of Springerville-Eagar, Casa Malpais Archaeological Park is a prehistoric pueblo site with construction characteristics of both the ancient Puebloan peoples to the north and the Mogollon peoples to the south. Today, both the Hopi and Zuni peoples hotly claim individual affiliations with the sacred ruins of Casa Malpais, thought to have been a prominent religious center with an impressive astronomical calendar and the largest kiva (sunken ceremonial chamber) ever discovered in the United States. Nearby Lyman Lake State Park has petroglyph trails with some of the region's more accessible rock art. West of Holbrook, Homolovi Ruins State Park is home to a large complex of Hopi ancestral pueblos. Petroglyphs and pueblos dating back more than 600 years can be found at stops along the 28-mi park road in the Petrified Forest National Park.

Skiing & Snowmobiling

Famous regionally for winter skiing, the 11,000-ft White Mountains offer hilly, wooded landscapes that invite downhill and cross-country skiing adventurers. Greer is an ideal hub for cross-country skiers: The nearby Pole Knoll Trail System and surrounding Forest Service roads make for 33 mi of cross-country trails. No matter where you stay in the White Mountains, the drive to Sunrise Park Resort—the state's largest ski resort—with 65 trails on three mountains—is never more than an hour away, and equipment-rental facilities are located throughout the region. Snowmobilers enjoy the area's dense forest and expansive meadows; the more adventurous enjoy the long-distance routes connecting Sunrise Ski Area to Williams Valley (near Alpine) or Hannagan Meadow.

THE WHITE MOUNTAINS

With elevations climbing to more than 11,000 ft, the White Mountains of east-central Arizona are a winter wonderland and a summer haven from the desert heat. In the 1870s John Gregory Bourke labeled the region "a strange upheaval, a freak of nature, a mountain canted up on one side; one rides along the edge and looks down two or three thousand feet into . . . a weird scene of grandeur and rugged beauty." It is still grand and rugged, carved by deep river canyons and tall cliffs covered with ponderosa pine. It is also much less remote than it was in Bourke's time, with a full-scale real-estate boom now under way.

Winter travelers through the White Mountains should be aware that weather conditions can change without notice in these higher elevations. Call for weather information before heading out to White Mountains highways.

Salt River Canyon

❶ *40 mi north of Globe on U.S. 60.*

Fodor'sChoice
★

Exposing a time lapse of 500 million years, these multicolored spires, buttes, mesas, and canyon walls have inspired this canyon's nickname, the mini–Grand Canyon. Approaching the Salt River Canyon from Phoenix, U.S. 60 climbs through rolling hills, and the terrain changes to forests of ponderosa pine. After entering the San Carlos Indian Reservation, the highway drops 2,000 ft—from the Natanes Plateau into the canyon's vast gorge—and makes a series of hairpin turns down to cross the Salt River. Stop at the viewing and interpretive display area before crossing the bridge to stretch your legs. Wander along the banks below and enjoy the rock-strewn rapids (on hot Arizona days you can slip your shoes off and dip your feet into the chilly water for a cool respite). The river and canyon are open to a variety of activities, including hiking, camping, fishing, and white-water rafting. For information on Salt River Canyon and the activities it supports, contact the **Greater Globe-Miami Chamber of Commerce** (☎ 800/804–5623 ⊕ www.globemiamichamber.com).

en route

The road out of the Salt River Canyon climbs along the canyon's northern cliffs, providing views of this truly spectacular chasm, unfairly overlooked in a state full of world-famous gorges. The highway continues some 50 mi northward to the **Mogollon Rim**—a huge geologic ledge that bisects much of Arizona—and its cool upland pine woods.

Show Low

② *60 mi north of the Salt River Canyon on U.S. 60.*

Why, yes, Show Low *is* an odd name for a town. Local legend has it that two partners, Clark and Cooley, homesteaded the surrounding 100,000 acres in 1870 but found themselves wanting to dissolve the partnership some years later after an argument. The two decided to play cards, after which the winner would buy out the loser. On the last hand of the night, Cooley was a point behind when Clark allegedly offered "show low and you win." Cooley cut the deck and came up with the deuce of clubs, thereby winning the game and the land. Part of the partners' then-ranch is now the town of Show Low, and the main drag through town is called Deuce of Clubs.

Show Low has little of the charm of its neighboring White Mountains communities, but it is the main commercial center for the High Country. Additionally, the city is a crossing point for east–west traffic along the Mogollon Rim and traffic headed for Holbrook and points north. If you're heading up to the Painted Desert and Petrified Forest from Phoenix, you might want to spend the night here.

Where to Stay & Eat

¢–$$ ✕ **Licano's Mexican Food and Steakhouse.** You'll find everything here from nachos to prime rib and lobster tail. It's open seven days a week. The spacious but cozy lounge, with a weekday happy hour 4:30–6, stays open to 10 PM nightly. ⊠ *573 W. Deuce of Clubs* ☎ *928/537–8220* ▭ *AE, D, DC, MC, V.*

¢–$ ✕ **High in the Pines Deli.** A block east of Deuce of Clubs, this quaint deli and coffeehouse has tasty specialty sandwiches—the roasted pork tenderloin sandwich is out of this world. European-style charcuterie boards include fine selections of pâtés, meats, and cheeses served with a fresh baguette. Box lunches are available for those planning to hit the road or spend the day exploring the local surroundings. ⊠ *1191 E. Hall* ☎ *928/537–1453* ▭ *AE, D, MC, V* ☉ *Closed Sun. No dinner.*

¢–$ ▦ **Best Western Paint Pony Lodge.** Guest rooms here have traditional stucco, wood accents, and large picture windows overlooking Arizona's pine-studded high country. Suites and some rooms include fireplaces, and use of an off-property gym is free for hotel guests. ⊠ *581 W. Deuce of Clubs, 85901* ☎ *928/537–5773* ⊕ *www.bestwestern.com* ⟿ *46 rooms, 4 suites* ⚹ *In-room data ports, cable TV, refrigerators, some microwaves, bar, no-smoking rooms* ▭ *AE, D, DC, MC, V* ⦿| *CP.*

¢ ▦ **KC Motel.** Victorian decor, including four-poster beds, makes this a not-so-typical motel. All rooms have cable TV and refrigerators. ⊠ *60 W. Deuce of Clubs, 85901* ☎ *928/537–4433 or 800/531–7152* ⟿ *37 rooms* ⚹ *Refrigerators, cable TV, hot tub* ▭ *AE, D, DC, MC, V* ⦿| *CP.*

Sports & the Outdoors

FISHING **Show Low Lake** (⊠ Show Low Lake Rd. ☎ 928/537–4126), south of town and 1 mi off AZ 260, holds the state record for the largest walleye catch and is well stocked with largemouth bass, bluegill, and catfish. Facilities include a bait shop, marina with boat rentals, and campsites with bathrooms and showers. **Fool Hollow Lake Recreational Area** (⊠ 2 mi north of U.S. 60 off AZ 260 ☎ 928/537–3680), is open year-round for camping, fishing, and boating. Set amid a picturesque, piney 800 acres, the lake is stocked with rainbow trout, walleye, and bass, and the surrounding area provides wonderful opportunities for wildlife viewing. **Troutback Flyfishing** (⊠ Box 864, Show Low 85902 ☎ 928/532–3473 or 800/903–4092 ⊕ www.troutback.com) has access to some of the most scenic lakes and private waters in the region. From April through Oc-

Eastern
Arizona

TO FLAGSTAFF

KEY
► Start of itinerary

tober, this fishing guide company specializes in fly-fishing instruction, guided walk-wades, and float tube and boating trips.

GOLF **Show Low Golf Club** (⊠ 860 N. 36th Dr., at AZ 260 ☎ 928/537–4564 ⊕ www.showlowgolf.com) is a par-70 course with a back 9 in the pines and a front 9 in a more open meadow setting. Need to practice driving

Fodor'sChoice or putting? You can do it here. It's closed in winter. **Silver Creek Golf Club** ★ (⊠ 2051 Silver Lake Blvd. ☎ 928/537–2744 ⊕ www.silvercreekgolfclub. com), 5 mi east of town on U.S. 60, then 7½ mi north on Bourdon Ranch Road, is an 18-hole championship golf course. Voted by the PGA as one of the top 10 golf courses in Arizona, it's also one of the most affordable.

Pinetop-Lakeside

► **❸** *15 mi southeast of Show Low on AZ 260.*

At 7,200 ft, the community of Pinetop-Lakeside is known for its proximity to the world's largest stand of ponderosa pine. Two towns, Pinetop and Lakeside, were incorporated in 1984 to form this municipality—although they still retain separate post offices. The modest year-round population is 4,500, but in summer months it can jump as high as 40,000, so the secret about this mountain resort town is now officially out. Once popular only with the retirement and summer-home set, the city now lures thousands of "flatlanders" up from the Valley of the Sun with its gorgeous scenery, excellent multi-use trails, premier golf courses, and temperatures rarely exceeding 85°F. The main drag is known as both AZ 260 and White Mountain Boulevard.

Where to Stay & Eat

$–$$$ ✕ **Christmas Tree.** Year-round festive lights and displays of colorful ornaments inside this restaurant highlight a theme that's been at work here since 1977. Chicken and dumplings are the house specialty, but beef Stroganoff and honey duck served with fried apples are also highly recommended. A variety of steaks, chops, lamb, and seafood is also available, as well as a children's menu. Save room for a piece of the Christmas Tree's famous fresh-baked fruit cobbler or Texas sheet cake à la mode. Reservations are a good idea. ⊠ *455 N. Woodland Rd., near AZ 260, Lakeside* ☎ *928/367–3107* ▤ *D, MC, V* ☉ *Closed Mon.–Tues. in Nov. No lunch.*

$–$$$ ✕ **Phineas T's.** Word has it that the stuffed jumbo prawns, rack of lamb, and Creole cioppino here have no equal in the White Mountains. You'll also find a high-end wine list and a bar selling premium liquors and beers; the separate cigar and no-smoking bars are perfect for catching live, Santana-based music every Tuesday night. ⊠ *1450 E. White Mountain Blvd., Pinetop* ☎ *928/367–7400* ▤ *AE, D, MC, V.*

★ $–$$ ✕ **Annie's Gift Shop and Tea Room.** Across the highway from the Lakeside Fire Department, this genteel sandwich shop has specialty sandwiches, quiches, salads, and other delectables that make it the local "in" spot for lunch. ⊠ *2849 White Mountain Blvd., Lakeside* ☎ *928/368–5737* ▤ *AE, D, MC, V* ☉ *Closed July–Dec.*

¢ ✕ **Khadija's Bakery & Bistro.** You won't find a more perfect spot for breakfast. Khadija's (pronounced ha-*dee*-sha's) offers scrumptious, expertly prepared eggs, bacon, hash browns, and buttermilk pancakes. If you're en route to the slopes or hiking trails, order Breakfast on the Run—a gourmet answer to the Egg McMuffin. After 11 AM, sample daily-made soups and gourmet sandwiches on fresh-baked breads, and make sure to save room for pastries. ⊠ *4945 White Mountain Blvd., Lakeside* ☎ *928/537–7776* ▤ *AE, D, MC, V* ☉ *Closed Sun.–Tues. No dinner.*

¢ ✕ **MorMor Library Coffee House.** Coffee here is widely regarded as the best in town, and a browsing library and attached pottery store (operated by the owner's daughter) make this a lively gathering place. Weekend entertainment ranges from comedy to poetry readings to opera a cappella. ⊠ *1450 E. White Mountain Blvd., Pinetop* ☎ *928/367–3931* ▤ *MC, V* ☉ *Closed Mon. May–Sept.*

¢ ✕ **Zombies.** This self-styled "nouveau bistro" opens at 6 AM and has a great breakfast burrito and B.Y.O.B (build your own bagel), not to mention a lunch selection that includes mouthwatering gyros, burgers, and Philly cheese-steak sandwiches. As you head off for a day of fishing or hiking, call ahead with your order and it'll be waiting at the drive-through window. ⊠ *544 E. White Mountain Blvd., Pinetop* ☎ *928/367–0002* ▤ *AE, D, DC, MC, V.*

$–$$$ 🏨 **Hon-Dah Resort.** Guests are welcomed by a surreal staircase tableau of stuffed high-country creatures atop a mountain of boulders. The main draw here is the casino, with a small poker room, video blackjack, and hundreds of slot machines. Large rooms all have coffeemakers and wet bars. A high-roof atrium holds the pool and hot tub. Because the hotel is connected to the casino, you might pop out to fill the ice bucket but wind up at a slot machine instead. The casino offers weekend entertainment, and the Indian Pine Restaurant serves daily buffet meals. Beside the hotel lobby, be sure to check out the small Heritage Museum where the White Mountain Apache are featured in rotating exhibits. ⊠ *777 AZ 260, Pinetop 85935* ☎ *928/369–0299 or 800/929–8744* 🖷 *928/369–7405* ⊕ *www.hon-dah.com* ➥ *128 rooms, 2 suites* ⌂ *Restaurant, refrigerators, cable TV, indoor pool, hot tub, sauna, shop, 2 bars, casino, nightclub, meeting rooms* ▤ *AE, D, MC, V.*

$–$$$ ▦ **Northwoods Resort.** Each of the 14 cottage-cabins at this mountain retreat has its own covered porch and barbecue. Inside, natural wood paneling, brick fireplaces, and wall-to-wall carpeting add to the homey feel. Full electric kitchens have full-size refrigerators, ovens, microwave ovens, and adjacent dinette sets. Proprietors here keep their promise to provide "meticulously maintained" accommodations, all the way down to a daily replenishment of firewood. The honeymoon cabin features an indoor spa, and the two-story cabins can accommodate up to 18 people. ⊠ *AZ 260, Milepost 352* ✑ *Box 397N, Pinetop 85935* ☎ *928/ 367–2966 or 800/813–2966* ⊟ *928/367–2969* ⊕ *www.northwoodsaz. com* ⌨ *14 cabins* ⚮ *Kitchens, cable TV, outdoor hot tub, volleyball, playground, laundry facilities; no smoking* ⊟ *D, MC, V.*

$–$$ ▦ **Pinetop Country Inn.** This inn, on 4 acres surrounded by tall ponderosa pines, has three large guest rooms. A common room has a cozy fireplace, a library, and an extensive video selection; a 1950s-style game room is loaded with entertaining diversions including a jukebox, pool table, and Pac-Man game. A full breakfast gives you 10 items to choose from, and homemade desserts are served in the evening. Some rooms have fireplaces and small balconies, and there's a private, gazebo-covered hot tub. ⊠ *2444 Jan La., Pinetop 85935* ☎ *928/367–0479 or 888/521–5044* ⊟ *928/367–0479* ⊕ *www.pinetopcountry.com* ⌨ *3 rooms* ⚮ *Refrigerators, outdoor hot tub, bicycles, recreation room, no-smoking rooms* ⊟ *MC, V* ❙❙ *BP.*

¢–$$ ▦ **Whispering Pines Resort.** These well-maintained cabins have fireplaces, grills, and double sofa beds. One-, two-, and three-bedroom units— some with second bathrooms—have either handsome knotty-pine or more modern wood-paneled interiors. The four log cabins, three of them studio units, have that rustic hideaway vibe. Couples may want to request one of the alpine suites, with whirlpool tubs. On 12 acres bordering the Apache National Forest, cabins are within walking distance of Woodland Lake and Walnut Creek. There's a four-night minimum stay in summer and during holidays. ⊠ *AZ 260, just beyond Milepost 352* ✑ *Box 1043, Pinetop 85935* ☎ *928/367–4386 or 800/840–3867* ⊟ *928/367– 3702* ⊕ *www.whisperingpinesaz.com* ⌨ *36 cabins* ⚮ *Some in-room hot tubs, some kitchens, some kitchenettes, cable TV, hot tub, laundry facilities, some pets allowed (fee)* ⊟ *AE, D, MC, V.*

Nightlife & the Arts

LOUNGES **Charlie Clark's Steakhouse** (⊠ 1701 E. White Mountain Blvd., Pinetop ☎ 928/367–4900) has been around since 1938; the cook knows how to produce a mouthwatering prime rib and other specialties over mesquite. The lounge, with a full bar, pool tables, and a bouncing jukebox, stays open until 10 PM on the weekends, which is about as late as nightlife lasts in Pinetop. Major credit cards are accepted.

Sports & the Outdoors

BIKING & HIKING Named one of the country's "Top Ten Trail Towns" by the American Hiking Society, Pinetop-Lakeside is the primary trailhead for the White Mountains Trails System, roughly 180 mi of interconnecting multi-use loop trails spanning the White Mountains. All these trails are open to mountain bikers, horseback riders, and hikers.

Half a mile off AZ 260 on Woodland Road, **Big Springs Environmental Study Area** is a ½-mi loop trail that wanders by riparian meadows, two streams, and a spring-fed pond. A series of educational signs is devoted to the surrounding flora and fauna. The trailhead for **Country Club Trail** is at the junction of Forest Service Roads 182 and 185; these 3½ mi of moderate-difficulty mountain-biking and hiking trails can be spiced up by following the spur-trail to the top of Pat Mullen Mountain and back.

The well-traveled and very easy **Mogollon Rim Interpretive Trail** follows a small part of the 19th-century **Crook Trail** along the Mogollon Rim; the ¼-mi path, with a trailhead just west of the Pinetop-Lakeside city limits, is well marked with placards describing local wildlife and geography. The 8-mi **Panorama Trail** affords astonishing views from the top of extinct double volcanoes known as the Twin Knolls and passes though a portion of designated wildlife habitat area; the trailhead is 6 mi east on Porter Mountain Road, off AZ 260.

You can get individual trail brochures or other information from the **Apache-Sitgreaves National Forest** (✉ Lakeside Ranger Station, 2022 W. White Mountain Blvd. ✆ R.R. 3, Box B-50, Lakeside 85929 ☎ 928/ 368–5111 ⊕ www.fs.fed.us/r3/asnf), including a $2 booklet on the White Mountains Trail System.

FISHING East of Pinetop-Lakeside and 9 mi south of AZ 260, 260-acre **Hawley Lake** (✉ AZ 473, Hawley Lake) sits on Apache territory and yields mostly rainbow trout; rental boats are available in the marina. Tribal permits are required for all recreational activities. **Bob's Bang Room Sporting Goods & Pawn Shop** (✉ 3973 AZ 260, Lakeside ☎ 928/368– 5040 or 800/368–5040 ⊕ www.bobsbangroom.com) deals in hunting, archery, and pawned fishing equipment.

GOLF **Pinetop Lakes Golf & Country Club** (✉ 4643 Buck Springs Rd., Pinetop ☎ 928/369–4184 ⊕ www.pinetoplakesgolf.com) has fewer trees than other area courses, but it offers several water hazards by way of compensation. This shorter course is wonderful for public play. The club has a driving range, putting greens, and tennis courts, not to mention a restaurant and lounge. It's open April–October.

HORSEBACK RIDING **Porter Mountain Stables** (✉ 4048 Porter Mountain Rd., Lakeside ☎ 928/ 368–5306) offers one-hour to all-day horseback trips in the summer.

SKIING & SNOWBOARDING **Action Ski Rental** (✉ 857 E. White Mountain Blvd., Pinetop ☎ 928/367– 3373 ⊕ www.actionski.com) sells and rents skis and snowboards and offers special seasonal rental packages for children 12 and under. It's open December–March 15.

The **Skier's Edge** (✉ 560 W. White Mountain Blvd., Pinetop ☎ 928/367– 6200 or 800/231–3831 ⊕ www.skiersedgepinetop.com) has cross-country and downhill skis as well as snowboards and boots. At the same location, Paradise Creek Anglers sells fly-fishing and hiking supplies.

Shopping

Orchard Antiques (✉ 1664 W. White Mountain Blvd., Lakeside ☎ 928/ 368–6563), open from April to October and on all major holidays, is a reliable purveyor of high-quality furniture, glass, china, and sterling and deals in some quilts and vintage clothing. **Antique Mercantile Company** (✉ 2106 W. White Mountain Blvd., Lakeside ☎ 928/368–9090) has a variety of upscale-quality glass, china, furniture, militaria, vintage sports and camera equipment, and century-old collectibles ranging from first-edition law encyclopedias to working Victrolas. The log-cabin **Harvest Moon Antiques** (✉ 392 W. White Mountain Blvd., Pinetop ☎ 928/367–6973), open Memorial Day through Thanksgiving weekend, specializes in Old West relics, ranging from buckskins and Apache wares to old guns and U.S. Cavalry items. This is an excellent place to find affordable Indian jewelry and Navajo rugs; look for the tepees set up outside.

Sunrise Park Resort

🐾 ❹ *17 mi southeast of McNary, 7 mi south of AZ 260 on AZ 273.*

In winter and early spring, skiers and other snow lovers flock to this ski area. There's plenty more than downhill and cross-country skiing here, including snowboarding, snowmobiling, snowshoeing, ice-fishing, and sleigh rides. The resort has 10 lifts and 65 trails on three mountains rising to 11,000 ft. Eighty percent of the downhill runs are for beginning or intermediate skiers, there's a "ski-wee" hill for youngsters, and many less-intense trails begin at the top so skiers of varying skill levels can enjoy riding the chairlifts together. The Sunrise Express high-speed chairlift anchors the 10 lifts and has an uphill skier capacity of 16,000 skiers per hour. One-day lift tickets are $38. In summer, a marina is open for boat rentals on beautiful Sunrise Lake. Sunrise's Snowboard Park features jumps of all difficulty levels and its own sound system. Restricted to snowboarders only, the area—between the Pump House and Fairway runs—can support enthusiasts' quests to "get a great ollie, hit the kicker, and go big," while simultaneously lessening tension on the hill between boarders and skiers. Cross-country skiers enjoy 13½ mi of interconnecting trails, and snowmobilers have their own 25 mi of separate, designated trails. If you don't have your own equipment, you can rent it at the resort's ski shop. ⊠ *AZ 273, 7 mi south of AZ 260* ⬠ *Box 117, Greer 85927* ☎ *928/735–7669, 800/772–7669 hotel reservations and snow reports* ⊟ *AE, D, MC, V.*

Where to Stay

¢–$$$ 🏨 **Sunrise Park Lodge.** Catering to those who want to be as close as possible to the slopes, this hotel runs a shuttle to the slopes every half hour, has comfortable rooms with ski racks, and offers lodging and lift-ticket packages. The VIP Suite, with its wet bar, refrigerator, microwave oven, and hot tub, comes with two lift tickets that grant the holders line-cutting privileges on the slopes. Master suites feature Queen Anne–style beds, sleeper sofas, and satellite TVs. In the summer, you can enjoy boating on Sunrise Lake, "3-D" archery, scenic chairlift rides, horseback riding, and mountain biking on designated trails. ⊠ *AZ 273, 7 mi south of AZ 260* ⬠ *Box 117, Greer 85927* ☎ *928/735–7669 or 800/772–7669* 🖷 *928/735–7315* ⊕ *www.sunriseskipark.com* ⇆ *95 rooms, 6 suites* ⚑ *Restaurant, some in-room hot tubs, some microwaves, some refrigerators, indoor pool, lake, outdoor hot tub, sauna, boating, marina, volleyball, ski shop, lounge, recreation room, meeting rooms, no-smoking rooms* ⊟ *AE, D, DC, MC, V.*

Greer

★ ❺ *35 mi southeast of Pinetop-Lakeside and 15 mi southwest of Eagar on AZ 260; 8 mi east of AZ 273 turnoff, via AZ 373 south.*

The charming community of Greer sits just south of AZ 260 among pine, spruce, willow, and aspen on the banks of the Little Colorado River. At an elevation of 8,500 ft, Greer offers a variety of four-season diversions, especially for nature lovers. This portion of gently sloping National Forest land is covered with meadows and reservoirs and dominated by 11,590-ft Baldy Peak. Much of the surrounding area remains under the control of the Apache tribe, so visitors must take care to respect Apache law and land. AZ 373 is also Greer's "Main Street"; it winds through the village and crosses the Little Colorado River, eventually coming to a dead end. It's affectionately called the Road to Nowhere.

Listed on the National Register of Historic Places, the picturesque **Butterfly Lodge Museum** was built as a hunting lodge in 1914 by John Butler, the husband of "Aunt Molly" (of Molly Butler Lodge fame) for author James Willard Schultz and his artist son, Lone Wolf, a prolific painter of Indian and Western scenes. There's a small gift shop. In spring and summer, take time to watch the surrounding meadow come to life with beautiful butterflies, from which the lodge got its name. ⊠ *AZ 373 at CR 1126* ☎ *928/735–7514* ⊕ *www.wmonline.com/butterflylodge.htm* 🎫 *$2* ☉ *Memorial Day–Labor Day, Fri.–Sun. 10–5.*

Where to Stay & Eat

¢–$ ✕**Greer Mountain Resort Country Cafe.** This plant-hung diner-café is open daily from 7 AM to 3 PM year-round. Grab a seat by the fireplace and sample the homemade ranch beans, a signature grilled-cheese sandwich with green chilies and tomato, or a piece of fresh-baked cobbler. ⊠ *AZ 373, 1½ mi south of AZ 260,* ☎ *928/735–7560* ☐ *MC, V* ☉ *No dinner.*

¢–$ ✕**Rendezvous Diner.** Previous reincarnations of this cozy, colorful eatery
Fodor'sChoice include a family home as well as Greer's main post office. This diner
★ has earned a reputation for serving up some of Greer's tastiest dishes, not to mention the area's best hot, spiced cider. Of particular note are the pineapple teriyaki and green-chili burgers, 8-ounce sirloin steak with shrimp, and generous portions of homemade desserts. It's open year-round for breakfast, lunch, and dinner. ⊠ *117 Main St.* ☎ *928/735— 7483* ☐ *MC, V* ☉ *Closed Tues.*

¢ ✕▦ **Molly Butler Lodge.** Colorful quilts and barn-wood furnishings fill the comfortable rooms at Arizona's oldest lodge. There are no phones or TVs in the rooms, but both are available in the main lodge. The menu in the Molly Butler Lodge restaurant ($–$$) is divided between entrées "upstream" (sautéed scallops, halibut, trout amandine) and "downstream" (prime rib au jus, "hot dang" chili), but it's the hand-cut, aged steaks that draw locals. Sweeping views of Greer's pristine wilderness are enjoyed amid the lodge's cozy, rustic decor, with kerosene lamps on the tables and mounted hunting trophies on the walls. There is a two-night minimum. ⊠ *109 Main St., 85927* ☎ *928/735–7226* ⊕ *www. mollybutlerlodge.com* ⇴ *11 rooms* ♢ *Bar, video game room, some pets allowed (fee); no room phones, no room TVs* ☐ *D, MC, V.*

$$–$$$$ ▦ **Red Setter Inn.** From the vaulted ceiling in the breakfast room to the
Fodor'sChoice player piano in the gathering room, this hand-hewn-log inn is rich in
★ detail. Some rooms have fireplaces and private decks; the cottage rooms share a full kitchen. A spacious deck has Adirondack chairs and permits excellent wildlife viewing—don't be surprised to see mountain lions or black bear around the stream below, stopping to have a drink or to catch unsuspecting trout. Weekend guests who set out to hike or fish during the day are sent off with gourmet sack lunches. Weekends, there is a two-night minimum stay (three nights over holidays). ⊠ *8 Main St.* ☐ *Box 133, 85927* ☎ *928/735–7441 or 888/994–7337* 🖷 *928/735– 7425* ⊕ *www.redsetterinn.com* ⇴ *13 rooms, 3 cottages* ♢ *Some in-room hot tubs, some kitchens, some in-room VCRs, fishing, hiking, cross-country skiing, recreation room; no kids under 16, no smoking* ☐ *AE, D, MC, V* ⦿❙ *BP.*

$–$$$ ▦ **White Mountain Lodge.** On the banks of the Little Colorado River, this charming lodge is the oldest building in Greer. Most of the individually decorated rooms are country-cozy. Separate housekeeping cabins have gas fireplaces, and several have whirlpool tubs. An always-accessible sideboard in the lodge's great room is stocked with homemade cookies and spiced cider, as well as teas and cocoa. A full breakfast is included in the room rates. If you'd like a bit of sleuthing with your stay, be sure to ask about Murder Mystery Weekends. ⊠ *140 Main St.* ☎ *928/735–*

7568 or 888/493–7568 ⌂ *928/735–7498* ⊕ *www.wmlodge.com* ↗ *7 rooms, 6 cabins* ⟡ *Some in-room hot tubs, some kitchens, cable TV, some in-room VCRs, outdoor hot tub, hiking; no smoking* ⊟ *AE, D, DC, MC, V* ⊙ *BP.*

¢–$$ ▣ **Greer Mountain Resort.** Budget travelers and families appreciate these cabin-style accommodations. Each unit is different, but most can sleep up to six people and contain either a fireplace or a gas- or wood-burning stove. The smallest, one-bedroom, knotty-pine units have no fireplaces, but they're reasonably priced and good for couples. You may want to enjoy breakfast or lunch at the resort's roadside restaurant, but the fully equipped kitchens appeal to those wanting to whip up their own feast. ⊠ *AZ 373, 1½ mi south of AZ 260* ⌑ *Box 145, Greer 85927* ☎ *928/735–7560* ⊕ *www.wmonline.com/greermountain* ↗ *8 units* ⟡ *Kitchens; no room phones, no room TVs* ⊟ *MC, V.*

$ ⚠ **Rolfe C. Hoyer Campgrounds.** Nestled among pristine stands of ponderosa pine, these choice campsites in the Apache-Sitgreaves National Forest have no utility hook-ups but are proximate to equipment rentals, gas, groceries, and restaurants in the town of Greer. A $9 surcharge (per booking, not per night) is added by the company that handles the reservations. The abundant local wildlife is one of this site's draws, but remember to secure campsites from foraging four-legged friends. There's a $3 fee to use the dump stations or to take a shower. ⟡ *Flush toilets, dump station, drinking water, showers, fire pits, grills, picnic tables* ↗ *100 sites* ⊠ *AZ 373* ☎ *928/333–4372 or 877/444–6777* ⊕ *www.reserveusa.com* ✉ *$14* ⊙ *Open May 15–Oct. 15.*

Nightlife

Tiny Greer's nightlife can be found in the bar and lounge of the **Molly Butler Lodge** (⊠ 109 Main St. ☎ 928/735–7226), where you can listen to vintage tunes on the jukebox, sink into a cozy seat near the fireplace, play an arcade game, or challenge a "local" to a game of pool or darts.

Sports & the Outdoors

The **Circle B Market** (⊠ 38940 AZ 373 ☎ 928/735–7540) rents cross-country skis and sells sleds in winter and tackle and inner tubes the rest of the year. Fishing licenses and reservation permits are also for sale.

FISHING   The three Greer Lakes are actually the Bunch, River, and Tunnel reservoirs. Bait and fly-fishing options are scenic and plentiful, and there are several places to launch a boat. Winding through Greer, the Little Colorado River's West Fork is well stocked with brookies and rainbows and has 23 mi of fishable waters.

HIKING   The difficult but accessible **Mt. Baldy Trail** begins at **Sheeps Crossing**, southwest of Greer on AZ 273. In just under 8 mi (one-way), the trail climbs the northern flank of 11,590-ft Mt. Baldy, the second-highest peak in Arizona, where spectacular views of the Salt River Canyon and Mogollon Rim can be had. Note that the very summit of Baldy is on the White Mountain Apache reservation. Considered sacred land, this final ¼ mi is off-limits to non-Apaches. The boundary is clearly marked; please respect it, regardless of how much you might wish to continue on to the peak.

SKIING   Cross-country skiers find Greer an ideally situated hub for some of the mountain's best trails. About 2½ mi west of AZ 373 on AZ 260, a trailhead marks the starting point for the **Pole Knoll Trail System**, nearly 30 mi of well-marked, groomed cross-country trails interlacing through the Apache Sitgreaves National Forest and color-coded by experience level. Trail maps are available from the **Apache-Sitgreaves National Forest** (⊠ Springerville Ranger District, 165 S. Mountain Ave., Springerville 85938 ☎ 928/333–4372 ⊕ www.fs.fed.us/r3/asnf).

Shopping

Calamity Janet's (✉ 96 Main St. ☎ 928/735–7610) specializes in antiques and Western collectibles, and its mid-20th-century Navajo jewelry merits a special look. This shop also has a number of impressive paintings and wood-turning pieces by well-known regional artists, and the original James Muir sculptures are breathtaking. It's open from April through October, or by appointment only the rest of the year.

Lyman Lake State Park

❻ *18 mi north of Springerville on U.S. 180/191, 55 mi southeast of Petrified Forest National Park on U.S. 180.*

Created in 1915, when the Little Colorado River was dammed for irrigation purposes, the 3-mi-long **Lyman Lake** reservoir is popular for boating, waterskiing (a permit is required for the exclusive waterskiing course on the dam end), windsurfing, and sailing. Designated swimming beaches accommodate those who prefer to stick closer to shore.

A buoyed-off "no-wake" area at the lake's west end ensures that fishing efforts there won't be disturbed by passing speedboats and waterskiers. Contributions to the creel here include largemouth bass as well as the "good size" (6 to 8 pounds) channel catfish that can be pulled up from May to August. Locals recommend early spring as prime season for walleye—the tastiest catch of all; Lyman Lake also has lots of crawfish, a.k.a. "poor man's shrimp."

Between early May and late October, ranger-led pontoon-boat tours go across Lyman Lake to the **Petroglyph Trail,** where some of the state's most wondrous and accessible Native American rock art lies chiseled in basalt. Check out the Pueblo site, which dates to the 14th century and has three rooms and a kiva.

Other attractions in the 1,200-acre park include a volleyball court, horseshoe pits, a water-ski slalom course, and the rare chance to observe the park's resident small herd of buffalo. There is also a campground, along with several log cabins and yurts for rent, and a camping supply and boat rental store. In nearby St. Johns, there's lodging, restaurants, and an airfield and fuel for planes. ✉ *U.S. 180/191, 18 mi north of Springerville/Eagar ✉ Box 1428, St. Johns 85936 ☎ 928/337–4441 ⊕ www.pr.state.az.us.*

en route   The junction of U.S. 180/191 and U.S. 60, just north of Springerville, is the perfect jumping-off spot for a driving tour of the **Springerville Volcanic Field.** On the southern edge of the Colorado Plateau, it covers a total area larger than the state of Rhode Island and is spread across a high-elevation plain similar to the Tibetan Plateau. Six miles north of Springerville on U.S. 180/191 are sweeping westward views of the **Twin Knolls**—double volcanoes that erupted twice here about 700,000 years ago. As you travel west on U.S. 60, Green's Peak Road and various south-winding Forest Service roads make for a leisurely, hour-long drive past **St. Peter's Dome** and a stop for impressive views from **Green's Peak,** the topographic high point of the Springerville Field. A free detailed driving-tour brochure of the Springerville Volcanic Field is available from the **Springerville-Eagar Regional Chamber of Commerce** (✉ 318 Main St. ✉ Box 31, Springerville 85938 ☎ 928/333–2123).

Springerville-Eagar

❼ *45 mi east of Pinetop-Lakeside on AZ 260, 67 mi southeast of Petrified Forest National Park on U.S. 180.*

Christened "Valle Redondo," or Round Valley, by early Basque settlers of the late 1800s, sister cities Springerville and Eagar are tucked into a circular, high mountain basin. Nestled on the back side of massive 10,912-ft Escudilla Mountain, this self-proclaimed "Gateway to the White Mountains" sits in a different climate belt from nearby Greer and Sunrise Resort; insulated by its unique geography, Springerville-Eagar has markedly less severe winter temperatures and lighter snowfall than neighboring mountain towns. Geographically, the Round Valley also served as a unique Old West haven for the lawless—a great place to conceal stolen cattle and hide out for a while. Butch Cassidy, the Clantons, and the Smith gang all spent time here. So did the late John Wayne, whose former 26-Bar Ranch lies just west of Eagar off AZ 260.

The Round Valley is the favorite of skiers in the know, who appreciate the location as they commute to the lifts at Sunrise with the sun always at their back—important when you consider the glare off those blanketed snowscapes between the resort and Pinetop-Lakeside—and the dramatically lighter traffic on this less-icy stretch of AZ 260.

The 14½-acre **Casa Malpais Archaeological Park** pueblo complex is piquing the interest of a growing number of world-class anthropologists and astronomers. The "House of the Badlands" (a sobriquet for the rough-textured ground's effect on bare feet) has a series of narrow terraces lining eroded edges of basalt (hardened lava flow) cliff, as well as an extensive system of subterranean rooms nestled within the Earth's fissures underneath. Strategically designed gateways in the walls of the complex allow for streams of sunlight to precisely illuminate significant petroglyphs prior to the setting equinox or solstice sun. Perhaps most important, Casa Malpais is home to the 55-ft-diameter Great Kiva—one of the largest Native American ceremonial chambers known to exist in North America. Strong evidence suggests that these sacred ruins were once inhabited solely by a class of scholars and holy men among the ancient Mogollon peoples. ⊠ *318 E. Main St., Springerville* ☎ *928/333–5375* ⊕ *www. casamalpais.com* ☒ *Guided tour $5* ☉ *Museum Mon.–Thurs. 8–5, Fri.–Sun. 8–4; guided tours of ruins daily at 9, 11, and 2.*

The 120,000-square-ft **Ensphere** may convince you that something from a galaxy far, far away landed in Eagar (especially at night, when a wafflelike grid of lights radiates eerily from its rooftop), but in fact it is the only domed high school football stadium in the country. The dome is a gift of Tucson Power & Electric, which moved into these parts and vowed to contribute something to the community. The then-absurd proposal was placed on the ballot, alongside a host of other less-extravagant options, and passed. The shocked TPE, after demanding a recount, made good on its promise. ⊠ *590 N. Butler St., Eagar.*

This **Little House Museum** has an interesting collection of local pioneer and ranching memorabilia, but it's the mesmerizing tones from a rare collection of automatic musical instruments that you'll come away remembering—that, and the museum's colorful curator, Wink Crigler, with her lore of this region's lively past. To reach the ranch, go 10 mi southwest of Eagar on AZ 260, turn south onto South Fork Road, and go 3 mi. ⊠ *X Diamond Ranch, South Fork Rd., 10 mi southwest of Eagar,* ☎ *928/333–2286* ⊕ *www.xdiamondranch.com* ☒ *$5* ☉ *Labor Day–Oct., tours Thurs.–Sat. at 11 and 1:30, Sun.–Wed. by reservation only.*

The **Renée Cushman Art Collection Museum** is open to the public only by special appointment, but a visit here is worth the extra effort. Renée Cushman's extensive collection of objets d'art—some acquired on her travels, some collected with the accumulated resources of three wealthy husbands, some willed to her by her artistic father—is administered by the Church of Latter-day Saints. Her treasure of goods includes a Rembrandt engraving, Tiepolo pen-and-inks, and an impressive collection of European antiques, some dating back to the 15th century. Call the **Springerville-Eagar Regional Chamber of Commerce** (☎ 928/333–2123) to arrange your visit to the Renée Cushman Art Collection Museum.

Where to Stay & Eat

¢–$$ ✕ **Booga Reds.** The delicious home-style cooking here is worth a stop. Fish-and-chips and roast beef dinners with homemade mashed potatoes and gravy top the menu; should your palate demand something spicier, however, try one of the many Mexican dishes. Save room for an unforgettable piece of the daily fruit or cream pie. Booga Reds opens at 5:30 AM for an early breakfast but closes relatively early—at 9 PM—so make your dinner an early one, too. ⊠ *521 E. Main St., Springerville* ☎ *928/333–2640* ⊟ *AE, D, MC, V.*

$–$$$ ⊞ ✕ **Diamond & MLY Ranch.** This magnificent ranch has log cabins complete with porches, fireplaces, and full kitchens. Most sleep two to six, but the Butler House sleeps eight and has an atrium and private yard. Ranch activities include horseback riding, participating in the excavation of the Little Bear and Kokopelli archaeological sites, and fly-fishing on a private section of the Little Colorado. You don't have to be a ranch guest to participate in activities. Horse boarding is also available. ⊠ *South Fork Rd., 10 mi southwest of Eagar off AZ 260* ⊘ *Box 791, Springerville 85938* ☎ *928/333–2286* ⊟ *928/333–5009* ⊕ *www.xdiamondranch.com* ➴ *7 cabins* △ *Kitchens, fishing, hiking, horseback riding, no-smoking rooms* ⊟ *AE, D, MC, V.*

★ $ ⊞ **Paisley Corner Bed & Breakfast.** From embossed-tin ceilings and stained-glass windows in the parlor to an authentic "soda shop" re-creation replete with Wurlitzer jukebox, not a detail has been overlooked in this restored 1910 colonial revival–style home. Rooms have antique beds and armoires, old-fashioned showers, and pull-chain commodes. Lush terry robes, wine, fresh fruit, and homemade munchies are included. Breakfast is served as early as you want and is prepared on a 1910 stove rescued from the Bisbee Grand Hotel. In the summer, if you time your visit right, you may even catch a vintage fashion show in the garden. ⊠ *287 N. Main St., Springerville 85938* ☎ *928/333–4665* ⊕ *www.paisleycorner.com* ➴ *4 rooms* △ *No smoking, no TV in some rooms* ⊟ *MC, V* ⎟O⎟ *BP.*

¢   ⊞ **Reed's Lodge.** The rooms of this mostly single-story motel have Western accents such as knotty-pine paneling and Navajo-print bedspreads. Thoughtful touches include a recreation room with pool table, video games, and a pinball machine; movie rentals for a nominal fee; a gift shop; and complimentary bicycles for guests. Proprietor Roxanne Knight, who has a wealth of local knowledge, will arrange "shared ranch" visits for guests on an actual working cowboy-style (not dude) ranch, cattle drives, customized horseback adventures, four-wheel-drive tours, wildlife-viewing trips, or fossil-hunting expeditions. ⊠ *514 E. Main St., Springerville 85938* ☎ *928/333–4323 or 800/814–6451* ⊟ *928/333–5191* ➴ *45 rooms, 5 suites* △ *In-room VCRs, some microwaves, some refrigerators, outdoor hot tub, bicycles, recreation room, shop* ⊟ *AE, D, DC, MC, V.*

FodorsChoice ★

¢   ⊞ **Rode Inn.** Don't let the John Wayne motif scare you away—two cardboard figures of "The Duke," in full cowboy regalia, are perched on a walkway above the lobby, and his photos decorate the walls; the rooms and service here are excellent. John Wayne did in fact stay here (when it was a Ramada Inn), and the room in which he slept has been converted into a plush suite. ⊠ *242 E. Main St., Springerville 85938* ☎ *928/ 333–4365* ⊕ *www.rodeinn.com* ↩ *60 rooms, 3 suites* ⚹ *Some microwaves, some refrigerators, hot tub, laundry facilities, Internet, nosmoking rooms* ⊟ *AE, D, DC, MC, V.*

$ 　⚠ **Big Lake Campgrounds.** On the southeast shore of Big Lake, 30 mi southwest of the Round Valley, these campgrounds are along the shore of a popular White Mountains summer destination. The lake supplies more than 300,000 trout to fishermen each year. The civilized Rainbow site offers paved loops to its more developed units. The lake's smaller sites, Grayling, Cutthroat, and Brookchar, are less swank but are within easy walking distance of Rainbow's amenities and share the picturesque tableau of looming 11,590-ft Mt. Baldy. The lake has a marina where boats and motors are available for rent. ⚹ *Flush toilets, dump station, drinking water, showers, general store, swimming (lake)* ↩ *152 sites at Rainbow* ⊠ *AZ 273, Big Lake, 24 mi south of AZ 260,* ☎ *928/735– 7313* ✍ *$12–$22* ⊘ *Open mid-May–early Sept.*

Nightlife

Out on the edge of town, where U.S. 60/180 enters Springerville, the bright yellow **Little River Lounge** (⊠ 262 W. Main St., Springerville ☎ 928/333–5790) is a cowboy bar with pool tables, darts, and live music and dancing on the weekends. Behind Booga Red's restaurant, **Tequila Red's** (⊠ 521 E. Main St., Springerville ☎ 928/333–5036) is a popular watering hole and the best place to catch a sporting event.

Sports & the Outdoors

For all your mountain-sport needs, stop in at the **Sweat Shop** (⊠ 74 N. Main St., Eagar ☎ 928/333–2950), which rents skis, snowboards, and mountain bikes.

FISHING   **Becker Lake** (⊠ U.S. 60, 2 mi northwest of Springerville, Becker Lake ☎ 928/367–4281) is a "specialty lake" for trout fishing; call for seasonal bait requirements. **Big Lake** (⊠ AZ 273, 24 mi south of AZ 260, Big Lake ☎ 928/735–7313), known to many as the "queen of all trout lakes," is stocked each spring and fall with rainbow, brook, and cutthroat trout. **Nelson Reservoir** (⊠ U.S. 191, Nutrioso), between Springerville-Eagar and Alpine, is well stocked with rainbow, brown, and brook trout. The **Speckled Trout** (⊠ 224 E. Main St., Springerville ☎ 928/333–0852 ⊕ www.cybertrails.com/~cltrout) is probably the only fly-fishing store attached to a law office anywhere. The store offers Orvis-licensed fly-fishing guide services and sells fly-fishing equipment. Springerville-Eagar's only commercial espresso machine sparkles behind a small coffee bar here. **Sport Shack** (⊠ 329 E. Main St., Springerville ☎ 928/333–2222) sells camping equipment, fishing tackle, and hunting and fishing licenses. **Troutback** (⊡ Box 864, Show Low 85901 ☎ 928/532–3474 ⊕ www.troutback.com) is a fly-fishing guide service that will create half- or full-day fishing trips for novices and seasoned anglers alike throughout the White Mountains. Equipment, including boats, waders, fly rods and reels, and float tubes, is available for rent. **Western United Drug** (⊠ 105 E. Main St., Springerville ☎ 928/333– 4321) stays open 365 days a year and has a well-stocked sportinggoods and outdoor-equipment section.

Shopping

K-5 Western Gallery (⊠ Reed's Lodge, 514 E. Main St., Springerville ☎ 928/333–4323) sells wares created by White Mountains artists and local craftspeople, including those from nearby reservations (check out the rustic elk-antler furniture). The gallery teems with Western-themed paintings, stocks books on local history and wildlife, and has a selection of cowboy poetry.

Coronado Trail

FodorsChoice *The 127-mi stretch of U.S. 191 from Springerville to Clifton.*
★

Surely one of the world's curviest roads, this steep, winding portion of U.S. 191 was referred to as the Devil's Highway in its prior incarnation as U.S. 666. More significantly, the route parallels the one allegedly followed more than 450 years ago by Spanish explorer Francisco Vásquez de Coronado on his search for the legendary Seven Cities of Cíbola, where the streets were reputedly paved of gold and jewels.

This 127-mi stretch of highway is renowned for the transitions of its spectacular scenery over a dramatic 5,000-ft elevation change—from rolling meadows to spruce- and ponderosa pine–covered mountains, down into the Sonoran Desert's piñon pine, grassland savannas, juniper stands, and cacti. A trip down the Coronado Trail crosses through Apache Sitgreaves National Forest, as well as the White Mountain Apache and San Carlos Indian reservations.

Cautious switchback-navigating will result in stretches on which motorists barely exceed 10 mph; allow a good four hours to make the drive, more if you plan to stop and leisurely explore—which you should.

Pause at **Blue Vista,** perched on the edge of the Mogollon Rim, about 30 mi outside Alpine, to take in views of the Blue Range Mountains to the east and the succession of tiered valleys dropping some 4,000 ft back down into the Sonoran Desert. Still above the rim, this is one of your last opportunities to enjoy the blue spruce, ponderosa pine, and high-country mountain meadows.

About 17 mi south of Blue Vista, the Coronado Trail continues twisting and turning, eventually crossing under 8,786-ft **Rose Peak.** Named for the wild roses growing on its mountainside, Rose Peak is also home to a fire lookout tower—staffed during the May–July dry-lightning season—from which peaks more than 100 mi away can be seen on a clear day. This is a great picnic-lunch stop.

After Rose Peak, enjoy the remaining scenery some 70 more miles until reaching the less picturesque towns of Clifton and Morenci, homes to a massive Phelps Dodge copper mine. U.S. 191 then swings back west, links up with U.S. 70, and provides a fairly straight shot through Safford and across rather uninteresting desert toward Globe. ⊠ *U.S. 191 between Springerville and Clifton.*

Alpine

❽ *27 mi south of Springerville-Eagar on U.S. 191.*

Known as the Alps of Arizona, the tiny, scenic village of Alpine promotes its variety of winter recreation opportunities, but outdoors enthusiasts will also find that the town, sitting on the lush plains of the San Francisco River, is centrally located for many excellent hiking, fishing, and mountain-biking excursions during the warmer months.

Where to Stay & Eat

$ ✕▦ **Tal-Wi-Wi Lodge.** This lodge draws many repeat visitors to its lush meadows. Standard motel-style rooms are simple and clean, with either two doubles or one king-size bed, and three of the most popular rooms have wood-burning fireplace-stoves, indoor hot tubs, or both. In the evening, stroll the grounds and gaze at the Milky Way in the brilliant night sky. With satellite TV and live country music on weekends, the lodge saloon draws a loyal local following. The cozy, casual restaurant is open May–December and serves breakfast on weekends and dinner Wednesday through Saturday. Tal-Wi-Wi is popular with car and motorcycle clubs and hosts an annual car show in August. ⊠ *U.S. 191* ⅅ *Box 169, Alpine 85920* ☎ *928/339–4319 or 800/476–2695* ⊞ *928/339–1962* ⊕ *www.talwiwilodge.com* ⤴ *20 rooms* ఉ *Restaurant, some in-room hot tubs, bar, some pets allowed (fee)* ⊟ *AE, MC, V.*

Sports & the Outdoors

BIKING   The 8-mi **Luna Lake Trail** (⊠ U.S. 180, Alpine), 5 mi east of U.S. 191, is a good two-hour cruise for beginning and intermediate cyclists. The trailhead is on the north side of the lake, just before the campground entrance.

FISHING   A divergence of the San Francisco River's headwaters, 80-acre **Luna Lake** (⊠ U.S. 180, Alpine), 5 mi east of U.S. 191, is well stocked with rainbow, cutthroat, and brook trout.

GOLF   **Alpine Country Club** (⊠ Off U.S. 180, 3 mi east of U.S. 191 ⅅ Box 526, 85920, ☎ 928/339–4944 ⊕ www.geocities.com/alpinecountryclub), at 8,500 ft above sea level, is one of the highest golf courses in the Southwest. Even if you don't play golf, stop in for Mexican food and breathtaking scenery at the club's Aspen Room Restaurant. It's 1 mi south of Alpine on Blue River Road.

HIKING   The **Escudilla National Recreation Trail** (⊠ U.S. 191, Hulsey Lake) is more picturesque than arduous; the 3-mi trail wends through the Escudilla Wilderness to the summit of towering 10,912-ft **Escudilla Mountain**, Arizona's third-tallest peak. From Alpine, take U.S. 191 north and follow the signs to Hulsey Lake (about 5 mi).

SKIING   **Williams Valley Winter Sports Area** (⊠ Forest Service Rd. 249, Alpine ☎ 928/339–4384), 2½ mi west of town, has 12½ mi of cross-country trails of varying difficulty maintained by the Alpine Ranger District. Toboggan Hill is a favorite place for families, with sleds, toboggans, and tubes. New shelters, picnic facilities, and toilets enhance the experience.

SNOWMOBILING   Trails begin just off Forest Service Road 249, on the west side of **Williams Valley Winter Sports Area** (⊠ Forest Service Rd. 249, Alpine ☎ 928/339–4384), and the network of snow-covered Forest Service roads extends for miles. Snowmobilers are asked to respect marked boundaries to the adjacent Bear Wallow Wilderness area, where all motorized equipment is prohibited. Pick up an Apache Sitgreaves National Forest map and Winter Sports brochure from the Alpine Ranger District, and call for conditions prior to heading out, as weak links in longer routes sometimes "burn out."

Hannagan Meadow

★ ❾   *50 mi south of Springerville-Eagar on U.S. 191, 23 mi south of Alpine on U.S. 191.*

Surely one of the state's most remote places, Hannagan Meadow is a pastorally mesmerizing location for several splendid camping areas. Lush and isolated at a 9,500-ft-plus elevation, the meadow is home to elk, deer, and range cattle, as well as blue grouse, wild turkey, and the occasional eagle. Adjacent to the meadow, the Blue Range Primitive Area gives access to miles of untouched wilderness and some beautiful rugged terrain, and it is a designated recovery area for the endangered Mexican gray wolf. It is believed that Francisco Vásquez del Coronado and his party came through the Meadow on their famed expedition in 1540 to find the Seven Cities of Cíbola.

<table>
<tr><td>

off the
beaten
path

</td><td>

BLUE RANGE PRIMITIVE AREA – Directly east of Hannagan Meadow, this unspoiled 170,000-acre area, lovingly referred to by locals as "The Blue," is the last designated primitive area in the United States. The area's diverse terrain surrounds the Blue River and is crossed by the Mogollon Rim from east to west. No motorized or mechanized equipment is allowed—including mountain bikes; passage is restricted to foot or horseback. Many trails interlace the Blue: prehistoric paths of the ancient native peoples, cowboy trails to move livestock between pastures and water sources, access routes to lookout towers and fire trails. Avid backpackers and campers may want to spend a few days exploring the dozens of hiking trails. Even though trail access is fairly good, hikers need to remember that this is primitive, rough country and to carry adequate water supplies. Contact **Apache-Sitgreaves National Forest** (✉ Alpine Ranger District, U.S. 191 🗗 Box 469, Alpine 85920 ☎ 928/339–4384 ⊕ www.fs.fed.us/r3/asnf) for trail maps and information for the Blue Range Primitive Area.

</td></tr>
</table>

Where to Stay & Eat

★ ¢–$$ ✕🏨 **Hannagan Meadow Lodge.** Antiques and floral prints impart a genteel, Victorian feel to this lodge. Log cabins are more rustic; some have full kitchens and fireplaces, while others are equipped with microwaves, stove tops, and wood-burning stoves. The lodge's dining room is the pièce de résistance, with hewn-log beams and a glass wall that overlooks a pristine meadow. The general store sells sundries as well as fishing supplies and rents snowshoes, cross-country skis, and mountain bikes. From November through April there's a 20% discount Sunday to Thursday. Children are welcome. ✉ *U.S. 191, Hannagan Meadow 🗗 HC 61, Box 335, Alpine 85920, 22 mi south of Alpine ☎ 928/339–4370 ⊕ www.hannaganmeadow.com ➫ 8 rooms, 10 cabins ⚃ Restaurant, some kitchens, some kitchenettes, biking, hiking, horseback riding, cross-country skiing, snowmobiling; some pets allowed ▤ MC, V ⧖ CP.*

¢ ⛺ **Hannagan Campground.** This intimate collection of Forest Service campsites sits under a canopy of spruce, fir, and aspen trees and is surrounded by tall, mature forest. The area is rich in wildlife, such as elk, wild turkey, and bear, and at night you might hear the howling of wolves. Although there are no bathing facilities here, nearby Hannagan Meadow Lodge provides hot showers for $5. ⚃ *Pit toilets, drinking water, fire pits, grills, picnic tables ➫ 8 campsites ✉ U.S. 191, Hannagan Meadow, ¼ mi past Hannagan Meadow Lodge ⊕ www.fs.fed.us/r3/asnf ⧖ Free ⊙ Open May–Oct.*

¢ ⛺ **KP Cienega.** These single-unit campsites in a lush meadow are a prime site for viewing the local wildlife. There are no developed facilities. ⚃ *Pit toilets, drinking water, fire pits, grills, picnic tables ➫ 5 campsites ✉ U.S. 191 and Forest Service Rd. 25, Hannagan Meadow ⊕ www.fs.fed.us/r3/asnf ⧖ Free ⊙ Open May–Oct.*

Sports & the Outdoors

FISHING Down in the Blue Range, anglers will want to cast into KP Creek and Grant Creek, both of which rush through spectacular scenery. **Bear Wallow Wilderness Area** (✉ west of U.S. 191 and bordered by Forest Service Rds. 25 and 54) has a network of cool, flowing streams that are sure bets for native Apache trout.

HIKING Twenty-one miles of maintained trail wind through the 11,000 acres of the **Bear Wallow Wilderness Area** (✉ west of U.S. 191 and bordered by Forest Service Rds. 25 and 54 ☎ 928/339–4384 Alpine Ranger District office ⊕ www.fs.fed.us/r3/asnf). The **Rose Spring Trail** is a pleasant 5½-

mi hike with a moderate gradient and magnificent views from the Mogollon Rim's edge; the trailhead is at the end of Forest Service Road 54. **Reno Trail** and **Gobbler Trail** both drop into the main canyon from well-marked trailheads off Forest Service Road 25. Reno Trail meanders 2 mi through conifer forest and aspen stands, while Gobbler Trail is 2½ mi in length and offers views overlooking the Black River and Fort Apache Indian Reservation. This designated wilderness (and some of its trails) borders the San Carlos Indian Reservation, where an advance permit is required for entry.

SKIING The 8½ mi of groomed cross-country trails of the **Hannagan Meadow Winter Recreation Area** (✉ U.S. 191, Hannagan Meadow ☎ 928/339–4384 Alpine Ranger District office ⊕ www.fs.fed.us/r3/asnf) are narrower than the trails of neighboring Williams Valley. The 4½-mi **Clell Lee Loop** is an easy route, partially following U.S. 191; the advanced-level, ungroomed **KP Rim Loop** traverses upper elevations of the Blue Primitive Range and provides some of the most varied (and tranquil) remote skiing in the state.

SNOWMOBILING The area just northeast of U.S. 191 is a snowmobile playground. Trailheads are located at U.S. 191 and Forest Service Road 576. Snowmobile trail maps are available at the Alpine Ranger District office and Hannagan Meadow Lodge.

PETRIFIED FOREST NATIONAL PARK & THE PAINTED DESERT

Only about 1½ hours from Show Low and the lush, verdant forests of the White Mountains, Arizona's diverse and dramatic scenery transforms itself from pine-crested mountains to the sunbaked terrain of the Petrified Forest and lunarlike landscape of the Painted Desert.

Homolovi Ruins State Park

⑩ *53 mi east of Flagstaff, 33 mi west of Holbrook. Exit 257 off of I–40.*

Fodor'sChoice
★ Homolovi (a Hopi word meaning "place of the little hills") is 5 mi northeast of Winslow off AZ 87 along the Little Colorado River. These pueblo sites are thought to have been occupied between AD 1200 and 1425 and include 40 ceremonial kivas and two pueblos containing more than 1,000 rooms each. The Hopi believe their immediate ancestors inhabited this place and still hold the site to be sacred. Monday through Friday in June and July, you can see archaeologists working the site. The Homolovi Visitor's Center has a small museum with Hopi pottery and Anasazi artifacts and also hosts workshops on native art, ethnobotany, and traditional foods. Mobility-impaired persons should check with the ranger station for alternate access information; rangers conduct guided tours. ✉ AZ 87, 5 mi northeast of Winslow ⑤ HCR 63, Box 5, Winslow 86047 ☎ 928/289–4106 ⊕ www.pr.state.az.us.

Camping

$ ⚠ **Homolovi Ruins State Park Campground.** At an elevation of 4,900 ft, this campsite is a short walk from Homolovi I pueblo and the Little Colorado River and close to several other archaeological sites and trails leading to petroglyphs and evidence of prehistoric habitations. ♿ *Pit toilets, partial hook-ups (electric and water), dump station, drinking water, showers, fire pits, grills, picnic tables* ⚐ *53 campsites* ✉ *AZ 87, 5 mi northeast of Winslow,* ☎ *928/289–4106* ☉ *Open year-round.*

Petrified Forest National Park

54 mi east of Homolovi Ruins State Park and 27 mi east of Holbrook on I–40; 18 mi east of Holbrook on U.S. 180.

A visit to the Petrified Forest is a trip back in geological time. In 1984 the fossil remains of one of the oldest dinosaurs ever unearthed—dating from the Triassic period of the Mesozoic era 225 million years ago—were discovered here; other plant and animal fossils in the park date from the same period. Remnants of ancient human beings and their artifacts, dating back 10,000 years, have been recovered at more than 500 sites in this national park.

The park derives its name from the fact that the grounds are also covered with petrified tree trunks whose wood cells were replaced over centuries by brightly hued mineral deposits—silica, iron oxide, manganese, aluminum, copper, lithium, and carbon—which contributed to their fossilization. In many places, petrified logs scattered about the landscape resemble a fairy-tale forest turned to stone. The park's 93,000 acres include portions of the vast, pink-hue lunarlike landscape known as the **Painted Desert.** In the northern area of the park, this colorful but essentially barren series of windswept plains, hills, and mesas is considered by geologists to be part of the Chinle formation, deposited at an early stage of the Triassic period.

You can easily spend most of a day on the park's 28 mi of paved roads and walking trails. Lookouts on the north end of the park provide beautiful Painted Desert vistas. Fascinating Native American petroglyphs survive on boulders at **Newspaper Rock** and **Puerco Ruins,** which also has a partially stabilized 100-room pueblo more than 600 years old. The area around **Jasper Forest** contains stunning hunks of petrified trees scattered on the desert floor. Near the southern end of the park, **Agate House** is a pueblo structure assembled from pieces of petrified wood. The self-guided **Giant Logs Trail** starts at the Rainbow Forest Museum and Visitor Center and loops through ½ mi of huge fallen trees. One of the ancient, fallen trunks is more than 9 ft in diameter.

Because so many looters hauled away large quantities of petrified wood in the early years of the 20th, President Theodore Roosevelt made the area a national monument in 1906. Since then, it has been illegal (not to mention bad karma) to remove even a small sliver of petrified wood from the park. Plenty of souvenir pieces are available from the park's visitor-center gift shop and surrounding trading posts. The removal of pieces from the park is a federal offense and carries with it a hefty fine and potential imprisonment. Additionally, don't miss the "Guilt Books" in each entrance's museum. There you'll find letters from guilt-riddled former visitors anxiously returning their purloined souvenirs and detailing directly attributable hexes—from runs of bad luck to husbands turning into "hard-drinking strangers."

At the north entrance of the park, the **Painted Desert Visitor Center** shows a 20-minute movie entitled *Timeless Impressions,* tracing the natural history of the area. The **Rainbow Forest Museum and Visitor Center** (⊠ near the south entrance, off U.S. 180) displays skeletons from the Triassic period, including that of "Gertie"—the ferocious phytosaur, a crocodile-like carnivore. The museum has numerous exhibits relating to the world of cycads (tropical plants), ferns, fish, and other early life, as well as artifacts and tools of ancient humans. Within the park's boundaries, visitors also have access to a restaurant and a service station at the north end of the park. Those interested in purchasing books or slides should know that many of the same titles are offered at the gift shops (there's one at each end of the park) and at the Painted Desert Visitor Center (at the north end of the park). Only those books purchased from the visitor center will fund the continued research and interpretive activities for the park.

Picnicking is allowed inside the park. You may hike into the nearby wilderness areas to camp overnight, but you must obtain a Wilderness Permit. Free permits are issued at both visitor centers.

Visitors can begin the 28-mi drive through the park either from the northern I–40 entrance or the southern entrance off U.S. 180. Those continuing on to New Mexico should enter from the park's south entrance, ending up with I–40's straight shot over the border toward Albuquerque. Visitors with accommodations in Holbrook should tour the park from south end to north end, saving dramatic sunset vistas of the Painted Desert for last. As you leave the park, rangers will question you to be certain you haven't been tempted to collect a souvenir of petrified wood. *North Entrance ⊠ I–40, Milepost 311, Petrified Forest, 27 mi east of Holbrook, ☎ 928/524–6228 ⊕ www.nps.gov/pefo ⊠ South Entrance ⊠ U.S. 180, 18 mi southeast of Holbrook ⌖ Box 2217, Petrified Forest 86028 ⊠ $10 per vehicle, valid for 1 wk ⊙ Mid-Oct.–May, daily 8–5; June–mid-Oct., daily 7–7.*

Where to Stay & Eat

Petrified Forest National Park has neither dining nor lodging facilities. The closest restaurants and motels are in Holbrook, which is 27 mi west of the park's northern entrance on I–40.

$–$$$ ✕ **Mesa Italiana Restaurant.** The chef here uses the finest herbs, spices, and other ingredients to create an authentic taste of old Italy. Fresh pastas, calzones, spaghetti with Italian mushrooms, and homemade salads are featured fare. Don't forget the spumoni for dessert. *⊠ 2318 E. Navajo Blvd., Holbrook 86025 ☎ 928/524–6696 ⊟ AE, D, MC, V ⊙ No lunch.*

¢–$ ⊞ **Best Western Arizonian Inn.** Each of the large, handsome rooms here is furnished with a suite of formal, ersatz–cherrywood furniture. A 24-hour diner is just steps across the parking lot. *⊠ 2508 E. Navajo Blvd., Holbrook 86025 ☎☎ 928/524–2611 ⊕ www.bestwestern.com ⇌ 70 rooms, 3 suites ⌂ Some in-room data ports, some microwaves, some refrigerators, pool ⊟ AE, D, DC, MC, V ⏀ CP.*

¢ ⊞ **Holbrook Days Inn.** This modern Southwestern-style structure of stucco walls and Spanish-tile roofs stands amid petrified wood landscaping. Inside, rooms are in Southwestern teal hues with whitewashed furniture. Free Continental breakfast, local phone calls, a heated indoor pool and hot tub, plus nearby restaurants, make this a pleasant, convenient choice. *⊠ 2601 Navajo Blvd., Holbrook 86025 ☎ 928/524–6949 ⊕ www.daysinn.com ⇌ 51 rooms, 3 suites ⌂ Some microwaves, some refrigerators, cable TV, indoor pool, hot tub ⊟ AE, D, DC, MC, V ⏀ CP.*

$ ⊞ **Wigwam Motel.** This motel is classic Route 66. The Wigwam consists of 15 bright white, roadside concrete tepees where you can sleep inexpensively in a surreal environment. As you might expect, wigwams are phoneless, but—ode to Mother Progress—these have cable TV. A small lobby museum exhibits Mexican, Native American, and military relics collected by the owner's family. *⊠ 711 W. Hopi Dr., Holbrook 86025 ☎ 928/524–3048 ⇌ 15 rooms ⌂ Cable TV; no room phones ⊟ MC, V.*

Fodor'sChoice
★

Shopping

McGees Beyond Native Tradition (⊠ 2114 N. Navajo Blvd., Holbrook ☎ 928/524–1977 ⊕ www.hopiart.com) is the area's premier source of high-quality Native American jewelry, rugs, Hopi baskets, and katsina dolls. You may have heard the dolls referred to as kachina, but because the Hopi have no "ch" sound in their language, they are more accurately known as *katsina* dolls. The owners have long-standing, personal relationships with reservation artisans and a knowledgeable staff that adroitly assists first-time buyers and seasoned collectors alike.

EASTERN ARIZONA A TO Z

To research prices, get advice from other travelers, and book travel arrangements, visit www.fodors.com.

BUS TRAVEL

White Mountain Passenger Lines has service between Phoenix and Show Low; one-way fares are around $44. Greyhound Lines travels from Phoenix to Winslow, 50 mi west of Petrified Forest National Park, for around $40.

🚌 **Greyhound Lines** ⊠ 2201 N. Park Dr., Winslow ☎ 928/289–2171. **White Mountain Passenger Lines** ⊠ 1041 E. Hall St., Show Low ☎ 928/537–4539 ⊠ 319 S. 24th St., Phoenix ☎ 602/275–4245.

CAMPING

Call or write the Apache-Sitgreaves National Forest for a brochure listing all public camping facilities in the region, most of which operate from April to November. To assure a site at a fee campground, call the National Recreation Reservation Service, which charges a reservation fee of $10 per transaction. Book your campground site well in advance with the Game and Fish Division of the White Mountain Apache Tribe.

🏕 **Apache-Sitgreaves National Forest** ⊠ 2022 White Mountain Blvd., Pinetop-Lakeside 85929 ☎ 928/368–5111 ⊕ www.fs.fed.us/r3/asnf. **National Recreation Reservation Service** ☎ 877/444–6777 ⊕ www.reserveusa.com. **White Mountain Apache Tribe** ⊡ Box 700, Whiteriver 85941 ☎ 928/338–4385 ⊕ www.wmat.nsn.us.

CAR RENTALS

🚗 **Enterprise Rent-A-Car** ⊠ 980 E. Deuce of Clubs, Show Low 85901 ☎ 928/537–5144. **Hatch Motor Company** ⊠ 260 W. Deuce of Clubs, Show Low 85901 ☎ 928/537–8887.

CAR TRAVEL

A car is essential for touring eastern Arizona, especially because most of the region's top scenic attractions are between towns. Rental facilities are few and far between in these parts, so you'll do well to rent a car from your departure point, whether it's Phoenix, Flagstaff, or Albuquerque.

If you're arriving from points west via Flagstaff, I–40 leads directly to Holbrook, where drivers can take AZ 77 south into Show Low or U.S. 180 southeast to Springerville-Eagar. Those departing from the metropolitan Phoenix area should take the scenic drive northeast on U.S. 60, or the only slightly faster AZ 87 north to AZ 260 east, both of which lead to Show Low. From Tucson, AZ 77 north connects with U.S. 60 at Globe and continues through Show Low up to Holbrook. From New Mexico, drivers can enter the state on I–40 and take U.S. 191 south into Springerville-Eagar, or continue on to Holbrook and reach the White Mountains via AZ 77. For those who want to drive the Coronado Trail south-to-north, U.S. 70 and AZ 78 link up with U.S. 191 from Globe to the west and New Mexico to the east, respectively.

ROAD CONDITIONS
In winter, motorists should travel prepared, with jumper cables, a shovel, tire chains, and—for tire traction on icy roads—a bag of cat litter. Chain requirements apply to all vehicles, including those with four-wheel drive. Bridges and overpasses freeze first and are often slicker than normal road surfaces; never assume sufficient traction simply because a road appears to be sanded. If you must travel in poor visibility conditions, drivers should turn on the headlights and always keep the highway's white reflectors to their right. For road conditions through the region, call the White Mountains Road and Weather Information Line.

White Mountains Road and Weather Information Line ☎ 928/537-7623.

EMERGENCIES

Ambulance & Fire **Ambulance and Fire Emergencies** ☎ 911.
Hospitals **Navapache Regional Medical Center** ✉ 2200 E. Show Low Lake Rd., Show Low ☎ 928/537-4375 ⊕ www.nrmc.org. **White Mountain Regional Medical Center** ✉ 118 S. Mountain Ave., Springerville ☎ 928/333-4368.
Police **Police Emergencies** ☎ 911.

TRAIN TRAVEL

Amtrak trains depart daily at 6:15 AM from Flagstaff to Winslow. There is no train service to Phoenix; those traveling from Phoenix will need to take the Amtrak shuttle—which departs Phoenix-area stations four times daily bound for Flagstaff—and stay overnight in Flagstaff to catch the early-morning train to Winslow. From Albuquerque, Winslow is only a three-hour ride, leaving daily at 5:28 PM. Schedules are subject to change.

Amtrak ☎ 928/774-8679 in Flagstaff.

VISITOR INFORMATION

Alpine Chamber of Commerce ✆ Box 410, Alpine 85920 ☎ 928/339-4330. **Holbrook Chamber of Commerce** ✉ 100 E. Arizona St., Holbrook 86025 ☎ 928/524-6558 or 800/524-2459 ⊕ www.ci.holbrook.az.us. **Pinetop-Lakeside Chamber of Commerce** ✉ 102-C W. White Mountain Blvd., Lakeside 85929 ☎ 928/367-4290 or 800/573-4031 ⊕ www.pinetoplakesidechamber.com. **Show Low Chamber of Commerce** ✉ 951 W. Deuce of Clubs ✆ Box 1083, Show Low 85902, ☎ 928/537-2326 or 888/746-9569 ⊕ www.showlowchamberofcommerce.com. **Springerville-Eagar Regional Chamber of Commerce** ✉ 318 E. Main St., Springerville 85938 ☎ 928/333-2123 ⊕ www.az-tourist.com. **White Mountain Apache Office of Tourism** ✆ Box 710, Fort Apache 85926 ☎ 928/338-1230 ⊕ www.wmat.nsn.us.

LAND-MANAGEMENT AGENCIES
Apache Sitgreaves National Forest Forest Supervisor's Office ✆ Box 640, Springerville 85938 ☎ 928/333-4301 ⊕ www.fs.fed.us/r3/asnf ✉ Alpine Ranger District ✆ Box 469, Alpine 85920 ☎ 928/339-4384 ✉ Lakeside Ranger District ✉ 2022 W. White Mountain Blvd., Lakeside 85929 ☎ 928/368-5111 ✉ Springerville Ranger District ✆ Box 760, Springerville 85938 ☎ 928/333-4372. **Arizona Game & Fish Department** ✉ 2878 E. White Mountain Blvd., Pinetop 85935 ☎ 928/367-4281 ⊕ www.gf.state.az.us. **San Carlos Apache Tribe** ✆ Box 0, San Carlos 85550 ☎ 928/475-2361. **White Mountain Apache Fish & Game Department** ✆ Box 220, Whiteriver 85941 ☎ 928/338-4385.

TUCSON

FODOR'S CHOICE

Arizona Inn, *University*

Arizona–Sonora Desert Museum, *Westside*

Café Poca Cosa, *Downtown*

Casa Tierra, *Westside*

Clarion Hotel & Suites Santa Rita, *a budget hotel in Downtown*

Janos, *a restaurant in the Foothills*

The Lodge at Ventana Canyon Golf Course, *Northeast*

Mi Nidito, *a budget restaurant in South Tucson*

Mission San Xavier del Bac, *southwest of Tucson*

Randolph Park Golf Course–North Course, *Central*

Saguaro National Park West, *Westside*

White Stallion Ranch, *Northwest*

HIGHLY RECOMMENDED

SIGHTS   Center for Creative Photography, *University*

Pima County Courthouse, *Downtown*

Sabino Canyon, *Foothills*

Tubac, *a town south of Tucson*

Tucson Museum of Art and Historic Block, *Downtown*

Many other great hotels and restaurants enliven this area. For other favorites, look for the black stars as you read this chapter.

Updated by
Mara Levin

TUCSON FEELS LIKE A SMALL TOWN, but in fact it's Arizona's second-largest city. Enriched by its deep Native American, Spanish, Mexican, and Old West roots, it is at once a bustling center of business and a relaxed university and resort town. Metropolitan Tucson has more than 800,000 residents, including thousands of part-time "snowbirds" who flee colder climes to enjoy the warm sun that shines on the city more than 340 days a year. Winter temperatures hover around 65°F during the day and 38°F at night. Summers are unquestionably hot—July averages 104°F during the day and 75°F at night—but, as Tucsonans are fond of saying, "it's a dry heat" (Tucson averages only 12 inches of rain a year).

In a part of the world where everything seems new and buildings built before 1950 or so are viewed as historic places, Tucson is an exception. Native Americans have lived along the waterways in this valley for thousands of years. During the 1500s, Spanish explorers arrived to find Pima Indians enjoying the mild weather and growing crops. Father Eusebio Francisco Kino, a Jesuit missionary whose influence is still strongly felt throughout the region, first visited the area in 1687 and returned a few years later to build missions.

The name Tucson came from the Native American word *stjukshon* (pronounced *stook*-shahn), meaning "spring at the foot of a black mountain." (The springs at the foot of Sentinel Peak, made of black volcanic rock, are now dry.) The name became Tucson (originally pronounced *tuk*-son) in the mouths of the Spanish explorers who built the *presidio* (fortified city) of San Augustin del Tuguison in 1776 to keep Native Americans from reclaiming the city. At the time it was the northernmost Spanish settlement in the area known as the Pimeria Alta, and current-day Main Street is a quiet reminder of the former Camino Real, the royal road, that stretched from this tiny walled fort all the way to Mexico City.

Four flags have flown over Tucson—Spanish, Mexican, Confederate, and, finally, the Stars and Stripes. Tucson's allegiance changed in 1820 when Mexico declared independence from Spain, and again in 1853 when the Gadsden purchase made it part of the United States (Arizona didn't officially become a state until 1912). In the 1850s the Butterfield stage line was extended to Tucson, bringing adventurers, a few settlers, and more than a handful of outlaws. The arrival of the railroad in 1880 marked another spurt of growth, as did the opening of the University of Arizona in 1891.

Tucson's 20th-century growth occurred after World War I, when veterans with damaged lungs sought the dry air and healing power of the sun, and again during World War II with the opening of Davis-Monthan Air Force Base and the rise of local aeronautical industries. It was also around this time that air-conditioning made the desert climate hospitable year-round. Today, many transplants come from the Midwest and nearby California because of the lower housing costs, cleaner environment, and spectacular scenery. And despite the ubiquitous strip malls (Speedway Boulevard was once dubbed the "ugliest street in America" by *Life* magazine) and tract-home developments, this college town has Mexican and Native American cultural influences, a striking landscape, and all the amenities of a resort town. High-tech industries have moved into the area, but the economy still relies heavily on tourism and the university, although, come summer, you'd never guess. When the snowbirds and students depart, Tucson can be a pretty sleepy place, which reminds you just how much the desert still determines the city's pace.

If you have
1 day
With only one day and a lot of ground to cover, you would be better off experiencing a taste of both the wild and developed parts of Tucson. A good way to experience the natural wonders of the area is to drive out to **Saguaro National Park West** and the **Arizona–Sonora Desert Museum.** Children may enjoy a stop at the **Old Tucson Studios,** nearby. On your way back, drive through downtown's **Barrio Historico** neighborhood and **El Presidio Historic District** for a glimpse into the city's past, but with just a day, you won't have time to do much stopping.

If you have
3 days
Follow the first day's itinerary, through Old Tucson Studios. The next morning, drive out to the **Mission San Xavier del Bac** and have some Indian fry bread for lunch in the plaza. You might wish to continue south to the **Titan Missile Museum** and then continue on to **Tubac** or **Nogales** for some shopping. On the third day, head **Downtown** to explore Tucson's early history and, in the afternoon, visit one of the several museums at the **University of Arizona.** While near the U of A, you might also want to consider heading to 4th Avenue between 2nd and 9th streets, where boutiques and used-book stores await.

If you have
4 days
What you do on the fourth day depends on the weather: if it's hot, visit **Mt. Lemmon** to cool off; if it's not, you might enjoy breakfast at **Tohono Chul Park,** followed by a visit to **Biosphere 2 Center** or beautiful **Sabino Canyon.**

EXPLORING TUCSON

The metropolitan Tucson area covers more than 500 square mi in a valley ringed by mountains—the Santa Catalinas to the north, the Santa Ritas to the south, the Rincons to the east, and the Tucson Mountains to the west. Needless to say, you'll need a car to explore the city. And while Tucson doesn't yet have as wide a range of resorts as its neighbor to the north, you will not be lacking in activities and diversions to keep you busy during your stay. The city has a tri-cultural (Hispanic, Anglo, Native American) population, and the chance to see how these cultures interact—and to sample their cuisines—is one of the pleasures of a visit to Tucson. The city is particularly popular among golfers, but the area's many hiking trails will keep non-duffers busy, too. And if the weather is too hot to stay outdoors comfortably, Tucson is also known as the home of world-class museums like the Arizona State Museum. An influx of both new residents and visitors has given the city some growing pains, including questions regarding development and pollution control, but these problems are being addressed by city planners.

Getting Your Bearings

The central portion of town, where you'll find most of the shops, restaurants, and businesses, is roughly bounded by Craycroft Road on the east, Oracle Road on the west, River Road to the north, and 22nd Street to the south. The older downtown section, east of I–10 off the Broadway-Congress exit, is much smaller and easy to navigate on foot. Streets downtown don't run true to any sort of grid, however, and many are one-way, so it's best to get a good, detailed map. The city's Westside area is the vast region west of I–10 and I–19, which includes the western section of Saguaro National Park and the San Xavier Indian Reservation.

Remember, too, that the old cliché is reversed here: it's not the humidity—it's the heat. If you are accustomed to humid conditions, then chances are you'll be unprepared for Tucson's dry climate, so use lip balm and skin moisturizer, and drink water or other noncaffeinated fluids frequently, whether you're active or not. Also, the strong solar radiation here (Tucson is second only to Cape Town, South Africa, in skin cancer incidence) makes sunscreen a must.

Downtown

The area bordered by Franklin Street on the north, Cushing Street on the south, Church Avenue on the east, and Main Avenue on the west encompasses more than two centuries of the city's architectural history, dating from the original walled El Presidio de Tucson, a Spanish fortress built in 1776, when Arizona was still part of New Spain. A good deal of Tucson's history was destroyed in the 1960s, when large sections of the downtown's barrio were bulldozed to make way for the Tucson Convention Center, high-rises, and parking lots. However, within the areas' three small historic districts it's still possible to explore parts of the original Spanish settlement and to see a number of the posh residences that accompanied the arrival of the railroad.

El Presidio Historic District, north of the Convention Center and the government buildings that dominate downtown, is a representative mixture of Tucson's historic architecture, a thumbnail of the city's former self. The north–south streets Court, Meyer, and Main are sprinkled with traditional adobe houses. These typical Mexican structures sit cheek by jowl with territorial-style houses, with wide attics and porches. Paseo Redondo, once called Snob Hollow, is the wide road along which wealthy merchants built their homes.

The area most closely resembling 19th-century Tucson is the **Barrio Historico,** where El Tiradito shrine is located. The narrow streets of this neighborhood, including Convent Avenue, have a good sampling of the thick-wall adobe houses positioned close to the street, hiding the yards and gardens within. Ongoing gentrification has made this area an attractive, yet affordable, place to live.

To the east of the Barrio Historico, across Stone Avenue, lies the **Armory Park** neighborhood, mostly constructed by and for the railroad workers who settled here after the 1880s. The brick or wood territorial-style homes here were the Victorian era's adaptation to the desert climate.

Numbers in the text correspond to numbers in the margin and on the What to See in Downtown Tucson map.

<table>
<tr><td>

a good
tour

</td><td>

Drive up to **"A" Mountain (Sentinel Peak)** ❶ ▶ for a great perspective of downtown Tucson. Come down from on high and head east along Congress Street, crossing the **Santa Cruz River** ❷. Continue east along Congress; then head south on Granada to the **Sosa-Carillo-Frémont House** ❸ (park at the adjacent Convention Center lot if no events are in progress). Continue south on Granada to the flashing signal and turn left on Cushing Street to the shrine of **El Tiradito (The Castaway)** ❹, next to El Minuto's parking lot. One-way streets require you to drive east on Cushing, north on Church, east on Broadway Boulevard, and then south on Stone Avenue to **St. Augustine Cathedral** ❺. To reach the **Tucson Children's Museum** ❻, head east on McCormick to 6th Avenue. To get to the **Tucson Museum of Art and Historic Block** ❼, take Church Avenue north to Alameda, then west to Main, where you'll find parking. The complex includes **La Casa Cordova** ❽, the **J. Knox Corbett House** ❾, and the **Stevens**

</td></tr>
</table>

6

Mexican- & Native-American Culture
Mexican Americans make up about 30% of Tucson's population and play a major role in all aspects of daily life. The city's south-of-the-border soul is visible in everything from the city's tile-roof architecture to its mariachi festivals and abundance of Mexican restaurants. Native Americans have a strong presence in the area as well: the Tohono O'odham—the name means "desert people who have come from the Earth"—reservation borders Tucson, and the Pascua Yaqui have their villages within the city limits. Local events, especially religious festivals around Christmas and Easter, celebrate the culture of these and other Arizona tribes. Crafts range from exquisite jewelry and basketry to the more pedestrian (but still authentic) tourist trinkets.

Getting Outdoors
A warm, dry climate and a varied terrain make the Tucson area wonderfully suited for outdoor sports throughout the year. The city has miles of bike paths (shared by joggers and walkers) and plenty of wide-open spaces with memorable desert views. Those same expanses contain some of the best golf courses in the country, with options ranging from well-manicured links at posh resorts to reasonably priced, excellent municipal courses. In the winter, hikers enjoy the myriad desert trails; during the summer, they go on cooler treks in nearby mountain ranges: Saguaro (pronounced suh-*war*-oh) National Park (both east and west), Sabino Canyon, and Catalina State Park are all within 20 minutes of central Tucson by car. Both equestrians and ersatz cowboys and -girls will find scenic trails and horseback riding options to suit them at one of the many area stables. City ordinances against "light pollution"—laws designed to minimize the amount of man-made light emitted into the atmosphere—allow viewing of the usually clear desert skies, even in the city center.

Home ⑩. Finally, walk east on Alameda and then south on Church to reach the **Pima County Courthouse** ⑪, downtown's architectural jewel.

Timing

You can see most of the highlights of downtown, including the Tucson Museum of Art, in about four hours. Although it is all accessible by car, the one-way streets can be frustrating and time-consuming, so you might consider parking your car and walking between destinations if the weather is not too hot. It's a good way to take in downtown, stopping for lunch or a snack along the way. On weekends, the area is less crowded and parking is easier, but some businesses and restaurants are closed.

What to See

▶ ❶ **"A" Mountain (Sentinel Peak).** The original name of this mountain west of downtown was derived from its function as a lookout point for the Spanish. In 1915, fans of the University of Arizona football team whitewashed a large "A" on its side to celebrate a victory, and the tradition has been kept up ever since. The Pima village and cultivated fields that once lay at the base of the peak are long gone, although John Warner's renovated 19th-century house at the base still stands. During the day,

What to See in Downtown Tucson

KEY

▶ *Start of walk*

the peak's a great place to get an overview of the town's layout; at night the city lights below form a dazzling carpet, but the teenage hangout/make-out scene may make some uncomfortable. ⊠ *Congress St. on Sentinel Peak Rd., Downtown.*

❹ El Tiradito (The Castaway). No one seems to know the details of the story behind this little shrine, but everyone agrees a tragic love triangle was involved. A bronze plaque indicates only that it is dedicated to a sinner who is buried here on unconsecrated ground. The many candles that line the cactus-shrouded spot attest to its continuing importance in local Catholic lore. People light candles and leave *milagros* (literally, "miracles"; little icons used in prayers for healing) for their loved ones. A modern-day miracle: the shrine's inclusion on the National Register of Historic Places helped prevent a freeway from plowing through this section of the Barrio Historico. ⊠ *Main Ave., south of Cushing St., Downtown.*

❾ J. Knox Corbett House. Built in 1906–07, this house was occupied by members of the Corbett family until 1963. Tucson's Hi Corbett field (the Major League Colorado Rockies use this field for spring training) is named for the grandnephew of the original occupants: J. Knox Corbett, a businessman, and Elizabeth Hughes Corbett, daughter of Tucson pioneer Sam Hughes. The two-story, Mission Revival–style residence has been furnished with Arts and Crafts pieces: Stickley, Roycroft, Tiffany, and Morris are among the more famous manufacturers represented. ⊠ *180 N. Main Ave., Downtown* ☎ *520/624-2333* ⊕ *www.tucsonarts.com* ✉ *Included in $5 admission to Tucson Museum of Art* ☉ *Mon.–Sat. 10–4, Sun. noon–4. Free guided tour Tues. at 11.*

❽ La Casa Cordova. One of the best examples of the simple but elegant Sonoran row house, a Spanish style adapted to adobe construction, La Casa

Cordova is also one of the oldest buildings in Tucson. The oldest section, constructed around 1848, has been restored to its original appearance and is now the Mexican Heritage Museum. Inside you'll find furnishings of the Native American and pioneer settlers and an exhibit on the presidio's history. After visiting the museum, you'll understand why adobe—brick made of mud and straw, cured in the hot sun—was so widely used in early Tucson. It provides a natural insulation from the heat and cold, and it is durable in Tucson's dry climate. ⊠ *175 N. Meyer Ave., Downtown* ☎ *520/624–2333* ⊕ *www.tucsonarts.com* ✉ *Included in $5 admission to Tucson Museum of Art* ☉ *Mon.–Sat. 10–4, Sun. noon–4.*

need a break? On the patio of Stevens Home, a 19th-century adobe building adjacent to the Tucson Museum of Art, **Cafe A La C'Arte** (⊠ 150 N. Main Ave., Downtown ☎ 520/628–8533) serves fanciful salads, soups, and sandwiches. For a tasty frittata (omelet) or panini (pressed sandwich), try **Caffé Milano** (⊠ 46 W. Congress St., Downtown ☎ 520/628–1601), an Italian deli open weekdays until 3 PM.

★ ⑪ **Pima County Courthouse.** This Spanish colonial–style building with a mosaic-tile dome is among Tucson's most beautiful historic structures. It was built in 1927 on the site of the original single-story adobe court of 1869; a portion of the old presidio wall can be seen in the south wing of the courthouse's second floor. To the side of the building, the county assessor's office has a diorama depicting the area's early days (if the location seems odd, remember that the Spanish were big on taxation, too). The courthouse, still in use, is on the eastern side of El Presidio Park, a modern square once occupied by the Plaza de las Armas, the largest of El Presidio's plazas. ⊠ *115 N. Church Ave.; between Alameda and Pennington Sts., Downtown* ⊕ *jp.co.pima.az.us* ✉ *Free* ☉ *Weekdays 8–4:30, Sat. 8–noon.*

❷ **Santa Cruz River.** This is a dry wash, or arroyo, most of the year, but sudden summer thunderstorms and rainwater from upper elevations can turn it into a raging river in a matter of hours. The river has been the location of a settlement for thousands of years, and most of the archaeological finds in the valley are along its banks. When Europeans arrived, the Santa Cruz was a permanent river with wide banks suitable for irrigation. Over time its banks have been narrowed and contained and are now lined by the River Park. A favorite spot for walkers, joggers, bicyclists, and horseback riders, the park now sports a bike path, rest rooms, drinking fountains, and sculptures created by local artists.

❸ **Sosa-Carillo-Frémont House.** One of Tucson's oldest adobe residences, this was the only building spared when the surrounding barrio was torn down to build the Tucson Convention Center. Originally purchased by José Maria Sosa in 1860, it was owned by the Carillo family for 80 years and leased at one time to territorial governor John C. Frémont. The restored house, now a branch of the Arizona Historical Society, is furnished in 1880s fashion and has changing displays of territorial life. The house is in the Convention Center complex, between the Music Hall and the Arena. ⊠ *151 S. Granada Ave., Downtown* ☎ *520/622–0956* ⊕ *www. ahs.state.az.us* ✉ *Free; guided walking tours of the Presidio and Tucson Historic District $10* ☉ *Wed.–Sat. 10–4; walking tours Nov.–Mar., Thurs. and Sat. at 10.*

❺ **St. Augustine Cathedral.** Construction began in 1896 on one of downtown's most striking structures, in what had earlier been the Plaza de Mesilla. Although the imposing white and beige Spanish-style building was modeled after the Cathedral of Queretaro in Mexico, a number of its details reflect the desert setting: above the entryway, next to a bronze statue of St. Augustine, are carvings of local desert scenes with saguaro cacti, yucca, and prickly pears (look closely for the horned toad). Compared with the magnificent facade, the modernized interior is a bit disappointing. For a unique Southwestern experience, attend the mariachi mass celebrated Sunday at 8 AM. ⊠ *192 S. Stone Ave., Downtown* 🎫 *Free* ⊘ *Daily 7–6.*

⑩ Stevens Home. It was here that wealthy politician and cattle rancher Hiram Stevens and his Mexican wife, Petra Santa Cruz, entertained many of Tucson's leaders—including Edward and Maria Fish—during the 1800s. A drought brought the Stevenses' cattle ranching to a halt in 1893, and Stevens killed himself in despair, after unsuccessfully attempting to shoot his wife (the bullet was deflected by the comb she wore in her hair). The 1865 house, just north of the Edward Nye Fish House, was restored in 1980 and now houses the Tucson Museum of Art's permanent collections of pre-Columbian, Spanish colonial, and Latin American folk art. A café on the porch and patio of this home serves lovely sandwiches, soups, and pastries to the downtown crowd weekdays 11–3, and it's a great place to fortify yourself against museum fatigue. ⊠ *150 N. Main Ave., Downtown* ⊕ *www.tucsonarts.com* 🎫 *Included in $5 admission to Tucson Museum of Art* ⊘ *Mon.–Sat. 10–4, Sun. noon–4.*

☕ ⑥ Tucson Children's Museum. Youngsters are encouraged to touch and explore the exhibits here, which are oriented toward science, language, and history. They can key in on Little Tikes IBM computers or turn on the electricity in the streets of a model town. There's Dinosaur Canyon, with mechanical prehistoric creatures, and a bubble room where children can place themselves in the middle of a large vertical soap bubble. For smaller fry there's a toddler's playroom; a pretend grocery store and musical instruments add to the fun. ⊠ *200 S. 6th Ave., Downtown* ☎ *520/ 792–9985* ⊕ *www.tucsonchildrensmuseum.org* 🎫 *$5.50* ⊘ *Tues.–Sat. 10–5, Sun. noon–5.*

★ ⑦ Tucson Museum of Art and Historic Block. Tucson's past is chronicled in downtown's main cultural center. The five historic buildings on this block are listed in the National Register of Historic Places; you can enter La Casa Cordova, the Stevens Home, the J. Knox Corbett House, and the Edward Nye Fish House. The Romero House, believed to incorporate a section of the presidio wall, is not open to the public. In the center of the museum complex is the Plaza of the Pioneers, honoring Tucson's early citizens.

The museum building, the only modern structure of the complex, houses a permanent collection of modern and contemporary art and hosts some interesting traveling shows. The museum's permanent and changing exhibitions of Western art fill an 1868 adobe, the Edward Nye Fish House, which belonged to an early merchant, entrepreneur, and politician, and his wife, Maria Wakefield Fish, a prominent educator. The building is notable for its 15-ft beamed ceilings and saguaro cactus–rib supports. Take one of the free docent tours for a more complete understanding of the museum's rich history. Those interested in exploring the El Presidio district further can also get a self-guided tour map from the museum. Parking is in a large lot at North Main Avenue and Paseo Redondo. ⊠ *140 N. Main Ave., Downtown* ☎ *520/624–2333* ⊕ *www. tucsonarts.com* 🎫 *$5, Sun. free; tours free* ⊘ *Mon.–Sat. 10–4, Sun. noon–4. Guided tours Wed.–Thurs. and Sat. at 11. Closed Mon. late May–early Sept. (no guided tours during that period).*

The University of Arizona

A university might not seem to be the most likely spot for a vacation visit, but this one is unusual. Not only is the institution itself of historical importance, but it also supports several museums with exhibitions ranging from astronomy to photography. Call ahead to verify hours for the university's museums, as yearly budget revisions often cause schedule changes. If you drive, leave your car in a university garage or lot; those on 2nd Street at Mountain Avenue, on Speedway Boulevard at Park Avenue, on Tyndall Avenue south of University Boulevard, and on 2nd Street at Euclid Avenue are the most centrally located. Parking costs $2 for the first hour and $1 for each additional hour, with free parking on weekends and holidays.

The U of A, as the University of Arizona is known locally (as opposed to ASU, its rival state university in Tempe), covers 353 acres and is a major economic influence with a student population of more than 34,000. The land for the university was "donated" by a couple of gamblers and a saloon owner in 1891 (their benevolence was reputed to have been inspired by a bad hand of cards), and $25,000 of territorial money was used to build Old Main (the original building) and hire six faculty members. Money ran out before Old Main's roof was placed, but a few enlightened local citizens pitched in funds to finish it. Most of the city's populace was less enthusiastic about the institution: they were disgruntled when the 13th Territorial Legislature granted the University of Arizona to Tucson and awarded rival Phoenix with what was considered to be the real prize—an insane asylum and a prison.

The university's flora is very impressive—the campus has been designated an arboretum. Its outstanding plants include extremely rare mutated, or "crested," saguaro at the northeast corner of the Old Main building. The long, grassy Mall in the heart of campus—itself once a vast cactus garden—sits atop a huge underground student activity center, and makes for a pleasant stroll or bike ride on a balmy evening.

Although the U of A prides itself on its achievements in the fields of academics (the astronomy department, medical school, and anthropology program are top-rated), undergrads seem more interested in their school's renown on the fields of athletics. The movie *Revenge of the Nerds*, filmed on campus, further contributed to the university's reputation as a "party school."

Numbers in the text correspond to numbers in the margin and on the What to See in University of Arizona map.

a good tour

Start your tour on the northwestern corner of campus, at the junction of Speedway Boulevard and Park Avenue, where you'll find a large parking garage. Walk south on Park to the **Arizona Historical Society's Museum** 12 ▶. One block farther south on University Boulevard, just inside the main gate of the university, is the **Arizona State Museum** 13. As you head farther east and deeper into the campus, you'll pass by Old Main, and University Boulevard turns into the University Mall; continue on to Cherry Avenue to reach the **Flandrau Science Center and Planetarium** 14. Walking north on Cherry, then turning west onto 2nd Street, will take you past several fraternity and sorority houses. Turn north on Olive Road to find the **Center for Creative Photography** 15 in a gray concrete building on the right. Most of the photographer Ansel Adams's negatives are here. Across from the center is the **University of Arizona Museum of Art** 16. From here, it's a short walk under Speedway Boulevard via a pedestrian tunnel to the parking lot.

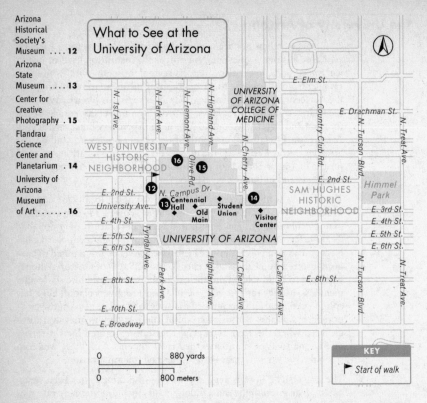

What to See at the
University of Arizona

TIMING   To see this huge university campus in a single day takes careful planning. During the school semesters, you're better off visiting on the weekend when university parking is free and plentiful; there's no problem in
summer when most of the students leave campus. Visit the Web site **University of Arizona** (⊕ www.arizona.edu), for parking maps and the latest visitor information.

What to See

🖑 ⏐ **⑫ Arizona Historical Society's Museum.** Flanking the entrance to the museum
are statues of two men: Father Kino, the Jesuit who established San Xavier
del Bac and a string of other missions, and John Greenaway, indelibly
linked to Phelps Dodge, the copper-mining company that helped Arizona earn statehood in 1912. The museum houses the headquarters of
the state Historical Society, originally the Society of Arizona Pioneers,
and has exhibits exploring the history of southern Arizona, the Southwest United States, and northern Mexico, starting with the Hohokam
Indians and Spanish explorers. Check out the interesting yet harrowing
"Life on the Edge: A History of Medicine in Arizona" exhibit and you'll
be thankful that there are more than 30 Walgreens drugstores in present-
day Tucson. Children will enjoy the large exhibit on copper mining (complete with an atmospheric replica of a mine shaft and camp), the
stagecoaches in the transportation area, and the pioneer clothing in the
costume exhibit. The library houses an extensive collection of historic
Arizona photographs and sells inexpensive reprints of most of them. (If
you're driving and this is your first stop, park your car in the garage at
the corner of 2nd and Euclid streets and then get a free parking pass in
the museum.) ⊠ 949 E. 2nd St., University ☎ 520/628–5774 ⊕ www.
arizona.edu ☜ $5 ⊘ Mon.–Sat. 10–4, Sun. noon–4; library weekdays
10–4, Sat. 10–1.

⑬ Arizona State Museum. Inside the main gate of the university is Arizona's oldest museum, dating from territorial days (1893) and recognized as one of the world's most important resources for the study of Southwestern cultures. Exhibits in the original (south) building focus on the state's ancient history, including fossils and a fascinating sample of tree-ring dating. "Paths of Life: American Indians of the Southwest" is a permanent exhibit that explores the cultural traditions, origins, and contemporary lives of 10 native tribes of Arizona and Sonora, Mexico. ⊠ *Park Ave. at University Ave., University* ☎ *520/621–6302* ⊕ *www.statemuseum. arizona.edu* ⊡ *Free* ⊙ *Mon.–Sat. 10–5, Sun. noon–5.*

need a break? Just outside the campus gate, University Boulevard is lined with student-oriented eateries. **Café Paraiso** (⊠ 800 E. University Blvd., University ☎ 520/624–1707) is a home-grown establishment (as opposed to the nearby Starbucks) serving salads, sandwiches, and other lunch items, and it has a great patio with a view of the passing university scene. Beer aficionados should head over to **Gentle Ben's** (⊠ 865 E. University Blvd., University ☎ 520/624–4177), one of Tucson's brewpubs. The patio upstairs affords a good view of the sunset.

★ **⑮ Center for Creative Photography.** Ansel Adams conceived the idea of a photographer's archive and donated the majority of his negatives to this museum. In addition to its superb collection of his work, the center has works by other major 20th-century photographers including Paul Strand, W. Eugene Smith, Edward Weston, and Louise Dahl-Wolfe. Changing exhibits in the main gallery highlight various holdings of the collection, but if you'd like to see the work of a particular photographer in the archives, call to arrange an appointment. ⊠ *1030 N. Olive Rd., north of 2nd St., University* ☎ *520/621–7968* ⊕ *www.creativephotography. org* ⊡ *$5 suggested donation* ⊙ *Weekdays 9–5, weekends noon–5.*

⑭ Flandrau Science Center and Planetarium. Attractions here include a 16-inch public telescope; the impressive Star Theatre, where a multimedia show brings astronomy to life; an interactive meteor exhibit; and, in the basement, a Mineral Museum, which exhibits more than 2,000 rocks and gems, some rather rare. Bring a camera—special adapters allow you to take pictures through the telescopes. ⊠ *Cherry Ave. and University Blvd., University* ☎ *520/621–4515, 520/621–7827 recorded message* ⊕ *www.flandrau.org* ⊡ *Exhibits $3; planetarium shows $5; observatory free* ⊙ *Exhibits Tues. and Thurs.–Sat. 9–5 and 7–9, Wed. 9–5, Sun. 1–5. Planetarium show times vary. Observatory Aug. 15–May 15, Wed.–Sat. 6:40 PM–10 PM; May 16–Aug. 14, Wed.–Sat. 7:30 PM–10 PM.*

⑯ University of Arizona Museum of Art. This small museum houses a collection of European paintings from the Renaissance through the 17th century. One of the museum's highlights is the Kress Collection's Retablo from Ciudad Rodrigo: 26 panels of an altarpiece made in 1488 by Fernando Gallego. The museum also houses the world's second-largest collection of bronze, plaster, and ceramic sculpture by Jacques Lipschitz. ⊠ *Fine Arts Complex, Bldg. 2 (southeast corner of Speedway Blvd. and Park Ave.), University* ☎ *520/621–7567* ⊕ *artmuseum.arizona.edu* ⊡ *Free* ⊙ *Sept.–mid-May, weekdays 9–5, Sun. noon–4; mid-May–Aug., weekdays 10–3:30, Sun. noon–4.*

off the beaten path UNIVERSITY NEIGHBORHOODS – When the University of Arizona was built, it stood in the desert on the east side of town, and students either lived at home or boarded with residents. Drive slowly along University Boulevard west from the Main Gate of campus through

West University Neighborhood, a wonderful mixture of stately homes built by former prominent Tucsonans and bungalows constructed for rental to students. On the other side of campus, off Campbell Avenue between Speedway and Broadway Boulevard, lies Sam Hughes Neighborhood, which saw its first homes in the 1920s. Meander along 3rd Street, one of Tucson's many bike paths, to see an eclectic mix of Spanish mission revival, bungalow, adobe, and brick homes.

East of I–10 and Central Tucson

The U of A, built in 1891, determined the direction in which the city would grow: many of the city's major attractions are east of its only major freeway, I–10. Sights worth seeing in central Tucson, as the area near the university is called, include a city park, a zoo, and botanical gardens. Farther to the north lie the imposing Santa Catalina Mountains, and to the far east cacti and caverns rule. Those interested in World War II should take a detour south to see a huge repository of old military aircraft.

Numbers in the text correspond to numbers in the margin and on the What to See in Greater Tucson map.

a good drive

Start your drive at the **Tucson Botanical Gardens** ⑰ ▶. One kids' option is close by: the **Reid Park Zoo** ⑱, less than 10 minutes to the southeast. From here, distances get a bit greater, so some decisions need to be made. You can head north, stopping off at your choice of **Fort Lowell Park and Museum** ⑲, **Sabino Canyon** ⑳, or **De Grazia's Gallery in the Sun** ㉑ en route to **Tohono Chul Park** ㉒ or **Mt. Lemmon** ㉓ (Sabino Canyon and Mt. Lemmon are the most time-consuming of these). Or you can go east to **Saguaro National Park East** ㉔ and **Colossal Cave Mountain Park** ㉕, and south to **Pima Air and Space Museum** ㉖.

TIMING If it's warm, visit outdoor attractions such as the Tucson Botanical Gardens, Sabino Canyon, and Saguaro National Park East in the morning. The elevation of Mt. Lemmon, on the other hand, makes it significantly cooler than the rest of the city. Colossal Cave stays at a constant, comfortable temperature, making it a nice year-round adjunct to a Saguaro National Park East tour.

What to See

☝ ㉕ **Colossal Cave Mountain Park.** This limestone grotto 20 mi east of Tucson (take Broadway Boulevard or 22nd Street East to Colossal Cave Road) is the largest dry cavern in the world. Informed guides discuss the fascinating crystal formations and relate the many romantic tales surrounding the cave, including the legend that an enormous sum of money stolen in a stagecoach robbery is still hidden here. Forty-five-minute cave tours begin every 30 minutes and require a ½-mi walk and 363 stairs. The park includes a ranch area with trail rides ($20 per hour), a gemstone-sluicing area, a small museum, nature trails, a butterfly garden, a snack bar, and a gift shop. ⊠ *Colossal Cave Rd. at Old Spanish Trail Rd., Eastside* ☎ *520/647-7275* ⊕ *www.colossalcave.com* ☎ *Park $3 per car; cave tour $7.50 per person* ☼ *Oct.–mid-Mar., Mon.–Sat. 9–5, Sun. 9–6; mid-Mar.–Sept., Mon.–Sat. 8–6, Sun. 8–7.*

㉑ **De Grazia's Gallery in the Sun.** Arizonan artist Ted De Grazia, who depicted Southwest Native American and Mexican life in a manner some find kitschy and others adore, built this sprawling, spacious single-story museum with the assistance of Native American friends, using only natural material from the surrounding desert. You can visit De Grazia's workshop, former home, and grave. Although the original works are not for

What to See in
Greater Tucson

sale, the museum's gift shop has a wide selection of prints, ceramics, and books by and about the colorful artist. ⊠ 6300 N. Swan Rd., Foothills ☎ 520/299–9191 ⊕ www.degrazia.org ⊠ Free ☉ Daily 10–4.

⑲ Fort Lowell Park and Museum. Because of its fertile soil and proximity to the Rillito River, this restful city park was once the site of a Hohokam village. Centuries later, a fort was built here to protect the fledgling city against the Apaches (1873–91). The former commanding officer's quarters displays artifacts from military life in territorial days. Some of the descendants of the inhabitants of El Fuerte, a Mexican village that arose among the abandoned fort buildings in the 1890s, live in El Callejón, a narrow alley near the museum. ⊠ 2900 N. Craycroft Rd., Central ☎ 520/885–3832 ⊠ Free ☉ Wed.–Sat. 10–4.

23 Mt. Lemmon. This peak is one of the Santa Catalina Mountains. It's named after Sara Lemmon, who in 1881 became the first woman to ascend to its top. Mt. Lemmon is the southernmost ski slope in the continental United States, but you don't have to be a skier to enjoy a visit. In spring and fall you can picnic and hike among the 150 mi of clearly marked and well-maintained trails; in summer the mountain's 9,157-ft elevation brings welcome relief from the heat. There are no gas stations on Mt. Lemmon Highway, the road that winds and twists its way for 28 mi up the mountainside, so be sure to check the road conditions in winter and to gas up before you leave town any time of year. To reach the highway, take Tanque Verde Road to Catalina Highway, which becomes Mt. Lemmon Highway as you head north. Even if you don't make it to the top, you'll find stunning views of Tucson at Windy Point, about halfway up the mountain. Look for a road on your left between the Windy Point and San Pedro lookouts; it leads to Rose Canyon Lake, a lovely little reservoir.

The journey up the mountain is interesting in itself: every 1,000-ft climb in elevation is equivalent to traveling 300 mi north, so you'll move from typical Sonoran Desert plants in the foothills to vegetation similar to that found in southern Canada at the top. Along the way, you'll see rock formations that look as though they were carefully balanced against each other by sculptors from another planet.

At milepost 18 of your ascent, on the left-hand side of the road, the Palisades Ranger Station of **Coronado National Forest** (☎ 520/749–8700 for information) can give you current information on the mountain's campgrounds, hiking trails, and picnic spots. It's open weekends 8:30–4:30 in winter, daily 9–6 in summer.

Just before you reach the ski resort, you'll pass through the tiny alpine-style village of **Summerhaven,** which has a couple of casual restaurants, gift shops, and a few pleasant lodges.

Mt. Lemmon Highway ends at **Mt. Lemmon Ski Valley.** Skiing here depends on natural conditions—there's no artificial snow—so call ahead. There are 16 runs, open daily, ranging from beginner to advanced. Lift tickets cost $28 weekdays ($32 weekends and holidays) for an all-day pass and $23 weekdays ($27 weekends and holidays) for a half-day pass (starting at 1 PM). Ski equipment can be rented, and instruction is available. In off-season you can take a ride ($7.50) on the double chairlift that whisks you to the top of the slope—some 9,100 ft. Many ride the lift and then head out hiking on one of several trails that crisscross the summit. ✉ *Mt. Lemmon Hwy., Northeast* ☎ *520/576–1400 recorded snow report, 520/547–7510 winter road conditions* ▣ *$5 per vehicle per day or $20 for an annual pass (includes Sabino Canyon)* ☉ *Daily (depending on snow during ski season).*

26 Pima Air and Space Museum. This huge facility ranks among the largest private collections of aircraft in the world, with more than 200 airplanes on display. You'll see a full-scale replica of the Wright brothers' 1903 Wright Flyer and a mock-up of the X-15, the world's fastest aircraft. You can tour a presidential plane used by both John F. Kennedy and Lyndon B. Johnson. Those with a special interest in World War II find the museum particularly worthwhile, but many others should enjoy this walk through U.S. aviation history. Hour-long van tours of the nearby Aerospace Maintenance and Regeneration Center (AMARC) at Davis-Monthan Air Force Base provide an eerie glimpse of hundreds of mothballed aircraft lined up in long rows on a vast tract of desert; you must reserve a place in advance for this tour. ✉ *6000 E. Valencia Rd. (I–10,*

Exit 267), South ☎ *520/574–0462* ⊕ *www.pimaair.org* ✈ *$7.50, tram $3, AMARC tour $6* ⊙ *Daily 9–5 (last admission at 4); AMARC tours weekdays only.*

🐾 ⑱ **Reid Park Zoo.** This small but well-designed zoo won't tax the children's—or your—patience. There are plenty of shady places to sit, a wonderful little gift shop, and a snack bar to rev you up when your energy is flagging. The youngsters will love the zoo's adorable newborns and the South American enclosure with its rain forest and exotic birds. If you're visiting in summer, go early in the day when the animals are active. ⊠ *Reid Park, Lake Shore La. off 22nd St. between Alvernon Way and Country Club Rd., Central* ☎ *520/791–3204* ⊕ *www.tucsonzoo. org* ✈ *$4* ⊙ *Daily 9–4.*

★ ⑳ **Sabino Canyon.** Year-round, but especially during summer, locals flock to this oasis in Coronado National Forest to hike, picnic, and enjoy the waterfalls, streams, swimming holes, and shade trees that provide a respite from the heat. No cars are allowed, but a narrated tram ride (about 45 minutes round-trip) takes you up a WPA-built road to the top of the canyon; you can hop off and on at any of the nine stops. There's also a tram ride to adjacent Bear Canyon, where you can take a much more rigorous but rewarding hike to the popular Seven Falls (it'll take about 1½ hours each way from the drop-off point, so carry plenty of water). If you're in Tucson near a full moon, take the special night tram and watch the desert come alive. ⊠ *Sabino Canyon Rd. at Sunrise Dr., Foothills* ☎ *520/749–2861 recorded tram information, 520/749–8700 visitor center* ⊕ *www.fs.fed.us/r3/coronado/scrd* ✈ *$5 per vehicle per day or $20 for an annual pass (includes Mt. Lemmon), tram $6, Bear Canyon tram $3* ⊙ *Visitor center weekdays 8–4:30, weekends 8:30–4:30; call for tram schedules.*

㉔ **Saguaro National Park East.** About 16 mi from the town center is the eastern portion of the national park that sandwiches in Tucson. This section covers more than 67,000 acres and climbs through five climate zones, which makes for some dramatic hikes through the foothills of the Rincon Mountains. Eight-mile paved Cactus Forest Drive leads to trailheads and picnic areas. Ask for a detailed map at the visitor center for more information about the unique cacti that are concentrated here. To get here, take Speedway Boulevard or 22nd Street East. ⊠ *3693 S. Old Spanish Trail, Eastside* ☎ *520/733–5153* ⊕ *www.nps.gov/sagu* ✈ *$6 per vehicle or $3 per person on foot or bike* ⊙ *Visitor center daily 8:30–5; park roads daily 7 AM–sunset.*

㉒ **Tohono Chul Park.** A 48-acre retreat designed to promote the conservation of arid regions, Tohono Chul—the name means "desert corner" in the language of the Tohono O'odham—uses a demonstration garden, greenhouse, and geology wall that help explain this unique desert area. Enjoy the shady nooks, nature trails, small art gallery, great gift shop, and tearoom at this peaceful spot; note that only the tearoom and gift shop can be entered at no charge. ⊠ *7366 N. Paseo del Norte, Northwest* ☎ *520/742–6455* ⊕ *www.tohonochulpark.org* ✈ *$5* ⊙ *Park daily 8 AM–sunset; building Mon.–Sat. 9–5, Sun. 11–5.*

➤ ⑰ **Tucson Botanical Gardens.** On 5 acres are a tropical greenhouse; a sensory garden, where you can touch and smell the plants and listen to the abundant bird life; historical gardens, which display the Mediterranean landscaping that the property's original owners planted in the 1930s; a garden designed to attract birds; and a cactus garden. Other special gardens showcase wildflowers, Australian plants, and Native American crops and herbs, so call to find out what's blooming. All of the paths are wheel-

CloseUp

THE DESERT'S FRAGILE GIANT

EASY TO ANTHROPOMORPHIZE because they have "arms," saguaros are thought to be the descendants of tropical trees that lost their leaves and became dormant during drought. Carnegiea gigantea (the saguaro's scientific name) grows nowhere else on earth than the Sonoran Basin, an area that includes southern Arizona and northern Mexico.

Tourists are often amazed to find that these odd-looking plants actually bloom each May or June. Each bloom opens only for a few evening hours after sunset. The next afternoon, the creamy-white chalice closes forever. Each adult saguaro produces six or seven flowers a day for about a month. They are cross-pollinated by bees, Mexican white-winged doves, and brown bats.

Because the saguaro stores massive quantities of water (enough conceivably to last two years), it is often called the "cactus camel." New saguaros are born when the seeds of the flower take root, an arduous process. Late freezes and even high heat can kill a seedling in its first days. Once a seed is established, it grows up under the protection of a "nurse" tree, such as a paloverde. Fully grown, a saguaro can weigh as much as 7 tons.

The saguaro, like many other wild plants, is protected by Arizona law. Without an Arizona Department of Agriculture permit, it is illegal to move a saguaro or sell one from private property. And the saguaro has its own means of protecting itself from would-be poachers or vandals. In the early 1980s, a hunter fired a shotgun at a large saguaro near Phoenix. It collapsed onto him, killing him instantly.

---

chair accessible, and there is a little gift shop near the entrance. ✉ 2150 N. Alvernon Way, Central ☎ 520/326–9686 ⊕ www.tucsonbotanical. org 💲 $4 ⊘ Daily 8:30–4:30.

> **off the beaten path**

BIOSPHERE 2 CENTER – In the little town of Oracle, some 30 minutes north of central Tucson, eight scientists walked into a self-contained, sealed ecosystem in 1992, intending to remain inside for two years. The experiment was not a complete success, but the structure itself remains an interesting phenomenon, and those interested in the earth sciences will find the ongoing experiments fascinating. Biosphere 2 Center is now managed by Columbia University's Earth Institute, which directs all of the current scientific, educational, and visitor-center operations.

The miniature world within Biosphere includes tropical rain forest, savanna, desert, thorn scrub, marsh, ocean, and agricultural areas, including almost 3,000 plant and animal species. A film and a large, rotating cutaway model in the visitor center explain the project. Guided walking tours, which last about two hours and cover ¾ mi, don't enter most of the sealed sphere, but observation areas let you peer in at the rest. The one-hour, guided World of Discovery Tour takes you inside the biomes for an additional charge. The Canada del Oro restaurant, overlooking the Santa Catalina Mountains, has a full menu of sandwiches and hearty entrées; there are also several snack bars. Reasonably priced hotel suites with excellent views are available on Biosphere's premises. ✉ AZ 77, Milepost 96.5, Oracle ☎ 520/896–6200 ⊕ www.bio2.edu 💲 $12.95, World of Discovery Tour $10 ⊘ Daily 8:30–5; guided tours every ½ hr.

Westside

If you're interested in the flora and fauna of the Sonoran Desert—as well as some of its appearances in the cinema—heed the same advice given the pioneers: go west.

a good tour

From central Tucson, take Speedway Boulevard west; when the houses begin to thin and stands of cacti begin to thicken, you'll see the **International Wildlife Museum** ㉗ ⌐. Continue west on Speedway to where it joins Anklam Road and becomes Gates Pass Road; at the juncture of Gates Pass and Kinney roads, you'll see signs directing you south to **Old Tucson Studios** ㉘. Return to this juncture and continue north on Kinney Road for about 10 mi until you come to the **Arizona–Sonora Desert Museum** ㉙. It's a short drive farther north along the same road to the Red Hills Visitor Center, which will introduce you to **Saguaro National Park West** ㉚. Note: The Gates Pass Road can be daunting to a nervous driver, and the pass itself is not navigable for large campers, RVs, or cars towing campers. As an alternative, take I–10 to I–19 south to Ajo Road, go west to Kinney Road, and follow the signs. Regardless of which route you choose, take Kinney Road back to I–19 and continue south again. You'll soon come to the turnoff for **Mission San Xavier del Bac** ㉛.

TIMING Although the attractions in this area are not close together, it's easy to tour all the sights in one day, as they're on a fairly direct route to one another. The best plan is to set out in the cooler early morning to Saguaro National Park, which has no shaded areas (it's also the best time to see the wildlife at its liveliest). Spend the rest of the morning at the Desert Museum, where you can have lunch at the Ironwood Terrace or the more upscale Ocotillo Café (in any case, allow at least two hours for your visit). The hottest time of the afternoon can be spent ducking in and out of attractions at Old Tucson, visiting the air-conditioned International Wildlife Museum, or enjoying the indoor sanctuary of San Xavier mission.

What to See

㉙ **Arizona–Sonora Desert Museum.** The name "museum" is misleading; this delightful site is a beautifully planned zoo and botanical garden featuring the animals and plants of the Sonoran Desert. Hummingbirds, cactus wrens, rattlesnakes, scorpions, bighorn sheep, and prairie dogs all busy themselves in ingeniously designed habitats. An Earth Sciences Center has an artificial limestone cave and a hands-on meteor and mineral display. The coyote and javelina exhibits have "invisible" fencing that separates humans from animals, and the Riparian Corridor section affords great underwater views of otters and beavers. The gift shop carries an impressive selection of books about Arizona and the desert, plus jewelry and crafts. ✉ *2021 N. Kinney Rd., Westside* ☎ *520/883–2702* ⊕ *www.desertmuseum.org* ✇ *$9.95* ☉ *Mar.–Sept., daily 7:30–5; Oct.–Feb., daily 8:30–5.*

FodorsChoice ★

㉗ **International Wildlife Museum.** Dubbed by some locals as the International Plush Toy Museum, this imposing structure has no real wildlife in it at all: almost 400 species of animals are stuffed and mounted in re-creations of their natural habitats. Some of the exhibits are quite naturalistic, but the "trophy room" full of mounted animal heads reminds you that hunter-conservators supplied the specimens. A "petting" menagerie allows children to touch different animal skins; they can also learn about birds and mammals from all over the world via interactive computers. ✉ *4800 W. Gates Pass Rd., Westside* ☎ *520/629–0100* ⊕ *www.thewildlifemuseum.org* ✇ *$7* ☉ *Weekdays 9–5, weekends 9–6.*

③① Mission San Xavier del Bac. The oldest Catholic church in the United States
Fodor'sChoice still serving the community for which it was built, San Xavier was
★ founded in 1692 by Father Eusebio Francisco Kino, who established 22
missions in northern Mexico and southern Arizona. The current structure was constructed out of native materials by Franciscan missionaries between 1777 and 1797 and is owned by the Tohono O'odham tribe.

The beauty of the mission, with elements of Spanish, Baroque, and
Moorish architectural styles, is highlighted by the stark landscape against
which it is set, inspiring an early-20th-century poet to dub it White Dove
of the Desert. Inside, there's a wealth of painted statues, carvings, and
frescoes. Paul Schwartzbaum, who helped restore Michelangelo's mas-
terwork in Rome, supervised Tohono O'odham artisans in the restora-
tion of the mission's artwork, completed in 1997; he has called the mission
the Sistine Chapel of the United States. Mass is celebrated at 8:30 AM
daily in the church and three times on Sunday morning. Call ahead for
information about special celebrations.

Across the parking lot from the mission, San Xavier Plaza has a number of Native American crafts shops where you'll find the handiwork
of the Tohono O'odham tribe, including jewelry, pottery, friendship bowls,
and baskets with man-in-the-maze designs. ⊠ *San Xavier Rd., South,
9 mi southwest of Tucson on I–19,* ☎ *520/294–2624* ⊕ *www.
sanxaviermission.org* ☞ *Free* ☉ *Church daily 7–5, gift shop daily 8–5.*

**need a
break?**
For wonderful Indian fry bread—large, round pieces of dough taken
fresh from the hot oil and topped with all sorts of delicious sweet or
savory additions like honey, powdered sugar, beans, meats, or green
chilies—stop in the **Wa:k Snack Shop** (☎ no phone) at the back of
San Xavier Plaza. You can also have breakfast or a lunch of Mexican
food here, and if you're lucky, local dancers will be performing for
one of the many tour groups that stop here.

☺ ②⑧ Old Tucson Studios. This film studio–cum–theme park, originally built
for the 1940 motion picture *Arizona,* has been used to shoot countless
movies from *Rio Bravo* (1959) to *The Quick and the Dead* (1994) and
TV shows from *Gunsmoke* and *Bonanza* to *Highway to Heaven.* Ac-
tors in Western garb perform and roam the streets talking to visitors.
Youngsters enjoy the simulated gunfights, rides, stunt shows, and petting farm, while adults might appreciate the screenings of old Westerns
and the little-bit-bawdy Grand Palace Hotel's Dance Hall Revue. There
are plenty of places to chow down and to buy souvenirs. ⊠ *Tucson Mountain Park, 201 S. Kinney Rd., Westside* ☎ *520/883–0100* ⊕ *www.
oldtucson.com* ☞ *$14.95* ☉ *Daily 10–6.*

③⓪ Saguaro National Park West. This is the smaller (24,000 acres), more heav-
Fodor'sChoice ily visited section of the national park that flanks Tucson; the other unit
★ is east of the city. Together, the sections have the world's largest concentration of the saguaro cactus.

A native to the Sonoran Desert, the saguaro is known for its towering
height (often 50 ft) and arms that reach out in weird configurations. The
cactus is ribbed vertically with accordionlike pleats that expand to store
water gathered through its shallow roots during the infrequent desert
rain showers. In spring (usually April or May), the giant succulent's top
is covered with tiny white blooms. At any time of year, the sight of these
kings of the desert ruling over their quiet domain is awe-inspiring. The
slow-growing cacti (they can take up to 15 years to grow a foot and 75
years to grow their first arm) are protected by state and federal laws,
so enjoy but don't disturb them.

Before you venture into the desert, it's worth stopping in at the impressive Red Hills Visitor Center. A slide show (given every half hour from 8:30 to 4:30) offers a Native American perspective of the saguaro cactus, and a lifelike display simulates the flora and fauna of the region. A drive through the park on an unpaved loop takes ½–2 hours depending on how many stops you make. Ask how to get to Signal Hill, where you can inspect petroglyphs (rock drawings) left by the Hohokam Indians centuries ago. ✉ *2700 N. Kinney Rd., Westside, 2 mi north of Arizona–Sonora Desert Museum entrance* ☎ *520/733-5158* ⊕ *www.nps. gov/sagu* ✍ *Free* ⊙ *Visitor center daily 8:30–5, park roads daily sunrise–sunset.*

WHERE TO EAT

Residents have long boasted about Tucson's Mexican food, boldly proclaiming their town "Mexican Food Capital of the U.S." Most of the Mexican food in town is Sonoran style—native to the adjoining Mexican state of Sonora—a cuisine now familiar to most Americans, since it uses cheese, mild peppers, corn tortillas, pinto beans, and beef or chicken. Tucson is the birthplace of the *chimichanga* (Spanish for "whatchamacallit"), a flour tortilla filled with meat or cheese, rolled and deep-fried. All traditional Mexican restaurants serve mild and hot salsa, but test carefully, because Southwesterners have liberal ideas regarding spices. Southwestern cuisine ranges from barbecue and cowboy steaks to light nouvelle dishes, and you'll also find good ethnic restaurants, from Japanese to Cajun.

Although the city's selection of restaurants is impressive, Tucson doesn't offer much in the way of late-night dining. Most restaurants in town are shuttered by 10 PM; some spots that keep later hours are noted below.

Costs

WHAT IT COSTS				
$$$$	**$$$**	**$$**	**$**	**¢**
AT DINNER over $30	$20–$30	$12–$20	$8–$12	under $8

Prices are per person for a main course. The final tab will include sales tax of 7%.

Northwest Tucson

Contemporary

$$–$$$ ✕ **Soleil.** Watch the sun set over the Tucson Mountains from either the outdoor terrace or the panoramic picture window inside—then gaze at the twinkling city lights below as you feast on contemporary French fare. Try a selection from the champagne bar, even if you don't usually indulge in bubbly. After dinner, take a stroll into the surrounding fine art galleries in this imaginatively designed shopping complex. ✉ *3001 E. Skyline Dr., Northwest* ☎ *520/299-3345* ▤ *AE, D, MC, V* ⊙ *Closed Mon.*

★ **$$–$$$** ✕ **Wildflower Grill.** This airy, bright restaurant is well known for its creative American fare and stunning presentation. Everything tastes as good as it sounds on the menu, which offers compelling choices like warm Maine lobster salad; bow-tie pasta with grilled chicken, tomatoes, spinach, and pine nuts; and rack of lamb with a Dijon crust (this dish pairs well with an accompaniment from the bar's popular martini menu). Desserts are equally top-notch. ✉ *7037 N. Oracle Rd., Northwest* ☎ *520/219-4230* ▤ *AE, D, DC, MC, V* ⊙ *No lunch Sun.*

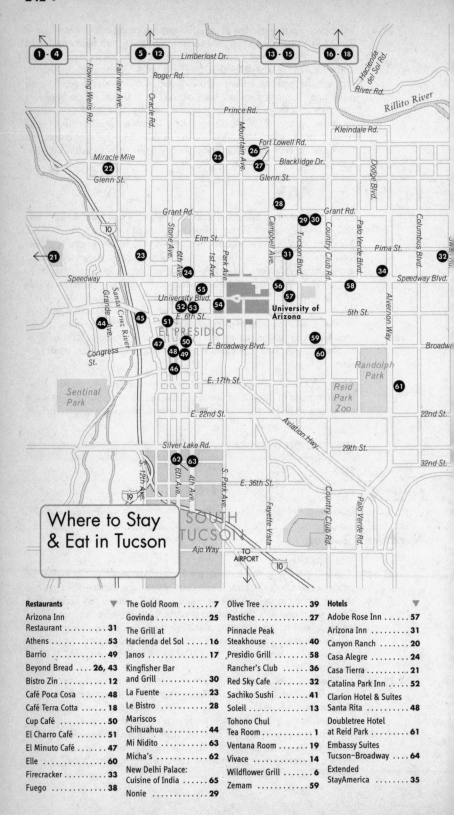

Where to Stay & Eat in Tucson

Southwestern

$$–$$$$ ✕ **The Gold Room.** Every seat in this spacious, elegant, and quiet dining room affords a spectacular view of the city below. The creative fare includes such classics as sautéed halibut and roasted rack of lamb in truffle port sauce as well as regional specialties such as mesquite-grilled buffalo sirloin. Many of the herbs and vegetables that flavor and garnish the artistically presented dishes are grown on site. ⊠ *Westward Look Resort, 245 E. Ina Rd., Northwest* ☎ *520/297–1151* ⊟ *AE, DC, MC, V.*

¢–$ ✕ **Tohono Chul Tea Room.** The food is fine, but what stands out here is the tearoom's location—inside a wildlife sanctuary and surrounded by a cactus garden. The interior is typically Southwestern, with Mexican tile, light wood, and a cobblestone patio, and the menu covers Southwestern, Mexican, and American dishes. House favorites include tortilla chicken soup with avocado, served with bread and scones baked on the premises, and grilled raspberry chipotle chicken. Open daily 8 to 5, the Tea Room is popular for Sunday brunch—which can mean long waits in high season. ⊠ *Tohono Chul Park, 7366 N. Paseo del Norte, Northwest* ☎ *520/797–1222* ⊟ *AE, MC, V* ☉ *No dinner.*

Catalina Foothills (North)

Italian

$$–$$$ ✕ **Vivace.** This nouvelle Italian bistro in the lovely St. Philip's Plaza is a consistent favorite with Tucsonans. Wild mushrooms and goat cheese in puff pastry is hard to resist as a starter. For a lighter alternative to such entrées as a rich osso buco, try the fettuccine with grilled salmon. For dessert, the chocolate molten cake, served with spumoni ice cream, is worth the 20 minutes it takes to create. Patio seating, which overlooks an expansive garden, is especially inviting on warm evenings. ⊠ *4310 N. Campbell Ave., Foothills* ☎ *520/795–7221* ⊟ *AE, D, MC, V* ☉ *No lunch Sun.*

Southwestern

★ $$$–$$$$ ✕ **The Grill at Hacienda del Sol.** Tucked into the foothills and surrounded by flowering gardens, this special-occasion restaurant provides a welcome alternative to the chili-laden dishes of Southwestern nouvelle cuisine. The steamed chicken dumplings with Havarti cheese are well done; the pecan-grilled double breast of duckling with thyme on wild rice pilaf is a popular house specialty, and deservedly so. Save room for a selection of intense desserts. ⊠ *Hacienda del Sol Guest Ranch Resort, 5601 N. Hacienda del Sol Rd., Foothills* ☎ *520/529–3500* ⊟ *AE, DC, MC, V.*

$$$–$$$$
Fodor'sChoice
★
✕ **Janos.** Chef Janos Wilder was one of the first to reinvent Southwestern cuisine, and the menu, wine list, and service place this restaurant among the finest in the West. The hillside location is a stunning backdrop for such sumptuous selections as sweet and spicy glazed quail with butternut-squash cannelloni, salmon with a scallop mousse served on mascarpone polenta, and venison loin with chili-lime paste and pecans. Have a drink or a more casual meal of Caribbean fare next door at J Bar, a lively and lower-priced venue for Janos's innovative cuisine. ⊠ *Westin La Paloma, 3770 E. Sunrise Dr., Foothills* ☎ *520/615–6100* ⊟ *AE, DC, MC, V* ☉ *Closed Sun. No lunch.*

$$–$$$ ✕ **Café Terra Cotta.** Everything about this restaurant says Southwest— from the bright orange and purple walls, large windows and exposed beams to the contemporary art—but especially the food. Café Terra Cotta's specialties include duck two ways (grilled breast and duck *carnitas* spring roll), chiles rellenos, tortilla soup, and creative pizzas with toppings like goat cheese, artichokes, and herbed mozzarella. This is the ultimate casual yet classy place to dine in town. ⊠ *3500 E. Sunrise Dr., Foothills* ☎ *520/577–8100* ⊟ *AE, D, DC, MC, V.*

Downtown Tucson and 4th Avenue

Contemporary

$$–$$$ ✕ **Barrio.** This trendy grill serves the most innovative cuisine in the downtown area and is at its liveliest at lunchtime. Try a "little plate" of black tiger shrimp rubbed with tamarind paste, or stuffed Anaheim chile in red bell pepper cream. Entrées range from simple but delicious fish tacos to linguine with chicken, dried papaya, and mango in a chipotle chardonnay cream sauce. Save room for an elegant dessert of fresh berries drenched in crème anglaise or a chilled chocolate custard topped with caramel. ⊠ *135 S. 6th Ave., Downtown* ☎ *520/629–0191* ⊟ *AE, D, DC, MC, V* ☉ *Closed Mon. No lunch weekends.*

¢–$$ ✕ **Cup Café.** This charming spot off the lobby of Hotel Congress is at the epicenter of Tucson's hippest downtown scene, but it's also a down-home, friendly place. Try Eggs in Hell (with green chile, salsa, and cayenne pepper) for breakfast or the Queer Steer Burger (a veggie burger) for lunch. The Heartbreaker appetizer (Brie melted over artichoke hearts and apple slices on a baguette) complements such entrées as chicken satay or grilled salmon. Open until 11 PM, until midnight on weekends, it becomes interestingly crowded in the evening with patrons from the Club Congress, the hotel nightclub. ⊠ *Hotel Congress, 311 E. Congress St., Downtown* ☎ *520/798–1618* ⊟ *AE, D, MC, V.*

Greek

$–$$ ✕ **Athens.** The dining room in this Greek oasis of tranquillity off bustling 4th Avenue is furnished with lace curtains, wooden wainscoting, white stucco walls, and potted plants. Order a dish of creamy *taramasalata* (a Greek dip made with roe) followed by *kotopoulo stin pita* (grilled chicken breast with a yogurt-cucumber sauce on freshly baked pita). If it's Greek comfort food you're after, order the moussaka or the *pastitsio* (a casserole made with pasta, meat, and béchamel). The house favorite is braised lamb shoulder in red wine sauce over pasta—call to reserve your order ahead of time. ⊠ *500 N. 4th Ave., at 6th St., University* ☎ *520/624–6886* ⊟ *AE, D, DC, MC, V* ☉ *Closed Sun. No lunch.*

Mexican

$$ ✕ **Café Poca Cosa.** In what is arguably Tucson's most innovative Mex-

FodorsChoice ican restaurant, chef-owner Susana Davila creates exciting recipes in-

★ spired by different regions of her native Mexico. The menu, which changes daily, might include *pollo à mole* (chicken in a spicy chocolate-based sauce) or pork *pibil* (made with a tangy Yucatán barbecue seasoning). Servings are plentiful, and each table gets a stack of warm corn tortillas and a bowl of beans to share. Order the daily Plato Poca Cosa, and the chef will select one beef, one chicken, and one vegetarian entrée for you to sample. ⊠ *88 E. Broadway Blvd., beside the Clarion Santa Rita, Downtown* ☎ *520/622–6400* ⊟ *MC, V* ☉ *Closed Sun.*

¢–$$ ✕ **El Charro Café.** Started by Monica Flin in 1922 and run by her grandniece today, El Charro still serves excellent versions of the Mexican-American staples Flin claims to have originated, most notably chimichangas (deep-fried flour tortillas filled with seasoned beef or chicken) and cheese crisps. Daily "fitness-fare" specials such as seafood enchiladas are delicious as well as healthful. The *carne seca* chimichanga, made with meat that is dried on the premises—on the roof, actually—is delicious. ⊠ *311 N. Court Ave., Downtown* ☎ *520/622–1922* ⊟ *AE, D, DC, MC, V.*

¢–$ ✕ **El Minuto Café.** This brightly decorated, bustling restaurant in Tucson's historic barrio is where local families come to eat, and it's equally popular with the business crowd at lunch. Open until midnight Friday and Saturday and until 10 PM the rest of the week, it's also a good bet for those seeking a late meal downtown. For more than 50 years, El Minuto has served up *topopo* salads (a crispy tortilla shell heaped with beans, guacamole, and many other ingredients); huge burritos; and green-corn tamales (in season) made just right. The spicy *menudo* (tripe soup) is reputed to be a great hangover remedy. ⊠ *354 S. Main Ave., Downtown* ☎ *520/882–4145* ⊟ *AE, D, DC, MC, V.*

¢–$$ ✕ **Mariscos Chihuahua.** Brightly lit, cheerful, and scrupulously clean, this Mexican restaurant is popular with the Tucsonans looking for a break from the usual Sonoran offerings. This one specializes in fresh—by which they mean uncooked—seafood cocktails. Tostadas seviche–style loads diced seafood atop a corn tortilla, with plenty of salsa to spice it up. There is a sizable menu of well-prepared cooked seafood as well, highlighted by the Seven Seas Soup, with all manner of fish and shellfish, and by the *camarones al mojo de ajo* (sautéed shrimp sautéed in a garlic sauce). Open 9–9 daily, it draws a significant crowd noon and night. ⊠ *1009 N. Grande Ave., Downtown* ☎ *520/623–3563* ⊟ *AE, D, DC, MC, V.*

South Tucson

Mexican

¢–$ ✕ **Mi Nidito.** A perennial favorite among locals (be prepared to wait awhile
FodorsChoice at dinnertime), Mi Nidito has also hosted its share of visiting celebri-
★ ties. Following President Clinton's lunch here, the rather hefty "Presidential Plate" (bean tostada, taco with barbecued meat, chile relleno, chicken enchilada, and beef tamale with rice and beans) was added to the menu. Top that off with the mango chimichangas for dessert, and you're talkin' executive privilege. ⊠ *1813 S. 4th Ave., South* ☎ *520/622–5081* ⊟ *AE, DC, MC, V* ☉ *Closed Mon.–Tues.*

¢–$ ✕ **Micha's.** Family-owned for 24 years, this local institution, though a simple Mexican diner (don't expect much atmosphere), serves some of the best Sonoran classics this side of the border. House specialties include *machaca* (shredded beef) enchiladas and chimichangas, and *cocido,* a hearty vegetable beef soup. Homemade chorizo spices up breakfast, which is served daily. ⊠ *2908 S. 4th Ave., South* ☎ *520/623–5307* ⊟ *AE, DC, MC, V* ☉ *No dinner Mon.*

Central Tucson

American

$$–$$$ ✕ **Kingfisher Bar and Grill.** Chic yet cozy and serving imaginative American cuisine, Kingfisher is a standout. Brightly colored panels of turquoise and terra-cotta combine with neon lighting and black banquettes to lend a feeling of intimacy as well as sophistication. Although the emphasis is on fresh seafood (including oysters and mussels), the kitchen does baby-back pork ribs and New York steak with equal success. Try the delicately battered fish-and-chips or the clam chowder on the late-night menu, served from 10 PM to midnight. ⊠ *2564 E. Grant Rd., Central* ☎ *520/323–7739* ⊟ *AE, D, DC, MC, V* ☉ *No lunch weekends.*

American Casual

¢ ✕ **Beyond Bread.** This bakery bustles with a morning and afternoon crowd and bakes 27 varieties of bread. Highlights from the huge sandwich menu include Annie's Addiction (hummus, tomato, sprouts, red onion, and cucumber on a roll) and Brad's Beef (roast beef, provolone, onion, green chilies, and Russian dressing on white bread). Eat inside or on the patio, or order takeout and munch on daily samples while you wait. Be sure to splurge on at least one of the incredible desserts. Popular demand has extended shop hours through dinner. ⊠ *3026 N. Campbell Ave.,*

Central ☎ *520/322–9965* ✉ *6260 E. Speedway Blvd., Eastside* ☎ *520/747–7477* ▭ *AE, D, MC, V.*

Cajun/Creole

¢–$$ ✕ **Nonie.** Owned by author Elmore Leonard's son, Chris, who named it for his grandmother, this restaurant has the flamboyant style of a New Orleans bistro with the good food to match. Add friendly, fast service and a hopping dose of Cajun music, and you get the idea. Try the tail gators (minced alligator tail meat, breaded and deep-fried) even if you've never eaten alligator, and you'll wish your local market carried them. It may be hard to save room for dessert, but the pecan pie and bread pudding are the standouts. ✉ *2526 E. Grant Rd., Central* ☎ *520/319–1965* ▭ *AE, MC, V* ✆ *Closed Mon. No lunch weekends.*

Contemporary

$$–$$$ ✕ **Bistro Zin.** French cooking meets American comfort food here at the hip sister restaurant to Wildflower Grill. While lunch hums with the business crowd, at night it's a place to see and be seen for a wide range of folks—everyone from singles in their twenties and thirties to a good number of older couples, too. Indulge in their delicately flaky chicken pot-pie and french fries, or the succulent maple leaf duck in drunken-cherry sauce. One hundred wines are available by the glass or "flight"—three tastes of the same type of wine from various vintners. ✉ *1865 E. River Rd., Central* ☎ *520/299–7799* ▭ *AE, D, DC, MC, V* ✆ *No lunch Sun.*

$$–$$$ ✕ **Pastiche.** With local artists' colorful work lining the walls, this popular spot for lunch and dinner is bright and airy. As is appropriate for a place named Pastiche, the menu has an eclectic mix of dishes. A favorite starter is the mushroom soufflé, made with an Asiago cream sauce and topped with fried leeks. Other highlights include the Canadian crab cakes and the thyme-crusted sea bass with smoked tomatoes and capers. The full menu is served until midnight; come in after 10 PM for half-price appetizers. ✉ *3025 N. Campbell Ave., Central* ☎ *520/325–3333* ▭ *AE, D, DC, MC, V* ✆ *No lunch weekends.*

$–$$$ ✕ **Elle.** This self-described "wine country restaurant" is influenced by northern Californian, French, and Italian cuisines. The dining area is open and expansive, with contemporary furniture and slate floors. Choose from a long list of pasta dishes, including squash ravioli with spinach, mushrooms, and sage butter, or, if you're game, try the grilled venison in roasted garlic sauce with rosemary polenta. Your server can provide expert assistance in selecting the perfect wine to complement your meal. ✉ *3048 E. Broadway Blvd., Central* ☎ *520/327–0500* ▭ *AE, DC, MC, V* ✆ *Closed Sun. No lunch Sat.*

$–$$ ✕ **Red Sky Cafe.** Trained in Paris at La Varenne, chef-owner Steve Schultz returned to Tucson to create his own contemporary cuisine, a fusion of French, Californian, and Southwestern flavors. The result is well-prepared, exquisitely presented meals for half the price you'd pay elsewhere. Schultz's enthusiasm pervades the Red Sky—you're made to feel like you have personally inspired every dish brought out from the kitchen. For a starter, try the foie gras with a potato pancake. All main courses include soup or salad made with fresh (and often exotic) produce from the U of A's greenhouses. ✉ *1661 N. Swan Rd., Central* ☎ *520/326–5454* ▭ *AE, MC, V* ✆ *Closed Sun.*

Continental

$$$–$$$$ ✕ **Arizona Inn Restaurant.** Executive chef Odell Baskerville presides over one of Tucson's most elegant restaurants. Dine on the patio overlooking the lush grounds of this inn, or enjoy the view from the dining room, a light, airy place with Southwestern details from the 1930s. The culinary range is broad, from bouillabaisse to a vegetarian corn and but-

ternut squash cannelloni with a carrot beurre blanc. Locals come in for Sunday brunch or a civilized afternoon high tea in the library (late November–mid-April only). There is no dress code, but men may feel most comfortable in a jacket. ⊠ *Arizona Inn, 2200 E. Elm St., Central* ☎ *520/325–1541* ▭ *AE, MC, V.*

Ethiopian

¢ ✕ **Zemam.** It can be hard at most times of the year to get a table in this small, humble eatery (in the summer, the lack of air-conditioning presents a challenge). The sampler plate of any three items allows you to try such dishes as *yesimir wat* (a spicy lentil-based dish) and *lega tibs* (a milder beef dish with a tomato sauce). Most of the food has a stew-like consistency; don't come if you feel the need to crunch. Everything is served on a communal platter topped with *injera,* a spongy bread, and eaten with the hands. Prices are incredibly low, considering the food quality and quantity. ⊠ *2731 E. Broadway Blvd., Central* ☎ *520/323–9928* ⌨ *Reservations not accepted* ▭ *MC, V* 🍴 *BYOB* ⊘ *Closed Mon.*

French

★ $$–$$$ ✕ **Le Bistro.** Art nouveau–etched mirrors and potted palms grace the walls of this French restaurant. The elegant yet unpretentious dining room is matched by the splendid creations of chef-owner Laurent Reux, a native of Brittany. House specialties include escargots cooked in garlic butter under a dome of puff pastry, ginger-crusted salmon in lime butter, and roasted quail flambéed with cognac. Lunch is reasonably priced, and many Tucsonans claim that the desserts here—proudly displayed as you walk in—are the best in town. ⊠ *2574 N. Campbell Ave., Central* ☎ *520/327–3086* ▭ *AE, D, MC, V* ⊘ *No lunch weekends, no dinner Mon.*

Mexican

¢–$$ ✕ **La Fuente.** Frank Davis owns and plays host at this family-run restaurant, long a staple of Tucson nightlife. The plain exterior belies the extravagant gardenlike interior, which bursts with color, plants, light, and the sound of quality mariachi music nightly. Diners can enjoy traditional Sonoran cuisine, including sea bass Yucatán style and enchiladas *a la bandera,* with green (guacamole), white (sour cream), and red (chili) representing the Mexican flag. The chicken mole poblano—with a spicy, dark sauce based on nuts and chocolate—is an authentic new-world dish. ⊠ *1749 N. Oracle Rd., Central* ☎ *520/623–8659* ▭ *AE, DC, MC, V.*

Pan-Asian

$–$$ ✕ **Firecracker.** Splitting the difference between Chinese and Pacific Rim fare, this restaurant enjoys a popularity with those who like their Asian food a little on the nouvelle side. The *ahi katsu*—fresh ahi tuna wrapped in spinach and seaweed, then breaded and flash-fried—makes for a flavorful opening. Wasabi-cream chicken breast with Thai chili soy sauce is zesty and hot; the flavorful Beijing pork is roasted with sweet plum sauce. Bananas Firecracker (Foster to the rest of us) or a dense, flourless chocolate torte brings a fitting end to the meal. ⊠ *2990 N. Swan Rd., Central* ☎ *520/318–1118* ▭ *AE, D, MC, V.*

Steak

$$–$$$ ✕ **Rancher's Club.** Wood-burning grills are the key to the success of this upscale Western-style restaurant, where the walls have side saddles, dark-wood paneling, and old photos of real cowboys. The attentive staff will help you choose the right timber—different woods impart different flavors—for your taste buds: mesquite, apple wood, and wild cherrywood are your choices. Sauces and condiments offer more traditional

flavorings for the excellent and very large steaks (sharing is encouraged). Good fish and poultry dishes are also available, and local movers and shakers like to gather here for lunch. ⊠ *Sheraton Tucson Hotel, 5151 E. Grant Rd., Central* ☎ *520/321–7621* 🖃 *AE, D, DC, MC, V* ⊗ *Closed Sun. No lunch Sat., no dinner Mon.*

Vegetarian

¢–$ ✕ **Govinda.** One of the few places in town with a strictly meatless menu, this Hare Krishna–run restaurant has reasonably priced all-you-can-eat lunch and dinner buffets, which include vegan options. Hot and cold dishes vary daily, but ingredients are consistently fresh, and the food is tasty if not spicy. Choose from three seating areas, including an outdoor patio with a koi pond and an aviary, where you can hear the calls of the resident peacocks. No alcohol is served or permitted. ⊠ *711 E. Black-lidge Dr., Central* ☎ *520/792–0630* ⚑ *Reservations not accepted* 🖃 *MC, V* ⊗ *Closed Sun.–Mon. No lunch Tues.*

Northeast Tucson

Continental

$$$$ ✕ **Ventana Room.** This very formal restaurant is a triumph of dining elegance: muted colors, a see-through fireplace, grand views of the city lights, a classical guitarist, and waiters who attend to every detail. The contemporary Continental menu contain such entrées as a mixed grill of game (venison, quail, and buffalo) with black barley and huckleberries, and potato-wrapped striped sea bass with spinach, tomato timbale, and sweet-basil beurre blanc. There's also a spa tasting menu ($55) for those watching fat and calories. ⊠ *Loews Ventana Canyon Resort, 7000 N. Resort Dr., Northeast* ☎ *520/299–2020 Ext. 5194* 🏛 *Jacket required* 🖃 *AE, D, DC, MC, V* ⊗ *No lunch.*

Greek

$$–$$$ ✕ **Olive Tree.** In a modern Santa Fe–style building, the Olive Tree serves up fine versions of such Greek standards as moussaka, shish kebab, and stuffed grape leaves, but it has more unusual dishes on its menu as well. The Lamb Bandit is baked in foil with two types of cheese, potatoes, and vegetables. Leg of lamb is roasted in wine and served with a well-prepared orzo. Daily fresh-fish specials are broiled or sautéed in garlic, oregano, and olive oil. This is not light cuisine. If you don't have room for super-sweet baklava, a cup of strong Greek coffee makes for a satisfying finish. ⊠ *7000 E. Tanque Verde Rd., Northeast* ☎ *520/298–1845* 🖃 *AE, DC, MC, V* ⊗ *No lunch.*

Southwestern

$$ ✕ **Fuego.** The "fire" of Alan Zeman's cooking refers not so much to hot and spicy fare but to the flambéed chorizo and tequila shrimp appetizer, which can start your meal off with tableside pyrotechnics. Fresh oysters and seafood, prickly-pear pork tenderloin, and ostrich (served according to the chef's mood that day) are all tasty selections at this comfortable bar and grill with knotty-pine floors and cozy brick fireplace. Many children will find the kids' menu here more appealing than most, with tacos and pastas as well as the usual burger and chicken-finger fare. ⊠ *6958 E. Tanque Verde Rd., Northeast* ☎ *520/886–1745* 🖃 *AE, MC, V* ⊗ *No lunch.*

Eastside

Indian

$–$$ ✕ **New Delhi Palace: Cuisine of India.** Vegetarians, carnivores, and seafood lovers will all find something to enjoy at this savory Indian restaurant, where the rich scent of curry greets you upon arrival. The congenial staff is helpful in explaining the menu, which includes lots of tandoori dishes, curries, rice, and breads. The "heat" of each dish can be adjusted to individual preference by the chef. ⊠ *6751 E. Broadway Blvd., Eastside* ☎ *520/296–8585* ⊟ *AE, MC, V.*

Japanese

$–$$ ╳ **Sachiko Sushi.** Perfectly prepared sushi, generous combinations of tempura and teriyaki, and friendly service greet you at what many locals consider the best Japanese restaurant in Tucson. Sit at the sushi bar and chat with owner-chef Tomio while you dine. Try a bowl of udon noodles, served in broth with assorted meat, seafood, or vegetables. The dish is a satisfying meal in itself. ⊠ *1101 Wilmot Rd., Eastside* ☎ *520/886–7000* ⊟ *AE, DC, MC, V* ☉ *No lunch Sun.*

Steak

¢–$$ ╳ **Pinnacle Peak Steakhouse.** Anybody caught eating newfangled foods like fish tacos or cactus jelly here would probably be hanged from the rafters—along with all the ties snipped from city slickers who overdressed. This cowboy steak house serves excellent mesquite-broiled steak (and chicken and grilled fish) with salad and pinto beans. The restaurant is part of Trail Dust Town, a re-creation of a turn-of-the-20th-century town, complete with a working antique carousel, a narrow-gauge train, and souvenir shops. Gunfights are staged in the street outside nightly at 7, 8, and 9. ⊠ *6541 E. Tanque Verde Rd., Eastside* ☎ *520/296–0911* ⚘ *Reservations not accepted* ⊟ *AE, D, DC, MC, V* ☉ *No lunch.*

WHERE TO STAY

In Tucson you can choose from luxurious desert resorts, basic accommodations offered by small- to medium-size hotels and motels, or area bed-and-breakfasts ranging from bedrooms in modest homes to private cottages nestled on wildlife preserves. Southwestern-style "dude" ranches—some of them former cattle ranches from the 1800s—are on the outskirts of town. Unless otherwise indicated, price categories for guest ranches include all meals and most activities.

Summer rates (April 15–September) are up to 60% lower than those in the winter. Note that unless you book months in advance, you'll be hard-pressed to find a Tucson hotel room at any price the week before and during the huge gem and mineral show, which is usually held in February.

Costs

WHAT IT COSTS				
$$$$	**$$$**	**$$**	**$**	**¢**
FOR 2 PEOPLE	over $250	$175–$250	$100–$175	$80–$100	under $80

Prices are for two people in a standard double room in high season.

Northwest Tucson

$$$$ ▦ **Lazy K Bar Guest Ranch.** In the Tucson Mountains, 16 mi northwest of town at an altitude of 2,300 ft, this family-oriented guest ranch accommodates both greenhorns and more experienced riders. Guest rooms are in eight *casitas*, or cottages. Those in the older structures, made of Mexican stucco, have fireplaces and wood-beam ceilings; rooms in the newer, adobe-brick buildings are larger and more modern. Rides are twice-daily, but you can also enjoy guided hikes, cookouts, hayrides, and rock climbing. There are plenty of hammocks, a heated pool, and a hot tub to relax those post-equestrian muscles. There's a three-night minimum stay. ⊠ *8401 N. Scenic Dr., Northwest, 85743* ☎ *520/744–3050 or 800/ 321–7018* 🖷 *520/744–7628* ⊕ *www.lazykbar.com* 🖙 *19 rooms, 4 suites* ♿ *Picnic area, pool, outdoor hot tub, hiking, horseback riding, library, meeting rooms, airport shuttle, no-smoking rooms; no room phones, no room TVs* ⊟ *AE, D, MC, V* ⏍ *FAP.*

★ **$$$$** 🖭 **Miraval.** Giving Canyon Ranch a run for its money, this New Age health spa 30 mi north of Tucson has a secluded desert setting and beautiful Southwestern rooms. The majority of its myriad spa services and wellness programs are based on Eastern philosophies. Whether you prefer to be pampered with a hot stone massage, seaweed body mask, Dead Sea salt scrub; get involved in the many fitness and nature activities; or just do yoga and meditate, it's all here. All gratuities and meals, including tasty buffets (with calories and fat content noted, of course), are included. ⊠ *5000 E. Via Estancia Miraval, Northwest, Catalina 85739* ☎ *520/825–4000 or 800/825–4000* 🖷 *520/825–5163* ⊕ *www. miravalresort.com* 🖙 *106 rooms* ♿ *2 restaurants, 2 tennis courts, 3 pools, gym, spa, bicycles, croquet, horseback riding, bar* ⊟ *AE, D, DC, MC, V* ⏍ *FAP.*

$$$$ 🖭 **Hilton Tucson El Conquistador.** You'll know you're in the Southwest when you enter the lobby of this golf and tennis resort, where there's a huge copper mural of cowboys and cacti and a wide view of the rugged Santa Catalina Mountains. This friendly resort draws families and conventioneers, some taking advantage of lower summer rates for the excellent sports facilities. Rooms, either in private one-bedroom casitas or the main hotel building, are decorated in desert tones of taupe, sand, and gold, and some suites have kiva-style fireplaces. ⊠ *10000 N. Oracle Rd., Northwest, 85737* ☎ *520/544–5000 or 800/325–3525* 🖷 *520/ 544–1224* ⊕ *www.hiltonelconquistador.com* 🖙 *328 rooms, 57 suites, 43 casitas* ♿ *5 restaurants, 2 18-hole golf courses, 31 tennis courts, 3 pro shops, 4 pools, 2 gyms, spa, bicycles, basketball, horseback riding, racquetball, volleyball, piano bar, shops, business services, meeting rooms* ⊟ *AE, D, DC, MC, V.*

$$$$ 🖭 **White Stallion Ranch.** A 3,000-acre working cattle ranch run by the
FodorsChoice warm, hospitable True family since 1965, this place is the real deal. You
★ can ride up to four times daily, hike in the mountains, enjoy a hayride cookout, and even compete in team cattle penning. Most rooms retain their original Western furniture, and newer deluxe rooms have whirlpool baths or fireplaces. Rates include all meals, riding, and daily entertainment such as weekend rodeos, country line dancing, telescopic stargazing, and singing cowboy songs around a campfire. ⊠ *9251 W. Twin Peaks Rd., Northwest, 85743* ☎ *520/297–0252 or 888/977– 2624* 🖷 *520/744–2786* ⊕ *www.wsranch.com* 🖙 *24 rooms, 17 suites* ♿ *2 tennis courts, pool, hot tub, massage, basketball, billiards, horseback riding, horseshoes, Ping-Pong, shuffleboard, volleyball, bar, library, piano, recreation room, business services, airport shuttle; no room phones, no room TVs* ⊟ *No credit cards* ☾ *Closed June–Aug.* ⏍ *FAP.*

$$$–$$$$ 🖭 **Westward Look Resort.** Originally the 1912 homestead of William and Mary Watson, this laid-back place offers Southwestern character and all the amenities you expect at a major resort. The Watsons' original living room, with beautiful, dried ocotillo branches draped along the ceiling and antique furnishings, is now a comfortable lounge off the main lobby. The couple probably never envisioned anything like the New Age wellness center, offering hot desert stone massages and three-mud body masks. Spacious rooms have wrought-iron beds and Mission-style furniture. Borrow a bike or take a stroll along the beautiful and well-marked nature trails. ⊠ *245 E. Ina Rd., Northwest, 85704* ☎ *520/297–1151* *or 800/722–2500* 🖨 *520/297–9023* ⊕ *www.westwardlook.com* ⊅ *244 rooms* ♿ *2 restaurants, 8 tennis courts, 3 pools, gym, spa, mountain bikes, horseback riding, shop, concierge, business services, meeting rooms* ☰ *AE, D, DC, MC, V.*

$$ 🏨 **La Tierra Linda Guest Ranch Resort.** Off a quiet dirt road, this 30-acre ranch sits adjacent to Saguaro National Park West. Its adobe casitas, furnished in typical Southwestern style, range from standard double rooms to two-bedroom suites. Riding and hiking trails lead right into the park, and a stable offers horseback riding, roping instruction, and hayrides (for an additional fee). Check out the original fireplace with antique cannonballs and cave stalactites embedded in its masonry. Dinner is available for an additional fee. ⊠ *7501 N. Wade Rd., Northwest, 85743* 🕾 *520/744–7700 or 888/872–6241* 🖨 *520/579–9742* ⊕ *www. latierralinda.com* ⊅ *7 rooms, 7 suites* ♿ *Restaurant, room service, refrigerators, tennis court, pool, outdoor hot tub, hiking, horseback riding, bar, meeting rooms* ☰ *AE, D, DC, MC, V* ⦿ *BP.*

$$ 🏨 **Marriott TownePlace Suites.** With full kitchens in all of its studio, one-bedroom, and two-bedroom suites, this fresh newcomer is suitable for short or extended stays. In fact, the longer you stay, the lower your nightly rate. Its location is extremely handy, yet the interior hallways and the way the buildings are set back from the road make for a quiet retreat. Some suites have a view of the neighboring golf course, and a half-dozen are thoughtfully designed for wheelchair access. ⊠ *405 W. Rudasill Rd., Northwest, 85704* 🕾 *520/292–9697 or 800/257–3000* 🖨 *520/292–9884* ⊕ *www.towneplacesuites.com* ⊅ *77 suites* ♿ *Kitchens, pool, exercise equipment, laundry, Internet, no-smoking rooms* ☰ *AE, MC, V.*

¢–$ 🏨 **Quail's Vista Bed and Breakfast.** Innkeeper and former concierge Barbara Bauer and her husband, Richard, can direct you to all the best things to see and do in Tucson; some activities, include bird-watching or soaking in a hot tub on a redwood deck that looks out on the dramatic west face of the Santa Catalina Mountains, can be done right in the inn's backyard. Inside, peeled spruce columns support the beamed ceiling and thick, rounded walls of this rammed-earth adobe home. Fiesta dinnerware, Native American pottery, and bright Mexican blankets decorate the common area, which has cozy nooks for reading or watching the wildlife out the windows. ⊠ *826 E. Palisades Rd., Northwest, 85737* 🕾 *520/ 297–5980* ⊕ *www.quails-vista-bb.com* ⊅ *3 rooms, 1 with bath* ♿ *Hot tub, laundry facilities, Internet; no smoking* ☰ *No credit cards* ⊘ *Closed June–Sept.* ⦿ *CP.*

Catalina Foothills (North)

★ $$$$ 🏨 **Westin La Paloma.** Vying with the Hilton La Conquistador and Loews Ventana for convention business, this sprawling, pale pink resort offers views of the Santa Catalina Mountains above and the city below. It specializes in relaxation with an emphasis on fun: the golf, tennis, and spa facilities are top-notch, and the huge pool complex has an impressively long water slide, as well as a swim-up bar and grill for those who can't bear to leave the water. On-site child care and adults- and children-only pools make for a vacation the whole family will enjoy. Janos, one of Tucson's top restaurants, is also here. ⊠ *3800 E. Sunrise Dr., Foothills, 85718* 🕾 *520/742–6000 or 888/625–5144* 🖨 *520/577–5878* ⊕ *www. starwood.com* ⊅ *455 rooms, 32 suites* ♿ *4 restaurants, room service, in-room data ports, cable TV with movies and video games, 3 9-hole golf courses, 12 tennis courts, 3 pools, gym, hair salon, 3 outdoor hot tubs, spa, croquet, racquetball, volleyball, 2 bars, shops, children's programs (ages 6 months–12 years), business services, meeting rooms, no-smoking rooms* ☰ *AE, D, DC, MC, V.*

$$–$$$ ⊞ **Hacienda del Sol Guest Ranch Resort.** This 32-acre hideaway in the Santa Catalina foothills is part guest ranch, part resort, and entirely gracious. It's a charming and lower-priced alternative to the larger resorts. Designed in classic Mexican hacienda style, this former finishing school for girls attracted stars like Clark Gable, Katharine Hepburn, and Spencer Tracy when it was converted to a guest ranch during World War II. Some of the one- and two-bedroom casitas have fireplaces and private porches, where you can watch the sun set over the Tucson Mountains. The superb Grill at Hacienda del Sol is part of the resort. ⊠ *5601 N. Hacienda del Sol Rd., Foothills, 85718* ☎ *520/299–1501 or 800/ 728–6514* 🖷 *520/299–5554* ⊕ *www.haciendadelsol.com* 🖘 *22 rooms, 8 suites* ♢ *Restaurant, tennis court, pool, outdoor hot tub, horseback riding, shuffleboard, library, business services, meeting rooms* ☴ *AE, D, MC, V* ⊣⊙⊢ *CP.*

$$ ⊞ **Windmill Inn at St. Philip's Plaza.** This all-suite hotel is in a chic shopping plaza filled with glitzy boutiques and good restaurants. Each 500-square-ft suite has a small sitting area, wet bar, two TVs, and three telephones (local calls are free). A few dollars extra will buy you a view of the pool and fountain rather than the parking lot. Complimentary coffee, muffins, juice, and a newspaper are delivered to your door; additional breakfast goodies are set up in the lobby. The Windmill is centrally located, and free passes to a nearby gym are included. There are also bicycles available for excursions along the nearby Rillito River. ⊠ *4250 N. Campbell Ave., Foothills, 85718* ☎ *520/577–0007 or 800/ 547–4747* 🖷 *520/577–0045* ⊕ *www.windmillinns.com* 🖘 *122 suites* ♢ *Microwaves, refrigerators, pool, hot tub, bicycles, library, laundry facilities, business services* ☴ *AE, D, DC, MC, V* ⊣⊙⊢ *BP.*

West of Tucson

$$ ⊞ **Casa Tierra.** For a real desert experience, head out to this B&B on 5 acres near the Arizona–Sonora Desert Museum and Saguaro National Park West. For the last 1½ mi you'll be on a dirt road. All rooms have private patio entrances and look out onto a lovely central courtyard with a paloverde tree, desert foliage, and a fountain. The Southwestern-style furnishings include Mexican *equipales* (chairs with pigskin seats), tiled floors, and beamed ceilings. A full vegetarian breakfast served on fine china is included in the room rate, and there is a media room for those who can't stand the quiet. There's a minimum stay of two nights. ⊠ *11155 W. Calle Pima, Westside, 85743* ☎ *520/578–3058 or 866/ 254–0006* 🖷 *520/578–8445* ⊕ *www.casatierratucson.com* 🖘 *3 rooms, 1 suite* ♢ *Microwaves, refrigerators, gym, hot tub, recreation room; no room TVs* ☴ *AE, MC, V* ⊙ *Closed mid-June–mid-Aug.* ⊣⊙⊢ *BP.*

FodorsChoice ★

Downtown Tucson & University of Arizona

$$$ ⊞ **Arizona Inn.** Although close to the university and many sights, the beautifully landscaped lawns and gardens of this 1930 inn seem far away from it all. The spacious, individually decorated rooms are spread out over 14 acres in pink adobe-style casitas—most have private patios and some have fireplaces. The resort also has two luxurious two-story houses, which come with their own heated pools and full hotel service. The main building houses an elegant library, a fine restaurant, and a cocktail lounge, where an excellent jazz pianist plays. ⊠ *2200 E. Elm St., University, 85719* ☎ *520/325–1541 or 800/933–1093* 🖷 *520/881– 5830* ⊕ *www.arizonainn.com* 🖘 *70 rooms, 16 suites, 3 casitas* ♢ *2 restaurants, room service, 2 tennis courts, pool, gym, sauna, croquet, Ping-Pong, bar, library, dry cleaning, business services, meeting rooms* ☴ *AE, DC, MC, V.*

FodorsChoice ★

★ $$ ⊞ **Casa Alegre.** You'll enjoy poking around the knickknacks and antiques—everything from a hand-hewn Mexican mine shovel to an ornate 19th-century French clock—in Phyllis Florek's "Happy House," which is as comfortable as it is fascinating. The 1915 Arts and Crafts–style bungalow is near the university, 4th Avenue, and downtown, and it's a straight shot west from here to the Desert Museum and other attractions. Resting in the shade of the ramadas (the Southwest's version of a trellis or arbor) or taking a plunge into the pool or hot tub is an ideal end to a day of sightseeing. Breakfasts are copious and delicious. ⊠ *316 E. Speedway Blvd., University, 85705* ☎ *520/628–1800 or 800/628–5654* ☐ *520/792–1880* ⊕ *www.casaalegreinn.com* ⇨ *7 rooms* ⚐ *Pool, outdoor hot tub* ☐ *D, MC, V* ❙⊘❙ *BP.*

$$ ⊞ **Catalina Park Inn.** Classical music plays softly in the living room of this beautifully restored 1927 neoclassical house behind a gate in the West University neighborhood. The original art nouveau tile work and a butler's pantry are among many charming architectural details, and there's a lovely collection of blue-and-white china displayed in glass cabinets. All rooms include robes, irons, and hair dryers. You may be tempted to fill your suitcase with the papaya and lime scones that are part of breakfast. ⊠ *309 E. 1st St., University, 85705* ☎ *520/792–4541 or 800/792–4885* ⊕ *www.catalinaparkinn.com* ⇨ *6 rooms* ☐ *AE, D, MC, V* ❙⊘❙ *BP.*

$$ ⊞ **Four Points Sheraton Tucson University Plaza.** Formerly the Plaza Hotel, this high-rise has a prime location, across the street from the University of Arizona, two blocks from the University Medical Center, and at the intersection of two major bus routes. A favorite of visiting faculty, prospective students, and parents, as well as the spring training home of the Chicago White Sox, it is a no-nonsense hotel with an average restaurant. Fortunately, there are many other places to eat within walking or driving distance along Speedway or Campbell. ⊠ *1900 E. Speedway Blvd., University, 85719* ☎ *520/327–7341 or 888/625–5144* ☐ *520/327–0276* ⊕ *www.starwood.com* ⇨ *150 rooms* ⚐ *Restaurant, room service, cable TV, pool, gym, bar, lounge, meeting rooms, free parking* ☐ *AE, D, MC, V.*

$$ ⊞ **The Royal Elizabeth Bed and Breakfast Inn.** Fans of Victoriana will adore this B&B built in 1878 and owned for more than 100 years by the prominent Blenman family. Beautifully furnished with period antiques, the six rooms are spacious and are outfitted with ceiling fans. Two of the larger rooms have separate sitting areas and pull-out sofa beds. Gracious Southern hosts Robert and Jack take turns in the kitchen, preparing eye-opener Southwestern breakfasts that might include chiles rellenos and baked eggs in tomato shells. ⊠ *204 S. Scott Ave., Downtown, 85701* ☎ *520/670–9022* ☐ *520/679–9710* ⊕ *www.royalelizabeth.com* ⇨ *6 rooms* ⚐ *In-room VCRs, pool, hot tub, Internet; no smoking* ☐ *AE, MC, V* ❙⊘❙ *BP.*

★ $$ ⊞ **Tucson Marriott University Park.** With the University of Arizona less than a block from the front door, the Marriott is an ideal place to stay when visiting the campus. This immaculately clean and well-appointed hotel has a lush atrium lobby area that can be enjoyed from both the restaurant and bar. Visit the university shopping district's cafés, pubs, bookstores, and clothes stores—all within a short stroll. ⊠ *880 E. 2nd St., University, 85719* ☎ *520/792–4100 or 888/236–2427* ☐ *520/882–4100* ⊕ *www.marriott.com* ⇨ *234 rooms, 16 suites* ⚐ *Restaurant, room service, in-room data ports, some refrigerators, cable TV with movies, pool, gym, outdoor hot tub, sauna, lounge, laundry service, concierge floor, Internet, business services, meeting rooms* ☐ *AE, D, DC, MC, V.*

$–$$ ⊞ **Adobe Rose Inn.** In the historic Sam Hughes neighborhood just east of the university, this 1933 adobe offers three lodgepole pine–furnished rooms, two of which have beehive fireplaces and stained-glass windows. Two cottages also grace this property, which is within easy walking distance of shops, restaurants, and two major bus lines. Owner Joy Andrews's breakfasts, with dishes like Italian omelets or pecan pancakes, are enjoyed in a dining room overlooking the bougainvillea-draped pool area. ⊠ *940 N. Olsen Ave., University, 85719* ☎ *520/318–4644 or 800/328–4122* 📠 *520/325–0055* ⊕ *www.aroseinn.com* 🛏 *4 rooms, 1 suite* ⟑ *Dining room, cable TV, pool, outdoor hot tub; no smoking* 🖃 *AE, MC, V* ⦿ *BP.*

$–$$ 🏨 **Peppertrees B&B Inn.** This restored 1905 Victorian just east of the U of A campus affords a degree of privacy along with B&B camaraderie. Two appealing, contemporary-style guest houses at the rear of the tree-shaded main house have full kitchens, separate phone lines, washers and dryers, and individual patios. The antiques-filled main house (furnished with pieces from innkeeper Jill Light's family in England) has several guest rooms, as well as a separate one-bedroom apartment. Light, an award-winning pastry chef, prepares elaborate breakfasts for her visitors. ⊠ *724 E. University Blvd., University, 85719* ☎ *520/622–7167 or 800/348–5763* ⊕ *www.peppertreesinn.com* 🛏 *3 rooms, 1 suite, 2 guest houses* ⟑ *Some kitchens; no smoking* 🖃 *D, MC, V* ⦿ *BP.*

$
🏨 **Clarion Hotel & Suites Santa Rita.** The modest but lush, plant-filled lobby of this historic hotel has gleaming marble floors and a sunken lounge area with comfortable overstuffed couches and chairs. The rooms are standard, but breakfast, newspapers, and local phone calls are all on the house. Ask for a room with a view of the outdoor pool and waterfall, a lovely remnant of the original hotel. It's also where you'll find the excellent Café Poca Cosa. ⊠ *88 E. Broadway Blvd., Downtown, 85701* ☎ *520/622–4000 or 877/424–6423* 📠 *520/620–0376* ⊕ *www. clarionsantarita.com* 🛏 *139 rooms, 22 suites* ⟑ *Restaurant, microwaves, refrigerators, cable TV with movies, pool, gym, outdoor hot tub, sauna, library, dry cleaning, laundry service, some pets allowed (fee), no-smoking rooms* 🖃 *AE, D, DC, MC, V* ⦿ *CP.*

¢–$ 🏨 **Inn Suites Hotel & Resort.** Just north of downtown and the historic district, this hotel is next to I–10 but is nevertheless quiet. The large, peach-and-green Southwestern-theme rooms, circa 1980, face a lush interior courtyard with a sparkling pool and *palapas* (thatched open gazebos). Free daily extras such as a breakfast buffet, newspaper, and happy-hour cocktails, as well as a free barbecue every Wednesday night, help make this a haven in the center of the city. ⊠ *475 N. Granada Ave., Downtown, 85701* ☎ *520/622–3000 or 877/446–6589* 📠 *520/623–8922* ⊕ *www.innsuites.com* 🛏 *265 rooms, 35 suites* ⟑ *Restaurant, room service, microwaves, refrigerators, cable TV with movies and video games, pool, hot tub, volleyball, bar, playground, business services, meeting rooms, some pets allowed (fee)* 🖃 *AE, D, DC, MC, V* ⦿ *BP.*

¢ 🏨 **Hotel Congress.** This downtown hotel built in 1919 has been artfully restored to its original Western version of art deco. The gangster John Dillinger was almost caught here in 1934 (his luggage, filled with guns and ammo, was suspiciously heavy; he was captured later near the university). Each room has black-and-white tile baths and the original iron beds. Its convenient location downtown means it can be noisy: don't get a room over the popular Club Congress or you'll be up until the wee hours. A great place to stay for younger or more adventurous visitors, it's also a youth hostel and the center of Tucson's hippest scene. ⊠ *311 E. Congress St., Downtown, 85701* ☎ *520/622–8848 or 800/722–8848* 📠 *520/792–6366* ⊕ *www.hotcong.com* 🛏 *40 rooms* ⟑ *Restaurant, hair salon, bar, lobby lounge, nightclub* 🖃 *AE, D, MC, V.*

Central Tucson

$$ ▦ **Doubletree Hotel at Reid Park.** Convenient to the airport and to the center of town, this sprawling, contemporary-style hotel and conference center is across the road from the 36-hole municipal golf course at Randolph Park, which hosts the LPGA tournament every year. Most of the participants stay here. The park also has a pleasant jogging trail and a zoo; the large El Con shopping mall is nearby. ⊠ *445 S. Alvernon Way, Central, 85711* ☎ *520/881–4200 or 800/222–8733* 🖷 *520/323–5225* ⊕ *www.doubletree.com* ⤴ *295 rooms ⚲ 2 restaurants, room service, in-room data ports, cable TV with movies, 3 tennis courts, pool, gym, hair salon, hot tub, bar, video game room, dry cleaning, laundry service, business services, meeting rooms ⊟ AE, D, DC, MC, V* ⭐ *BP.*

$$ ▦ **Embassy Suites Tucson–Broadway.** Towering palms, red-tile roofs, and a hot-pink exterior greet you from the front of this centrally located property. The older but spacious two-room suites open onto a plant-filled atrium. Among the extras are a free cooked-to-order breakfast and nightly happy hour, passes to a local gym, and complimentary shuttle service to anywhere within 5 mi. The lounge has a large-screen television and billiard tables. ⊠ *5335 E. Broadway Blvd., Central, 85711* ☎ *520/745–2700 or 800/362–2779* 🖷 *520/790–9232* ⊕ *www. embassysuites.com* ⤴ *142 suites ⚲ In-room data ports, kitchenettes, pool, hot tub, billiards, recreation room, laundry facilities, business services, meeting rooms, some pets allowed ⊟ AE, D, DC, MC, V* ⭐ *BP.*

$$ ▦ **Varsity Clubs of America.** This time-share facility also doubles as a hotel, so it may have any or all of its suites available for rental at any given time. Its handy location is also a rather busy and noisy one. One- and two-bedroom suites have whirlpool tubs and full kitchens; alternatives to cooking include the Stadium Sports Grill downstairs or any of the several restaurants within walking distance. There's a billiard room and a cozy library with a fireplace. ⊠ *3855 E. Speedway Blvd., Central, 85716* ☎ *520/318–3777 or 888/594–2287* 🖷 *888/410–9770* ⊕ *www.ilxresorts.com* ⤴ *59 suites ⚲ Restaurant, kitchens, cable TV with movies and video games, pool, gym, hot tub, billiards, library ⊟ AE, D, MC, V.*

$ ▦ **Ghost Ranch Lodge.** A neon cow-skull sign lights up the entrance to the former Hotel Pack, which opened in 1941 on what was then the main road into Tucson. The single-story, Spanish tile-roof units are spread out over 8 acres that encompass an orange grove and cactus garden. Rooms are decorated with modern motel furnishings but retain original brick walls and sloped wood-beam ceilings. The cottages, with a separate kitchen, sitting area, and carport, are a bargain. While this retro property has been well maintained, it's a bit west of city central, and its neighbors now include strip clubs and hourly motels. ⊠ *801 W. Miracle Mile, Central, 85705* ☎ *520/791–7565 or 800/456–7565* 🖷 *520/791–3898* ⊕ *www.ghostranchlodge.com* ⤴ *72 rooms, 11 cottages ⚲ Restaurant, in-room data ports, some kitchenettes, cable TV, pool, hot tub, shuffleboard, bar, no-smoking rooms ⊟ AE, D, DC, MC, V* ⭐ *CP.*

¢ ▦ **Extended StayAmerica.** If you're seeking convenience and value (and don't mind a certain blandness), this modern chain property will suffice. All rooms have queen-size beds and recliner chairs. Don't expect a view or coffee in the lobby, but local calls are free, and you're two blocks' walk to the Crossroads Shopping Center, where there are restaurants, a Starbucks, a grocery store, shops, and a cinema. ⊠ *5050 E. Grant Rd., Central 85712* ☎ *520/795–9510 800/398–7829* 🖷 *520/795–9504* ⊕ *www.extendedstay.com* ⤴ *120 rooms ⚲ In-room data ports, kitchens, laundry facilities ⊟ AE, D, MC, V.*

Northeast Tucson

★ **$$$$** ▣ **Canyon Ranch.** The Canyon Ranch draws an international crowd of well-to-do health seekers to its superb spa facilities on 70 acres in the desert foothills. Two activity centers include an enormous spa complex and a Health and Healing Center, where dietitians, exercise physiologists, behavioral-health professionals, and medical staff attend to body and soul. Just about every type of physical activity is possible, from Pilates to guided hiking, and the food is plentiful and healthy. Rates include all meals, activities, taxes, and gratuities. There's a four-night minimum. ⊠ *8600 E. Rockcliff Rd., Northeast, 85750* ☎ *520/749–9000 or 800/742–9000* 🖷 *520/749–1646* ⊕ *www.canyonranch.com* ⇨ *240 rooms* ⚬ *Dining room, 8 tennis courts, pool, health club, spa, basketball, racquetball, squash, laundry facilities, airport shuttle* ⊟ *AE, D, MC, V* ¶◐ *FAP.*

★ **$$$–$$$$** ▣ **Loews Ventana Canyon Resort.** This is one of the most luxurious of the big resorts, with dramatic stone architecture and an 80-ft waterfall cascading down the mountains. Rooms, facing either the Catalinas or the golf course and city, are modern and elegantly furnished in muted earth tones and light woods; each bath has a miniature TV, a double-wide tub, and bubble bath. Dining options include everything from poolside snacks at Bill's Grill to fine Continental cuisine at the Ventana Room. The scenic Ventana Canyon trailhead is steps away, and there's a free shuttle to nearby Sabino Canyon. ⊠ *7000 N. Resort Dr., Northeast, 85750* ☎ *520/299–2020 or 800/234–5117* 🖷 *520/299–6832* ⊕ *www. loewshotels.com* ⇨ *384 rooms, 14 suites* ⚬ *4 restaurants, room service, in-room data ports, minibars, 2 18-hole golf courses, 8 tennis courts, pro shop, 2 pools, health club, spa, mountain bikes, croquet, hiking, bar, lobby lounge, shop, children's programs (ages 4–12), business services, meeting rooms* ⊟ *AE, D, DC, MC, V.*

$$ ▣ **Ramada Inn Foothills.** Families and business travelers stay in this Ramada on the northeastern side of town, close to many restaurants and Sabino Canyon. An attractive light stucco building with a Spanish tile roof and a fake bell tower, this property has serviceable, if generic, rooms and small suites. Complimentary beer and wine is served in the afternoon. The Southwestern restaurant next door, Fuego, provides room service. Free passes to a local health club are available, and golf and tennis facilities are nearby. ⊠ *6944 E. Tanque Verde Rd., Northeast, 85715* ☎ *520/886–9595 or 800/228–2828* 🖷 *520/721–8466* ⊕ *www.ramada. com* ⇨ *50 rooms, 63 suites* ⚬ *Room service, pool, sauna, laundry facilities, business services, meeting rooms, some pets allowed* ⊟ *AE, D, DC, MC, V* ¶◐ *CP.*

Eastside

$$$$ ▣ **Tanque Verde Ranch.** The most upscale of Tucson's guest ranches and one of the oldest in the country, the Tanque Verde sits on 640 beautiful acres in the Rincon Mountains next to Saguaro National Park East. Rooms in one-story casitas have tasteful Western-style furnishings, fireplaces, and picture-window views of the desert. Breakfast and lunch buffets are huge, and barbecues add variety to the daily dinner menu. Horseback excursions are offered for every skill level (lessons are included in rates), and children can participate in daylong activity programs, from riding to tennis to crafts, leaving parents to their leisure. ⊠ *14301 E. Speedway Blvd., Eastside, 85748* ☎ *520/296–6275 or 800/ 234–3833* 🖷 *520/721–9426* ⊕ *www.tanqueverderanch.com* ⇨ *49 rooms, 23 suites, 2 casitas* ⚬ *5 tennis courts, 2 pools (1 indoor), gym, hot tub, fishing, basketball, bicycles, hiking, horseback riding, horse-*

shoes, volleyball, children's programs (ages 4–11) ☰ *AE, D, MC, V* ⧈ *FAP.*

$$ ⬚ **The SunCatcher.** The four rooms in this B&B have been whimsically decorated in the style of four of the original owner's favorite hotels— the Connaught in London, the Regent in Hong Kong, the Oriental in Bangkok, and the Four Seasons in Chicago. All are charming. Focal points in the spacious living room are a large sunken seating area facing a copper-hooded fireplace and the mirrored mesquite wood bar where happy-hour snacks are served. If you're in the mood for watching a video, you can select from more than 100. All in all, it's a nice retreat after a day of sightseeing or hiking in nearby Saguaro National Park East. ✉ *105 N. Avda. Javelina, Eastside, 85748* ☎ *520/885–0883* ⊕ *www. thesuncatcher.com* ⬚ *4 rooms* ♨ *In-room VCRs, pool, hot tub, Internet; no kids, no smoking* ☰ *AE, D, MC, V* ⧈ *BP.*

$$ ⬚ **Tucson Hilton East.** This high-rise hotel and conference center is set comfortably back off a main road on the suburban side of town. An airy atrium lobby takes full advantage of the view of the Santa Catalina Mountains; better yet, push "6" in the glass elevator for a spectacular vista. The rooms are spacious and well tended but not particularly distinctive. ✉ *7600 E. Broadway Blvd., Eastside, 85710* ☎ *520/721–5600 or 800/774–1500* ⊟ *520/721–5696* ⊕ *www.hilton.com* ⬚ *225 rooms, 8 suites* ♨ *Restaurant, in-room data ports, cable TV, 2 pools, gym, outdoor hot tub, bar, business services, meeting rooms* ☰ *AE, D, DC, MC, V.*

¢ ⬚ **Smuggler's Inn.** At the corner of Wilmot Street and Speedway Boulevard, this comfortable suburban hotel, where you can park by your door, has easy access to Eastside activities and restaurants. A lushly landscaped central courtyard is the focus for the serviceable rooms, which have either a balcony or patio. A full, hot breakfast is included; you might also want to stock up on delectable treats from the Trader Joe's Market and Beyond Bread Bakery across the street. ✉ *6350 E. Speedway Blvd., Eastside, 85710* ☎ *520/296–3292 or 800/525–8852* ⊟ *520/722–3713* ⊕ *www.smugglersinn.com* ⬚ *150 rooms* ♨ *Restaurant, in-room data ports, cable TV with movies and video games, pool, outdoor hot tub, bar* ☰ *AE, D, MC, V* ⧈ *BP.*

NIGHTLIFE & THE ARTS

The Arts

Tucson, full of cultural activity for its size, is one of only 14 cities in the United States with a symphony as well as opera, theater, and ballet companies. Wintertime, when Tucson's population swells with vacationers, is the high season, but the arts are alive and well year-round. The low cost of Tucson's cultural events comes as a pleasant surprise to those accustomed to paying East or West Coast prices: symphony tickets are as little as $5 for some performances, and touring Broadway musicals can often be seen for $22. Parking is plentiful and frequently free.

The free *Tucson Weekly* (⊕ www.tucsonweekly.com), which hits the stands on Thursday, and the Friday "Caliente" section of the *Arizona Daily Star* (⊕ www.azstarnet.com) have complete listings of what's going on in town.

Downtown Saturday Night, an event held the first and third Saturday night of every month, keeps downtown art-district galleries, studios, and cafés hopping from 7 to 10. There's often dancing in the street—everything from calypso to square dancing—and musical performances ranging from jazz to gospel. Most of the activity takes place along Congress Street and Broadway Boulevard (from 4th Avenue to Stone Street) and along 5th and 6th avenues. You can also explore this area via such free guided tours as the Thursday Night Artwalk, or self-guided tours of art galleries and the historic districts. For more information contact the **Tucson Arts District Partnership, Inc.** (☎ 520/624–9977 ⊕ tucsonartsdistrict.org).

Much of the city's cultural activity takes place at or near the **Tucson Convention Center** (✉ 260 S. Church St., Downtown ☎ 520/791–4101, 520/791–4266 box office ⊕ www.ci.tucson.az.us/tcc) in the El Presidio neighborhood. Dance, music, and other kinds of performances take place at the University of Arizona's **Centennial Hall** (✉ 1020 E. University Blvd., University ☎ 520/621–3341 ⊕ uapresents.arizona.edu).

Each season brings visiting companies of opera, theater, and dance to Tucson, and tickets to many events can be purchased through **Ticketmaster** (✉ Robinsons-May, El Con Mall, 3435 E. Broadway Blvd., Central ☎ 520/795–3950 ✉ Robinsons-May, Tucson Mall, 4470 N. Oracle Rd., Central ☎ 520/292–0345 ⊕ www.ticketmaster.com) directly or from its outlets in the Robinsons-May stores.

Dance

Tucson shares its professional ballet company, **Ballet Arizona** (☎ 888/322–5538 ⊕ www.balletaz.org), with Phoenix. Performances, which range from classical to contemporary, are held at the Music Hall in the Tucson Convention Center. Tucson's most established modern dance company, **Orts Theatre of Dance** (✉ 930 N. Stone Ave., Downtown ☎ 520/624–3799 ⊕ www.orts.org) incorporates trapeze flying into the dances. Outdoor and indoor performances are staged throughout the year.

Music

A Wednesday-night chamber-music series is hosted by the **Arizona Friends of Chamber Music** (☎ 520/577–3769 ⊕ arizonachambermusic.org) at the Leo Rich Theater in the Tucson Convention Center from October through April. It also presents a weeklong festival the first week of March. The **Arizona Opera Company** (☎ 520/293–4336 ⊕ www.azopera.com), based in Tucson, puts on five major productions each year at the Tucson Convention Center's Music Hall.

The **Arizona Symphonic Winds** (✉ Tanque Verde and Sabino Canyon Rds., Northeast ⊕ www.azsymwinds.org) has both a winter and spring-summer schedule of performances. Many of the spring-summer performances are in Morris T. Udall Park. Performances are usually at 7 PM, but you need to arrive at least an hour early. From late February through late June, the **Tucson Pops Orchestra** (✉ Lake Shore La. off 22nd St. between Alvernon Way and Country Club Rd., Central ⊕ www.theriver.com/public/tucsonpops) gives free concerts each Saturday evening at the De Meester Outdoor Performance Center in Reid Park. Arrive about an hour before the music starts (usually at 7 PM) to stake your claim on a prime viewing spot.

The **Tucson Symphony Orchestra** (✉ 443 S. Stone Ave., Downtown ☎ 520/882–8585 box office, 520/792–9155 main office ⊕ www.tucsym.org), part of Tucson's cultural scene since 1929, holds concerts in the Music Hall in the Tucson Convention Center and at sites in the Foothills and the northwest as well.

Tucson's small but vibrant jazz scene encompasses everything from afternoon jam sessions in the park to Sunday jazz brunches at resorts in the Foothills. Call the **Tucson Jazz Society Hot Line** (☎ 520/743–3399) for information. Blues aficionados appreciate the **Tucson Blues Society Hot Line** (☎ 520/887–2126) for its recorded updates on local concerts.

One of Tucson's hottest rock music venues, the **Rialto Theatre** (✉ 318 E. Congress St., Downtown ☎ 520/798–3333 ⊕ www.rialtotheatre.com), was once a silent movie theater but now reverberates with the sounds of jazz, folk, and world music concerts, although the emphasis is on hard rock. The Rialto hosts dance and dramatic productions as well.

Poetry

Spring brings the **Tucson Poetry Festival** (☎ 520/620–2045 ⊕ www. tucsonpoetryfestival.org) and its three days of readings and related events. Such internationally acclaimed poets as Jorie Graham and Sherman Alexie have participated.

The **University of Arizona Poetry Center** (✉ 1216 N. Cherry Ave., University ☎ 520/626–3765 ⊕ www.coh.arizona.edu/poetry) runs a free series open to the public. Check during fall and spring semesters for information on scheduled readings.

Theater

Arizona's state theater, the **Arizona Theatre Company** (✉ Temple of Music and Art, 330 S. Scott Ave., Downtown ☎ 520/622–2823 box office, 520/884–8210 company office ⊕ www.aztheatreco.org), performs everything from classical to contemporary drama to musical comedy at the historic Temple of Music and Art from September through May. It's worth coming just to see the beautifully restored historic Spanish colonial/Moorish–style theater; dinner at the adjoining Temple Café makes a tasty prelude to any performance.

The University of Arizona's **Arizona Repertory Theatre** (✉ Speedway Blvd. and Olive St., University ☎ 520/621–1162 ⊕ http://arts.music.arizona.edu/theatre) has performances during the academic year, in both the fall and spring semesters. **Borderlands Theater** (✉ 373 S. Meyer Ave., Downtown ☎ 520/882–7406) presents new plays—often multicultural and bilingual—at various venues throughout Tucson, usually from late June through April. Children of all ages love the old-fashioned and cleverly written melodramas at the **Gaslight Theatre** (✉ 7010 E. Broadway Blvd., Eastside ☎ 520/886–9428 box office), where hissing the villain and cheering the hero are part of the audience's duty. **Invisible Theatre** (✉ 1400 N. 1st Ave., Central ☎ 520/882–9721) presents contemporary plays and musicals.

Nightlife

Bars & Clubs

Although Tucson doesn't have the huge selection of bars and clubs available in some major cities, there's something here to suit nearly every taste. In addition to the places listed below, most of the major resorts have late spots for drinks or dancing.

COUNTRY & WESTERN An excellent house band gets the crowd two-stepping every night except Sunday and Monday at the **Maverick** (✉ 4702 E. 22nd St., Eastside ☎ 520/748–0456).

GAY & LESBIAN BARS **Ain't Nobody's Bizness** (✉ 2900 E. Broadway Blvd., Central ☎ 520/318–4838) is the most popular lesbian bar in town. It has a karaoke night where you'll hear more than your fair share of Melissa Etheridge. **IBT's (It's 'Bout Time)** (✉ 616 N. 4th Ave., University ☎ 520/882–3053) is Tucson's most popular gay men's bar, with a nice patio, rock and disco DJ music, and Sunday-night drag shows. Expect long lines on weekends.

JAZZ There's usually a lively jazz pianist at the **Arizona Inn** (✉ 2200 E. Elm St., University ☎ 520/325–1541). **Old Pueblo Grille** (✉ 60 N. Alvernon Way, Central ☎ 520/326–6000) has live jazz on Tuesday, Saturday, and Sunday nights. **Ric's Café** (✉ 5605 E. River Rd., Northeast ☎ 520/577–7272) features jazz musicians outside in the courtyard every Saturday night.

ROCK, BLUES &
MORE **Berky's** (✉ 5769 E. Speedway Blvd., Central ☎ 520/296–1981) has live R&B and rock and roll every night. The **Cactus Moon Café** (✉ 5470 E. Broadway Blvd., Central ☎ 520/748–0049) offers an eclectic mix that draws on Top 40, hip-hop, and modern country, often with free appetizer buffets during happy hour. The **Chicago Bar** (✉ 5954 E. Speedway Blvd., Central ☎ 520/748–8169) is a good place to catch Tucson blues legend Sam Taylor; other nightly shows include reggae and rock. **Club Congress** (✉ Hotel Congress, 311 E. Congress St., Downtown ☎ 520/622–8848) is the main Friday venue for cutting-edge rock bands, with a mixed-bag crowd of jaded alternative rockers, international travelers, and college kids. Saturday brings a more outrageous crowd dancing to a big electronic beat. **Plush** (✉ 340 E. 6th St., University ☎ 520/798–1298) hosts bands like Camp Courageous and Greyhound Soul, as well as local performers with a loyal following. Go totally retro at the **Shelter** (✉ 4155 E. Grant Rd., Central ☎ 520/326–1345), a former bomb shelter decked out in plastic 1960s kitsch, lava lamps, and JFK memorabilia, which plays Elvis videos and music by the likes of Burt Bacharach and Martin Denny.

Casinos

After a long struggle with the state of Arizona, two Native American tribes now operate casinos on their Tucson-area reservations west of the airport. The casinos are virtually the same, and quite unlike their distant and much grander cousins in Las Vegas and Atlantic City. Don't expect much glamour, ersatz or otherwise; these casinos are more like glorified video arcades, although you can lose money much faster. You'll be greeted by a wall of cigarette smoke (the reservation is exempt from the city's antismoking laws) and the wail of hundreds of slot machines and video poker, blackjack, roulette, and craps machines. The only "live" gaming is keno, bingo, and certain types of poker. The crowd is mostly older smokers, and because the casinos are on reservation lands, alcohol is neither sold nor permitted at either location.

The Pascua Yaqui tribe's **Casino of the Sun** (✉ 7406 S. Camino de Oeste, South, off W. Valencia Rd. about 5 mi west of I–19, ☎ 520/883–1700 or 800/344–9435 ⊕ www.casinosun.com) has slot and video-gambling machines, high-stakes bingo, and live poker. Food selections include an all-you-can-eat prime rib buffet (washed down with nonalcoholic beer). This is the less crowded of Tucson's two casinos, but free shuttle buses operate from points all over Tucson; call for a schedule. It's closed most of the week before Easter. The Tohono O'odham tribe operates the dizzying **Desert Diamond Bingo and Casino** (✉ 7350 S. Old Nogales Hwy., South 1 mi south of Valencia, just west of the airport, ☎ 520/294–7777 ⊕ www.desertdiamondcasino.com), which has 500 one-arm bandits and video poker in addition to live keno, bingo, and Stud High, Texas Hold'em, Omaha, and Stud Lo poker. Players are served free beverages and can order tacos, burritos, sandwiches, and several varieties of Native American fry bread as they play.

SPORTS & THE OUTDOORS

Ballooning

Two companies in Tucson offer hot-air-balloon flights from September to May, flown by FAA-certified pilots. **Balloon Rides USA** (✉ Box 31255, Tucson 85751 ☎ 520/299–7744 ⊕ www.balloonridesusa.com) has daily champagne tours (passengers toast with crystal flutes), departing from the east side of Tucson. **Southern Arizona Balloon Excursions** (✉ Box 5265, Tucson 85703 ☎ 520/624–3599 ⊕ www.tucsoncomefly.com) offers daily sunrise flights over northwest Tucson.

Baseball

While it doesn't have as many teams as Phoenix, Tucson does have its share of baseball spring training action. Spring training brings the Arizona Diamondbacks, the Chicago White Sox, and the Colorado Rockies to the Tucson area, from the middle of February until the end of March. The Diamondbacks and White Sox play at Tucson Electric Park. The Rockies play at Hi Corbett Field, which is adjacent to Reid Park and most easily reached by driving south at the junction of East Broadway Boulevard and Randolph Way; parking is tight at Hi Corbett, so arrive early to enjoy a picnic lunch at one of the many nearby ramadas (wooden shelters that supply shade for your table). Not surprisingly, some people plan vacations around scheduled training dates; there are plenty of local fans, too. The **Pacific Coast League** (⊕ www.pclbaseball.com) includes the Tucson Sidewinders, the AAA team of the Arizona Diamondbacks, who play in Tucson Electric Park from April through July.

Arizona Diamondbacks (✉ Tucson Electric Park, 2400 E. Ajo Way, South ☎ 520/434–1000, 520/683–3900 for tickets ⊕ www.tucsonbaseball.com).
Chicago White Sox (✉ Tucson Electric Park, 2400 E. Ajo Way, South ☎ 520/434–1000, 520/683–3900 for tickets ⊕ www.tucsonbaseball.com).
Colorado Rockies (✉ Hi Corbett Field, 3400 E. Camino Campestre, Central ☎ 520/327–9467 box office ⊕ colorado.rockies.mlb.com).
Tucson Sidewinders (☎ 520/325–2621, 520/434–1021 for tickets ⊕ www.tucsonsidewinders.com).

Bicycling

Tucson, ranked among America's top five bicycling cities by *Bicycling* magazine, has well-maintained bikeways, routes, lanes, and paths all over the city. Scenic loop roads in both sections of Saguaro National Park offer rewarding rides for all levels of cyclists. Most bike stores in Tucson carry the monthly newsletter of the Tucson chapter of **GABA** (Greater Arizona Bicycling Association; ✉ Box 43273, Tucson 85733 ⊕ www.bikegaba.org), which lists rated group rides. You can pick up a map of Tucson-area bike routes at the **Pima Association of Governments** (✉ 177 N. Church St., Suite 405, Downtown ☎ 520/792–1093).

Mountain bikes, comfort bikes, and road bikes can be rented by the day or week at **Fair Wheel Bikes** (✉ 1110 E. 6th St., University ☎ 520/258–0118). **Sabino Cycles** (✉ 7131 E. Tanque Verde Rd., Northeast ☎ 520/885–3666) offers a broad selection of rentals, including road bikes and mountain bikes with front or full suspension.

Bird-Watching

The naturalist and illustrator Roger Tory Peterson (1908–1996) considered Tucson one of the country's top birding spots, and avid "life listers"—birders who keep a list of all the birds they've sighted and identified—soon see why. In the early morning and early evening, Sabino Canyon is alive with cactus and canyon wrens, hawks, and quail. Spring and summer, when species of migrants come in from Mexico, are great hummingbird seasons. In the nearby Santa Rita Mountains and Madera Canyon, you can see elegant trogons nesting in early spring. The area also supports species usually found only in higher elevations.

You can get the latest word on the bird by phoning the 24-hour line at the **Tucson Audubon Society** (☎ 520/798–1005 ⊕ www.tucsonaudubon.org); sightings of rare or interesting birds in the area are recorded regularly.

The society's **Audubon Nature Shop** (⊠ 300 E. University Blvd., Suite 120, University ☎ 520/629–0510) carries field guides, bird feeders, binoculars, and natural history books. The **Wild Bird Store** (⊠ 3526 E. Grant Rd., Central ☎ 520/322–9466) is an excellent resource for bird-watching books, maps, and trail guides.

Several companies offer birding tours in the Tucson area. **Borderland Tours** (⊠ 2550 W. Calle Padilla, Northwest, Tucson 85745 ☎ 520/882–7650 or 800/525–7753 ⊕ www.borderland-tours.com) leads bird-watching tours in Arizona and all over the world. **Wings** (⊠ 1643 N. Alvernon Way, Suite 105, Central, Tucson 85712 ☎ 520/320–9868 ⊕ www.wingsbirds.com), a Tucson-based company, leads ornithological expeditions locally and worldwide.

Camping

The closest public campground to Tucson is at **Catalina State Park** (⊠ 11570 N. Oracle Rd., Northwest ☎ 520/628–5798 ⊕ www.pr.state.az.us/parkhtml/catalina.html), about 14 mi north of town on AZ 77 in the foothills of the Santa Catalinas. The campground has 48 sites, about half with electrical hook-ups, accommodating both tents and RVs. Sites cost $15 with electric hook-ups, $10 without, and the cash-or check-only facility operates on a first-come, first-served basis.

Golf

For a detailed listing of the state's courses, contact the **Arizona Golf Association** (⊡ 7226 N. 16th St., Phoenix 85020 ☎ 602/944–3035 or 800/458–8484 ⊕ www.azgolf.org). The **Golf Stop Inc.** (⊠ 1830 S. Alvernon Way, South ☎ 520/790–0941), a shop owned and run by two LPGA pros, can fit you with custom clubs, repair your old irons, or give you lessons. For a local golf package based on your budget, interests, and experience, contact **Tee Time Arrangers** (⊠ 6979 E. Broadway Blvd., Eastside ☎ 520/296–4800 or 800/742–9939). If you're planning to stay a week or more, **Tucson's Resort Golf Card** (☎ 520/886–8800), offering discounts at 13 of the area's best courses, is a good deal.

MUNICIPAL COURSES One of Tucson's best-kept secrets is that the city's five low-priced, municipal courses are maintained to standards usually found only at the best country clubs. To reserve a tee time at one of the city's courses, call the **Tucson Parks and Recreation Department** (☎ 520/791–4653 general golf information, 520/791–4336 automated tee time reservations ⊕ www.tucsoncitygolf.com) at least a week in advance.

Dell Urich Golf Course (⊠ 600 S. Alvernon Way, Central ☎ 520/791–4161), adjacent to Randolph and formerly known as Randolph South, is a par-70 course with tall trees and dramatic elevation changes.
El Rio Golf Course (⊠ 1400 W. Speedway Blvd., Westside ☎ 520/791–4229) has tight fairways, small greens, and two lakes on fairly flat terrain.
Fred Enke Golf Course (⊠ 8251 E. Irvington, Eastside ☎ 520/791–2539) is a hilly, semiarid course, meaning that it has less grass and more native vegetation. It's southeast of town.

Fodor'sChoice ★ **Randolph Park Golf Course–North Course** (⊠ 600 S. Alvernon Way, Central ☎ 520/791–4161), a long, scenic course that has hosted the LPGA Tour for many years, is the flagship of Tucson's municipal courses.
Silverbell Golf Course (⊠ 3600 N. Silverbell Rd., Northwest ☎ 520/791–5235), with spacious fairways and ample greens, is set along the west bank of the Santa Cruz River.

PUBLIC COURSES **Dorado Golf Course** (⊠ 6601 E. Speedway Blvd., Eastside ☎ 520/885–6751) has an 18-hole executive course that's good for those who want to play just a few short rounds.

Raven Golf Club at Sabino Springs (✉ 9777 E. Sabino Greens Dr., Eastside ☎ 520/749–3636) is a gorgeous 18-hole, par-71 course.

Rio Rico Resort & Country Club (✉ 1069 Camino Carampi, Tubac ☎ 800/288–4746), south of Tucson, near Nogales, was designed by Robert Trent Jones Jr. It's one of Arizona's lesser-known gems.

San Ignacio Golf Club (✉ 4201 S. Camino del Sol, Green Valley ☎ 520/648–3468) was designed by Arthur Hills and is a challenging 18-hole desert course.

Tubac Golf Resort (✉ 1 Otero Rd., Tubac ☎ 520/398–2021), 45 minutes south of Tucson, will look familiar to you if you've seen the movie *Tin Cup.*

RESORTS   Avid golfers check into one of Tucson's many tony resorts and head straight for the links. Those who don't mind getting up early to beat the heat will find some excellent golf packages at these places in the summer.

Hilton Tucson El Conquistador (✉ 10000 N. Oracle Rd., Northwest ☎ 520/544–5000) has 45 holes of golf in the Santa Catalina foothills. The course has some panoramic views of the city.

Fodor'sChoice   **Lodge at Ventana Canyon** (✉ 6200 N. Clubhouse La., Northeast ☎ 520/
★   577–1400 or 800/828–5701) has a 36-hole Tom Fazio–designed course.

Omni Tucson National Golf Resort (✉ 2727 W. Club Dr., Northwest ☎ 520/575–7540), cohost of an annual PGA winter open, offers 27 holes and beautiful, long par 4's. The resort's orange and gold courses were designed by Robert Van Hagge and Bruce Devlin.

Starr Pass Golf Resort (✉ 3645 W. Starr Pass Blvd., Westside ☎ 520/670–0400), with 18 magnificent holes in the Tucson Mountains, was developed as a Tournament Player's Course. Managed by Arnold Palmer, Starr Pass has become a favorite of visiting pros; playing its No. 15 signature hole has been likened to threading a moving needle.

Westin La Paloma (✉ 3800 E. Sunrise Dr., Foothills, 85718 ☎ 520/742–6000), in the Tucson foothills, is rated among the top resort courses by *Golf Digest.* The 27-hole layout was designed by Jack Nicklaus.

Health Clubs

FIT Center (✉ 5555 E. 5th St., Eastside ☎ 520/571–7000) has an indoor swimming pool, sauna, hot tub, gym, and aerobics classes, as well as massage services available. A day pass costs $8. **Gold's Gym** (✉ 110 S. Church Ave., Suite 5030, Downtown ☎ 520/623–6300 ✉ 7315 N. Oracle Rd., Northwest ☎ 520/297–8000 ✉ 5851 E. Speedway Blvd., Eastside ☎ 520/751–0303) charges $10 per day to use an indoor swimming pool, Nautilus equipment, free weights, racquetball courts, aerobics classes, sauna, and a steam room. **Tucson Racquet & Fitness Club** (✉ 4001 N. Country Club Rd., Central ☎ 520/795–6960) has extensive facilities, including 32 tennis courts, 11 racquetball courts, 2 lap pools, martial arts classes, and a restaurant; it's open 24 hours a day and charges $10 per day.

Hiking

For hiking inside Tucson city limits, you can test your skills climbing trails up Sentinel Peak ("A" Mountain), but there are also hundreds of other trails in the immediate Tucson area. Sabino Canyon and Saguaro National Park East and West beckon hikers with waterfalls, birds, critters, and huge saguaro cacti. **Catalina State Park** (✉ 11570 N. Oracle Rd., Northwest ☎ 520/628–5798 ⊕ www.pr.state.az.us) is crisscrossed by hiking trails. One of them, a relatively easy two-hour (5-mi round-trip) walk, leads to the Romero Pools, a series of natural *tinajas,* or stone "jars," filled with water much of the year.

The local chapter of the **Sierra Club** (⊠ 738 N. 5th Ave., University, Tucson ☎ 520/620–6401) welcomes out-of-towners on weekend hikes around Tucson. The **Southern Arizona Hiking Club** (☎ 520/751–4513 ⊕ www.sahcinfo.org) leads weekend hikes of varying difficulty. For hiking on your own, a good source is **Summit Hut** (⊠ 5045 E. Speedway Blvd., Central ☎ 520/325–1554), which has a collection of hiking reference materials and a friendly staff who will help you plan and outfit your trip. Packs, tents, bags, and climbing shoes can be rented here.

Horseback Riding

Pusch Ridge Stables (⊠ 13700 N. Oracle Rd., Northwest ☎ 520/825–1664), adjacent to Catalina State Park, can serve up a cowboy-style breakfast on your trail ride; gentle children's horse walks, one-hour, and overnight rides are also available. **Colossal Cave Stables** (⊠ 16600 Colossal Cave Rd., Eastside ☎ 520/647–3450) takes riders into Saguaro National Park East on one-hour or longer guided trail rides.

Rodeo

In the last week of February, Tucson hosts **Fiesta de Los Vaqueros**, the largest annual winter rodeo in the United States, a five-day extravaganza with more than 600 events and a crowd of more than 44,000 spectators a day at the **Tucson Rodeo Grounds** (⊠ 4823 S. 6th Ave., South ☎ 520/294–8896 ⊕ www.tucsonrodeo.com). The rodeo kicks off with a 2-mi parade of horseback riders (Western and fancy-dress Mexican *charro*), wagons, stagecoaches, and horse-drawn floats; it's touted as the largest nonmotorized parade in the world. Local schoolkids especially love the celebration—they get a two-day holiday from school. Daily seats at the rodeo range from $8 to $14.

Tennis

Excellent tennis facilities can be found at area resorts, among them Loews Ventana Canyon, Hilton Tucson El Conquistador, Westin La Paloma, Westward Look, and Canyon Ranch. **Catalina High School** (⊠ 3645 E. Pima, Central), singer Linda Ronstadt's alma mater, is a favorite among local tennis enthusiasts for its well-lighted, no-charge courts, which are open to the public when school's out. **Fort Lowell Park** (⊠ 2900 N. Craycroft Rd., Central ☎ 520/791–2584) has eight lighted courts and tennis instruction for all ages. **Himmel Park** (⊠ 1000 N. Tucson Blvd., University ☎ 520/791–3276), a mile east of the university, has eight lighted tennis courts and low prices. The **Randolph Tennis Center** (⊠ 50 S. Alvernon Way, Central ☎ 520/791–4896) has 24 tennis courts (and 10 racquetball courts), all of them lighted, at very reasonable rates.

SHOPPING

Much of Tucson's retail activity is focused around malls, but you'll find shops with more character and some unique wares in the city's open plazas: St. Philip's Plaza (River Road and Campbell Avenue), Plaza Palomino (Swan and Fort Lowell roads), and Casas Adobes Plaza (Oracle and Ina roads).

The 4th Avenue neighborhood near the University of Arizona—especially 4th Avenue between 2nd and 9th streets—is fertile ground for unusual items in artsy boutiques and galleries and secondhand-clothing stores. You may experience some aggressive panhandling here.

Hard-core bargain hunters usually continue south to the Mexican border town of Nogales, for jewelry, liquor, home furnishings, and leather goods.

Malls & Shopping Centers

Casas Adobes Plaza (✉ Oracle and Ina Rds., southwest corner, Northwest ☎ no phone ⊕ www.casasadobesplaza.com) originally served the ranchers and orange grove owners in this once remote part of town, which is now the fastest-growing area. This Mediterranean-style shopping center has a full-service grocery with outstanding meats and produce, the superb Wildflower Grill, a bagel shop, and several upscale clothes stores and gift shops.

El Con Mall (✉ 3601 E. Broadway Blvd., Central at Alvernon Way, ☎ 520/795–9958) has a 20-screen movie theater and a large food court. Stores here include JCPenney and Robinsons-May; a renovation, in progress at this writing, is due to be completed in mid-2004.

Foothills Mall (✉ 7401 N. La Cholla Blvd. at Ina Rd., Northwest ☎ 520/742–7191 ⊕ www.shopfoothillsmall.com) has a Barnes & Noble Superstore and a Saks Fifth Avenue outlet store; many other outlets including Samsonite, Nike, and Adidas; as well as boutiques, a 16-screen cineplex, and several restaurants, most notably the Italian restaurant Gavi.

Historic Broadway Village (✉ Country Club Rd. and Broadway Blvd., Central ☎ no phone) was the first shopping center in Tucson, and although small, it houses interesting shops such as the Clues Unlimited mystery bookstore, Zocalo for colonial Mexican furniture, Yikes! for off-the-wall toys, and Picante for Mexican clothing and crafts (get your Day of the Dead merchandise here).

Old Town Artisans Complex (✉ 186 N. Meyer Ave., Downtown ☎ 520/623–6024), across from the Tucson Museum of Art, has a large selection of Southwestern wares, including Native American jewelry, baskets, Mexican handicrafts, pottery, and textiles.

Park Place (✉ 5870 E. Broadway Blvd., Eastside ☎ 520/747–7575), a thriving mall, has plush chairs and couches throughout, a toddler play area, an extensive food court, a 20-screen cineplex, and more than 120 stores, including Dillard's, Macy's, and Borders.

Plaza Palomino (✉ 2980 N. Swan Rd., at Ft. Lowell Rd., Central ☎ 520/795–1177), an outdoor mall, has many shops, galleries, and clothing boutiques, including Dark Star Leather and the Strand. On Saturdays, you can sample locally grown produce, baked goods, salsas, and tamales at the farmers' market. La Placita Cafe serves tasty Mexican food.

St. Philip's Plaza (✉ 4280 N. Campbell Ave., at River Rd., Foothills ☎ 520/886–7485) arranges its chic shops around a series of Spanish-style outdoor patios. You can shop away at more than a dozen boutiques and eye some outstanding art at Obsidian Gallery and Philabaum Contemporary Glass. When it's time to recuperate, the nearby restaurants Vivace and Ovens can provide chic sustenance.

Tucson Mall (✉ 4500 N. Oracle Rd., at Wetmore Rd., Central ☎ 520/293–7330) is the busiest mall in town, with Robinsons-May, Dillard's, Macy's, Mervyn's, Sears, JCPenney, more than 200 specialty shops, and a carousel for the kids. For tasteful Southwestern-style T-shirts, belts, jewelry, and prickly-pear candies, try Señor Coyote, Morning Singer, or any of the other shops on Arizona Avenue, a section of the first floor that's devoted to regional items.

Specialty Shops

ART GALLERIES If you're seeking out work by regional artists, you might want to drive down to Tubac, a community 45 mi south of Tucson. **Art Life in Southern Arizona** (✉ Box 36777, Tucson 85740 ☎ 520/797–1271 ⊕ artlifearizona.com), published annually, lists galleries and artists statewide.

Dinnerware Artists Cooperative (✉ 135 E. Congress St., Downtown ☎ 520/792–4503) is a cutting-edge downtown gallery.

Etherton Gallery (✉ 135 S. 6th Ave., Downtown ☎ 520/624–7370) specializes in photography but also represents artists in other media.

Obsidian Gallery (✉ 4340 N. Campbell Ave., Suite 90, Central ☎ 520/577–3598) has exquisite glass, ceramic, and jewelry pieces.

Philabaum Contemporary Glass (✉ 4280 N. Campbell Ave., Suite 105, Foothills ☎ 520/299–1939) sells magnificent handblown vases, artwork, table settings, and the jewelry of Tom Philabaum and others.

Rosequist Galleries (✉ 1615 E. Ft. Lowell Rd., Central ☎ 520/327–5729) has represented regional artists working in all media for more than 50 years.

BOOKS **Antigone** (✉ 411 N. 4th Ave., University ☎ 520/792–3715) specializes in books by and about women and also sells creative feminist cards and T-shirts.

Barnes & Noble (✉ 5130 E. Broadway Blvd., Eastside ☎ 520/512–1166 ✉ Foothills Mall, 7325 N. La Cholla Blvd., Northwest ☎ 520/742–6402) is capacious but comfortable, with a well-stocked children's section.

Bookman's (✉ 1930 E. Grant Rd., Central ☎ 520/325–5767 ✉ 3733 W. Ina Rd., Northwest ☎ 520/579–0303 ✉ 6230 E. Speedway Blvd., Eastside ☎ 520/748–9555) carries an eclectic selection of used and new books, music, magazines, and software in three spacious locations. The **Book Stop** (✉ 2504 N. Campbell Ave., Central ☎ 520/326–6661) is a wonderful browsing place for used and out-of-print books.

Borders Books and Music (✉ Park Place Mall, 5870 E. Broadway Blvd., Eastside ☎ 520/584–0111 ✉ 4235 N. Oracle Rd., Northwest ☎ 520/292–1331) has a vast selection of books and music, plus an above-average café.

Clues Unlimited (✉ 3000 E. Broadway Blvd., Central ☎ 520/326–8533) specializes in mysteries.

Crescent Tobacco and Newsstand (✉ 200 E. Congress St., Downtown ☎ 520/622–1559 ✉ 7037 E. Tanque Verde Rd., Northeast ☎ 520/296–3102) carries hundreds of daily newspapers and magazines from around the world, not to mention imported cigars and cigarettes.

Reader's Oasis (✉ 3400 E. Speedway Blvd., Central ☎ 520/319–7887), an independent bookstore, has frequent author readings and book signings. Some used books are also available.

Tucson's Map and Flag Center (✉ 3239 N. 1st Ave., Central ☎ 520/887–4234) is the place to pick up your topographical maps and specialty guides to Arizona.

Waldenbooks (✉ 4500 N. Oracle Rd., Tucson Mall, Central ☎ 520/293–6799) is handy if you need to take a break from souvenir shopping at the mall.

CACTI **B&B Cactus Farm** (✉ 11550 E. Speedway Blvd., Eastside ☎ 520/721–4687), which you'll pass en route to Saguaro National Park East, has a huge selection of cacti and other succulents and will ship anywhere in the country.

GIFTS **Del Sol** (✉ 435 N. 4th Ave., University ☎ 520/628–8765 ✉ 6536 E. Tanque Verde Rd., Eastside ☎ 520/298–3398) specializes in Mexican folk art, jewelry, and Southwest-style clothing.

Mrs. Tiggy Winkle's Toys (✉ 4811 E. Grant Rd., Central ☎ 520/326–0188) will probably remind you of the toy shops of the past—only better—with many items that are hard to find in the big-box toy stores.

United Nations Center (✉ 2911 E. Grant Rd., Central ☎ 520/881–7060) sells reasonably priced ethnic jewelry, apparel, and crafts from all over the world.

JEWELRY **Abbott Taylor** (✉ 6372 E. Broadway Blvd., Eastside ☎ 520/745–5080) creates custom designs in diamonds and other precious stones.

Beth Friedman (✉ Joesler Village, 1865 E. River Rd., Suite 121, Foothills ☎ 520/577–6858) sells unsurpassed designs in silver and semiprecious stones. Her store also carries an eclectic selection of ladies' apparel, fine art, and home furnishings.

Patania's Originals (✉ 3000 E. Broadway Blvd., Central ☎ 520/795–0086), formerly the Thunderbird Shop, is one of the best-known jewelers in the Southwest. The Patania family has been creating unique designs in silver, gold, and platinum here and in Santa Fe for three generations.

Turquoise Door (✉ 4340 N. Campbell Ave., Foothills ☎ 520/299–7787) creates innovative jewelry that amounts to a modern take on classic Southwestern designs.

MEXICAN FURNISHINGS **Antigua de Mexico** (✉ 3235 W. Orange Grove Rd., Northwest ☎ 520/742–7114) sells well-made furniture and crafts that you are not likely to find elsewhere in town.

Tres Encantos (✉ 6538 E. Tanque Verde Rd., Suite 110, Eastside ☎ 520/885–4522) carries hand-carved furniture and decorative accent pieces.

NATIVE AMERICAN ARTS & CRAFTS San Xavier Plaza, across from San Xavier mission and also part of the Tohono O'odham reservation, is a good place to find vendors and stores selling the work of this and other area tribes.

Bahti Indian Arts (✉ St. Philip's Plaza, 4300 N. Campbell Ave., Foothills ☎ 520/577–0290) is owned and run by Mark Bahti, whose father, Tom, literally wrote the book on Native American art, including an early definitive work on katsinas. The store sells high-quality jewelry, pottery, rugs, art, and more.

Grey Dog Trading Company (✉ Plaza Palomino, 2970 N. Swan Rd., Central ☎ 520/881–6888) has an ample selection of jewelry, katsinas, weaving, pottery, and Zuni fetishes.

Kaibab Courtyard Shops (✉ 2837 N. Campbell Ave., Central ☎ 520/795–6905) sells traditional Native American arts, along with Mexican imports and Nambé dinnerware.

Silverbell Trading (✉ Casa Adobes Plaza, 7007 N. Oracle Rd., Northwest ☎ 520/797–6852) carries the work of local and regional artists.

WESTERN WEAR Tucsonans who wear Western gear keep it simple for the most part—jeans, a Western shirt, maybe boots. This ain't Santa Fe.

Arizona Hatters (✉ 3600 N. 1st Ave., Central ☎ 520/292–1320) can fit you for that Stetson you've always wanted.

Corral Western Wear (✉ 4525 E. Broadway Blvd., Eastside ☎ 520/322–6001) sells shirts, hats, belts, jewelry, and boots, catering to both urban and authentic cowboys and cowgirls.

Stewart Boot Manufacturing (✉ 30 W. 28th St., South Tucson ☎ 520/622–2706) has been making handmade leather boots since the 1940s.

Western Warehouse (✉ 3030 E. Speedway Blvd., Central ☎ 520/327–8005 ✉ 3719 N. Oracle Rd., Northwest ☎ 520/293–1808 ✉ 6701 E. Broadway Blvd., Eastside ☎ 520/885–4385) is the place if you want to go where native Tucsonans shop for their everyday Western duds.

SIDE TRIPS NEAR TUCSON

There's something for nearly everyone—history buffs, bird-watchers, hikers, Mexican-food lovers, and hard-core shoppers—en route from Tucson to Nogales along I–19. The road roughly follows the Camino Real (King's Road), which the conquistadors and missionaries traveled from

Mexico up to what was once the northernmost portion of New Spain. Today, I–19 is the only U.S. highway to be signed in kilometers, the remnant of a failed attempt by the feds to convert U.S. roads to the metric system.

The Asarco Mineral Discovery Center

③② *15 mi south of Tucson off I–19.*

Operated by the American Smelting and Refining Co. (ASARCO), this facility is designed to elucidate the importance of mining to your everyday life. Exhibits in two connected buildings include a walk-through model of an ore crusher, video stations that explain various refining processes, and a theater that shows a film on extraction of minerals from the earth. The big draw, however, is the yawning open pit of the Mission Mine, some 2 mi long and 1¾ mi wide because a lot of earth has to be torn up to extract the 1% that is copper. It's an impressive sight, although it doesn't exactly bolster the case the center tries to make about how environmentally conscious mining has become. Tours of the Mission Mine open pit, which take about one hour, leave the center on the half hour; the last one starts at 3:30. ⊠ *1421 W. Pima Mine Rd.* ☎ *520/625–0879* ⊕ *www.mineraldiscovery.com* ⊠ *$6* ☽ *Tues.–Sat. 9–5.*

Titan Missile Museum

③③ *25 mi south of Tucson, off I–19.*

During the cold war, Tucson was ringed by 18 of the 54 Titan II missiles that existed in the United States. After the SALT II treaty with the Soviet Union was signed in 1979, this was the only missile launch site left intact. Now a National Historic Landmark, the Titan Missile Museum makes for a sobering visit. Guided tours last about an hour and take you down 55 steps into the command post, where a ground crew of four lived and waited. Among the fascinating sights is the 103-ft, 165-ton, two-stage liquid-fuel rocket. Now empty, it originally held a nuclear warhead with 214 times the explosive power of the bomb that destroyed Hiroshima. Guided tours run every half hour. ⊠ *1580 W. Duval Mine Rd. (I–19, Exit 69)* ☎ *520/625–7736* ⊕ *www.pimaair.org* ⊠ *$7.50* ☉ *Nov.–Apr., daily 9–5; May–Oct., Wed.–Sun. 9–4.*

Madera Canyon

34 *61½ mi southeast of Tucson; Exit 63 off I–19, then east on White House Canyon Rd. for 12½ mi (it turns into Madera Canyon Rd.).*

This is where the Coronado National Forest meets the Santa Rita Mountains—among them Mt. Wrightson, the highest peak in southern Arizona, at 9,453 ft. With approximately 200 mi of scenic trails, the Madera Canyon recreation area is a favorite destination for hikers. Higher elevations and thick pine cover make it especially popular with Tucsonans looking to escape the summer heat. Trails range from a steep trek up Mount Baldy to a paved, wheelchair-accessible path. Birders flock here year-round; about 400 avian species have been spotted in the area. The small, volunteer-run visitor center is open only on weekends. Nearby, the Bog Springs Campground has 13 sites, with toilets, potable water, and grills, available on a first-come, first-served basis. The cost is $10 per vehicle per night. ⊠ *Madera Canyon Rd., Madera Canyon* ☎ *520/281–2296 Nogales Ranger District office* ⊕ *www.fs.fed.us/r3/ coronado* ⊠ *Donation requested* ☉ *Daily.*

Tubac

★ **35** *45 mi south of Tucson at Exit 40 off I–19.*

Established in 1726, Tubac is the site of the first European settlement in Arizona. A year after the Pima Indian uprising in 1851, a military garrison was established here to protect early Spanish settlers, missionaries, and peaceful Native American converts of the nearby Tumacácori Mission from further attack. It was from here that Juan Bautista de Anza led 240 colonists across the desert—the expedition resulted in the founding of San Francisco in 1776. Arizona's first newspaper, the *Weekly Arizonian,* was printed here in 1859, and in 1860 Tubac was the largest town in Arizona. Today, the quiet little town is a popular art colony. Crafts sold in the more than 80 shops range from carved wooden furniture and hand-thrown pottery to delicately painted tiles and silk-screen fabrics. The annual **Tubac Festival of the Arts** has been held in February for more than 30 years.

There's an archaeological display of portions of the original 1752 fort at the **Tubac Presidio State Historic Park and Museum** in the center of town. In addition to the visitor center and the adjoining museum, which has detailed the history of the early colony, the park includes Tubac's 1885 schoolhouse and a pleasant picnic area. ⊠ *Presidio Dr.* ☎ *520/ 398–2252* ⊕ *www.pr.state.az.us* ⊠ *$2* ☉ *Daily 8–5.*

Where to Stay & Eat

¢ ✕ **Tubac Deli & Coffee Co.** Smack in the middle of Tubac village, this pleasant little eatery serves up generous sandwiches, salads, and soups—as well as cappuccinos and pastries—every day until 4 PM. ⊠ *6 Plaza Rd.* ☎ *520/398–3330* ▭ *No credit cards* ☉ *No dinner.*

★ $$ ▣ **Amado Territory Innand Cafe.** Although this quiet, friendly B&B is directly off the highway frontage road, it feels worlds away. Part of a ranch complex that includes a plant nursery, a gem and mineral shop, an antiques store, and an artist's studio, the inn resembles a late-19th-century ranch house, but a soaring ceiling and contemporary Southwestern art make the interior distinctly modern. Rooms are furnished with handcrafted Mexican pieces, and some have a pretty view of the garden and the Santa Rita Mountains. Breakfast is included at the inn (try the huevos rancheros); next door, the Amado Cafe serves savory Greek-style pasta, chicken, and fish specialties for lunch and dinner. ⊠ *3001 E. Frontage Rd., off Exit 48 of I–19* ⬭ *Box 81, Amado 85645* ☎ *520/398–8684 or 888/398–8684* 🖷 *520/398–8186* ⊕ *www.amado-territory-inn.com* ⮐ *9 rooms, 2 suites* ⟁ *Restaurant, putting green, meeting rooms; no room phones, no room TVs* ▤ *MC, V* ⦿⧉ *BP.*

$$ ⌂ **Burro Inn.** Leave the city behind and wake up to the sounds and sights of burros in the nearly untouched hills just west of Tubac. Although the inn appears to be rustic, the two-room suites have all the modern amenities, including king-size beds and sofa beds. The property is 20 ft from National Forest Service land. The *tanque* (reservoir) on the property is a drawing card for the burros, and you're likely to see other wildlife as well. ⊠ *70 W. El Burro La., 85646* ☎ *520/398–2281* ⮐ *4 suites* ⟁ *Restaurant, microwaves, refrigerators, bar* ▤ *MC, V.*

en route | You can tread the same road as the conquistadors: the first 4½ mi of the **Juan Bautista de Anza National Historic Trail** (⊕ www.nps.gov/juba) from Tumacácori to Tubac were dedicated in 1992. You'll have to cross the Santa Cruz River (which is usually pretty low) three times to complete the hike, and the path is rather sandy, but it's a pleasant journey along the tree-shaded banks of the river.

Tumacácori National Historic Park

❸❻ *3 mi south of Tubac; Exit 29 off I–19.*

The site where Tumacácori National Historic Park now stands was visited by missionary Father Eusebio Francisco Kino in 1691, but the Jesuits didn't build a church here until 1751. You can still see some ruins of this simple structure, but the main attraction is the mission of San José de Tumacácori, built by the Franciscans around 1799–1803. A combination of circumstances—Apache attacks, a bad winter, and Mexico's withdrawal of funds and priests—caused the remaining inhabitants to flee in 1848. Persistent rumors of wealth left behind by both the Franciscans and the Jesuits led treasure seekers to pillage the site; it still bears those scars. The site was finally protected in 1908, when it became a national monument.

Information about the mission and the Anza trail is available at the visitor center, and guided tours are offered daily (more in winter than in summer). A small museum displays some of the mission's artifacts, and sometimes fresh tortillas are made on a wood-fire stove in the courtyard. In addition to a Christmas Eve celebration, costumed historical high masses are held at Tumacácori in spring and fall. An annual fiesta the first weekend of December has arts and crafts and food booths. ⊠ *I–19, Exit 29, Tumacácori* ☎ *520/398–2341* ⊕ *www.nps.gov/tuma* 🖾 *$2* ⊙ *Daily 8–5.*

Where to Stay

$$ ⌂ **Rio Rico Resort.** Too close to Tucson to be a real getaway, this hotel languished for many years before finally coming into its own. In a three-story complex without much charm, the rooms are large and comfortable. Most people come for the golf course, designed by Robert Trent

Jones Sr.; the splendid views; and the isolation. Nogales is a short drive south. ⊠ *1069 Camino Caralampi, 85648, off I–19 at Rio Rico Rd. (Exit 17),* ☎ *520/281–1901 or 800/288–4746* 🖷 *520/281–7132* ⊕ *www. rioricoresort.com* 🖘 *166 rooms, 14 suites* ☖ *Restaurant, 18-hole golf course, 4 tennis courts, pool, gym, outdoor hot tub, sauna, hiking, horseback riding, bar, business services, meeting rooms* ▤ *AE, D, MC, V.*

Nogales

37 *15 mi south of Tumacácori; 63 mi south of Tucson, on I–19 at the Mexican border.*

Nogales, named for the walnut trees that grew along the river here, is actually two towns: the American town and the huge Mexican city over the border. The American side was once a focal point for cattle shipping between Sonora and the United States. Today, Nogales reaps the benefits of NAFTA, with warehouses and trucking firms dedicated to the distribution of Mexican produce, making it one of the world's busiest produce ports. The American side depends on the health of the peso and the number of shoppers who cross the border from Mexico to buy American goods. The Mexican side has grown with the economic success of *maquiladoras,* factories that manufacture goods destined for the United States. There is a great deal of commerce between the two sides of Nogales.

Unfortunately, some of this trade is in narcotics and undocumented workers, adding to the edgy quality of this border town and not representative of most other parts of Mexico. Security on the American side is very tight; don't even think about taking a firearm near the border. You'll also do better not to drive your car into Mexico: not only is there a very real possibility it may be stolen, but you'll face significant delays because of the thorough search you and your vehicle will receive upon returning. This hassle is unnecessary, though, because you can cover Nogales in a day trip, and the area of interest to tourists is within easy walking distance of the border crossing. Park on the Arizona side, either on the street or, better yet, in one of many guarded lots that cost about $4 or $5 for the day (use rest rooms on the U.S. side before you cross).

You should be prepared for aggressive selling tactics and sometimes-disorienting hubbub, but locals are always glad to point you in the right direction, and almost all speak English.

Where to Stay & Eat

$–$$ ✕ **La Roca.** East of the railroad tracks and off the beaten tourist path, La Roca is a favorite of Tucsonans. The setting—a series of tiled rooms and courtyards in a stately old stone house, with a balcony overlooking a charming patio—is lovely, the service is attentive and professional, and the food is considered the best in Nogales. If you like meat, try the *carne tampiqueña,* an assortment of grilled meats that comes with chiles rellenos and an enchilada. Chicken mole (with a chocolate-chili sauce) is also a favorite. ⊠ *Calle Elias 91, Mexico* ☎ *63½–07–60 or 888/527–0220* ▤ *AE, DC, MC, V.*

¢–$ ✕ **Elvira.** The free shot of tequila that comes with each meal will whet your appetite for Elvira's reliable fish dishes, chicken mole, and chiles rellenos. This large, friendly restaurant (divided into intimate dining areas) is at the foot of Avenida Obregón just south of the border and popular with those who visit Nogales often. Grandmother Elvira herself is no longer around, but her succulent signature dish, shrimp Elvira-style, steamed in white wine, lives on. ⊠ *Avda. Obregón 1, Mexico* ☎ *631/ 2–47–73* ☖ *Reservations not accepted* ▤ *DC, MC, V.*

¢–$ ✕ **Zula's.** Standard, old-fashioned border restaurant fare is served with Greek flair here on the Arizona side, with Sonoran food (tortillas, cheese, refried beans) alongside gyros and American selections such as burgers, steaks, and seafood entrées. It makes for an interesting combination. It's not as glitzy as the south-of-the-border places, but the food is just as tasty. ⊠ *982 N. Grand Ave.* ☎ *520/287–2892* ▤ *MC, V.*

¢ ▣ **Americana Motor Hotel.** A serviceable place that has seen better days, the Americana has large, Aztec-style stone sculptures scattered around the grounds. Spacious and decorated in a Southwest motif, rooms are comfortable but worn. The restaurant and lounge are casual places to eat American food. ⊠ *639 N. Grand Ave., 85621* ☎ *520/287–7211 or 800/874–8079* ▭ *97 rooms* ⚄ *Restaurant, pool, bar* ▤ *AE, MC, V.*

¢ ▣ **El Dorado Motel.** This typical motel offers casual, unpretentious border flavor. The small-town service, although friendly, is not particularly quick. ⊠ *884 N. Grand Ave., 85621* ☎ *520/287–4611* ▤ *520/287–0101* ▭ *100 rooms* ⚄ *Pool, outdoor hot tub* ▤ *AE, MC, V.*

Shopping

The main shopping area is on the Mexican side, on Avenida Obregón, which begins a few blocks west (to your right) of the border entrance and runs north–south; just follow the crowds. You'll find handicrafts, furnishings, and jewelry here, but if you go off on some of the side streets, you might come across more interesting finds at better prices. Except at shops that indicate otherwise, bargaining is not only acceptable but expected. Playing this customary game can save you, on average, 50%, so don't be shy. The shops listed below tend to have fixed prices, so either buy here if you don't want to bargain at all, or note their prices and see if you can do better elsewhere.

Casa Bonita (⊠ Avda. Obregón 134, Mexico ☎ 631/2–30–59) carries jewelry, a nice selection of tinwork mirrors, carved wooden chests, and interesting household items.

El Changarro (⊠ Calle Elias 93, Mexico ☎ 613/2–05–45) sells high-quality (and high-priced) furniture, antiques, pottery, and handwoven rugs. It's next door to El Balcón de la Roca.

El Sarape (⊠ Avda. Obregón 161, Mexico ☎ 631/2–03–09) specializes in sterling silver jewelry from Taxco and women's designer clothing.

Maya de México (⊠ Avda. Obregón 150, Mexico ☎ no phone) is the place to come for smaller folk-art items, including Day of the Dead displays, blue glass, painted dishes, and colorful clothing.

TUCSON A TO Z

To research prices, get advice from other travelers, and book travel arrangements, visit ⊕ www.fodors.com

AIR TRAVEL

Check plane fares carefully when planning your trip. Although you may not want to spend time in Phoenix, sometimes it's cheaper to fly into that city and then take a scenic 2½-hour drive down the Pinal Pioneer Parkway (U.S. 79), or a speedier (by ½-hour) trip on I–10, to Tucson.

Airlines operating out of Tucson include Aerocalifornia, Aeroméxico/ Aerolitoral, Alaska Airlines, America West, American, Continental, Delta/Skywest, Northwest, Southwest, and United/Lufthansa.

AIRPORTS & TRANSFERS

Tucson International Airport is 8½ mi south of downtown, west of I–10 off the Valencia exit.

🄵 **Tucson International Airport** ☎ 520/573–8000 ⊕ www.tucsonairport.org.

AIRPORT TRANSFERS Many hotels provide courtesy airport shuttle service; inquire when making reservations.

It makes sense to rent a car at the airport; all the major rental-car agencies—Avis, Budget, Hertz, and National—are represented, along with Alamo, Dollar, and Thrifty. The driving time from the airport to the center of town varies, but it's usually less than half an hour; add 15 minutes during rush hours (7:30 AM–9 AM and 4:30 PM–6 PM). Parking is not a problem in most parts of town.

For $9–$38, depending on the location, Arizona Stagecoach takes groups and individuals to all parts of Tucson and Green Valley. If you're traveling light and aren't in a hurry, you can take a city Sun Tran bus to central Tucson. Bus 11, which leaves every half hour from a stop at the left of the lower level as you come out of the terminal, goes north on Alvernon Way, and you can transfer to most of the east–west bus lines from this main north–south road; ask the bus driver which one would take you closest to the location you need. You can also transfer to several lines from Bus 6, which leaves less frequently from the same airport location and heads to the Roy Laos center at the south of town.
🚩 **Arizona Stagecoach** ☎ 520/889-1000. **Sun Tran** ☎ 520/792-9222.

BUS TRAVEL TO & FROM TUCSON
Buses to Los Angeles, El Paso, Phoenix, Flagstaff, Douglas, and Nogales (Arizona) depart and arrive regularly from Tucson's Greyhound Lines terminal. For travel to Phoenix, Arizona Shuttle Service, Inc., runs express service from three locations in Tucson every hour on the hour, 4 AM–9 PM every day; the trip takes about 2¼ hours. One-way fare is $24. Call 24 hours in advance for reservations.
🚩 **Arizona Shuttle Service, Inc.** ☎ 520/795-6771. **Greyhound Lines terminal** ✉ 2 S. 4th Ave., at E. Broadway Blvd., Downtown ☎ 520/792-3475.

BUS TRAVEL WITHIN TUCSON
Within the city limits, public transportation, which is geared primarily to commuters, is available through Sun Tran, Tucson's bus system. On weekdays, bus service starts around 5 AM; some lines operate until 10 PM, but most go only until 7 or 8 PM, and weekend service is limited. A one-way ride costs $1; transfers are free, but be sure to request them when you pay your fare, for which exact change is required. An all-day pass costs $2. Those with valid Medicare cards can ride for 40¢. Call for information on Sun Tran bus routes.

The city-run Van Tran has specially outfitted vans for riders with disabilities. Call for information and reservations.
🚩 **Sun Tran** ☎ 520/792-9222. **Van Tran** ☎ 520/620-1234.

BUSINESS HOURS
BANKS Banks are generally open 9–4 Monday through Thursday and 9–6 on Friday. Bank One branches inside Fry's Grocery stores are also open Saturday 9–5.

POST OFFICES Most post office stations are open weekdays 8:30–5. Some have Saturday-morning hours as well.

SHOPS Retail stores are typically open Monday through Saturday 10–5 and Sunday noon–5. Mall stores stay open until 9 PM weekdays and 6 PM weekends.

CAR RENTALS
You will need a car to get around Tucson and the surrounding area. If you haven't rented a car at the Tucson International Airport, or if you

want to save the 10% "airport concession fee" the airport imposes on renters there, several car-rental agencies also have pick-up and drop-off locations in the central, northwest, and east areas of town. In addition, Carefree Rent-a-Car rents reliable used cars at good rates. If you think you might be interested in driving farther into Mexico than Nogales (where you can park on the U.S. side of the border), check in advance to make sure that the rental company will allow this and that you are covered on your rental insurance policy: many rental insurance agreements do not cover accidents or thefts that occur outside the United States.

Alamo ☎ 520/573-4740. **Avis** ☎ 520/294-1494. **Budget** ☎ 520/889-8800. **Carefree Rent-a-Car** ☎ 520/790-2655. **Dollar** ☎ 520/573-8486. **Enterprise** ☎ 520/792-1602. **Hertz** ☎ 520/294-7616. **National** ☎ 520/573-8050. **Thrifty** ☎ 520/790-2277.

CAR TRAVEL

From Phoenix, 111 mi northwest, I–10 east is the road that will take you to Tucson. Also a major north–south traffic artery along the west side of town, I–10 has well-marked exits all along the route. At Casa Grande, 70 mi north of Tucson, I–8 connects with I–10, bringing travelers into the area from Yuma and San Diego. From Nogales, 63 mi south on the Mexican border, take I–19 into Tucson.

ROAD CONDITIONS — Much of the year, traffic in Tucson isn't especially heavy, but during the busiest winter months (December through March), streets in the central area of town can get congested during rush hour, between 4 and 6 PM.

RULES OF THE ROAD — If you drive on Broadway Boulevard or Grant Road, note that the center lanes change from left-turn lanes to through-traffic lanes during rush hour (watch the signage carefully). These are called "suicide lanes" by locals because unwitting drivers wander into them for left turns at the wrong time of day. There's a seat-belt law in the state, as well as one that requires children under the age of four to ride in a secure child-restraint seat.

Don't even think of drinking and driving; if you do, you may spend your vacation in jail. Arizona's strict laws against driving under the influence are strongly enforced.

EMERGENCIES

Ambulance, Fire, Police **Emergency Services** ☎ 911.

Hospitals **Columbia Northwest Medical Center** ✉ 6200 N. La Cholla Blvd., Northwest ☎ 520/742-9000. **St. Joseph's Hospital** ✉ 350 N. Wilmot Rd., Eastside ☎ 520/873-3000. **Tucson Medical Center** ✉ 5301 E. Grant Rd., Central ☎ 520/327-5461. **University Medical Center** ✉ 1501 N. Campbell Ave., University ☎ 520/694-0111; a teaching hospital with a first-rate trauma center.

Pharmacies **Walgreens 24-Hour Pharmacy** ✉ 4685 E. Grant Rd., Central ☎ 520/326-4341 ✉ 7114 N. Oracle Rd., Northwest ☎ 520/297-2826.

LODGING

Several of the larger, more professionally run inns in town have formed Premier Bed & Breakfast Inns of Tucson. Write or call for a brochure.

Premier Bed & Breakfast Inns of Tucson 316 E. Speedway Blvd., 85705 ☎ 520/628-1800 or 800/628-5654 🖷 520/792-1880.

SIGHTSEEING TOURS

ADVENTURE & ECOTOURS — Sunshine Jeep Tours and Trail Dust Adventures arrange trips into the Sonoran Desert outside Tucson in open-air, four-wheel-drive vehicles. Baja's Frontier Tours and Desert Path Tours explore the natural history of Tucson and the surrounding area.

Baja's Frontier Tours ☎ 520/887-2340 or 888/297-2508 ⊕ www.bajasfrontiertours. com. **Desert Path Tours** ☎ 520/327-7235. **Sunshine Jeep Tours** ☎ 520/742-1943

⊕ www.sunshinejeeptours.com. **Trail Dust Adventures** ☎ 520/747-0323 ⊕ www.traildustadventures.com.

ORIENTATION
TOURS

Great Western Tours takes individuals and groups to such popular sights as Old Tucson, Sabino Canyon, and the Arizona–Sonora Desert Museum; in-depth tours of the city and its neighborhoods are also available. Old Pueblo Tours, with a slightly different itinerary (including "A" Mountain and Mission San Xavier del Bac), provides a fine historical overview of the area. Many tour operators are on limited schedules (or close altogether) during the summer, but Off the Beaten Path Tours has excellent customized excursions year-round throughout the Southwest United States and Mexico.

🚩 **Great Western Tours** ☎ 520/572-1660 ⊕ www.greatwesterntours.com. **Off the Beaten Path Tours** ☎ 520/529-6090. **Old Pueblo Tours** ☎ 520/795-7448 ⊕ www.oldpueblotours.com.

SPECIAL-
INTEREST TOURS

In the spring and fall, those interested in visiting the area's historic missions can contact Kino Mission Tours, which has professional historians and bilingual guides on staff.

🚩 **Kino Mission Tours** ☎ 520/628-1269.

WALKING TOURS

The friendly, knowledgeable docents of the Arizona Historical Society conduct walking tours of El Presidio neighborhood (departing from the Sosa-Carillo-Fremont House) every Saturday at 10 from November through March; the cost is $5. Old Pueblo Walking Tours offers two-hour walking tours of the downtown historic districts led by Ken Scoville, a living encyclopedia of Tucson's history.

🚩 **Arizona Historical Society** ☎ 520/622-0956 ⊕ www.arizona.edu/KERN⁻azhist. **Old Pueblo Walking Tours** ☎ 520/323-9290.

TAXIS

Taxi rates vary widely; they are unregulated in Arizona. It's always wise to inquire about the cost of a trip before getting into a cab. You shouldn't pay much more than $18 from the airport to central Tucson. Two of the more reliable Tucson cab companies are Allstate Taxi and Yellow Cab, which also operates Fiesta Taxi, whose drivers speak both English and Spanish.

🚩 **Allstate Taxi** ☎ 520/798-1111. **Fiesta Taxi** ☎ 520/622-7777. **Yellow Cab** ☎ 520/624-6611.

TRAIN TRAVEL

Amtrak serves the city with westbound and eastbound trains six times a week.

🚩 **Amtrak** ✉ 400 E. Toole Ave., Downtown ☎ 520/623-4442.

VISITOR INFORMATION

🚩 **Metropolitan Tucson Convention and Visitors Bureau** ✉ 110 S. Church Ave., Downtown, 85701 ☎ 520/624-1817 or 800/638-8350 ⊕ www.visittucson.org.

SOUTHERN ARIZONA

7

FODOR'S CHOICE

Canyon Rose Suites, *Bisbee*

Chiricahua National Monument

Holiday Inn Express, *a budget hotel in Benson*

Kartchner Caverns State Park, *south of Benson*

Ruiz's Mexican Food & Cantina, *a budget restaurant in Benson*

School House Inn Bed & Breakfast, *a budget B&B in Bisbee*

Texas Canyon, *a scenic drive west of Willcox*

HIGHLY RECOMMENDED

RESTAURANTS   Café Roka, *Bisbee*

Café Sonoita, *Sonoita*

Parana's Bistro, *Bisbee*

HOTELS   Best Western Coronado Motor Hotel, *Yuma*

Grapevine Canyon Ranch, *a guest ranch near Chiricahua National Monument*

Ramsey Canyon Inn Bed & Breakfast, *Hereford*

Skywatcher's Inn, *Benson*

Updated by
Mara Levin

SOUTHERN ARIZONA CAN DO little to escape its cliché-ridden image as a landscape of cow skulls, tumbleweeds, dried-up riverbeds, and mother lodes—it doesn't need to. The area that evokes such American dime-novel notions as Indian wars, vast land grants, and savage shoot-'em-ups is not simply another part of the Wild West drunk on romanticized images of its former self; local farmers and ranchers here evoke the self-sufficiency and ruggedness of their pioneer ancestors and revel in the area's rowdy past. Abandoned mining towns and sleepy Western hamlets dot a lonely landscape of rugged rock formations, deep pine forests, dense mountain ranges, and scrubby grasslands.

South of Sierra Vista, just above the Mexican border, a stone marker commemorates the spot where the first Europeans set foot in what is now the United States. In 1540, 80 years before the Pilgrims landed at Plymouth Rock, Spanish conquistador Don Francisco Vásquez de Coronado led one of Spain's largest expeditions from Mexico along the fertile San Pedro River valley, where the little towns of Benson and St. David are found today. They had come north to seek the legendary Seven Cities of Cíbola, where Native American pueblos were rumored to have doors of polished turquoise and streets of solid gold.

The real wealth of the region, however, lay in its rich veins of copper and silver, not tapped until more than 300 years after the Spanish marched on in disappointment. Once word of this cache spread, these parts of the West quickly grew much wilder: fortune seekers who rushed to the region came face-to-face with the Chiricahua Apaches, led by Cochise and Geronimo, while from rugged mountain hideaways Indian warriors battled encroaching settlers and the U.S. Cavalry sent to protect them.

Although the search for mineral booty in southeastern Arizona is much more notorious, the western side of the state wasn't entirely untouched by the rage to plunder the earth. The leaching plant built by the New Cornelia Copper Company in 1917 transformed the sleepy desert community of Ajo into one of the most important mining districts in the state. Interest in going for the gold in California gave rise to the town of Yuma: the Colorado River had to be crossed to get to the West Coast, and Fort Yuma was established in part to protect the Anglo ferry business at a good fording point of the river from Indian competitors. The Yuma tribe lost that battle, but another group of Native Americans, the Tohono O'odham, fared better in this part of the state. Known for a long time as the Papago—or "bean eaters," a name given them by the Spanish—they were deeded a large portion of their ancestral homeland by the U.S. Bureau of Indian Affairs. The largest of their three reservations, stretching across an almost completely undeveloped section of southwestern Arizona, encompasses 2,774,370 acres.

Exploring Southern Arizona

The diverse geography of this region and the driving distances between sights require you to make some thoughtful decisions when planning your tour. With Tucson as a starting point, the rolling hills and grasslands of Sonoita and Patagonia are little more than an hour away, as are the underground marvels in Kartchner Caverns (to the southeast) and the starry skies above Kitt Peak Observatory (to the southwest). You can explore the Old West of Tombstone, Bisbee, and the surrounding ghost towns in one day, or more leisurely in two. To see hillsides covered with Organ Pipe Cactus National Monument, however, you'll need to drive about three hours southwest to reach the national monument and then take at least a full day to hike or drive around it

Numbers in the text correspond to numbers in the margin and on the Southeast Arizona and Southwest Arizona maps.

7

If you have
2 days

If you only have a short time to explore this region, you'll have to choose whether to tour the eastern or western section of southern Arizona. If you are headed east from Tucson, poke around the town of **Patagonia** ❷ ☞ and the Patagonia–Sonoita Creek preserve in the morning, and then continue east to **Tombstone** ❹ in the afternoon. After strolling the shoot-'em-up capital, head south to 🔲 **Bisbee** ❺, a good place to spend the night. Take the mine tour the next morning and devote the afternoon to exploring the shops on Main Street.

If you're going west, take a leisurely drive to **Kitt Peak National Observatory** ⓮ ☞. Stop at the Tohono O'odham Reservation capital, **Sells** ⓯, en route to 🔲 **Ajo** ⓰, where you'll sleep. Plan to spend most of the next day hiking or driving around **Organ Pipe Cactus National Monument** ⓱, but set aside a little time to explore the pleasant mining town.

If you have
4 days

Begin your tour in Arizona wine country. First, head to **Patagonia** ❷ ☞, where you can visit the vineyards around **Sonoita** ❶ and Elgin. Stay overnight here or in 🔲 **Sierra Vista** ❸ near Ramsey Canyon, where you're likely to be greeted by hummingbirds in the morning. Head out early for **Tombstone** ❹ so you can spend the morning exploring the town; in the afternoon head south to see the sights of 🔲 **Bisbee** ❺ and stay overnight. Head north the next day to **Chiricahua National Monument** ❼, hike or drive through the magnificent rock formations, and spend the night in the area. On your way back toward Tucson, stop in Dragoon at **Texas Canyon** ❿ and visit the Amerind Foundation's gallery and museum. A few miles farther west on I–10 is **Benson** ⓫, where you can have lunch and then tour the huge underground world of stalactites and stalagmites in **Kartchner Caverns State Park** ⓬.

If you have
7 days

If you have a week to explore only southern Arizona, follow the four-day southeastern Arizona tour, above, and spend the night in 🔲 **Benson** ⓫ after your Kartchner Caverns tour. Then set out the next morning on the two-day southwestern Arizona tour, continuing on to 🔲 **Yuma** ⓲, especially if desert hiking in Organ Pipe Cactus National Monument isn't to your liking.

---

and the town of Ajo. A trek through the stunning Chiricahua rock formations calls for an overnight stay, since the area is a 2½-hour drive southeast of Tucson; you may wish to make an overnight stop in Texas Canyon or Willcox.

About the Restaurants

In southern Arizona, cowboy fare is more common than haute cuisine. But there are exceptions to the rule, especially in the wine-growing area of Sonoita and in Bisbee, both popular for weekend outings from Tucson. And, of course, a region that shares its border with Mexico is bound to have a fair number of good taquerias.

About the Hotels

From historic hotels, bed-and-breakfasts, and guest ranches to Nature Conservancy casitas, southern Arizona has an increasing array of properties that let you lay down your head surrounded by nature and history. Still, it's easy to find the park-your-car-outside-the-room chain-variety lodgings. Prices for the "high" season (winter and spring) tend to be a bit higher than for the "low" season (summer to early fall).

	WHAT IT COSTS				
	$$$$	**$$$**	**$$**	**$**	**¢**
RESTAURANTS	over $30	$20–$30	$12–$20	$8–$12	under $8
HOTELS	over $250	$175–$250	$120–$175	$70–$120	under $70

Restaurant prices are per person for a main course at dinner. Hotel prices are for two people in a standard double room in high season, excluding taxes and service charges.

Timing

As you might expect, the desert areas are popular in winter, and the cooler mountain areas are more heavily visited in summer months. Southern Arizona has developed seasonal travel, causing area hotels to adopt "high-season" (winter and spring) and "low-season" (summer and early fall) prices. In general, however, prices tend to be lower here than in the more touristed areas to the north.

SOUTHEAST ARIZONA

From the rugged mountain forests to the desert grasslands of Sierra Vista, the southeast corner of Arizona is one of the state's most scenic regions. Much of this area is part of Cochise County, named in 1881 in honor of the chief of the Chiricahua Apache. Cochise waged war against troops and settlers for 11 years, and he was respected by Indian and non-Indian alike for his integrity and leadership skills. Today Cochise County is dotted by small towns, many of them much smaller—and all much tamer—than they were in their heyday. Cochise County encompasses 6 and part of the 7th of the 12 mountain ranges—including the Huachucas, Mustangs, Whetstones, and Rincons—that compose the 1.7-million-acre Coronado National Forest.

Sonoita

❶ *34 mi southeast of Tucson on I–10 to AZ 83, 57 mi west of Tombstone.*

Sonoita, once little more than a truck stop at the junction of AZ 83 and AZ 82, has come to life with the establishment of a few upscale B&Bs and restaurants, but the nearby wineries are what draw crowds. La Pradera, the hilly region around the town, has attracted Hollywood film crews with its natural, Tuscany-like beauty; a few miles to the east is Arizona's primary wine-producing region.

To explore the wineries of southern Arizona, head south on AZ 83 from Sonoita and then east on Elgin Road. Most of the growers are in and around the tiny village of Elgin, which is 9 mi southeast of Sonoita. You'll find quite a few good wineries as well as several horse farms in this scenic ranching region.

If you'd like to sample some local products and learn more about wine- and beer-making without traveling as far south as Sonoita, stop at **Dark Mountain Brewery and Winery** (⊠ 13605 E. Benson Hwy. [Frontage

Bird-Watching

Southern Arizona is one of the best areas for bird-watching in the United States; nearly 500 species have been spotted in the area. To the east, birders flock to the Patagonia-Sonoita Creek and Ramsey Canyon preserves, the San Pedro Riparian National Conservation Area, the ponds and dry lake beds south of Willcox, and the Portal-Cave Creek area in the Chiricahua Mountains near the New Mexico border. To the west, the Buenos Aires and Imperial national wildlife refuges are among the many places famed for their abundance of avian visitors.

Camping

Sleeping under the vast, starry desert sky reminds you that there are still huge swaths of undeveloped wilderness in the untrammeled southwest. You can find at least 100 camping areas set throughout southern Arizona. Though it can get chilly at night in the desert, the weather's usually good enough year-round to make sleeping out an appealing option. Summer is the time to camp in the state's cooler, higher-altitude campgrounds. Campgrounds in the rural areas of southern Arizona rarely come close to getting full except on holiday weekends, and even then, campers tend to stay close to major cities and towns. Keep in mind that you will find fairly primitive camping conditions (RV hook-ups are rare). It is advisable to bring your own fresh drinking water and be prepared to carry out what trash you bring in.

Ghost Towns

A number of the smaller mining communities in Cochise County died when their veins of ore ran out, and their adobe buildings gradually melted back into the desert under the summer monsoons. Some of what are termed ghost towns in the area are only heaps of rubble, but others show strong evidence of better days. In addition to Gleeson and Fairbank, a few holdouts remain—with enough residents to keep the post office open—in the town of Dos Cabezas, 15 mi southeast of Willcox, where you'll see the 1885 Wells Fargo station still standing. A tunnel through the mountaintop connects the eastern and western halves of the abandoned town of Hilltop, farther southeast of Willcox. Six miles northwest of Portal in the Chiricahua Mountains, Paradise was active in the 1900s, and a few old-timers still live here. Look for the old town jail among the ruined buildings.

Hiking

You can trek under, over, and through dramatic rock formations in both Chiricahua National Monument and the Dragoon Mountains. Grasslands and waterways abound in Nature Conservancy preserves such as Ramsey Canyon, Arivaipa Canyon, the Patagonia-Sonoita Creek Sanctuary, and Muleshoe Ranch. Organ Pipe National Monument offers sweeping vistas of the Sonoran Desert; and hiking trails in the Huachuca, Patagonia, Rincon, and Whetstone mountain ranges afford striking ridgetop views.

Wineries

The term "Arizona wine country" may sound odd, but the soil and climate in the Santa Cruz Valley southeast of Tucson are ideal for growing grapes. Connoisseurs debate the merits of the wines produced in this area since 1974, but if you want to decide for yourself, tour some of the region's wineries.

Southeast Arizona

Rd.], Vail ☎ 520/749–2298 ⊕ www.darkmountainbrewery.com). Take I–10 east from Tucson about 12 mi to Vail, Exit 279. This is the only brewery and winery on the same premises in the state, and it's about 24 mi farther north than most of the other wineries.

Callaghan Vineyards (⊠ 336 Elgin Rd., Elgin ☎ 520/455–5322 ⊕ www.callaghanvineyards.com), which is open Friday–Sunday 11–3, produces the best wine in Arizona. Its Buena Suerte Cuvee is highly regarded by the wine press. In the town of Elgin, stop in for tastings daily from 10 to 5 at **Village of Elgin Winery** (⊠ The Elgin Complex, Upper Elgin Rd., Elgin ☎ 520/455–9309 ⊕ www.elginwines.com), the largest producer of wines in the state. **Sonoita Vineyards** (⊠ Canelo Rd., Elgin, 3 mi southwest of town, ☎ 520/455–5893 ⊕ www.sonoitavineyards.com), known for its high-quality reds, offers tours and tastings daily 10–4.

Where to Stay & Eat

$–$$ ✕ **Steak Out Restaurant & Saloon.** A frontier-style design and weathered-wood exterior belie the newness of this structure, built and owned by the same family that operates the Sonoita Inn next door. The restaurant features tasty cowboy fare: mesquite-grilled steaks, ribs, chicken, and fish. ⊠ 3235 AZ 82 ☎ 520/455–5205 ⊟ AE, D, DC, MC, V ☾ No lunch weekdays.

★ **¢–$** ✕ **Café Sonoita.** Like Sonoita itself, the Café Sonoita combines big-city sophistication with small-town charm. A local favorite, the restaurant also draws day-trippers from Tucson and tourists from afar. The dinner menu, which changes daily, includes generous portions of fresh seafood, poultry, and meats in creative combinations with locally grown produce. You'll find lush sandwiches for lunch, plus local wines and beers. ⊠ 3280 AZ 82 ☎ 520/455–5278 ⊟ MC, V ☾ Closed Sun.–Tues.

$–$$ ⊞ **Sonoita Inn.** This inn, whose owner also owned the late, famous Triple Crown–winning race horse Secretariat, is centrally located at the intersection of AZ 82 and AZ 83. Spacious guest rooms, some with views of the Santa Rita mountains, feature what the owners call "luxurious rustic Western country living," complete with hardwood floors, colorful woven rugs, retro-cowboy bedspreads, and VCRs. ⊠ *3243 AZ 82* ⌂ *Box 99, 85637* ☏ *520/455–5935 or 800/696–1006* ⎙ *520/455–5069* ⊕ *www.sonoitainn.com* ⮐ *18 rooms* ⌂ *Cable TV, in-room VCRs* ▭ *AE, D, MC, V* ⏐◯⏐ *CP.*

$ ⊞ **Rainbow's End.** An old ranch manager's home atop a hill overlooking the Sonoita countryside, this B&B has been painstakingly renovated and furnished in period antiques. Four bedrooms, each with a modern bathroom, share a great room with fireplace and a big kitchen, where guests can assemble their own Continental breakfast and snacks (supplied by the hosts, who live in a separate house down the hill). A few stalls at this serious horse-breeding ranch are also available, for those who vacation with their trusty steeds. ⊠ *3088 AZ 83* ⌂ *Box 717, 85637* ☏ *520/455–0202* ⎙ *520/455–0303* ⊕ *www. gaitedmountainhorses.com* ⮐ *4 rooms* ⌂ *Library; no children under 12* ▭ *No credit cards* ⏐◯⏐ *CP.*

Patagonia

▶ ❷   *12 mi southwest of Sonoita via AZ 82.*

Served by a spur of the Atchison, Topeka, and Santa Fe Railroad, Patagonia was a shipping center for cattle and ore. The town declined after the railroad departed in 1962, and the old depot is now the town hall. Today, art galleries and boutiques coexist with real Western saloons in this tiny, tree-lined village in the Patagonia Mountains. Most of the town's shops and eateries are closed Monday.

The **Patagonia Visitors Center** (⊠ 307 McKeown Ave. ☏ 520/394–0060 or 888/794–0060) is a good first stop for an overview of the region; it's closed on Tuesday. **Mariposa Books & More** (⊠ 307 McKeown Ave. ☏ 520/394–9186), which shares quarters with the visitor center, is also worthy of a look around. It is closed Tuesday.

At the Nature Conservancy's **Patagonia–Sonoita Creek Preserve,** 1,400 acres of riparian habitat are protected along the Patagonia–Sonoita Creek. More than 275 bird species have been sighted here, along with deer, javelina, coatimundi, desert tortoise, snakes, and more. There is a self-guided nature trail; guided walks are given every Saturday at 9 AM. Three concrete structures near an elevated berm of the Railroad Trail serve as reminders of the land's former use. To reach the preserve from Patagonia, make a right on 4th Avenue; at the stop sign, turn left onto Blue Haven Road. This paved road soon becomes dirt and leads to the preserve in about 1¼ mi. ⊠ *150 Blue Haven Rd.* ☏ *520/394–2400* ⊕ *www.tncarizona.org* ⌑ *$5* ◷ *Wed.–Sun. 7:30–3:30.*

Eleven miles south of town, **Patagonia Lake State Park** is popular for water sports, picnicking, and camping. Formed by the damming of Sonoita Creek, the 265-acre reservoir lures fishers with its largemouth bass, crappie, bluegill, and catfish; it's stocked with rainbow trout in the wintertime. You can rent rowboats, paddleboats, canoes, and camping and fishing gear at the marina. Most swimmers head for Boulder Beach. ⊠ *400 Lake Patagonia Rd.* ☏ *520/287–6965* ⊕ *www.pr.state.az.us* ⌑ *$7 per vehicle* ◷ *Visitor center daily 9–4:30, gates closed 10 PM–4 AM.*

Sonoita Creek State Natural Area. Arizona State Parks has designated almost 5,000 acres surrounding Patagonia Lake as a state natural area.

This project, funded by the Arizona State Parks Heritage Fund (lottery monies) and the State Lake Improvement Fund, offers environmental educational programs and university-level research opportunities. The riparian area is home to giant cottonwoods, willows, sycamores, and mesquites; nesting black hawks; and endangered species. ⊠ *AZ 82, 5 mi south of town* ☎ *800/285–3703* ⊕ *www.pr.state.az.us.*

Where to Stay & Eat

$–$$ ╳ **Velvet Elvis Pizza Co.** There can't be too many places where you can enjoy a gourmet pizza heaped with organic veggies, a crisp salad of organic greens tossed with homemade dressing, and freshly pressed carrot juice, organic wine, and microbrewed and imported beer while surrounded by images of Elvis *and* the Virgin Mary. The desserts are homemade, too. ⊠ *292 Naugle Ave.* ☎ *520/394–2102* ⊟ *MC, V* ☉ *Closed Mon.–Wed.*

$ ╳ **Wagon Wheel Saloon.** The Wagon Wheel's restaurant, serving ribs, steaks, and burgers, is a more recent development, but the cowboy bar, with its neon beer signs and mounted moose head, has been around since the early 1900s. This is where every Stetson-wearing ranch hand in the area comes to listen to the country jukebox and down a long-neck, maybe accompanied by some poppers (deep-fried hot peppers stuffed with cream cheese). ⊠ *400 W. Naugle Ave.* ☎ *520/394–2433* ⊟ *AE, MC, V.*

¢   ╳ **Gathering Grounds.** This colorful little café and espresso bar serves up healthful breakfasts and imaginative soups, salads, and sandwiches through the late afternoon. Whole-grain muffins and organically grown fruits and veggies make for a great repast of earthy comfort food. ⊠ *319 McKeown Ave.* ☎ *520/394–2097* ⊟ *No credit cards* ☉ *No dinner.*

$$$$ ▦ **Circle Z Ranch.** Rimmed by giant sycamore, ash, and cottonwood trees and surrounded by the Patagonia–Sonoita Creek Preserve, this guest ranch has served as the setting of movies such as *Red River* and several episodes of *Gunsmoke.* Rooms in the adobe-style buildings are spacious, with hardwood floors and area rugs, king-size or twin beds, and antique Monterrey wooden chests. Meals are prepared to suit individual tastes, which might explain why more than 60% of business here comes from repeat customers. Riders from beginners through advanced can be accommodated on adventurous, scenic trails. All meals, riding, and amenities are included. ⊠ *AZ 82, 4 mi southwest of town* ⍟ *Box 194, 85624* ☎ *520/394–2525 or 888/854–2525* ⊕ *www.circlez.com* ⇱ *24 units* ⅙ *Dining room, tennis court, pool, billiards, hiking, horseback riding, Ping-Pong; no room phones, no room TVs* ⊟ *MC, V* ☉ *Closed mid-May–Oct.* ⅣⅠ *FAP.*

$ ▦ **Duquesne House Bed & Breakfast/Gallery.** The rooms of this corrugate tin–roof adobe B&B, built as a miner's boardinghouse at the turn of the 20th century, have been decorated with a wonderfully whimsical hand by owner-artist Regina Medley. Western-period furniture collected in the Patagonia area fills the house and the four high-ceilinged guest rooms, each with a private entrance. Breakfast may be enjoyed in your room, on the flower-filled screened porch, or in the Santa Fe–style great room. ⊠ *357 Duquesne Ave.* ⍟ *Box 772, 85624* ☎ *520/394–2732* ⇱ *4 suites* ⊟ *No credit cards* ⅣⅠ *BP.*

¢–$ ▦ **Stage Stop Inn.** Old territorial appearance notwithstanding, the building isn't historic and the rooms are standard motel issue, but this is still a decent place to lay your head for the night. The public areas have character, the center-of-town location is prime, and the price is right. ⊠ *303 W. McKeown Ave.* ⍟ *Box 777, 85624* ☎ *520/394–2211 or 800/923–2211* ⊟ *520/394–2212* ⇱ *43 rooms* ⅙ *Restaurant, pool, lounge* ⊟ *AE, D, DC, MC, V.*

¢ ⚠ **Patagonia Lake Campground.** This civilized campground in Patagonia Lake State Park has water, showers, rest rooms, a general store, and a marina, and even some boat-camping sites. Arizona has a surprising number of water-recreation lovers, so you can expect the campsites to fill up quickly—plus, you can't make reservations. ♿ *Flush toilets, partial hook-ups (electric and water), dump station, drinking water, showers, grills, picnic tables, public telephone, general store, lake ⬚ 72 tent sites, 34 RV sites, 13 boat sites* ✉ *AZ 82, 4 mi southeast of town,* ☎ *602/542-4174 or 800/285-3703* ⊕ *www.pr.state.az.us* ⬚ *Tent site $15, RV site $22* ⬚ *Reservations not accepted* ⊟ *MC, V* ☉ *Open year-round.*

Sierra Vista

❸ *42 mi southeast of Patagonia via AZ 82 to AZ 90.*

A temperate climate year-round has attracted retirees to this town, which is 4,620 ft above sea level. Although Sierra Vista is fairly characterless, with tract housing, RV parks, chain motels, and fast-food restaurants, it's a good base from which to explore the more scenic areas that surround it.

Historic Fort Huachuca, headquarters of the army's Global Information Systems Command, is the last of the great Western forts still in operation. It dates back to 1877, when the Buffalo Soldiers (yes, Bob Marley fans—*those* Buffalo Soldiers), the first all-black regiment in the U.S. forces, came to aid settlers battling invaders from Mexico, Indian tribes reluctant to give up their homelands, and assorted American desperadoes on the lam from the law back East. Three miles from the fort's main gate is the **Fort Huachuca Museum,** housed in a late-19th-century bachelor officers' quarters. The museum and its annex across the street provide a fascinating record of military life on the frontier. Enter the main gate of Fort Huachuca on AZ 90, west of Sierra Vista. ✉ *Grierson St., Fort Huachuca, off AZ 90, west of Sierra Vista* ☎ *520/533-5736* ⊕ *huachuca-www.army.mil* ⬚ *Free* ☉ *Weekdays 9–4, weekends 1–4.*

Those driving to **Coronado National Memorial,** dedicated to Francisco Vásquez de Coronado, will see many of the same stunning vistas of Arizona and Mexico the conquistador saw when he trod this route in 1540 seeking the mythical Seven Cities of Cíbola. It's a little more than 3 mi via a dirt road from the visitor center to Montezuma Pass, and another ½ mi on foot to the top of the nearly 7,000-ft Coronado Peak, where the views are best. Other trails include Joe's Canyon Trail, a steep 3-mi route (one-way) down to the visitor center, and Miller Peak Trail, 12 mi round-trip to the highest point in the Huachuca Mountains (Miller Peak is 9,466 ft). The turnoff for the monument is 16 mi south of Sierra Vista on AZ 92; the visitor center is 5 mi in. ✉ *4101 E. Montezuma Canyon Rd., Hereford* ☎ *520/366-5515* ⊕ *www.nps.gov/coro* ⬚ *Free* ☉ *Visitor center daily 8–5.*

Hikers and bird-watchers alike flock to the **Ramsey Canyon Preserve,** managed by the Nature Conservancy. The convergence of two mountain and desert systems—this spot marks the northernmost limit of the Sierra Madre and the southernmost limit of the Rockies, and it's at the edge of the Chihuahuan and Sonoran deserts—as well as the presence of the fresh water of the San Pedro River, makes it a mecca for bird life. Rare species such as the marvelously named elegant trogon nest here; between April and October, 14 species of hummingbird come to the area—more than get together anywhere else in the United States. Stop at the visitor center for maps and books on the area's natural history, flora, and fauna. To get here, take AZ 92 south from Sierra Vista for 6 mi, turn right on

Ramsey Canyon Road, and then go 4 mi to the preserve entrance. ✉ 27 *Ramsey Canyon Rd., Hereford* ☎ *520/378–2785* ⊕ *www.tncarizona. org* ☞ *$5* ⊙ *Daily 8–5.*

<table>
<tr><td>off the beaten path</td><td>

SAN PEDRO RIPARIAN NATIONAL CONSERVATION AREA – The San Pedro River, partially rerouted underground by an 1887 earthquake, may not look like much for most of the year, but it sustains an impressive array of flora and fauna. In order to maintain this fragile creek-side ecosystem, a 56,000-acre area along the river (extending about 40 mi north between the Mexican border and St. David) was designated a protected riparian area in 1988. (About 70%–80% of the state's wildlife depends on riparian habitats, which now constitute only 0.5% of Arizona's land.) More than 250 species of birds come here, as well as the occasional javelina, bobcat, and mountain lion. Forty thousand years ago, this was the domain of woolly mammoths and mastodons: many of the huge skeletons in Washington's Smithsonian Institute and New York's Museum of Natural History came from the massive fossil pits in the area. As evidenced by a number of small, unexcavated ruins, the various migratory Indian tribes who passed through centuries later also found this valley hospitable, in part because of its many useful plants. Information, guided tours, books, and gifts are available from the volunteer staff at San Pedro House, a visitor center operated by Friends of the San Pedro River. ✉ *San Pedro House, 9800 AZ 90* ☎ *520/458–3559 Sierra Vista BLM office* ⊕ *www.az.blm.gov* ☞ *Free* ⊙ *Visitor center daily 9:30–4:30, conservation area daily sunrise–sunset.*

</td></tr>
</table>

Where to Stay

★ **$$** 🏨 **Ramsey Canyon Inn Bed & Breakfast.** The Nature Conservancy's Ramsey Canyon Preserve is a bird haven, and the nearby Ramsey Canyon Inn is a bird-watcher's heaven. There are three housekeeping apartments and six guest rooms with private baths and antique furnishings, named for the hummingbirds that visit the inn's feeders and garden flowers. Guest-room rates include a full breakfast; coffee, tea, and homemade pies are served in the afternoon. Rooms are hard to get here during the spring, so advanced booking is a good idea. There's a two-night minimum from March through September. ✉ *29 Ramsey Canyon Rd., Hereford 85615* ☎ *520/378–3010* 🖶 *520/378–0487* ⊕ *www. ramseycanyoninn.com* ⏎ *6 rooms, two 1-bedroom cottages* ⟡ *Some kitchens; no phones in some rooms, no room TVs* ▭ *MC, V* ◉ *BP.*

$ 🏨 **Casa de San Pedro.** Bird-watchers are drawn to this contemporary hacienda-style B&B abutting the San Pedro Riparian National Conservation Area, and the hosts do everything they can to nourish it—they even provide a computer with Robert Tory Peterson software on it so that guests can identify the birds they spot from picture windows in the high-ceilinged common room. A number of hiking trails pass behind the house, and regular weekend birding courses and tours are offered. Guest quarters are bright and modern, and handcrafted wooden furnishings from northern Mexico lend local character. There's a two-night minimum. ✉ *8933 S. Yell La., Hereford 85615* ☎ *520/366–1300 or 888/257–2050* 🖶 *520/366–0701* ⊕ *www.bedandbirds.com* ⏎ *10 rooms* ⟡ *Library; no room phones, no room TVs* ▭ *AE, D, MC, V* ◉ *BP.*

$ 🏨 **Windemere Hotel & Conference Center.** This large hotel complex, across from the area's sprawling shopping mall, is on AZ 92 in what used to be the eastern outskirts of Sierra Vista but is now a rapidly growing commercial corridor. Despite all this development, it's not uncommon to see roadrunners dashing about the hotel grounds. The three-story hotel has large, comfortable rooms, and most offer sweeping views of the nearby Huachuca Mountains. Room rates include access to a nearby health club, complimentary breakfast buffet, and evening cocktails. ⊠ *2047 S. AZ 92, 85635* ☎ *520/459–5900 or 800/825–4656* 🖷 *520/458–1347* ⊕ *www.windemerehotel.com* ⊃ *149 rooms* ♨ *Restaurant, in-room data ports, microwaves, refrigerators, cable TV with movies and video games, pool, hot tub, lounge, dry cleaning, laundry facilities, laundry service, business services, meeting rooms, some pets allowed, no-smoking rooms* ⊟ *AE, D, DC, MC, V* ⦿ *BP.*

¢ 🛆 **Ramsey Vista.** Though not easy to reach—it's about 7,400 ft up the side of a mountain on an unpaved and winding road—this National Forest Service campground with bathrooms (no showers) but no hook-ups is never crowded and is well worth the trip. Reservations aren't accepted. The birding is excellent, and you are likely to see coatimundi, javelina, and deer. Go 7 mi south of Sierra Vista on AZ 92, then turn on Carr Canyon Road, and go 10 mi farther west. But RVs are not allowed on this road. ♨ *Pit toilets, fire pits, picnic tables* ⊃ *8 sites* ⊠ *Carr Canyon Rd.* ☎ *520/670–4552* ⊕ *www.fs.fed.us/r3/coronado* ⊠ *$10 per night* ⚰ *Reservations not accepted* ☉ *Open year-round, weather permitting.*

¢ 🛆 **Reef Townsite.** Named for the vanished mining town of Reef, this spot is a mile west of Ramsey Vista, high up on a mountainside in a ponderosa pine forest. It has rest rooms but no drinking water, showers, or hookups. Reservations are not accepted. Go 7 mi south of Sierra Vista on AZ 92, then turn on Carr Canyon Road, and go 11 mi farther west. ♨ *Toilets, fire pits, grills, picnic tables* ⊃ *14 sites* ⊠ *Carr Canyon Rd.* ☎ *520/670–4552* ⊕ *www.fs.fed.us/r3/coronado* ⊠ *$10 per night* ⚰ *Reservations not accepted* ☉ *Open year-round, weather permitting.*

Tombstone

❹ *28 mi northeast of Sierra Vista via AZ 90, 24 mi south of Benson via AZ 80.*

It's hard to imagine now, but Tombstone, headquarters for most of the area's gamblers and gunfighters, was once bigger than San Francisco. These days it derives most of its revenue from tourism. The legendary headquarters of Wild West rowdies, Tombstone was part of an area called Goose Flats in the late 1800s and was prone to attack by nearby Apache tribesmen. Ed Schieffelin, an intrepid prospector, wasn't discouraged by those who cautioned that "all you'll find there is your tombstone." In 1877 he struck one of the West's richest veins of silver in the tough old hills and gave the town its name as an ironic "I told you so." He called the silver mine Lucky Cuss, figuring that he fit the description himself.

The promise of riches attracted all types of folks, including outlaws. Soon gambling halls, saloons, and houses of prostitution sprang up all along Allen Street. In 1881 the Earp family and Doc Holliday battled to the death with the Clanton boys at the famous shoot-out at the OK Corral. Over the past century, scriptwriters and storytellers have done much to rewrite the exact details of the confrontation, but it's a fact that the town was the scene of several gunfights in the 1880s. On Sunday, you can witness replays of some of these on Allen Street.

Tombstone's rough-and-ready heyday was popularized by Hollywood in the 1930s and capitalized on by the local tourist industry in the decades that followed, but there's more to the town than the OK Corral, the souvenir shops on Allen Street, and the staged shoot-outs. "The town too tough to die" (it survived two major fires, an earthquake, the closing of the mines, and the moving of the county seat to Bisbee) was also a cultural center, and many of its original buildings remain intact.

Allen Street, the town's main drag, is lined with restaurants and curio shops. Many of the street's buildings still bear bullet holes from their livelier days, and some of the remaining artifacts are interesting.

The **Tombstone Chamber of Commerce and Visitor Center** (⊠ 4th and Allen Sts. ☎ 520/457–3929 ⊕ www.tombstone.org) is the best place to start your tour of this tiny town. You can take a self-guided walking tour and wander at your leisure, or hop aboard an authentic stagecoach or covered wagon for a tour narrated by a real Tombstone native.

Boot Hill Graveyard, where the victims of the OK Corral shoot-out are buried, is on the northwestern corner of town, facing U.S. 80. If you're put off by the commercialism of the place—you enter through a gift shop that sells novelty items in the shape of tombstones—remember that Tombstone itself is the result of crass acquisition, a trait that tends to be decried in the present while its manifestations in the past are romanticized. Chinese names in one section bear testament to the laundry and restaurant workers who came from San Francisco during the height of Tombstone's mining fever. About a third of the more than 350 graves dug here from 1879 to 1974 are unmarked. ⊠ *U.S. 80* ☎ *520/457–9344* ☞ *Free* ◷ *Daily 7:30–6.*

For an introduction to the town's—and the area's—past, visit the **Tombstone Courthouse State Historic Park.** Displays include a reconstruction of the original 1882 courtroom, area artifacts, and numerous photographs of prominent—and notorious—town figures. ⊠ *Toughnut and 3rd Sts.* ☎ *520/457–3311* ⊕ *www.pr.state.az.us* ☞ *$2.50* ◷ *Daily 8–5.*

Originally a boardinghouse for the Vizina Mining Company and later a popular hotel, the **Rose Tree Inn Museum,** with its 1880s period rooms and gargantuan rosebush (claimed to be the world's largest) in the backyard, displays the gentler side of life in Tombstone. ⊠ *Toughnut and 4th Sts.* ☎ *520/457–3326* ☞ *$2* ◷ *Daily 9–5.*

You'll get a dramatic version of the town's past, narrated by Vincent Price, in the **Historama**—a 26-minute multimedia presentation on Tombstone's history. At the adjoining **OK Corral,** a recorded voice-over details the town's famous shoot-out, while life-size figures of the gunfight's participants stand poised to shoot. Photographer C. S. Fly, whose studio was next door to the corral, didn't record this bit of history, but Geronimo and his pursuers were among the historic figures he did capture with his camera. Many of his fascinating Old West images may be viewed at the **Fly Exhibition Gallery.** ⊠ *Allen St., between 3rd and 4th Sts.* ☎ *520/457–3456* ⊕ *www.ok-corral.com* ☞ *Historama $2.50, OK Corral and Fly Exhibition Gallery $2.50* ◷ *Daily 8:30–5, Historama shows on the hr 9–4.*

You can see the original printing presses for the town's newspaper at the **Tombstone Epitaph Museum** (⊠ 9 S. 5th St. ☎ 520/457–2211). The newspaper was founded in 1880 and is still publishing. If you're looking to wet your whistle, stop by the **Crystal Palace** (⊠ Allen and 5th Sts. ☎ 520/457–3611), where a beautiful mirrored mahogany bar, wrought-iron chandeliers, and tinwork ceilings date back to Tombstone's heyday. Locals come here on weekends to dance to live country-and-western music.

A Tombstone institution, the **Bird Cage Theater** is a former music hall where Enrico Caruso, Sarah Bernhardt, and Lillian Russell—among others—performed. It was also the site of the longest continuous poker game recorded, started when the Bird Cage opened in 1881 and lasting eight years, five months, and three days. Some of the better-known players included Diamond Jim Brady, Adolphus Busch (of brewery fame), and William Randolph Hearst's father. The cards were dealt round the clock; players had to give a 20-minute notice when they were planning to vacate their seats, because there was always a waiting list of at least 10 people ready to shell out $1,000 (the equivalent of about $30,000 today) to get in. In all, some $10 million changed hands.

When the mines closed in 1889, the Bird Cage was abandoned and locked up, but the building has remained in the hands of the same family, who threw nothing out, through five generations. The basement, which served as a bordello, still has all the original furnishings and fixtures intact, and you can see the personal belongings left behind by the ladies of the night when the mines closed and they, and their clients, headed for California. ⊠ *6th and Allen Sts.* ☎ *520/457–3421* ⊠ *$5* ⊗ *Daily 8–6.*

Where to Stay & Eat

¢–$$ ✕ **Longhorn Restaurant.** Also home to Big Nose Kate's Saloon, named for Doc Holliday's girlfriend, this was formerly the Owl Cafe and originally the Bucket of Blood Saloon. Old-time saloon keepers may not have had a way with words, but they sure knew what to serve to keep the likes of the Earps, Bat Masterson, and Johnny Ringo coming back for more. Today it's noisier and definitely for the whole family, with American, Mexican, and Italian dishes available: hot dogs, burgers, steaks, ribs, tacos, enchiladas, and spaghetti should keep the children happy. It may not be "cuisine," but it is filling and fun and open for three meals a day. ⊠ *Allen and 5th Sts.* ☎ *520/457–3405* ⊟ *AE, MC, V.*

¢–$ ✕ **Nellie Cashman's.** You can order anything from a burger to a hearty dinner of juicy pork chops or chicken-fried steak in this homey spot, named for the original owner, a Tombstone pioneer who opened a hotel and restaurant in 1882. Old photographs and postcards decorate the walls. Nellie's is also a great place for a country breakfast complete with biscuits and gravy. ⊠ *5th and Toughnut Sts.* ☎ *520/457–2212* ⊟ *AE, D, MC, V.*

$ ▥ **Curly Bill's Bed & Breakfast.** Though named for one of the baddest outlaws in Tombstone Territory, this B&B is quite serene. Five blocks away from all the activity on Allen Street, the adobe hacienda has nice views of the Dragoon mountains from the screened sunporch and hot tub. Two rooms furnished with Victorian antiques share a bath, and two larger rooms have their own TV, VCR, and private bath. Coffee and juice are served in the morning, and a free breakfast awaits you in town at the OK Cafe, next door to the OK Corral. ⊠ *210 N. 9th St., 85638* ☎ *520/ 457–3858* ⊕ *www.curlybillsbandb.com* ⇆ *4 rooms, 2 with shared bath* ⌂ *Fans, some in-room VCRs, hot tub, massage; no TV in some rooms, no smoking* ⊟ *AE, MC, V* ⊧⊙⊧ *BP.*

¢ ▥ **Best Western Look-Out Lodge.** This small, circa-1960 motel a few miles outside of town has spectacular views of the Dragoon Mountains and desert valley below. Touches such as Western-print bedspreads, Victorian-style lamps, and locally made wood-hewn clocks give the rooms character. A Continental breakfast is included. The front desk and motel switchboard close at 10 PM, so you'll need to check in and receive any phone calls before then. ⊠ *AZ 80 W* ✦ *Box 787, 85638* ☎ *520/457– 2223 or 877/652–6772* ⎗ *520/457–3870* ⊕ *www.bestwestern.com* ⇆ *40 rooms* ⌂ *Cable TV, pool, no-smoking rooms* ⊟ *AE, D, DC, MC, V* ⊧⊙⊧ *CP.*

¢ ▥ **Tombstone Boarding House Bed & Breakfast.** This friendly B&B is actually two meticulously restored 1880s adobes that sit side by side in a quiet residential neighborhood: guests sleep in one house and go next door to have a hearty country breakfast (the restaurant there is open to the public). The spotless rooms, all with private entrances and bathrooms, have hardwood floors and period furnishings collected from around Cochise County. Those seeking a romantic evening should inquire about the inn's candlelight dinners. ⊠ *108 N. 4th St.* ⊘ *Box 906, 85638* ☎ *520/457–3716 or 877/225–1313* 🖶 *520/457–3038* ⊕ *www.tombstoneboardinghouse.com* 🕾 *8 rooms* ♨ *Restaurant; no room phones, no room TVs, no smoking* ⊟ *AE, D, MC, V* 🍴 *BP.*

¢ 🖼 **Tombstone Motel.** Catercorner from the offices of the *Tombstone Epitaph,* on the town's main through street, this comfortable and well-run motel will remind you of the motor courts of years past. The major attractions of Allen Street are a block away. ⊠ *502 E. Fremont St.* ⊘ *Box 837, 85638* ☎ *520/455–3478 or 888/455–3478* 🖶 *520/457–9017* ⊕ *www.tombstonemotel.com* 🕾 *12 rooms, 1 suite* ♨ *Some refrigerators, cable TV, some pets allowed* ⊟ *MC, V.*

Bisbee

⑤ *24 mi south of Tombstone.*

Like Tombstone, Bisbee was a mining boomtown, but its wealth was in copper, not silver, and its success was much longer lived. It wasn't until 1975 that the Phelps Dodge Company closed its last mine and the city went into decline. However, it was rediscovered in the early 1980s by burned-out city dwellers and revived as a kind of Woodstock West. The permanent population is a mix of retired miners and their families, aging hippie jewelry makers, and enterprising young restaurateurs and boutique owners. The latter two groups are currently ascendant, and the town is getting a bit touristy, but its complexion is likely to shift again soon: the Phelps Dodge Company has plans to reopen the area's old copper mines.

If you want to head straight into town from U.S. 80, get off at the Brewery Gulch interchange. You can park here and cross under the highway, taking Main, Commerce, or Brewery Gulch Street, all of which meet here.

About ¼ mi after AZ 80 intersects with AZ 92, you can pull off the highway into a gravel parking lot, where a short, typewritten history of the **Lavender Pit Mine** (⊠ U.S. 80) can be found attached to the hurricane fence surrounding the area (Bisbee isn't big on formal exhibits). The hole left by the copper miners is huge, with piles of lavender-hued "tailings," or waste, creating mountains around it. Arizona's largest pit mine yielded some 94 million tons of copper ore before the town's mining activity came to a halt.

For a lesson in mining history, take the **Copper Queen mine tour.** The mine is less than ½ mi to the east of the Lavender Pit, across AZ 80 from downtown at the Brewery Gulch interchange. Tours are led by Bisbee's retired copper miners, who are wont to embellish their official spiel with tales from their mining days. They're also very capable, safety-minded people (any miner who survives to lead tours in his older years would have to be), so don't be concerned about the precautionary dog tags (literally—they're donated by a local veterinarian) issued to each person on the tour.

The tours, which depart daily at 9, 10:30, noon, 2, and 3:30 (you can't enter the mine at any other time), last from 1 to 1½ hours, and visitors go into the shaft via a little open train, like those the miners rode when the mine was active. Before you climb aboard, you're outfitted in miner's garb—a yellow slicker and a hard hat with a light that runs off a battery pack strapped to your waist. You may want to wear a sweater or light coat under your slicker because the temperature in the mine is a brisk 47°F on average. You'll travel by train thousands of feet into the

A BRIEF GUIDE TO TEQUILA

THROUGHOUT SOUTHERN ARIZONA, the landscape is crowded with agave, the plant from which fine tequila is made. Many people think the agave is a cactus, but it isn't. It's a succulent, closely related to the lily or amaryllis. Only blue agave—just one of 136 species—is used to make true tequila, but other species are used to make mezcal, the more generic type of liquor. Tequila is a specific type of mezcal, just as bourbon or scotch are specific types of whiskey. Many of the cheap brands are actually mixtos, which means they aren't 100% agave; true tequila isn't cheap, and you can pay more than $50 per bottle for a premium brand.

Just across the border in Mexico, there are more than 50 tequila producers, so it's understandable that tequila is a popular drink in Arizona. In fact, more tequila is consumed in the United States than anywhere else, including Mexico. The heart of the tequila-making region is Tequila itself, some 30 mi west of Guadalajara, in the state of Jalisco. The hills around the town are responsible for its name, "tel" meaning "hill," and "quilla," a kind of lava around the dead volcanoes in the area.

To produce tequila, the bulb of the blue agave plant is harvested (it may weigh up to 150 pounds), heated to break down the sugars, and fermented. The best brands, Herradura and El Tesoro, are fermented with wild yeasts that add distinctive flavors to the final product. The fermented tequila is then placed into pot stills, where it is double-distilled to 90 proof or higher. Bottles designated "añejo" have been aged for a minimum of a year in oak barrels and these tequilas are the most expensive.

---

mine, up a grade of 30 ft (not down, as many visitors expect). Those who are a bit claustrophobic might consider taking one of the van tours of the surface mines and historic district that depart from the building at the same times as the mine tours (excluding 9 AM). ✉ 478 N. Dart Rd. ☎ 520/432–2071 ✉ Mine tour $10 ☉ Tours daily at 9, 10:30, noon, 2, and 3:30.

The **Bisbee Mining and Historical Museum** is in a redbrick structure built in 1895 to serve as the Phelps Dodge Company's general offices. The rooms today are filled with exhibits, photographs, and artifacts that offer visitors a fascinating glimpse into the everyday life of Bisbee's early mining community. This small museum enjoys the distinction of having been the first rural museum in the United States to become a member of the Smithsonian Institution Affiliations Program. ✉ 5 Copper Queen Plaza ☎ 520/432–7071 ✉ $4 ☉ Daily 10–4.

The venerable old **Copper Queen Hotel** (✉ 11 Howell Ave.), built a century ago, is behind the Mining and Historical Museum. It has housed the famous as well as the infamous: "Black Jack" Pershing, John Wayne, Teddy Roosevelt, and mining executives from all over the world made this their home away from home.

Brewery Gulch, a short street running north and south, is adjacent to the Copper Queen Hotel (walk out the front door of the Copper Queen, make a left, and you'll be there in about 20 paces). In the old days, the brewery housed there allowed the dregs of the beer that was being brewed to flow down the street and into the gutter. Once largely abandoned, these structures, like many others in the area, are gradually being renovated to accommodate the demands of Bisbee's growing tourist industry.

Bisbee's **Main Street** is alive and retailing. This hilly commercial thoroughfare is lined with appealing crafts shops, boutiques, and restaurants, many of them in well-preserved turn-of-the-20th-century brick buildings.

Where to Stay & Eat

★ $$ ✕ **Café Roka.** This is the deserved darling of the hip Bisbee crowd. The constantly changing northern Italian–style evening menu is not extensive, but you can count on whatever you order—chicken with ricotta and basil cannelloni, scallops with spinach pasta, or roasted duck with cranberry and merlot—to be wonderful. Portions are generous, and entrées include soup or salad. The dining room, with exposed-brick walls and the original 1906 tinwork ceiling, looks onto a central bar that offers a nice selection of wines and cognacs. ⌧ *35 Main St.* ☎ *520/432–5153* ▭ *AE, MC, V* ⊘ *Closed Sun.–Tues. No lunch.*

★ $$ ✕ **Parana's Bistro.** Named for the owner (not the fish), this sleek newcomer to Brewery Gulch offers diners quality nouvelle cuisine with their history lesson. The former Western Union building is divided into three exposed-brick dining rooms, one with an elegant bar featuring turn-of-the-20th-century Bisbee photos, the other two decorated with local art. Tapas, house-made pastas, meats, and fish are divinely prepared, and even the grilled cheese sandwich at lunch is a dressed-up affair, with buttered Parmesan cheese outside and sun-dried tomato aioli inside. Reservations for dinner are a good idea. ⌧ *1 Howell Ave.* ☎ *520/432–1832* ▭ *D, MC, V* ⊘ *Closed Sun.–Mon.*

$–$$ ▥ **Copper Queen Hotel.** Built by the Copper Queen Mining Company (which later became the Phelps Dodge Company) when Bisbee was the biggest copper-mining town in the world, this hotel in the heart of downtown has been operating since 1902. Some of the rooms are small or oddly laid out, and the walls between them are thin, but all have a Victorian charm. Ask for one that's been renovated. Peek into the quaint dining room, but eat elsewhere. ⌧ *11 Howell Ave.* ✑ *Drawer CQ, 85603* ☎ *520/432–2216 or 800/247–5829* 🖷 *520/432–4298* ⊕ *www. copperqueen.com* ➲ *47 rooms* ⚫ *Restaurant, pool, bar* ▭ *AE, D, DC, MC, V.*

$–$$ ▥ **Canyon Rose Suites.** Steps away from the heart of downtown Bisbee, FodorsChoice this all-suites B&B is in the masterfully restored Allen Block Building, ★ formerly a furniture store and miner's rooming house. This modern, sophisticated establishment upstairs has five spacious units, all with hardwood floors, 10-ft ceilings, and fully equipped kitchens, plus TVs, VCRs, and phones with answering machines. Local art (for sale) adorns the walls. In the spa downstairs you can pamper yourself with a hot-stone massage or herbal body wrap after a day in the mines. ⌧ *27 Subway St.* ✑ *Box 1915, 85603* ☎ *520/432–5098 or 800/296–7673* ⊕ *www.canyonrose.com* ➲ *5 suites* ⚫ *Kitchens, cable TV, in-room VCRs, spa, laundry facilities* ▭ *AE, D, DC, MC, V.*

¢–$ ▥ **Inn At Castle Rock.** Originally built as a miners' boardinghouse in 1890, this funky two-story B&B on Bisbee's main road has an acre of hillside gardens and a wonderfully eclectic decor. An unusual fishpond dominates the inn's Eccentricity Dining Room, where a "mighty big" breakfast is served. Casually and comfortably furnished guest rooms have various decorative themes, such as the Sultan's Harem, draped in colorful patterned fabrics, and the Map Room, wallpapered in maps. A shady patio, a garden bar, and a cozy parlor with books to read by the fireplace provide other relaxing options. ⌧ *112 Tombstone Canyon Rd.* ✑ *Box 1161, 85603* ☎ *520/432–4449 or 800/566–4449* 🖷 *520/432–7868* ⊕ *www.theinn.org* ➲ *15 rooms* ⚫ *Library; no room phones, no room TVs, no smoking* ▭ *D, DC, MC, V* ⦿ *BP.*

¢–$ 🏠 **School House Inn Bed & Breakfast.** You may flash back to your class-
Fodor'sChoice room days at this B&B, a schoolhouse built in 1918 at the height of
★ Bisbee's mining days. Perched on the side of a hill, the two-story brick
building has a pleasant outdoor patio shaded by an oak tree. In keeping with its educational past, the inn's rooms all have a theme—music,
history, geography, arithmetic—reflected in the decor (though, surprisingly, there is no writing desk in the writing room). Twelve-foot ceilings contribute to an overall airy effect, but the old floors can be creaky
at night. ✉ *818 Tombstone Canyon Rd.* 🖃 *Box 32, 85603* ☎ *800/537-
4333* 🖷🖷 *520/432–2996* ➷ *6 rooms, 3 suites* ⚭ *No room phones, no
room TVs, no smoking* ▤ *AE, D, DC, MC, V* ⏺ *BP.*

Douglas

❻ *23 mi southeast of Bisbee.*

This town on the U.S.–Mexico border was founded in 1902 by James
Douglas to serve as the copper-smelting center for the mines in Bisbee.
James Douglas's house, now owned by the Arizona Historical Society,
is open to the public as the **Douglas/Williams House Museum** (✉ 1001 D
Ave. ☎ 520/364–7370). There's not much to see here and hours are limited (it's open Tuesday–Thursday and Saturday 1–4), but there are some
interesting old photographs and mementos, and it's free.

The must-see historic landmark in town and still the center of much of
Douglas's activity is the **Gadsden Hotel** (✉ 1046 G Ave.), built in 1907.
The lobby contains a solid white Italian-marble staircase, two authentic Tiffany-vaulted skylights, and a 42-ft-long stained-glass mural. One
thousand ounces of 14-karat gold leaf were used to decorate the capi-
tals. The bar is lively all day long and still serves as a meeting place for
local ranchers. When you leave the hotel and walk out onto G Avenue,
Douglas's main thoroughfare, you'll be taking a stroll back through time.
A film company shooting here had to do very little to make the restaurants and shop fronts fit its 1940s plotline.

Before Douglas became the smelter for Bisbee, the site was the annual
roundup ground for local ranchers, Mexican and American—among them
John Slaughter, who was the sheriff of Cochise County after Wyatt
Earp. The 140-acre **John Slaughter Ranch/San Bernardino Land Grant**, a
National Historic Landmark, gives a glimpse of life near the border in
the late 19th and early 20th centuries. You can also visit ruins of a military outpost established here in 1911 during the Mexican civil unrest.
Much of the ride out to the ranch is via a graded dirt road that traverses
a strikingly Western landscape of rolling hills and desert scrub. The ranch
is 15 mi east of Douglas (from town, go east on 15th Street, which turns
into Geronimo Trail and leads to the ranch). ✉ *6153 Geronimo Trail*
☎ *520/558–2474* ⊕ *www.vtc.net/~sranch* 🎟 *$3* ☉ *Wed.–Sun. 10–3.*

Where to Stay & Eat

$–$$ ✕ **Grand Café.** The Marilyn Monroe tribute wall and red velvet–draped
dining niche in the back may be kitschy, but the Mexican cooking here
is taken very seriously. Soups range from a soothing *caldo de queso*, laced
with cheese and chunks of fresh potato, to a bracing, nicely spiced
menudo. The refried beans served on the side of such well-prepared Sonoran specialties as chiles rellenos are wonderfully flavorful. ✉ *1119 G
Ave.* ☎ *520/364–2344* ▤ *MC, V* ☉ *Closed Sun.*

¢ 🏠 **Gadsden Hotel.** This hotel makes no concessions to the modern idea
of what the West should look like: what you see is what you get. Most
of the rugs, drapes, and shower curtains look weary, and the old plumbing and fixtures aren't always well maintained. Still, the public areas

are comfortable and the prices are the best you'll find in Douglas. The bar is still where all the local ranchers hang out when they come into town. Suites and apartments with kitchenettes are available. ⊠ 1046 G Ave., 85607 ☎ 520/364–4481 ⊟ 520/364–4005 ⊕ www.theriver.com/gadsdenhotel ⇆ 160 rooms ☍ Restaurant, coffee shop, some kitchenettes, hair salon, bar ⊟ AE, DC, MC, V.

Chiricahua National Monument

7 58 mi northeast of Douglas on U.S. 191 to AZ 181; 36 mi southeast of
Fodor'sChoice Willcox.
★

Vast fields of desert grass are suddenly transformed into a landscape of forest, mountains, and striking rock formations as you enter the 12,000-acre Chiricahua National Monument. Dubbed the Land of the Standing-Up Rocks by the Chiricahua Apache—who lived in the mountains for centuries and, led by Cochise and Geronimo, tried for 25 years to prevent white pioneers from settling here—this is an unusual place for a variety of reasons. Enormous outcroppings of volcanic rock worn by erosion into strange pinnacles and spires are set in a forest where autumn and spring seem to occur at the same time. Because of the particular balance of sunshine and rain in the area, in April and May visitors will see brown, yellow, and red leaves coexisting with new green foliage. Summer in Chiricahua National Monument is exceptionally wet: from July through September there are thunderstorms nearly every afternoon. In addition, few other areas in the United States have such a variety of plant, bird, and animal life. Deer, coatimundis, peccaries, and lizards live among the aspen, ponderosa pine, Douglas fir, oak, and cypress trees—to name just a few. Well worth the driving distance, this is a prime area for bird-watchers, and hikers have more than 17 mi of scenic trails. Some of the most beautiful and untouched camping areas in Arizona are nearby, in the Chiricahua Mountains. ⊠ AZ 181, 36 mi southeast of Willcox, ☎ 520/824–3560 ⊕ www.nps.gov/chir ⊠ $5 ◷ Daily 8–5.

off the
beaten
path

PEARCE – The gold camp of Pearce, 1 mi off U.S. 191, 29 mi south of Willcox, has a post office and one viable store; the ruins of the mill, the mine, and many old adobes are very much in evidence. Gold was discovered here in 1894, and the town maintained a thriving population of 1,500 until the mine closed in the 1930s, turning Pearce into a ghost town.

Where to Stay

★ $$$$ 🏨 **Grapevine Canyon Ranch.** This guest ranch on the west side of the Chiricahuas adjoins a working cattle ranch. Visitors get the chance to watch—and, in some cases, participate in—real day-to-day cowboy activities. Riders of all levels of experience are welcome, and hiking trails crisscross this quintessentially Western terrain. Accommodations vary—some are rather plain, others have striking Southwestern-style furnishings—but all have spacious decks and porches. Rates include meals and all activities. There is a three-night minimum. ⊠ Highland Rd. ⊡ Box 302, Pearce 85625 ☎ 520/826–3185 or 800/245–9202 ⊟ 520/826–3636 ⊕ www.gcranch.com ⇆ 12 rooms ☍ Refrigerators, pool, hot tub, hiking, horseback riding, laundry facilities; no kids under 12 ⊟ AE, D, MC, V ⏀ FAP.

$$$ 🏨 **Sunglow Guest Ranch.** You can't beat this location in Cottonwood Canyon, about 15 mi south of Chiricahua National Monument. Though horseback riding is no longer offered, there are plenty of pigs, chickens, geese, and ranch dogs to entertain children. Rooms face a central courtyard, with views of the pond and the forest beyond. The quiet,

spacious setting makes it an ideal spot for family reunions or retreats. Rates include breakfast, afternoon tea, and a gourmet dinner, all served in a lovely dining room with a wraparound porch that's perfect for curling up with a good book or watching for white-tailed deer at sunset. ⊠ *Turkey Creek Rd.* ⬭ *HCR 1, Box 385, Pearce 85625* ☎ *520/824–3334 or 866/786–4569* ⊕ *www.sunglowranch.com* ⇨ *9 suites, 1 casita* ⅋ *Dining room, hiking, library, bicycles, birding, meeting room, some pets allowed (fee); no room phones, no room TVs, no smoking* ⊟ *AE, MC, V* ⵔ *MAP.*

¢ ⊞ **Portal Peak Lodge.** This barracks-style structure, just east of Chiricahua National Monument near the New Mexico border, is notable less for its rooms (clean and pleasant but nondescript) than for its winged visitors: the elegant trogon, 14 types of hummingbird, and 10 species of owl are among the 330 varieties of birds that flock to nearby Cave Creek Canyon. Decks outside each room provide a good vantage point. ⊠ *1215 Main St.* ⬭ *Box 364, Portal 85632* ☎ *520/558–2223* 🖷 *520/558–2473* ⊕ *www.portalpeaklodge.com* ⇨ *16 rooms* ⅋ *Restaurant, grocery, no-smoking rooms; no room phones* ⊟ *AE, D, MC, V.*

¢ ⬭ **Bonita Canyon Campground.** Just ½ mi from the visitor center at Chiricahua National Monument, this campground is nestled among oak and pine trees along a meandering creek. The dense vegetation gives campers a feeling of privacy, and each site has its own picnic table and grill. An assortment of wildlife, such as javelinas, fox squirrels, and coatimundis, may join you for breakfast. In spring and summer, evening naturalist programs are held at the campgrounds' amphitheater. Drinking water and flush toilets (no showers or hook-ups) are available at the 24 campsites; reservations are not accepted. ⅋ *Flush toilets, drinking water, grills, picnic tables* ⇨ *24 campsites* ⊠ *Bonita Canyon Dr., Willcox* ☎ *520/824–3560* ⊕ *www.nps.gov/chir* ⬭ *No reservations accepted* ⊙ *Open year-round.*

Fort Bowie National Historical Site

8 *8 mi northwest of Chiricahua National Monument. Take AZ 186 east from Chiricahua National Monument; 5 mi north of junction with AZ 181, signs direct you to road leading to fort.*

It's a bit of an outing to the location of Arizona's last battle between Native Americans and U.S. troops in the Dos Cabezas (Two-Headed) Mountains. After driving down a graded but winding gravel road, you'll come to a parking lot where a challenging trail leads 1½ mi to the historic site. The fort itself is virtually in ruins, but there's a small ranger-staffed visitor center with historical displays, rest rooms, and books for sale.

The various points of interest along the way, all indicated by historic markers, include the **Butterfield stage stop,** a crucial link in the journey from east to west in the mid-19th century that happened to be in the heart of Chiricahua Apache land. Chief Cochise and the stagecoach operators ignored one another until sometime in 1861, when hostilities broke out between U.S. Cavalry troops and the Apache. After an ambush by the chief's warriors at Apache Pass in 1862, U.S. troops decided a fort was desperately needed in the area, and Fort Bowie was built within weeks. There were skirmishes for the next 10 years, followed by a peaceful decade. Renewed fighting broke out in 1881. Geronimo, the new leader of the Indian warriors, finally surrendered in 1886. The fort was abandoned eight years later and fell into disrepair. ⊠ *Apache Pass Rd., 26 mi southeast of Willcox* ☎ *520/847–2500* ⊕ *www.nps.gov/fobo* ⊡ *Free* ⊙ *Daily 8–5.*

Willcox

9 *26 mi northwest of Fort Bowie National Historical Site on AZ 186.*

The small town of Willcox, in the heart of Arizona ranching country, began in the late 1870s as a railroad construction camp called Maley. When the Southern Pacific Railroad line arrived in 1880, the town was renamed in honor of the highly regarded Fort Bowie commander, General Orlando B. Willcox. Once a major shipping center for cattle ranchers and mining companies, the town has preserved its rustic charm; the downtown area looks like an Old West movie set. An elevation of 4,167 ft means moderate summers and chilly winters, which is an ideal climate for growing apples, and apple pie fans from as far away as Phoenix make pilgrimages just to sample the harvest. Don't miss the mile-high apple pies and hand-pressed cider at **Stout's Cider Mill** (⊠ 1510 N. Circle I Rd. ☎ 520/384–3696).

If you visit in winter, you can see some of the more than 10,000 sandhill cranes that roost at the **Willcox Playa,** a 37,000-acre area resembling a dry lake bed 12 mi south of Willcox. They migrate in late fall and head north to nesting sites in February, and bird-watchers migrate to Willcox the third week in January for the annual Wings over Willcox bird-watching event held in their honor.

Outside Willcox you'll find the headquarters for the **Muleshoe Ranch Cooperative Management Area** (⊠ 6502 N. Muleshoe Ranch Rd. ☎ 520/212–4295 ⊕ www.tnc.org), nearly 50,000 acres of riparian desert land in the foothills of the Galiuro Mountains that are jointly owned and managed by the Nature Conservancy, the U.S. Forest Service, and the U.S. Bureau of Land Management. It's a 30-mi drive on a dirt road to the ranch—it takes about an hour to get there—but the scenery, wildlife, and hiking are well worth the bumps. Backcountry hiking and mountain-biking trips can be arranged by the ranch, and overnight accommodations are available. To reach the ranch, take Exit 340 off I–10, turn right on Bisbee Avenue and continue to Airport Road, turn right again, and after 15 mi take the right fork at a junction just past a group of mailboxes and continue to the end of the road.

The **Rex Allen Arizona Cowboy Museum,** in Willcox's historic district, is a tribute to Willcox's most famous native son, cowboy singer Rex Allen. (As he requested, Allen's ashes were scattered on the grave of his horse, Koko, buried in Railroad Avenue Park across the street from the museum.) He starred in several rather average cowboy movies during the 1940s and '50s for Republic Pictures, but he's probably most famous as the friendly voice that narrated Walt Disney nature films of the 1960s. Check out the glittery suits the star wore on tour—they'd do Liberace proud. ⊠ 155 N. Railroad Ave. ☎ 520/384–4583 or 877/234–4111 ⊕ www.pinkbanana.com/rex ⊠ $2 ☉ Daily 10–4.

The **Willcox Commercial Store** (⊠ 180 N. Railroad Ave. ☎ 520/384–2448), near the Rex Allen Cowboy Museum, was established in 1881 and is the oldest retail establishment in Arizona. Locals like to boast that Geronimo used to shop here. Today it's a clothing store, with a large selection of Western wear.

The **Chiricahua Regional Museum and Research Center,** previously known as the Museum of the Southwest, is in downtown Willcox. Exhibits relating to Native American and military history and culture, including a separate Geronimo exhibit, were created by the Sulphur Springs Valley Historical Society. One oddity the museum points out is that the memoirs of Civil War general Orlando Willcox, for whom the town was named, don't even mention a visit to Arizona. ☒ *127 E. Maley St.* ☏ *520/384–3971* ☒ *Free* ⊙ *Daily 10–4.*

Where to Stay & Eat

$–$$$ ✕ **Desert Rose Café.** Enjoy lunch, dinner, or the Sunday buffet with the locals at this family-owned, family-friendly restaurant in Willcox. The food is as down-home as the atmosphere—mostly burgers, chicken, steak, and seafood standards—so it's just the place to go when you want a meal that's predictable, unpretentious, but also good. ☒ *706 S. Haskell Ave.* ☏ *520/384–0514* ☐ *AE, MC, V.*

¢–$ ✕ **Salsa Fiesta Mexican Restaurant.** You can't miss the bright neon lights of this little restaurant, just south of I–10 at Exit 340 in Willcox. The interior is cheerful and clean, with tables, chairs, and walls painted in a spicy medley of hot pink, purple, turquoise, green, and orange. The menu consists of Mexican standards, and the salsa bar runs the gamut from mild to super-hot. There is a modest selection of domestic and Mexican beers, and takeout is available. ☒ *1201 W. Rex Allen Dr.* ☏ *520/ 384–4233* ☐ *MC, V.*

$–$$ 🛏 **Muleshoe Ranch.** This turn-of-the-20th-century health spa is run by the Arizona chapter of the Nature Conservancy. Five furnished casitas with well-equipped kitchens, baths, and linens sit in a pristine setting in the grassland foothills of the Galiuro Mountains. There's a visitor center, 22 mi of hiking trails, and natural hot springs (for use by casita guests only). There's a two-night minimum from September to May, and a three-night minimum on holiday weekends. ☒ *6502 N. Muleshoe Ranch Rd.* ⓓ *R.R. 1, Box 1542, 85643* ☏ *520/212–4295* ⊕ *www. muleshoelodging.org* ⇝ *5 units* ⚐ *Kitchens, hiking, library, piano; no room phones, no room TVs* ☐ *AE, MC, V.*

¢ 🛏 **Willcox Days Inn.** A clean room and good value are what you'll find here, just off the highway and close to this small town's sights. It's a handy stopping point on your way to or from the Chiricahuas, and a plentiful Continental breakfast is included. ☒ *724 N. Bisbee Ave., 85643* ☏ *520/384–4222* 🖷 *520/384–3785* ⊕ *www.daysinn.com* ⇝ *73 rooms* ⚐ *In-room data ports, some microwaves, some refrigerators, cable TV with movies, pool, laundry facilities, some pets allowed (fee)* ☐ *AE, D, DC, MC, V* ⦿ *CP.*

Texas Canyon

10 *16 mi west of Willcox off I–10.*

A dramatic change of scenery along I–10 will signal that you're entering Texas Canyon. The rock formations here are exceptional—huge boulders appear to be delicately balanced against each other.

Texas Canyon is the home of the **Amerind Foundation** (a contraction of "American" and "Indian"), founded by amateur archaeologist William Fulton in 1937 to foster understanding about Native American cultures. The research facility and museum are housed in a Spanish colonial revival–style structure designed by noted Tucson architect H. M. Starkweather. The museum's rotating displays of archaeological materials, crafts, and photographs give an overview of Native American cultures of the Southwest and Mexico. The adjacent Fulton–Hayden Memorial Art Gallery displays an assortment of art collected by William Fulton. The museum's gift shop has a superlative selection of Native American art, crafts, and jewelry. ☒ *2100 N. Amerind Rd., Dragoon, 1 mi southeast of I–10 (Exit 318)* ☏ *520/586–3666* ⊕ *www.amerind.org* ☒ *$3* ⊙ *Sept.–May, daily 10–4; June–Aug., Tues.–Sun. 10–4.*

Benson

⑪ *12 mi west of Texas Canyon and 50 mi east of Tucson via I–10.*

Even in its historic heyday as a Butterfield stagecoach station, and later as the hub of the Southern Pacific Railroad, Benson was just a place to stop on the way to somewhere else, a sleepy little Western town. But that role changed beginning with the 1974 discovery of a pristine cave beneath the Whetstone Mountains west of Benson and culminating 25 years later with the opening of Kartchner Caverns State Park, one of the most remarkable living cave systems in the world. Benson today is a modern boomtown, in the process of evolving into a destination to travel to instead of through.

Though the city is undergoing dramatic changes, you can see the story of Benson's past at the little **San Pedro Valley Arts and Historical Society Museum** (✉ S. San Pedro Ave. at E. 5th St. ☎ 520/586–3070), a free museum that is closed in August.

As you pass Benson on I–10, watch for Ocotillo Avenue, Exit 304. Take a left and drive about 2¼ mi, where a mailbox with a backward SW signals that you've come to the turnoff for **Singing Wind Bookshop.** Make a right at the mailbox and drive ¼ mi until you see a green gate. Let yourself in, close the gate, and go another ¼ mi to the shop. If you don't see the proprietor, who also runs the ranch, ring the large gong out front and she's sure to come out and welcome you. This unique bookshop-on-a-ranch has a good selection of books on Arizona wildlife, history, and geology. She doesn't take credit cards, though. ✉ *700 W. Singing Wind Rd.* ☎ *520/586-2425* ☾ *Daily 9–5.*

Where to Stay & Eat

$–$$$ ✕ **Chute-Out Steakhouse & Saloon.** Don't be deceived by the unassuming exterior of this stucco steak house a block from Benson's main street. Once inside you can understand why it's one of the most popular restaurants in town. The atmosphere is warm and welcoming, the food is excellent, and the service is efficient and friendly. Mesquite-grilled steaks, ribs, chicken, and seafood, fresh-baked breads and desserts, and salads (the house dressing is superb) and a variety of seasonal and regional appetizers and vegetables make this spot well worth the visit. ✉ *161 S. Huachuca St.* ☎ *520/586-7297* ▭ *AE, D, MC, V.*

$–$$$ ✕ **Horseshoe Steakhouse & Cantina.** For a good green-chili burrito or a patty melt, stop in at this eclectic eatery, which has graced Benson's main street for more than 60 years. You'll know you're in cowboy country when you see the neon horseshoe on the ceiling, the macramés of local cattle brands, and the large Wurlitzer jukebox with its selection of sad country-and-western ballads. ✉ *154 E. 4th St.* ☎ *520/586-3303* ▭ *MC, V.*

$–$$ ✕ **Galleano's.** The kitchen at this upscale roadhouse, a favorite among locals, turns out traditional diner fare—including great burgers and fries—as well as pastas and salads. There's a big salad bar, too—unusual in these parts. ✉ *601 W. 4th St.* ☎ *520/586-3523* ▭ *MC, V* ☾ *No lunch.*

¢–$ ✕ **Reb's Cafe & Coffee Shop.** For a more traditional take on real Southwestern food—none of that newfangled nouvelle stuff—this unpretentious spot is of the cowboy variety. It serves Mexican food and what passes for Italian, but it really prides itself on steaks and hamburgers, and a darned good breakfast. ✉ *1020 W. 4th St.* ☎ *520/586-3856* ▭ *No credit cards.*

¢ ✕ **Ruiz's Mexican Food & Cantina.** In this part of the world, the name is
FodorsChoice   pronounced "Reese" and the food is just as regional as the name. Lo-
★   cated on Benson's main drag, this tiny spot accommodates a daily stream of lunch and dinner customers, hungry for green-corn tamales,

chiles rellenos, *topopo* (deep-fried tortilla) salads, and other specialties. The adjoining bar serves a full range of beers, wine, and cocktails. The atmosphere is casual, and the service is fast and pleasant. ⊠ *687 W. 4th St.* ☎ *520/586–2707* ☰ *MC, V.*

$ 🖫 **Holiday Inn Express.** The closest lodging to Kartchner Caverns State
Fodor'sChoice Park, this motel sits just off I–10 at the "Kartchner Corridor," a few
★ miles west of Benson. It has the comfort and amenities you'd expect but with a Southwestern elegance rarely found in chain motels around the area. Rooms have coffeemakers and hair dryers, and a Continental breakfast is included. There's no restaurant, but motel staff can direct you to the best places to eat in nearby Benson. ⊠ *630 S. Village Loop* ⚐ *Box 2252, 85602* ☎ *520/586–8800 or 888/263–2283* 🖷 *520/586– 1370* ⊕ *www.sixcontinentshotels.com* 🖙 *62 rooms* ♨ *In-room data ports, microwaves, refrigerators, pool, gym, laundry facilities, business services* ☰ *AE, D, DC, MC, V* †⊙† *CP.*

★ $ 🖫 **Skywatcher's Inn.** You don't have to be an astronomer to enjoy staying at this hilltop lodging on the grounds of the private Vega-Bray Observatory, but eight powerful telescopes are available for your universe-viewing pleasure. The B&B, built to accommodate sleepy stargazers, reflects the owners' delight in science: the comfortable rooms have such gadgets as lamps that simulate lightning and decorations (visible in black light) that resemble constellations painted on the ceiling. ⊠ *1311 Astronomers Rd., 2 mi southeast of I–10, Exit 306* ⚐ *5655 N. Via Umbrosa, Tucson 85750* ☎ *520/615–3886* 🖷 *520/733–0600* ⊕ *www.communiverse.com/skywatcher* 🖙 *5 rooms* ☰ *MC, V* †⊙† *BP.*

¢ 🖫 **Days Inn of Benson.** Like other businesses in the Benson area, this motel has seized the opportunity to capitalize on its proximity to Kartchner Caverns State Park, offering special package rates that include tickets for the cavern tour. The rooms are standard issue, large, clean, and comfortable, and a deluxe Continental breakfast is included in your stay. ⊠ *621 Commerce Dr., 85602* ☎ *520/586–3000 or 800/329–7466* ⊕ *www.daysinn.com* 🖙 *75 rooms* ♨ *In-room data ports, some microwaves, some refrigerators, cable TV with movies, pool, hot tub, laundry facilities* ☰ *AE, MC, V* †⊙† *CP.*

Kartchner Caverns State Park

⑫ *9 mi south of Benson on AZ 90.*
Fodor'sChoice
★

The publicity that surrounded the official opening of the Kartchner Caverns in November 1999 was in marked contrast to the secrecy that shrouded their discovery 25 years earlier and concealed their existence for 14 years. The two young men who stumbled into what is now considered one of the most spectacular cave systems ever found recognized the significance of their find and played a fundamental role in its protection and eventual development. Great precautions have been taken to protect the wet cave system—which comprises 13,000 ft of passages and two chambers as long as football fields—from damage by light and dryness. In the summer, a colony of bats roosts in a portion of the cave to raise their young; that area remains off-limits to visitors for the time being.

The sophisticated Discovery Center introduces visitors to the cave and its formations, and hour-long guided tours take small groups into the upper cave, including the large Rotunda and Throne rooms. Kartchner Caverns is a wet, "live" cave, meaning that water still rises up from the surface to increase the multicolored calcium carbonate formations already visible. The most spectacular is one of the world's longest "soda straws," measuring 21.16 ft in length and a mere fraction of an inch in diameter.

The total cavern size is 2⅖ mi long, but the explored areas cover an area of only 1,600 ft by 1,100 ft. The average relative humidity inside is 99%, so visitors are often graced with "cave kisses," water droplets that drip from above. Because the climate outside the caves is so dry, it is estimated that if air got inside, it could deplete the annual supply of moisture in only a few days, halting the growth of the speleothems that decorate its walls. To prevent this, there are 22 environmental monitoring stations that measure air and soil temperature, relative humidity, evaporation rates, air trace gases, and airflow inside the caverns. Tour reservations are required and should be made several months in advance; hiking trails, picnic areas, and campsites are available on the park's 550 acres. ⊠ *AZ 90, 9 mi south of Exit 302 off I–10* ☎ *520/586–4100 information, 520/586–2283 tour reservations* ⊕ *www.pr.state.az.us* ☒ *$10 per vehicle up to 4 people, $1 each additional person; tours $14* ☉ *Daily 7:30–6, cave tours (by reservation) daily 8:40–4:40.*

SOUTHWEST ARIZONA

Many people speed through southwest Arizona on their way to California, but the area has much to offer those willing to slow down for a closer look. The turbulent history of the West is writ large in this now-sleepy part of the state. It's home to the Tohono O'odham Indian Reservation (the largest in the country after the Navajo Nation's) and towns such as Ajo, created—and almost undone—by the copper-mining industry. Yuma, abutting the California border, was a major crossing point of the Colorado River as far back as the time of the conquistadors.

Natural attractions are a lure in this starkly scenic region: Organ Pipe Cactus National Monument provides a number of trails for desert hikers, and Buenos Aires and Imperial wildlife refuges—homes to many unusual species—are important destinations for birders and other nature watchers.

On warm weekends and especially during semester breaks, the 130-mi route from Tucson to Ajo is busy with traffic headed southwest to Puerto Penasco (Rocky Point), Mexico, the closest outlet to the sea for Arizonans. Much of the time, however, the only companions you'll have on this trek are the low-lying scrub and cactus and the mesquite, ironwood, and paloverde trees.

Buenos Aires National Wildlife Refuge

🔞 *66 mi southwest of Tucson; from Tucson, take AZ 86 west 22 mi to AZ 286; go south 40 mi to milepost 8, and it's another 3 mi east to the preserve headquarters.*

This remote nature preserve, in the Altar Valley and encircled by seven mountain ranges, is the only place in the United States where the Sonoran/savanna grasslands that once spread over the entire region can still be seen. The fragile ecosystem was almost completely destroyed by overgrazing, and a program to restore native grasses is currently in progress. In 1985 the U.S. Fish and Wildlife Service purchased the Buenos Aires Ranch—now headquarters for the 115,000-acre preserve—to establish a reintroduction program for the endangered masked bobwhite quail. Bird-watchers consider Buenos Aires unique because it's the only place in the United States where they can see a "grand slam" (four species) of quail: Montezuma quail, Gambel's quail, scaled quail, and masked bobwhite. If it rains, the 100-acre Aguirre Lake, 1½ mi north of the headquarters, attracts wading birds, shorebirds, and waterfowl—in all, more than 250 avian species have been spotted here. They share the turf with

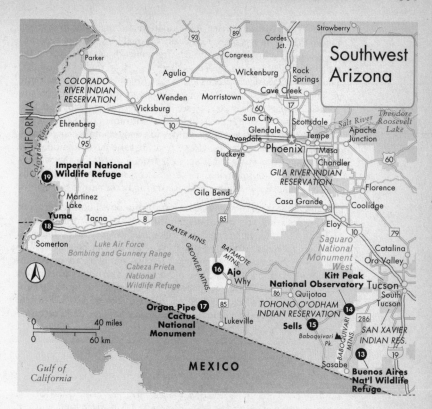

deer, antelope, coatimundi, badgers, bobcats, and mountain lions. Touring options include a 10-mi auto tour through the area, nature trails, a boardwalk through the marshes at Arivaca Cienega, and, by reservation only, weekend guided tours. ⊠ *AZ 286, Sasabe* ☎ *520/823–4251* 🖃 *Free* ☉ *Refuge headquarters and visitor center daily sunrise–sunset.*

Where to Stay

$$$$ 🏨 **Rancho de la Osa.** This historical ranch, set on 250 eucalyptus-shaded acres near the Mexican border and Buenos Aires preserve, was built in 1889, and two adobe structures were added in the 1920s to accommodate guests, among them Lyndon Johnson and Adlai Stevenson. The rooms have modern plumbing and fixtures, wood-burning fireplaces, and porches with Adirondack chairs. Bread baked on the premises, salads made with ingredients grown in the garden, and water drawn from the well all contribute to the back-to-basics serenity. Rates include all meals and horseback riding, and guests are expected to dress for dinner. ⊠ *AZ 286* 🖅 *Box 1, Sasabe 85633* ☎ *520/823–4257 or 800/872–6240* 🖷 *520/823–4238* 🌐 *www.guestranches.com/ranchodelaosa* 🛏 *18 rooms* ⚒ *Dining room, bar, pool, hot tub, bicycles, billiards, hiking, horseback riding, lounge, library, massage; no smoking* 🚭 *D, MC, V* 🍽 *FAP.*

Kitt Peak National Observatory

⑭ *56 mi southwest of Tucson; to reach Kitt Peak from Tucson, take I–10 to I–19 south, and then AZ 86. After 44 mi on AZ 86, turn left at AZ 386 junction and follow winding mountain road 12 mi up to observatory. (In inclement weather, contact the highway department to confirm that the road is open.)*

Funded by the National Science Foundation and managed by a group of more than 20 universities, Kitt Peak National Observatory is part of the Tohono O'odham Reservation. After much discussion back in the late 1950s, tribal leaders agreed to share a small section of their 4,400 square mi with the observatory's telescopes. Among these is the McMath, the world's largest solar telescope, which uses piped-in liquid coolant. From the visitors' gallery you can see into the telescope's light-path tunnel, which goes down hundreds of feet into the mountain. Kitt Peak scientists use these high-power telescopes to conduct vital solar research and observe distant galaxies. Likely to attract the most attention here is Skywatch—no, not a sci-fi spin-off from *Baywatch*—the world's largest asteroid-hunting telescope. The scientists and staff are friendly and knowledgeable, and their enthusiasm for astronomy is contagious.

The museum's visitor center has exhibits on astronomy, information about the telescopes, and free hour-long guided tours that depart daily at 10, 11:30, and 1:30. Complimentary brochures enable you to take self-guided tours, and there's a picnic area about 1½ mi below the observatory. The observatory buildings have vending machines, but there are no restaurants or gas stations within 20 mi of Kitt Peak. The observatory offers occasional stargazing dinner tours ($35 per person) for up to 20 people; reservations are necessary. ⊠ *AZ 386, Pan Tak* ☎ *520/318–8726, 520/318–7200 recorded message* ⊕ *www.noao.edu/kpno* ☑ *$2 suggested donation* ⊙ *Visitor center daily 9–3:45.*

Sells

⑮ *32 mi southwest of Kitt Peak via AZ 386 to AZ 86.*

The Tohono O'odham Reservation, the second-largest in the United States, covers 4,400 square mi between Tucson and Ajo, stretching south to the Mexican border and north almost to the city of Casa Grande. To the south of Kitt Peak, the 7,730-ft Baboquivari Peak is considered sacred by the Tohono O'odham as the home of their deity, I'itoi ("elder brother"). A little less than halfway between Tucson and Ajo, Sells, the tribal capital of the Tohono O'odham, is a good place to stop for gas or a soft drink. Much of the time there's little to see or do in Sells, but in winter an annual rodeo and fair attract thousands of visitors. If you want something more substantial than a snack, head for the Sells Shopping Center, where you'll see **Basha's Deli & Bakery** (⊠ Topawa Rd. ☎ 520/383–2546). It's a good-size market and can supply all the makings for a picnic, including a picnic table near the store's entrance. For traditional Indian and Mexican food like fry bread, tacos, and chili, try the **Papago Cafe** (⊠ AZ 86, near the Chevron Station ☎ 520/383–3510). The **Turquoise Turtle** (⊠ AZ 86 ☎ 520/383–2411) sells baskets and other crafts made on the reservation and beyond.

en route   At **Why,** about 60 mi from Sells, AZ 86 forks off into the north and south sections of AZ 85. Originally the name of the community at this Y-shape intersection was spelled, simply and descriptively, "Y," but in 1950 the town was told that it had to have a three-letter name in order to be assigned a postal code—hence the querulous appellation that has kept travelers wondering *Why* ever since.

Ajo

⑯ *90 mi northwest of Sells.*

"Ajo" (pronounced *ah*-ho) is Spanish for garlic, and some say the town got its name from the wild garlic that grows in the area. Others claim the word is a bastardization of the Indian word *au-auho,* referring to red paint derived from a local pigment.

For many years Ajo, like Bisbee to the east, was a thriving Phelps Dodge Company town. Copper mining had been attempted in the area in the late 19th century, but it wasn't until the 1911 arrival of John Greenway, general manager of the Calumet & Arizona Mining Company, that the region began to be developed profitably. Calumet and Phelps Dodge merged in 1935, and the huge New Cornelia pit mine produced millions of tons of copper until the mine finally closed in 1985. With the town's main source of revenue gone, Ajo looked for a time as though it might shut down, but many retirees are now being lured here by the warm climate and low-cost housing.

At the center of town is a sparkling white Spanish-style plaza, designed in 1917 by Isabella Greenway, wife of the Calumet mine manager and an important figure in her own right: in the 1930s she opened the Arizona Inn in Tucson, and her friends included such dignitaries as Eleanor Roosevelt. The shops and restaurants that line the plaza's covered arcade today are rather modest. Unlike Bisbee, Ajo hasn't yet drawn an artistic crowd— or the upscale boutiques and eateries that tend to follow.

You get a panoramic view of Ajo's huge open-pit mine, almost 2 mi wide, from the **New Cornelia Open Pit Mine Lookout Point.** Some of the abandoned equipment remains in the pit, and various stages of mining operations are diagrammed at the covered visitors' shelters, where there's a 30-minute film about Phelps Dodge's mining operations. ⊠ *Indian Village Rd.* ☎ *520/387–7746* 🖃 *$1 suggested donation* ☉ *Generally Nov.–Apr., Mon.–Sat. 10–4.*

The **Ajo Historical Society Museum** has collected a mélange of articles related to Ajo's past from local townspeople. The displays are rather disorganized, but some of the historical photographs and artifacts are fascinating, and the museum is inside the territorial-style St. Catherine's Indian Mission, built around 1916. ⊠ *160 Mission St.* ☎ *520/387–7105* 🖃 *Free* ☉ *Generally Nov.–Apr., Mon.–Sat. 10–4, Sun. noon–4; call ahead to confirm.*

The 860,000-acre **Cabeza Prieta National Wildlife Refuge,** about 10 minutes from Ajo, was established in 1939 as a preserve for endangered bighorn sheep and other Sonoran Desert wildlife. A permit is required to enter, and only those with four-wheel-drive vehicles, needed to traverse the rugged terrain, can obtain one from the refuge's office. ⊠ *1611 N. 2nd Ave., Ajo 85321* ☎ *520/387–6483* ⊕ *southwest.fws.gov* 🖃 *Free* ☉ *Office weekdays 9–5, refuge daily dawn–dusk.*

Where to Stay & Eat

¢–$ ✕ **Señor Sancho.** Just about everybody in Ajo comes to this unprepossessing roadhouse at the north end of town for generous portions of Mexican food, well prepared and very reasonably priced. This friendly spot has light-wood booths and colorful murals with a Mexican motif. All the standard favorites are on the menu—hearty combination platters, tacos, enchiladas, chiles rellenos, flautas, and good chicken mole. ⊠ *663 N. 2nd Ave.* ☎ *520/387–6226* 🖃 *No credit cards.*

$ 🏨 **Guest House Inn Bed & Breakfast.** Built in 1925 to accommodate visiting Phelps Dodge VIPs, this lodging is a favorite for birders: guests can head out early to nearby Organ Pipe National Monument or just sit on the patio and watch the quail, cactus wrens, and other warblers that fly in to visit. Rooms are furnished in a range of Southwestern styles, from light Santa Fe to rich Spanish colonial. The owners speak fluent French and Spanish, and a full gourmet breakfast is served. ⊠ *700 Guest*

House Rd., 85321 ☎ 520/387–6133 ⊕ www.guesthouseinn.biz ⟿ 4 rooms ⊟ DC, MC, V �10l BP.

Organ Pipe Cactus National Monument

⑰   *32 mi southwest of Ajo; from Ajo, backtrack to Why and take AZ 85 south for 22 mi to reach the visitor center.*

Anyone interested in exploring the flora and fauna of the Sonoran Desert should head for Organ Pipe Cactus National Monument, abutting Cabeza Prieta National Wildlife Refuge but much more accessible to visitors. The monument is the largest habitat north of the border for organ-pipe cacti. These multi-armed cousins of the saguaro are fairly common in Mexico but rare in the United States. Because they tend to grow on south-facing slopes, you won't be able to see many of them unless you take one of the two scenic loop drives: the 21-mi **Ajo Mountain Drive** or the 53-mi **Puerto Blanco Drive**, both on winding, graded one-way dirt roads. The latter trail, which takes half a day to traverse, brings you to Quitobaquito, a desert oasis with a flowing spring. Construction, which at this writing was scheduled to be completed by early 2004, will widen Puerto Blanco into a two-way road so that drivers can turn around at any point along the route.

Because Quitobaquito is literally on the Mexican border—only an open gate between barbed wire fencing separates Arizona and Mexico—safety concerns regarding illegal alien traffic and smuggling are a reality here. However, park officials emphasize that tourists have only occasionally been the victims of isolated property crimes—primarily theft of personal items from parked cars. Visitors are advised by rangers to keep valuables locked and out of plain view and not to initiate contact with groups of strangers whom they may encounter on hiking trails. ⊠ AZ 85 ☎ 520/387–6849 ⊕ www.nps.gov/orpi ⊡ $4 per vehicle ☉ Visitor center daily 8–5.

Yuma

⑱   *170 mi northwest of Ajo.*

Today, many people think of Yuma as a convenient stop between Phoenix or Tucson and San Diego—and this was equally true in the past. It's difficult to imagine the lower Colorado River, now dammed and bridged, as either a barrier or a means of transportation, but until the early part of the 20th century, this section of the great waterway was a force to contend with. Records show that since at least 1540 the Spanish were using Yuma (then the site of a Quechan Indian village) as a ford across a relatively shallow juncture of the Colorado.

Three centuries later, the advent of the shallow-draft steamboat made the settlement a point of entry for fortune seekers heading up through the Gulf of California to mining sites in eastern Arizona. Fort Yuma was established in 1850 to guard against Indian attacks, and by 1873 the town was a county seat, a U.S. port of entry, and an army quartermaster depot. The building of the Yuma Territorial Prison in 1876 helped stabilize the economy.

The steamboat shipping business, undermined by the completion of the Southern Pacific Railroad line in 1877, was finished off by the building of Laguna Dam in 1909, which controlled the overflow of the Colorado River and made agricultural development in the area possible. In World War II, Yuma Proving Ground was used to train bomber pilots, and General Patton readied some of his desert war forces for battle at classified areas near the city. Many who served here during the war returned to Yuma to retire, and the city's economy now relies largely on tourism. One very telling fact may shed some light on why: according to National Weather Service statistics, Yuma is the sunniest city in the United States.

Most of the interesting sights in Yuma are at the north end of town. Stop in at the **Yuma Convention and Visitors Bureau** (⊠ 377 S. Main St. ☎ 928/ 783–0071 ⊕ www.visityuma.com) and pick up a walking-tour guide to the historic downtown area. The adobe-style **Arizona Historical Society Museum,** housed in the Century House, was built around 1870 and exhibits artifacts from Yuma's territorial days and details the military presence in the area. ⊠ *240 S. Madison Ave.* ☎ *928/782–1841* ☟ *Free* ⊙ *Tues.–Sat. 10–4.*

If you cross the railroad tracks at the northernmost part of town, you'll come to **Yuma Crossing National Historic Landmark,** which consists of the Quartermaster Depot and Fort Yuma, on the California side of the Colorado River. The mess hall of Fort Yuma, later used as a school for Native American children, now serves as the small **Fort Yuma Quechan Indian Museum.** Historical photographs, archaeological items, and Quechan arts and crafts are on display. ⊠ *CA 24* ☎ *619/572–0661* ☟ *$1* ⊙ *Weekdays 8–5, Sat. 10–4.*

On the other side of the river from Fort Yuma, the Civil War–period quartermaster depot resupplied army posts to the north and east and served as a distribution point for steamboat freight headed overland to Arizona forts. The 1853 home of riverboat captain G. A. Johnson is the depot's earliest building and the centerpiece of the **Yuma Crossing State Historic Park.** The residence also served as a weather bureau and home for customs agents, among other functions, and the guided tour through the house provides a complete history. The complex was closed until the fall of 1997, when it reopened as a state park. The Transportation Museum has stagecoaches, Wells Fargo wagons, and antique surreys, as well as more "modern" modes of transportation like the 1909 Model T and the 1931 Model A pickup. You can also visit a re-creation of the Commanding Officer's Quarters, complete with period furnishings and servants' quarters: you'll find the dining-room table set with antique china and linens, as if the C. O. himself were expected for dinner. ⊠ *201 N. 4th Ave., between 1st St. and the Colorado River Bridge* ☎ *928/329– 0471* ⊕ *www.pr.state.az.us* ☟ *$3* ⊙ *Daily 8–5.*

The most notorious tourist sight in town, **Yuma Territorial Prison,** now an Arizona state historic park, was built for the most part by the convicts who were incarcerated here from 1876 until 1909, when the prison outgrew its location. The hilly site on the Colorado River, chosen for security purposes, precluded further expansion.

Visitors gazing today at the tiny cells that held six inmates each, often in 115°F heat, are likely to be appalled, but the prison—dubbed the Country Club of the Colorado by locals—was considered a model of enlightenment by turn-of-the-20th-century standards: in an era when beatings were common, the only punishments meted out here were solitary confinement and assignment to a dark cell. The complex housed a hospital as well as Yuma's only public library, where the 25¢ that visitors paid for a prison tour financed the acquisition of new books.

The 3,069 prisoners who served time at what was then the territory's only prison included men and women from 21 different countries. They came from all social classes and were sent up for everything from armed robbery and murder to violation of the Mexican Neutrality Act and polygamy. R. L. McDonald, incarcerated for forgery, had been the superintendent of the Phoenix public school system. Chosen as the prison bookkeeper, he absconded with $130 of the inmates' money when he left. Pearl Hart, convicted of stagecoach robbery, gained such notoriety for her crime that she attempted to launch a career in vaudeville after her release.

The mess hall opened as a museum in 1940, and the entire prison complex was designated a state historic park in 1961. ⊠ *1 Prison Hill Rd., near Exit 1 off I-8,* ☎ *928/783-4771* ⊕ *www.pr.state.az.us* ✉ *$3* ⊙ *Daily 8–5; free interpretive programs at 11, 2, and 3:30.*

Where to Stay & Eat

¢–$$ ✕ **Chretin's Mexican Food.** A Yuma institution, Chretin's opened as a dance hall in the 1930s before it became one of the first Mexican restaurants in town in 1946. Don't be put off by the nondescript exterior or the entryway, which leads back past the kitchen and cashier's stand into three large dining areas. The food is all made on the premises, right down to the chips and tortillas. Try anything that features *machaca* (shredded spiced beef or chicken). ⊠ *485 S. 15th Ave.* ☎ *928/782–1291* ▭ *D, MC, V* ⊙ *Closed Sun.*

¢–$ ✕ **Lutes Casino.** Almost always packed with locals at lunchtime, this large, funky restaurant and bar claims to be the oldest pool hall and domino parlor in Arizona. It's a great place for a burger and a brew. ⊠ *221 S. Main St.* ☎ *928/782–2192* ▭ *No credit cards.*

★ $–$$ 🏨 **Best Western Coronado Motor Hotel.** This Spanish tile–roofed motor hotel, convenient to both the freeway and downtown historical sights, was built in 1938 and is run by the son of the original owner. Bob Hope used to stay here during World War II, when he entertained the gunnery troops training in Yuma. The rooms have such extras as irons and ironing boards and hair dryers. Yuma Landing Restaurant & Lounge is on-site with an impressive collection of historical photos. ⊠ *233 4th Ave., 85364* ☎ *928/783–4453 or 800/528–1234* 🖷 *928/782–7487* ⊕ *www.bestwestern.com* 📲 *86 rooms* ⌂ *Restaurant, in-room data ports, microwaves, refrigerators, in-room VCRs, pool, lobby lounge, laundry facilities* ▭ *AE, D, DC, MC, V* ⏐◎⏐ *BP.*

🖑 $–$$ 🏨 **Shilo Inn.** This is an excellent family place to stay because of in-room facilities that come as close to a kitchen as you might want on a trip. Rooms are spacious, equipped with microwave ovens, irons and ironing boards, coffeemakers, and video games, and most have views of the courtyard and pool. A full breakfast is included in the rates and served in the restaurant. ⊠ *1550 S. Castle Dome Rd., 85365* ☎ *928/782–9511 or 800/222–2244* 🖷 *928/783–1538* ⊕ *www.shiloinns.com* 📲 *131 rooms, 15 suites* ⌂ *Restaurant, microwaves, refrigerators, business center, cable TV with video games, pool, gym, hot tub, sauna, lounge, some pets allowed (fee)* ▭ *AE, D, DC, MC, V* ⏐◎⏐ *BP.*

$ 🏨 **La Fuente Inn.** Keep in mind that Yuma's hotels have to compete with huge RV parks, and you begin to see why the rates are reasonable and so many extras are included. La Fuente is particularly popular with military personnel. The decor and setting may be unremarkable, but the rooms are large and very clean, and each is equipped with coffeemaker, iron, and ironing board. Room rates include Continental breakfast, happy-hour drinks, and access to a nearby fitness center. ⊠ *1513 E. 16th St., 85365* ☎ *928/329–1814 or 800/841–1814* 🖷 *928/343–2671* ⊕ *www.lafuenteinn.com* 📲 *96 rooms* ⌂ *Microwaves, refrigerators, pool, hot tub, laundry facilities* ▭ *AE, D, DC, MC, V* ⏐◎⏐ *CP.*

$ 🏨 **Radisson Suites Inn.** One wing of this sprawling hotel surrounds a well-manicured courtyard with a fountain and several orange trees; another faces the pool and Cabana Club, where the complimentary Continental breakfast and happy-hour drinks are served. This is an all-suites property, and each accommodation has a coffeemaker and a separate sitting area with a desk. ⊠ *2600 S. 4th Ave., 85364* ☎ *928/726–4830 or 800/ 333–3333* 🖷 *928/341–1152* 🌐 *www.radisson.com* ⇥ *164 suites* ⚘ *Microwaves, refrigerators, pool, hot tub, lobby lounge, laundry facilities, airport shuttle* ▤ *AE, D, DC, MC, V* ⊧ *CP.*

Imperial National Wildlife Refuge

⑲ *40 mi north of Yuma; from Yuma, take U.S. 95 north past the Proving Ground and follow the signs to the refuge.*

A guided tour is the best way to visit the 25,765-acre Imperial National Wildlife Refuge, created by backwaters formed when the Imperial Dam was built. Something of an anomaly, the refuge is home both to species indigenous to marshy rivers and to creatures that inhabit the adjacent Sonoran Desert—desert tortoises, coyotes, bobcats, and bighorn sheep. Most of all, though, this is a major bird habitat. Thousands of waterfowl and shorebirds live here year-round, and migrating flocks of swallows pass through in the spring and fall. During those seasons, expect to see everything from pelicans and cormorants to Canada geese, snowy egrets, and a variety of rarer species. Canoes can be rented at Martinez Lake Marina, 3½ mi southeast of the refuge headquarters. It's best to visit from mid-October through May, when it's cooler and the ever-present mosquitoes are least active. The well-marked Painted Desert Nature Trail, about a mile long, takes you through the different levels of the Sonoran Desert. From an observation tower at the visitor center you can see the river, as well as the fields being planted with rye and millet, on which the migrating birds like to feed. ⊠ *Martinez Lake Rd., Martinez Lake* ☎ *928/783–3371* 🌐 *refuges.fws.gov* ▣ *Free* ◷ *Visitor center mid-Apr.–mid-Oct., weekdays 7:30–4; mid-Oct.–mid-Apr., weekdays 7:30–4, weekends 9–4.*

SOUTHERN ARIZONA A TO Z

To research prices, get advice from other travelers, and book travel arrangements, visit www.fodors.com.

AIR TRAVEL
America West has regular flights from Phoenix to the Sierra Vista/Fort Huachuca Airport. America West Express has direct flights to Yuma International Airport from Phoenix. Sky West, a United subsidiary, flies nonstop from Los Angeles to Yuma.

AIRPORTS
🚺 Airport Information **Sierra Vista/Fort Huachuca Airport** ⊠ 2100 Airport Ave. ☎ 928/459-8575. **Yuma International Airport** ⊠ 2191 32nd St. ☎ 520/726-5882.

BUS TRAVEL
Greyhound Lines has service from Tucson to the stations in Ajo, Benson, and Willcox; the line uses Bridgewater Transport in Tucson for its runs to Bisbee, Douglas, and Sierra Vista. You'll need to book a tour if you want to take the bus to Tombstone. The Ajo Stage Line offers regular shuttle van service from Tucson and Phoenix to Ajo and Rocky Point, Mexico.

🚺**Ajo Stage Line** ☎ 800/942-1981 🌐 www.ajostageline.com. **Bridgewater Transport** ⊠ 7 Okay St., Bisbee ☎ 520/432-5359 ⊠ 538 14th St., Douglas ☎ 520/364-2233 ⊠ 28 Fab Ave., Sierra Vista ☎ 520/458-3471. **Greyhound Lines** ⊠ 242 E. 4th St., Benson ☎ 520/ 586-3141 ⊠ 622 N. Haskell Ave., Willcox ☎ 520/384-2183. **Yuma bus station** ⊠ 170 E. 17th Pl., Yuma ☎ 928/783-4403.

CAR RENTALS

You can rent a car from several national companies at Yuma International Airport.

⛛ Major Agencies Avis ☎ 520/726-5737. **Budget** ☎ 928/344-1822. **Enterprise** ☎ 928/325-8007. **Hertz** ☎ 928/726-5160.

CAR TRAVEL

You'll need a car to tour most of southern Arizona. The best plan is to fly into Tucson, which is the hub of the area, or Phoenix, which has the most flights, and pick up a car at the airport.

SOUTHEASTERN ARIZONA
From Tucson, take I–10 east. When you come to Benson, take AZ 80 south to reach Tombstone, Bisbee, and Douglas. If you want to go to Sonoita and Patagonia, or just take a pretty drive, turn off I–10 earlier, at the exit for AZ 83 south; you'll come to Sonoita, where this road intersects AZ 82. From here you can either continue south to Sierra Vista, head southwest on AZ 82 to Patagonia, or head east to Tombstone.

SOUTHWESTERN ARIZONA
Ajo lies on AZ 85 (north–south), Yuma at the junction of I–8 and U.S. 95. For a scenic route to Ajo from Tucson (126 mi), take AZ 86 west to Why and turn north on AZ 85. Yuma is 170 mi from San Diego on I–8, and it is 300 mi from Las Vegas on U.S. 95.

EMERGENCIES

⛛ Emergency Services Ambulance, Fire, or Police Emergencies ☎ 911.

⛛ Hospitals Ajo Community Health Center ✉ 410 Malacate St., Ajo ☎ 520/387-5651. **Benson Hospital** ✉ 350 S. Ocotillo St., Benson ☎ 520/586-2261. **Bisbee Copper Queen Hospital** ✉ 101 Cole St., Bisbee ☎ 520/432-5383. **Northern Cochise Community Hospital** ✉ 901 W. Rex Allen Dr., Willcox ☎ 520/384-3541 or 800/696-3541. **Sierra Vista Regional Health Center** ✉ 300 El Camino Real, Sierra Vista ☎ 520/458-4641 or 800/880-0088. **Yuma Regional Medical Center** ✉ 2400 S. Ave. A, Yuma ☎ 928/344-2000.

⛛ Pharmacies Bob's IGA Pharmacy ✉ 900 W. Rex Allen Dr., Willcox ☎ 520/384-2502. **Medicine Shoppe Pharmacy** ✉ 675 W. 4th St., Benson ☎ 520/586-1299. **Payless** ✉ 600 W. Catalina Dr., Yuma ☎ 928/726-7810. **Safeway Pharmacy** ✉ 101 Naco Hwy., Bisbee ☎ 520/432-5425. **Tom's Pharmacy** ✉ 40 W. Plaza St., Ajo ☎ 520/387-7080. **Walgreens** ✉ 1150 W. 8th St., Yuma ☎ 928/783-6834 ✉ 3121 S. 4th Ave., Yuma ☎ 928/344-0453.

SPORTS & THE OUTDOORS

CAMPING & HIKING
Douglas Ranger District and the Sierra Vista Ranger Station of the National Forest Service can give you information about camping and hiking in the Coronado National Forest, which covers most of the mountain ranges in southeastern Arizona. The Bureau of Land Management Yuma Field Office can give you details about outdoor recreational activities in that area.

⛛ Bureau of Land Management Yuma Field Office ⌖ 2555 E. Gila Ridge Rd., Yuma 85365 ☎ 928/317-3200 ⊕ www.az.blm.gov. **Coronado National Forest** Douglas Ranger District ✉ 3081 N. Leslie Canyon Rd., Douglas ☎ 520/364-3468 ⊕ www.fs.fed.us/r3/coronado ✉ Sierra Vista Ranger Station ✉ 5990 S. AZ 92, Hereford 85615 ☎ 520/378-0311.

SIGHTSEEING TOURS

BIRD-WATCHING
The Southeastern Arizona Bird Observatory is a nonprofit organization that offers guided tours, educational programs, and informational materials for bird-watchers visiting, or living in, Arizona. SABO has also collaborated with other private and public organizations to develop the Southeastern Arizona Birding Trail, slated for completion by 2005. A road guide and map to the best bird-watching sites has been published, and the trail system will eventually include highway signs, informational

markers, footpaths, boardwalks, observation platforms, and other bird-watching amenities. High Lonesome Ecotours offers birding tours with lodging.

High Lonesome Ecotours ✉ 570 S. Little Bear Trail, Sierra Vista ☎ 520/458-9446 ⊕ www.hilonesome.com. **Southeastern Arizona Bird Observatory** ✍ Box 5521, Bisbee 85603 ☎ 520/432-1388 ⊕ www.sabo.org.

BOAT TOURS You can take a boat ride up the Colorado with Yuma River Tours. You can book 12- to 45-person jet-boat excursions through Smokey Knowlton, who has been exploring the area for more than 36 years.

Yuma River Tours ✉ 1920 Arizona Ave., Yuma 85364 ☎ 928/783-4400 ⊕ www.yumarivertours.com.

GUIDED TOURS Southern Arizona Adventures offers a variety of ecotours, hiking, backpacking, mountain biking, and historical/cultural expeditions from its base in Bisbee. Ajo Stage Line leads tours of the historical Southwest, from ghost towns to pueblo ruins, as well as ecotours of the Sonoran Desert from its base in Ajo.

Ajo Stage Line ✉ 321 E. Taladro, Ajo ☎ 520/387-6467 or 800/942-1981 ⊕ www.ajostageline.com. **Southern Arizona Adventures** ✉ 22 Main St., Bisbee ☎ 520/432-9058 or 800/319-7377 ⊕ www.arizonatour.com.

TRAIN EXCURSIONS Ajo Stage Line offers a steam train tour of the Ajo environs. On weekends from October through June, you can take a two-hour round-trip jaunt on the Yuma Valley Railway. The 1922 coach, pulled by one of two historic diesel engines, departs at 1 PM from the 8th Street station in Yuma and runs south alongside the Colorado River for about 11 mi. Tickets cost $10.

Ajo Stage Line ✉ 321 E. Taladro, Ajo ☎ 520/387-6467 or 800/942-1981 ⊕ www.ajostageline.com. **Yuma Valley Railway** ✉ 2nd Ave. and 1st St., behind City Hall, Yuma ☎ 928/783-3466.

TAXIS

SOUTHEASTERN ARIZONA Benson Taxi offers transport services in the Benson area. In Bisbee, call Sun Arizona Taxi. In Sierra Vista, Angel Transport provides both local and regional transport.

Angel Transport ☎ 520/458-0027. **Benson Taxi** ☎ 520/586-1274. **Sun Arizona Taxi** ☎ 520/432-7899.

SOUTHWESTERN ARIZONA Ajo Stage Line offers local and regional transport and tour services. Friendly Taxi Service and Yuma City Cab have the newest, cleanest taxis in Yuma.

Ajo Stage Line ☎ 520/387-6467 or 800/942-1981. **Friendly Taxi Service** ☎ 928/783-1000. **Yuma City Cab** ☎ 928/782-0111.

TRAIN TRAVEL

Amtrak trains run three times a week from Tucson east to the Benson depot and west to Yuma. Both stations are unstaffed with Amtrak personnel; however, the Benson Visitor Center is located in the train depot.

Amtrak ☎ 800/872-7245. **Benson train station** ✉ 4th St. at San Pedro Ave., Benson. **Yuma train station** ✉ 281 Gila St., Yuma.

VISITOR INFORMATION

In Southeastern Arizona Benson Railroad Depot and Visitor Center ✉ 249 E. 4th St., Benson ☎ 520/586-4293 ⊕ www.cityofbenson.com. **Bisbee Chamber of Commerce** ✉ 31 Subway St., Bisbee ☎ 520/432-5421 ⊟ 520/432-3308 ⊕ www.bisbeearizona.com. **Douglas Visitor Center** ✉ 1125 Pan American, Douglas 85607 ☎ 520/364-2478 or 888/315-9999 ⊕ www.discoverdouglas.com. **Patagonia Visitors Center** ✉ 307 McKeown Ave., Patagonia ☎ 520/394-0060 or 888/794-0060 ⊕ www.patagoniaaz.com. **Sierra Vista Convention and Visitors Bureau** ✉ 21 E. Willcox Dr., Sierra Vista

85635 ☎ 520/458-6940 or 800/288-3861 ⊕ www.visitsierravista.com. **Tombstone Chamber of Commerce and Visitor Center** ⊠ 4th and Allen Sts., Tombstone 85638 ☎ 520/457-3929 or 888/457-3929 ⊕ www.cityoftombstone.com. **Willcox Chamber of Commerce & Agriculture** ⊠ 1500 N. Circle I Rd., Willcox 85643 ☎ 520/384-2272 or 800/200-2272 ⊕ www.willcoxchamber.com.

🚹 Contacts in Southwestern Arizona **Ajo Chamber of Commerce** ⊠ 400 Taladro St., Ajo 85321 ☎ 520/387-7742 ⊕ www.ajoinaz.com. **Tohono O'odham Nation office** ☎ 520/383-2221. **Yuma Convention and Visitors Bureau** ⊠ 377 S. Main St., Yuma ☎ 928/783-0071 or 800/293-0071 ⊕ www.visityuma.com.

UNDERSTANDING ARIZONA

THE NATIVE SOUTHWEST

BOOKS & MOVIES

THE NATIVE SOUTHWEST

ONSIDERING THE ARIDITY of the Southwest, the tremendous cultural productivity of its native civilizations is a fascinating case of people turning the challenges of nature into a meaningful existence. Within the compass of the state of Arizona, Native American pottery and cliff dwellings are the most apparent evidence of this. In fact, they are isolated phenomena on a vast trade route that spanned the continent from the Pacific coast all the way to Mesoamerica, an area in which not only goods but pottery-making techniques, agricultural technologies, and spiritual beliefs were transmitted.

Some 4,000 years ago—at least 8,000 years after humans crossed the Bering Strait land bridge that once allowed passage on foot between Asia and North America—a major transition in cultures around the world saw people shifting from nomadic hunting-and-gathering lifestyles to more settled agricultural existence. In the Southwest, ancient pioneers brought the practice of cultivating corn, squash, and beans north from Mesoamerica. One group in particular, the Hohokam, is believed to have fostered this. In an area straddling the Arizona–New Mexico border, the Hohokam developed a highly productive system. Some archaeologists believe that they migrated from northwestern Mexico with knowledge of planting, growing, and irrigating. Others picture an evolution of Archaic peoples who gradually took on Mesoamerican practices. Either way, they had great success and in turn influenced their northern and eastern neighbors for more than a thousand years. Their artisans produced ritual objects, jewelry, and stone and ceramic wares with great skill. They regularly traded with Mesoamerican tribes, and Pacific-coast exchange brought in raw materials for their own and other regional artisans.

The flowering of Hohokam culture began around 2,300 years ago. The period of their growth, expansion, and eventual decline, when they began to take new ideas in from the north, lasted about 1,500 years—twice as long as the Roman Empire. During that time, they cultivated corn, beans, squash, agave, and cotton, using remarkable irrigation methods. Some of their networks of canals stretched 3 mi from the Salt and Gila rivers to planted fields. Their contact with Mesoamerican cultures periodically brought new strains of corn to the Southwest, along with religious beliefs, ritual practices, and the ball game and ball courts well known from the Maya. The Hohokam culturally fertilized the region, providing a base for the Pueblo culture that has survived into the modern era.

The Mogollon (pronounced *muh*-gee-on) were another group, occupying an area stretching from eastern-central Arizona into New Mexico from 2,000 to 500 years ago. They took on Hohokam and so-called Anasazi cultural patterns, but they never fully embraced an agricultural lifestyle. They became skillful potters, especially those living near the Mimbres River. Their contact with the Anasazi resulted in the production of some of the Southwest's most outstanding pottery. The principle Mimbres Mogollon site is now the Gila Cliff Dwellings National Monument in New Mexico.

Romanticized, mythicized, and perhaps misunderstood, the so-called Anasazi left wondrous architectural remains, most notably at Mesa Verde in Colorado; Chaco Canyon in New Mexico; and Canyon de Chelly, Betatakin, and Keet Seel in Arizona. Composed of various groups living around the Four Corners area, they have generated the most intense interest. For centuries they lived semi-nomadically, hunting, gathering, and marginally cultivating corn, squash, and beans. They eventually settled into villages and adopted much of the Hohokam culture, more than their Mogollon neighbors did.

These various Ancestral Pueblo peoples were not pueblo dwellers yet, however. They were slow to establish year-round communities. Perhaps they weren't convinced that the Hohokam model would work in their rugged, dry canyonlands. With fewer and smaller rivers, they couldn't irrigate on the Hohokam scale. About 1,500 years ago the Pueblo cultural pattern called Anasazi began to take shape, owing, perhaps, to the introduction of a new, more productive strain of corn.

Ancestral Pueblo peoples made a significant contribution to Southwestern culture with their architecture. Their remarkable stone masonry evolved out of a pithouse style used by Archaic peoples. A precursor of the kiva, the pithouse was constructed around a shallow, circular dugout with mud walls packed around vertical pole supports. The new stone-and-mortar houses, on the other hand, were very often rectangular in plan. In small communities they were built on a scale to house groups of a few families. These groups would have individual clan *kivas* (the Hopi word for underground ceremonial chambers) or single great kivas.

The soaring cliff dwellings of Canyon de Chelly, Betatakin, Keet Seel, and Mesa Verde represented another type of settlement, more protected from the elements and, perhaps, from raiders. Villagers cultivated the land around them. All of these communities had kivas, ritual spaces central to the lives of deeply spiritual people.

Ancestral Pueblo culture reached its height about 1,000 years ago. Hitherto Puebloans had continued to refine their use of water, not actually irrigating but using sporadic rainfall to the greatest advantage. They would line stones across slopes and cut ditches to distribute rainfall and limit erosion. Occasionally they dug canals in order to channel rainwater into planted fields. Unquestionably, they were expert dry farmers, coaxing abundance out of a harsh environment.

At the time of this climax, some people began moving from smaller, widespread communities into larger, denser settlements—perhaps like today's migrations to cities. The volume of trade in nearly all directions was tremendous, and Pueblo artisans were making superb pottery. Decorative techniques varied from region to region: black-on-white, black-on-red, black-on-orange, red-on-orange, and expressive combinations of these. People also etched petroglyphs into, and painted pictograms onto, rock faces. Rock art is found at almost all Anasazi and Sinagua sites. The quantity of artifacts that they left behind—utility and ceremonial items

alike—is unparalleled among native North American groups.

Around 850 years ago, a cultural decline began. Drought and climatic change put pressure on the Pueblos' settled, agricultural lifestyles. Longer winters shortened growing seasons in which less rain fell. Villagers continued to move to more productive areas. By the late 1200s, Canyon de Chelly was unoccupied. Chaco Canyon had been vacant for 100 years. Settlements at Wupatki continued a little longer, into the 1300s. The Hopi Mesas, on the other hand, first built in the 1100s, were growing. They absorbed some of their migrating neighbors, and their traditions testify to their assimilation of ancient Pueblo culture.

There are also a great number of transitional settlements, many yet to be excavated, that accommodated groups leaving the immediate Four Corners area. Some of them are quite substantial. Considering these transitional settlements, what used to be a question of a culture's simply disappearing can now take a more human shape. The Anasazi didn't vanish—they chose to move. Over a couple of centuries they gradually migrated to new locations, slightly altering their lifestyles. (For some of them, that may have been part of a centuries-old practice.) In the process they passed on their knowledge to the people they joined: the Hopi, the New Mexican Zuñi, the Acoma, and other Pueblos. The Zuñi perspective on this migration is telling. As opposed to archaeologists' causes—drought, climatic change, deforestation, disease, warfare—they see it as a process of searching for "the center place," a place of spiritual rightness. And that center place is where present-day Pueblos are living.

The Sinagua, their name meaning "without water" in Spanish, belonged to a diverse group called the Hakataya, spread out across central Arizona. Wupatki, Walnut Canyon, Tuzigoot, and the inappropriately named Montezuma Castle are all Sinagua sites. These people absorbed Hohokam, Mogollon, and Anasazi cultural patterns: agriculture, village life, and the Mesoamerican ball game; stone masonry and cliff-dwelling architecture; and pottery. Situated in the middle of these three groups, they became a composite but separate culture.

As the so-called Anasazi waned, Hopi and Navajo cultures grew. The Navajo, an Apachean group from the north, gradually migrated southward along the Rocky Mountains about 5,000 years ago and settled in unoccupied places around Pueblo villages. Hunting and gathering were just about all that the land would support for them. Over time they learned farming techniques from the Pueblos and traded with them and as a result took on a character distinct from other Apachean groups, such as the 19th-century Chiracahua and Mescalero Apache. Living in small, dispersed groups, Navajos also raided Pueblo farms and villages—a practice in retrospect notoriously Apachean.

Soon after the Navajo came the Spanish, invading the Southwest early in the 16th century. Unlike Anglo-European conquerors, they allowed elements of native cultures to survive, provided that they accept a transfusion of Catholicism and alien governance. Of course, their intrusion into Southwestern life was far from cordial. Their first contact was with New Mexican Pueblos, whose understandable lack of interest in accepting Spanish rule met with the sword. Pueblo retaliation brought further hostility from the invaders, who murdered hundreds of natives and destroyed villages.

The Spanish didn't have the chance to overrun the Apacheans, whose scattered settlements were more difficult to locate than were pueblos. After the Pueblo Revolt of 1680, which drove the Spanish away, only to have them return 12 years later, the Navajo periodically housed Pueblos seeking refuge from reprisals. In return, the Pueblos taught them rituals, customs, agricultural techniques, and arts—in some of which, like weaving, they eventually surpassed their teachers. In the 1700s, drought led many Hopis to seek refuge among the Navajo in the formerly vacated Canyon de Chelly—a poignant example of the long-standing cooperative relationship of the two groups.

The Navajo also picked up European skills, some of them from the Pueblos. Directly from the Spanish they learned about silversmithing, raising cattle, and riding horses—and they became superior horsemen. Horses extended their gathering range and gave them greater mobility for trading and raiding. The Navajo were not nomadic, however. Many of them had different seasonal residences, log-and-earth hogans, as they continue to do today. These are maintained as permanent dwellings.

After independent Mexico ceded New Mexico to the United States in 1848, the Southwest's new proprietors decided to put an end to Indian raids. Over the next 16 years U.S. troops and the Navajo clashed repeatedly. The United States set up army posts within Navajo territory. They attempted to impose treaties, but U.S. agents often arranged treaties with individual headmen who had no authority that the Navajo as a whole could accept.

This misunderstanding of Navajo organization had tragic results. When raids continued, the U.S. territorial governor believed he had been betrayed. In order to safeguard the so-called frontier, he called in Colonel Kit Carson to destroy Navajo crops and livestock. Over the next few months, the People, as the Navajo call themselves, began to give themselves up. In 1864, as many as 8,000 Navajo made the forced Long Walk to captivity in Fort Sumner, 300 mi to the southeast.

The People were allowed to return to their land after four years of concentration-camp life. Fewer in number and greatly demoralized, they had to reconstruct their lives from scratch, rebuilding customs and lifestyles that had been impossible, if not forbidden, in the camps. Since then, Navajo ingenuity and an impressive ability to seize opportunities have gained them a measure of success in modern America. Their democratically governed community—Navajo Nation—numbers more than 250,000.

The Hopi didn't suffer such brutality. After conflicts with the Spanish—at the end of which they destroyed their own Christianized village of Awatovi in order to maintain the purity of Hopi ritual—their largely noncombative stance with the U.S. government afforded the Hopi more or less hands-off treatment.

In their proper observance of tradition and ritual, the Hopi are unique even among traditional Native Americans. In fact it was to Hopi spiritual leaders that many Native American traditionalists turned in the 1950s in what eventually became the Indian Unity Movement. Hopi beliefs focus on the relationship between the people, the land, and the Creator. In this strict moral order, prayer and ritual—which include the katsina rain power being dances—are necessary to keep the natural cycle in motion and to ensure the flow of life-sustaining forces. The earth is sacred, and they are its keepers.

The Hopi may well be the best dry farmers on the planet, successfully harvesting crops on a precarious 8 to 15 inches of rain per year—and no irrigation. Doubtless they manage this because they have perfected ancient Ancestral Pueblo techniques. The mesas on which they chose to live contain precious aquifers, particularly essential to life in such an arid territory. These vast water sources no doubt sustained them and their migrant guests when Pueblo peoples left places like Wupatki and Walnut Canyon and Canyon de Chelly 700 years ago. Unfortunately, the Hopi Tribal Council, which represents the progressive Christianized members of the Hopi, has sold sacred land to strip miners who in turn have destroyed parts of Black Mesa and depleted the aquifer. This is one indication of the rift between modernizers and those who continue to practice traditional ways. The traditionalists reside in the villages of Oraibi, Hotevilla, and Shungapovi. They are, understandably, intolerant of whites. They follow the Hopi Way even as contemporary life and the Tribal Council pose ever greater threats to it.

The present-day Tohono O'odham (called Papago by the Spanish) and the Pima, in central-southern Arizona, are descendants of the Hohokam. The Spanish first encountered them in the 17th century cultivating former Hohokam territory, using some of the ancient irrigation canals. Both tribes are Pimans, and both continue some Hohokam practices: living in rancherías along canals and performing costume dances and other rituals that link them to Uto-Aztecan language groups nearby in Mexico. The Pima live on the Salt River Reservation south of Phoenix, and the Tohono O'odham reservation stretches north from the Mexican border.

Like the Southwest's history, perspectives on Native American cultures are complex and fascinating—and have become confused in the clash of Euro-American and Native American ways. Take, for example, the enchanting and mysterious word *Anasazi,* which enters into almost any discussion of native Arizonans. This Navajo word, meaning both "ancient ones" and "enemy ancestors," automatically implies a Navajo perspective. Another of equal value is that of the Hopi, whose name for the ancient culture, *Hisatsinom,* means "people of long ago." Yet another perspective is that of the New Mexican Zuñi, who prefer the word *Enote:que,* "our ancient ones, our ancestors."

To scientifically trained Euro-American archaeologists, the term Anasazi conveniently groups together a variety of ancient Pueblo peoples who had similar lifestyles but often divergent adaptations to Southwestern conditions. In past decades researchers encouraged the myth of a lost Anasazi civilization and posed virtually unanswerable questions about who the people were and how and why they "vanished" from the scene. Had they taken the beliefs and statements of the Hopi and of New Mexican Pueblos seriously—acting as both archaeologists and anthropologists—the Hisatsinom–Enote:que–Anasazi would have fit seamlessly into the continuity of Native American life.

The perspective we can never know is that of the Ancestral Pueblos themselves—we don't even know what language they spoke. Yet we can try to get a sense of their world view by listening to contemporary Pueblos. If we project their uniquely American customs into the past, aspects of their ancestral culture come to life. And while Western tradition has its own ancient echoes, such as "know yourself" and "love your neighbor," traditional Pueblo ways speak of a life balanced in its relationship with the earth.

Sources

What Happened to the Anasazi? Why Did They Leave? Where Did They Go? A Panel Discussion at the Anasazi Heritage Center. Jerold G. Widdison, ed. Albuquerque: Southwest Natural and Cultural Heritage Association, 1990.

— Stephen Wolf

Stephen Wolf was formerly an editor at Fodor's.

BOOKS & MOVIES

Books

Essays and Fiction. *Going Back to Bisbee,* by Richard Shelton, *Frog Mountain Blues,* by Charles Bowden, and *The Mountains Next Day,* by Janice Emily Bowers, are all fine personal accounts of life in southern Arizona. The hipster fiction classic *The Monkey Wrench Gang,* by Edward Abbey, details an ecoanarchist plot to blow up Glen Canyon Dam. *Stolen Gods,* a thriller by Jake Page, is set largely on Arizona's Hopi reservation and in Tucson. Three novels by Tucson-based writers skillfully evoke the interplay between Native American culture and contemporary Southwest life: *Pigs in Heaven,* by Barbara Kingsolver, *Almanac of the Dead,* by Leslie Marmon Silko, and *Yes Is Better Than No,* by Byrd Baylor. Wild West adventure, with all of the mythological glory that Hollywood has tried to capture, abounds in Zane Grey's novels—buy a new copy or look for any of the charming illustrated hardcover editions in used- or out-of-print-book stores. Tony Hillerman's mysteries will put you in an equally Southwestern mood.

General History. *Arizona: A History,* by Thomas E. Sheridan, chronicles the Anglo, Mexican, and Native American frontier and details its transformation into the modern-day Sunbelt. *Arizona Cowboys,* by Dane Coolidge, is an illustrated account of the cowboys, Native Americans, settlers, and explorers of the early 1900s. Buried-treasure hunters will be inspired by *Lost Mines of the Great Southwest,* by John D. Mitchell, which is just enough of a nibble to start you sketching maps and planning strategy. First printed back in 1891, *Some Strange Corners of Our Country,* by Charles F. Lummis, takes readers on a century-old journey to the Grand Canyon, Montezuma Castle, the Petrified Forest, and other Arizonan "strange corners." For a dip into the back roads of the past, try *Arizona Good Roads Association Illustrated Road Maps and Tour Book,* a 1913 volume, replete with hotel ads, reprinted by *Arizona Highways* magazine. *Roadside History of Arizona,* by Marshall Trimble, will bring you up to date on many of the same thoroughfares. *Ghost Towns of Arizona,* by James E. and Barbara H. Sherman, gives historical details on the abandoned mining towns that dot the state and provides maps to find them. For an anthology that covers the entire state's literature, consult *Named in Stone and Sky: An Arizona Anthology,* edited by Gregory McNamee.

Native American History. Two books provide excellent surveys of the ancient and more recent Native American past and cover in more depth sites mentioned in this guidebook. *Those Who Came Before: Southwestern Archaeology in the National Park System,* by Robert Lister and Florence Lister, provides a well-researched and completely accessible summary of centuries of life in the region informed by both contemporary Indian and archaeological perspectives. David G. Noble's *Ancient Ruins of the Southwest* covers similar territory more briefly and portably and includes directions for driving to sites. *Hohokam Indians of the Tucson Basin,* by Linda Gregonis, offers an in-depth look at this prehistoric tribe. In *Hopi,* by Susanne Page and Jake Page, the daily, ceremonial, and spiritual life of the tribe is explored in detail. Study up on the history of Hopi silversmithing techniques in *Hopi Silver,* by Margaret Wright. The beautifully illustrated *Hopi Indian Kachina Dolls,* by Oscar T. Branson, details the different ceremonial roles of the colorful Native American figurines. Navajo homes, ceremonies, crafts, and tribal traditions are kept alive in *The Enduring Navajo,* by Laura Gilpin. Navajo legends and trends from early days to the present are collected in *The Book of the Navajo,* by Raymond F. Locke.

A superb collection of Native American stories, songs, and poems, *Coming to Light,* edited by Brian Swann, includes material from all over the country, not only the Southwest. *Paths of Life: American Indians of the Southwest and Northern Mexico,* edited by Thomas E. Sheridan and Nancy J. Parezo, offers both contemporary and historical portraits of Native Americans.

Natural History. *The Arizona Sonora Desert Museum Book of Answers,* by David

Lazaroff, covers hundreds of frequently asked natural-history questions. *Gathering the Desert,* by Gary Paul Nabhan, explores the Southwest from an ethnobotanist's viewpoint. *A Guide to Exploring Oak Creek and the Sedona Area,* by Stewart Aitchison, provides natural-history driving tours of this very scenic district. In *100 Desert Wildflowers in Natural Color,* by Natt N. Dodge, you'll find a color photo and brief description of each of the flowers included. Also written by Natt N. Dodge, *Poisonous Dwellers of the Desert* gives precise information on both venomous and nonvenomous creatures of the Southwest. *Venomous Animals of Arizona,* by Robert L. Smith, offers detailed information on venomous creatures of the Southwest. *Cacti of the Southwest,* by W. Hubert Earle, depicts some of the best-known species of the region with color photos and descriptive material. For comprehensive information on Grand Canyon geology, history, flora, and fauna, plus hiking suggestions, pick up *A Field Guide to the Grand Canyon,* by Steve Whitney. *Grand Canyon Country: Its Majesty and Lore,* by Seymour L. Fishbein, published by National Geographic Books, describes the Grand Canyon through photographs, maps, and firsthand accounts. *Common Edible and Useful Plants of the West,* by Muriel Sweet, gives the layperson descriptions of medicinal and other plants and shrubs, most of which were first discovered by Native Americans. *Roadside Geology of Arizona,* by Halka Chronic, is a good resource for finding the causes of the striking natural formations you'll see throughout the state.

Crafts. *The Traveler's Guide to American Crafts: West of the Mississippi,* by Suzanne Carmichael, gives browsers and buyers alike a useful overview of Arizona's traditional and contemporary handiwork.

General Interest. *Arizona Highways,* a monthly magazine, features exquisite color photography of this versatile state. Useful general travel information, fine pictures, and well-written historical essays all make the book *Arizona,* by Larry Cheek, a good pretrip resource.

Movies

The Arizona landscape has starred in a slew of films either as itself or as a stand-in for similar terrain—the Sahara, for instance—around the world. *The Postman* (1997), starring Kevin Costner, and *Buffalo Soldiers* (1997), starring Danny Glover, were filmed around Tucson. The Titan Missile Base near Green Valley was the locale for filming parts of *Star Trek: First Contact* (1996). Sun Devil Stadium in Tempe and Lost Dutchman State Park were featured in the blockbuster hit *Jerry Maguire* (1996). Parts of the Kevin Costner comedy *Tin Cup* (1996) were shot in Tubac. Much of director John Woo's bombastic *Broken Arrow* (1995), starring John Travolta and Christian Slater, was shot around Marble Canyon, which was also used, along with the Page–Lake Powell area, in the Mel Gibson–Jodie Foster vehicle *Maverick* (1994). Tom Hanks trotted through Monument Valley and Flagstaff in *Forrest Gump* (1994). The Tucson area served as the backdrop for much of *Boys on the Side* (1994), starring Whoopi Goldberg, Drew Barrymore, and Mary-Louise Parker. The nouveau Westerns *Tombstone* (1993), starring Val Kilmer and Kurt Russell, and Sharon Stone's *The Quick and the Dead* (1995) both made use of various sites in Mescal. Woody Harrelson and Juliette Lewis raged through Holbrook, Winslow, and other towns in *Natural Born Killers* (1994), and the Yuma area was used to otherworldly effect in the science-fiction film *Stargate* (1994). Yuma stands in for a lot of places, including Morocco in Joseph von Sternberg's *Morocco* (1930), starring the sultry Marlene Dietrich, and the Bob Hope comedy *Road to Morocco* (1942).

The famous canyon loomed large in *Grand Canyon* (1991), starring Kevin Kline, Steve Martin, and Danny Glover. The independent cult hit *Red Rock West* (1991), directed by John Dahl and starring Nicolas Cage, was filmed in Willcox and other southeastern Arizona locales. Cage also starred, with Holly Hunter, in *Raising Arizona* (1987). Footage for the Joel Coen–directed film was shot in Scottsdale, Phoenix, and other locations. Chevy Chase frolicked through the Grand Canyon, Monument Valley, and Flagstaff in *National Lampoon's Vacation* (1983). Clint Eastwood stared down all comers in *The Outlaw Josey Wales* (1976), which showcases Patagonia and Mescal. Italian director Michelangelo Antonioni's

Zabriskie Point (1968) includes scenes of Carefree and Phoenix. Marilyn Monroe dropped in on Phoenix in *Bus Stop* (1956). Gerd Oswald's noirish *A Kiss Before Dying* (1955), starring Robert Wagner and Joanne Woodward, filmed in Tucson. Parts of *The Bells of St. Mary's* (1954) take place in Old Tucson. Some Arizona locations worked better than the real thing in Fred Zinnemann's *Oklahoma!* (1954). Jean Harlow whooped it up as a harried movie superstar in Victor Fleming's very funny *Bombshell* (1933), which has scenes shot in Tucson proper.

Among the many classic Westerns shot in Arizona are *The Searchers* (1956), *She Wore a Yellow Ribbon* (1949), *Fort Apache* (1948), and *Stagecoach* (1939), all directed by John Ford and starring John Wayne, both of whom spent a lot of time filming in the state over the years; *Gunfight at the OK Corral* (1957), starring Burt Lancaster and Kirk Douglas; *Johnny Guitar* (1954), director Nicholas Ray's Freudian take on the Old West that features Joan Crawford in a gender-bending performance as a tough-gal gunslinger; director Howard Hawks's moody *Red River* (1948), which stars John Wayne and Montgomery Clift; and Ford's *My Darling Clementine* (1946), in which Henry Fonda plays a reluctant sheriff.

INDEX

NOTES

NOTES

NOTES

NOTES

NOTES

FODOR'S KEY TO THE GUIDES

America's guidebook leader publishes guides for every kind of traveler. Check out our many series and find your perfect match.

FODOR'S GOLD GUIDES

America's favorite travel-guide series offers the most detailed insider reviews of hotels, restaurants, and attractions in all price ranges, plus great background information, smart tips, and useful maps.

COMPASS AMERICAN GUIDES

Stunning guides from top local writers and photographers, with gorgeous photos, literary excerpts, and colorful anecdotes. A must-have for culture mavens, history buffs, and new residents.

FODOR'S CITYPACKS

Concise city coverage in a guide plus a foldout map. The right choice for urban travelers who want everything under one cover.

FODOR'S EXPLORING GUIDES

Hundreds of color photos bring your destination to life. Lively stories lend insight into the culture, history, and people.

FODOR'S TRAVEL HISTORIC AMERICA

For travelers who want to experience history firsthand, this series gives in-depth coverage of historic sights, plus nearby restaurants and hotels. Themes include the Thirteen Colonies, the Old West, and the Lewis and Clark Trail.

FODOR'S POCKET GUIDES

For travelers who need only the essentials. The best of Fodor's in pocket-size packages for just $9.95.

FODOR'S FLASHMAPS

Every resident's map guide, with 60 easy-to-follow maps of public transit, parks, museums, zip codes, and more.

FODOR'S CITYGUIDES

Sourcebooks for living in the city: thousands of in-the-know listings for restaurants, shops, sports, nightlife, and other city resources.

FODOR'S AROUND THE CITY WITH KIDS

Up to 68 great ideas for family days, recommended by resident parents. Perfect for exploring in your own backyard or on the road.

FODOR'S HOW TO GUIDES

Get tips from the pros on planning the perfect trip. Learn how to pack, fly hassle-free, plan a honeymoon or cruise, stay healthy on the road, and travel with your baby.

FODOR'S LANGUAGES FOR TRAVELERS

Practice the local language before you hit the road. Available in phrase books, cassette sets, and CD sets.

KAREN BROWN'S GUIDES

Engaging guides—many with easy-to-follow inn-to-inn itineraries—to the most charming inns and B&Bs in the U.S.A. and Europe.

BAEDEKER'S GUIDES

Comprehensive guides, trusted since 1829, packed with A–Z reviews and star ratings.

OTHER GREAT TITLES FROM FODOR'S

Baseball Vacations, The Complete Guide to the National Parks, Family Vacations, Golf Digest's Places to Play, Great American Drives of the East, Great American Drives of the West, Great American Vacations, Healthy Escapes, National Parks of the West, Skiing USA.